History of the Fylde of

Lancashire

John Porter

Alpha Editions

This edition published in 2019

ISBN : 9789353602031

Design and Setting By
Alpha Editions
email - alphaedis@gmail.com

HISTORY OF THE FYLDE

OF LANCASHIRE,

BY

JOHN PORTER, M.R.C.S.,L.S.A.

FLEETWOOD AND BLACKPOOL:
W. PORTER AND SONS, PUBLISHERS.
1876.

TO

BENJAMIN WHITWORTH, ESQUIRE, M.P.,

In admiration of his Enterprise, Generosity, and Philanthropy,

DISPLAYED IN THE FYLDE, AND ELSEWHERE,

AND AS

A TRIBUTE OF PERSONAL REGARD AND ESTEEM,

THIS VOLUME

IS RESPECTFULLY INSCRIBED, BY

THE AUTHOR.

PREFACE.

—:o:—

FEW, and only a few, words are needed to introduce the History of the Fylde to the public. In its preparation my aim has been to make the work as comprehensive in description and detail as the prescribed limits would allow, and I have endeavoured to write in a style free from any tendency to pedantry, and I hope, also, from dulness. How far these conditions have been fulfilled I must now leave to the judgment of the reader, doing so with some degree of confidence that at any rate the attempt will be generally appreciated, if the success be not universally acknowledged. In the course of my labours I have availed myself of the works of various authors, and desire to acknowledge my indebtedness, especially to Baines's Lancashire, Fishwick's Kirkham, Thornber's Blackpool, and many volumes of the Cheetham and other historical societies. My thanks for valuable aid are also due to the following gentlemen, amongst others, the Ven. Archdeacon Hornby, of St. Michael's-on-Wyre; the Rev. W. Richardson, of Poulton-le-Fylde; Col. Bourne, M.P., of Hackensall and Heathfield; John Furness, esq., of Fulwood; W. H. Poole, esq., of Fleetwood; and the Bailiffs of Kirkham.

JOHN PORTER.

Fleetwood, August, 1876.

ERRATA.

—:o:—

Page 7, line 15, after the word *crossing*, insert *the Main Dyke from*. This Dyke is crossed after leaving, and not before reaching, Staining, as stated.

Page 147, line 9 from the bottom, for *Gulph*, read *Gulf*.

Page 183, line 2, for 1857, read 1657.

· Page 256, dele the heading *Coasting*.

Page 286, line 2 from the bottom, for *fortified*, read *forfeited*.

Page 289, line 13 from the bottom, for the first *funds*, read *expenses*.

CONTENTS.

—:0:——

HISTORY OF THE FYLDE.

-------:o:-------

CHAPTER I.

THE ANCIENT BRITONS, ROMANS, ANGLO-SAXONS, AND DANES.

> "See! in what crowds the uncouth forms advance :
> Each would outstrip the other, each prevent
> Our careful search, and offer to your gaze,
> Unask'd, his motley features. Wait awhile,
> My curious friends ! and let us first arrange
> In proper order your promiscuous throng."

THE large district of western Lancashire, denominated from time immemorial the Fylde, embraces one third at least of the Hundred of Amounderness, and a line drawn from Ashton, on the Ribble, to Churchtown, on the Wyre, forms the nearest approach to an eastern boundary attainable, for although the section cut off by its means includes more land and villages than properly appertain to the Fylde, a more westerly division would exclude others which form part of it. The whole of the parishes of Bispham, Lytham, Poulton, and St. Michael's ; and the parish of Kirkham, exclusive of Goosnargh-with-Newsham and Whittingham, are comprised in the Fylde country.

The word Amounderness was formerly considered to signify the " Promontory of Agmund," or "Edmund," and this origin is alluded to in a treatise written some years since by Mr. Thomas

B

Baines on the "Valley of the Mersey," in which the following remarks occur :—"In the year 911 the Northumbrians themselves began the war, for they despised the peace which King Edward and his 'Witan' offered them, and overran the land of Mercia. After collecting great booty they were overtaken on their march home by the forces of the West Saxons and the Mercians, who put them to flight and slew many thousands of them. Two Danish Kings and five Earls were slain in this battle. Amongst the Earls slain was Agmund, the governor, from whom the Hundred of Agmunderness (Amounderness) was probably named." In order that the reader may properly comprehend why Mr. Baines should surmise that Amounderness received its title from the Danish Earl, Agmund, it may be stated that the extensive province of Northumbria, then colonised by the Northmen or Danes, embraced, amongst other territory, the district afterwards called Lancashire, and, consequently, the Hundred of Amounderness would be in a great measure under Danish governance. When, however, we call to mind that the Danes did not invade England until A.D. 787, and learn that this Hundred was entered in the Ripon grant in A.D. 705, as Hacmunderness, it becomes obvious that the name cannot have been conferred upon it by that nation, and some other source must be looked to for its origin. In Gibsons' Etymological Geography there is "Anderness" (for Ackmunderness) described as a "promontory sheltered by oaks, (ac, oak ; and mund, protection)." As many large trunks of trees have been discovered beneath the layers of peat in the extensive local mosses, whilst others have been laid bare along the shore by the action of the tides, it can be readily believed that at one time the greater share of the district was clothed with forests. Leyland, who was antiquary to Henry VIII., and surveyed the Hundred during the reign of that monarch, 1509-47, says :—"Al Aundernesse for the most parte in time paste hathe been full of woods, and many of the moores replenished with hy fyrre trees ; but now such part of Aundernesse as is towarde the se is sore destitute of woodde." With such irrefutable evidences of the early woodland condition of Amounderness, there need be no hesitation in accepting the signification which Messrs. Gibson have given to the name—the Ness or Promontory protected by oaks. The word Fylde is regarded simply as a corruption of

" Field." Camden in his "Britannia" of 1590, writes:—

> "Tota est campestris, unde Fild pro Field appellatur." [1]
> (The whole is champaign, whence it is called Fild for Field.)

In a subsequent edition of the same work Fild is spelt File, and the latter orthography was used inFileplumpton, in the Duchy records, afterwards called Fylde Plumpton, and now Wood Plumpton. The Fylde section of this Hundred is a level well-watered country, highly cultivated and richly productive, especially of grain, from which circumstance it was formerly designated the corn-field of Amounderness.

Anterior to the third invasion of the Romans in A.D. 43, the inhabitants of the Fylde and other portions of Lancashire lying between the range of mountains which separates this county from Yorkshire, and the coast about the Bay of Morecambe, were called the Setantii or Segantii, " the dwellers in the country of water," but at that date the whole tract populated by these people was included in the more extensive province of the Brigantes, comprehending what are now known as the six counties of York, Durham, Northumberland, Westmoreland, Cumberland, and Lancaster. The Fylde at that epoch would be composed chiefly of morasses and forests, interspersed with limited areas and narrow paths of more stable land, and there can be little doubt that the dwellers on such an uninviting spot must have been very few, but that it was traversed and, as far as practicable, inhabited by the ancient Setantii is evident from the several relics of them which have been discovered amongst the peat in modern days. Two or three canoes, consisting of light wooden frameworks, covered with hides, were found by a man named Jolly, about half a century ago, when cutting the " Main Dyke" of Marton Mere; [2] Celtic hammers, axes, and spears have also been taken out of the mosses in the district, all of which were doubtless originally the property of the aboriginal Britons. The bay of Morecambe and the river Wyre acquired their distinctive appellations from the Setantii, the one being

1. William Camden was born in London in 1551. His most celebrated publication is entitled " Britannia," and consists of a survey of the British isles, written in elegant Latin. He died in 1623, at Chiselhurst, in Kent.

2. The reader must not confound these canoes with some others found in Martin Meer, North Meols.

derived from the Celtic *gwyr*, pure or fresh, and the other from *mawr*, great, and *cam*, winding or bent.

The hardihood of the native Britons of these parts is attested by Dion Cassius, who informs us that they lived on prey, hunting, and the fruits of trees, and were accustomed to brave hunger, cold, and all kinds of toil, for they would " continue several days up to their chins in water, and bear hunger many days." In the woods their habitations were wicker shelters, formed of the branches of trees interwoven together, and, in the open grounds, clay or mud huts. They were indebted to the skins of animals slain in the chase for such scanty covering as they cared to wear, and according to Cæsar and other writers, dyed their bodies with woad, which produced a blue colour, and had long flowing hair, being cleanly shaved except the head and upper lip. That the power of endurance possessed by the Setantii, and the neighbouring Brigantes is not to be understood literally as expressed by Cassius may, we venture to think, be taken for granted. It can scarcely be credited that the human frame could ever be reduced or exalted to such an amphibious condition as to be indifferent whether it passed a number of days on dry land or under water ; it seems more probable that in his description Cassius referred to the hunting and other expeditions of the inhabitants into the forests and morasses of the Fylde and similarly wooded and marshy tracts, where there is no question the followers of the chase would be more or less in a state of immersion during the whole time they were so engaged.

The religion of the Setantii was Druidical, and their deities resembled those of other heathen nations, such as the Romans and Greeks of that era, but differed in their names. Cæsar tells us that this order of priesthood was presided over by a superior, who was known as the chief Druid, and had almost unlimited authority over all the rest. The Druids were settled at various points of the island, where they erected their temples, but in addition to these principle stations, many of their order were scattered amongst the native tribes of Britain, over which they appear to have exercised the functions and power of judges, arranging both public and private disputes, and deciding all criminal cases. It was part of the creed professed by the Setantii, to vow, when they were engaged in warfare, that they would, through the agency of the Druids, immolate human victims as an atonement for slaughtered enemies, believing that unless man's life were given for man's life, the divine anger of the immortal Gods could not be appeased. There were other sacrifices of the same kind instituted at regularly appointed seasons and on special occasions. The Setantii also believed in an immortal soul, but seem to have had no idea of a higher state, as their priests inculcated the doctrine that after death the soul was transported to another body, " imagining that by this the men were more effectually roused to valour, the fear of death being taken away."[1] Ornaments called " Druids' eggs," and worn only by these priests, have been found in the Fylde.

How Cæsar, in B.C. 54 and 55, invaded Britain a first and a second time, achieving at best an empty conquest, and how, after his death, the emperor Claudius sent over an army with a determination to exterminate the Druids, and after thirty pitched battles, subdued province after province, is beyond the limits of this work to state, but as a connecting link of the history of the country with that of our own county, and that portion of it especially under examination, it may be stated that Britain was finally conquered by the Romans under Julius Agricola, and that the best investigation of the subject leads to the opinion that the district which we call Lancashire, was brought into subjection to the Roman conqueror in A.D. 79. A vigorous resistance was for long offered to the army of invaders in the territory of the Setantii by the natives under the Brigantine chief Venutius, but the well drilled legions of the Romans, when commanded by Agricola, proved too formidable to be checked or broken by the wild, undisciplined valour of the Setantii. Tacitus, the son-in-law of the general, informs us that early in the summer of A.D. 79, Agricola personally inspected his soldiers, and marked out many of the stations, one of which, either made at that time or later by the same people, was situated at Kirkham, on the line of the Roman road running from the mouth of Wyre, which will be described hereafter. He explored the estuaries and woods along the western coast of Lancashire, and harassed the enemy by sudden and frequent incursions. When the Brigantes and

1. Cæcar's Bell. Gall., v. 14.

Setantii had been thoroughly overawed and disheartened by the invincible Romans, Agricola stayed his operations in order to shew them the blessings of peace, and in that way many towns which had bravely held out were induced to surrender and give hostages.   These places he surrounded with guards and fortifications.   The following winter was passed in endeavouring, by various incentives to pleasure, to subdue the warlike nature of the Britons, thereby diminishing the danger of an outbreak, especially amongst such tribes as the Setantii, whose intrepid spirits had been so difficult to quell, and who were not likely to submit quietly to the yoke of the conqueror, unless some means were adopted to allure them by the charms of civilised luxury from their free field and forest mode of existence.   Temples, courts of justice, and comfortable habitations were first erected ; the sons of the petty chiefs were next instructed in the liberal arts, and Agricola professed to prefer the genius of the Britons to the attainments of the Gauls.   The Roman dress became the fashion, and the *toga* was frequently worn.   The " porch, luxurious baths, and elegant banquets" were regularly instituted, and by degrees the crafty design of the Roman general was accomplished, and the vanquished Britons had ceased to be the hardy warriors of old.

About one century after the subjugation of Britain by Agricola no less than seven important Roman stations, or garrisoned places, had risen up in the county of Lancaster, and were situated at Manchester, Colne, Warrington, Lancaster, Walton-le-dale, Ribchester, and Overborough.   The minor ones, such as Kirkham, supposing their sites to have been first built upon in a season of warfare, subsequently became small settlements only, and were, in all probability, unused as military depots.   The rivers which flowed in the neighbourhood of the several encampments, terminated in three estuaries, denominated by Ptolemy,[1] the ancient geographer, in his book, completed in A.D. 130, the Seteia Æstuarium, the Moricambe Æstuarium, and the Belisama

---

1.   Ptolemy was a native of Egypt, and lived at Alexandria during the first half of the second century.   He was an astronomer, chronologer, and geographer. His geographical work was in use in all schools until the 15th century, when it was supplanted by another treatise containing the more recent discoveries of Venetian and other navigators.

Æstuarium. The first of these estuaries is generally regarded as the mouth of the Dee, the second is identified with Morecambe Bay, and the third with the Ribble by some historians and the Mersey by others. The same authority mentions also a Portus Setantiorum, which has been located on the banks of the Ribble, Lune, and Mersey, by different antiquarians, but in the opinion of the most recent writers the ancient harbour of the Setantii was situated at the mouth of the river Wyre. Further reference to the Setantian port will be made in a later page of the present chapter.

At the shore margin of the warren at Fleetwood there was visible, about forty years ago, the abrupt and broken termination of a Roman road, which could be traced across the sward, along the Naze below Burn Hall, and onward in the direction of Poulton. From that town it ran in a southerly line towards Staining, crossing Marton Mere, on its way, in the cutting of which its materials were very apparent, and lying on the low mossy lands to the depth of two yards in gravel. From Staining it proceeded to Weeton, and in a hollow near to the moss of that township, consisted of an immense stony embankment several yards in height ; in the moss itself the deep beds of gravel were distinctly observable, and from there the road continued its course up the rising ground to Plumpton, the traces as usual being less obvious on the higher land. From Plumpton it travelled towards the elevated site of a windmill between Weeton moss and Kirkham, at which point it turned suddenly, and joined the public road, running in a continuous straight line towards the latter town. The greater part of the long street of Kirkham is either upon or in the immediate vicinity of the old Roman road. From Kirkham the road directed its course towards Lund church, somewhere in the neighbourhood of which it was joined by another path formed by the same people and commencing at the Neb of the Naze near Freckleton.[1] Leaving Lund it ran through Lea on to Fulwood moor, where it took the name of Watling street, and proceeded on to Ribchester. This road has always been known in the Flyde as the Danes' Pad, from a tradition that those pirates made use of it at a later period in their incursions into our district, visiting and ransacking Kirkham, Poulton, and

1. Mr. Thornber mentions this path in his History of Blackpool.

other towns or hamlets of the unfortunate Saxons. Numerous
relics, chiefly of the Roman soldiery, have been dug or ploughed
up at different times out of the soil, bordering on the road, or
found amongst the pebbles of which it was composed, and
amongst them may be mentioned spears, both British and Roman,
horse shoes in abundance, several stone hammers, a battle axe,
a broken sword, and ancient Roman coins, all of which were
picked up along its line between Wyre mouth and Weeton.
Several half-baked urns marked with dots, and pieces of rudely
fashioned pottery were discovered in an extensive barrow or cairn
near Weeton-lane Heads, which was accidentally opened, and is
now pointed out as the abode of the local hairy ghost or boggart.
In the neighbourhood of Kirkham there have been found many
broken specimens of Roman pottery, stones prepared for building
purposes, eight or ten urns, some containing ashes and beads,
stone handmills for corn grinding, ancient coins, " Druids' eggs,"
axes, and horse shoes; in the fields near Dowbridge, where several
of the above urns were discovered, there was found a flattened
ivory needle, about five or six inches long with a large eyelet.
A cuirass was also picked up on the banks of the Wyre ; but the
most interesting relic of antiquity is the boss or umbo of a shield,
taken out of a ditch near Kirkham, which will be fully described
in the chapter devoted to that township. The Romans were
accustomed to make three kinds of roads, the first of which,
called the Viæ Militares, were constructed during active warfare,
when they were engaged in pushing their way into the territory
of the enemy, and easy unobstructed communication between
their various encampments became a matter of the utmost
importance. The second, or public roads, were formed to facilitate
commerce in time of peace ; and the third were narrower paths,
called private roads. The county of Lancaster was intersected by
no less than four important Roman routes, two of which ran from
north to south, and two traversed the land from west to east.
The course of one road, and perhaps the best constructed of the
whole four, we have just followed out ; of the remainder, the first,
commencing at Carlisle, passed near Garstang and Preston, crossed
the Irwell at Old Trafford, and maintaining its southerly direction,
ultimately arrived at Kinderton, in Cheshire. The second
extended from Overborough to Slack, in Yorkshire, passing on its

way through Ribchester, the Ribble, Radcliffe, Prestwich, and Newton Heath ; whilst the third had its origin at a ford on the Mersey, in close proximity to Warrington, and from that spot could be traced through Barton, Eccles, Manchester, Moston, Chadderton, Royton, and Littleborough, thence over Rumbles Moor to Ilkley, where was located the temple of the goddes Verbeia. It is conjectured that these roads, which consisted for the most part of pavement and deep beds of gravel, were begun, or at least marked out, by Agricola during the time he was occupied in the subjugation of Lancashire, and if this very probable hypothesis be correct the course taken by that general in his exploration of the woods of the Fylde, and the estuaries of Morecambe and the Ribble is clearly indicated by the direction of the ancient path communicating with the mouth of Wyre and the Naze.

At the opening of the third century the Roman governor of Britain found it necessary to obtain the personal co-operation of Severus, in order to put an effectual check to the repeated outbreaks of the natives ; in A.D. 207, that emperor having landed and established his head-quarters at York, a considerable force marched northwards under his leadership to punish the revolting tribes, and it is surmised that the curious road, running across the mosses of Rawcliffe, Stalmine, and Pilling, was constructed by the legionaries whilst on this tour. The pathway alluded to, and commonly known as Kate's Pad, was deeply situated in the mosses, and had apparently been formed by fastening riven oak planks on to sleepers of the same material, secured and held stationary by means of pins or rivets driven into the marl a little above which they rested. Its width was about twenty inches, but in some places rather more.[1] Herodian, in describing the expedition of Severus to quell the insurrection of the Briton, says :—" He more especially endeavoured to render the marshy places stable by means of causeways, that his soldiers, treading with safety, might pass them, and having firm footing fight to advantage. In these the natives are accustomed to swim and traverse about, being immersed as high as their waists : for going

---

1. " In the memory of man large portions of Kate's Pad existed with various, but irregular interruptions : these, however, the moss cutter yearly removes, and shortly no remains of it will be found."—Rev. W. Thornber, Blackpool, 1837.

naked as to the greater part of their bodies they contemn the
mud. His army having passed beyond the rivers and fortresses
which defended the Roman territory, there were frequent attacks
and skirmishes, and retreats on the side of the barbarians. To
these indeed flight was an easy matter, and they lay hidden in the
thickets and marshes through their local knowledge ; all which
things being adverse to the Romans served to protract the war."
There can be no doubt that, when the path, which consisted in
some parts of one huge tree and in others of two or more, was
formed, timber must have been very plentiful in the vicinity, and
at the present day numbers of tree trunks of large size are to be
found in the mosses, further corroborating the conclusions arrived
at by Leyland, whose words have already been quoted, and
Holinshed, who wrote :—" The whole countrie of Lancaster has
beene forests heretofore." An iron fibula, a pewter wine-strainer,
a wooden drinking bowl, hooped with two brass bands and having
two handles, a brass stirrup, and other relics have been taken out
of the moss fields ; and in the same neighbourhood an anvil,
several pieces of thin sheet-brass, and a pair of shears were
discovered in a ditch.

About the year 416 the Romans finally removed themselves
from our island, taking with them many of the brave youths of
Britain, and leaving the country in the hands of a people whose
inactive habits, acquired under their dominion, had rendered
them ignorant of the art and unfit for the hardships of warfare.
According to Ethelwerd's Chronicle, in the year 418 those few of
the Roman race who were left in Britain, not being able to put
up with the manifold insults of the natives, buried their treasure
in pits, hoping that at some future day, when all animosity had
subsided, they would be able to recover it and live peaceably, but
such a fortunate consummation never arrived, and weary at
length of waiting, they assembled on the coasts and " spreading
their canvass to the wind, sought an exile on the shores of Gaul."
The Saxon Chronicle says :—" This year, A.D. 418, the Romans
collected all the treasures that were in Britain, and some they hid
in the earth so that no one since has been able to find them ; and
some they carried with them into Gaul." It is far from unlikely
that the silver denarii, discovered in 1840 by some brickmakers
near Rossall, and amounting to four hundred coins of Trajan,

Hadrian, Titus, Vespasian, Domitian, Antonius, Severus, Sabina, etc., were deposited in that spot for security by one of those much harassed Romans, previous to his departure from our coast.

A prize so easily to be obtained as Britain in its practically unprotected state appeared, was not long in attracting the covetousness of the neighbouring Picts and Scots, who came down in thousands from the north, forced their way beyond the Roman Wall erected by Hadrian, occupied the fortresses and towns, and spread ruin and devastation in their track. The northern counties were the chief sufferers from these ruthless marauders. Cumberland, Yorkshire, and Lancashire, were ravaged and plundered to such an extent that had it not been for the seasonable assistance of the Saxons, the whole country they embrace would have been utterly devastated and almost depopulated. Gildas, the earliest British historian[1], born about 500, described our land before the incursions of the Picts and Scots as abounding in pleasant hills, spreading pastures, cultivated fields, silvery streams, and snow-white sands, and spoke of the roofs of the buildings in the twenty-eight cities of the kingdom as "raised aloft with threatening hugeness." We may readily conceive how this picture of peace and prosperity was marred and ruined, as far as the three counties above-named were concerned, by the destroying hand of the northern nation. The British towns were still surrounded by the fortified walls and embattled towers, built by the Romans, but the unfortunate inhabitants, so long unaccustomed to

"The close-wedged battle and the din of war,"

and deprived of their armed soldiers and valiant youth, were panic stricken by the fierce onslaughts of the Scottish tribes, and fled before their advancing arms. Some idea of the critical and truly pitiable condition to which they were reduced may be gleaned from the tenor of an appeal for help sent by them to their old rulers, which the author last quoted has preserved as follows :—

The Lamentation of the Britons unto Agitius, thrice Consul.

"The barbarians drive us to the sea, the sea drives us back to the barbarians. Thus of two kinds of death, one or other must be our choice, either to be swallowed up by the waves or butchered by the sword."

1. Gildas, the wise, as he was styled, was the son of Caw, Prince of Strathclyde, and was born at Dumbarton.

The Romans were fully occupied with enemies of their own, the Goths, and consequently were unprepared to offer any assistance to the Britons, whose position was shortly afterwards rendered additionally wretched by famine and its attendant evils. At that period both the state of Lancashire itself and of its inhabitants must have been exceedingly deplorable—the country ravaged and still exposed to the depredations and barbarities of the enemy, had now become a prey to a fearful dearth. Many of the descendants of the old Setantii, unable any further to support the double contest, yielded themselves up to the Picts and Scots in the hope of obtaining food to appease the fierce cravings of hunger, whilst others, more hardy, but outnumbered and weakened by long fasts, sought refuge in the woods and such other shelters as the neighbourhood afforded. Disappointed in the Romans, the Britons applied for aid to the Saxons, or Anglo-Saxons, a mixed and piratical tribe, dwelling on the banks of the German Ocean, and composed of Jutes, Angles, and pure Saxons. The men of this race are described as determined, fearless, and of great size, with blue eyes, ruddy complexions, and yellow streaming hair. They were well practised in warfare, and armed with battle-axes, swords, spears, and maces. Their chief god was Odin, or Woden, and their heaven Valhalla. About one thousand of these warriors, under the command of Hengist and Horsa, embarked in three vessels, built of hides, and called *Cyulæ* or *Ceols*. They landed on the coast of Kent, about the year 449, and by the direction of Vortigern, king of the Island, marched northwards until they arrived near York, where an encounter of great moment took place, terminating in the utter defeat of the Picts and Scots. Inspirited by so early and signal a success the Saxons followed up their advantage with alacrity, drove the baleful marauders out of the counties of Lancaster and York, and finally compelled them to retreat across the frontier into their own territory. After having rescued the kingdom from these invaders the Saxons settled at York and Manchester, and not only evinced no sign of returning to their own country, but even despatched messengers for fresh troops. This strange and suspicious conduct on the part of their allies excited considerable alarm and anxiety amongst the Britons, who practically expressed their disapproval by refusing to make any provision for the reinforcements. After a short interval a mandate was issued to the Saxon leader ordering him to withdraw his army from the soil of Britain. Incensed and stimulated by such decisive action Hengist determined at once to carry out the object he had cherished from the first—the subjugation of the people and the seizure of the island. Having procured a further supply of men under his son Octa, he established them in the country of the Brigantes, and almost immediately invited the native nobles to a friendly conference with his chiefs on Salisbury plain. The Britons, who were far from suspecting his treacherous design, attended the assembly unarmed, and in that defenceless state fell an easy prey to their Saxon hosts, who in the midst of feasting and revelry, brutally massacred the whole of their guests. Successful in his cowardly and murderous stratagem, Hengist took possession of the southern counties, whilst his son Octa maintained his sway over the Brigantine province of Northumbria, in which the Fylde was included, as intimated at the beginning of the chapter.

The ancient warlike spirit of the Setantii, which had lain almost dormant for centuries, was once more thoroughly aroused in the natives of Lancashire, and a determined and valiant opposition offered by them to Octa and his army. Overborough capitulated only when its inhabitants were worn out by fatigue and famine, whilst Warrington and Manchester sustained severe and protracted sieges before they fell into the hands of the enemy. Nennius, another early historian, who was born towards the end of the sixth century, informs us that the famous King Arthur and his sixty Knights of the Round Table worsted the Saxons in twelve successive battles, four of which were fought on the banks of the Douglas, near Wigan. In those conflicts our county was well and effectively represented in the person of Paulinus, the commander of the right wing of the army, who after many brave and sanguinary struggles overthrew the hitherto unconquered Octa, and for a time, at least, delivered the Fylde and other parts of Northumbria from the rule of the Saxons. This gallant soldier was the offspring of a union between a Roman warrior and a British maiden, who had established themselves in Manchester. The chieftain Ella, however, compelled the Britons to submission, and assumed the government over part of Northumbria. Clusters of Saxon huts, soon growing into villages, now sprang up on the soil of the Fylde, which under the wood-levelling and marsh-draining Romans had lost much of its swampy and forest characters and been transformed into a more habitable locality. We need have little hesitation in conjecturing that the valour displayed by the inhabitants of our county was greatly increased, and often rendered almost desperate, by the knowledge that if their land were subdued and occupied by the Saxons the key, if it may so be called, to their mountainous strongholds would be lost, and the line of communication between them impassably and irretrievably obstructed ; for the venerable Bede[1] tells us that a portion of the Britons fled to the hills and fells of Furness, and we are aware that a much larger share sought refuge amongst the mountains of Wales, lying to the south-west, and visible from the shores of the Fylde. Others escaped over to Armorica in France, and from them it acquired the name of Brittany. Additional evidence that Furness was peopled by the Britons, even for more than two centuries after the arrival of the Saxons, is to be found in the writings of Camden, who says :—"The Britons in Furness lived securely for a long time, relying upon those fortifications, wherewith nature had guarded them ; for that the Britons lived here in the 228th year after the coming of the Saxons, is plain from hence; that at that time Egfrid, the king of the Northumbrians, gave to St. Cuthbert the land called Cartmell, and all the Britons in it ; for so it is related in his life."

The Saxons were great idolaters, and soon crowded the country with their temples and images. The deities they worshipped have furnished us with names for the different days of the week, thus Sunday is derived from *Sunan* the sun, Monday from *Monan* the moon, Tuesday from *Tuisco* a German god, Wednesday from *Woden*, Thursday from *Thor* or *Thur*, Friday from *Friga*, and Saturday from *Seater*.

When the nation was once more at peace, all the towns and castles which had been damaged during the wars were repaired, and others, which had been destroyed, rebuilt. The Britons were brought by degrees to look with less disfavour on their conquerors, and as time progressed adopted their heathenish faith and offered up prayer at the shrines of the same idols, drifting back into

---

1. Bede died in A.D. 734. His chief work was an Ecclesiastical History.

darkness and forgetting or ignoring those true doctrines which, it is said, had been declared and expounded to them at the very commencement of the Christian era. According to Clemens Romanus and Theodoret, the Apostle Paul was one of the earliest preachers of the Gospel in Britain, but whatever amount of truth there may be in this statement, it is certain that at the Council of Arles in A.D. 314, and ten years later at that of Nicene, three British bishops were present. All traces of their former religion quickly vanished from amongst the native population of Lancashire under the pagan influence of their rulers ; and it was during that unhallowed age that Gregory, surnamed the Great, and afterwards pontiff, being attracted by the handsome appearance of some youths exposed for sale in the market-place at Rome, and finding, on inquiry, that they came from the kingdom of Deira, in Britain, determined to send over Augustine and Paulinus to Christianise the inhabitants. In 596 Augustine landed with forty missionaries on the coast of Kent, the king became a convert, and the new faith spread rapidly throughout the island. Thousands were baptised by Paulinus in the river Swale, then called the Northumbrian Jordan, and the waters of Ribble were also resorted to for the performance of similar ceremonies.

The advent of the Roman mission initiated a fresh epoch in the ecclesiastical history of the county, monasteries and religious houses sprang up in different parts, and at the consecration of the church and monastery of Ripon, lands bordering on the Ribble, in Hacmundernesse (Amounderness), in Gedene, and in Duninge were presented amongst other gifts to that foundation. Paulinus was created bishop of Northumbria in 627, and it is to his ministrations and pious example that the conversion of the inhabitants of the Fylde and vicinal territory is generally attributed. The Saxon Chronicle records, however, that in 565 Columba "came from Scotia (Ireland) to preach to the Picts." Columba was born at Garten, a village in county Donegal, and according to Selden and other learned writers, the religion professed by him and the Culdees, as the priests of his order were called, was strictly Presbyterian. Bede writes :—" They preached only such works of charity and piety as they could learn from prophetical, evangelical, and apostolic writings." Columba established a monastery at Iona. Dr. Giles states that " the ancient name of Iona was I or Hi, or Aoi, which was Latinised into Hyona, or Iona ; the common name of it now is I-colum-kill, the Island of Colum of the Cells." Bishop Turner affirms that "the lands in Amounderness, on the Ribble," were first presented to a Culdee abbot, named Eata, on the erection of a monastery at Ripon, but that before the building was finished he was dismissed and St. Wilfred made abbot of Ripon, sometime before 661. If the foregoing assertion be correct there is certain evidence that the Culdee doctrines were also promulgated in Lancashire, and doubtless in our own district, at that early date. Bede seems to support such an assumption when he states that the Ripon lands were originally granted to those who professed the creed of the Picts to build a monastery upon, and did not pass to St. Wilfred, bishop of Northumbria, until afterwards, in 705, when he re-edified the monastery. Whatever discrepancies may exist as to the exact period and manner in which Christianity was introduced or revived in the bosoms of our forefathers, there is ample and reliable proof that the majority of them had embraced the true faith about the middle of the seventh century, when churches were probably erected in the hamlets of Kirkham and St. Michael's-on-Wyre.

About the year 936 the Hundred of Amounderness was granted by Athelstan to the See of York :—"I, Athelstan, king of the Angles, etc., freely give to the Omnipotent God, and to the blessed Apostle Peter, at his church in the diocese of York, a certain section of land, not small in extent, in the place which the inhabitants call Amounderness," etc. The Hundred of Amounderness when this grant was made must have been pretty thickly peopled, for Athlestan states that he " purchased it at no small price," and land at that date was valued chiefly by the number of its residents. Here it will be convenient to observe that in some instances, as in that of Amounderness, the Hundreds acquired the additional titles of Wapentakes, and, in explanation of the origin of the term, we learn from "Thoresby Ducat Leodiens," that when a person received the government of a Wapentake, he was met, at the appointed time and usual place, by the elder portion of the inhabitants, and, after dismounting from his horse, he held up his spear and took a pledge of fealty from all according to the usual custom. Whoever came touched his spear with theirs, and by such contact of arms they were confirmed in one common interest. So from *wœpnu*, a weapon, and *tac*, a touch, or *taccare*, to confirm, the Hundreds were called *Wapentakes.* Traces of the above antique ceremony are still to be met with in the peculiar form of expression used when the tenantry and others are summoned by the manorial lords of Amounderness to attend their court-barons and court-leets.

The Heptarchy, established about 550, and consisting of seven sovereign states, was finally abolished in 830, and Egbert became king over the whole island. The province of Northumbria, more especially the Fylde and tracts of adjoining territory, had at that date been the scene of irregular and intermittent warfare during the previous forty years. Lancashire had suffered cruelly from the visitations of the Northmen, or Danes, who spared neither age, sex, nor condition in their furious sallies. In the years 787, 794, and 800, these pirates invaded the soil, ravaged the country, butchered the inhabitants, and on the last occasion shot Edmund, the king of the West Saxons, to death with arrows, because he refused to renounce the Christian faith and embrace the errors of heathenism. Egbert was no sooner seated on the throne than the Danes re-appeared off the coasts, and there can be little doubt that some of their bands made their way down the western shore of the island, entered the Bay of Morecambe, and, guided by the old Roman road near the mouth of the Wyre, pushed onwards into and through the heart of the Fylde, plundering and laying waste villages, hamlets, and every trace of agriculture in their path. "The name of the *Danes' Pad*," says Mr. Thornber, "given to the Roman agger is and ever will be an everlasting memorial of their ravages and atrocities in this quarter."[1] In addition it may be stated that many warlike relics of the Danes have been found along the road here indicated, and that the names of the Great and Little Knots in the channel of Wyre, opposite Fleetwood, were of pure Scandinavian derivation, and signified "round heaps," probably, of stones. These mounds were, during the formation of the harbour entrance, either destroyed or disfigured beyond recognition. Several localities, also, along the sea boundary of the Fylde bear Danish denomin-

1. History of Blackpool and Neighbourhood.

C

ations, which will be treated of hereafter. In 869 Lancashire was
again visited by a dreadful famine, and many of the people in every
part of the county fell victims either to the dearth itself or the fatal
disorders following in its train. Those who were fortunate enough
to escape the wholesale destruction of the scourge suffered so
severely from the merciless massacres of the Danes that at the
accession of Alfred the Great, in 871, our Hundred was but
sparsely populated. During the reign of that illustrious monarch
England was divided into counties, which again were subdivided
into Hundreds. Each Hundred was composed of ten Tithings,
and each Tithing of ten Freeholders and their families. When
this division of the kingdom was effected the south-western
portion of the old province of Northumbria was separated from
the remainder, and received the name of *Lonceshire*, from the
capital *Loncaster*, the castle on the *Lone*, or Lune. Alfred, as we
are told by his biographer Asser, did much to improve the
condition of his subjects both for peace and war ; referring to
their illiterate state, on his accession the king himself says :—
" When I took the kingdom there were very few on the south
side of the river Humber, the most improved portion of England,
who could understand their daily prayers in English, or translate
a letter from the Latin. I think they were not many beyond the
Humber. There were so few that I cannot, indeed, recollect one
single instance on the south of the Thames."[1] After suffering a
defeat at Wilton almost at the outset of his career, Alfred
surprised and overthrew the Danish camp at Eddington ;
Guthrum, their leader, and the whole of his followers were taken
prisoners, but afterwards liberated and permitted to colonise East
Anglia, and subsequently Northumbria, an act of clemency which
entailed most disastrous consequences upon the different sections
of the latter province. The Fylde now became the legalised
abode of numbers of the northern race, between whom and the
Saxon settlers perpetual strife was carried on ; in addition the
restless and covetous spirit of the new colonists constantly
prompted them to raids beyond the legitimate limits of their
territory, rebellions amongst themselves, and conspiracies against
the king ; insurrection followed insurrection, and it was not until

1. Alfred's Preface, p. 33.

Athelstan had inflicted a decisive blow upon the Danish forces, and brought the seditious province of Northumbria under his own more immediate dominion, that a short lull of peace was obtained. In the reign of his successor, however, they broke out again, and having been once more reduced to order, agreed to take the name of Christians, abjure their false gods, and live quietly henceforth. These promises, made to appease the anger of Edmund, were only temporarily observed, and their turbulent natures were never tranquilised until Canute, the first Danish king, ascended the throne of England in 1017. The Norse line of monarchs comprised only three, and terminated in 1041. Reverting to Athelstan and the Danes we find that about ten years after the subjugation of the latter in 926, as recorded in the Saxon Chronicle, Anlaf, a noted Danish chieftain, made a vigorous attempt to regain Northumbria. The site of the glorious battle where this ambitious project was overthrown and the army of Anlaf routed and driven to seek refuge in flight from the shore, on which they had but a short time previously landed exulting in a prospect of conquest and plunder, is a matter of dispute, and nothing authentic can be discovered concerning it beyond the fact that the name of the town or district where the forces met was Brunandune or Brunanburgh, and was situated in the province of Northumbria. The former orthography is used in Ethelwerd's Chronicle :—" A fierce battle was fought against the barbarians at Brunandune, whereof that fight is called great even to the present day ; then the barbarian tribes were defeated and domineer no longer ; they are driven beyond the ocean." Burn, in Thornton township, is one of the several rival localities which claim to have witnessed the sanguinary conflict. In the Domesday Survey, Burn was written *Brune*, and it also comprises a rising ground or *Dune*, which seem to imply some connection with *Brunandune*. From an ancient song or poem, bearing the date 937, it is clear that the battle lasted from sunrise to sunset, and that at night-fall Anlaf and the remnant of his followers, being utterly discomfited, escaped from the coast in the manner before described. This circumstance also upholds the pretentions of Burn, as it is situated close to the banks of the Wyre, and at a very short distance both from the Irish Sea and Morecambe Bay, as well as being in the

direct line of the road called Danes' Pad, the track usually taken
by the Northmen in former incursions into the Fylde and county.
In addition it may be mentioned that tradition affirms that a large
quantity of human bones were ploughed up in a field between
Burn and Poulton about a century ago.   Sharon Turner says :—
"It is singular that the position of this famous battle is not yet
ascertained.   The Saxon song says it was at Brunanburgh ;
Ethelwerd, a contemporary, names the place Brunandune.   These
of course are the same place, but where is it ? "[1]   Having done our
best to suggest or rather renew an answer presenting several
points worthy of consideration to Mr. Turner's query, we will,
before bidding farewell to the subject, give our readers a
translated extract from the old song to which allusion has been
made :—

Athelstan king,
Of earls the Lord,
Of Heroes the bracelet giver,
And his brother eke,
Edmund Atheling,
Life-long glory,
In battle won,
With edges of swords,
Near Brunanburgh.
The field was dyed
With warriors blood,
Since the sun, up
At morning tide,
Mighty planet,
Gilded o'er grounds,
God's candle bright,
The eternal Lord's,
Till the noble creature
Sank to her rest.
        *   *   *
West Saxons onwards
Throughout the day,
In numerous bands
Pursued the footsteps

Of the loathed nations.
They hewed the fugitives,
Behind, amain,
With swords mill-sharp.
Mercians refused not
The hard-hand play
To any heroes,
Who with Anlaf,
Over the ocean,
In the ship's bosom,
This land sought.
        *   *   *
There was made to flee
The Northmens' chieftain,
By need constrained,
To the ships prow
With a little band.
The bark drove afloat.
The king departed.
On the fallow flood'
His life he preserved.
The Northmen departed
In their nailed barks
On roaring ocean.

Athelstan, in order to encourage commerce and agriculture,
enacted that any of the humbler classes, called Ceorls, who had
crossed the sea thrice with their own merchandise, or who,

_____

1. History of the Anglo-Saxons.

individually, possessed five hides of land, a bell-house, a church, a kitchen, and a separate office in the king's hall, should be raised to the privileged rank of Thane. Sometime in the interval between the death of this monarch, in 941, and the arrival of William the Conqueror, the Hundred of Amounderness had been relinquished by the See of York, probably owing to frequent wars and disturbances having so ruined the country and thinned the inhabitants that the grant had ceased to be profitable.

During the earlier part of the Saxon era the clergy claimed one tenth or tithe of the produce of the soil, and exemption for their monasteries and churches from all taxations. These demands were resisted for a considerable period, but at length were conceded by Ethelwulf " for the honour of God, and for his own everlasting salvation." [1] In 1002, it is recorded in the Saxon Chronicle, that " the king (Ethelred) ordered all the Danish men who were in England to be slain, because it was made known to him that they would treacherously bereave him of his life, and after that have his kingdom without any gainsaying." In accordance with the royal mandate, which was circulated in secret, the Anglo-Saxon populace of the villages and farms of the Fylde, as elsewhere, rose at the appointed day upon the unprepared and unsuspecting Northmen, barbarously massacring old and young, male and female alike. Great must have been the slaughter in districts like our own, where from the Danes having been established for so many generations and its proximity to the coast and the estuaries of Wyre and Ribble, a safe landing and a friendly soil would be insured, and attract numbers of their countrymen from Scandinavia. The vengeance of Sweyn, king of Denmark, was speedy and complete ; the country ot Northumbria was laid waste, towns and hamlets were pillaged and destroyed, and for four years all that fire and sword, spurred on by hatred and revenge, could effect in depopulating and devastating a land was accomplished in Lancashire, and the neighbouring counties, by the enraged Dane. Half a century later than the events just narrated, earl Tosti, the brother ot Harold, who forfeited his life and kingdom to the Norman invaders on the field of Hastings, was chosen duke of Northumbria.

1. Saxon Chronicle.

The seat of the new ruler has not been discovered, but as far as his personal association with the Fylde is concerned it will be sufficient to state that almost on its boundaries, in the township of Preston, he held six hundred acres of cultivated soil, to which all the lands and villages of Amounderness were tributary.   As a governor Tosti proved himself both brutal and oppressive.   In a very limited space of time his tyrannical and merciless conduct goaded his subjects to rebellion, and with one consent they ejected him from his dukedom and elected earl Morcar in his stead, a step commended and confirmed by Harold, when the unjust severity of his brother had been made known to him.   Tosti embraced the Norman cause, and fell at the head of a Norwegian force in an engagement which took place at Standford a few months before the famous and eventful battle of Hastings.

We have now traced briefly the history of the Fylde through a period of eleven hundred years, and before entering on the era which dates from the accession of William the Conqueror, it will be well to review the traces and influences of the three dissimilar races, which have at different epochs usurped and settled on the territory of the old Setantii ; our reference is, of course, to the Romans, Anglo-Saxons, and Danes.   Under the first, great advances were made in civilisation ; clearings were effected in the woods, the marshes were trenched, and lasting lines of communication were established between the various stations and encampments.   The peaceful arts were cultivated, and agriculture made considerable progress, corn even, from some parts of Britain, being exported to the continent.   Remains of the Roman occupation are to be observed in the names of a few towns, as Colne and Lincoln, from *Colonia*, a Colony, also Chester and Lancaster, from *Castra*, a Camp, as well as in relics like those enumerated earlier.   The word "street" is derived from *Stratum*, a layer, covering, or pavement.   Their festival of Flora originated our May-day celebrations, and the paraphernalia of marriage, including the ring, veil, gifts, bride-cake, bridesmaids, and groomsmen, are Roman ; so also are the customs of strewing flowers upon graves, and wearing black in time of mourning. That the Romans had many stations in the Fylde is improbable, but that they certainly had one in the township of Kirkham is shown by the number and character of the relics found there.

This settlement would seem to have been a fairly populous one, if an opinion may be formed from the quantity of cinereal urns discovered at various times, in which had been deposited the cremated remains of Romans, who had spent their days and done good service in levelling the forests and developing the resources of the Fylde. The traffic over the Roman road through the district must have been almost continuous, to judge from the abundance of horse-shoes and other matters picked up along its route, and whether the harbour of the Setantii was on Wyre, Ribble, or elsewhere, it is evident from the course taken by the well constructed path that something of importance, say a favourable spot for embarcation or debarcation, attracted the inhabitants across the soil of the Fylde towards its north-west boundary. Now arises the question what was the boundary here denoted, and in reply we venture to suggest that the extent of this district, in both a northerly and westerly direction, was much greater in ancient days than it is in our own, and that the Lune formed its highest boundary, whilst its seaward limits, opposite Rossall, were carried out to a distance of nearly eight miles beyond the existing coast, and comprised what is now denominated Shell Wharf, a bank so shallowly covered at low water spring tides that huge boulders become visible all over it. Novel as such a theory may at first sight appear, there is much that can be advanced in support of it. From about the point in Morecambe Bay, near the foot of Wyre Lighthouse, where the stream of Wyre meets that of Lune at right angles, there is the commencement of a long deep channel, apparently continuous with the bed of the latter river as defined by its sandbanks, which extends out into the Irish Sea for rather more than seven miles west of the mouth of Morecambe Bay, at Rossall Point. This channel, called "Lune Deep," is described on the authorised charts as being in several places twenty-seven fathoms deep, in others rather less, and at its somewhat abrupt termination twenty-three fathoms. Throughout the entire length its boundaries are well and clearly marked, and its sudden declivity is described by the local mariners as being "steep as a house side." Regarding this curious phenomenon from every available point of view, it seems more probable to us that so long and perfect a channel was formed at an early period, when the river Lune was, as we conjecture, continued from its present mouth, at Heysham Point, through green plains, now the Bay of Lancaster, in the direction and to the distance of "Lune Deep," than that it was excavated by the current of Lune, as it exists to-day, after mingling with the waters of Morecambe and Wyre. The course and completeness of Wyre channel from Fleetwood, between the sandbanks called Bernard's Wharf and North Wharf, to its point of junction with the stream from Lancaster, prove satisfactorily that at one time the former river was a tributary of the Lune. Other evidence can be brought forward of the theory we are wishful to establish—that the southern portion of Morecambe Bay, from about Heysham Point, bearing the name of Lancaster Bay, as well as "Shell Wharf" was about the era of the Romans, dry or, at least, marshy land watered by the Wyre and Lune, the latter of which would open on the west coast immediately into the Irish Sea. If the reader refer to a map of Lancashire he will see at once that the smaller bay has many appearances of having been added to the larger one, and that its floor is formed by a continuous line of banks, uncovered each ebb tide and intersected only by the channels of Wyre and Lune. The Land Mark, at Rossall Point, has been removed several times owing to the incursions of the sea, and within the memory of the living generation wide tracts of soil, amounting to more than a quarter of a mile westward, have been swallowed up on that part of the coast, as the strong currents of the rising tides have swept into the bay; and in such manner would the land about the estuary of "Lune Deep," that is the original river of Lune, be washed away. As the encroachments of the sea progressed, the channel of the river would be gradually widened and deepened to the present dimensions of the "Deep"; the stream of Wyre would by degrees be brought more immediately under the tidal influence, and in proportion as the Lune was absorbed into the bay, so would its tributary lose its shallowness and insignificance, and become expanded to a more important and navigable size. About the time that "Lune Deep" had ceased to exist as a river, and become part of the bay, the overcharged banks of the Wyre would have yielded up their super-abundance of waters over the districts now marked by Bernard's Wharf and North Wharf, and subsequently, as the waves continued their incursions, inundations would increase, until finally the whole territory, forming the site of Lancaster Bay, would be submerged and appropriated by the rapacious hosts of Neptune. The "Shell Wharf" would be covered in a manner exactly similar to the more recently lost fields off Rossall ; and as illustrations of land carried away from the west coast in that neighbourhood, may be instanced a farm called Fenny, at Rossall, which was removed back from threatened destruction by the waves at least four times within the last fifty years, when its re-building was abandoned, and its site soon swept over by the billows ; also the village of Singleton Thorp, which occupied the locality marked by "Singleton Skeer" off Cleveleys until 1555, when it was destroyed by an irruption of the sea. Numerous other instances in which the coast line has been altered and driven eastward, between Rossall Point and the mouth of Ribble, during both actually and comparatively modern days might be cited, but the above are sufficient to support our view of the former connection of "Shell Wharf" with the main-land, and its gradual submersion. If on the map, the Bay of Lancaster be detached from that of Morecambe, the latter still retains a most imposing aspect, and its identity with the Moricambe Æstuarium of Ptolemy is in no way interfered with or rendered less evident. The foregoing, as our antiquarian readers will doubtless have surmised, is but a prelude to something more, for it is our purpose to endeavour to disturb the forty years of quiet repose enjoyed by the Portus Setantiorum on the banks of the Wyre and hurl it far into the Irish Sea, to the very limits of the "Lune Deep," where, on the original estuary of the river Lune, we believe to be its legitimate home. No locality, as yet claiming to be the site of the ancient harbour, accords so well with the distances given by Ptolemy. Assuming the Dee and the Ribble to represent respectively, as now generally admitted, the Seteia Æstuarium and the Belisama Æstuarium, the Portus Setantiorum should lie about seven miles[1] to the west and twenty-five to the north of the Belisama. The position of the "Lune Deep" termination is just about seven miles to the west of the estuary of the Ribble, but is, like most other places whose stations have been mentioned by Ptolemy, defective in its latitudinal measurement according to

1. Ptolemy gives the longitude as ten minutes, but at such a height a minute would scarcely represent a mile.

the record left by that geographer, being only fifteen instead of twenty-five miles north of the Belisama or Ribble estuary. Rigodunum, or Ribchester, is fully thirty miles to the east of the spot where it is wished to locate the Portus, and thus approaches very nearly to the forty-mile measurement of Ptolemy, whose distances, as just hinted, were universally excessive. As an instance of such error it may be stated that the longitude, east from Ferro, of Morecambe Bay or Estuary given by Ptolemy, is 3° 40' in excess of that marked on modern maps of ancient Britannia, and if the same over-plus be allowed in the longitude of the Portus Setantiorum a line drawn in accordance, from north to south, would pass across the west extremity of the "Lune Deep," showing that its distance from the Bay corresponds pretty accurately with that of the Portus from the Morecambe Æstuarium as geographically fixed by Ptolemy. In describing the extent and direction of the Roman road, or Danes' Pad, in his "History of Blackpool and Neighbourhood," Mr. Thornber writes: —" Commencing at the *terminus*, we trace its course from the Warren, near the spot named the 'Abbot's walk'; " but that the place thus indicated was not the *terminus*, in the sense of *end* or *origin*, is proved by the fact that shortly after the publication of this statement, the workmen engaged in excavating for a sea-wall foundation in that vicinity came upon the road in the sand on the very margin of the Warren. Hence it would seem that the path was continued onwards over the site of the North Wharf sand bank, either towards the foot of Wyre where its channel joins that of Lune, and where would be the original mouth of the former river, or, as we think more probable, towards the Lune itself, and along its banks westward to the estuary of the stream, as now marked by the termination of " Lune Deep." The Wyre, during the period it existed simply as a tributary of the Lune, a name very possibly compounded from the Celtic *al*, chief, and *aun*, or *un*, contractions of *afon*, a river, must have been a stream of comparatively slight utility in a navigable point of view, and even to this day its seaward channel from Fleetwood is obstructed by two shallows, denominated from time out of mind the Great and Little Fords. The Lune, or "Chief River," on the contrary, was evidently, from its very title, whether acquired from its relative position to its tributary, or from its favourable comparison with other rivers of the neighbourhood, which is less likely, regarded by the natives as a stream of no insignificant magnitude and importance. As far as its navigability was concerned the Portus may have been placed on its banks near to the junction of Wyre, but the distances of Ptolemy, which agree pretty fairly, as shown above, with the location of the Portus on the west extremity of the present "Lune Deep," are incompatible with such a station as this one for the same harbour. The collection of coins discovered near Rossall may imply the existence in early days of a settlement west of that shore, and many remains of the Romans may yet be mingled with the sand and shingle for centuries submerged by the water of the still encroaching Irish Sea. Leaving this long-argued question of the real site of the Portus Setantiorum, in which perhaps the patience of our readers has been rather unduly tried, and soliciting others to test more thoroughly the merits of the ideas here thrown out, we will hasten to examine the traces of the Anglo-Saxons and Danes.

Many, in fact most, of the towns and villages of the Fylde were founded by the Anglo-Saxons, and have retained the names, generally in a modified form, bestowed upon them by that race, as instance Singleton, Lytham, Mythorp, all of which have Saxon terminals signifying a dwelling, village, or enclosure. The word *hearb*, genitive *hearges*, indicates in the vocabulary of the same people a heathen temple or place of sacrifice, and as it is to be traced in the endings of Goosnargh, and Kellamergh, there need be no hesitation in surmising that the barbarous and pagan rites of the Saxons were celebrated there, before their conversion to Christianity. Ley, or lay, whether at the beginning of a name, as in Layton, or at end, as in Boonley, signifies a field, and is from the Saxon *leag*; whilst Hawes and Holme imply, respectively, a group of thorps or hamlets, and a river island. Breck, Warbreck, and Larbreck, derive their final syllables from the Norse *brecka*, a gentle rise; and from that language comes also the terminal *by*, in Westby, Ribby, and other places, as well as the *kirk* in Kirkham, all of which point out the localities occupied by the Danes, or Norsemen. Lund was doubtless the site of a sacred grove of these colonists and the scene of many a dark and cruel ceremony, its derivation being from the ancient Norse *lundr*, a consecrated grove, where such rites were performed.

At the present time it is difficult, if indeed possible, to determine from what races our own native population has descended, and the subject is one which has provoked more than a little controversy. Palgrave, in his "History of the Anglo-Saxons," says :—"From the Ribble in Lancashire, or thereabouts, up to the Clyde, there existed a dense population composed of Britons, who preserved their national language and customs, agreeing in all respects with the Welsh of the present day ; so that even to the tenth century the ancient Britons still inhabited the greater part of the west coast of the island, however much they had been compelled to yield to the political supremacy of the Saxon invaders." Mr. Thornber states that he has been "frequently told by those who were reputed judges" that the manners, customs, and dialect of the Fylde partook far more of the Welsh than of the Saxon, and that this was more perceptible half a century ago than now (1837). "The pronunciation," he adds, "of the words—laughing, toffee, haughendo, etc., the Shibboleth of the Fylde—always reminds me of the deep gutterals of the Welsh,[1] and the frequent use of a particular oath is, alas ! too common to both." Another investigator, Dr. Robson, holds an entirely different opinion, and maintains in his paper on Lancashire and Cheshire, that there is no sufficient foundation for the common belief that the inhabitants of any portion of those counties have been at any time either Welsh, or Celtic ; and that the Celtic tribes at the earliest known period were confined to certain districts, which may be traced, together with the extent of their dominions, by the Celtic names of places both in Wales and Cornwall. From another source we are informed that at the date of the Roman abdication the original Celtic population would have dwindled down to an insignificant number acting as serfs and tillers of the land, and not likely to have much influence upon future generations. Mr. Hardwick, in his History of Preston, writes :—"Few women would accompany the Roman colonists, auxillaries, and soldiers into Britain ; hence it is but rational to conclude, that during the long period of their dominion, numerous intermarriages with the

---

1. The Welsh language is the oldest of all living languages, and is of Celtic origin, being in fact the tongue spoken by the ancient Britons but little altered by modern innovations.

native population would take place." Admitting the force of reasoning brought forward by the last authority, it can readily be conceived that the purity of the aboriginal tribes would in a great measure be destroyed at an early epoch, and that subsequent alliances with the Anglo-Saxons, Danes, and Normans, have rendered all conjectures as to the race of forefathers to which the inhabitants of the Fylde have most claim practically valueless.

The dense forests with which our district in the earliest historic periods abounded must have been well supplied with beasts of chase, whereon the Aborigines exercised their courage and craft, and from which their clothing and, in a great measure, their sustenance were derived. The large branching horns of the Wild Deer have been found in the ground at Larbrick, and during the excavations for the North Union and East Lancashire Railway Bridges over the Ribble, in 1838 and 1846 respectively, numerous remains of the huge ox, called the *Bos primigenius*, and the *Bos longifrons*, or long-faced ox, as well as of wild boars and bears, were raised from beneath the bed of the river, so that it is extremely likely that similar relics of the brute creation are lying deeply buried in our soil. Such a supposition is at least warranted by the discovery, half-a-century ago, of the skull and short upright horns of a stag and those of an ox, of a breed no longer known, at the bottom of a marl pit near Rossall. Bones and sculls, chiefly those of deer and oxen, have been taken from under the peat in all the mosses, and two osseous relics, consisting each of skull and horns, of immense specimens of the latter animal, have been dug up at Kirkham. In the "Reliquiæ Diluvianæ" of Mr. Buckland is a figure of the scull of a rhinoceros belonging to the antediluvian age, and stated to have been discovered beneath a moss in Lancashire.

CHAPTER II.

WHEN the battle of Hastings, in 1066, had terminated in favour of William the Conquerer, and placed him on the throne of England, he indulged his newly acquired power in many acts of tyranny towards the vanquished nation, subjecting the old nobility to frequent indignities, weakening the sway of the Church, and impoverishing the middle and lower classes of the community. This harsh policy spread dissatisfaction and indignation through all ranks of the people, and it was not long before rebellion broke out in the old province of Northumbria. The Lancastrians and others, under the earls Morcar and Edwin, rose up in revolt, slew the Norman Baron set over them, and were only reduced to order and submission when William appeared on the scene at the head of an overwhelming force. The two earls escaped across the frontier to Scotland, and for some inexplicable reason were permitted to retain their possessions in Lancashire and elsewhere, while the common insurgents were afterwards treated with great severity and cruelty by their Norman rulers. Numerous castles were now erected in the north of England to hold the Saxons in subjection, and guard against similar outbreaks in future. Those at Lancaster and Liverpool were built by a Norman Baron of high position, named Roger de Poictou, the third son of Robert de Montgomery, earl of Arundel and Shrewsbury. When William divided the conquered territory amongst his followers, the Honor[1] of Lancaster and the Hundred

---

1. An Honor has a castle or mansion, and consists of demesnes and services, to which a number of manors and lordships, with all their appurtenances and other regalities, are annexed. In an Honor an Honourable Court is held once every year at least.

of Amounderness fell, amongst other gifts, amounting in all to
three hundred and ninety-eight manors,[1] to that nobleman, and,
as he resided during a large portion of his time at the castle
erected on the banks of the Lune, our district would receive a
greater share of attention than his more distant possessions.

After the country had been restored to peace, William determined to institute an inquiry into the condition and resources of
his kingdom. The records of the survey were afterwards bound
up in two volumes, which received the name of the Domesday
Book, from *Dome*, a census, and *Boc*, a book.

The king's commands to the investigators were, according to
the Saxon Chronicle, to ascertain—"How many hundreds of
hydes were in each shire, what lands the king himself had, and
what stock there was upon the land ; or what dues he ought to
have by the year from each shire. Also he commissioned them
to record in writing, how much land his archbishops had and his
diocesan bishops, and his abbots and his earls ; what or how much
each man had, who was an occupier of land in England, either in
land or stock, and how much money it was worth. So very
narrowly, indeed, did he commission them to trace it out, that
there was not one single hide, nor a yard of land ; nay, moreover
(it is shameful to tell, though he thought it no shame to do it),
not even an ox, nor a cow, nor a swine, was there left that was
not set down in his writ." The examination was commenced in
1080, and six years afterwards the whole of the laborious task was
accomplished. In this compilation the county of Lancaster is
never once mentioned by name, but the northern portion is joined
to the Yorkshire survey, and the southern to that of Cheshire.

The following is a translation of that part of Domesday Book
relating to the Fylde :—

AGEMUNDERNESSE UNDER EVRVIC—SCIRE (YORKSHIRE).

Poltun (Poulton), two carucates;[2] *Rushale* (Rossall), two carucates; *Brune* (Burn),
two carucates ; *Torentun* (Thornton), six carucates; *Carlentun* (Carleton), four

1. A Manor is composed of demesne and services, to which belong a three
weeks Court, where the freeholders, being tenants of the manor, sit covered, and
give judgement in all suits that are pleading. To every manor a Court Baron is
attached.

2. A *carucate* was generally about one hundred acres of arable soil, or land in
cultivation ; this word superseded the Saxon *hyde*, which signified the same thing.

carucates; *Meretun* (Marton), six carucates; *Staininghe* (Staining), six carucates.
Biscopham (Bispham), eight carucates; *Latun* (Layton), six carucates.

Chicheham (Kirkham), four carucates; *Salewic* (Salwick), one carucate; *Cliftun* (Clifton), two carucates; *Newtune* (Newton-with-Scales), two carucates; *Frecheltune* (Freckleton), four carucates; *Rigbi* (Ribby-with-Wray), six carucates; *Treueles* (Treales), two carucates; *Westbi* (Westby), two carucates; *Pluntun* (Plumptons), two carucates; *Widetun* (Weeton), three carucates; *Pres* (Preese), two carucates; *Midehope* (Mythorp), one carucate; *Wartun* (Warton), four carucates; *Singletun* (Singleton), six carucates; *Greneholf* (Greenhalgh), three carucates; *Hameltune* (Hambleton), two carucates.

Lidun (Lytham), two carucates.

Michelescherche (St. Michael's-on-Wyre), one carucate; *Pluntun* (Wood Plumpton) five carucates; *Rodecliff* (Upper Rawcliffe), two carucates; *Rodecliff* (Middle Rawcliffe), two carucates; a third *Rodecliff* (Out Rawcliffe), three carucates; *Eglestun* (Ecclestons), two carucates; *Edeleswic* (Elswick), three carucates; *Inscip* (Inskip), two carucates; *Sorbi* (Sowerby), one carucate.

All these vills belong to *Prestune* (Preston); and there are three churches (in Amounderness). In sixteen of these vills[1] there are but few inhabitants—but how many there are is not known.

The rest are waste. *Roger de Poictou* had [the whole].

When we read the concluding remark—"The rest are waste," and observe the insignificant proportion of the many thousands of acres comprised in the Fylde at that time under cultivation, we are made forcibly cognizant of the truly deplorable condition to which the district had been reduced by ever-recurring warfare through a long succession of years. There is no guide to the number of the inhabitants, excepting, perhaps, the existence of only three churches in the whole Hundred of Amounderness, and this can scarcely be admitted as certain evidence of the paucity of the population, as in the harassed and unsettled state in which they lived it is not very probable that the people would be much concerned about the public observances of religious ceremonials or services. The churches alluded to were situated at Preston, Kirkham, and St. Michael's-on-Wyre. The parish church at Poulton was the next one erected, and appears to have been standing less than ten years after the completion of the Survey, for Roger de Poictou, when he founded the priory of St. Mary, Lancaster, in 1094, endowed it with—"Pulton in Agmundernesia, and whatsoever belonged to it, and the *church*, with one carucate of land, and all other things belonging to it."[2] The terminal paragraph

1. The whole of the *vills* of Amounderness, here signified, amounted to sixty-one.
2. Regist. S. Mariæ de Lanc.

of the foundation-charter of the monastery states that Geoffrey, the sheriff, having heard of the liberal grants of Roger de Poictou, also bestowed upon it—"the tithes of Biscopham, whatever he had in Lancaster, some houses, and an orchard." It is difficult to determine whether a church existed in the township of Bispham at that date or not, but as no such edifice is included in the above list of benefactions, we are inclined to believe that it was not erected until later. The earliest mention of it occurs in the reign of Richard I., 1189 to 1199, when Theobald Walter quitclaimed to the abbot of Sees "all his right in the advowson of Pulton, with the *church of Biscopham*."[1]

The rebellious and ungrateful conduct of Roger de Poictou ultimately led to his banishment out of the country, and the forfeiture of the whole of his extensive possessions to the crown. The Hundred of Amounderness was conveyed by the King on the 22nd of April, 1194, being the fifth year of his reign, to Theobald Walter, the son of Hervens, a Norman who had accompanied the Conqueror. "Be it known," says the document, "that we give and confirm to Theobald Walter the whole of Amounderness with its appurtenances by the service of three Knights' fees, namely, all the domain thereto belonging, all the services of the Knights who hold of the fee of Amounderness by Knight's service, all the service of the Free-tenants of Amounderness, all the Forest of Amounderness, with all the Venison, and all the Pleas of the Forest." His rights "are to be freely and quietly allowed," continues the deed, "in wood and plain, in meadows and pastures, in highways and footpaths, in waters and mills, in mill-ponds, in fish-ponds and fishings, in peat-lands, moors and marshes, in wreck of the sea, in fairs and markets, in advowsons and chapelries, and in all liberties and free customs." Amongst the barons of Lancashire given in the MSS. of Percival is— "Theobald Walter, baron of Weeton and Amounderness," but, as Weeton never existed as a barony, it is clear that the former title is an error. The "Black Book of the Exchequer," the oldest record after the "Domesday Book," has entered in it the tenants and fees *de veteri feoffamento*[2] and *de novo feoffamento*,[3] and amongst others is a statement that Theobald Walter held

1. Regist. S. Mariæ de Lanc.   2. Held in the reign of Henry I., 1100-1135.
    3. Held in the reigns of Stephen and Henry II., 1135-1189.

D

Amounderness by the service of one Knight, thus the later charter, just quoted, must be regarded as a confirmation of a previous grant, and not as an original donation. He was an extensive founder of monastic houses, and amongst the abbeys established by him was that of Cockersand, which he endowed with the whole Hay of Pylin (Pilling) in Amounderness. He was appointed sheriff of the county of Lancaster by Richard I. in 1194, and retained the office until the death of that monarch five years afterwards. His son, Theobald, married Maud, sister to the celebrated Thomas à Becket, archbishop of Canterbury, and assumed the title of his office when created *Chief Butler* of Ireland. The family of the same name which inhabited Rawcliffe Hall until that property was confiscated through the treasonable part played by Henry Butler and his son Richard in the rebellion of 1715, was directly descended from Theobald Walter-Butler. The Butlers of Kirkland, the last of whom, Alexander Butler, died in 1811, and was succeeded by a great-nephew, were also representatives of the ancient race of Walter, and preserved the line unbroken. Theobald Walter, the elder, died in 1206, and Amounderness reverted to the crown.

Richard I. a few years before his death presented the Honor of Lancaster to his brother, the earl of Moreton, who subsequently became King John, and it is asserted that this nobleman, when residing at the castle of Lancaster, was occasionally a guest at Staining Hall, and that during one of his visits he so admired the strength and skill displayed by a person called Geoffrey, and surnamed the Crossbowman, that he induced him to join his retinue. How far truth has been embellished and disguised by fiction in this traditional statement we are unable to conjecture, but there are reasonable grounds for believing that the story is not entirely supposititious, for the earl of Moreton granted to Geoffrey l'Arbalistrier, or the Crossbowman, who is said to have been a younger brother of Theobald Walter, senior, six carucates of land in Hackinsall-with-Preesall, and a little later, the manor of Hambleton, most likely as rewards for military or other services rendered to that nobleman. John, as earl of Moreton, appears to have gained the affection and respect of the inhabitants of Lancashire by his liberal practices during his long sojourns in their midst. He granted a charter to the knights, thanes, and freeholders of the county, whereby they and their heirs, without challenge or interference from him and his heirs, were permitted to fell, sell, and give, at their pleasure, their forest woods, without being subject to the forest regulations, and to hunt and take hares, foxes, rabbits, and all kinds of wild beasts, excepting stags, hinds, roebucks, and wild hogs, in all parts within his forests beyond the desmesne hays of the county.[1]   On ascending the throne, however, he soon aroused the indignation of all sections of his subjects by his meanness, pride, and utter inability to govern the kingdom.   His indolent habits excited the disgust of a nobility, whose regular custom was to breakfast at five and dine at nine in the morning, as proclaimed by the following popular Norman proverb :—

> Lever à cinque, diner à neuf,
> Souper à cinque, coucher à neuf,
> Fait vivre d'ans nonante et neuf.[2]

Eventually his evil actions and foolish threats so incensed the nation, that the barons, headed by William, earl of Pembroke, compelled him, in 1215, to sign the Magna Charta, a code of laws embodying two important principles—the general rights of the freemen, and the limitation of the powers of both king and pope.

About that time it would have been almost, if not quite, impossible to have decided or described what was the national language of the country.   The services at the churches were read in Latin, the aristocracy indulged only in Norman-French, whilst the great mass of the people spoke a language, usually denominated Saxon or English, but which had been so mutilated and altered by additions from various sources that the ancient "Settlers on the shores of the German Ocean" would scarcely have recognized it as their native tongue.   Each division of the kingdom had its peculiar dialect, very much as now, and from the remarks of a southern writer, named Trevisa, it must be inferred that the *patois* of our own district, which he would include in the old province of Northumbria,[3] was far from either elegant or

---

1. Duchy Rolls, Rot. f. 12.
2. To rise at five, to dine at nine, to sup at five, to bed at nine, makes a man live to ninety-nine.
3. Although England had been divided into counties the different districts were for long classified under the names of the old provinces or petty kingdoms of the Heptarchy.

musical. " Some," he says, " use strange gibbering, chattering, waffling, and grating ; then the Northumbre's tongue is so sharp, flitting, floyting, and unshape, that we Southron men may not understand that language." Such a list of curious and uncomplimentary epithets inclines us at first sight to doubt the strict impartiality of their author, but when it is remembered that, in spite of the greatly increased opportunities for education and facilities for intercommunion amongst the different classes, the provincialisms of some of our own peasantry would be utterly unintelligible to many of us at the present day, we are constrained to admit that Trevisa may have had just reason for his remarks.

In 1268 the Honor of Lancaster, the Wapentake of Amounderness, and the manors of Preston, Ribby-with-Wray, and Singleton were given by Henry III. to his son Edmund Crouchback, and in addition the king published an edict forbidding the sheriffs of neighbouring counties to enter themselves, or send, or permit their bailiffs to enter or interfere with anything belonging to the Honor of Lancaster, or to the men of that Honor, unless required to do so by his son. Edmund was also created earl of Lancaster, and became the founder of that noble house, whose possessions and power afterwards attained to such magnitude as to place its representative, Henry IV., upon the throne, although nearer descendants of his grandfather Edward III. were still living.

We have now arrived at the unsettled era, comprising the reigns of the three Edwards and Richard II., and during the whole of the time these monarchs wore the crown, a period of one hundred and twenty-six years, the nation was engaged in continual wars—with the Welsh under Llewellyn, the Scotch under Bruce and Wallace, and the French under Philip. The reign of Richard II. was additionally agitated by the insurrection of Wat Tyler. Looking at that long uninterrupted season of excitement, we cease to wonder at the riotous and disorganized state into which society was thrown. The rulers, whether local and subordinate, or those of a higher grade, were too actively engaged in forwarding the efficiency of the army, to devote much attention to the welfare and proper government of the people. Crimes and disturbances were allowed to pass unpunished, and evil-doers, being thus encouraged to prosecute their unlawful purposes, carried their outrages to the very confines of open rebellion against all power and order. It was not until such a dangerous climax had been reached that a commission, consisting of the following judges, Peter de Bradbate, Edmund Deyncourt, William de Vavasour, John de Island, and Adam de Middleton, was appointed to deal summarily and severely with all offenders in the counties of Lancaster and Westmoreland. During those troublesome times Sir Adam Banastre and a number of others assaulted Ralph de Truno, prior of Lancaster, and his train of attendants at Poulton-le-Fylde, seized and carried him off to Thornton, where they brutally ill-used and finally imprisoned him. An inquiry into the disgraceful proceeding was instituted by order of Edward I., but the result has not been preserved, at least no record of it has as yet been discovered amongst any of the ancient documents concerning this county. Leyland, who was antiquary to Henry VIII., alluding to the death of the disorderly knight, says,—"Adam Banastre, a bachelar of Lancastershire, moved ryot agayne Thomas of Lancaster by kraft of kynge Edward II., but he was taken and behedid by the commandment of Thomas of Lancaster." The first part of the quotation has reference to a quarrel between the earl of Lancaster and Sir Adam, who for his own aggrandizement and to curry favour with the king, as well as to divert the attention of that monarch from his own misdeeds, declared that Thomas of Lancaster wished to interfere with the royal prerogative in the choice of ministers; and, professedly, to punish such presumption he invaded the domains of that nobleman. An encounter took place in the valley of the Ribble, not far from Preston, in which the followers of Sir Adam were vanquished and put to flight. Their leader secreted himself in a barn on his own lands, but, being discovered by the soldiers of his opponent, was dragged forth and beheaded with a sword. Subjoined is an account of a disturbance which occurred at Kirkham during the same period, transcribed from the Vale Royal[1] register :—" A narrative of proceedings in a dispute between the abbot of Vale Royal, and Sir Will. de Clifton, knt., respecting the tithes in the manor of Clifton and Westby, in the parish of Kirkham, A.D. 1337, in the time of Peter's abbacy.

1. Vale Royal, Cheshire, obtained a grant of the manor, etc., of Kirkham in 1296.

The charges alleged against Sir William state, that he had
obtained twenty marks[1] due to the abbot ; had forcibly obstructed
the rector in the gathering of tithes within the manor of Clifton
and Westby ; seized his loaded wain, and brought ridicule on his
palfrey : that he had also burst, with his armed retainers, into the
parish church of Kirkham, and thereby deterred his clerks from
the performance of divine service ; had prevented the parishioners
from resorting to the font for the rite of baptism ; and that,
having seized on Thomas, the clerk of the abbot of Vale Royal,
he had inflicted on him a flagellation in the public streets of
Preston. After a complaint, made to the abbot of Westminster, a
conservator of the rights and privileges of the order to which
Vale Royal belonged, Sir William confessed his fault and threw
himself on the mercy of the abbot of the Cheshire convent, who
contented himself, after receiving a compensation for his rector's
losses, with an oath from the refractory knight, that he would in
future maintain and defend the privileges of the abbey, and would
bind himself in forty shillings to offer no further violence to the
unfortunate secretary of the abbot."

During the reign of Edward III., Henry, earl of Lancaster, was
created duke of the county with the consent of the prelates and
peers assembled in parliament.   This nobleman, whose pious and
generous actions earned for him the title of the "Good duke of
Lancaster," received a mandate from the king during the war with
France, when there were serious apprehensions of an invasion by
that nation, to arm all the lancers on his estates, and to set a strict
watch over the seacoasts of Lancashire.   These precautions,
however, proved unnecessary, as the French made no attempt to
cross the channel.   In his will, bearing the date 1361, (the year of
his death), Duke Henry bequeathed the Wappentakes or Hundreds
of Amounderness, Lonsdale, and Leyland, with other estates, to
his daughter Blanche, who had married John of Gaunt, the earl
of Richmond and fourth son of Edward III.   John of Gaunt
succeeded to the dukedom in right of his wife.

"In the "Testa de Nevill'," a register extending from 1274 to
1327, and containing, amongst other matters, a list of the fees and
serjeanties holden of the king and the churches in his gift, it is

1. £13 6s. 3d.

stated under the latter heading :—"St. Michael upon Wyre ; the son of Count Salvata had it by gift of the present king, and he says, that he is elected into a bishoprick, and that the church is vacant, and worth 30 marks[1] per an. Kyrkeham ; King John gave two parts of it to Simon Blundel, on account of his custody of the son and heir of Theobald Walter. Worth 80 marks[2] per an." In another part of these records it is named that Richard de Frekelton held fees in chief in Freckleton, Newton, and Eccleston ; Alan de Singilton, in Singleton, Freckleton, Newton, and Elswick ; and Adam de Merton, in Marton ; also that Fitz Richard held serjeanties in Singleton, by serjeanty of Amounderness.

The earliest intimation of members being returned to represent our own district, in conjunction with the other divisions of the county, is to the parliament of Edward I., assembled in 1295, when Matthew de Redmand and John de Ewyas were elected knights of the shire for Lancaster, and in his report the sheriff adds—"There is no city in the county of Lancaster." The members of parliament in 1297 were Henricus de Kigheley and Henricus le Botyler ; in 1302 Willielmus de Clifton and Gilbertus de Singleton ; and in 1304 Willielmus de Clifton and Willielmus Banastre. Henricus le Botyler, or Butler, belonged to the family of the Butlers of Rawcliffe ; Gilbertus de Singleton was probably connected with the Singletons whose descendants resided at Staining Hall ; Willielmus de Clifton was an ancestor of the Cliftons of Lytham, and here it may be stated that Lancashire was represented in 1383 by Robt. de Clifton, of Westby, and Ric'us de Hoghton ; and in 1844 by J. Wilson Patten, now Lord Winmarleigh, and Jno. Talbot Clifton, esq., of Lytham Hall. Thos. Henry Clifton, esq., son of the last gentleman, and the Hon. F. A. Stanley are the present members for North Lancashire.

During the Scottish wars of Edward III., John de Coupland, of Upper Rawcliffe, valiantly captured David II., king of Scotland, at the battle of Durham, and although that monarch dashed out Coupland's teeth and used every means to incite the latter to slay him, the brave soldier restrained his wrath and delivered up his

---

1. £20 0s. 0d.   2. £53 6s. 8d.

prisoner alive. For that signal service Edward rewarded him with a grant of £500 per annum, until he could receive an equivalent in land wherever he might choose, and created him a knight banneret.[1] "I have seen," says Camden, "a charter of King Edward III., by which he advanced John Coupland to the state of a banneret in the following words, because in a battle fought at Durham he had taken prisoner David the Second, King of Scots :—'Being willing to reward the said John, who took David de Bruis prisoner, and frankly delivered him unto us, for the deserts of his honest and valiant service, in such sort as others may take example by his precedent to do us faithful service in time to come, we have promoted the said John to the place and degree of a banneret ; and, for the maintenance of the same state, we have granted, for us and our heirs, to the same John, five hundred pounds by the year, to be received by him and his heirs," etc.

For some time after a truce had been concluded with Scotland, the war, in which the incident narrated occurred, continued with little abatement, and in 1322 this county with others was called upon to raise fresh levies. These constant drains upon its resources, and the devastations committed by riotous companies of armed men, so impoverished our district that the inhabitants of Poulton forwarded a petition to the Pope, praying him to forego his claims upon their town on account of the deplorably distressed condition to which they had been reduced. The taxations of all churches in the Fylde were greatly lowered in consideration of the indigency of the people ; that of Kirkham from 240 marks per annum to 120, and the others in like proportion. Further evidence of the poverty of this division may be gathered from a census taken in 1377, which states, amongst other things, that— "There is no town worthy of notice anywhere in the whole of the county " ; and again, twenty years later, when a loan was raised to meet the enormous expenditure of the country, Lancashire furnished no contributors.

In 1389, during the reign of Richard II., it was enacted, with a

---

1. Knights banneret were so called from a privilege they possessed of carrying a small banner. This privilege and the title of " Sir" were conferred as a reward for distinguished military service, and were usually accompanied by a pecuniary provision.

view to the preservation and improvement of the salmon fisheries throughout the kingdom, "that no young salmon be taken or destroyed by nets, at mill-dams or other places, from the middle of April to the Nativity of St. John Baptist"; and special reference is made to this neighbourhood in the following sentence of the bill :—"It is ordained and assented, that the waters of Lone, Wyre, Mersee, Ribbyl, and all other waters in the county of Lancaster, be put in defence, as to the taking of Salmons, from Michaelmas Day to the Purification of our Lady (2nd of February), and in no other time of the year, because that salmons be not seasonable in the said waters in the time aforesaid ; and in the parts where such rivers be, there shall be assigned and sworn good and sufficient conservators of this statute." The foregoing is the earliest regulation of the kind, and the wisdom and utility of its provisions are evinced by the existence of similar measures at the present day.

From the annals of the Duchy may be learnt some interesting particulars relative to changes in ownership at that period of certain portions of the territory comprised in the Fylde. In 1380 John of Gaunt, duke of Lancaster, issued a "precept to the Escheator to give seisin of the Lands of William Botyler in Layton Magna, Layton Parva, Bispham, Warthebrek, and Great Merton," etc. ; and shortly afterwards gave orders to "seize the Lands of William Botyler." In 1385 mandates were issued by the same nobleman to his Escheator to "seize into the Hands of the King and himself the Lands of Thomas Banastre, (deceased, 1384), in Ethelswyk, Frekculton, Claughton in Amoundernes, Syngleton Parva, Hamylton, Stalmyn," etc. ; also those of "Emund Banastre, (deceased, 1384), in Wodeplumpton, Preston," etc. In the Rolls the subjoined entries also occur :—

1381.

GRANTORS.	GRANTEES.	MATTERS AND PREMISES.
John Botyler, Knt.	Henry de Bispham, Richard de Carleton, Chaplains.	Enrolment of the Grant of the Manors of Great Layton, Little Layton, Bispham, and Wardebrek ; lands in Great Merton, and the whole Lordship of Merton Town.
Henry de Bispham, Richard de Carleton.	John Botyler, Knt., and Alice his wife.	Enrolment of the Grant of the above Manors, Lands, and Lordship, in Fee Tail special.

1382.

Robert de Wasshyngton.	William de Hornby, Parson of St. Michael-upon-Wyre, and William le Ducton.	Enrolment of Grant of Lands, etc., in Carleton in Amounderness, for a Rose Rent per ann. 8 years, and increased rent £20 per ann.

There is nothing of interest or importance to recount affecting the Fylde from the death of Richard II. until the year 1455, when the battle of St. Albans, resulting in the defeat of Henry VI. and the royal forces by the Duke of York, initiated those lamentable struggles between the rival houses of York and Lancaster ; and the inhabitants of our section shared, like the rest, in the ruin and bloodshed of civil war. Those contests, which lasted no less than thirty years, and included thirteen pitched battles, were finally terminated in 1485, by the union of Henry VII. with Catherine of York, daughter of Edward IV.

In 1485 a malady called the "Sweating Sickness" visited the different districts of Lancashire, and so rapid and fatal were the effects, that during the seven weeks it prevailed, large numbers of the populace fell victims to its virulence. Lord Verulam, describing the disease, says :—" The complaint was a pestilent fever, attended by a malign vapour, which flew to the heart and seized the vital spirits ; which stirred nature to strive to send it forth by an extreme sweat."

In 1487 the impostor Lambert Simnel, who personated Edward, earl of Warwick, the heir in rightful succession to Edward IV., landed at the Pile of Fouldrey, (Peel harbour) in Morecambe Bay, with an army raised chiefly by the aid of the Duchess of Burgundy, and marched into the country. At Stoke, near Newark, he was defeated and taken prisoner, and subsequently the adventurer was made a scullion in the king's kitchen, from which humble sphere he rose by good conduct to the position of falconer. Henry VIII., soon after his accession in 1509, became embroiled in war with France, and whilst he was engaged in hostilities on the continent, James IV. of Scotland crossed the border, and invaded England with a force of fifty thousand men. To resist this aggression large levies were promptly raised in Lancashire and other northern counties, and on the field of Flodden, in Northumberland, a decisive battle took place in 1513, in which the Scottish monarch was slain, and his army routed. The

Lancashire troops were led by Sir Edward Stanley, and their patriotism and valour are celebrated in an ancient song call the " Famous Historie or Songe of Floodan Field." In the following extract certain localities in and near the Fylde are mentioned as having furnished their contingents of willing soldiers :—

> " All Lancashire for the most parte
> The lusty Standley stowte can lead,
> A stock of striplings stronge of heart
> Brought up from babes with beef and bread,
> From Warton unto Warrington,
> From Wiggen unto Wyresdale,
> From Weddecon to Waddington.
> From Ribchester to Rochdale,
> From Poulton to Preston with pikes
> They with ye Standley howte forthe went,
> From Pemberton and Pilling Dikes
> For Battell Billmen bould were bent
> With fellowes fearce and fresh for feight
> With Halton feilds did turne in foores,
> With lusty ladds liver and light
> From Blackborne and Bolton in ye moores."

The office of High Sheriff is one of considerable antiquity, and in early times it was no uncommon thing for the elected person to retain the position for several years together. Annexed is a list of gentlemen connected with the Fylde who have been High Sheriffs of the county of Lancaster at different times, with their years of office :—

1194 to 1199. Theobald Walter, of Amounderness.
1278. Gilbert de Clifton, of Clifton and Westby.
1287. Gilbert de Clifton, of Clifton and Westby.
1289. Gilbert de Clifton, of Clifton and Westby.
1393. Sir Johannes Butler, Knt., of Rawcliffe.
1394. Sir Johannes Butler, Knt., of Rawcliffe.
1395. Sir Johannes Butler, Knt., of Rawcliffe,
1397. Sir Richard Molyneux, Knt., of Larbrick (for life).
1566. Sir Richard Molyneux, Knt., of Larbrick.
1606. Edmund Fleetwood, of Rossall.
1677. Alexander Rigby, of Layton.
1678. Alexander Rigby, of Layton.
1691. Sir Alexander Rigby, Knt., of Layton.
1740. Roger Hesketh, of Rossall.
1797. Bold Fleetwood Hesketh, of Rossall.

1820. Robert Hesketh, of Rossall.
1830. Peter Hesketh Fleetwood, of Rossall.
1835. Thomas Clifton, of Lytham.
1842. Thomas Robert Wilson ffrance, of Rawcliffe.
1853. John Talbot Clifton, of Lytham.

It may be here noticed that Edmund Dudley, so notorious in English history as the infamous agent of Henry VII. in the wholesale and scandalous extortions that monarch practised upon his subjects, held many and large territorial possessions in the county of Lancashire, the reward in all probability of his unscrupulous services to the king. After the death of his royal patron a loud outcry for the punishment of Dudley was raised by the nation, and in the first year of Henry VIII. a proclamation was issued inviting those subjects who had been injured by Dudley and his fellow commissioner, Sir Richard Empson, to come forward and state their complaints; the number of complainants who appeared was so great that it was found impossible to examine all their claims, so in order to pacify the universal indignation, the two obnoxious agents were thrown into prison on a charge of treason. From the Inquisition for the Escheat of the Duchy of Lancaster taken on the attainder of Edmund Dudley, in 1509, it is discovered that amongst his numerous estates, were lands in Elswick, Hambleton, Freckleton, Thornton, Little Singleton, Wood Plumpton, Whittingham, Goosnargh, and Claughton. Stow, writing about the circumstances alluded to, says :—" Thereupon was Sir Richard Empson, Knight, and Edmund Dudley, Esquire, by a politicke mean brought into the Tower, where they were accused of treason, and so remained there prisoners, thereby to quiet men's minds, that made such suit to have their money restored. On the seventeenth of July Edmund Dudley was arraigned in the Guildhall of London, where he was condemned, and had judgement to be drawn, hanged, and quartered.   *   *   *   Henry VIII. sent commandment to the Constable of the Tower, charging him that Empson and Dudley should shortly after be put to execution. The Sheriffs of London were commanded by a special writ to see the said execution performed and done, whereupon they went to the Tower and received the prisoners on the 17th of August, 1510, and from thence brought them unto the scaffold on Tower Hill, where their heads were stricken off."

The most conspicuous event which happened during the sovereignty of Henry VIII. was the Protestant Reformation. Henry, having quarrelled with the Supreme Head of the Church at Rome, determined to suppress all religious houses in his kingdom whose incomes amounted to less than £200 per annum. Doctors Thomas Leigh and Thomas Layton were appointed to inspect and report on those in Lancashire ; and amongst the number condemned on their visit was a small Benedictine Cell at Lytham. This Cell owed its origin to Richard Fitz Roger, who towards the latter part of the reign of Richard I. granted lands at Lytham to the Durham Church, in order that a prior and Benedictine monks might be established there to the honour of St. Mary and St. Cuthbert. Its yearly revenue at the time of suppression was only £55. A little later, in 1540, the larger monastic institutions suffered the fate of the smaller ones ; and amongst the chantries closed were two at St. Michael's-on-Wyre. All Catholic places of worship were closed by a proclamation, bearing the date September 23rd, 1548, and issued by the lord protector Somerset on behalf of the young king Edward VI. On the death of that monarch in 1553 the crown descended to his sister Mary, only daughter of Catherine of Arrogan ; and one of her first acts was to re-establish the old faith and re-open the churches and chantries which her predecessors had closed. Mass was again celebrated in the churches of St. Michael's-on-Wyre, Kirkham, and Singleton, as in former days, the officiating priests being :—

Kirkham	...	...	...	Thomas Primbet, annual fee £2 10s. 0d.
Singleton	...	...	...	Richard Goodson, „ „ £2 9s. 0d.
St. Michael's-on-Wyre,		Thomas Cross	„ „ £4 13s. 10d.

In the early part of this reign a grand military muster was ordered to be made in the county palatine of Lancaster, and towards the 300 men raised in the Hundred of Amounderness the Fylde townships contributed as follows :—

Warton	4 men.	Thornton	8 men.
Carleton	8 „	Out Rawcliffe	4 „
Hardhome with Newton..	8 „	Upper Rawcliffe and Tornecard	1 „
Much Eccleston	5 „	Pulton	3 „
Clifton	6 „	Weton	3 „
Bispham and Norbreke ...	5 „	Threleyle	6 „
Freckleton	5 „	Little Eccleston and Larbreke	6 „
Thilston	8 „	Little Singleton and Grange...	5 „

Newton with Scales	...	3 men.	Westbye and Plumpton...	...	8 men.
Layton with Warbrick	...	8 „	Rigby with Wraye... ...	...	8 „
Elliswicke	...	5 „	Lithum	...	5 „
Kelmyne and Brininge	...	5 „	Much Singleton	...	7 „
Kirkham	...	3 „	Plumpton	...	11 „

The commanders of the regiment were—Sir Thomas Hesketh, Sir Richard Houghton ; George Browne, John Kitchen, Richard Barton, William Westby (of Mowbreck), and William Barton, Esquires.

Dodsworth, who lived in the latter part of the sixteenth and early part of the seventeenth centuries, informs us that sometime during the year 1555 "a sudden irruption of the sea" took place near Rossall grange, and a whole village, called Singleton Thorp, was washed away by the fury of the waves. "The inhabitants were driven out of their ancient home, and erected their tents at a place called Singleton to this day." It has been surmised that Singleton Thorp was the residence of Thomas de Singleton, who opposed Edward I. in a suit to recover from that king the manors of Singleton, Thornton, and Brughton. The site formerly occupied by the ancient village is now called Singleton Skeer. Dodsworth also declares that the Horse-bank lying off the shores of Lytham was, in 1612, during the reign of James I., a pasture for cattle, and that, in 1601, a village called Waddum Thorp existed between it and the present main-land.

In January, 1559, about two months after the accession of Elizabeth, another muster took place throughout the several counties of the kingdom, and subjoined are enumerated the bodies of soldiers furnished by the different Hundreds of Lancashire :—

BLACKEBURNE HUNDRED—407 harnessed men, 406 unharnessed men.
AMOUNDERNES HUNDRED—213 harnessed men, 369 unharnessed men.
LONDESDALL HUNDRED—356 harnessed men, 114 unharnessed men.
LEYLONDE HUNDRED—80 harnessed men, 22 unharnesed men.
SALEFORDE HUNDRED—394 harnessed men, 649 unharnessed men.
WEST DERBY HUNDRED—459 harnessed men, 413 unharnessed men.
Sum Total of harnessed men 1919.
Sum Total of unharnessed men 2073.[1]

An epidemic, described by Hollinworth as a "sore sicknesse," prevailed in this county during some months of 1565, and carried off many of the inhabitants.

1. Harl. Mss. cod. 1926, fol. 4 b.

Queen Elizabeth on her accession wrought another change in the national religion, but taking warning from the outcries and disturbances produced by the sudden and sweeping policies of Henry VIII. and Mary, proceeded to affect her purpose in a more deliberate manner. She retained some of her Catholic ministers, taking care, however, to have sufficient of the reformed faith to outvote them when occasion required, and appointed a commission to inquire into the persecutions of the last reign, with orders to liberate from prison all those who had been confined on account of their attachment to Protestant principles. In her own chapel she forbade several Popish practices, and commanded that certain portions of the services should be read in the English tongue. Shortly afterwards a proclamation was issued, ordering that all chantries should conduct their services after the model of her own chapel. This comparative moderation was succeeded at a later period of her sovereignty by sterner measures, and many Catholic recusants were placed in confinement, being subjected to heavy penalties and degradations. During the same reign the military strength of the nation was again ascertained by a general muster. The gathering took place in 1574, when six gentlemen of our neighbourhood were thus rated :—

Cuthbert Clifton, esq., to furnish :—Light horse 1, Plate-coate 1, Pyke 1, Long bows 2, Sheaves of arrows 2, Steel caps 2, Caliver 1, Morion 1.

James Massey, George Alane to furnish :—Plate-coat 1, Long bow 1, Sheaf of arrows 1, Steel cap 1, Caliver 1, Morion 1, Bill 1.

William Hesketh to furnish of good will :—Caliver 1, Morion 1.

William Singleton, John Veale to furnish :—The same as William Hesketh doth.

The whole complement raised in the Hundred of Amounderness consisted of—5 Light horse, 1 Demi-lance, 2 Corslets, 17 Plate-coats, 11 Pykes, 22 Long bows, 22 Sheaves of arrows, 27 Steel caps, 15 Calivers, 20 Morions, and 10 Bills.

Father Edmund Campion, the notorious Jesuit, was apprehended in 1581, immediately after travelling through Lancashire endeavouring to spread the doctrines of his faith, and imprisoned in the Tower. Under the cruel influence of the rack he divulged the names of several persons by whom he had been received and entertained whilst on his journey, and amongst them were Mrs.

Allen of Rossall Hall, the widow of Richard Allen, and John Westby of Mowbreck and Burn Halls. Shortly before his execution Campion deplored his compulsory confession in a letter to a friend in these words :—" It grieved me much to have offended the Catholic cause so highly, as to confess the names of some gentlemen and friends in whose houses I have been entertained ; yet in this I greatly cherish and comfort myself, that I never discovered any secrets there declared, and that I will not, come rack, come rope."

The following extracts are taken from some manuscripts in the Harleian collection, and will explain themselves :—

" Names of such as are detected for receiptinge of Priests, Seminaries, etc., in the County of Lancashire.

" This appeareth by the presentment of the Vicar of Garstang.

One named little Richard receipted at Mr. Rigmaden's of Weddicar by report.

" This appeareth by the presentment of the Vicar of Kirkham.

Ricard Cadocke, a seminary priest, also Deiv. Tytmouse conversant in the Company of two widows—viz. Mistress Alice Clyfton and Mistress Jane Clyfton, about the first of October last, 1580, by the report of James Burie.

" This also appeareth by the presentment of the Vicar of Kirkham.

Richard Brittain, a priest receipted in the house of William Bennett of Westby, about the beginning of June last, from whence young Mr. Norrice of Speke conveyed the said Brittain to the Speke, as the said Bennett hath reported.

" The said Brittain remayneth now at the house of Mr. Norrice of the Speke, as appeareth by the deposition of John Osbaldston.

" Diocese of Chester
" Amounderness Deanery
Cuthb. Clifton, Esq. - - - Obstinate.
Will. Hesketh, gent. - - - Obstinate.
John Singleton, gent. - - - Obstinate."

At that period it was customary to levy a tax of live stock and different articles of food on each county, for the supply of the royal larder, and Sir Richard Sherburn, of Carleton and Hambleton, and Alexander Rigby, of Middleton, near Preston,[1] ratified an agreement with the treasurer and controller of Elizabeth's household, that Lancashire should provide annually

1. Alexander Rigby was related to the branch of that family residing at Layton Hall.

forty great oxen, to be delivered alive at her majesty's pasture at Crestow. Afterwards the sums to be contributed by each Hundred for the purchase of these animals was arranged, and Amounderness rated at £16 10s. 0d. per year. The latter agreement was ratified by Sir Richard Sherburne and Edward Tyldesley, of Myerscough, amongst others. Grievous complaints were made in the Fylde and other parts of the county of the desecration of the Sabbath by "Wakes, fayres, markettes, bayrebaytes, bull baits, Ales, Maygames, Resortinge to Alehouses in tyme of devyne service, pypinge and dauncinge, huntinge and all manner of unlawfull gamynge." A letter praying that these profanations might be reformed was signed by the magistrates of the several districts, amongst whom were Edmund Fleetwood of Rossall, and R. Sherburne of Carleton, etc., and forwarded to London. A commission of inquiry was appointed, and after an investigation, the commissioners charged all mayors, bailiffs, and constables, as well as other civil officers, churchwardens, etc., to suppress by all lawful means the said disorders of the Sabbath, and to present the offenders at the quarter sessions, that they might be dealt with for the same according to law. They also directed that the minstrels, bearwards, and all such disorderly persons, should be immediately apprehended and brought before the justices of the peace, and punished at their discretion ; that the churchwardens should be enjoined to present at the sessions all those that neglected to attend divine service upon the Sabbath day, that they might be indicted and fined in the penalty of twelve pence for every offence ; that the number of alehouses should be abridged, that the ale-sellers should utter a full quart of ale for one penny, and none of any less size, and that they should sell no ale or other victuals in time of divine service ; that none should sell ale without a license ; that the magistrates should be enjoined not to grant any ale-licenses except in public sessions ; that they should examine the officers of the commonwealth to learn whether they made due presentment at the quarter sessions of all bastards born or remaining within their several precincts ; and that thereupon a strict course should be taken for the due punishment of the reputed parents according to the statute, as also for the convenient keeping and relief of the infants.[1]

1. Harl. MSS. cod. 1926, fol. 80.

E

In 1588, the year following the execution of Mary, Queen of Scots, Philip of Spain, urged on by an ambition to conquer the kingdom of England and re-establish the Romish religion, equipped an immense fleet, consisting of seventy-two galliasses and galleons, forty-seven second-class ships of war, and eleven pinnaces, to which he gave the name of the " Invincible Armada." The rumour of this invasion spread great alarm throughout the country ; and the magistrates, gentry, and freeholders of Lancashire were summoned to meet Lord Strange at Preston, to consider what steps should be taken for the defence of their coast, on which, at Peel in Morecambe Bay, it was deemed probable the Spaniards would attempt a landing. So doubtful does Elizabeth appear to have been of the loyalty of her Lancashire subjects that Lord Strange was commanded to append to his summonses the words,—" Fayle not at your uttermost peril." Nor were these suspicions on the part of the queen without good reason, for the principal landed proprietors and gentry of the county were members of the Romish Church, and it was to be feared that they would be only lukewarm in repelling, if not, indeed, active in encouraging, an enemy whose professed object was the restoration of their religion. Baines, in reviewing the Reformation, says,— " In the county of Lancashire it was retrograde. The Catholics multiplied, priests were harboured, the book of common prayer and the service of the Church, established by law, were laid aside ; many of the churches were shut up, and the cures unsupplied, unless by the ejected Catholics." Numerous crosses on the highways, as well as the names of several places, as Low-cross, High-cross, Norcross, etc., also testify to the Romish tendency of the inhabitants. Cardinal Allen, who had for many years been living on the continent at Douai and elsewhere[1] was suspected of having, in conjunction with Parsons, the Jesuit, instigated Philip to this invasion. The harbour of " Pille," (Peel) is described in the Lansdowne manuscripts as the " very best haven for landings with great shyppes in all the west coast of England, called St. George's Channel," and further in the same folio we read :—" What the Spanyerd means to do the Lord knows, for all the countrie being known to Doctor Allen, who was born harde by

---

1. See " Allen of Rossall," in Chapter vi.

the pyle," (Rossall Hall was the birth-place of Allen,) "and the inhabytentes ther aboutes all ynfected with the Romish poyson, it is not unlike that his directione will be used for some landinge there. * * * One Thomas Prestone (a papyshe atheiste) is deputye steward, and commandes the menrede, and lands ther, wch were sometyme appertayning to the Abbeye of Fornes."

Whilst preparations for resisting the Spaniards were being pushed forward with as much expedition as possible, the "Invincibles" appeared in the English Channel, and arranged themselves for battle in the form of a crescent. The British fleet, numbering only thirty-four ships of war, and sundry private vessels equipped for the occasion, under the command of Lord Howard, sailed out to engage them. A series of actions took place, and although nothing decisive had been effected, the advantage seemed to be leaning towards the English fleet, when eight fire-ships drifted in amongst the Armada and threw them into utter confusion. This *coup de maître* took place on the 29th of July, 1588. The panic-stricken Spaniards, fearing that the whole of their ships would be destroyed in a general conflagration, severed their cables, and fled. A westerly gale, however, sprang up, and wrecked many of the vessels on the coast between Ostend and Calais ; the shores of Scotland and Ireland were also covered with fragments of their ships and bodies of their mariners, while tradition asserts that one of the galleons was stranded on the Point of Rossall, where it was attacked by the country people, either for the sake of pillage or in the hope of capturing it. Whether one or both of these desires actuated the rustics they were doomed to disappointment, for the Spaniards successfully resisted their first attempt, and escaped on the returning tide, before further efforts could be made by the little band on shore. Two cannon balls were formerly to be seen at Rossall Hall, and it was stated that they were the identical ones fired by this vessel, as a parting salute, when she sailed away. They were found on removing some of the walls belonging to the old mansion.

The annexed is a list of free-tenants residing in the Fylde district about the year 1585, the 27th of the reign of Queen Elizabeth :—

Molyneux, Sir Richard, of Larbrick, knight.
Clifton, Thomas, of Westby, esq.

Rigby, Edward, of Layton and Burgh, esq.
Veale, John, of Mythorp, esq.
Butler, Henry, of Out-Rawcliffe, esq.
Parker, William, of Bradkirk, esq.
Westby, John, of Mowbreck, esq.
Kirkby, William, of Upper Rawcliffe, esq.
Singleton, George, of Staining, esq.
Hesketh, William, of Little Poulton, esq.
Stanley, Thomas, of Great Eccleston, esq.
Warren, ———, of Plumpton, esq.
White, Nicholas, of Great Eccleston, gent.
Rogerly, George, of Lytham, gent.
Banister, William, of Carleton, gent.
Sharples John, of Freckleton, gent.

The dress of the priests previous to the Protestant Reformation is
thus described by Harrison :—" They went either in divers colours
like plaiers, or in garments of light hew, as yellow, red, greene,
etc., with their shoes piked, their haire crisped, and their girdles
armed with silver ; their shoes, spurs, bridles, etc., buckled with
like mettall ; their apparell chiefly of silke, and richlie furred,
their cappes laced and buttoned with gold ; so that to meet a
priest in those days, was to beholde a peacocke that spreadeth his
taile when he danseth before the henne." " The manners and
customs of the inhabitants of Lancashire," writes John de
Brentford, "are similar to those of the neighbouring counties
except that the people eat with two pronged forks[1] ; the men are
masculine, and in general well made, they ride and hunt the same
as in the most southern parts, but not with that grace, owing to
the whip being carried in the left hand ; the women are most
handsome, their eyes brown, black, hazel, blue, or grey ; their
noses, if not inclined to the aquiline, are mostly of the Grecian
form, which gives a most beautiful archness to the countenance,
such indeed as is not easy to be described, their fascinating
manners have long procured them the name of Lancashire
witches." Leyland in his "Itinerary" says :—" The dress of the
men chiefly consists of woollen garments, while the women wear
those of silk, linen, or stuff. Their usual colours are those of

1. Table forks were introduced into England from Italy at the close of the
Tudor dynasty ; previously the people of all ranks used their fingers for the
purposes to which we now apply a fork. A kind of fork was used as far back as
the Anglo-Saxon times, but only to serve articles from the dish.

green, blue, black, and sometimes brown. The military are dressed in red, which is vulgarly called scarlet." In the time of Henry VIII. the custom of placing chimneys on the tops of the houses was first introduced amongst the English; before that period the smoke usually found its way through an opening in the roof or out of the doorway. The houses of the middle classes were for the most part formed of wood, whilst those of the peasantry were built of wattles plastered over with a thick coating of clay. The few stone mansions existing in Lancashire were the residences of the nobility or of the most opulent gentry. Harrison, referring to the improvements in accommodation gradually gaining ground, remarks :—"There was a great, although not general, amendment of lodging; for our fathers, yea, and we ourselves also, have lien full oft upon straw pallets, on rough mats, onelie covered with a sheet under coverlets made of dagswam or hopparlots, and a good round log under the head instead of a bolster or pillow, which was thought meet onelie for women in childbed; as for servants, if they had anie sheets above them, it was well, for seldome had they anie under their bodies to keep them from the prickly straws that ran oft through the canvas of the pallet, and raised their hardened hides." Holinshed, also, notices the better style of entertainment at the inns of Lancaster, Preston, etc.; at which he tells us the guests were well provided with "napierie, bedding, and tapisserie," and each was sure of resting "in cleane sheets wherein no man had been lodged since they came from the laundress." Camden, writing of our more immediate neighbourhood a little later than the period we are now discussing, says :—"The goodly and fresh complexion of the natives does sufficiently evince the goodness of the county; nay and the cattle too, if you will; for in the oxen, which have huge horns and proportionate bodies, you will find nothing of that perfection wanting that Mago, the Carthagenian, in Columella required. This soil (Amounderness) bears oats pretty well, but is not so good for barley; it makes excellent pasture especially towards the sea, where it is partly Champain; whence a great part of it is called the File, probably for the Field. But being in other places Fenny 'tis reckoned less wholesome. In many places along the coast there are heaps of sand, upon which the natives now and then pour water, till it grows saltish, and then with turf boyl it into white salt." Several of these salt manufacturies were located near Lytham, and it is very likely that the two brass pans and an ancient measure, discovered about forty years since deeply imbedded in the peat not far from Fox Hall, were used in the production of salt somewhere in that vicinity.

CHAPTER III.

JAMES THE FIRST TO QUEEN VICTORIA.

ON the accession of James I., in 1603, the crowns of England and Scotland became legally united, although it was not until a considerable time afterwards that they could be regarded as practically so. This monarch was the first to assume the title of King of Great Britain.

A custom prevailed in former days of relieving the secular portion of the community by imposing exclusive taxes on the clergy, and hence it is seen, that in 1608 a rate was levied upon the latter by the Right Reverend George Lloyd, D.D., the eighth bishop of Chester. The following is a copy of the impost so far as the Hundred of Amounderness was concerned :—

"*Archid. Decanatus* } A Rayte imposed by me George Bushoppe of Cestrie *in Com.* Lancastrie } Chest^r upon the Clergie within the Countye of Chesshyre and Lancashyre within the Dyoces of Chest,^r By vertue of lres from the lordes grace of Yorke grounded upon + from the lordes and others of his ma^{tes} most honorable privye counsell for the fyndinge of horses, armes, and other furniture, the xxviiith of October 1608.

Amounderness Decanatus Archid. Richm.

Mr. Porter, vicar of Lancast^r		... a corslet furnished.
Mr. Paler, vicar of Preston	}	... a musket furnished.
Mr. Norcrosse, vicar of Ribchest^r		
Mr. Whyt, vicar of Poulton &	}	... a musket furnished.
Mr. Greenacres, vicar of Kirkham		
Mr. Aynsworth, vicar of Garstange	}	... a musket furnished.
Mr. Woolfenden, vicar of St. Michael's upon Wyre		
Mr. Calver, vicar of Cockerham	}	... a caliver furnished.
Mr. Parker, vicar of Chippin		

George Cestriensis."[1]

Here it may be mentioned that, although about 636, Honorus, archbishop of Canterbury, attempted to divide the kingdom into parishes, it was not until many years later, in the reign of Henry

1. Harl, MSS.

VIII., that the diocese to which Lancashire belonged was clearly
defined. At that date Chester was created a distinct bishopric,
and the southern part of our county included in the archdeaconry
of Chester, whilst the northern portion was attached to the
archdeaconry of Richmond.

In 1617 James I., on his return journey from Scotland to
London, was entertained at Myerscough Lodge, near Garstang, by
Edward Tyldesley, the grandfather of the gentleman who erected
Fox Hall, at Blackpool. Thomas Tyldesley, a cousin of the owner
of Myerscough Lodge, and attorney-general of the county of
Lancaster, had been knighted by the monarch at Wimbleton in
the previous year. From Myerscough the King proceeded to
Hoghton Tower, where a petition was presented to him by the
agricultural labourers, petty tradesmen, and ordinary servants in
this and other districts lying near Preston, praying that the edict
of the late queen, whereby sports and games had been prohibited
on the Sabbath, might be repealed. The prayer of the petitioners
found favour with James, and shortly afterwards he caused it to
be proclaimed—"that his majesty's pleasure was, that the bishops
of the diocese should take strict order with all the puritans and
precisians within the county of Lancaster, and either constrain
them to conform themselves, or to leave the countrie, according
to the laws of this kingdom and the canons of the church ; and
for his good people's recreation his pleasure was, that after the
end of divine service, they be not disturbed, letted, or discouraged
from any lawful recreation, such as dancing, either men or women ;
archery for men, leaping, vaulting, or any such harmless
recreation ; nor having of May-games, Whitson-ales, and Morice-
dances, and the setting up of May-poles, and other sports
therewith used ; so as the same be had in due and convenient
time, without impediment or neglect of divine service ; and that
women should have leave to carry rushes to the church, for
decorating of it according to the old custom ; but withal his
majesty did here account still as prohibited, all unlawful games to
be used on Sundays only, as bear and bull-baitings, interludes,
and, at all times, in the meaner sort of people, by law prohibited,
bowling." A few months after this concession to the wishes of a
portion of his subjects, James issued a publication designated the
" Book of Sports," in which he explained what were to be

considered lawful sports to be indulged in on "Sundays and Festivals."

The gentlemen enumerated below were free-tenants, residing in the Fylde, during his reign :—

> Clifton, Sir Cuthbert, of Westby, knight.
> Banister, Sir Robert, of Plumpton, knight.
> Fleetwood, Edward, of Rossall, esq.
> Westby, Thomas, of Mowbreck, esq.
> Kirkby, William, of Upper Rawcliffe, esq.
> Veale, Edward, of Whinney Heys, esq.
> Burgh, Richard, of Larbrick, esq.
> Leckonby, John, of Great Eccleston, esq.
> Longworth, Richard, of St. Michael's, esq.
> Parker, John, of Bradkirk, esq.
> Hesketh, William, of Mains, esq.
> Singleton, Thomas, of Staining, esq.
> Brown James, of Singleton, gent.
> Leigh, Robert, of Plumpton, gent.
> Smith, John, of Kirkham, gent.
> Sharples, Henry, of Kirkham, gent.
> ffrance, John, of Eccleston, gent.
> Thompson Wm., of Little Eccleston, gent.
> Dobson, William, of Bispham, gent.
> Hornby, Henry, of Bankfield, gent.
> Bradley, James, of Bryning, gent.
> Taylor, James, of Poulton, gent.
> Bamber, Thomas, of Poulton, gent.
> Bailey, Lawrence, of Layton, gent.
> Bonny, Robert, of Kirkham, gent.
> Whiteside, Robt., of Thornton, gent.

In the Registers of Kirkham is the annexed statement, from which it appears that a few years from the death of James I. the Fylde, or at least a considerable tract of it, was visited by some fatal epidemic, but its peculiar nature cannot be ascertained :— "A.D. 1630. This year was a great plague in Kirkham, in which the more part of the people of the town died thereof. It began about the 25th of July and continued vehemently until Martinmas, but was not clear of it before Lent ; and divers towns of the parish was infected with it, and many died thereof out of them, as Treales, Newton, Greenall, Estbrick, Thistleton. N.B.—The great mortality was in the year 1631 ; 304 died that year, and were buried at Kirkham, of whom 193 in the months of August and September." Charles I. soon after ascending the throne in

1626, provoked a breach with his parliament by endeavouring to enforce subsidies, with which to carry on his foreign wars, and further, he alienated the affections and respect of the Puritan section of his subjects by confirming the regulations of the "Book of Sports." Dissatisfaction and murmurings were quickly fermented into rebellion, and the closing of the gates of Hull against the king in 1642 initiated those fearful wars, which desolated and disorganised the country for so many years. In 1641, Alexander Rigby,[1] esq., of Layton Hall, Sir Gilbert de Hoghton, with eight other gentlemen, were removed from the commission of the peace, by order of parliament, on suspicion of being favourably disposed towards the royal party. The chief supporters of the king in the ensuing conflicts were the nobility, in great numbers; the higher orders of the gentry, and a considerable portion of their tenantry; all the High-churchmen; and a large majority of the Catholics. The parliamentarian army, on the other hand, was mainly composed of freeholders, traders, manufacturers, Puritans, Presbyterians, and Independents. An engagement near Wigan roused up the people in our vicinity to a sense of the dangers menacing them, and a public meeting of royalists was called at Preston under the presidency of the earl of Derby. Amongst other gentlemen who took a prominent part in the assembly were Thomas Clifton, esq., of Lytham, and Alexander Rigby, esq., of Layton. Several resolutions were adopted, the most important being that a sum of money, amounting to £8,700, should be raised and devoted to the payment of a regiment, consisting of 2,000 foot and 400 horse, in the following scale of remuneration :—

DRAGOONERS.

Captain	12s. 0d.	per diem.	
Lieutenant	6s. 0d.	,,	,,
Cornet	4s. 0d.	,,	,,
Sergeant	3s. 0d.	,,	,,
Corporal	2s. 0d.	,,	,,
Dragooner	1s. 6d.	,,	,,
Kettle-drum	2s. 0d.	,,	,,

1. This Alex. Rigby must not be confounded with the gentleman of that name mentioned in the former chapter, and who in the civil contests was a parliamentary general. A. Rigby here denoted, was a royalist officer.

FOOT.		HORSE.	
Captain	10s. od. per diem.	Captain	16s. od. per diem.
Lieutenant	4s. od. ,, ,,	Lieutenant	8s. od. ,, ,,
Sergeant	1s. 6d. ,, ,,	Cornet	6s. od. ,, ,,
Drummer	1s. 3d. ,, ,,	Corporal	4s. od. ,, ,,
Corporal	1s. od. ,, ,,	Trumpeter	5s. od. ,, ,,
Private	os. 9d. ,, ,,	Private	2s. 6d. ,, ,,

And to every Commissary .... 5s. od. per diem.

Parliamentary commissioners were sent this year, 1642, into all parts of Lancashire to visit the churches and chapels and to remove therefrom all images, superstitious pictures, and idolatorous relics, which any of them might contain.

Preston and Lancaster were amongst the earliest towns to fall into the hands of the Roundheads, and about ten days after the surrender of the former place, when the people of this district were labouring under the excitement of war on their very frontier, Alexander Rigby, of Layton Hall, accompanied by Captain Thomas Singleton, of Staining, and other officers, appeared near Poulton at the head of a number of horsemen, and threw the inhabitants into a state of great consternation and alarm, fortunately proving unnecessary, for the cavalcade had other designs than that of bringing devastation and bloodshed to their own doors, and continued their journey peacably northward. A few weeks later a Spanish vessel was seen at the entrance of Morecambe Bay, off Rossall Point, and as it evinced no signs of movement, either towards the harbour of Lancaster or out to sea, the yeomen and farm servants of that neighbourhood at once surmised that some sort of an invasive attack was meditated on their coast, nor were these fears in any way allayed by the constant firing of a piece of cannon from the deck of the ship, and it was not until the discharges had been repeated through several days that they realised that distress and not bombardment was intended to be indicated. On boarding the vessel they found that she contained a number of passengers, all of whom, together with the crew, were reduced to a pitiable and enfeebled condition through exposure and scarcity of provisions, for, having lost their way in the heavy weather which prevailed, they had been detained much over the time expected for the voyage, blindly cruising about in the hope of discovering some friendly haven or guide. The craft was piloted round into the mouth of the river Wyre, opposite the

Warren, and relief afforded to the sufferers. Rumour of the presence of the ship was not long in reaching the ears of the earl of Derby, who, with promptitude determined to march down and seize it in the king's name. On the Saturday he arrived at Lytham Hall with a small troop of cavalry, where he sojourned for the night, with the intention of completing his journey and effecting his purpose the following day before the parliamentarians had got word of the matter ; but here his calculations were at fault, for the parliamentary leader had already dispatched four companies of infantry, under Major Sparrow, to take possession of the prize, and on the same Saturday evening they took up their quarters at Poulton and Singleton, having arrived by a different route to the earl, who had forded the river at Hesketh Bank. On the Sunday Major Sparrow, who throughout showed a lively horror of risking an encounter with the renowned nobleman, posted scouts with orders to watch the direction taken by the latter, and convey the information without delay to the chief station at Poulton, where the soldiers were in readiness, not for action, as it subsequently turned out, but to put a safe barrier between themselves and the enemy, for no sooner was it ascertained that the earl, "all his company having their swords drawn," was marching along Layton Hawes towards Rossall, than Sparrow conducted his force across the Wyre, at the Shard, and followed the course of the stream towards its outlet "until he came over against where the shipp lay, being as feared of the earle as the earle was of him."[1] The earl of Derby advanced along the shore line and across the Warren to the mouth of the river without the naked weapons of his followers being called into service, but finding when he boarded the ship that two parliamentary gentlemen had forestalled his intention by seizing her for the powers they recognized, he unhesitatingly took them prisoners, and set fire to the vessel, whilst Sparrow and his men stood helplessly by, on the opposite side of the water, where the gallant major perhaps congratulated himself on his caution in having avoided a collision with so prompt and vigorous a foe. Some of the Spaniards attached themselves to the train of the earl, whilst others were scattered over the neighbourhood, depending for subsistence upon

1. A Discourse of the Warr in Lancashire, edited by William Beamont (Cheetham Society.)

the charity of the cottagers and farmers, but their final destiny is unknown. The noble general, enraged at the unlooked for frustration of the main object of his journey, determined that it should not be altogether fruitless, and on his return forced admittance into the mansion of the Fleetwoods, at Rossall, and bore off all the arms he could lay hands upon. Resuming his march he re-passed through Lytham, forded the Ribble, and finally made his way to Lathom House, his famous residence.

Inactivity, however temporary, was ill suited to the temperament of the earl, and on receiving the news that the solitary piece of artillery belonging to the luckless Spanish vessel had been appropriated by the parliamentary officials before he appeared upon the scene, and transferred to their stronghold at Lancaster, he conceived the idea of reducing the ancient castle on the Lune, and so taking vengeance on those who had anticipated him in the Wyre affair, as well as removing a formidable obstacle to the success of the royal arms. Before entering on an undertaking of such importance it was necessary that his small body of troops should be materially increased, and after exhausting the districts south of the Ribble, he crossed it, in search of recruits amongst the yeomanry and peasantry of the Fylde. The earl lodged his soldiers in and about Kirkham, and fixed his own quarters at Lytham Hall. Dreadful stories are related by the old historian, from whose work we have already quoted, of the doings of the troops for the short time they remained in the neighbourhood, but it is only fair to state that their rapacity was directed exclusively against the property of those whose sympathies were with their opponents, whose houses and farms they plundered most mercilessly, driving off their horses, and carrying away ornaments, bedding, and everything which could either be turned to immediate use or offered a prospect of future gain. Warrants were issued on the first day of their arrival, from the head quarters at Lytham, over the whole of our section, calling upon every male above sixteen years of age and under sixty, "upon payne of death to appear before his Honor at Kirkham the next morning by eight of the clock, in their best weapons, to attend the King's service."[1] The officers to whom fell the task of heralding the mandate over the

---

1. A Discourse of the Warr in Lancashire, edited by William Beamont.

large area in the brief interval allowed, fulfilled their duties with
energy, and a goodly company responded to the arbitrary summons of the commander. After having seen that the fresh levies
were as suitably equipped for warfare as means would permit, the
earl appointed John Hoole, of Singleton, and John Ambrose, of
Wood Plumpton, as captains over them, and gave the order to
march.   On reaching Lancaster Lord Derby summoned the
mayor and burgesses to surrender the town and castle into his
hands, to which the chief magistrate replied that the inhabitants
had already been deprived of their arms and were unresisting, but
that the fortress, now garrisoned by parliamentary troops, was out
of his keeping, an answer so far unsatisfactory to the besieger
that he set fire to the buildings, about one hundred and seventy
of which were destroyed, and inflicted other injury on the place.
Colonel Ashton, of Middleton, who had been sent to relieve the
castle, arrived too late, when the earl was some distance on his
return towards Preston, from which town he dislodged the enemy.
A little later the tide of fortune turned against the royalists, and
the earl of Derby was one of the earliest to suffer defeat.   Colonel
Thomas Tyldesley, a staunch partizan of the king, and the father
of Edward Tyldesley, of Fox Hall, Blackpool, retreated before
Colonel Ashton, from Wigan to Lathom, and afterwards to Liverpool, where he was beseiged and forced again to fly by his indefatigable opponent. (Later he distinguished himself at Burton-on-
Trent, by the desperate heroism with which he led a cavalry
charge over a bridge of thirty-six arches, and for that display of
valour as well as his faithful adherence to Charles, he received
the honour of knighthood.)   Driven from Liverpool, Tyldesley,
in company with Lord Molyneux, withdrew the remnant of his
regiment towards the Ribble, crossed that stream, and quartered
his men in Kirkham, whilst Molyneux occupied the village of
Clifton.   In these places they rested a night and a day, keeping a
vigilant look out for their pursuer, Ashton, from the old windmill,
situated at the east end of Kirkham.   About one o'clock on the
day succeeding the evening of their arrival the soldiers, acting
under orders, repaired to their several lodgings to further refresh
themselves after their prolonged fatigues, but before four hours
had elapsed, a report came from the outpost that the enemy was
approaching.   An alarm spread through the camp, and with

difficulty Lord Molyneux and Colonel Tyldesley assembled their forces in the town of Kirkham, where they elected once more to make a stand against the victorious Ashton. Command was given that all the women and children should confine themselves within doors, and preparations were hurried forward to offer the parliamentarians a vigorous resistance ; but as daylight waned and the besiegers were momentarily expected, the courage of the royal troops seems to have oozed away, and they precipitately vacated the town, fording the Wyre, and flying towards Stalmine, whence they continued their retreat to Cockerham, and so on northwards. When Colonel Ashton entered Kirkham he found the enemy gone and the inhabitants in a state of extreme trepidation, but their fears were soon dismissed by the action of the gallant soldier who, on learning the course taken by Tyldesley and Molyneux, pushed on without delay. Ashton followed up the pursuit as far as the boundaries of Lancashire, without overtaking any of the royalists, and then returned to Preston. The rear of his troops diverged from the main road at Garstang, unknown to their leader, and marched into the Fylde for plunder. They passed through St. Michael's, and visiting the residence and estate of Christopher Parker, of Bradkirk, drove away many of his cattle, and stripped his house of everything of value. In Kirkham they laid the people under heavy toll, and even spared not those who were notoriously well affected towards parliament. At Clifton they found more herds of cattle, which were joined to those already with them ; but at Preston they fell to quarrelling over the booty, and it is questionable whether their ill-gotten stores did not prove rather a curse than a blessing to them.

Towards the end of 1643, the year in which the events just narrated occurred, Thurland Castle, the seat of Sir John Girlington, was captured by the parliamentary colonel, Alexander Rigby, of Middleton, near Preston. In the engagement the Lancashire troops were under the command of Alexander Rigby, of Layton, who allowed his small regiment to be surprised and routed by his namesake. After his success at Thurland, Colonel Rigby, of Middleton, proceeded to raise fresh levies in Amounderness. Mr. Clayton, of Fulwood Moor, was appointed to superintend the whole of the recruiting and directed to place himself at the head of the new regiment. Mr. Patteson, of

Ribby, and Mr. Wilding, of Kirkham, were each apportioned half of the parish bearing the latter name, in which they were respectively ordered to raise a company. In the parishes of Poulton and Bispham, Mr. Robert Jolly, of Warbreck, Mr. William Hull, of Bispham, Mr. Richard Davis, of Newton, and Mr. Rowland Amon, of Thornton, were made captains, and had similar duties imposed upon them. In Lytham parish, Mr. George Sharples, of Freckleton, received a commission, but was unable to muster more than a very few followers, as the people of that neighbourhood reflected the loyal sentiments of the lord of the manor, and could neither be coerced nor seduced from their allegiance to the king. Captains Richard Smith and George Carter, of Hambleton, raised companies in Stalmine, Hambleton, and the adjacent townships and villages. Mr. William Swarbrick recruited a company in his native parish of St. Michael's, and Mr. Duddell obtained another in Wood Plumpton.

At the siege of Bolton, in May, 1644, when the town was stormed and surrendered after a valiant resistance, to Prince Rupert, with an army of over nine thousand royalists, Duddell and Davis were amongst the officers slain, whilst their companies were literally cut to pieces. Captain George Sharples, of Freckleton, was taken prisoner, and dragged, almost naked and barefooted, through the miry and blood-stained streets to the spot where Cuthbert, the eldest son of Thomas Clifton, of Lytham, was standing after the carnage, in which he had led a party of the besiegers. Captain Clifton and others near him were in a mood for a somewhat rude and ungenerous entertainment, and placed the hapless Sharples, in his dilapidated attire, in a prominent position and, thrusting a Psalter into his hand, compelled him to sing a Psalm for their delectation. After they had amused themselves in such fashion for some time the prisoner was handed over to the guard, from whom he ultimately made his escape. Captain Cuthbert Clifton was elevated to the rank of colonel as an acknowledgment of his gallant services at Bolton, after which he returned for a few days into the Fylde, where he engaged himself in procuring a fresh detachment of soldiers, who readily flocked to his standard. For their provision and comfort he did not hesitate or scruple to appropriate a number of cattle on Layton Hawes, and to relieve some of the Puritans of Kirkham, Bispham, and

Poulton, of their bedding, etc. Having fully supplied his commissariat department by these means, he marched to Liverpool, and joining Prince Rupert, was present at the sacking of that town.

The Civil War had proved most disastrous to Lancashire, where the constant movements and frequent collisions of the contending parties had ruined the towns, destroyed almost all attempts at agriculture, and reduced the inhabitants to a state of wretchedness and poverty, in many instances to the verge of starvation ; and notwithstanding the fact that in not one single instance had the Fylde been the scene of an encounter, the people of this section were in as lamentable a condition of penury and suffering as those of the less fortunate districts, a circumstance not to be wondered at when the incessant plunderings are taken into consideration, and when it is remembered that the youth and strength of the neighbourhood were serving as volunteers or recruits, either under the banner of parliament or that of the king. The 12th of September, 1644, was appointed by the Puritans as a day of solemn prayer and fasting throughout the country, and parliament decreed that half of the money collected " in all the churches within the cities of London and Westminster and within the lines of communication," should be devoted to the relief of the distressed and impoverished in this county.

Sir Thomas Tyldesley accompanied the army of Prince Rupert to York, near to where the sanguinary and famous battle of Marston Moor, in which no less than sixty thousand men were engaged on both sides, was fought on the 2nd of July, 1644. Oliver Cromwell commanded the parliamentarians in person, and after a fierce struggle discomfited the troops of Prince Rupert and drove them in confusion from the field. Sir Thomas Tyldesley retreated with his shattered regiment in hot haste towards Amounderness, where he made diligent search for arms and ammunition, but hearing that the enemy, under Sir John Meldrum, was marching in quest of him he hurried to the banks of the Ribble, and crossed the ford into the Fylde. This latter incident happened towards the end of the week, and on Saturday he was joined in his ambush by the immense royalist force of Colonel Goring, so great indeed that " before the last companies had marched over the bridge at St.

F

Michael's Church the first company was judged to be at Kirkham."[1] There is probably some little exaggeration in the quoted statement, but even allowing it to be verbally correct, there can be no doubt that it is unintentionally misleading, as the extreme length of road covered would be due more to the wide intervals between the companies and the straggling manner in which they proceeded than to their actual numerical strength.　Nevertheless the detachment, chiefly composed of cavalry, was enormous, and completely inundated the towns and villages in the parishes of Poulton, Kirkham, and Lytham.　The men were lodged twenty, thirty, forty, fifty, and even sixty in a house, and on the Sunday morning they set out on an errand of pilfering without respect to persons, pillaging those who were friendly with as much eagerness and apparent satisfaction as others who were inimical to their cause, an impartiality so little appreciated by the inhabitants that they are said to have blessed the Roundheads by comparison with these insatiate freebooters.　Horses, money, clothes, sheets, everything that was portable or could be driven, was greedily seized upon, and, in spite of threats and entreaties, remorselessly borne away.　Hundreds of households were stripped not only of their ornaments, bedding, etc., but even of the very implements on which the family depended for subsistence.　It is in truth no figure of speech to state that by far the larger share of the people were reduced to utter and seemingly hopeless destitution, and grateful indeed were they when their portion of the parliamentary grant of collections in the metropolis, before mentioned, was distributed amongst them, coming like manna from the heavens to comfort their desolated homes.　To add insult to injury the graceless troopers compelled their entertainers to employ the Sabbath in winnowing corn in the fields for their chargers, and even refused to allow them to erect the usual curtains to protect the grain from being carried away by the high wind, so that the loss and waste amounted to barely less than the quantity utilised as fodder, and completely exhausted the fruits of their harvest.　Sir Thomas Tyldesley, Lord Molyneux, and others of the leaders, fixed their lodgment near the residence of a gentleman named Richard Harrison, and were supplied with necessaries from Mowbreck Hall.　Freckleton

---

1. A discourse of the Warr in Lancashire, edited by William Beamont.

marsh was the rendezvous, and there the entire forces assembled on the morning of Monday, but were compelled to remain until one o'clock at noon before the Ribble was fordable, when they took their departure, to the intense joy of all those who had trembled for their lives and suffered ruin in their small properties during their brief sojourn. Sir John Meldrum appeared in the district only a few hours after the royalists had left, and thus the Fylde had again a narrow escape of adding one more to the long list of unnatural battles, most truly described as suicidal massacres of the nation, where men ignoring the ties of friendship or kinship imbrued their swords in the blood of each other with a relentless and inhuman savagery, reviving as it seemed the horrid butcheries of the dark ages. Sir John Meldrum hastened in the direction of the retreating foe, but failed to overtake them.

"In 1645," writes Rushworth, "there remained of unreduced garrisons belonging to the king in Lancashire only Lathom House and Greenhalgh Castle."[1] This castle was erected about half a mile eastward of Garstang, overlooking the Wyre, by Thomas, the first earl of Derby, in 1490, after the victory of Bosworth Field, as a protection from certain of the outlawed nobles, whose estates in that vicinity had rewarded the services of the earl to Henry VII. The castle was built in a rectangular form almost approaching to a square, with a tower at each angle. The edifice was surrounded and protected by a wide moat. The garrison occupying the small fortress at the date under consideration held out until the death of the governor, when a capitulation was made, and, about 1649, the castle was dismantled. In 1772 Penant spoke of the "poor remains of Greenhalgh Castle."[2]

The fall of Lathom House and other strongholds of the king and the surrender of Charles himself to the Scotch army of Puritans, brought the contests for a time to a close in 1647, and Sir Thomas Tyldesley, with several more, received instructions to disband the troops under his command. During the foregoing struggles parliament, in order to provide the necessary funds for the increased expenditure, had allowed "delinquents, papists, spies, and intelligencers" to compound for their sequestered estates, and amongst those connected with this locality who had taken

1, Hist. Collect. P. 4, vol. 1, p. 22.   2. Tour, p. 20.

advantage of the permission were :—

Brown, Edward, of Plumpton, compounded for		£127	8s.	0d.
Breres, Alexander, of Marton, gent.,	,,	£82	4s.	5d.
Bate, John, of Warbreck,	,,	£11	0s.	0d.
Leckonby, Richard, of Elswick, esq.,	,,	£58	6s.	0d.
Nicholson, Francis, of Poulton, yeoman	,,	£133	3s.	4d.
Rigby, Alexander, of Layton, esq.,	,,	£381	3s.	4d.
Walker, William, of Kirkham, gent.,	,,	£175	0s.	0d.
Westby, John, of Mowbreck, esq.,	,,	£1,000	0s.	0d.

Presbyterianism became the national, or at least, the state religion, and for the regulation of ecclesiastical matters the Assembly of Divines, at Westminster, suggested that the country should be divided into provinces, whose representatives should hold annual conferences at the larger towns. The county of Lancaster was divided into nine Classical Presbyteries, and the seventh Classis, embracing the parishes of Preston, Kirkham, Garstang, and Poulton, consisted of—

> Mr. Isaac Ambrose, of Preston, minister.
> Mr. Robert Yates, of Preston, minister.
> Mr. Ed. Fleeetwood, of Kirkham, minister.
> Mr. Thos. Cranage, of Goosnargh, minister.
> Mr. Chr. Edmondson, of Garstang, minister.
> Mr. John Sumner, of Poulton, minister.

LAYMEN.

Alexander Rigby, of Preston, Esq.
William Langton, Esq.
Alderman Matt. Addison, of Preston, gent.
Alderman Wm. Sudall, of Preston, gent.
Alderman Wm. Cottam, of Preston, gent.
Edward Downes, of Wesham, gent

Thomas Nickson, of Plumpton, gent.
Robt. Crane, of Layton, gent.
Wm. Latewise, of Catterall, gent.
Wm. Whitehead, of Garstang, gent.
Edward Veale, of Layton, Esq.
Rd. Wilkins, of Kirkham, yeoman.

Edmund Turner, of Goosnargh, yeoman.

One of the duties of these Classes was to examine, ordain, and appoint ministers, or presbyters, as they were called, whenever vacancies occurred in the district over which, respectively, they had jurisdiction ; subjoined is the certificate given in the case of Cuthbert Harrison, B.A., when selected and appointed presbyter of Singleton chapel :—

"Whereas Cuthbert Harrison, B.A., aged 30 years, hath addressed himself to us, authorised by ordinance of parliament of 22 Aug. 1646, for ordination of ministers, desiring to be ordained a presbyter, being chosen by the inhabitants within the chapelry of Singleton to officiate there ; and having been examined by us the ministers of the Seventh Classis, and found sufficiently qualified for the ministerial functions, according to the rules preserved in the said ordinance, and thereupon approved—we have this day solemnly set him apart to the office of presbyter and work of the ministry of the gospel, by laying on of hands by us present, with fasting and prayer, by virtue whereof we declare him to be a lawful and sufficiently authorised minister of Jesus Christ. In testimony whereof we have hereunto put our hands the 27th Nov., 1651."

(Here follow the signatures.)

In 1648 General Langdale, a royalist officer, appealed to the loyalty of the northern counties to attempt a rescue of the imprisoned monarch from the hands of his enemies. Many rushed to his standard, and the parliamentarians of the Fylde shared the general consternation which pervaded Lancashire at the success of his effort to rekindle the still smouldering embers of civil war. There is no necessity to trace the steps of this ill-judged enterprise to its disastrous issue, but suffice it to say that the defeat and routing of the little army was followed at a very short interval by the execution of Charles I., after a formal trial in which he disclaimed the jurisdiction of the court.

On the 22nd of June, 1650, a meeting of Commissioners under the Great Seal of England was held at Preston—" for inquiring into and certeifying of the certeine numbers and true yearely value of all parsonages and vicariges presentative, of all and every the sp'uall and eccli'call benefices, livings, and donatives within the said countye"; and after examining the good and lawful men of Kirkham and Lytham, it was recommended by the assembly that Goosnargh and Whittingham should be formed into a separate parish on account of their great distance from the church at Kirkham. At this inquiry it was also stated that—" the inhabitants of Newsham desired to be annexed to Woodplumpton; the inhabitants of Clifton and Salwick, together with the inhabitants of Newton-cum-Scales, and the upper end of Treales, desired to be united in one parish. Singleton chappell, newly erected, desired that it might be made a parish. The inhabitants of Weeton-cum-Preese desired that that township might be made a parish, and the inhabitants of Rawcliffe desired to be annexed to it. The townships of Rigby-cum-Wraye, and of Warton, and of Kellamore-cum-Bryning, and Westbye-cum-Plumpton, all humbly desired to be made a parish. The several townships of Eccleston Parva-cum-Labrecke, and the inhabitants of Medlar and Thistleton, and the inhabitants of Rossaker-cum-Wharles, desired to be annexed to Elswick, and that it might be made a parish." Although at that time these petitions failed in obtaining their objects, much the same thing has been accomplished in more recent years by Lord Blandford's Act, by which separate parochial districts, as far as ecclesiastical matters are concerned, have been appropriated to each church, thus rendering it independent of the mother-church of the ancient parish in which it might happen to be situated.

In 1651 the son of the unfortunate monarch, who had been proclaimed king by the Scotch under the title of Charles II., crossed the frontier and invaded England with a force of fourteen thousand men. That year the earl of Derby, Sir Thomas Tyldesley, and several other officers, sailed from the Isle of Man, whither they had retired, in obedience to the call of the young prince, and landed either on the Warren, at the mouth of the river Wyre, or at Skippool higher up the stream, with a regiment of two hundred and fifty infantry and sixty cavalry. Two of the vessels grounded during the operation of disembarking the horses, and in the heavy winds that ensued were reduced to total wrecks. As soon as the news of the earl of Derby's arrival on the banks of the Wyre was rumoured abroad, "all the ships," says the *Perfect Diurnall*, "were wafted out of the rivers of Liverpool, and set sail with a fair wind fore Wirewater, where the Frigots rid that brought the Lord Derby over with his company, to surprise them and prevent his Lordship escaping any way by water." The earl marched through the Fylde, but the martial ardour of the inhabitants was not so readily excited as on former occasions, for the recollection of their abusive and piratical treatment by the troopers of Colonel Goring, in 1644, was still fresh in their minds, and effectually checked any feelings of enthusiasm at seeing the royal banners once again unfurled in their midst. A scattered few, however, there were who were willing to forget the misdeeds of the agents in their eagerness for the success of the cause, and with such meagre additions to his strength the earl hastened on. At Preston he raised six hundred horse, and shortly afterwards encountered the parliamentarians, under Colonel Lilburne, at Wigan-lane, where the royalists were defeated with great slaughter. Sir Thomas Tyldesley was slain, and the gallant earl escaped from the field only to be taken prisoner in Cheshire and suffer the fate of his late regal master, Charles I. Alexander

Rigby, the grandson of the Alexander Rigby, of Layton, before mentioned, and only seventeen years of age, also took part in this eventful engagement, and twenty-eight years subsequently, when High Sheriff of the county of Lancaster, erected a monument to the memory of Major-General Sir Thomas Tyldesley near the spot where he fell. So universally esteemed was the valiant knight for his bravery and honourable conduct that the title of "Chevalier sans peur et sans reproche" was conferred upon him alike by friends and enemies. Charles II., after the overthrow of his army by Cromwell, adopted the disguise of a peasant, and having narrowly escaped detection by hiding himself amidst the foliage of an oak tree, fled at the first opportunity over to France. Cromwell was now installed in the chief seat of authority and held the reins of government under the style of Lord Protector.

In 1660, two years after the death of Cromwell, Charles II. was recalled and placed upon the throne; and in 1662 a law was passed by which it was enacted that before St. Bartholomew's Day of that year, all ministers should arrange their services according to the rules contained in the new book of Common Prayer, under pain of dismissal from their preferments. The following letter was received by the churchwardens of Garstang, ordering the ejectment of the Rev. Isaac Ambrose, who was a member of the family of Ambrose of Ambrose Hall, in Wood Plumpton, from his benefice on account of his refusal to conform to the arbitrary regulation :—

"Whereas in a late act of Parliament for uniformitie, it is enacted that every parson, vicar, curate, lecturer, or other ecclesiasticall person, neglecting or refusing, before the Feast Day of St. Bartholomew, 1662, to declare openly before their respective congregations, his assent and consent to all things contained in the book of common prayer established by the said act, *ipso facto*, be deposed, and that every person not being in holy orders by episcopall ordination, and every parson, vicar, curate, lecturer, or other ecclesiasticall person, failing in his subscription to a declaration mentioned in the said act to be subscribed before the Feast Day of St. Bartholomew, 1662, shall be utterly disabled, and *ipso facto* deprived, and his place be void, as if the person so failing be naturally dead. And whereas Isaac Ambrose, late Vicar of Garstang, in the county of Lancaster, hath neglected to declare and subscribe according to the tenor of the said act, I doe therefore declare the church of Garstang to be now void, and doe strictly charge the said Isaac Ambrose, late vicar of the said church, to forbear preaching, lecturing, or officiating in the said church, or elsewhere in the diocese of Chester. And the church-wardens of the said parish of Garstang are hereby required (as by duty they are bound) to secure and preserve the said parish church of Garstang from any

invasion or intrusion of the said Isaac Ambrose, disabled and deprived as above
said by the said act, and the churchwardens are also required upon sight hereof to
show this order to the said Isaac Ambrose, and cause the same to be published
next Sunday after in the Parish Church of Garstang, before the congregation, as
they will answer the contrary.—Given under my hand this 29th day of August,
1662.

"Geo. Cestriens.

" To the Churchwardens of Garstang, in the County Palatine of Lancaster."

In this county sixty-seven ministers refused to submit to the
mandate, and were removed from their churches by the authority
of documents similar to the above, and prohibited from officiating
in their priestly capacity anywhere within the diocese. Amongst
the number, so interdicted, were the Rev. W. Bullock, of
Hambleton, the Rev. Joseph Harrison, of Lund chapel, and the
Rev. Nathaniel Baxter, M.A., of St. Michael's-on-Wyre. The
Nonconformists were subsequently subjected to even greater
harshness and injustice by an act which decreed that no
clergyman, belonging to any of their sects, should reside within
five miles of the town or place at which he had last preached,
unless he took an oath as under :—

"I do swear that it is not lawful, upon any pretence whatsoever, to take arms
against the king, and that I do abhor the traitorous position of taking arms
against his authority ; against his person ; or against those that are commissioned
by him, in pursuance of such commissions ; and that I will not at any time
endeavour any alteration of government either in church or state."

The sufferings experienced by those ministers who had been
deprived of their benefices are described as having been extreme,
nay, almost intolerable, and it was doubtless owing to the great
severity practised towards the body of Nonconformists that the
old creed gained such little popularity for some time after its
re-establishment.

Charles II., soon after the restoration of monarchy at his
coronation, determined to create a new order of knighthood, to
be called the " Royal Oak," as a reward to some of the more
distinguished of his faithful adherents, and amongst the number
selected for the honour were Col. Kirkby, of Upper Rawcliffe,
Richard Butler, of Out Rawcliffe, and Edward Tyldesley, of Fox
Hall, Blackpool.[1] The design was shortly abandoned by the advice

1. From a M.S. of Peter Le Neve., Norroy, among the collection of Mr. Joseph
Ames. The knights of this order were to wear a silver medal ornamented with a
device of the King in the Oak, suspended by a ribbon from their necks. The

of the crown ministers, who foresaw that the necessarily limited distribution of the distinction would give rise to jealousy and animosity amongst those who had been active in the late wars.

In 30 Charles II. a statute was passed entitled "An act for lessening the importation of linen from beyond the seas, and the encouragement of the woollen and paper manufactories of the kingdom"; and by it was provided, under a penalty of £5, half of which was to be distributed to the poor of the parish, that at every interment throughout the country a certificate should be presented to the officiating minister stating that the winding sheet of the deceased person was composed of woollen material and not of linen, as heretofore. The certificate ordered to be used at every burial ran thus :—

"A, of the parish of B, in the county of C, maketh Oath that D, of the parish of B, in the county of C, lately deceased, was not put in, wrapt or wound up or Buried, in any Shirt, Shift, Sheet, or Shroud, made or mingled with Flax, Hemp, Silk, Hair, Gold, or Silver, or other than that which is made of Sheep's Wool only. Nor in any Coffin lined or faced with any cloth, stuff, or anything whatsoever, made or mingled with Flax, Hemp, Silk, Hair, Gold, or Silver, or any other material but Sheep's Wool only.

"Dated the * * day of * * in the xxxth year of the reign of our Sovereign Lord, Charles the second, king of England, Scotland, France, and Ireland, etc.

"Sealed and Subscribed by us, who were present and witnesses to the Swearing of the above said affidavit

(Signatures of two witnesses.)

"I, * * , esq., one of the King's Majesties Justices of the Peace for the County above said, do hereby certify that the day and year above said A came before me and made such affidavit as is above specified according to the late Act of Parliament, entitled An Act for burying in Woollen.

(Signature.)"

The foregoing statute was amended two years later, and the modified enactment continued in force for some time, when it was

following is a list of persons in the county of Lancashire who were considered fit and qualified to be made Knights of this Order with the value of their estates :—

Thomas Holt	per annum	£1000	John Girlington	per annum	£1000
Thomas Greenhalgh	„	1000	Thomas Preston	„	2000
Colonel Kirkby	„	1500	Thomas Farrington of Worden		1000
Robert Holt	„	1000	Thomas Fleetwood of Penwortham		1000
Edmund Asheton	„	1000	William Stanley	„	1000
Christopher Banister	„	1000	Edward Tyldesley	„	1000
Francis Anderton	„	1000	Thomas Stanley	„	1000
Col. James Anderton	„	1500	Richard Boteler (Butler)	„	1000
Robert Nowell	„	1000	John Ingleton, senior	„	1000
Henry Norris	„	1200	— Walmsley of Dunkenhalgh		2000

repealed. In the registers of old churches, such as Bispham, Poulton, Kirkham, and St. Michael's-on-Wyre, where they have been preserved, notices of burials according to this regulation during the two years it was in operation, may be seen ; and amongst the records of the Thirty-men, or governing body of Kirkham, is an entry of expenses incurred when they went "to justice Stanley" to obtain his authority to "demand 50s. for Tomlinson's wife buried in linen," contrary to the law.

Three years from the accession of James II., his repeated attempts to curtail the civil and religious liberties of his subjects had so far incensed them against him that William, Prince of Orange, was invited over to free them from his rule. In 1688 James abdicated the throne, and the following year William and Mary were crowned at Westminster. Annexed is a list of the gentry residing in the Fylde from the reign of Henry VIII, to their accession, as prepared from original records and private manuscripts :—

Allen of Rossall Hall.	Lowde of Kirkham.
Ambrose of Ambrose Hall.	Massey of Carleton.
Bradley of Bryning.	Molyneux of Larbrick Hall.
Bradshaw of Preese and Scales.	Parker of Bradkirk Hall.
Butler of Rawcliffe Hall.	Rigby of Layton Hall.
Butler of Layton and Hackensall.	Sharples of Freckleton.
Clifton of Westby.	Shuttleworth of Larbrick.
Eccleston of Great Eccleston Hall.	Singleton of Singleton.
Fleetwood of Plumpton.	Singleton of Staining Hall.
Fleetwood of Rossall Hall.	Stanley of Great Eccleston Hall.
Hesketh of Mains Hall.	Tyldesley of Fox Hall, Blackpool.
Kirkby of Upper Rawcliffe.	Veale of Whinney Heys.
Kirkby of Mowbreck.	Westby of Rawcliffe.
Leigh of Singleton.	Westby of Mowbreck and Burn
Longworth of St. Michael's Hall.	Halls.

James II., when force of circumstances had driven him into exile, left a considerable number of supporters behind him, chiefly amongst the Roman Catholics, who were not dilatory in devising schemes for his re-establishment. On the 16th of May, 1690, Robert Dodsworth deposed upon oath, before Lord Chief Justice Holt, that the following Popish gentry of the Fylde, amongst others, had entered into a conspiracy to restore James, and that they had received commissions as indicated for the purpose of raising troops to carry out the enterprise :—Colonel Thomas

Tyldesley, son of the late Sir Thomas ; Captains Ralph Tyldesley, son of the late Sir Thomas ; Thomas Tyldesley, of Fox Hall, nephew to the two preceeding ; Richard Butler, of Rawcliffe Hall, and Henry, his eldest son ; Thomas Westby, of Mowbreck Hall, and William, his third son, who was designated a lieutenant ; and Lieutenant Richard Stanley, of Great Eccleston Hall. Nothing is recorded as to the result of the above information, but in 1694 Sir Thomas Clifton, brother to Cuthbert Clifton, of Lytham, was arraigned, with several more, on a charge of treason in connection with a reported Jacobite plot, but was acquited, as also were those with him. During the course of the trial, Thomas Patten, of Preston, as witness to the loyalty of Sir Thomas Clifton to the existing government, stated that "in 1689 he received orders from the Lord Lieutenant to secure several Popish gentlemen, and that amongst them Sir Thomas Clifton was one who was taken and brought prisoner to Preston upon the 16th day of June in that year ; that Sir Thomas being a very infirm man and unfit to be carried so far as Manchester, which was the place where the rest of the Popish gentlemen then made prisoners were secured, he undertook for Sir Thomas, and prevailed to have him kept at his (Patten's) own house in Preston, where he continued prisoner, and was not discharged until the January following, at which time all the gentlemen were set at liberty ; that during Sir Thomas Clifton's confinement he expressed to him much zeal and affection to the present government, saying how much the persons of his religion ought to be satisfied with their usage, as putting no difference betwixt them and other subjects save the public exercise of their religion, so long as they themselves would be quiet, and protested for himself that he could never endure to think of practising any change." Further Mr. Patten affirmed "that he knew Sir Thomas's disposition to have always been peaceful and quiet." During the time that James II. was engaged in inciting the Irish nation to espouse his cause and furnish him with an army to invade England and regain his throne, Thomas Tyldesley, of Fox Hall, prepared a secret chamber in that mansion for his reception. The disastrous battle of the Boyne, however, in which James was vanquished by William, Prince of Orange, and King of England, crushed all hope of future success in the fallen monarch, and at the earliest opportunity he escaped to France.

In 1715, during the reign of George I., his son, the Chevalier de
St. George was proclaimed king in Scotland under the title of
James III. The earl of Mar and several other influential supporters of the Stuarts assembled a large force and marched southwards ; on arriving at the border five hundred of the Highlanders
refused to proceed further, but the remainder passed through the
northern counties as far as Preston. Here they were besieged by
the loyal troops under Generals Carpenter and Wills, who
stormed the town and forced the rebels to an unconditional
surrrender. Many of the leaders were executed, whilst others
were incarcerated for various terms ; the general treatment of
their unfortunate followers may be gleaned from the journal of
William Stout, of Lancaster, in which it is written :—" After the
rebellion was suppressed about 400 of the rebels were brought to
Lancaster Castle, and a regiment of Dragoons was quartered in
the town to guard them. The king allowed them each 4d. a day
for maintenance, viz., 2d. in bread, 1d. in cheese, and 1d. in small
beer. And they laid on straw in stables most of them, and in a
month's time about 100 of them were conveyed to Liverpool to be
tried, where they were convicted and near 40 of them hanged at
Preston, Garstang, Lancaster, etc. ; and about 200 of them continued a year, and about 50 of them died, and the rest were
transported to America." Thomas Tyldesley, of Fox Hall, died in
1715, just before the outbreak of the rebellion, but his son Edward,
who succeeded him, joined the rebels. For this act of treason he
was put on his trial, but escaped conviction and punishment
through the favour of the jury, by whom he was acquitted
in spite of clear and reliable evidence that he had entered
Preston at the head of a company of insurgents with a
drawn sword in his hand. After the capitulation, when
the king's troops had entered the town and were marching
along the streets, many men from our district, who had
congregated on Spital's Moss, armed with fowling pieces and
implements of husbandry, joined their ranks, and a huge duck-gun
belonging to a yeoman named Jolly, from Mythorp, near Blackpool, was instrumental in doing good service to the besiegers by
slaying one Mayfield, of the Ashes, Goosnargh. The rebel had
secreted himself behind a chimney on one of the houses, and was
engaged in picking off the loyal soldiers as they made their way

along the thoroughfare below. His murderous fire was at length put an end to by a charge from the famed gun of Jolly, whose keen eye had detected the assassin in his hiding place. Jolly himself appears to have had an aversion to causing the death of a fellow-creature in cold blood, even though a rebel, and the credit of the shot is due to a soldier, whose own weapon failed in reaching the object. The Rev. W. Thornber tells us in his History of Blackpool, that the family of the Jollys, for many years, treasured up the wonderful gun, and that the tale of its exploit was circulated far and wide in the neighbourhood of their home. From the remarks of the Rev. — Patten, who accompanied the army of the Chevalier, as chaplain to General Forster, we learn that those who joined the insurgents in Lancashire were chiefly Papists, and that the members of the High-church party held aloof, much to the disappointment and chagrin of General Forster, who, in his anger, declared " that for the time to come he would never again believe a drunken tory." Edward Tyldesley, Henry Butler, of Rawcliffe Hall, and his son Richard Butler, were the most distinguished personages amongst the small body of men belonging to this section who openly espoused the cause of the Pretender. The paucity of the recruits attracted by the insurgent standard from our neighbourhood is easily to be accounted for, when it is remembered that for many years the county of Lancashire had enjoyed an inmunity from strifes and disturbances, so that the inhabitants of the rural districts, such as the Fylde, had settled down to the cultivation of the soil, and would care little to assist in a work which as far as they were privately concerned, could only terminate in the devastation of their fields, and, probably, in the ruin of many of their households. Especially, in 1715, would the people be disinclined to take part in or encourage insurrectionary and warlike proceedings, for in that year extraordinarily bountiful harvests had rewarded their labours, and general prosperity had taught them the blessings of peace.[1] After the rebellion of 1715 many Papists registered their estates and the respective yearly values thereof, according to an Act of Parliament passed in the reign of George I., and amongst the number may be observed the

---

1. " This year (1715) provisions were plentiful and cheap, as also corn and hay " —the Journal of W. Stout of Lancaster.

names of sundry local personages as :—

		Annual Value.		
Sherburne, Sir Nicholas,	of Carleton, Hambleton, and Stonyhurst,	£1210	6s.	3½d.
Butley, Mary, }	wife and only child of Rich. Butler,	100	0	0
Butler, Catherine, }	who died in gaol,	537	0	0
Butler, Elizabeth,	of Kirkland, afterwards the third wife of Henry Butler, of Rawcliffe,	11	10	0
Butler, Christopher	second son of H. Butler, of Rawcliffe,	10	19	6
Brockholes, John,	of Claughton, etc.,	522	19	1
Clifton, Thomas,	of Lytham, Clifton, etc.,	1548	16	10½
Clifton, Bridget,		3	10	0
Blackburne, Thomas	of Wood Plumpton,	1	6	0
Blackburne, Richard,	of Stockenbridge, near St. Michael's,	21	2	0
Hesketh, William,	of Mains,	198	3	4½
Hesketh, George,	brother to W. Hesketh,	13	6	8
Hesketh, Margaret,	widow of Thos. Hesketh, of Mains,	57	0	0
Singleton, Anne,	of Staining and Bardsea,	76	15	10
Stanley, Anne,	widow of Richard Stanley of Great Eccleston,	118	15	0
Swartbreck, John,	of Little Eccleston,	23	15	0
Tyldesley, Edward,	of Fox Hall, and Myerscough,	720	9	2
Tyldesley, Agatha,	half-sister of Edward Tyldesley,	52	10	0
Threlfall, Cuthbert,	of Wood Plumpton,	31	12	6
Westby, John,	of White Hall, St. Michael's,	119	11	1
Westby, John,	of Mowbreck,	230	5	1½
Westby, Thomas, }	bros. of J. Westby, of Mowbreck,	20	0	0
Westby, Cuthbert, }		20	0	0
Leckonby, William,	of Leckonby House, Elswick, etc.,	79	11	6
Walley, Thurstan,	of Kirkham,	12	0	8
Charnock, Anne,	of Salwick,	1	4	0
Knott, Thomas,	of Thistleton,	20	0	0

Prince Charles Edward, the son of the former Pretender, landed in the Hebrides, in 1745, with a well-officered force of two thousand men, and after defeating Sir John Cope, seized the city of Edinburgh and commenced his march southwards. Crossing the border, he passed through Lancashire, and arrived at Preston with an army barely six thousand strong. At Preston he met with an enthusiastic welcome, the church bells were rung, and loud cheers greeted the proclamation of his father, the Chevalier, as king of Great Britain and Ireland. His sojourn in the town was brief, and on the 27th of November the rebel troops set out for Manchester, inspirited by the lively strains of "The King shall have his own again." Arriving at that city, they continued

their march towards Derby, where, on receiving the news that the
Duke of Cumberland was at Lichfield on his way to intercept
them, Prince Charles Edward hastened to beat a retreat, and on
the 12th of December re-passed through the streets of Preston,
the wearied feet of his followers keeping time to the doleful but
appropriate air of " Hie the Charlie home again."

The battle on the moor of Culloden, in which the rebel army
was defeated by the Duke of Cumberland, finally decided the fate
of the House of Stuart, and after experiencing many hardships,
Prince Charles Edward escaped across the channel into France.
James, the son of Edward Tyldesley who took part in the
insurrection of 1715, served in the army of the Young Pretender.
During the excitement and alarm produced by these rebellions,
silver spoons, tankards, and other household treasures, were
deposited for safety in a farm house at Marton ; cattle and other
farm-stock were driven to Boonley, near Blackpool, whilst money
and articles of jewelry were buried in the soil of Hound Hill in
that town. The Scots who accompanied Prince Charles were so
renowned for their voracious appetites that the householders of
the Fylde prepared for their expected visit by laying in an
abundant supply of eatables, hoping that a good repast, like a soft
answer, would turn away wrath. Mr. Physic, of Poulton, was an
exception to the general rule, and having barricaded his house,
determined vigorously to resist any attack of the rebels either
on his larder or his purse. Hotly pursued by the Duke of
Cumberland in their retreat towards Scotland, the insurgents
were quickly hurried through the country, but some of the
stragglers found their way to Mains Hall, where they were
liberally provided with food by Mrs. Hesketh. It is probable that
these rebels formed part of the number of Highlanders, who were
afterwards captured at Garstang, and that one of them was the
bare-footed Scot who seized the boots of John Miller, of Layton,
dragging them from his feet with the cool remark—" Hout mon,
but I mon tak' thy brogues." William Hesketh, of Mains, had
considered it prudent to secrete himself on the warren at Rossall
until the excitement had subsided, as in some way or other he
had been mixed up with the former outbreak, and wished to
avoid any suspicion of having been implicated in this one also.
At the sanguinary and decisive battle of Culloden, two notorious

characters from Layton and Staining were present ; one of them,
named Leonard Warbreck, served in the capacity of hangman at
the executions following the rebellion, whilst the other, James
Kirkham, generally known as Black Kirkham, was a gallant
soldier, remarkable for his giant-like size and immense strength.
The country people near his home were wont to declare that,
for a small wager, this warrior carried his horse and accoutrements
round the cross at Wigan to the astonishment and admiration of
the by-standers.   One incident of these times, reflecting little
credit on this neighbourhood, but which, as faithful recorders,
we are bound to relate, was the journey of Henry Hardicar, of
Little Poulton, to London, a distance of two hundred and thirty-
three miles, all of which he travelled on foot, solely to gratify a
morbid taste by witnessing the legal tragedies performed on
Tower Hill.   "I saw the lords heided" was his invariable
answer to all inquiries as to the wonders he had seen in the
metropolis.   In this rising, as in the earlier one, the inhabitants
of the Fylde evinced their prudence and good sense by remaining
as nearly neutral as their allegiance to the reigning monarch
would permit them.   Those insurgents who found their way into
the district were treated with kindness, but no encouragement
was given them to prolong their stay, either by professions of
sympathy or offers of assistance in their insurrectionary enterprise.

We have at last come to the end of the long chain of wars and
disturbances which from the period of the struggles between the
Houses of York and Lancaster, had exercised their baneful
influence on the territory and population of the Fylde, and are
now entering on an era of peace and unbroken prosperity.   The
small water-side hamlets of Blackpool and Lytham put forth
their rival claims to the patronage of the inland residents,—

                "And had their claims allow'd."

In 1788, Mr. Hutton described the former place as consisting of
about fifty houses and containing four hundred visitors in the
height of the season.   This historian also informs us, that the
inhabitants were remarkable for their great longevity, and relates
the anecdote of a woman who, forming one of a group of
sympathising friends around the couch of a dying man, exclaimed
—"Poor John! I knew him a clever young fellow four score
years ago."   Lytham, also, attracted a considerable number of

visitors during the summer, and for many years was a more popular resort than Blackpool. In Mr. Baines's account of Lytham, published in 1825, we read as follows :—" This is one of the most popular sea-bathing places in the county of Lancashire ; and if the company is less fashionable than at Blackpool, it is generally more numerous, and usually very respectable."

A list of the Catholic Chapels and Chaplains, together with the number of their respective congregations, in the county of Lancaster, was collected in 1819, and subjoined are enumerated those situated in the Hundred of Amounderness :—

Place.	Chapels.		Priest.	No. of Congregation.
Preston	2	Revd.	— Dunn	
,,		,,	— Morris	
,,		,,	— Gore	 6,000
,,		,,	— Bird	
Alston Lane	1	,,	— Cowburne	400
Fernyhalgh	1	,,	— Blakoe	500
The Hill	1	,,	— Martin	450
Claughton	1	,,	— Gradwell	800
Scorton	1	,,	— Lawrenson	350
Garstang	1	,,	— Storey	600
New House	1	,,	— Marsh	600
Cottam	1	,,	— Caton	300
Lea	1	,,	— Anderton	400
Willows	1	,,	— Sherburne	600
Westby	1	,,	— Butler	300
Lytham	1	,,	— Dawson	500
Poulton	1	,,	— Platt	400
Great Eccleston	1	,,	— Parkinson	450
Total	16			12,650 1.

In 1836 the first house of Fleetwood was erected, and in a few years the desolate warren at the mouth of the Wyre was converted into a rising and prosperous town. The rapidity of its early growth may be inferred from the following paragraph, extracted from a volume on Lancashire, published during the infancy of this new offspring of the Fylde :—" As a bathing place, it possesses very superior attractions : hot water baths, inns, and habitations of all kinds have sprung as if by magic on one of the most agreeable sites it is possible to imagine, very superior to any other

1. A tract in the library of the British Museum, entitled " Catholic Chapels, Chaplains," etc., and bearing the date 1819.

in Lancashire, admitting, as from a central point, excursions by
land and water in all directions, amongst some of the most
beautiful scenery in the empire.   A couple of hours steaming takes
the tourist across Morecambe Bay to the Furness capital, and into
the heart of a district of surpassing interest.   Charming indeed
is Fleetwood in the height of the summer, with its cool sands,
northern aspect, and delightful prospects.   First there is a noble
bay in front, an ocean of itself when the tide is in ; and when it
is out offering firm sands of vast extent, for riding or walking."
Sir Peter Hesketh Fleetwood, bart., of Rossall Hall, lord of the
manor, and founder of the town to which he gave his name, was
returned on four occasions as one of the parliamentary representatives of Preston :—

MEMBERS OF PARLIAMENT FOR PRESTON.

1832.—Peter Hesketh Fleetwood, and the Hon. Henry Thos. Stanley.
1835.—Peter Hesketh Fleetwood, and the Hon. Henry Thos. Stanley.
1837.—Peter Hesketh Fleetwood, and Robert Townley Parker.
1841.—Sir Peter Hesketh Fleetwood, Bart., and Sir Geo. Strickland, Bart.

The year 1840 was an auspicious one in the history of the Fylde.
On the 25th of July, the Preston and Wyre Railway, running
through the heart of this district, was completed and declared
open for traffic.   By its means the farmer became enabled to
convey his produce to the extensive market of Preston ; and
Kirkham, Poulton, and Garstang were no longer the only towns
accessible to our agriculturists for the sale of their crops.   The
early appreciation of the utility and benefit of the line is apparent
from the rapid increase of its traffic, as shown by the annexed
tables, in which the official returns of passengers and goods for
the week ending Dec. 14th, 1842, and the corresponding weeks
of the four succeeding years are stated :—

Week ending Dec. 14th, 1842.	911 Passengers.	£65 10s. 5d.
	Goods.	62 8 1
		127 18 6
Corresponding week in 1843.	1105 Passengers.	88 1 6
	Goods.	140 11 9
		228 13 3

Corresponding week in 1844.	1601 Passengers	139	4	6
	Goods.	163	18	11
		303	3	5
Corresponding week in 1845.	1997 Passengers.	144	12	1
	Goods.	234	13	4
		379	5	5
Corresponding week in 1846.	2820 Passengers.	243	19	0
	Goods.	308	18	5
		552	17	5

At the present date, 1876, the average weekly traffic on this railway and its branches to Lytham and Blackpool, amounts in round numbers to £1,200 for passengers, and £800 for goods.

The Preston and Wyre Railway was amongst the earliest formed, and the impression made on the natives of this district, who had been accustomed to the slow-going coaches, must have been one of no little amazement, when, for the first time, they beheld the "iron horse" steaming along the rails at a speed which their past experience of travelling would make them regard as impossible. The following lines were written by a gentleman named Henry Anderton, a resident in the Fylde, on the opening of the railway:

> "Some fifty years since and a coach had no power,
> To move faster forward than six miles an hour,
> Till Sawney McAdam made highways as good,
> As paving-stones crushed into little bits could.
> The coachee quite proud of his horse-flesh and trip,
> Cried, 'Go it, ye cripples!' and gave them the whip,
> And ten miles an hour, by the help of the thong,
> They put forth their mettle and scampered along.
> The Present has taken great strides of the Past,
> For carriages run without horses at last!
> And what is more strange,—yet it's truth I avow,
> Hack-horses themselves have turned passengers now!
> These coaches alive go in sixes and twelves,
> And once set in motion they travel themselves!
> They'll run thirty miles while I'm cracking this joke,
> And need no provisions but pump-milk and coke!
> And with their long chimneys they skim o'er the rails,
> With two thousand hundred-weight tied to their tails!

> While Jarvey in stupid astonishment stands,
> Upturning both eyes and uplifting both hands,
> ' My nags,' he exclaims, betwixt laughing and crying,
> ' Are good 'uns to go, but yon devils are flying.'"

The fares on the Preston and Wyre Railway at its commencement were :—

	1st class.	2nd class.	3rd class.
Preston to Fleetwood or Blackpool	4s. 6d.	3s. 0d.	2s. 0d.
Preston to Poulton	3s. 6d.	2s. 6d.	1s. 6d.
Preston to Kirkham	2s. 0d.	1s. 3d.	0s. 9d.
Preston to Lytham	3s. 0d.	2s. 6d.	1s. 6d.

Until the opening of the branch lines to Lytham and Blackpool respectively, in 1846, passengers completed their journies from Kirkham and Poulton to those watering places by means of coaches. Three trains ran from the terminus at Fleetwood to Preston on each week-day, and one on Sunday, a similar number returning.

In consequence of the severe distress prevailing throughout the country, a proclamation was issued by Her Majesty for a General Fast to be held on Wednesday, the 24th of March, 1847 ; and from the public prints of that date it is evident that the occasion was observed with great solemnity in our division—the shops of the different towns were closed during the whole of the day, the streets were quiet, the hotels deserted, whilst the churches were crowded even to overflowing. This distress was caused by an almost complete failure in the potatoe harvests ; and at that time these necessary articles of diet were sold at 26s. per load in the local markets, whilst meal, also scarce, rose to 52s. per load.

In September of the same year, the Fylde was honoured by a passing visit from Queen Victoria and the late Prince Consort, who arrived at Fleetwood in the Royal Yacht on their return journey from Scotland to London. An address was presented by Sir P. H. Fleetwood, bart., the Rev. St. Vincent Beechey, Frederick Kemp, esq., James Crombleholme, esq., and Daniel Elletson, esq., on behalf of the inhabitants of Fleetwood, and received by Lord Palmerston, who promised that it should be laid before the Queen. In the course of a few days an acknowledgment was received from the metropolis. In Her Majesty's book, published in 1868, and entitled "Leaves from our Highland Journal," these diarian entries relating to the above event appear :—

" Monday, September 20th, 1847.

" We anchored at seven in Fleetwood Harbour ; the entrance was extremely narrow and difficult. We were lashed close to the pier, to prevent our being turned by the tide ; and when I went on deck there was a great commotion, such running and calling, and pulling of ropes, etc. It was a cheerless evening, blowing hard."

" Tuesday, September 21st, 1847.

" At ten o'clock we landed, and proceeded by rail to London."

In 1860, a project was launched for a comprehensive scheme of water supply for the towns of this district ; a company was established, and, in the session of 1861, an act of parliament was obtained " for incorporating the Fylde Waterworks Company, and for authorising them to make and maintain waterworks, and to supply water at Kirkham, Lytham, Blackpool, Fleetwood, Poulton, Rossall, Garstang, South-shore, and Bispham, in the county palatine of Lancaster, and to shipping at Fleetwood and Lytham." The act granted power to take the water from Grizedale Brook, a tributary of the Wyre, which rises in Grizedale Fell, one of the Bleasdale range, and, flowing through the gorge or pass, called Nickey Nook, divides the township of Nether-Wyersdale and Barnacre-with-Bonds, and falls into the Wyre a mile or so before that river reaches Garstang. A dam or embankment, upwards of 20 feet high, 70 feet wide at the base, and 12 feet wide at the top, was raised across the valley, converting the upper portion of it into a reservoir. At the west end of the reservoir, below the embankment, is a culvert, through which the water passes to a guage, where a stipulated quantity is turned into the brook, and the rest enters the pipe for the Fylde. Twelve miles of twelve inch pipes carry the water to the service reservoir at Weeton. The course is down Grizedale, under the railway, through Greenhalgh Green, Bowgrave, leaving Garstang to the right, then past Catterall Mill, through the grounds of Catterall Hall, and onward to the east of St. Michael's, through Elswick, to Weeton. The service reservoir, situated on the most elevated ground, called Whitprick Hill, in the township of Weeton, has a diameter at the base of 400 feet, and at the top 468 feet. The embankment is at the base 70 feet in diameter, and 12 feet at the top, with a puddle trench in it, varying from 8 feet 8 inches to 6 feet wide. To the south a 10 inch main takes the supply of water for Kirkham and Lytham ; and from the west side a main of similar size takes the water for Fleetwood and Blackpool, the supply for the former place branching off near Great Marton, and going by Bispham and Rossall. The Weeton reservoir was formed capable of containing fifteen million gallons of water. An additional pipe, running from Weeton through Singleton, Skippool, and Thornton, to join the Fleetwood main at Flakefleet, near Rossall, was laid in 1875 ; and a new reservoir, to hold 190,000,000 gallons, is in course of formation at Barnacre, above Grizedale.

CHAPTER IV.

CONDITION, CUSTOMS, AND SUPERSTITIONS OF THE PEOPLE.

THERE is little to be remarked, because little is known, respecting the social and moral aspects of the untutored race which, in the earliest historic age, sought a domicile or refuge amidst the forests of the Fylde, or invaded its glades in search of prey. The habits of the Setantii were simply those of other savage tribes who depended for their daily sustenance upon their skill and prowess in the chase, and whose intercommunion with the world beyond their own limited domains, was confined to hostile or friendly meetings with equally barbarous races whose frontiers adjoined their own. Certain disinterred roots were necessary adjuncts to their repasts, and indeed, on many occasions, when outwitted by the wild tenants of the woods, formed the sole item. Their Druidical faith and the supreme power of the priesthood over their almost every action, both secular and religious, have already been referred to in an earlier page. The remorseless sacrifice of fellow beings on their unhallowed altars, and the general spirit of cruelty and inhumanity which pervaded all their rites, are not to be regarded as disclosing a naturally callous and brutal disposition on the part of the Setantii, but as indications of the deplorable ignorance in which they existed, and the blind obdedience which they yielded to the principles indoctrinated by the Druids. That the Setantii, however submissive to the dictates and requirements of their priests, were far from passively allowing the encroachments of others on their liberties is shown by the promptitude and fierceness with which they combatted the progress of the Roman legions through their territory. No portion of the British conquest cost the conquerors more trouble, time, and bloodshed, than did the land peopled by the hardy and valorous Brigantes with their comparatively small, but equally intrepid, neighbours and allies the Setantii. The two most striking characteristics of the aboriginal Fylde inhabitants were their ignorance and bravery, and whilst the former rivetted the chains which held them in subjection to the priesthood, the latter incited them to oppose to the death the usurpations of the stranger. There is nothing of local interest to recount during the period the Romans held the soil, but after their abdication, when the Anglo-Saxons violated their faith and traitorously seized a land which they had come professedly to protect, the Fylde began to evince symptoms of greater animation ; villages sprang up in different spots on the open grounds or clearings in the woods ; the solitary Roman settlement at Kirkham was appropriated and renamed by the new arrivals, and, perhaps, for the first time a population of numerical importance was established in the district.

During the earlier part of this era the inhabitants were graziers rather than agriculturists or ploughmen. Three quarters, even, of the entire kingdom were devoted to rearing and feeding cattle, so that the grain produce of the country must have been extremely small when compared with the superabundance of live stock, and as a consequence of such a condition of things, those animals which could forage for themselves and exist upon the wild herbage of the waste lands or the fallen fruits of the trees, as acorns and beech-mast, were to be purchased at prices almost nominal, whilst others which required the cultivated products of the fields, as corn and hay, for their sustenance, were disproportionately dear ; thus about the end of the tenth century the values of the former were :—

One Ox	7s.	0½d.
„ Cow	5s.	6d.
„ Pig	1s.	10½d.
„ Sheep	1s.	2d.
„ Goat	0s.	5½d.

The latter commanded these comparatively high prices—

One Horse	£1	5s.	2d.
„ Mare, or Colt	£1	3s.	5d.
„ Ass, or Mule	£0	14s.	1d.

Trees were valued not by the circumference or magnitude of their trunks, but by the amount of shelter their branches would afford to the cattle, which seem to have lived almost entirely in the open pastures ; and bearing that in mind we are not surprised to read in the Saxon Chronicle of periodical plagues or murrains breaking out amongst them. " In 1054," says that journal, "there was so great loss of cattle as was not remembered for many winters before." This, however, is only one extract from frequent entries referring to similar misfortunes in different years, both before and after the date quoted. Swine were kept in immense herds throughout the kingdom, and there is every probability that in a locality like the Fylde, where trees would still abound and provender be plentifully scattered from the oaks and beeches, hogs would be extensively bred. Indeed immediately after the close of the Saxon empire, Roger de Poictou conveyed his newly acquired right to pawnage (swine's food) in the woods of Poulton, amongst other things, to the monastery of St. Mary, in Lancaster, a circumstance strongly favourable to the existence of swine there in considerable numbers. Kine, also, are usually reported to have been a favourite stock with the breeders of Lancashire, whilst sheep were rare in proportion, although in other places they were exceedingly popular and profitable, chiefly from the sale of their wool.

The Saxon inhabitants of the small villages in the Fylde who were engaged in agriculture had no knowledge of any manure beyond marl, which they mixed with lighter and finer soils ; nor were their farm-lands cultivated all at one time, but a portion only of the estate was subjected to the action of the plough, and when its fertility had been thoroughly exhausted, the remainder was tilled and brought into service, the first plot being allowed to lie fallow for a few years until its productive powers had been renewed. Grain was not, as now, purchased from the growers by dealers and stored up in warehouses, but each of the neighbouring people, as soon as the crops had been gathered into the barns, bought whatever quantity he thought would suffice for his household wants until the ensuing harvest, and removed it to his own residence. The universal waste and improvident consumption of grain during this season of abundance, led frequently to famines in other parts of the year, and many instances of that punishment following such prodigality are related in the chronicle before named. One notice, bearing the date 1044, says :—" This year there was very great hunger all over England, and corn so dear as no man ever remembered before ; so that a sester of wheat rose to sixty pence and even further."

The ploughs of our forefathers were, as would naturally be supposed, somewhat rude and clumsy in construction, differing considerably in appearance, although not in their *modus operandi*, from those which may be seen furrowing the same land in the present day. Each plough was furnished with an iron share, in front of which, attached to the extremity of a beam projecting anteriorly, was a wheel of moderate diameter, its purpose being to relieve the labour of the oxen and to facilitate the guiding of the instrument, especially in turning. The oxen employed were ordinarily four, and yoked to the plough by means of twisted willow bands. Horses were prohibited by law from being used on the land, but there must have been little need, one would imagine, for a legal prohibition in the matter when it is remembered that horses were nearly four times as valuable as oxen, and that the latter were fully efficient at the task. The month of January commenced their season for preparing the ground, and during the period thus occupied the labours of the ploughman began each morning at sunrise, when the oxen were tethered and conducted to the fields, where the duty of the husbandman was lightened by the assistance of a boy, who superintended the cattle, driving or leading them whilst at work. In the inclement months of winter these oxen were fed and tended in sheds under the special care of the ploughman, but during summer they shared a common lot with the other cattle and were turned out to pasture in the fields, being transferred to the charge of the cowherd. Other implements of husbandry in use, in addition to the plough, were scythes, sickles, axes, spades, pruning-hooks, forks, and flails, besides which the farmers possessed carts and waggons of rather a cumbersome pattern. It is doubtful whether the harrow was known here so early, but opinion usually refers its introduction to a later date.

Of the moral tone of our Saxon settlers it is difficult to judge, but that there business transactions were not always governed by a very strict sense of honour is intimated by the following enactment, apparently framed to check repudiations of bargains and, perhaps, to insure fair dealing :—" No one shall buy either what is living or what is dead to the value of four pennies without four witnesses either of the borough or of the village." William of Malmesbury, who wrote about a century after the Norman Conquest, informs us that " excessive eating and drinking were the common vices of the Saxons, in which they spent whole nights and days without intermission." It may, however, with much probability be conjectured that not only is the statement in some degree exaggerated, but that its application was designed more particularly for the inhabitants of the larger towns than those of comparatively sparsely populated districts like our own. Nevertheless it cannot be claimed, with any show of reason, that the small section of the nation established in the Fylde was entirely uninfected by the vices which enervated and degraded the wealthier and more populous regions of the kingdom. The evil of intemperance in both food and drink, especially the latter, pervaded the whole community, but as its indulgence required both means and opportunity, its loathsome features were less prominently visible in localities where these were scarce than in others where they abounded. The Church used every effort to awaken a better feeling in the minds of her degenerate sons, and liberate them from the chains of a passion which had so thoroughly enslaved them. Canons were directed against the " sin of drunkenness," and in order that no plea of ignorance could be urged by any who had overstepped the bounds of sobriety, a curious and minute description of the condition of body and brain which constituted inebriation was appended to one of them, as here quoted :—" This is drunkenness—when the state of the mind is changed, the tongue stammers, the eyes are disturbed, the head is giddy, the belly is swelled, and pain follows." Ale and mead were the beverages on which these excesses were committed, and cow-horns the drinking cups. It would seem that there was yet another national blemish, that of gambling, which even invaded the cloister and threw its veil of fascination over the clergy themselves, for a canon of the reign of Edgar ordered —" That no priest be a hunter, or fowler, or player at tables, but let him play upon his books, as becometh his calling."

Water-mills, planted on the banks of streams and consisting of square weather-boarded structures, usually open at the top, were the means possessed during the Saxon era for grinding the cereal products of the Fylde. The wheel which received the pressure of the current, and conveyed its motive power to the simple machinery within the fabric, differed little from those still in use in various parts of the country, one of which until recently was connected with a small mill on the brink of the brook which drains the mere at Marton into the river Wyre, and less than a century ago another mill, situated in the township of Marton and worked on a similar principle, was turned by a stream from the same mere. A water-mill is at present in use near Great Eccleston. After the grinding process had been completed the bran and flour were separated by hand-sieves. About seventy or eighty years after the Normans had settled in the district these primitive sheds were superseded by a fresh species of mill, in which sails supplied the place of the wheel, and another element was called into service. The new erections were of wood, and separated from the ground by a pivot of slight altitude, on which they turned bodily in order to be fixed in the most favourable position for their sails to reap a full harvest of wind. Solitary specimens of this early piece of mechanical ingenuity are still visible hereabouts, but most of the old mills were pulled down about a hundred years ago, or less, and rebuilt with more stable material, whilst the modern improvement of a revolving top only, did away with the necessity for the venerable pivot, and allowed the foundations of the edifices to be more intimately associated with mother earth than formerly.

Throughout the whole of the Saxon dynasty the mass of the inhabitants would be what were termed the "villani," that is, a class forming a link between abject slavery and perfect independence. They were not bound to any master but to the soil on which they happened to be born, and on no plea were they permitted to leave such localities. To the lord of the manor each of the "villani" gave annually a certain portion of the produce of the ground he tilled, but beyond that they acknowledged no claim to the proceeds of their thrift by the large territorial proprietors. When a manor changed ownership the "villani" were transferred with it in exactly the same condition as before, so that really they seem to have occupied the position of small tenants paying rent in kind, with the important addition that they were forced to pass their lives in the district where they had first seen the light of day. It should be noted that any "villani" not having domiciles of their own were compelled to enter the service of others who were more fortunately situated in that respect.

During the twelfth century the house-wife's plan of preparing bread for the table, in the absence of public bakehouses, common in some neighbourhoods, was to knead the dough into large flat cakes and lay them on the hearth in full glare of the fire, where they were permitted to remain until thoroughly baked. Bread from pure wheat of the best quality was a luxury unattainable except by those of high station or wealth, the bulk of the people having to content themselves with an inferior quality, brownish in colour and made from rye, oats, and barley. The amount of this indispensable commodity to be sold at a specified price was regulated by law, and the punishments for not supplying the proper measure, or for "lack of size" as it was termed, were—for the first offence, loss of the bread; for the second, imprisonment; and for the third, the pillory or tumbrel.[1] In 1185 the maximum charges to be made for certain provisions were settled by an act which decreed that the highest price for a hen should be $\frac{1}{2}$d., a sheep 5$\frac{1}{2}$d., a ram 8d., a hog 1s., an ox 5s. 8d., and a cow 4s. 6d.

In the ensuing century no restrictions were placed upon the tenants of the Fylde as to the course of husbandry to be pursued, but each on renting his farm or parcel of ground cultivated it according to the dictates of his own inclination or experience, the only stipulation being that the soil should suffer no deterioration from any ignorant or imprudent action on the part of the holder. Oats and barley mixed, and a light description of wheat, very inferior to the best grain, were the favourite crops, the former being known as "draget," and the latter as "siligo." Arable land was let at 4d. per acre, and the annual yield of each acre sown with wheat, usually amounted to 12 bushels, the value of the grain itself averaging about 4s. 6d. per quarter. Demand notices were sent in two days after the rent had become due, and if not complied with in two weeks the landlord distrained without further

1. A kind of Ducking Stool.

ceremony ; after an interval of another fortnight, if the money
still remained unpaid, the tenant was summarily ejected, and the
owner seized both farm and stock.

The meals consumed by the peasantry comprised only two during
the twenty-four hours, one, called dinner, being eaten at nine in
the morning, and the other, supper, at five in the afternoon.   It
is very possible, however, that during the summer those farm
servants whose arduous duties were entered on at daybreak, partook
of some slight repast at an early hour of the morning, but the only
meals for which regular times were appointed were the two mentioned.   During harvest the diet of the labourers consisted for the
most part of herrings, bread, and an allowance of beer, whilst
messes of pottage were far from uncommon objects on the rustic
boards.   Between the year 1314 and 1326 the prices of live stock
were again arranged, as under :—

The best grass fed ox	16s. 0d.
The best cow (fat)	12s. 0d.
The best short-horn sheep	1s. 2d.
The best goose	0s. 3d.
The best hen.............................	0s. 1½d.
The best chickens, per couple	0s. 1½d.
Eggs, twenty for	0s. 1d.

In 1338 no domestic or husbandry servant residing in the
Hundred of Amounderness was allowed to pass beyond the
boundaries of the Wapentake on profession of going to dwell or
serve elsewhere, or of setting out on a pilgrimage, without bearing
with him a letter patent stating the reason of his departure and the
date of his return. This law, which applied to all Hundreds alike,
was intended to prevent the threatened decay of agriculture from
a dearth of labourers, who heretofore had been in the habit of
deserting their employment and wandering away into other
divisions of the country, where they supported an idle and
frequently vicious existence by soliciting alms and by petty thefts.

It will scarcely surprise the reader to learn that superstition was
rife amongst the populace during the periods so far noticed, and
that nothing was too absurd to be accepted as an omen, either of
good or evil, by our credulous forefathers. A timid hare encountered
in their walks abroad announced the approach of some unforeseen
calamity, as also did a blind or lame man, a woman with dis-
hevelled hair, or even a monk ; whilst the visions of a wolf

crossing the path, St. Martin's birds flying from left to right, a humpbacked man, or the sound of distant thunder, were welcomed as heralds of prosperity. All amusements were of an athletic kind, and consisted of archery, casting heavy stones, spear darting, wrestling, running, leaping, and sword and buckler playing. On festivals, and occasionally at other seasons, the barbarous and cruel sports of bull and bear-baiting were indulged in,[1] but cock-fighting was considered, until a later epoch, an entertainment only suitable for children, and on Shrove Tuesday each boy took his pet bird to the school-house, which was for that day converted into a cock-pit, superintended by the master.

In 1444, the wages received by different classes of agricultural servants were :—

A bailiff .... £1 3s. 4d. per year, and 5s. for clothing, with board.
A chief hind ⎫
  „ carter ⎬ £1 0s. 0d. „ and 4s. for clothing, „
  „ shepherd ⎭
A woman servant £0 10s. 0d. „ and 4s. for clothing, „
A boy under 14 £0 6s. 0d. „ and 3s. for clothing, „
A common husbandman £0 15s. 0d. and 4od. for clothing, „

At harvest time, when special labour was required, the scale of remuneration was :—

A mower .... 4d. per day, with board.
  „ .... 6d. „ without „
A reaper or carter......... 3d. „ with „
  „ .... 5d. „ without „
A woman labourer, or
  other labourer ....2½d. „ with „
  „ ....4½d. „ without „

The statute which arranged the above rates of payment concluded by saying that "such as deserve less shall take less, and also in places where less is used to be given less shall be given from henceforth ;" so that the table just completed would seem to represent the maximum rather than the ordinary scale of wages. This statute also enacted that farm servants who purposed leaving their employers, must engage themselves to other masters and give reasonable warning before leaving their present ones, by which idleness and mendicancy were effectually guarded against.

The common pastimes of the inhabitants during the fifteenth and sixteenth centuries, in addition to some of those already

1. A bear was baited at Weeton fair less than a century ago.

enumerated which still held their sway, were club, and trap-ball, bowling, prisoners'-bars, hood-man blind, (a game similar to the modern blindman's-buff, but entered into by adults alone,) battle-dore and shuttlecock, and during hard frosts skating, at first by means of the shank bone of a sheep fastened on to the sole of the boot and afterwards with iron-shod skates. Hawking and hunting were confined to the familes of position who resided at the ancient Halls of the Fylde and to others of similar social standing, forming but a small proportion of the entire population. At Christmas the largest log obtainable was lighted on the hearth and denominated the yule log. If the mass burned throughout the night and the whole of the next day, it was regarded as an omen of good fortune by the members of the household, but if it were consumed or extinguished before that time had expired, it was looked upon as auguring adversely for their prosperity. The first Monday after Twelfth Day was called Plough Monday, a name still familar to many an old Fylde man, and was observed as a general holiday by the men whose labours were associated with that instrument, who on this day went about the villages from house to house asking for plough-money to spend in ale. Their processions, if such they could be called, consisted of a plough, which was dragged along by a number of sword-dancers ; a labourer, dressed to resemble an old woman ; and another, who was clothed in skins, and wore the tail of some animal hanging down his back. These two oddly garbed individuals solicited small contributions from the people whilst the remainder were engaged in dancing, and if anyone refused to disburse some trifling sum when requested, they turned up the ground fronting his doorway with the plough. During Christmas week the country people blackened their faces, and thus disguised committed all sorts of frolics and absurdities amongst their neighbours. The chief rustic festival, however, was appointed for the first of May, on which day the May-pole was drawn to the village green by several oxen, whose horns were decorated with bunches of flowers, and accompanied by a joyous band of revellers, who after its erection on the accustomed site held their jubilee of feasting and dancing around it. The pole itself was covered with floral garlands, and streamed with flags and handkerchiefs from its summit. A Lord and Lady, or Queen, of May were elected by a general vote, and to them belonged the honour of presiding over the festivities. The costumes of these pseudo-regal personages were liberally adorned with scarfs and ribbons, so that their appearances should be in unison with the rest of the gay preparations. The morris-dance formed an important feature of the festival, and the performers in that somewhat vigorous exercise wore richly decorated habits on to which small bells, varying in tone, had been fastened. The new year was ushered in with feasting and joviality, whilst friendly interchanges of presents took place amongst all classes. In the evening, a huge wassail-bowl filled with spiced ale was carried to the different houses of the villages, and all who quaffed its exhilerating contents drank prosperity to the coming year, and rewarded the cup-bearers, usually female farm-servants, with some small donation ; the following carol in a more antique form, or some similar one, was sung on the occasion :—

> "Good Dame, here at your door,
>   Our Wassel we begin,
> We are all maidens poor,
>   We pray now let us in,
>   With our Wassel.

> "Our Wassel we do fill,
>   With apples and with spice,
> Then grant us your good will
>   To taste here once or twice
>   Of our Wassel.
>   *   *   *   *   *
> "Some bounty from your hands
>   Our Wassel to maintain.
> We'll buy no house nor lands
>   With that which we do gain,
>   With our Wassel.

On Shrove Tuesday a barbarous custom prevailed of tying cocks to a stake driven into the ground, and throwing at them with sticks, until death ensued from repeated blows. St. Valentine's day received a merry welcome from the country swains and maidens, who at that auspicious time made choice of, or more properly speaking were mated to, their true loves for the year The all important selection was made by writing the names of an equal number of each sex on separate slips of paper, and then dividing them into two lots, one of which represented the males

H

and the other the females. The women drew from the male heap, and the men from that of the females, so that each person became possessed of two sweethearts, and the final pairing was really the only element of real choice in the matter ; in this the men usually claimed the girl whom each of them had drawn, and thus an amicable settlement was soon arrived at. After the mirthful ceremony had been completed and each happy couple duly united, the men gave treats and dances to their sweethearts, and wore their billets for several days pinned on to their breasts or coat sleeves. Another, and much simpler, plan of choosing a valentine was to look out of the door or window on the eventful morning, and the first person seen was regarded as the special selection of the patron Saint, provided always the individual was of the opposite sex, and unfettered by the silken bonds of Hymen. Whitsun-ales and Easter-ales were assemblies held within, or in the immediate neighbourhood of, the church-yards, at which the beverage, giving the title to these festivities, was sold by the clergy or their assistants, and consumed by the country people, the proceeds being devoted to ecclesiastical purposes and the relief of the poor. Wakes originated in an ancient custom of gathering together on the evening before the birthday of a Saint or the day appointed for the dedication of a church, and passing the night in devotion and prayer. These watches, however, were soon altered in character, and instead of religious exercises employing the period of vigil, feasting and debauchery became the recognized occupations.

The festival of Rush-bearing is of such antiquity that its origin has become in a great measure obscured, but there is a strong probability that the practice arose from a recommendation given by Pope Gregory IV. to Mellitus, who was associated with St. Augustine in christianising the inhabitants of England, to cele-brate the anniversaries of the dedications of those places of wor-ship, which they had rescued from Pagan influences, "by building themselves huts of the boughs of trees about such churches, and celebrating the solemnities with religious feastings." The rush-cart, decorated with flowers and ribbons, was paraded through the village streets, accompanied by morris-dancers and others bearing flags or banners. One of the mummers, dressed in a motley suit, somewhat resembling that of a circus jester, jingled a horse-collar hung with bells, and kept up a constant succession of small jokes at the expense of the bystanders as the procession advanced. In early days before churches were flagged it was the annual custom to strew their floors with rushes on the day of the dedication of the sacred edifice, and in the parish register of Kirkham we find, as follows :—" 1604. Rushes to strew the church cost this year 9s. 6d." From the register at Poulton church we have also extracted an entry, at random, from similar ones occurring each year :—" Aug. 6th, 1784. To Edward Whiteside for rushes, 6s. 8d." The practice appears to have arisen simply from a desire to promote warmth and comfort within the churches by providing a covering for the bare earth, and its connection with rush-bearing, when it existed, must be regarded as having been purely accidental. Brand has discovered another motive for rush-strewing, more especially in private houses, and one not very flattering to our forefathers :—" As our ancestors," writes he, "rarely washed their floors, disguises of un-cleanliness became very necessary." Erasmus, also, a Greek Professor at Oxford in the time of Henry VIII., in describing the hovels in which the agricultural labourers and others of the lower classes lived, says :—" The floors are commonly of clay strewed with rushes ; under which lies unmolested an ancient collection of beer, grease, fragments, bones, spittle, and everything that is nasty."

From 1589 to 1590 inclusive, the daily wages, without board, of a ditcher were 4d., a thresher 6d., a hedger 4d., a gardener 10d., and a master-mason 14d. In 1533 it was enacted that no tenant should hold more than two farms at once ; and fifty-five years later sundry penalties were imposed upon any one erecting cottages for the agricultural population without attaching four acres of land to each, also for allowing more than one family to occupy a cottage at the same time.[1] A law was passed in 1597, directing that all houses of husbandry which had fallen into decay within a period of seven years should be rebuilt, and from twenty to forty acres of ground apportioned to each.[2] The average yields of grain per acre on well-cultivated soils during the latter half of the sixteenth century were—wheat 20 bushels, barley 32 bushels,

---

1. 25 Henry VIII. c. 13, and 31 Elizabeth, c. 7.   2. 39 Elizabeth, c. 1.

and oats 40 bushels.   The subjoined tables contain the average prices of some of the common articles of consumption :—

	In 1500.	In 1541.	In 1590.	In 1597.
12 Pigeons	... 4d.	... 0s. 10d.	1s. 0d. ...; ...	4s. 3d. .
100 Eggs	... 7d.	... 1s. 6d.	... ...	3s. 6d.
1 Goose...	... 4d.	... 0s. 8d.	... ...	... ...
1 Chicken	... 1d.	... ...	... ...	0s. 8d.
1 Lb. of Butter		... 0s. 3d.	0s. 4d.	... ...

In 1581, the charge for shoeing a horse was 10d., and some-times 12d. Here it may be noticed, although perhaps rather digressive, that the herb tobacco was introduced into this country sometime during the summer of 1586, by a party of Englishmen, who for a short time colonised the island of Roanoak, near the coast of Virginia, but, having quarrelled with the aborigines, were removed home in the ships of Sir Francis Drake. Camden, writing of these men, says :—"They were the first that I know of that brought into England that Indian plant which they called *tabacca* and *nicotia*, or *tobacco*, which they used against crudities, being taught it by the Indians. Certainly, from that time forward, it began to grow into great request, and to be sold at a high rate; whilst in a short time many men, everywhere, some for wantonness, some for health sake, with insatiable desires and greediness, sucked in the stinking smoke thereof through an earthen pipe, which presently they blew out again at their nostrils; insomuch that tobacco-shops are now as ordinary in most towns as tap-houses and taverns."

The following rhymes, descriptive of the games and recreations common in Lancashire amongst the youth of both sexes, were written in 1600, by Samuel Rowland :—

"Any they dare challenge for to throw the sledge,
To jump or leap over ditch or hedge ;
To wrestle, play at stool-ball, or to run,
To pitch the bar or to shoot off a gun ;
To play at loggats, nine-holes, or ten-pins,
To try it out at foot-ball by the shins ;
At tick-tacke, seize-noddy, maw, and ruff ;
At hot-cockles, leap-frog, or blindman's buff ;
To drink the halper-pots, or deal at the whole can ;
To play at chess, or pue, and inkhorn ;
To dance the morris, play at barley-brake ;
At all exploits a man can think or speak :
At shove-groat, venter-point, or cross and pile ;

> At 'beshrew him that's last at any style';
> At leaping over a Christmas bonfire,
> Or at 'drawing the dame out of the mire';
> At shoot-cock, Gregory, stool-ball, and what-not;
> Pick-point, top and scourge, to make him hot."

Many of these games have long since become obsolete. Tick-tacke resembled backgammon, but was rather more complicated; seize-noddy, maw, and ruff were games of cards, the first being somewhat similar to cribbage, while the two latter have no modern representatives, although the expression *to ruff* is frequently used at the whist-table; 'cross and pile' is merely an earlier name of 'pitch and toss'; and shoot-cock has been modernised into shuttlecock.

During the seventeenth century occasional village fairs were held in the Fylde, at which such uncouth games as "grinning through a horse-collar," as well as trials in whistling, etc., were common amusements, while pedlars' stalls, puppet shows, raffling tables, and drinking booths were well attended by the holiday-makers. At that period any damsel, wishing to learn something, be it ever so little, of her future mate, was directed to run until out of breath on hearing the first notes of the cuckoo, and on removing her shoe she would find a hair of the same colour as that of the husband whom fate had selected for her. On May-day a snail placed upon the ashes of the hearth would trace the initial letter, or letters, of the lover's name; or the rind, peeled from an apple and thrown backwards over the head, would by its arrangement on falling to the ground effect a similar purpose:—

> "Last May-day fair I search'd to find a snail
> That might my secret lover's name reveal:
> Upon a gooseberry bush a snail I found,
> For always snails near sweetest fruit abound.
> I seiz'd the vermin; home I quickly sped,
> And on the hearth the milk white embers spread,
> Slow crawled the snail, and if I right can spell
> In the soft ashes marked a curious L."[1]

This couplet was recited by young maidens after capturing an insect called a Lady-bird, and on releasing it:—

> "Fly, Lady-bird, fly south, east, or west;
> Fly where the man is that I love best."

The following extracts from an "inventarye of all the goods and

1. Gay.

chattels of Peter Birket, late of Borrands," taken after his decease in 1661, will furnish a pretty accurate idea of the monetary worth of certain articles of farming stock at that time :—"One outshoote of hay, £1 6s. 8d.; one stack of hay without dores, 10s. ; one scaffold of hay, 10s. ; one mare and one colt, £3 ; five geese, 4s. ; 13 sheepe, £3 ; one cock and five hens, 2s. ; one calfe, 10s. ; two heiffers, £3 ; one heiffer, £2 ; one cow, £2 10s. ; another cow, £3 10s." Whether this gentleman was a fair representative of his class or not we are unable to say, but if so, the small farmers of Lancashire, to whom he appears to have belonged, were not over indulgent in articles of dress or comfort, for the whole of his wearing apparel was valued at no more than £1, whilst his bedding realised only 5s.

In 1725 the Lancashire justices arranged and ordered that the rate of wages in all parts of this county should be :—

A bailiff in husbandry, or chief hind	£6	0s.	0d.	per year, with board.
A chief servant in husbandry, able to mow or sow	5	0	0	" "
A common servant in husbandry of 24 years of age and upwards	4	0	0	" "
A man servant from 20 to 24 years of age ...	3	10	0	" "
A man servant from 16 to 20 years of age ...	2	10	0	" "
The best woman servant, able to cook	2	10	0	" "
Dairy man, or lower servant	2	0	0	" "
Woman servant under 16 years of age	1	10	0	" "
The best of millers	5	0	0	" "

They also appointed the hours of labour for those hired by the day to be, between the middle of March and the middle of September, from five in the morning until half-past seven in the evening, and during the remainder of the year from sunrise to sunset, resting half-an-hour at breakfast, an hour at dinner, and half-an-hour at "drinking," as the meal corresponding to our "tea" was termed. "In the summer half," added the magisterial mandate, "the labourers may sleep each day half-an-hour ; else for every hour's absence to defaulk a penny ; and every Saturday afternoon or eve of a holiday, that they cease to work, is to be accounted but half a day." The day wages, as fixed by the same authorities, were :—

The best kind of husbandry labourer	12d.	without, and 6d. with board.
An ordinary labourer	10d.	" and 5d. "
A male haymaker	10d.	" and 6d. "

A woman haymaker	7d. without	and 3d. with board.
A mower	15d. „	and 9d. „
A man shearer	12d. „	and 6d. „
A woman shearer	10d. „	and 6d. „
Hedgers, Ditchers, Threshers, and persons employed in task work	10d. „	and 6d. „
Masons, Joiners, Plumbers, Tilers, Slaters, Coopers, and Turners	12d. „	and 6d. „
Master workman, acting as foreman	14d. without board.	

From 1660 to 1690, the average price of mutton was 2d. per pound; from 1706 to 1730, 2½d.; and from 1730 to 1760, 3d. per pound. The prices of beef, veal, and lamb in 1710, were respectively $1\frac{1}{10}$d., $2\frac{3}{8}$d., and $2\frac{0}{10}$d., per pound.

During the eighteenth and earlier part of the nineteenth centuries there was perhaps no pastime more popular amongst the adult members of all classes than the callous sport of cock-fighting; every village and hamlet in the Fylde had its pit, where mains were held at all times and seasons. The following were the rules pretty generally adopted in this neighbourhood for the regulation of the contests :—

"1.—To begin the main by fighting the lighter pair of cocks which fall in match first, proceeding upwards towards the end, that every lighter pair may fight earlier than those that are heavier.

"2.—In matching, with relation to the battles, after the cocks of the main are weighed, the match bills are to be compared.

"3.—That every pair of equal weight are separated, and fight against others; provided it appears that the main can be enlarged by adding thereto."

Skippool was one of the favourite resorts for the gentry of our district when wishful to indulge in their favourite amusement, and frequent allusions to the cockpit there are to be found in the journal of Thomas Tyldesley, of Fox Hall, as—" June 9, 1714, * * * thence to Skipall, where at a cockin I meet with a deal of gentlemen. Gave Ned M——y 1s. for his expenses; spent 1s., and won 2s. 6d. of Dr. Hesketh's cockes." In 1790 a notice appeared in Liverpool that "The great main of cocks between John Clifton, Esq., of Lytham, and Thomas Townley Parker, Esq., of Cuerden, would be fought on Easter Monday, the 5th of April, and the three following days, at the new cockpit in Cockspur Street—to show forty-one cocks each. Ten guineas each battle, and two hundred guineas the main." The great-grandfather of the present Lord Derby compelled each of his tenants to maintain a game-cock for his benefit, and many were the birds supplied from the Fylde to uphold his great reputation as a successful cock-fighter.

One of the most ancient punishments amongst our forefathers was that of the Brank or Scolds' Bridle, a specimen of which was possessed by Kirkham, and doubtless many others existed in the Fylde. This instrument was but little removed in severity from those implements of torture in vogue at the time of the Inquisition, but differed from them in one important particular—it was intended to control or silence, and not to stimulate, the tongue of its victim. The Brank consisted of an iron framework, which was fitted on to the head of the offender, usually some woman whose intemperate language had incensed her husband ; and a metal spike, attached to the front of it, was so inserted into the mouth that the slightest movement of the tongue brought that sensitive organ in contact with its sharp edge or point. Doctor Plott, who appears to have held the Brank in high estimation, and to have considered it greatly superior to another mode of correction, much in fashion during his day, says :—"This artifice is much to be preferred to the ducking-stool, which not only endangers the health of the party, but gives liberty of tongue betwixt every dip."

The Ducking-stool or Cuck-stool consisted of a substantial chair, fastened to the extremity of a long pole, and suspended over a pool of water. The middle of the pole rested on an upright post near the edge of the pond, and was attached to it by means of a pivot-hinge, so that the chair could be swung round to the side to receive its victim, and, after being freighted and restored to its original position, plunged into the water by raising the other end of the shaft as often as those on the bank deemed it necessary to cool the anger of the unfortunate scold. Several pools in different parts of the Fylde still retain their names of Cucking-ponds, and the last person condemned to suffer the barbarous punishment was a young woman at Poulton, but she was happily rescued by the kindly intervention of Madam Hornby, who became surety for her good conduct in future.

In the belfry of Bispham church there formerly stood a plain-looking wooden frame, which in earlier times had done duty as a pennance-stool, but some years since the chair was removed, and probably destroyed, as no trace of its existence has since been discovered. The last to perform pennance in this church and sit upon the stool was a woman, who seems to have been living as recently as 1836. A public pennance was exacted by the Church from all frail maidens, who desired to obtain pardon for the sins into which they had fallen. The ceremony consisted of parading the aisles of the parish church with a candle in each hand, barefooted, and clothed in white. Jane Breckal, of Poulton, was the last to undergo the ceremony at that place, some time during the ministry of the Rev. Thos. Turner, 1770 to 1810. The sobs and cries of the unfortunate girl aroused the indignation of the inhabitants against the pennance, and the cruel and degrading exhibition was never repeated.

Riding Stang was another plan of punishment formerly inflicted on quarrelsome or adulterous persons, and a woman named Idle, of Great Layton, is mentioned as being the last of its victims in that locality, and very likely in the whole of the Fylde. There seem to have been two ways adopted of Riding Stang, one of which was to mount the offending party or parties on a ladder, supported at each end on the shoulders of one or sometimes two men, and carry them about the neighbourhood for several hours, accompanied by a band of men and boys beating tin kettles, frying-pans, etc.; the other mode, and perhaps the more antique one, was to place a youth astride a ladder, borne as in the previous case, and arm him with a hand-bell, so that he was fully equipped to undertake the duties of town crier. A procession was then formed, and, amidst the discordant sounds of the instruments just alluded to, paraded through the streets of the village, whilst the crier, who usually did his part with great gusto, shouted out the following doggrel rhymes, varying some portions of them when occasion required :—

"Ran a dan, ran a dan, dan, dan,
But for * * * has been banging his good dame.
He banged her, he banged her, he banged her, indeed,
He banged her, poor woman, before she stood need ;
For neither wasting his substance nor spending his brass,
But she was a woman, and he was an ass.
Now, all good people that live in this row,
I would have you take warning, for this is our law,
And if you do your good wives bang,
For you three nights we will ride this stang.
         Hurrah ! hurrah !"

When the offender happened to be some woman, who had
inflicted chastisement on the person of her spouse, the rhyme
was altered to suit her sex, and asserted that " he was a coward,
and she was an ass." The remains of stocks in various states of
preservation, are still to be seen in many old villages, and
their use is of too recent a date to require any elucidation in this
volume.

On the fifth Sunday in Lent, Carling Sunday, the villagers
prepared a feast, consisting chiefly of peas, first steeped in water,
and afterwards fried in butter, which were eaten on the
afternoon of that day. Small troops or companies of pace-
egg mummers went from house to house in Passion week
enacting a short dramatic piece, and afterwards soliciting
money, or, in some cases, eggs, from their audience. The
dramatis personæ usually represented St. George, the cham-
pion of England ; a Turk, dressed in national costume ; the
Doctor, of the quack fraternity ; the Fool ; and one or two others.
In the play, the Turk was wounded by St. George, and being left
for dead upon the field, guarded by the Fool, was restored to
health and strength by the Doctor, who opportunely arrived, and
concluded his self-laudatory harangue over the body of the
apparently defunct Turk, thus :—

> " Here, Jack, take a little out of my bottle,
> And let it run down thy throttle ;
> If thou be not quite slain,
> Rise, Jack, and fight again."

Easter mumming is now rapidly becoming obsolete, and at
present amounts to nothing more entertaining than the recital of
a few weak, almost meaningless, rhymes, by, usually, five young
boys, decorated with ribbons and coloured paper, and supposed to
represent Lord Nelson, a Jack-Tar, a Lovely Youth, Old Toss-pot,
and Old Bessy Branbags.

"Lifting at Easter" was an old-established practice, existing in
the villages, of hoisting individuals in the air, either in a chair
or by any other means that might be convenient, until they
purchased their release by payment of a forfeit, generally some
small coin. On Ascension-day the parochial schoolmaster
conducted his pupils, armed with peeled willow wands, round
the limits of the parish, and each pupil struck the various

boundary marks with his stick as he passed them. All-Hallows'
E'en was the time when the young people tested the durability of
love or friendship by burning nuts:—

> " Two hazel nuts I threw into the flame,
> And to each nut I gave a sweetheart's name :
> This with the loudest bounce, me sore amazed,
> That in a flame of brightest colour blazed ;
> As blazed the nut, so may thy passion grow,
> For 'twas thy nut that did so brightly glow ! "[1]

Other pastimes contributed to the evening's amusement, such
as "ducking for apples," and "snatch apple"—a tub, in the
former case, having been nearly filled with water, and the fruit
placed in it, each in turn, with hands bound behind them,
endeavoured to seize the prize with the teeth ; in the latter game,
an apple was fastened to one extremity of a rod and a lighted
candle to the other, the whole being suspended by a string from
the ceiling, and the players, bound as before, snapped at the
apple, and avoided the flame as well as they were able.

Until within the last fifty or sixty years, the mosses of Marton
and the hills in the vicinity of the Fylde were illuminated with
bonfires on All-Hallows' Eve, or Teanlay-night, as it was called,
kindled by the country people with the avowed object of suc-
couring their friends who were lingering in the imaginary regions
of a middle state. A field near Poulton received the name of
"Purgatory" from the mummery of the "Teanlays" having, on
one occasion at least, been celebrated there.[2] This ceremony was
simple in its performance, and consisted merely of a circle of men
raising masses of blazing straw on high with pitch-forks. On All
Souls' Day our Catholic forefathers were accustomed to bake cakes
of oatmeal and aromatic seeds, named Soul-cakes, and these,
together with pasties and furmety, formed a feast invariably eaten
at that season. Remnants of this custom existed even in late
years amongst the youths of Marton and some other townships and
villages, who on the day of ancient festival solicited money, under
the name of Soul-pence, from their neighbours.

We will now enumerate some of the superstitions and beliefs
that have prevailed in the Fylde more recently than those to

1. Gay. The Spell.
2. Hist. of Blackpool and Neighbourhood, by W. Thornber, B.A.

which allusion has been made in the earlier part of the chapter.

The following adage, showing the signification of certain marks on the nails, will probably be familiar to many of our readers, and it is questionable whether, even yet, it is not regarded by a few of the less enlightened of the peasantry as something more than a mere saying :—

> " Specks on the fingers,
> Fortune often lingers ;
> Specks on the thumbs,
> Fortune surely comes."

No sick person could die if the bed or pillow upon which he lay contained a pigeon's feather ; and, at an earlier date, the dwellers near the coast firmly believed that life could only depart with the ebbing tide.   A horse-shoe nailed against the stable or barn-door, or a broom-stick placed across the threshold of the dwelling, prevented the entrance of witches or evil persons ; also a hot heater placed in the churn, and the mark of a cross, protected respectively the cream and baking of dough from their presence. The advent of guests was made known to the family circle by certain conditions of the fire-grate ; thus, a flake of soot hanging from the topmost bar foretold a boy visitor, from the second a man, from the third a woman, and from the fourth a girl.   Cats were popularly supposed to have the power of drawing the breath, and as a natural consequence the life, out of children when asleep, and for this reason great care was taken to exclude them from bedchambers.   Should a dark complexioned person be the first to enter a dwelling on New Year's morning, the household looked forward with confidence to a prosperous year ; but if the person happened to be light, more especially if he had red hair, the omen was regarded as unpropitious.   Moon-beams shining through the windows of bedrooms were considered injurious to the sleepers, and even capable of distorting their features, or rendering them imbecile.   Children were taught to recite these simple lines whenever the moon shone into their chambers :—

> " I see the moon,
> The moon sees me ;
> God bless the priest
> That christened me."

A tooth, after extraction, was sprinkled with salt and thrown into the fire in order to insure peace and comfort to the person from whose mouth it had been removed. A pair of shoes placed under the bed so that the tips of the toes alone were visible, formed a certain remedy for cramp. Warts were removed by rubbing them with a piece of stolen beef, which was afterwards carefully and secretly buried to render the charm complete ; a snail hung on to a thorn was equally efficacious in removing these excrescences, which gradually faded away as the snail itself melted and vanished. A bag, containing small stones of the same number as the warts, thrown over the left shoulder, transmitted them to the person who had the misfortune to pick up the pebbles. People labouring under attacks of ague, jaundice, or other ailments, applied for relief to the wise-men of the neighbourhood, who professed to cure them by incantations. The two following receipts are taken from an old medical work, published as early as 1612, and in its time a highly popular authority on matters of " Phisicke and Chirurgerie " amongst our rural populations :—

" A good Medicine to staunch the bleeding of the Nose, although it bleed never so freely.

" Take an egg and breake it on the top, in such sorte that all the white and yolke may issue cleane forthe of it ; then fill the egg-shell with some of the bloud of the party which bleedeth, and put it in the fire, and there let it remaine until it be harde, and then burne it to ashes, and it will staunch the bleeding immediately without all doubt."

"A very good Medicine to staunch bloud when nothing else will do it, by reason the veine is cut, or that the wound is greate.

" Take a Toade and dry him very well in the sunne, and then put him in a linen Bagge, and hang him about the necke of him that bleedeth with a stringe, and let it hange so low that it may touch his breaste on the left side neere unto his hart, and commonly this will stay all manner of bleeding at the mouth, nose, wound, or otherwise whatever. Probatum est."

A woman named Bamber, living at Marton, attained to con-considerable celebrity amongst the peasantry and others by her skill in checking bleeding, which she is reported to have accomplished by the utterance of some mystic words.

The people of the Fylde were not exempt from the common belief in the miraculous power of the Royal touch in that particular form of disease known as king's evil, for amongst the records of the Thirty-men of Kirkham is a notice that in 1632 a sum of money was "given to Ricd. Barnes's child, that had the king's evil, to help him up to London," to be touched by Charles I.

The fairies of the Fylde were supposed, like those of other localities, to reside in the earth ; the vicinity of a cold spring, situated between Hardhorn and Newton, was one of their legendary resorts, and from such reputation acquired the name of " Fairies' well." Many stories are told of the mischievous, or good-natured doings of these imaginary beings ; one or two of which we will here narrate :—A poor woman when filling her pitcher at the above well, in order to bathe the weak eyes of her infant, was gently addressed by a handsome man, who gave her a small box of ointment, and told her at the same time that it would prove an infallible remedy for the ailment of her child. The woman, although grateful for the present, either overcome by that irresistible curiosity which is commonly, but perhaps erroneously, supposed to attach itself to her sex, or doubtful of the efficacy which the stranger had assigned to the drug, applied it to one of her own eyes. A few days afterwards she had occasion to go to Preston, and whilst there detected her benefactor in the act of stealing corn from the open mouths of some sacks exposed for sale, and, having accosted him, began to remonstrate with him on the wickedness of his proceedings, when he inquired with evident surprise, how she became enabled to observe him, as he was invisible to all else. She explained the use that had been made of his ointment, and pointed to the powerful eye ; but hardly had the words been uttered and the organ of supernatural vision indicated, before he raised his clenched hand, and with one blow struck out the offending optic, or rather reduced it to a state of total and irrecoverable blindness. Another anecdote refers to a milkmaid, who, whilst engaged in her avocation, perceived a jug and sixpence placed near to her by some invisible means ; but no way disconcerted by the singular event, and probably attributing it to the agency of one of the elvan tribes, she filled the pitcher with milk, and, having watched its mysterious disappearance and, with unerring commercial instinct, pocketed the silver coin, took her departure. This episode was repeated for many successive mornings, until the maiden, overjoyed at her good fortune, revealed the curious adventures to her lover, and from that hour the hobgoblins appear either to have grown less thirsty, or, annoyed at what they might consider the betrayal of their secret, to have removed their custom to some other dairy, for neither jug nor sixpence ever gladened the morning labours of the milk-maid again. A ploughman had his good nature, in cheerfully repairing the broken "spittle" of a lady liberally rewarded. The fairy, for such she proved to be, made known her presence to the agriculturist by suddenly crying in a distressed tone—"I have broken my speet," and then held out in her hands the useless instrument with a hammer and nails. No sooner had she received her property, restored to a state of utility, than she vanished into the earth, but not, however, without leaving a substantial acknowledgment of his skill and kindness in the palm of the astonished husbandman.

We can only discover a record of one witch in the Fylde ; this person of unenviable notoriety is stated to have had her abode in Singleton, and to have been known to the villagers as Mag Shelton. Her food, according to local tradition, was composed of boiled groats mixed with thyme or parsley, and numerous are the anecdotes related of her evil machinations and doings in the neighbourhood—the cows of the country people were constantly milked by her, whilst the pitcher walked before her in the form of a goose ; lives were blighted and prosperity checked by the influence of her evil eye. Once, however, she was foiled by a girl, who fastened her to a chair by sticking a bodkin, crossed with two weavers' healds, about her dress when seated before a large fire.

Some idea of the spiritual condition of the peasantry may be obtained from the perusal of the following prayer, a common one amongst the children of the Fylde about one hundred years ago :—

> "Matthew, Mark, Luke, and John,
> Bless the bed that I lie on ;
> There are four corners to my bed,
> And four angels overspread,
> Two at the feet and two at the head.
> If any ill thing me betide,
> Beneath your wings my body hide.
> Matthew, Mark, Luke, and John,
> Bless the bed that I lie on."

Bacon was considered to prove the finest and best if the hogs were slaughtered before the moon began to wane, and in some month whose name contained the letter R :—

> "Unless your bacon you would mar
> Kill not your pig without the R."

The dumb-cake was made by unmarried women who wished to divine the selection of fate as to their future husbands. The cake was baked in strict silence by two maidens on Midsummer's eve, and afterwards broken into three pieces by another, who placed one under each of their pillows; during sleep the expectant fair ones were rewarded with a vision of their lovers, but the charm was ruined if only a single word were spoken. Hemp-seed, also, was sown by young maidens, who whilst scattering it recited the words "Hemp-seed I sow, hemp-seed I hoe, and he that is my true-love come after me and mow." After repeating the rhyme three times it was only necessary to look over the shoulder, and the apparition of the destined swain would never fail to appear:—

> "At eve last Midsummer no sleep I sought,
> But to the field a bag of hemp-seed brought;
> I scattered round the seed on every side,
> And three times, in a trembling accent cried :
> 'This hemp-seed with my virgin hand I sow,
> Who shall my true love be the crop shall mow.'
> I straight looked back, and, if my eyes speak truth,
> With his keen scythe behind me came a youth."[1]

A spinster who fasted on Midsummer's eve, and at midnight laid a clean cloth, with bread, cheese, and ale, and sat down to the table as though about to eat, would be gratified with a sight of the person to whom she would be married. This individual was supposed to pass through the doorway, left open for the purpose, as the clock struck twelve, and, approaching the table, to salute his future partner with a bow and a pretence of drinking her health, after which he vanished, and the maid retired to her couch to rejoice or mourn, according as she admired or contemned the prospect in store for her. Cuttings or combings from the hair were thrown into the fire, and upon their blazing brightly or smouldering away depended the duration of life likely to be enjoyed by the person from whose head they had been taken. Wishing-wells and gates were visited by credulous rustics, who were anxious to make use of their mysterious power in obtaining their desires in matters of love or business. The forefinger was deemed venomous, and on that account children were instructed not to spread salve or ointment with it.

About a century ago oats formed the chief production, and

1. Gay.

nearly, if indeed not quite, the only grain crop cultivated in the Fylde. When reaped, in harvest time, this commodity was carried on the backs of pack-horses to the markets of Poulton, Kirkham, Garstang, and Preston. The "horse bridge" between Carleton and Poulton was originally a narrow structure, capable only of affording passage to a single horse at once, and it was from the practice of the farmers, with their laden cattle, crossing the stream by its aid, when journeying to market, that the bridge derived its name. These horses followed a leader ornamented with a bell, and after they had arrived at their destination and been relieved of their burdens, returned home in the same order without a driver, leaving him to attend to his duties at the market. The old bridge in use at the period to which we allude, still exists, but is built over and hidden by the present erection. Later experience has taught the agriculturist that the soil of the Fylde is capable of producing, under proper tillage, other crops, equal in their abundance to the one to which it appears formerly to have been mainly devoted, and it would be difficult at the present day to enumerate with accuracy the many and varied fruits of the earth that have fonnd a home in the Corn-field of Amounderness.

We mentioned about the commencement of the chapter that marl was in general use as a manure in the Anglo-Saxon era, and here it is perhaps hardly necessary to state that this substance, so rich in lime and so adapted for giving consistency to the sandy soils, is still occasionally had recourse to by the husbandman. Guano was first introduced into this country about the year 1842, but it is probable that it was not commonly used in our district until the beginning of 1845, when a cargo was imported from Ichaboe to Fleetwood by Messrs. Kemp and Co., and offered for sale to the farmers of the neighbourhood. Other cargoes followed. Subjoined are arranged some tables showing the average market values of certain productions of the Fylde in the two years given:—

	1847. Inclusive.		1867. Inclusive.	
	Jan. to June.	July to Dec.	Jan. to June.	July to Dec.
Wheat, per windle	39s. 6d.	25s. 6d.	31s. 8d.	32s. – 6d.
Meal, per load	52s. 6d.	41s. 6d.	37s. 0d.	37s. 6d.
Beans, per windle	25s. 6d.	22s. 6d.	....	....
Oats, per bushel	5s. 10½d.	4s. 8d.	4s. 5d.	4s. 6d.

I

	Jan. to June.	July to Dec.	Jan. to June.	July to Dec.
Potatoes, per windle	21s. 6d.[1]	7s. od.	12s. 8d.	11s. 6d.
Butter, per pound	1s. 1d.	1s. 1½d.	1s. 5d.	1s. 3d.
Eggs, per dozen	os. 10d.	os. 10d.	os. 11d.	1s. od.
Pork, per pound	os. 6d.	os. 6d.	os. 5½d.	os. 6d.
Beef ,,	os. 6½d.	os. 7½d.	os. 7¾d.	os. 6¾d.
Mutton ,,	os. 6¾d.	os. 8½d.	os. 8d.	os. 7d.
Geese ,,	os. 6¾d.	....	....	..........[2]

1. This high price was owing to an almost complete failure in the potatoe crops.
2. Obtained by striking an average of the weekly market quotations in the local periodicals, published weekly during the respective years.

CHAPTER V.

COSTUMES, COUNTRY, RIVERS, AND SEA.

HE history of the dresses and costumes of the inhabitants of the Fylde is interesting not only on account of the multifarious changes and peculiarities which it exhibits, but also as a sure indication of the progress in civilisation, wealth, and taste, made in our section at different eras. To Julius Cæsar we are indebted for our earliest knowledge of the scanty dress worn by the aborigines of this district, and from that warrior it is learnt that a slight covering of roughly prepared skins, girded about the loins, and the liberal application of a blue dye, called woad, to the rest of the body constituted the sole requisites of their primitive toilets. Cæsar conjectures that the juice or dye of woad was employed by the people to give them a terror-striking aspect in battle, but here he seems to have fallen into error, for the wars engaged in by the Setantii would be confined to hostilities with neighbouring tribes, stained in a similar manner, and it is scarcely reasonable to suppose that either side would hope to intimidate the other by the use of a practice common to both. A more probable explanation of the custom is, that it was instituted for the ornamental qualities it possessed in the eyes of the natives. Such a view is supported by the remarks of Solinus, a Roman author, who informs us that the embellishments usually consisted of the figures of animals, " which grew with the growth of the body " ; and from this it is evident that before the frame had arrived at maturity, in either youth or childhood, the skin was subjected to the painful and laborious process of tattooing, for such according to Isidore, appears to have been the nature of the operation. The

latter asserts that the staining was accomplished by squeezing out
the juice of the plant on to the skin, and puncturing it in with
sharp needles. When the Romans established a station at
Kirkham, and opened out the Fylde by means of a good road-way
to the coast, the Setantii modified their wild uncultivated habits,
and, taking pattern from the more civilised garb of their
conquerors, adopted a covering for the lower limbs, called *brachæ*,
hence the modern breeches, whilst many of the chiefs were not
long before they strutted about in all the pride of a *toga*, or gown.
About four hundred years later, when the Anglo-Saxons had
taken possession of· the soil of the Fylde, and had either
appropriated the deserted settlements and renamed them, or
reared small and scattered groups of dwellings of their own, a
marked change became visible in the nationality, character,
and costumes of the people. No longer the semi-civilised and
half-clad Briton was lord of the domain, but the more refined
Saxon with his linen shirt, drawers, and stockings, either of
linen or woollen, and bandaged crosswise from the ankle to the
knee with strips of leather ; over these a tunic of the same
material as the stockings was thrown, and reached as low as the
knees, being plain or ornamented according to the means or rank
of the wearer. This garment was open at the neck and for a
short distance over the chest ; the sleeves, extending to the wrists,
were generally tight, and a girdle frequently, but not universally,
confined the gown round the waist. In addition a small cloak
was worn for out-door purposes over the tunic, and fastened on
the breast or shoulder with brooches or clasps. The shoes of the
Saxon settlers were open down the instep, where they were laced
or tied with two thongs. Even the very lowest of the population,
although poverty might reduce them to miserable straits, seldom,
if ever, went barefooted. Caps, on the contrary, were not in great
request, and rarely to be seen, unless on the heads of some of
the more affluent. Our female ancestors at that era were habited
in a close-fitting dress, falling to the feet and furnished with tight
sleeves, reaching as far as the wrists, over which was placed a
shorter gown with loose open sleeves. Their head-dress was
simply a strip of linen of sufficient length to wrap round the
temples and fall on the neck. Amongst the wealthiest of the
nation a flowing mantle, ornaments of precious metal, and sable,

beaver, and fox furs were common, but the inhabitants of the
Fylde, being of less exalted social standing, were obliged to
content themselves with the skins of lambs and cats by way of
adornment. The inferior farm servants, called serfs, amongst
whom many of the vanquished Britons would be classed, were
seldom indulged by their masters with more than a coat, a pair
of drawers, and sandals, the shirt, we presume, being deemed ill
suited to their positions of servitude and dependence.

The colonisation of the Danes, whatever effect it may have had
upon the habits and condition of the people, exercised no lasting
influence upon their dress, and it was not until half a century after
the Norman baron, Roger de Poictou, had parcelled out the
land amongst his tenants, that the bulk of the males were induced,
by the example of the new-comers, to display their taste in the
choice of a head-covering.   Many varieties were daily open to
their inspection on the brows of the Norman landholders and
servants, but the diffidence, let us hope, of the now humbled
Saxons suggested the adoption of an exceedingly plain flat species
of bonnet, which speedily became the common cap of the district.
The ladies, however, with a greater aptitude for rising superior to
disappointment and affliction, were not dilatory in benefitting by
the superior style of the fair partners of their conquerors, and
soon, putting aside all semblance of depression, appeared in long
cuffs, hanging to the ground from their upper dress sleeves and
tied in a large knot ; their kerchiefs, also, whose modest pro-
portions had formerly served only to encircle the forehead, were
now extravagantly lengthened and fastened in a similar manner.
As years rolled on and fashion began to assert her sway with a
greater show of authority, the shoes of the men underwent certain
changes, becoming more neat in workmanship and having the
toes somewhat elongated and pointed, whilst the richer of the
gentry, chiefly Normans, wore short boots reaching a little
distance up the calf.   In the early part of the thirteenth
century the female head-dresses consisted of nets, made from
various materials, in which the hair was confined ; and the trains
of the gowns were lengthened.   Later in the same era cowls or
hoods, twisted and pinned in fanciful shapes, adorned the heads
of the ladies, and formed the main feature of their walking
costumes.   Aprons also came up at that period.   The dress of

the men underwent no alteration of any moment until the first
half of the fourteenth century, when the manorial lords of the
neighbourhood, and others of the inhabitants, discarded the cloaks
and tunics of their forefathers, and substituted in their stead a
close-fitting outer garment of costly and handsome material,
scarcely covering the hips, immediately above which it was
surrounded by a girdle. The sleeves usually terminated at the
elbows, and from there long white streamers depended, whilst the
sleeves of an under dress reached to the wrists, and were ornamented with rows of buttons. A long cape and cowl was the
general overcoat. The most characteristic dress of the ladies was
a habit cut away at the sides so as to expose the under skirt,
which was invariably of rich and fine texture. The long white
streamers, just alluded to, were part of the female as well as the
male attire, and the borders of the habit were bound with fur or
velvet. We may mention that an English beau of that era wore
long pointed shoes, the toes of which were connected with the
knees by gold or silver chains, a long stocking of different colour
on each leg, short trowsers, barely extending to the middle of the
thigh, a coat, half of which was white and the other blue or some
equally bright colour, and a silken hood or bonnet, fastened under
the chin, embroided with grotesque figures of animals, and
occasionally decked with gold and precious stones. Lest,
however, the reputations of our ancestors should suffer in the
eyes of the present generation from the existence in their age
of the absurdity here pictured, it is our duty and pleasure to
assure all readers that such parodies on manhood were strictly
confined to the populous cities, and that there is no probability of
even a solitary specimen ever having desecrated the modest soil
of the Fylde.

During the greater portion of the succeeding cycle of a hundred
years a species of cloth turban was much in favour amongst the
male sex of the middle and upper classes, from one side of which
a lengh of the same material hung down below the waist, and was
either thrust between the girdle and the coat, or wrapped round
the neck as a protection from cold. Faces were cleanly shaved,
and hair cut as close to the scalp as possible ; hitherto, from about
the date of the first arrival of the Normans, the practice had been
to allow the latter to grow long and to wear the beard. The hose

were long and tight. The boots were either short, or reached
half-way up the thighs, both kinds being long toed. Occasionally
a single feather relieved the plainness of the turban-shaped cap.
The ordinary dress of the gentlewomen was a full trained robe or
gown, made high in the neck, and sometimes, with a fur or velvet
turn-over collar, its folds at the short-waist being confined by
means of a simple band and buckle. Coiffures were mostly heart-
shaped, but in some rare instances horned. The sleeves of the
above costume were, shortly after its institution, lengthened and
widened to a ridiculous extent. Towards the end of the particular
era of which we are writing trains were discontinued, and broad
borders of fur substituted, whilst round tapering hats, two feet
in height, with loose kerchiefs floating from the apex, came
much into favour. The last few years of the fifteenth and the
earliest ones of the sixteenth centuries were marked by great
changes in the male attire ; the Butlers, Cliftons, Carletons,
Westbys, Allens, Molyneux, and many others of the gentry of
the neighoourhood, figured at that period in fine shirts of long
lawn, embroidered with silk round the collar and wristbands, a
doublet with sleeves open at the elbows to allow the shirt to
protrude, a stomacher, over which the doublet was laced ; a long
gown or cloak, with loose or hanging sleeves and broad turn-over
collar of fur or velvet ; long hose or stockings ; broad-toed shoes
for ordinary use, and high boots, reaching to the knees, for riding
purposes ; and broad felt hats, or variously shaped caps of fur or
velvet, adorned with ostrich or other feathers. The hair was
permitted to grow enormously long and fall down the back and
over the shoulders, but the face was still cleanly shaved, with the
exception of military and aged persons, who wore mustaches or
beards. The wives and daughters, belonging to such families as
those alluded to, were habited in upper garments, cut square at
the neck, and stomachers, belts, and buckles, or costly girdles
with long pendants in front. The sleeves were slit at the elbows
in a manner similar to those of the men. High head-dresses were
abandoned, and a cap or caul of gold net or embroidery, which
allowed the hair to flow beneath it half way to the ground, took
their place. Turbans, also, were fashionable for a brief season.
The females of a humbler sphere wore plain grey cloth gowns,
ornamented with lambs' skin or wool, and cloaks of Lincoln

green ; the appearance of such an one upon a holiday is described
by Skelton, the laureate of Henry VII., as under :—

> " Her kirtle bristow red,
> With cloths upon her head,
> They weigh a ton of lead.
> She hobbles as she goes,
> With her blanket hose,
> Her shoone smeared with tallow."

In the following reign, the commonalty, in imitation of the
example set by the resident squires in this and other parts of the
kingdom, became so extravagant in their ideas of suitable habiliments that Henry VIII. issued an edict, prohibiting them from
wearing ornaments of even the most simple description, and
confining them to the use of cloth at a certain fixed price, and
lambs' fur only. At the same time, velvets of any colour, furs of
martens, chains, bracelets, and collars of gold were allowed only
to those who possessed an income of not less than two hundred
marks per annum ; but the sons and heirs of such were permitted
to wear black velvet or damask, and tawny-coloured russet or
camlet. None but those in the yearly receipt of one hundred
marks could venture on satin or damask robes. The dress which
may be taken as the most characteristic garb under the sovereignty of the last Henry and of his two immediate successors,
comprised a doublet with long bases, or skirts, and extensive
sleeves, over which was thrown a short cloak, provided with arm-
holes for the passage of the doublet sleeves. The cloak had a
wide rolling collar, made of velvet, fur, or satin, according to
taste. The shirt was plaited, and embroidered with gold, silver,
or silk. The hose were closely fitted to the limb, being in some
cases long and entire, and in others divided, under the names of
the upper and nether stocks. Slashed shoes, or buskins of velvet
and satin, with broad toes, and a cap of one of sundry forms,
either simply bordered, or laden with feathers, completed the
costume of every male member of the numerous families inhabiting the ancient halls of this section. Sir Walter Scott, who is
generally allowed to have been pretty correct in the costumes of
his heroes and minor characters, has described the appearance of
a yeoman of our county about the middle of the sixteenth century
as follows :—

" He was an English yeoman good,
And born in Lancashire.

*　　*　　*　　*　　*

His coal-black hair, shorn round and close,
　Set off his sun-burnt face ;
Old England's sign, St. George's cross,
　His barret-cap did grace ;
His bugle horn hung from his side,
　All in a wolf-skin baldric tied ;
And his short falchion, sharp and clear,
　Had pierced the throat of many a deer.
His kirtle, made of forest green,
　Reached scantly to his knee ;
And at his belt, of arrows keen
　A furbished sheaf bore he." .

Shortly after the accession of Queen Elizabeth in 1558, remarkable alterations became evident in the fashions of the inhabitants. The skirts of the doublet were reduced to much smaller dimensions, so as thoroughly to expose the upper stocks, which, under the new title of trunk-hose, had risen to a very important place in the toilet. French trunk-hose were the first to render themselves conspicuous in our locality, and consisted of two varieties, the former of which were short, round, and full, becoming, in fact, in course of time, so swollen by padding that their use was abandoned by universal consent; and the second variety, going to the other extreme and fitting tightly to the limb, introduced. The next to arrive were the Gallic hose, very large and wide, and extending to the knee only ; after which came the Venetian hose, reaching below the knee to the garter, where they were secured with silken bands. The trunk-hose, of every kind, were made of silk, velvet, satin, or damask. The nether stocks, or stockings, were of jarnsey, thread, fine yarn, and later, of silk, whilst the shoes partook more of the nature of slippers, and were variously decorated. Ruffs encircled the necks of the males as well as the females. Above the doublet was worn in the Spanish style a cloak of silk, velvet, or taffeta, and of a red, black, green, yellow, tawny, russet, or violet colour, many being bordered with long glass beads. Hats were conical and high, flat and broad, and flat and round, but in all cases were made of velvet or sarcenet, and ornamented with bunches of feathers. The robes of the ladies, made of bright-coloured velvet, silk, or fine cloth, had both tight and wide sleeves, and were branched or opened at the front of the skirt to expose the handsome petticoat beneath. The farthingale distended the dresses of our female ancestry from just below the bodice or stomacher, in a manner that few, we opine, of the fair sex would care to see revived at the present day. The ruff was of cambric or lawn, and when first introduced, moderate in its proportions, but like many other fashions of that epoch, became enlarged into an absurdity as years passed on. The hair of the ladies was curled, crisped, and arranged with most elaborate care; indeed, so curious and changeable were the coiffures that it would be tedious to our readers to offer more than this general description of them. Capes falling but a short way beyond the shoulders, and faced with fringe or velvet, were also worn. The costume of the gentlewomen during the seventeenth century, if the sombre garbs of the Roundhead families be excepted, consisted of an upper gown, which comprised a bodice and short skirt, the former being open over a laced stomacher, and the latter divided anteriorly, and its sides drawn back and looped up behind; a petticoat or under-dress, of expensive material, reaching to the ground; a yellow starched neckerchief, overspreading the shoulders and terminating on the bosom in two pointed ends; and a high crowned hat, beneath which long ringlets escaped and flowed down the back. The peasant girls or female farm servants had plain dresses, falling to the ankles, and usually tight sleeves and aprons. The bodices of some were open to the waist, but the stomachers, although laced, were of a very inferior kind, and the starched neckerchiefs were wanting. The gentlemen of the Fylde were influenced in their choice of garments according as their sympathies were with the King or Parliament, but there can be little question that in a locality so staunchly loyal as our own, the picturesque garb of the Cavaliers would predominate over the affectedly modest and plain attire of the partizans of Cromwell. The existence on the soil of such men as Sir Thomas Tyldesley, Thomas Singleton of Staining Hall, Thomas Hesketh of Mains Hall, who laid down their lives in the service of the crown, and numbers of others, who drew the sword in the cause of the throneless monarch, are fair evidence that the above conjecture is not hazarded without good reason. A doublet of silk, satin, or velvet, with large wide sleeves slashed

up the front ; a collar covered by a band of rich point lace, with
Vandyke edging ; a short cloak, thrown on one shoulder ; short
trousers, fringed and reaching to the wide tops of the high boots ;
a broad-leaved Flemish beaver hat, with a plume of feathers and
band ; and a sword belt and rapier, constituted the full costume
of a Cavalier. Instead of the velvet doublet, a buff coat, richly
laced, and encircled by a broad silk or satin scarf, fastened in a
bow, was substituted when the inhabitants were under the
excitement produced by actual war, in which so many took part.
The hair, it should be mentioned, was worn long by the Cavaliers,
and closely cropped by the Roundheads, whose dress offers no
special features to our notice.

In the earlier part of last century the occupiers of Layton,
Lytham, Fox, Burn, Mains, Rawcliffe, Rossall, Larbrick, etc.,
Halls, and others of equal social standing, who formed the gentry
of the Fylde, and who consequently must be taken as our mirror
of fashion, were clothed in straight square-cut waistcoats, extending to the knees, and of very gorgeous patterns ; velvet breeches
fastened below the knees ; long silk stockings ; buckled shoes,
with high red heels ; periwigs of monstrous size ; hats, cocked on
three sides ; long lace neckerchiefs ; and lastly, but far from the
least important, a coat of rich material, having long stiff skirts
and wide cuffs, turned back and adorned with gold or silver lace.
The ladies had laced stomachers beneath a bodice with straight
sleeves, ending at the elbow in moderately wide cuffs. The skirt
of the dress was divided in front and looped up behind, disclosing
a petticoat equalling or surpassing the richness of the upper
garment, and trimmed with flounces and furbelows. The boots
resembled those just described, but were more delicate in workmanship. The head-dress was composed of a species of cap, the
lace material of which rose in three or four tiers, placed one above
another, almost to a point, whilst the hair was brushed up and
arranged in stiff curls, somewhat resembling a pyramid. This
coiffure had only a brief reign, and was superseded by one less
exalted, and of more elegant appearance. Hoops were introduced
about 1720, and thirty years later silk aprons and gipsy straw hats,
or small bonnets, were worn. In 1765 periwigs were discarded, and
the natural hair was allowed to grow, being profusely sprinkled
with powder, both by males and females. The country people

were habited in long, double-breasted coats, made from frieze or homespun, and of a dark brown, grey, or other quiet shade ; a light drugget waistcoat, red shag or plush breeches, and black stockings. There is no necessity to trace the costumes of our ancestors further than the point here reached, as their varieties present few phases of special interest, and probably the most striking are already sufficiently familiar to our readers. A sure, though somewhat unsteady, decline was shortly inaugurated in the sumptuous and elaborate dresses of the people, which continued its course of reform until the more economical and unostentatious dress of modern days had usurped the place of the showy habiliments of the eighteenth century.

THE COUNTRY or district of the Fylde may be briefly described as broad and flat, for although in many places it is raised in gentle undulations, no hill of any altitude is to be seen upon its surface. The fertility of its soil has long been acknowledged, and a visit to its fruitful fields during the warm months of summer would disclose numbers of rich acres yellow with the ripening grain, while potatoe and bean-fields, meadow and pasture-lands, orchards and fruit gardens, are scattered over the wide area. Our design in the present instance is not, however, to enlarge upon these cultivated features, but to notice some of the more striking natural peculiarities, and to arrange in a classified list sundry of the rarer wild plants growing in the neighbourhood, enumerating also the different birds and sea-fowl, which are either natives or frequenters of the locality.

The features most calculated by their singularity to attract the attention of the stranger on surveying this division of the county are the moss-lands, the sand-hills, the mere at Marton, and the stunted appearance and inclination from the sea of those trees situated anywhere in the vicinity of the coast.

The great moss of the Fylde lies in the township of Marton, and extends six miles from north to south, and about one mile from east to west. On examining the structure of this moss, below the coarse herbage covering its surface, is discovered a substance called peat, brown and distinctly fibrous at its upper part, but becoming more and more compact as we descend, until at the bottom is presented a firm, dark-coloured, or even black mass, betraying less evidence, in some cases barely perceptible, of its fibrous formation.   Beneath the peaty layer is a thick bed of clay, having imbedded in it, either partially or wholly, large trunks of trees—oak, yew, fir, etc., which, by their frequency and arrangement, show that at some period the extensive tract must have been a dense woodland, but at what particular era it is impossible, with any degree of exactness, to determine.   The disinterment, however, of certain Celtic relics from the substance of the peat, which may be supposed to have belonged to the aboriginal Britons of the section, inclines us to the opinion that the lower layers of the moss were formed, and consequently the forest overthrown, anterior to the Roman occupation of our island, but how long before that time it was standing, must remain purely a matter of conjecture, unless some reliable proofs of its more precise antiquity are disclosed during operations in the turf. The manner in which the demolition of the forest was effected is also somewhat wrapt in obscurity, although it is probable that the noble trees of which it was composed were overturned and uprooted by the fury of some wide-spread inundation or the violence of some terrific hurricane.   The fearful devastations, both or either of the elements here brought into action can accomplish, are too well marked in the histories of other countries for us to hesitate in ascribing to them the power of overthrowing, under similar turbulent conditions, even so substantial an obstruc-tion as the forest must have been ; but a careful study of the locality and of the several sudden incursions of the tide which have occurred during recent years, leads to the belief that the sea was the chief destructive agent, and that the gale which hurled the raging volumes of water over the low-lying lands at the south of Blackpool, and the then level wooded tract beyond, assisted only in the ruinous work.   In support of such a hypothesis may be instanced the flood of 1833, when a tide, only estimated to rise to a height of sixteen feet, but greatly swollen by a furious storm from the south-west, burst over at that spot, swept away several dwelling-houses in its course, battered down the hedges, and laid waste the fields far into the surrounding country.   Had this inundation occurred during the high spring tides, it is impossible to say to what extent its ravages might have been carried, but the incident as it stands, being within the recollection of many still living, and by no means a solitary example of the usual direction

taken by the storm-driven waves, furnishes an apt illustration of
the most natural way in which the downfall of the forest may
have been accomplished.   The Rev. W. Thornber, who has
bestowed much time and labour on the subject, says :—" There
are some facts that will go far to prove that these forests, once
standing on Marton Moss, were overthrown by an inundation of
the sea, viz., every tree on the Moss, as well as the Hawes, lies
in a south-eastern direction from the shore ; and the bank, which
appears to have been the extent of this irruption, commencing at
the Royal Hotel, runs exactly in the same direction.   The shells,
similar to those collected on the shore, intermixed with wrack of
the sea, which are found in abundance under the peat, also
corroborate this supposition.   Moreover the tide is constantly
depositing a marine silt similar to that which lies beneath the
peat, and in some instances upon it."

The wreck of such a vast number of trees would cause a great
but gradual alteration in the surface of the ground.   The masses
of fallen timber, blocking up the streamlets and obstructing
drainage, would create a more or less complete stagnation of
water upon the land ; the bark, branches, and leaves undergoing
a process of decay would form the deepest layers of the peat ;
rank herbage and aquatic plants springing up and dying in endless
succession, would form annual accumulations of matter, which in
course of time would also be assimilated into peat, and in this
manner the moss overlaying the original clayey surface and
burying the ancient forest, would grow step by step to its present
dimensions.   Again, each layer of peat, as they were successively
formed, would press upon those beneath, so that the weight of its
own increase would give firmness and solidity to the substance of
the moss.   Thus we see that the whole secret of the creation or
formation of the moss is simply a process of growth, decay, and
accumulation of certain vegetable products annually repeated.
The huge moss of Pilling and Rawcliffe owes its existence to
similar phenomena.

The large mounds, or star-hills as they are called, which
undulate the coast line from Lytham to South-Shore, are composed simply and purely of sand, covered over with a coarse
species of herb, bearing the name of star-grass. Similar eminences
at one time occupied the whole of the marine border of the Fylde,

but in many places the encroaching tide has not only annihilated the hills themselves, but even usurped their sites. The town of Fleetwood is erected on a foundation of sand, and several extensive mounds of that nature exist in its vicinity. Below this light superficial substance, in some places very deep and thrown into its elevated forms by the long-continued action of the wind, is a subsoil resembling that found in other parts of the Fylde, and consisting of a clayey loam and alluvial matter. The diminutive size of those trees growing near the coast is due both to the openness and bleakness of the site, and the deleterious effects of the saline particles contained in the air ; whilst the peculiar leaning from the water of their branches, and in many instances their trunks, is caused by the mechanical action or pressure of the strong winds and sea breezes prevailing from the west during three-fourths of the year.

Marton Mere, situated in the township indicated by its name, was formerly a lake of no inconsiderable extent, but drainage and the accumulation within its basin of sediment have reduced it to its present comparatively unimportant dimensions. Traces of the more extensive boundaries of the sheet of water in former days are still discernible along its banks, and at one time, it is stated, the wheel of a water-mill near to the village of Great Marton, was turned by a stream from the mere. The right of fishery in the lake, for such it was in the earlier periods, was the subject of legal contest in the reign of Edward III., and in 1590 John Singleton, of Staining Hall, held the privilege.

There are few districts of similar area which can boast so many and such interesting varieties of the feathered tribes, either natives or visitants, as the Fylde. Some of the rarest sea-fowl are occasionally seen along the coasts, while the fields and hedge-rows abound with most of the melodious songsters of our island. Amongst the number of both land and sea birds which have been observed in the neighbourhood, either during the whole year or only in certain parts of it, may be mentioned the following :—

ORDER—RAPTORES OR RAPACIOUS BIRDS.

FALCONIDÆ OR FALCON FAMILY.

Tinnunculus Alaudarus	Kestrel	Common
Accipiter Nisus	Sparrow Hawk	Common
Circus ceruginosus	Moor Buzzard	Very rare

Strix flammea	Barn Owl	Common
Otus vulgaris	Long-eared Owl	Common
Otus brachyotus	Short-eared Owl	Common

ORDER—PASSERES OR PERCHERS.

HIRUNDINIDÆ OR SWALLOW FAMILY.

Hirundo rustica	Common Swallow	Common
Cotyle riparia	Sand Martin	Common
Chelidon urbica	House Martin	Common

LUSCINIDÆ OR WARBLER FAMILY.

Sylvia undata	Whitethroat	Common
Sylvia trochilus	Willow Warbler	Rare
Sylvia curruca	Lesser Whitethroat	Common
Sylvia sibilatrix	Wood Warbler	Rare
Calamodyta phragmitis	Sedge Warbler	Rare
Saxicola œnanthe	Wheatear	Common
Pratincola rubetra	Whinchat	Common
Pratincola rubicola	Stonechat	Rare
Ruticilla phœnicura	Redstart	Rare
Parus major	Great Titmouse	Common
Parus cœruleus	Blue Titmouse	Common
Parus caudatus	Long-tailed Titmouse	Rare
Parus ater	Cole Titmouse	Rare
Motacilla Yarrellii	Pied Wagtail	Common
Motacilla sulphurea	Yellow Wagtail	Common
Motacilla campestris	Grey Wagtail	Rather rare
Anthus pratensis	Meadow Titlark	Common
Anthus arboreus	Tree Titlark	Rare
Regulus cristatus	Golden-crested Wren	Rare
Regulus ignicapillus	Fire-crested Wren	Very rare

TURDIDÆ OR THRUSH FAMILY.

Turdus musicus	Song Thrush	Very common
Turdus viscivorus	Missel Thrush	Common
Turdns pilaris	Fieldfare	Common
Turdus iliacus	Redwing	Rather rare
Turdus merula	Blackbird	Common
Turdus torquatus	Ring Ousel	Rather rare

LANIIDÆ OR SHRIEK FAMILY.

Lanius collurio	Red-backed Shriek	Rare

CORVIDÆ OR CROW FAMILY.

Corvus Corone	Carrion Crow	Very common
Corvus cornix	Hooded Crow	Rare
Corvus frugilegus	Rook	Very common
Pica caudata	Magpie	Rather rare

STURNIDÆ OR STARLING FAMILY.

Sturnus vulgaris	Common Starling	Common

FRINGILLIDÆ OR FINCH FAMILY.

Fringilla carduelis	Goldfinch	Common
Fringilla cælebs	Chaffinch	Common
Fringilla spinus	Siskin	Rare
Fringilla chloris	Greenfinch	Common
Fringilla cannabina	Linnet	Common
Emberiza citrinella	Yellow Bunting	Common
Emberiza schæniculus	Reed Bunting	Common
Emberiza miliaris	Common Bunting	Common
Emberiza nivalis	Snow Bunting	Rare
Pyrrhula rubicilla	Bullfinch	Rare
Alauda arvensis	Skylark	Very common
Alauda arborea	Woodlark	Rare

ORDER—SCANSORES OR CLIMBERS.

CUCULIDÆ OR CUCKOO FAMILY.

Cuculus canorus	Cuckoo	Common

ORDER—COLUMBÆ OR DOVES.

COLUMBIDÆ OR DOVE FAMILY.

Columba palumbus	Ring Dove	Rare
Columba ænas	Stock Dove	Common

ORDER—GALLINÆ OR FOWLS.

PHASIANIDÆ OR PHEASANT FAMILY.

Phasianus Colchicus	Common Pheasant	Common

TETRAONIDÆ OR TETRAO FAMILY.

Perdix cinereus	Common Partridge	Common
Coturnix communis	Quail	Common

ORDER—GRALLATORES OR WADERS.

CHARADRIADÆ OR PLOVER FAMILY.

Charadrius pluvialis	Golden Plover	Common
Charadrius hiaticula	Ringed Plover or Dotterel	Common
Charadrius morinellus	Common Dotterel	Common
Vanellus griseus	Grey Plover	Common
Vanellus cristatus	Common crested Lapwing	Common
Hæmatopus ostralegus	Oyster-catcher	Very common
Cinclus interpres	Turnstone	Common

ARDEIDÆ OR HERON FAMILY.

Ardea cinerea	Common Heron	Common
Nycticorax Europæus	Common Night Heron	Rare
Botaurus stellaris	Bittern	Very rare indeed

SCOLOPACIDÆ OR WOODCOCK FAMILY.

Tringoides hypoleuca	Common Sandpiper	Common
Totanus ochropus	Green Sandpiper	Rare
Totanus Calidris	Redshank Sandpiper	Common
Numenius arquata	Curlew or Whaup	Common
Numenius phæopus	Whimbrel	Common
Limosa vulgaris	Common Godwit	Rare

J

SCOLOPACIDÆ OR WOODCOCK FAMILY—*continued*.

Philomachus pugnax	Ruff	Rare
Tringa Canutus	Knot	Rare
Tringa Temminckii	Temminck's Stint	Rare
Tringa minuta	Little Stint	Very rare
Tringa cinclus	Dunlin	Common
Phalaropus fulicarius	Grey Phalarope	Rare
Scolopax rusticola	Woodcock	Common
Gallinago media	Common Snipe	Common
Gallinago gallinula	Jack Snipe	Common

RALLIDÆ OR RAIL FAMILY.

Rallus aquaticus	Water Rail	Common
Ortygometra crex	Land Rail	Common
Gallinula chloropus	Water Hen	Common
Fulica atra	Common Coot	Common

ORDER—NATORES OR SWIMMERS.

ANATIDÆ OR DUCK FAMILY.

Anser ferus	Grey-lag Goose	Rare
Anser segetum	Bean Goose	Common
Bernicla leucopsis	Bernicle Goose	Common
Cygnus ferus	Whistling Swan	Rare
Tadorna vulpanser	Common Shieldrake	Common
Mergus Castor	Goosander	Rare
Anas boschas	Mallard	Common
Querquedula Crecca	Common Teal	Common
Spatula clypeata	Shoveller Duck	Rare
Moreca Penelope	Common Wigeon	Common
Myroca Terina	Common Pochard	Rather rare
Margellus albellus	Smew	Occasional visitor
Fuligula cristata	Tufted Duck or Pochard	Rather common
Fuligula marila	Scaup Duck or Pochard	Rather rare
Oidemia fusca	Velvet Scoter	Rare
Oidemia nigra	Black Scoter	Very rare
Clangula vulgaris	Golden-eye Duck or Garrot	Rather common
Clangula albeola	Buffel-headed Duck	Common

COLYMBIDÆ OR DIVER FAMILY.

Colymbus glacialis	Great Northern Diver	Very rare
Colymbus arcticus	Black-throated Diver	Rare
Colymbus septentrionalis	Red-throated Diver	Rather common
Chaulelasmus strepera	Gadwall	Very rare
Podiceps minor	Little Grebe	Common

ALCIDÆ OR AUK FAMILY.

Fratercula artica	Puffin	Common
Alca torda	Razor-bill	Rare
Uria Troile	Common Guillemot	Rare

PROCELLARIDÆ OR PETRRL FAMILY.

Thalassidroma pelagica	Stormy Petrel	Common
Thalassidroma Leachii	Fork-tailed Petrel	Rather rare

LARIDÆ OR GULL FAMILY.

Larus canus	Common Gull	Very common
Larus ribibundus	Black-headed Gull	Very common
Larus fuscus	Little Black-headed Gull	Common
Larus tridactylus	Kittiwake Gull	Very common
Larus Glaucus	Glaucus Gull	Rare
Larus argentatus	Herring Gull	Very common
Sterna hirundo	Sea-swallow or Tern	Common
Sterna fuliginosa	Sooty Tern	Rare
Sterna minuta	Lesser Tern	Common

PELECANIDÆ OR PELICAN FAMILY.

Graculus Carbo	Common Cormorant	Common
Graculus Cristata	Crested Cormorant	Rather rare
Sula Bassanea	Gannet or Solan Goose	Common

The fertile fields and sunny lanes of the Fylde afford ample opportunity for the botanist to indulge in his favourite pursuit, and a short ramble over any portion of the pleasant country will unfold to his inquiring gaze many of Nature's most beautiful and interesting offsprings. Specimens, especially of the maritime varieties of several of the floral families, unobtainable in the inland districts, may here be found lightly planted on the loose, sandy margins of the shore. In the context it is not intended to enter into a description of the different plants or of the localities in which they may most commonly be found, but merely to enumerate some of the more important ones ; and in the following list all those inhabitants of the district, which are likely to interest the student of Botany or lover of Nature, are arranged in their various groups or orders :—

RANUNCULACEÆ OR BUTTERCUP ORDER.

Ranunculus aquatilis	Water Crowcroft
„ Lingua	Spearwort
„ acris	Meadow Crowfoot
„ arvensis	Corn „
Thalictrum minus	Lesser Meadow-rue
Delphinium consolida	Field Larkspur

NYMPHÆACEÆ OR LILY ORDER.

Nymphœa Alba	White Water-lily

PAPAVERACEÆ OR POPPY ORDER.

Papaver dubium	Long Smooth-headed Poppy
„ Rhœas	Corn Poppy
Chelidonium majus	Common Celandine

CRUCIFERÆ OR CABBAGE ORDER.

Nasturtium officinale	Common Water-cress
Hesperis matronalis	Common Damewort
Cochlearia officinalis	Common Scurvy-grass
„ Danica	Danish „
Cakile maritima	Purple Sea Rocket
Crambe „	Sea Kale
Sisymbrium Irio	Broad-leaved Hedge-mustard
„ Sophia	Fine-leaved „

VIOLACEÆ OR VIOLET ORDER.

Viola odorata	Sweet Violet
„ tricolar	Heartsease

RESEDACEÆ OR MIGNONETTE ORDER.

Reseda Luteola	Yellow Weed

DROSERACEÆ OR SUNDEW ORDER.

Drosera rotundifolfa	Sundew
Parnassia pallustris	Grass of Parnassus

CARYOPHYLLACEÆ OR CLOVEWORT ORDER.

Saponaria officinalis	Common Soapwort
Lychnis Diocia	White Campion
„ Floscuculi	Cuckoo-flower
Silene inflata	Bladder Catchfly
„ maritima	Sea „
Arenaria marina	Sea Sandwort
„ serpyllifolia	Thyme-leaved Sandwort
Adenaria peploides	Sea Chickweed

LINACEÆ OR FLAX ORDER.

Linnm usitatissimum	Common Flax
„ catharticum	Purging „

MALVACEÆ OR MALLOW ORDER.

Malva rotundifolia	Dwarf Mallow
Althæa officinalis	Marsh Mallow

GERANIACEÆ OR CRANESBILL ORDER.

Geranium sanguimeum	Bloody Crane's-bill
Geranium pratense	Meadow Crane's-bill
Geranium purpurea	Odoriferous Cranes-bill
Erodium cicutarium	Hemlock Stork's-bill

LEGUMINOSÆ LEGUMINOUS ORDER.

Anthyllis vulneraria	Common Kidney-vetch
Vicia lathyroides	Spring Vetch
Ononis procurrens	Procurrent Restharrow
„ spinosa	Spinous „
Melilotus officinalis	Common Melilot
Trifolium arvense	Hare's-foot Trefoil

ROSACEÆ OR ROSE ORDER.

Rosa canina	Dog rose
„ spinosissima	Burnet-leaved Rose
„ eglantaria	Sweet Briar
Agrimonia Eupatoria	Agrimony
Spiræa ulmaria	Meadow Sweet
Rubus fruticosus	Blackberry Brambles

ONAGRACEÆ OR ŒNOTHERA FAMILY.

Epilobium hirsutum	Great Willow-herb
„ montanum	Small „

LYTHRACEÆ OR LYTHRUM FAMILY.

Lythrum salicaria	Spiked purple Loosestrife

HALORAGEACEÆ OR THE MARE'S TAIL ORDER.

Hippuris vulgaris	Common Mare's-tail

PORTULACACEÆ OR PURSLANE ORDER.

Montia foutana	Water Blinks

CRASSULACEÆ OR THE CRASSULA ORDER.

Sedum acre	Biting Stonecrop
„ allbum	White „
Sempervivum tectorum	Houseleek

SAXIFRAGACEÆ OR SAXIFRAGE ORDER.

Saxifraga granulata	White Saxifrage
„ stellaris	Starry „
„ aizoides	Yellow „

UMBELLIFERÆ OR UMBELLIFEROUS ORDER.

Crithmum maritimum	Samphire
Hydrocotyle vulgaris	Marsh Pennywort
Conium maculatum	Hemlock
Cicuta virosa	Cowbane
Eryngium maritimum	Sea-holly
Apium graveolens	Wild Celery
Bupleurum tenuissimum	Slender Hare's-ear
Œnanthe Crocata	Dead-tongue
Peucedanum ostruthium	Master-wort
„ officinale	Sea Sulphurwort
Daucus Carato	Wild Carrot
Anthriscus sylvestris	Wild beaked Parsley
Scandix Pecten-Veneris	Venus' Comb

CAPRIFOLIACEÆ OR HONEYSUCKLE ORDER.

Louicera Periclymenum	Pretty piped Woodbine
„ Caprifolium	Common Woodbine
Sambucus Nigra	Elder

RUBIACEÆ OR MADDER ORDER.

Galium verum	Yellow Bedstraw
„ mollugo	Hedge „
Sherardia arvensis	Little Spurwort

VALERIANACEÆ OR VALERIAN ORDER.

Valeriana officinalis	Common Valerian
Valerianella olitoria	Lamb's Lettuce

DIPSACACEÆ OR TEAZEL ORDER.

Dipsacus sylvestris	Wild Teazel

COMPOSITÆ OR COMPOSITE ORDER.

Aster Tripolium	Sea Starwort
Apargia hispida	Rough Hawkbit
Hieracium pallidum	Hawkweed
„ umbellatum	Narrow-leaved Hawkweed
Carduus tenuiflorus	Slender-flowered Thistle
„ palustris	Marsh Thistle
Chysanthemum maritimum	Sea Feverfew
Tanacetum vulgare	Common Tansey
Centaurea Cyanus	Corn Bluebottle
Pryethrum parthenium	Common Feverfew
„ inodorum	Corn „
Senecio vulgaris	Common Groundsell
„ aquaticus	Marsh Groundsell
Silybum Marianum	Milk Thistle
Tragopogon pratense	Yellow Goatsbeard
Helminthia echioides	Bristly Oxtongue

VACCINIACEÆ OR CRANBERRY ORDER.

Oxycoccus palustris	Cranberry

CAMPANULACEÆ OR HAREBELL ORDER.

Campanula rotundifolia	Harebell

PYROLACEÆ OR WINTERGREEN ORDER.

Pyrola media	Intermediate Wintergreen

APOCYNACEÆ OR DOGBANE ORDER.

Vinca major	Greater Periwinkle

GENTIANACEÆ OR GENTIAN ORDER.

Gentiana Pneumonanthe	Marsh Gentian
„ Campestris	Field „
Chironia Centaurium, var.	White-flowered Centaury
„ latifolia	Broad-leaved „
„ pulchella	Dwarf-branched „

CONVOLVULACEÆ OR CONVOLVULUS ORDER.

Convolvulus Soldanella	Sea Bindweed
„ Sepium, var.	Great Ditto, Pink-flowered
„ arvensis	Small Bindweed

SCROPHULARIACEÆ OR FIGWORT ORDER.

Veronica Anagallis	Water Speedwell
„ arvensis	Wall „
„ Beccabunga	Brooklime
„ Serpyllifolia	Thyme-leaved Speedwell

SCROPHULACEÆ OR CONVOLVULUS ORDER—*continued.*

Digitalis purpurea	Purple Foxglove
Linaria vulgaris	Yellow toadflax
Antirrhinum Cymbalaria	Ivy-leaved Snapdragon
Scrophularia vernalis	„ figwort

LABIATÆ THE DEAD-NETTLE ORDER.

Thymus Serpyllum	Wild Thyme
Marrubium vulgare	White Horehound
Prunella vulgaris	Selfheel
Mentha viridis	Spearmint
„ arvensis	Corn mint
Betonica officinalis	Wood Betony
Lamum album	White Dead-nettle
„ purpureum	Red „
Galeopsis ladanum	Red Hemp-nettle
Scutellaria galericulata	Skullcap

PLUMBAGINACEÆ OR LEADWORT FAMILY.

Armeria vagaris	Common Thrift
Statice Limonium	Lavender „

BORAGINACEÆ OR BORAGE ORDER.

Myosotis palustris	Forget-me-not
„ cæspitosa	Water Scorpion-grass
„ arvensis	Field „
„ versicolor	Yellow and Blue „

LENTIBULARIACEÆ OR BLADDERWORT ORDER.

Utricularia vulgaris	Greater Bladderwort

PRIMULACEÆ OR PRIMROSE ORDER.

Primula vnlgaris	Primrose
„ veris	Cowslip
Glaux maritima	Black Saltweed
Samolus Valerandi	Brookweed
Anagallis cærula	Blue Pimpernel
„ tenella	Bog „
Hottonia palustris	Water Featherfoil
Lysimachia vulgaris	Yellow Loosestrife

PLANTAGINACEÆ OR RIBGRASS ORDER.

Plantago major	Plantain
„ media	Hoary Plantain
„ maritima	Sea-side Platain
Littorella lacustris	Plantain Shoreweed

POLYGONACEÆ OR BUCKWHEAT ORDER.

Rumex crispus	Curled Dock
„ acetosa	Common Sorrel

EUPHORBIACEÆ OR SPURGEWORT ORDER.

Euphorbia paralias	Sea purge

URTICACEÆ OR NETTLE ORDER.

Humulus Lupulus	Hop
Urtica pilulifera	Roman nettle
Parietaria officinalis	Common Wall-pellitory

SALICACEÆ OR WILLOW ORDER.

Salix argentea	Silky Sand Willow
„ repens	Dwarf Willow
Myrica Gale	Sweet Gale

IRIDACEÆ OR IRIS ORDER.

Iris Pseudacorus	Yellow water-iris

AMARYLLIDACEÆ OR THE AMYRILLIS ORDER.

Narcissus Pseudo-narcissus	Common Daffodil
Galanthus nivalis	Snowdrop

ALISMACEÆ OR WATER-PLANTAIN ORDER.

Butomus umbellatus	Flowering-rush
Alisma ranunculoides	Lesser Thrumwort

POTAMOGETONACEÆ OR PONDWEED ORDER.

Ruppia maritima	Sea Tasselgrass
Zannichellia palustris	Common Lakeweed

ORCHIDACEÆ OR ORCHID ORDER.

Orchis morio	Green-winged Orchis
„ pyramidalis	Pyramidal „
Epipactis latifolia	Broad-leaved Helleborine
„ palustris	Marsh „

JUNCACEÆ OR RUSH ORDER.

Juncus effesus	Soft Rush
„ filiformis	Threadrush
„ squarrosus	Heathrush
Narthecium ossifragrum	Bog Asphodel

ARACEÆ OR ARUM ORDER.

Lenna minor	Lesser Duckweed

CRONTIACEÆ OR SWEET-FLAG ORDER.

Acorus Calamus	Sweet-flag

CYPERACEÆ OR SEDGE ORDER.

Carex limosa	Mud Sedge
„ flava	Yellow „
„ arenaria	Sea „
Eriophorum polystachyon	Broad-leaved Cotton-grass

EQUISETACEÆ OR HORSETAIL ORDER.

Equisetum arvense	Corn Horsetail
„ variegatum	Variegated Horsetail

THE RIVER WYRE rises in the hills of Wyersdale and Bleasdale ; running in a south-westerly direction and passing the towns of Garstang and Church Town, it arrives at St. Michael's, from which point its tortuous course is continued almost due west as far as Skippool. Thence winding past the ancient port of Wardleys, the stream, much widened, flows north and a little inclined towards the west, until it reaches the harbour of Fleetwood, situated at its mouth. From that seaport, the channel of the river, unaltered in direction, lies for a distance of nearly two miles between the sand-banks of North Wharf and Bernard's Wharf, and finally terminates in Morecambe Bay, meeting the well-defined bed of the Lune at right angles. The origins of the Wyre in the hills consist of two small rivulets, and the stream formed by their union is joined near Scorton by the Grizedale Brook, whilst lower down, about two miles beyond the town of Garstang, it receives the Calder, rising on the slopes of Bleasdale. Before leaving the parish of Garstang, the Wyre is further increased by the brook springing from Fairsnape and Parlick Pike, which passes Claughton and Myerscough, not far from where it receives a small tributary from the south. At Skippool also a brook, the Skipton, which springs from the mere and marshy grounds of Marton Moss, pours its contents into the river.

The Wyre is crossed at Garstang by the aqueduct of the Preston, Lancaster, and Kendal canal, and at St. Michael's, near the Church, it is spanned by a rather narrow but substantial stone bridge. For a distance of about six miles in the neighbourhood of the latter place the stream is enclosed within artificial banks, which in some parts have a descent of thirty feet. In spite of these precautions, however, high floods occasionally occur, when the swollen waters burst over the embankments and inundate the adjoining country. At Cart Ford there is a wooden structure of very limited width, connecting the opposing banks; and a few miles further down is the Shard Bridge, built of iron, and presenting a neat and elegant appearance. The river at that spot is 500 yards in breadth, and until the erection of the bridge in 1864, was crossed by means of a ferry-boat, or forded at low water by carts and conveyances. The ancient name of this ford was Ald-wath, and we learn from the following entry in the diary of Thomas Tyldesley, that in 1713 the charge for crossing by boat was 6d. each journey:—"September 14, 1713.—Went after dinr. to ffox Hall ; pd. 6d. ffor boating att Sharde ; saw ye ferry man carry out of ye boat a Scot and his pack, a sight I never saw beffor, beeing 56 years off age."

About three hundred years since the venerable Harrison described the principal rivers of Lancashire, and from his writings at that time we quote as under :—

"The Wire ryseth eight or ten miles from Garstan, out of an hill in Wiresdale, from whence it runneth by Shireshed chappell, and then going by Wadland, Grenelaw Castle (which belongeth to the erle of Darbie), Garstan and Kyrkeland hall, it first receiveth the seconde Calder, that commeth down by Edmersey chappell, then another chanel increased with sundrie waters, the first water is called Plympton brooke. It riseth south of Gosner, and commeth by Craweforde hall, and eare long receyving the Barton becke, it proceedeth forward till it joyneth with the Brooke rill that commeth from Bowland Forest by Claughton hall, where M. Brokehales doth live, and so throw Mersco forest. After this confluence the Plime or Plimton water meeteth with the Calder, and then with the Wire, which passeth forth to Michael church and the Rawcliffes, and above Thorneton crosseth the Skipton, that goeth by Potton, then into the Wire rode, and finally into the sea, according to his nature."

Drayton also has left the subjoined versified account of the Wyre, and as in addition to its poetic merit, it possesses the virtue of being a faithful description, we need not apologise for giving it unabridged :—

> " Arising but a rill at first from Wyersdale's lap,
> Yet still receiving all her strength from her full mother's pap,
> As downe to seaward she her serious course doth ply,
> Takes Calder coming in, to beare her company,
> From Woolscrag's cliffy foot, a hill to her at hand,
> By that fayre forest knowne, within her Verge to stand.
> So Bowland from her breast sends Brock her to attend,
> As she a Forest is, so likewise doth she send
> Her child, on Wyresdale Flood, the dainty Wyre to wayte,
> With her assisting Rills, when Wyre is once repleat ;
> She in her crooked course to Seaward softly glides,
> Where Pellin's mighty Mosse, and Merton's on her sides
> Their boggy breasts outlay, and Skipton down doth crawle
> To entertain this Wyre, attained to her fall." [1]

White Hall, (formerly Upper Rawcliffe Hall,) Rawcliffe Hall, and Mains Hall, each of which will claim our attention more particularly hereafter, are seated on the banks of the Wyre, so also is the ancient house of Preesall-with-Hackensall, and although not properly comprised within the limits of this work, it has a right from its association with the river, to some description—a right the more readily conceded when it is known that in point of antiquity and interest, the hall and domain are well deserving

1. Faerie Land, Song, edit. A.D. 1622.

of our consideration. The site of the mansion is a little removed from the brink of the stream, and almost directly opposite the southern extremity of Fleetwood. The present building is of considerable age, having been erected by Richard Fleetwood, of Rossall, in 1656, as indicated by an inscription over the main entrance, but there can be no question that the origin of its predecessor was co-eval, at least, with the grant of the manor by King John, when earl of Moreton, to Geoffrey, the Crossbowman, who, with his descendants, resided there. The whole of the large estate remained in the family of Geoffrey until the fifteenth century, when it was conveyed in marriage to James Pickering, of Layton, by Agnes, the sole offspring and heiress of the last male Hackensall, the title assumed, according to custom, by the Crossbowman. James Pickering left at his decease four daughters, co-heiresses, and married to Richard Butler, of Rawcliffe, Thomas Aglionby, Nicholas Aglionby, and James Leybourne, each of whom inherited one-fourth of the manor in right of his wife. In 1639 Sir Paul Fleetwood, of Rossall, held three-fourths of Hackensall, whilst the remaining quarter had descended to Henry Butler. Under the will of Richard Fleetwood, the re-erector of the hall, at that time occupied by his brother Francis, the three-fourths just named were sold by his trustees, being purchased, in part, for the Hornbys, of Poulton. Geoffrey Hornby, vicar of Winwick, and Robert Loxham, vicar of Poulton, held between them three-quarters of the manor in 1729, and William Elletson, of Parrox Hall, had possession of the other fourth, which is now the hereditary estate of Daniel Hope Elletson, esq., justice of the peace, residing at the same seat. At the end of the last century the Hornbys disposed of their share to John Bourne, gentleman, of Stalmine, from whom it descended to his second son, James Bourne, of Stalmine, and from him to his nephews, Thomas, James, and Peter, successively. The other portion of the manorial rights of the three-fourths was subsequently acquired by the last-surviving nephew, Peter Bourne, of Heathfield and Liverpool. Peter Bourne, esq., of Hackensall, married Margaret, the only daughter of James Drinkwater, esq., of Bent, in Lancashire, and left issue James, who is the present lord of three-quarters of the manor, and owner of the ancient Hall. James Bourne, esq., M.P., of Hackensall, and of Heathfield, near

Liverpool, is Col.-Comdt. of the Royal Lancashire regiment of Militia Artillery, a deputy-lieutenant, and a justice of the peace of this county. Colonel Bourne has recently restored the old manor house, but in such a way as to preserve, and not obliterate, its links with a bygone age. The antique fire-places, one of which was protected by a massive arch of stone sweeping across the whole width of the room, have been renewed as before, and although the main doorway has been removed to another part of the building, the stone with the initials F. R. A., being those of Richard Fleetwood and Anne, his wife, has been reinstated in its original position above the newly-constructed lintel. Rumour affirms that during certain alterations two or three skeletons, supposed to be those of females, were found bricked up in a narrow chamber in one of the walls, and whilst confirming the discovery of a long secret recess, we dare not venture, for the evidence is somewhat contradictory, to hold ourselves responsible for the strict accuracy of the other part of the story, which suggests the enactment of a scene of revolting cruelty, similar to that introduced by Sir Walter Scott in the following lines :—

> " Yet well the luckless wretch might shriek,
> Well might her paleness terror speak !
> For there was seen in that dark wall,
> Two niches, narrow, deep, and tall.
> Who enters at such grisly door
> Shall ne'er I wean find exit more.
> In each a slender meal was laid
> Of roots, of water, and of bread.
>
> *   *   *   *
>
> Hewn stones and mortar were display'd,
> And building tools in order laid."

The moat has now been nearly filled up, but its extent and direction can still be pointed out. There are no indications of a chapel having formerly constituted part of the residential building, but several years since, when an outhouse was destroyed, at a short distance, about twenty yards, two gravestones were discovered, and it is probable that they were somewhere near, if not actually on the site of, the private chapel or oratory. One of the stones was broken up immediately, and the other is practically illegible, although three or four words, still preserved, prove that the inscription has not been in raised characters. The rights to wreckage, etc. on the foreshore of the manor have pertained to

the lords of Hackensall from time immemorial, and still continue
to be held and exercised as portion of the lordship.

Anterior to the establishment of a port at Fleetwood, or more
correctly speaking, to the foundation of a town and the erection
of wharfage, etc., on the warren forming the western boundary of
Wyre estuary, Wardleys and Skippool, almost facing each other,
were the harbours to which all commercial traffic on the river
was directed. Ships of considerable size, freighted with cargoes
of various sorts, found their way to those secluded havens, and
even within the last few years, during high tides, vessels laden
with grain have been berthed and unloaded in the narrow creek
leading from Skippool bay, while bags of guano have often terminated their sea-voyages at Wardleys. A solitary warehouse,
however, undated, but bearing on its battered exterior and decaying timbers the unmistakable stamp of time, is, at the present
day, almost the only remaining witness to the former pretentions
of the first named place. At Wardleys, three or four spacious
warehouses, in a similarly dilapidated condition and now partially .
converted into shippons, the remainder being unused except as
lumber-rooms or temporary storehouses for guano or some local
agricultural produce, together with a stone wharf, are evidences
of a fair amount of business having once been carried on at that
little port.

In 1825 Baines described Wardleys as "a small seaport on the
river Wyre, where vessels of 300 tons register may discharge their
burdens, situated in the township of Stalmine with Stainall, in
the hundred of Amounderness;" but in the year 1708 customs
were established at Poulton in connection with Wardleys and
Skippool. Nor should we be justified in limiting the antiquity of
the ports to that date, for as early as 1590—1600, William and
James Blackburne, of Thistleton, carried on an extensive trade
with Russia, and there can be no doubt that their cargoes of merchandise, most likely flax and tallow, were landed on the banks
of the Wyre at those ancient harbours. The father of the above
merchants was the first of the family to take up his residence in
this neighbourhood, and appears to have settled at Garstang,
about 1550, from Yorkshire. That the commercial dealings of
the partners were both large and successful is shown in the property acquired by William Blackburne, the elder brother, who

purchased Newton, lands in Thistleton, and several other estates
of considerable magnitude in the Fylde, all of which he bequeathed
to his son and heir, Richard.   Richard Blackburne married Jane,
the daughter of John Aynesworth, of Newton, and had issue John
of Eccleston ; Richard, of Goosnargh ; Thomas, of Orford and
Newton ; Edward, of Stockenbridge, near St. Michael's-on-Wyre ;
Robert, who was suspected of being implicated in the Gunpowder
Plot, but acquitted, the evidence being insufficient ; Annie, who
married — Nickson ; and Elizabeth, the wife of William Standish.
When the Singletons of Staining became extinct, the Hall and
estate of that name passed to a William Blackburne, as heir-at-
law, and there is great probability that he was a descendant of one
of the sons of Richard Blackburne of Thistleton, Newton, etc.—
most likely of John Blackburn, of Eccleston.

During the years more immediately previous to the opening of
the new port at the mouth of the river, a great many large ships
from America, laden with timber, and brigs from Russia, with flax
and tallow, were discharged at Wardleys.   A three masted vessel,
for the foreign trade, was also constructed in the ship-yard
attached to that place, but as far as can be learnt this was the
only vessel of equal dimensions ever built there, repairs being the
chief occupation of the workpeople.

Several of the officers connected with the Custom House at
Poulton, were stationed at Knot End, opposite the Warren,
living in the small cottage standing near the shore, in order to
board the different craft as they entered the river, and pilot them
up the stream to Wardleys.   A large hotel is situated behind
the site of the old ship-yard, and during the summer months is
generally well patronised by visitors, to whom, as well as to the
pleasure-parties arriving by water from Fleetwood, and by road
from Blackpool, the hamlet is now mainly indebted for support.
Some large mussels, the " Mytili angulosi," but known amongst
the natives of those parts as " Hambleton hookings," were found
formerly in large quantities a little lower down the river, but lately
specimens of this fine shell-fish have been growing much scarcer.
Dr. Leigh, in his Natural History of our county, informs us that
pearls have frequently been discovered enclosed within the shells
of these molluscs, and also that their popular name arises from the
manner in which they are taken, the feat being accomplished " by

plucking them from their Skeers, or Beds, with Hooks." The tidal estuary of the Wyre embraces an area of three miles by two, and it is near to its termination that the port and town of Fleetwood are situated. Our purpose now is not to enter into a description of the harbour, which will be found in the chapter specially devoted to the seaport itself, but a few words as to the advantages derived from the nature of the river's current and its bed, will not be out of place. Captain Denham, R.N., F.R.S., after inspecting the site of the proposed port on behalf of the promoters, issued a report in the month of January, 1840, and amongst other things, stated that during the first half of the ebb-tide, a reflux of backwater was produced which dipped with such a powerful under-scour as to preserve a natural basin, capable of riding ships of eighteen or twenty feet draught, at low water, spring tides; also that the anchorage ground, both within and without the harbour, was excellent. These facts alone seemed sufficient to warrant the gallant officer's prediction that the undertaking would be successful and remunerative, but when in addition it is called to mind, that " as easy and safe as Wyre water " had for long been a proverb amongst the mariners of our coast, and that the harbour was, and is, perfectly sheltered from all winds, as well as connected with a railway terminus which communicates with Preston, Manchester, etc., we are astonished that comparatively so little encouragement has been given to it, and that now, thirty-five years from the date of this survey, the first dock is only approaching completion.

The river Wyre is plentifully supplied with fish of various sorts; in the higher parts of the stream trout and smelts may be found, whilst the lower portion and estuary contain codling, flounders, sea-perch, conger, sand eels, and occasionally salmon. The earliest enactments with regard to the fisheries connected with the last-named fish related to the Wyre, Ribble, and other rivers of Lancashire. In 1389, during the reign of Richard II., a law, which arranged the times and seasons when the fisheries in these rivers should be closed, and other matters affecting them, was passed and brought into force, being the first regulation of its kind.

The Ribble is associated with the Fylde only in so much as its tidal estuary is concerned, which forms the southern boundary of

the district. Since 1837 great alterations have been effected in
the channel of the river by the Ribble Navigation Improvement
Company. The stream for the larger portion of its extent from
Preston to the Naze Point has been confined within stone
embankments, and its bed considerably deepened by dredging.
During the progress of these improvements wide tracts of land
have been reclaimed both north and south of the current.
From Freckleton the river rapidly widens as it approaches
the sea, so that a direct line drawn from Lytham to Southport
across its mouth would pass over a distance of seven or
eight miles. The channel here is shallow, while the sands on
each side are flat and extensive, and midway in the estuary, at its
lowest part, lies the far-famed Horse-bank, which divides the
stream into a north and south current, scarcely discernible,
however, after the tide has risen above the level of the bank.
About one mile from the town of Lytham, in the direction of
Preston, is a pool of moderate dimensions, having an open communication with the river, and formed into a small harbour or
dock for yachts and vessels connected with the coasting trade.
In the bed of the river, a little higher up than that locality,
trunks of large trees are occasionally observed at low water, and
many such remains of a once noble forest, which is believed to
have extended from near the Welsh coast as far even as Morecambe, have been raised at different times during the operation of
dredging.

The following descriptions of the Ribble, its source, course, and
tributaries, were written, respectively, by the ancient topographer
Harrison, and the poet Drayton, whose accounts of the Wyre
have been previously quoted :—

"The Rybell, a river verie rich of Salmon and Lampreie, dooth in manner
inviron Preston in Andernesse, and it riseth neere to Ribbesdale above Gisburne.
It goeth from thence to Sawley or Salley, Chatburne, Woodington, Clitherow
Castell, and beneath Mitton meeteth with the Odder, which ryseth not farre from
the Cross of Grete in Yorkshire, and going thence to Shilburne, Newton,
Radholme parke, and Stony hirst, it falleth ere long into Ribble water. From
thence the Ribble hath not gone farre, but it meeteth with the Calder. Thys
brooke ryseth above Holme Church, goeth by Townley and Burneley (where
it receiveth a trifeling rill), thence to Higham, and ere long crossing one
water that cometh from Wicoler, by Colne, and another by and by named Pidle
brooke that runneth by Newechurch, in the Pidle : it meeteth with ye Calder,
which passeth forth to Padiam, and thence (receyving a becke on the other side)

it runneth on to Altham, and so to Martholme, where the Henburne brooke doth joyn with all, that goeth by Alkington chappell, Dunkinhalge, Rishton, and so into ye Calder as I have sayde before. The Calder therefore being thus inlarged, runneth forth to Reade (where M. Noell dwelleth), to Whalley, and soon after into Ribell, that goeth from this confluence to Salisbury hal, Ribchester, Osbaston, Sambury, Keuerden, Law, Ribles bridge, and then taketh in the Darwent, before it goeth by Pontwarth or Pentworth into the sea. The Darwent devideth Leland shire from Andernesse,[1] and it ryseth by east above Darwent Chappell, and soone after uniting it selfe with the Blackeburne, and Rodlesworthe water it goeth thorowe Howghton Parke, by Howghton towne, to Walton hall, and so into the Ribell. As for the Sannocke brooke, it ryseth somewhat above Longridge Chappell, goeth to Broughton towne, Cotham, Lee hall, and so into Ribell."

> " From Penigent's proud foot as from my source I slide,
> That mountain, my proud sire, in height of all his pride,
> Takes pleasure in my course as in his first-born flood,
> And Ingleborrough too, of that Olympian brood,
> And Pendle, of the north, the highest hill that be,
> Do wistly me behold, and are beheld of me.
> These mountains make me proud, to gaze on me that stand,
> So Longridge, once arrived on the Lancastrian strand,
> Salutes me, and with smiles me to his soil invites,
> So have I many a flood that forward me excites,
> As Hodder that from Home attends me from my spring,
> Then Calder, coming down from Blackstonedge doth bring
> Me easily on my way to Preston, the greatest town
> Wherewith my banks are blest, where, at my going down,
> Clear Darwen on along me to the sea doth drive,
> And in my spacious fall no sooner I arrive,
> But Savock to the north from Longridge making way
> To this my greatness adds, when in my ample bay,
> Swart Dulas coming in from Wigan, with her aids,
> Short Taud and Dartow small, two little country maids,
> In these low watery lands and moory mosses bred,
> Do see me safely laid in mighty Neptune's bed,
> And cutting in my course, even through the heart
> Of this renowned shire, so equally it part,
> As nature should have said, lo ! thus I meant to do,
> This flood divides this shire, thus equally in two."

The beautiful scenery and historical associations of the Ribble render it the most interesting and charming of the several rivers which water the county of Lancaster. The quietude of its fair valley has on more than one occasion been rudely broken by the clash of arms, and students of our country's history will readily

1. This is incorrect, as the Ribble and not the Darwent separates the Hundreds of Leyland and Amounderness.

K

call to mind that calamitous day to the Duke of Hamilton, when Cromwell routed the Highlanders under his command, near Preston,

"And Darwen stream with blood of Scots imbrued."

Other instances of war-like doings along the banks of this river might be recounted, but as the neighbourhoods in which they occurred are not enclosed within the Fylde boundaries, we are perforce obliged to exclude them from this volume, and must refer those of our readers who are anxious to learn more both of them and of the river itself to other sources for the required information. The chief fish of the Ribble is of course its salmon, but in addition the estuary contains numbers of flounders and other varieties of the finny tribes similar to those found in the tidal portion of the Wyre. During the sixteenth century sturgeons seem to have been captured occasionally in the Ribble, and amongst the records of the duchy in 1536, there is a complaint that when "one certain sturgeon was found within the township of Warton and seized for the use of the King (who held the right of fishery there), and laid up in a house in Warton, one Christopher Bone, of Warton, and James Brad'ton, of the ley, with divers riotous persons, about the 6th of May last, did then and there take out of the said house the said sturgeon, and the said Bone hath at divers times and in like manner taken sturgeons and porpoises to his own use and the injury of his majesty."[1]

As such a small part, and that far from the most important, of of Ribble stream is really connected with the Fylde, and as it is not our intention to trespass beyond the limits of that district,—at least not knowingly, and the margin in the present instance is so clearly defined that no excuse could be offered for overstepping it, —we are compelled to content ourselves with this brief account, leaving much unsaid that is of considerable historical and general interest.

THE SEA which washes over the westerly shore of the Fylde forms part of St. George's Channel or the Irish Sea, whilst the narrow northern boundary of the same district is limited by the waters of Morecambe Bay. The main peculiarities to be noticed

1. Record Office, 28 Henry VIII., V. S., c. 6.

along the extensive line of this coast swept over by the billows of
the Irish Sea, are the almost entire absence of seaweeds and the
levelness of the sands ; indeed, so gentle is the slope of the latter
that its average declivity has been estimated at no more than one
foot in every fifty yards, and to the flatness of this surface it is
due that the beach is in a very great measure freed from putrifying
heaps of fish and seaweed, for the rising tides glide with such
swiftness over the level sandy beds that most driftmatters and
impurities are left behind in the depths beyond low water mark.
An analysis, made by Dr. Schweitzer, of the waters of the English
coast, furnishes the following result :—

	No. of grains.
Water	964.74
Chloride of Sodium (Table salt)	27.06
Chloride of Magnesium	3.67
Sulphate of Magnesia (Epsom Salts)	2.30
Sulphate of Lime	1.40
Carbonate of Lime	0.03
Carbonate of Magnesia	
Carbonic Acid	
Potash	Traces
Iodine	
Extractive matter	
Bromide of Magnesium	

1,000

There are few, we imagine, who have not at one time or
another admired the luminous appearance of the sea on certain
evenings. This astonishing and beautiful phenomenon is brought
about by the presence in the water of myriads of tiny beings,
called Noctilucæ, which possess the power of emitting a phos-
phorescent light, and seemingly convert the bursting waves into
masses of liquid fire. The immense expanse of sea spreading out
from the westerly border of the Fylde has, independently of its
association with the Gulph Stream, a marked influence in
equalising the climate and averting those sudden and extreme
degrees of heat and cold commonly experienced inland. The
atmosphere over water does not undergo such rapid alterations in
its temperature as that over land, and hence it happens that
localities situated near the coast are cooler in summer and
warmer in winter than others far removed from its vicinity.
Most people will have observed that after a calm sunny day at
the seaside, a breeze from the land invariably arises after sunset,

due to the fact that the air over the earth being cooled and condensed much sooner than that over the sea, the heavier body of atmosphere endeavours to displace the warmer and lighter one. A gentle evaporation is daily taking place from the surface of the sea, by which the air becomes loaded with moisture, remaining suspended until the coolness of evening sets in, when it is deposited on the ground as dew. The water thus obtained from the deep is not pure brine, as might at first sight appear, but is freed from its salts by the process of natural distillation which has been undergone. Similar evaporation also goes on from the surfaces of the Ribble and Wyre, and it is doubtless chiefly owing to the Fylde being almost environed by water, constantly disseminating dew, that its fecundity is not only so great, but also so constant. The following is a list of the seaweeds to be found on the coast :—

MELANOSPERMEÆ OR OLIVE GREEN SEAWEEDS.

TRIBE—FUCACEÆ.

Fucus nodosus	Knobbed Wrack
„ serratus	Serrated „
„ canaliculatus	Channelled „
„ vesiculosus	Bladder „

TRIBE—SPOROCHNACEÆ.

Desmarestia aculeata	Spring Desmarestia
„ viridis	Green „

TRIBE—LAMINARIEÆ.

Alaria esculenta	Edible Alaria
Laminaria digitata	Tangle
„ saccharina	Sweet Laminaria
„ bulbosa	Sea-furbelows
Chorda filum	Thread Ropeweed

TRIBE—DICTYOTEÆ.

Dictyosiphon fæniculaceus	Tubular Netweed
Asperococcus echinatus	Wooly Rough-weed
„ compressus	Compressed

TRIBE—CHORDARIEÆ.

Chordaria flagelliformis	Whiplash weed
Mesogloia virescens	Verdant Viscid-weed
„ vermicularis	Wormy „

TRIBE—ECTOCARPEÆ.

Cladostephus verticillatus	Whorled Cladostephus
„ spongiosus	Spongy „
Sphacellaria scoparia	Brown-like Sphacellaria
„ plumosa	Feathered „
„ Cirrhosa	Nodular „

TRIBE—ECTOCARPEÆ—*continued.*

Ectocarpus litoralis	Shore Ectocarpus
„ siliculosus	Podded „
„ tomentosus	Feathered „

RHODOSPERMEÆ OR RED SEAWEEDS.

TRIBE—RHODOMELEÆ.

Polysiphonia fastigiata	Tufted Polysiphonia
„ urceolata	Hair-like „
„ nigrescens	Dark „

TRIBE—LAURENCIEÆ.

Bonnemaisonia asparagoides	Asparagus-like Bonnemaisonia
Laurentia pinnatifida	Pinnatifid Pepper-dulse
„ cæspitosa	Tufted „
„ dasyphylla	Sedum-leaved „

TRIBE—CORRALLINEÆ.

Corallina officinalis	Officinal Coralline
Jania	Jania
Melobesia	Melobesia

TRIBE—DELESSERIEÆ.

Delesseria alata	Winged Delesseria

TRIBE—RHODYMENIEÆ.

Rhodymenia palmata	Dulse
„ ciliata	Ciliated Rhodymenia
Hypnea purpurescens	Purple Hypnea

TRIBE—CRYPTONEMIEÆ.

Gelidium	Jellyweed
Gigartina mamillosa	Papillary Grape-stone
Chondrus crispus	Irish moss
Polyides rotundus	Round Polyides
Furcellaria fastigiata	Slippery Forkweed
Halymenia rubens	Red Sea-film
„ membranifolia	Membranous Sea-film
„ edulis	Edible „
„ palmata	Palmated „
„ lacerata	Lacerated „
Catanella opuntia	Catanella opuntia

TRIBE—CERAMIEÆ.

Ceramium rubrum	Red Hornweed
„ diaphanum	Diaphanous „
„ ciliatum	Hairy „
„ echionotum	Irregularly-spined Hornweed
„ acanthonotum	Spined „
„ nodosum	Nodose „
Callithamnion tetragonum	Square-branched Callithamnion
„ plumula	Feathery „
„ polyspermum	Many-spermed „

CHLOROSPERMEÆ OR GRASS GREEN SEAWEEDS.

TRIBE—CONFERVEÆ.

Couferva rupestris	Rock Crowsilk
„ lanosa	Woolly „
„ fucicola	Wrack „
„ tortuosa	Twisted „

TRIBE—ULVEÆ.

Ulva latissima	Oyster Green or Laver
„ Lactuca	Lettuce Laver
Entermarpha intestinalis	Intestinal Entermorpha
„ compressa	Branched „

The subjoined table contains the names of some of the crustaceous animals and molluscs commonly met with in the neighbourhood :—

Arctopsis tetraodon	Four-horned Spider-crab
Hyas araneus	Great Spider-crab, or Sea-toad
Portunus puber	Velvet Fiddler-crab
Corystes dentata	Toothed Crab
Gonoplax angulata	Angular Crab
Pinnotheres pisum	Pea-crab
Porcellana platycheles	Broad-claw porcelain Crab
Cancer pagurus	Edible crab
Cancer mænas	Common Crab
Pagurus Bernhardus	Hermit-crab
Pilumnus hirtellus	Hairy-crab
Palæmon serratus	Common Prawn
Crangon vulgaris	Common Shrimp
Corophium longicorne	Long-horned Corophium
Orchestia littorea	Shore-hopper
Talitrus saltator	Sand-hopper
Sulcator arenarius	Sand-screw
Mytilus edulis	Edible Mussel
Cardium edule	Cockle
Buccinum undatum	Whelk
Litorina litorea	Periwinkle
Calyptra vulgaris	Common Limpet

CHAPTER VI.

THE PEDIGREES OF ANCIENT FAMILIES.

ALLEN OF ROSSALL HALL.

THE Allens who resided at Rossall Hall for a period of more than half a century, and by intermarriage became connected with the Westbys of Mowbreck, the Heskeths of Mains, and the Gillows of Bryning, sprang from the county of Stafford. At the time of the Protestant Reformation, George Allen, of Brookhouse, in the division just mentioned, held a long lease of the Grange and Hall of Rossall from a kinsman of his family, one of the abbots of Deulacres, a Staffordshire monastery, to which the estate had been granted by King John. George Allen at his death left one son, John, who resided at the Hall, and subsequently married Jane, the sister of Thomas Lister, of Arnold Biggin, in Yorkshire. The offspring of this marriage were Richard, William, Gabriel, George, who espoused Elizabeth, the daughter of William Westby, of Mowbreck; Mary, afterwards the wife of Thomas Worthington, of Blainscow; Elizabeth, subsequently the wife of William Hesketh, of Mains Hall; and Anne, who married George Gillow, of Bryning. Richard Allen, of Rossall Hall, the eldest son, left at his demise a widow with three daughters, named respectively, Helen, Catherine, and Mary, who were deprived of their possessions and rights in the Grange in the year 1583 by Edmund Fleetwood, whose father had purchased the reversion of the lease from Henry VIII., at the time when the larger monastic institutions were dissolved in

England. The widow and her daughters fled to Rheims to escape
further persecution, where they were hospitably received by their
near relative, Cardinal William Allen, who interested the princely
family of Guise in their behalf and so obtained for them the means
of subsistence.

William Allen, the second son of John Allen, of Rossall Hall,
was born in 1532, and at the early age of fifteen entered Oriel
College, Oxford, under the tutorship of Morgan Philips, perhaps
the most eminent logician of his day. Three years later he was
elected to a fellowship. Upon the accession of Mary he entered
the church, and in 1556 was made principal of St. Mary's Hall,
acting as Proctor for the two succeeding years. In 1558 he was
created canon of York, but on the accession of Elizabeth, he
refused the Protestant oaths, was deprived of his fellowship, and,
in 1560, retired to Louvaine, where he wrote his first work,
entitled "A Defence of the Doctrine of Catholics, concerning
Purgatory and Prayers for the Dead," in answer to an attack on
those dogmas by Bishop Jewell. In 1565, the year in which this
publication appeared and fermented great excitement both here
and abroad, William Allen determined, in spite of the extreme
dangers of such an act, to visit his native country, more
especially the home of his fathers at Rossall. Religious zeal
prevented his active spirit from being long at rest; after residing
in England about three years and visiting different parts of
Lancashire, seeking converts to his creed, he was obliged to
secrete himself from the eye of the law amongst his friends,
Layton Hall and Mains Hall being two of his hiding places,
until a suitable opportunity occurred for escaping over to the
continent. Flanders was his destination, and from there he went
to Mechlin, afterwards taking up his abode at Douai, where he
obtained a doctor's degree, and established an English seminary.
This college, we learn from the " Mem: Miss: Priests: Ed. 1741,"
was founded in 1568 "to train up English scholars in virtue and
learning, and to qualify them to labour in the vineyard of the
Lord, on their return to their native country; it was the first
college in the Christian world, instituted according to the model
given by the council of Trent."

Whilst engaged at the above scholastic institution, William
Allen was appointed canon of Cambray; subsequently when the

English council applied to the ruling powers of the Spanish Netherlands to suppress the college of Douai, the Doctor and his assistants were received under the protection of the house of Guise. Afterwards Doctor Allen, on being appointed canon of Rheims, established another seminary in that city. At that time perhaps no one was more admired and revered by the Catholic party abroad, and detested by the Protestant subjects of England, than William Allen. He was even accused by his countrymen at home of having traitorously instigated Philip II. of Spain, to attempt the invasion and conquest of England, and although he strenuously denied any agency in that matter, it is certain that after the defeat of the Armada, he wrote a defence of Sir William Stanley and Sir Rowland York, who had assisted the enemy. In 1587, he was made cardinal of St. Martin in Montibus by Pope Sectus V., and a little later was presented by the king of Spain to a rich abbey in Naples with promises of still higher preferment. In 1588 he published the " Declaration of the Sentence of Sixtus the Fifth," which was directed against the government of the British queen, whom he declared an usurper, obstinate and impenitent, and for these reasons to be deprived. As an appendix to the work he issued shortly afterwards an "Admonition to the Nobility and People of England and Ireland," in which he pronounced the queen an illegitimate daughter of Henry VIII. Although the effect of these publications on the English nation was not, as he hoped, to arouse the people to open rebellion, or in any way to advance the Catholic cause, the efforts of the cardinal were so far appreciated by the king of Spain that he promoted him to the archbishopric of Mechlin. He lived at Rome during the remainder of his life in great luxury and magnificence. On October 6th, 1594, this remarkable man expired at his palace, in the 63rd year of his age, and was buried with great pomp at the English church of the Holy Trinity in the ancient imperial city.

BUTLER OF RAWCLIFFE HALL.

The name of Butler, or as it was formerly written Botiler, belonged to an office in existence in earlier times, and was first assumed by Theobald Walter, who married Maud, the sister of Thomas á Becket, on being appointed *Butler* of Ireland.

Theobald Walter-Botiler gave to his relative Richard Pincerna, or Botiler, as the family was afterwards called, the whole of Out Rawcliffe and one carucate of land in Staynole. This gentleman was the founder of that branch of the Butlers which was established at Rawcliffe Hall for so many generations. Sir Richard Botiler, of Rawcliffe, married Alicia, in 1281, the daughter of William de Carleton, and thus obtained the manor of Inskip. He had issue—William, Henry, Richard, Edmund, and Galfrid. Richard Botiler, the third son, who had some possessions in Marton, left at his death one son, also named Richard, who was living in 1323, and became the progenitor of the Butlers of Kirkland. William, the eldest son, espoused Johanna de Sifewast, a widow, by whom he had Nicholas de Botiler, who was alive in 1322, and had issue by his wife Olivia, one son, William Botiler, living in 1390. William Botiler had three children—John, Richard, and Eleanor. John Botiler was created a knight, and in 1393-4-5 was High Sheriff of the county of Lancaster. Sir John Botiler left at his death, in 1404, three sons and one daughter, the offspring of his marriage with Isabella, his second wife, who was the widow of Sir John Butler, of Bewsey. Nicholas, the eldest son, was also twice married, and had issue by his first wife, Margeria, the daughter of Sir Richard Kirkeby,—John and Isabella Botiler. John Botiler espoused, in 1448, Elizabeth, the daughter of William Botiler, of Warrington, and had issue— Nicholas and Elizabeth Botiler. Nicholas Botiler married Alice, the daughter of Sir Thomas Radcliffe, knt., and was succeeded by his eldest son John Botiler, who subsequently espoused Elizabeth, the daughter and heiress of Sir John Lawrence, knt., and had issue—William, James, Richard, and Robert Botiler. James Botiler, the second son, inherited the estates, most probably owing to the death of William, his elder brother, and married Elizabeth, the daughter of Sir Thomas Molyneux, knt., of Larbrick Hall. James Botiler, or Butler, was living in 1500, but died shortly afterwards, leaving two sons and two daughters— John, Nicholas, Isabella, and Elizabeth. John, the elder son, had issue four daughters, whilst Nicholas, the second son, had issue by his first wife, the daughter of Richard Bold, of Bold, two sons, Richard and Henry, and by his second wife, Isabel, the daughter and co-heiress of John Clayton, of Clayton, one daughter, who died in 1606. Richard Butler married Agnes, the daughter of Sir Richard Houghton, knt., but having no offspring, the estates of Rawcliffe passed to William Butler, the eldest son of his younger brother, Henry Butler, somewhere about 1627. William Butler espoused Elizabeth, the daughter of Cuthbert Clifton, of Westby, by whom he had one son, Henry, who was thrice married, and had numerous offspring. Richard, the eldest son of Henry Butler by his first wife, Dorothy, the daughter of Henry Stanley, of Bickerstaffe, died before his father, but left several sons, one of whom, also named Richard, succeeded to the Rawcliffe property, and was thirty-two years of age in 1664; another, Nicholas, was a colonel in the time of Charles I.; and another, John, was a citizen of London. Richard Butler espoused Katherine, the daughter of Thomas Carus, of Halton, by whom he had a large family, the eldest of which, Henry, was six years of age in 1664. Henry Butler, of Rawcliffe, espoused as his first wife, Katherine, the granddaughter, and subsequently heiress, of Sir John Girlington, knt., of Thurland Csstle, and had issue—Richard, Christopher, Philip, Mary, and Katherine. Henry Butler, and Richard, his eldest son, took part with the Pretender in the rebellion of 1715, and for this piece of disaffection their estates were confiscated by the crown, and afterwards sold. Henry Butler made his escape over to France, but Richard was seized, tried, and condemned to death. He died in prison, however, in 1716, before the time appointed for his sentence to be carried out, leaving an only child, Catherine, by his wife, Mary, the daughter of Henry Curwen, of Workington, who married Edward Markham, of Ollarton, in the county of Nottingham, and died a minor without issue. Henry Butler lived in the Isle of Man for several years, and espoused Elizabeth Butler, of Kirkland, his third wife, but had no further issue.

CLIFTON OF CLIFTON, WESTBY, AND LYTHAM.

The family of the Cliftons, whose present seat is Lytham Hall, has been associated with the Fylde for many centuries. The earliest ancestor of whom there exists any authentic record, was Sir William de Clyfton, who lived in the time of William II., surnamed Rufus, and during the last year of that monarch's reign, A.D. 1100, gave certain lands in Salwick to his son William upon his marriage. In 1258 a namesake and descendant of this William de Clyfton held ten carucates of land in Amounderness, and was a collector of aids for the county of Lancaster. His son Gilbert de Clyfton was lord of the manors of Clifton, Westby, Fylde-Plumpton, etc., and High Sheriff of the county in the years 1278, 1287, and 1289. He died in 1324, during the reign of Edward II., and was succeeded by his eldest son, Sir William de Clifton, who was Knight of the Shire for Lancaster 1302-1304. Sir William de Clifton,[1] knt., the son of the latter gentleman, came into possession of the estates on the demise of his father, and married in 1329, Margaret, the daughter of Sir R. Shireburne, knt., of Stonyhurst, by whom he had issue one son, Nicholas, afterwards knighted. He also entailed the manors of Clifton and Westby on his male issue, and settled the manor of Goosnargh upon his son and heir. He died in 1365. Sir Nicholas de Clifton, during one portion of his life, held the post of Governor of the Castle of Ham, in Picardy. He married Margaret, the daughter of Sir Thomas West, of Snitterfield, in Warwickshire, and had issue two sons—Robert and Thomas. The former, who succeeded him, was Knight of the Shire 1382-1383, and espoused Eleyne, the daughter of Sir Robert Ursewyck, knt., by whom he had three sons—Thomas, Roger, and James. In course of time, Thomas, the eldest, became the representative of the family, and married Agnes, the daughter of Sir Richard Molyneux, of Sefton. This gentleman (Thomas Clifton), accompanied the army of Henry V., when that monarch invaded France in 1415. He settled Goosnargh and Wood-Plumpton upon his second son, James, while the other portion of the estates passed, on his death in 1442, to Richard, his heir. Richard Clifton formed a matrimonial alliance with Alice, the daughter of John Butler, of Rawcliffe, from which sprang one child, James Clifton, who afterwards espoused Alice, the daughter of Robert Lawrence, of Ashton. The offspring of the latter union were Robert and John Clifton. The former on inheriting the property married Margaret,

---

1. This Sir William de Clifton was accused in the year 1337 of having taken possession of twenty marks belonging to the Abbot of Vale Royal, and of having forcibly obstructed the rector in the collecting of tithes within the manors of Clifton and Westby ; also with having inflicted certain injuries upon the hunting palfrey of the latter gentleman.

the daughter of Nicholas Butler, of Bewsey, in Lancashire. His children were Cuthbert and William; and now, for a few generations, we have two separate branches, the descendants of these gentlemen, which afterwards became united in the persons of their respective representatives :—

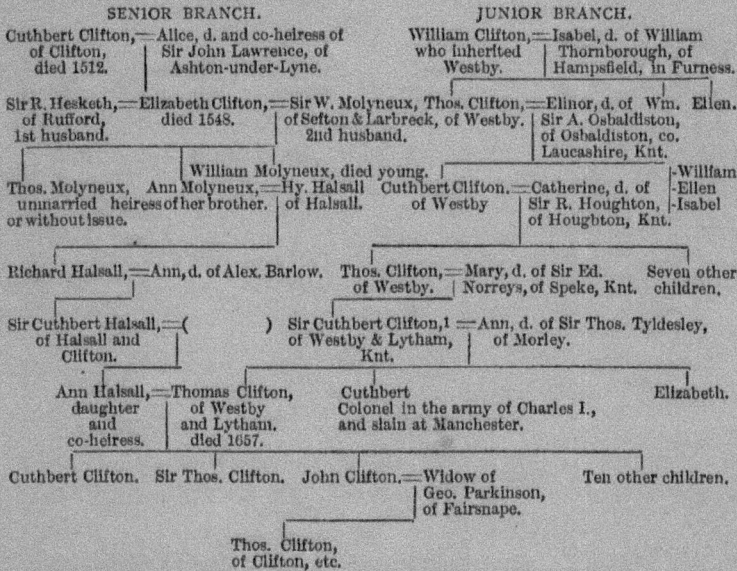

SENIOR BRANCH.		JUNIOR BRANCH.	
Cuthbert Clifton,══Alice, d. and co-heiress of		William Clifton,══Isabel, d. of William	
of Clifton,	Sir John Lawrence, of	who inherited	Thornborough, of
died 1512.	Ashton-under-Lyne.	Westby.	Hampsfield, in Furness.

Sir R. Hesketh,══Elizabeth Clifton,══Sir W. Molyneux,		Thos. Clifton,══Elinor, d. of Wm.	Ellen.	
of Rufford,	died 1548.	of Sefton & Larbreck,	of Westby.	Sir A. Osbaldiston,	
1st husband.		2nd husband.		of Osbaldiston, co.	
				Laucashire, Knt.	

	William Molyneux, died young.			┌William
Thos. Molyneux,	Ann Molyneux,══Hy. Halsall	Cuthbert Clifton.══Catherine, d. of	├Ellen
unmarried	heiress of her brother.	of Halsall.	of Westby	Sir R. Houghton,	├Isabel
or without issue.				of Houghton, Knt.	

Richard Halsall,══Ann, d. of Alex. Barlow.	Thos. Clifton,══Mary, d. of Sir Ed.	Seven other
	of Westby.	Norreys, of Speke, Knt.	children.

Sir Cuthbert Halsall,══(	) Sir Cuthbert Clifton,[1] ══Ann, d. of Sir Thos. Tyldesley,	
of Halsall and	of Westby & Lytham,	of Morley.
Clifton,	Knt.	

Ann Halsall,══Thomas Clifton,	Cuthbert		Elizabeth.
daughter	of Westby	Colonel in the army of Charles I.,	
and	and Lytham,	and slain at Manchester.	
co-heiress.	died 1657.		

Cuthbert Clifton.	Sir Thos. Clifton.	John Clifton.══Widow of	Ten other children.
		Geo. Parkinson,	
		of Fairsnape.	

Thos. Clifton,
of Clifton, etc.

This Thomas Clifton retained the Fairsnape estates, which he had inherited from his mother, during his lifetime, but on his decease they passed to his uncle. He marrried Eleanora Alathea, the daughter of Richard Walmsley, of Dunkenhalgh, in Lancashire. At his death he left a family of five daughters and two sons, the eldest of whom, Thomas Clifton, of Clifton, Westby, and Lytham, subsequently espoused Mary, the daughter of the fifth Viscount Molyneux. His heir, also Thomas, and born in 1728, rebuilt Lytham Hall, and allied himself to the noble house of Abingdon by marrying, as his third wife, Lady Jane Bertie,

---

1. Sir Cuthbert Clifton espoused as his second wife, Dorothy, daughter of Sir Thomas Smyth, of Wotton Walwyns, in Warwickshire, and had three sons, Lawrence, Francis, and John, captains in the royal army, and slain in the civil war, besides seven other children. Sir Cuthbert purchased Little Marton and the monastic portion of Lytham from Sir John Holcroft in 1606. He was knighted by James I. at Lathom House.

the daughter of the third earl. The children of this union were seven, and John, the eldest, born in 1764, inherited the estates, and married Elizabeth, the daughter of Thomas Horsley Widdrington-Riddell, of Felton Park, Northumberland. John Clifton was succeeded by his eldest son, Thomas, who had four brothers and three sisters—John, William, Charles, Mary, Harriet, and Elizabeth. Thomas Clifton, of Clifton and Lytham, born in 1788, was a justice of the peace, a deputy-lieutenant, and in 1835, High Sheriff of the county of Lancaster. He married Hetty, the daughter of Pellegrine Trevis, an Italian gentleman of ancient lineage, by whom he had issue John Talbot, born in 1819; Thomas Henry, lieut.-colonel in the army, and knight of the Legion of Honour and of the Mejidie; Edward Arthur, died abroad in 1850; Charles Frederick, who espoused Lady Edith Maud, eldest daughter of the second Marquis of Hastings, and assumed in 1859, by act of parliament, the arms and surname of Abney Hasting; and Augustus Wykenham, late captain in the Rifle Brigade, who married Lady Bertha Lelgarde Hastings, second daughter of the second Marquis of Hastings. John Talbot Clifton, esq., is still living, and is the present lord of Lytham, Clifton, etc. He was for some years colonel of the 1st. Royal Lancashire Militia, and sat in Parliament from 1844 to 1847 as Member for North Lancashire. In 1844 he married Eleanor Cicily, the daughter of the Hon. Colonel Lowther, M.P., and has one son, Thomas Henry Clifton, esq., who was born in 1845, and is now one of the Members of Parliament for North Lancashire. John Talbot Clifton, esq., is a justice of the peace, and deputy-lieutenant of this county. Thomas Henry Clifton, esq., M.P., espoused, in 1867, Madeline Diana Elizabeth, the eldest daughter of Sir Andrew Agnew, bart., and has issue several children.

In 1872 Henry Lowther succeeded his uncle as third earl of Lonsdale, and at the same time his sisters Eleanor Cicily, the wife of John Talbot Clifton, esq., of Lytham Hall, and Augusta Mary, the wife of the Right Hon. Gerard James Noel, M.P., younger son of the first earl of Gainsborough, were elevated to the rank of earl's daughters.

FLEETWOOD OF ROSSALL HALL.

This family sprang originally from Little Plumpton in the Fylde. Henry Fleetwood being the first of whom there is any reliable record, and of him nothing is known beyond the place of his residence, and the fact that he had a son named Edmund. Edmund Fleetwood married Elizabeth Holland, of Downholme, and was living about the middle and earlier portion of the latter half of the fifteenth century. From that marriage there sprang one son, William Fleetwood, who subsequently espoused Ellyn, the daughter of Robert Standish, and had issue John, Thomas, and Robert Fleetwood. Of these three sons, Thomas, the second, resided at Vach in the county of Buckingham, and at the dissolution of the monasteries by Henry VIII., about 1536, purchased from that monarch the reversion of the lease of Rossall Grange, then held by the Allens from the Abbot and convent of Deulacres, in Staffordshire. Thomas Fleetwood married Barbara, the cousin and heiress of Andrew Frances, of London, and had issue five sons, the second and third of whom were knighted later in life, whilst the eldest, Edmund, came into possession of Rossall Hall and estate in 1583, after the demise of Richard Allen, whose widow and daughters were ejected. Thus Edmund Fleetwood was the first of the name to reside at Rossall, where he died about forty years later. This gentleman married Elizabeth, the daughter of John Cheney, of Chesham Boys, in Buckinghamshire, and had issue several sons and daughters. Paul, the eldest son and heir, who succeeded him, was knighted by either James I. or Charles I., and married Jane, the daughter of Richard Argall from the county of Kent, by whom he had three sons and two daughters. Edmund, the eldest son, had no male issue, and at his death, in 1644, Richard, his brother, succeeded to the property and resided at Rossall Hall. Richard Fleetwood, who was only fifteen years of age when the death of his predecessor occurred, subsequently espoused a lady, named Anne Mayo, from the county of Herts, by whom he had only two children, a son and a daughter, and as the former died in youth, the estate passed to the next male heir on his demise. The heir was found in the person of Francis, of Hackensall Hall, the brother of Richard Fleetwood and the third son of Sir Paul Fleetwood. Francis Fleetwood, of Rossall, married Mary, the daughter of C. Foster, of Preesall, and had issue Richard Fleetwood, who succeeded him, and a daughter. Richard Fleetwood resided at Rossall Hall, and married Margaret, the daughter of Edwin Fleetwood, of Leyland, in 1674. The offspring of that union were two sons, Edward and Paul, and a daughter Margaret. Edward, the heir, was born in 1682, and practised for some time as an attorney in Ireland. On the death of his father, however, he inherited the property, and took up his abode at the ancestral Hall. He espoused Sarah, the daughter of Edward Veale, of Whinney Heys. Thomas Tyldesley, of Fox Hall, Blackpool, was on terms of friendship and intimacy with the Fleetwoods of Rossall at that period, and on the fourteenth of April, 1714, the following entry occurs in his diary, referring to Edward Fleetwood, the lord of the manor, and his brother Paul, also Edward Veale, the father of Mrs. Ed. Fleetwood, whom, for some reason unknown, the diarist invariably designated Captain Veale :—" Went to Rosshall. Din^d with the trustys, ye Lord & his lady, Mr. Paull, and Cap^{tt} Veal. Gave I. Gardiner 1s., and a boy 6d. ; soe to ffox Hall."

Paul Fleetwood, the younger brother of the " Lord " died in 1727 and was buried at Kirkham, where some of his descendants still exist in very humble circumstances.

The offspring of Edward Fleetwood consisted only of one child, a daughter, named Margaret, who was born in 1715, and to whom the estates appear to have descended on the decease of her father. On the sixteenth of February, 1733, she married, at Bispham church, Roger Hesketh, of North Meols and Tulketh. Roger Hesketh and his lady resided at Rossall Hall until their respective demises, which happened, the latter in 1752, and the former in 1791. Fleetwood and Sarah Hesketh were the children of their union. On the decease of his father at the ripe age of 81 years, the son and heir, Fleetwood, had already been dead 22 years, and consequently his son, Bold Fleetwood Hesketh, the eldest offspring of his marriage, in 1759, with Frances, the third daughter of Peter Bold, of Bold Hall, in the county of Lancaster, succeeded his grandfather Roger Hesketh. Bold Fleetwood Hesketh, who was born in 1762, died unmarried in 1819, and was buried at Poulton, his younger brother, Robert Hesketh, inheriting the Hall and estates. Robert Hesketh was in his 55th year when he became possessed of the property, and had already been married 29 years to Maria, the daughter of Henry Rawlinson, of Lancaster, by whom he had a numerous family. His four eldest sons died in youth and unmarried, the oldest having only attained the age of twenty three, so that at his decease in 1824 he was succeeded by his fifth son, Peter Hesketh. This gentleman, who was born in 1801, espoused at Dover, in 1826, Eliza Delamaire, the daughter of Sir Theophilus J. Metcalf, of Fern Hill, Berkshire, by whom he had several children, who died in early youth. As his second wife he married, in 1837, Verginie Marie, the daughter of Senor Pedro Garcia, and had issue one son, Peter Louis Hesketh. In 1831, Peter Hesketh obtained power by royal license to adopt the surname of Fleetwood in addition to his own, and in 1838 he was created a baronet. In 1844, Sir Peter Hesketh Fleetwood vacated Rossall Hall, and the site is now occupied by a large public educational institution, denominated the Northern Church of England School. Sir P. H. Fleetwood died, at Brighton, in 1866, leaving one son and heir, the Rev. Sir Peter Louis Hesketh Fleetwood, bart., M.A., of Sunbury on Thames, in the county of Middlesex. The Rev. Charles Hesketh, M.A., rector of North Meols, is the younger brother of the late Sir P. H. Fleetwood, and consequently uncle to the present baronet.

FFRANCE OF LITTLE ECCLESTON HALL.

William, the son of John ffrance, who married the younger daughter of Richard Kerston, of Little Eccleston, was the first of this family to reside at the Hall, and he was living there at the beginning of the seventeenth century. William ffrance had two sons and a daughter—John, born 1647 ; Henry, born 1649 ; and Alice, born 1653. John, the eldest son, succeeded to the Hall and estates on the demise of his father, and married Deborah Elston, of Brockholes, by whom he had issue—Robert, who died in 1671 ; Anne, died 1672 ; Thomas, died 1672 ; Deborah, died 1673 ; John, born 1675 ; William, died 1680 ; Henry, died 1676 ; Mary, died 1701 ; and Edward, died 1703. John ffrance, sen^r., survived all his sons except John and Edward, and on his death, in 1690, was succeeded by the former and elder of the two brothers. John ffrance, like his father, resided at the Hall, and espoused Joan, daughter of John Cross, of Cross Hall, by whom he had issue—John, born 1699 ; Anne, died 1702 ; and Henry, died 1707. John ffrance died in 1762, and his eldest son, John,

L

inherited the estates.   This John ffrance married Elizabeth, daughter and heiress of Thomas Roe, of Out Rawcliffe, and by that union became possessed, later, of Rawcliffe manor and Hall, to which the family of ffrance removed.   John ffrance, of Rawcliffe Hall, the son and heir of John and Elizabeth ffrance, of Little Eccleston Hall, and subsequently of Rawcliffe, died childless in 1817, aged 91 years, and bequeathed his property to Thomas Wilson, of Preston, who assumed the name of ffrance.[1]

HESKETH OF MAINS HALL.

This family was descended from the Heskeths, of Rufford, through William Hesketh, of Aughton, the sixth son of Thomas Hesketh, of Rufford.   Bartholomew, the son of William Hesketh, of Aughton, succeeded to his father's estates, and married Mary, the daughter of William Norris, of Speke, by whom he had one son, George, residing at Little Poulton Hall in 1570.   George Hesketh married Dorothy, the daughter of William Westby, of Mowbreck, and had issue a son, William, who, on his father's death, somewhere about 1571, inherited considerable property, comprising possessions in no less than twenty-eight different townships in Lancashire.   William Hesketh, who was living in 1613, married Elizabeth, the daughter of John Allen, of Rossall Hall, and sister to Cardinal Allen.   The children springing from that union were William and Wilfrid.   William, the elder son, is the first of the Heskeths mentioned as inhabiting Mains Hall, and he appears to have been living there in 1613.   We have no documents throwing any certain light upon the way in which he gained possession of the seat, but it is most probable that he purchased it.   William Hesketh, of Mains Hall, espoused Anne, the daughter of Hugh Anderton of Euxton, and had issue— Thomas, Roger, John, William, Hugh, George, Anne, Alice, and Mary.   Thomas, the eldest son, was nine years old in 1613, hence it is extremely likely that he was the first representative of the family born at Mains Hall.   Thomas Hesketh was twice married ; the first time to Anne, the daughter of Simon Haydock, of Hezantford, and after her decease, to Mary, the daughter of John Westby,

1. See Out Rawcliffe in the chapter on St. Michaels' parish for the Wilson-ffrance descent.

of Westby and Mowbreck. The children of his first marriage were William ; Thomas, an officer in the royalist army, and slain at Brindle in 1651 ; Anne, who became the wife of Thomas Nelson, of Fairhurst ; and Margaret, afterwards the wife of Major George Westby, of Upper Rawcliffe. William, the elder son, married Perpetua, the daughter of Thomas Westby, of Mowbreck, and had issue—Thomas, born in 1659 ; William, who died in infancy ; John ; Anne, married to Richard Leckonby, of Leckonby House, Great Eccleston ; Helen ; Dorothy, married to Thomas Wilkinson, of Claughton ; Perpetua, died in infancy ; and six other daughters, all of whom died in youth. Thomas Hesketh, the eldest son, left four sons and three daughters— William ; Thomas, who was a priest ; John ; George ; Mary ; Perpetua ; and Anne. William Hesketh, the eldest of these sons, was living at the same time as Thomas Tyldesley, who died in 1714, and was a frequent visitor at Fox Hall. He married Mary, the daughter of John Brockholes, of Claughton, and heiress to her brother. William Brockholes, of Claughton, and had issue— Thomas, Roger, William, Joseph, James, Catherine (an abbess), Margaret, Anne, Mary (a nun), and Aloysia (a nun). Thomas, the eldest son, inherited the property of his deceased uncle, William Brockholes, and assumed the name and arms of Brockholes. He died in 1766. Roger, the second son, also died in 1766. William, the third son, was born in 1717, and in later years entered the "Society of Jesus," dying in 1741. Joseph succeeded to the Brockholes' estates on the death of his brother Thomas, and, like him, assumed the name of Brockholes. He married Constantia, the daughter of Bazil Fitzherbert, of Swinnerton, and dying in a few years without issue, was succeeded by his sole remaining brother, James, who also assumed the name and arms of Brock-holes, and some years afterwards died unmarried. The Brock-holes' property now passed, under the will of Joseph Hesketh-Brockholes, to William Fitzherbert, the brother of his widow; and that gentleman, after the manner of his predecessors, assumed the name of Brockholes. He espoused Mary, the daughter and co-heiress of James Windsor Heneage, of Cadeby, Lincolnshire, and had issue—Thomas Fitzherbert-Brockholes, of Claughton ; Catherine, abbess of the Benedictines at Ghent; Margaret; Ann; Mary, who became a nun ; and Frances.

HORNBY OF POULTON.

The Hornbys, of Poulton, were descended from Hugh Hornby, of Singleton, who died about 1638, after having so far impoverished himself during the civil wars, as to be obliged to dispose of his estate at Bankfield, inherited from his sister, and purchased from him by the Harrisons. Geoffrey Hornby, the son of this gentleman, practised very successfully as a solicitor in Preston, and probably was the first to acquire property in Poulton. Edmund Hornby, his eldest son, of Poulton, where he also practised as a solicitor, and Scale Hall, married Dorothy, the daughter of Geoffrey Rishton, of Antley, in Lancashire, Member of Parliament for Preston, and had issue—Geoffrey, George, and Anne. George, the second son, went into holy orders, became rector of Whittingham, and subsequently died without surviving offspring. Anne Hornby married Edmund Cole, of Beaumont Cote, near Lancaster; and Geoffrey Hornby, who inherited the Poulton property, as well as Scale Hall, espoused Susannah, the daughter and heiress of Edward Sherdley, of Kirkham, gentleman, by whom he had issue—Edmund and Geoffrey, the latter dying unmarried in 1801. Geoffrey Hornby, who died in 1732, was buried in Poulton church, being succeeded by his son Edmund, who came into the possessions at Poulton and Scale. Edmund Hornby, born in 1728, married Margaret, the daughter of John Winckley, of Brockholes, and had issue one son, Geoffrey, and three daughters. At his decease, in 1766, the estates descended to his only son and heir, Geoffrey, born at Layton Hall in 1750, who, after being High Sheriff of Lancashire in 1774, and for some time colonel of a Lancashire regiment of militia, entered the church and became rector of Winwick. The Rev. Geoffrey Hornby espoused the Hon. Lucy Smith Stanley, daughter of Lord Strange, and sister of the twelfth earl of Derby, and had issue; but the departure of this representative of the family from the homes of his fathers severed the close connection between the town of Poulton and the name of Hornby, after an existence of about a century.

HORNBY OF RIBBY HALL.

Richard Hornby, of Newton, who was born in 1613, married Elizabeth, the daughter of Christopher Walmsley, of Elston, and had issue a son, William Hornby, also of Newton. That gentleman had several children by his wife Isabel, the eldest of whom, Robert Hornby, was born in 1690, and espoused Elizabeth Sharrock, of Clifton, leaving issue by her at his decease in 1768, three sons—Hugh, William, and Richard. Hugh Hornby took up his abode at Kirkham, where he married Margaret, the daughter and heiress of Joseph Hankinson, of the same place, and had issue—Joseph, born in 1748 ; Robert, born in 1750, and died in 1776 ; Thomas, of Kirkham, born in 1759, married Cicely, the daughter of Thomas Langton, of that town, and died in 1824, having had a family of two sons and five daughters ; William, of Kirkham ; John, of Blackburn and Raikes Hall, Blackpool, born in 1763 ; Hugh, vicar of St. Michael's-on-Wyre, born in 1765 ; Alice, who became the wife of Richard Birley, of Blackburn ; and Elizabeth. Joseph Hornby was a deputy-lieutenant of the county of Lancaster, and erected Ribby Hall. He married Margaret, the daughter of Robert Wilson, of Preston, by whom he had Hugh ; Margaret, who espoused William Langton, of Manchester ; and Alice, who died a spinster. Hugh Hornby, the only son, born in 1799, succeeded to the Hall and lands on the death of his father in 1832, and left issue at his own demise, in 1849, Hugh Hilton, Margaret Anne, and Mary Alice. Hugh Hilton Hornby, of Ribby Hall, esq., who married his relative, Georgina, the daughter of the Rev. Robert Hornby, M.A., J.P., in 1868, is the present representative of the family, and was born in 1836.

John Hornby, of Blackburn and Raikes Hall, married Alice Kendal, a widow, and the daughter of Daniel Backhouse, of Liverpool, by whom he had four sons—Daniel, born in 1800, who espoused Frances, daughter of John Birley, of Manchester, and dying in 1863, left issue, Fanny Backhouse and Margaret Alice Hornby ; Robert, born in 1804, M.A., a clergyman and justice of the peace, who married Maria Leyland, daughter of Sir William Fielden, bart., and had issue, Robert Montagu, William St. John Sumner, Leyland, Frederick Fielden, Henry Wallace, Hugh, and ten daughters, the first and third sons being captains in the army, and the second in the royal navy ; William Henry, of Staining Hall, J.P. and D.L., born in 1805, and Member of Parliament for Blackburn from 1857 to 1869, married

Susannah, only child of Edward Birley, of Kirkham, by whom
he had John, Edward Kenworthy, Henry Sudell, William Henry,
Cecil Lumsden, Albert Neilson, Charles Herbert, Elizabeth
Henriana, Frances Mary, Augusta Margaret, and Caroline
Louisa, of whom Edward Kenworthy Hornby, esq., has sat as
M.P. for Blackburn ; John, M.A., formerly M.P. for Blackburn,
and born 1810, married Margaret, daughter of the Rev. Chris-
topher Bird, having issue, John Frederick, Wilfrid Bird, Edith
Diana, and Clara Margaret. The Rev. Hugh Hornby, M.A.,
sixth son of Hugh Hornby, of Kirkham, was vicar of St.
Michael's-on-Wyre, and espoused Ann, daughter of Dr. Joshua
Starky, a physician, of Redbales, having issue one son, William,
now the Venerable Archdeacon Hornby, M.A., and the present
vicar of St. Michael's, born in 1810.   Archdeacon Hornby
married, firstly, Ellen, daughter of William Cross, esq., of Red
Scar, and four years after her decease, in 1844, Susan Charlotte,
daughter of Admiral Sir Phipps Hornby, K.C.B. The offspring
of the earlier union were two—William Hugh and Joseph Starky,
both of whom died young ; whilst those of the second marriage
are—William, Hugh Phipps, Phipps John, James John, William
Starky, Susan, and Anne Lucy, the eldest of whom, William,
died in 1858, aged thirteen years.

LECKONBY OF LECKONBY HOUSE.

John Leckonby, the earliest of the name we find mentioned
as connected with Great Eccleston, on the borders of which stood
Leckonby House, was living in 1621, and was twice married—
first to Alice, the daughter of Thomas Singleton, of Staining
Hall, and subsequently, in 1625, to Marie, the daughter of Henry
Preston, of Preston. Richard Leckonby, the eldest son and heir,
was the offspring of his first marriage, and like his father, became
involved in the civil wars on the royal side. Richard succeeded
to the family estates sometime before 1646, for in that year he
compounded for them with Parliament. He left issue at his
death in 1669, by his wife, Isabel, a numerous family—John ;
Richard, of Elswick ; George ; William, of Elswick ; Sarah ;
Martha ; and Mary, who married Gilbert Whiteside, of Marton,
gentleman. John Leckonby inherited the estate, and resided at
the ancestral mansion—Leckonby House. He married Ann, the

daughter of William Thompson, gent., of Little Eccleston, but dying without offspring, was succeeded by his brother Richard, who had espoused Ann, the daughter of William Hesketh, of Mains Hall. The children of Richard Leckonby, of Leckonby House, were William ; Richard, who was born in 1696, and afterwards became a Romish missionary ; and Thomas, also a missionary, who died at Maryland in 1734. William Leckonby, the eldest son, occupied Leckonby House, after the decease of his father, as holder of the hereditary estates. He espoused Anne, the daughter of Thomas Hothersall, of Hothersall Hall, and sister and co-heiress of John Hothersall, and had issue—Richard ; Thomas, born in 1717, who entered the Order of Jesus ; William, of Elswick, who died in 1784 ; Anne, born in 1706 ; Bridget ; and Mary, who became the wife of Thomas Singleton, of Barnacre-with-Bonds, gent. Richard Leckonby, who succeeded his father in 1728, inherited, in addition to the lands in Great Eccleston and Elswick, the extensive manor of Hothersall, and by his marriage with Mary, the daughter of William Hawthornthwaite, of Catshaw, gent., came into possession, on the death of her brother John Hawthornthwaite in 1760, of Catshaw, Lower Wyersdale, Hale, Luddocks, and Stockenbridge. Notwithstanding these large accessions to the original family domain, Richard Leckonby managed, by a long career of dissipation and extravagance, to run through his resources, mortgaging his estates, and bringing himself and his family to comparative poverty. He died in 1783, at about 68 years of age, having survived his wife many years, and was buried at St. Michael's-on-Wyre. His offspring were two sons, the elder of whom was thrown from a pony and killed in early youth ; whilst the second, William, met with a fatal accident when hunting in Wyersdale the year before the death of his father. William Leckonby, left, at his untimely death, by his wife, Elizabeth, the daughter of James Taylor, of Goosnargh, gent., two sons and a daughter. Of these children, Richard, the eldest, died in 1795, when only sixteen years of age ; James, the second son, died in infancy ; and Mary, their sister, married in 1799, at the age of twenty-two years, Thomas Henry Hale Phipps, of Leighton House, Wiltshire, a justice of the peace and deputy-lieutenant of his county, by which union, Leckonby of Leckonby House, became a title of the past.

LEYLAND OF LEYLAND HOUSE AND KELLAMERGH.

Leyland House was occupied during the latter half of the seventeenth and part of the eighteenth centuries by a family of wealth and position, named the Leylands of Kellamergh. Christopher Leyland, the first of the line recorded, resided at Leyland House in 1660, and married in 1665, Margaret Andrew, of Lea, by whom he had issue—John ; Ralph, died in 1675 ; Anne, born 1671 ; Ellen, born 1679 ; Susan, died 1670 ; another Ralph, born 1680 and died 1711 ; Francis, died 1674 ; Bridget, died 1687 ; Roger, died 1678 ; and Thomas, who died in 1682.

John Leyland, who succeeded to the Kellamergh property and Leyland House on the death of his father in 1716, married, in 1693, Elizabeth Whitehead, and had offspring—Christopher, born 1694 ; Thomas, born 1699, afterwards in holy orders ; Joseph, died 1709 ; Ralph, born 1712 ; John, died 1716 ; and William, who espoused Cicely, widow of Edward Rigby, of Freckleton, and daughter of Thomas Shepherd Birley, by whom he had two daughters, one of whom, Jane Leyland, subsequently married Thomas Langton.

Christopher Leyland inherited Kellamergh and the mansion on the demise of his father, John Leyland, in 1745, and at his own death, some years later, left one child, Elizabeth, who married, as her second husband, the Rev. Edward Whitehead, vicar of Bolton.

LONGWORTH OF ST. MICHAEL'S HALL.

The family of Longworths, inhabiting St. Michael's Hall until the early part of the eighteenth century, was descended from the Longworths, of Longworth, through Ralph, a younger son of Christopher Longworth, of Longworth, by his wife Alice, the daughter of Thomas Standish, of Duxbury. Ralph Longworth married Anne, the daughter of Thomas Kitchen, and had issue two sons and one daughter. Robert, the younger son, espoused Helen Hudson, whilst Elizabeth, his sister, married Richard Blackburne, and afterwards Thomas Bell, of Kirkland. Richard, the elder son and heir, is the first of the Longworths, described as of St. Michael's Hall, in Upper Rawcliffe. He married Margaret, the daughter of George Cumming, of Upper Rawcliffe, and had issue—Ralph, Thomas, Lawrence, Christopher, Anne,

Elizabeth, and Katherine. Ralph, the eldest son, espoused Jane, the daughter of Richard Cross, of Cross Hall, in Chorley parish, but further than this fact, we have no information concerning him. The family of the Crosses, into which he married, belonged to Liverpool, and their old country seat, Cross Hall, is now converted into cottages and workshops. Thomas Longworth, the second son, born in 1622, resided at St. Michael's Hall, and married Cicely, the daughter of Nicholas Wilkinson, of Kirkland, by whom he had one son—Richard Longworth. The latter representative, having succeeded in course of time to the Hall and estates, was a justice of the peace for the county of Lancaster, and on terms of intimacy with Thomas Tyldesley, of Fox Hall, Edward Veale, of Whinney Heys, William Hesketh, of Mains Hall, and a number of other leading gentry in the district. He married Fleetwood, the daughter of Edward Shutteworth, of Larbrick, and Thornton Hall, and left at his demise one son— Edward Longworth, who became a doctor of medicine, and resided at St. Michael's Hall until 1725, about which time he removed to Penrith, in the county of Cumberland.

PARKER OF BRADKIRK HALL.

The Parkers, who inhabited Bradkirk Hall for over a hundred years, were relatives of the Derby family, and came originally from Breightmet Hall, near Bolton, where they had lived for many centuries. William Parker, of Bradkirk Hall, who died in 1609, and was buried at Kirkham, is the first of whom we have any authentic account, and he is stated to have married Margaret, the daughter of Robert Shaw, of Crompton. The children springing from that union were—John, who inherited Bradkirk Hall ; Thomas, of Bidstone, in the county of Chester ; and Henry, who espoused, in 1609, Alice Threlfall, and became the founder of the family of Parkers of Whittingham. John Parker, of Bradkirk Hall, married Margaret, the daughter and co-heiress of Anthony Parker, of Radham Park, Yorkshire ; and after her decease he espoused Alice, the daughter of Richard Mason, of Up-Holland, near Wigan, by whom he had three sons and one daughter— William, Richard, John, and Margaret. The offspring of his first marriage were Anthony, Elizabeth, Jennet, Anne, Alice, and Christopher. Anthony died unmarried, and Christopher, the second son, born in 1625, succeeded to Bradkirk Hall on the demise of his father. He was a justice of the peace for the county of Lancaster, and married Katherine, sister to James Lowde, of Kirkham, and daughter of Ralph Lowde, of Norfolk. His children were Anthony ; Alexander, who married Dorothy, the daughter of Thomas Westby, of Mowbreck ; John, William, Gerrard, Christopher, Margaret, Mary, and Jane, the last married John Westby, of Mowbreck, at Poulton church, in 1688. Anthony Parker, the eldest son, born in 1657, lived at Bradkirk Hall, and espoused Mary, the daughter of Sir Thomas Stringer, sergeant-at-law, by whom he had issue—Christopher, Catherine, and Rebecca, who died young. Christopher Parker inherited Baadkirk Hall, and was Member of Parliament for Clitheroe in 1708. He died unmarried about 1713, and the Hall and estates passed by will to his sister Catherine, the wife of Thomas Stanley, of Cross Hall, in Ormskirk Parish, conjointly with her uncle Alexander Parker. In 1723 the possessions of the deceased Christopher Parker in Lancashire and Yorkshire were sold by Catherine Stanley and Alexander Parker. The latter, however, resided at Bradkirk Hall for some time after that date with his wife Dorothy, the daughter, as before stated, of Thomas Westby of Mowbreck, by whom he had nine sons and two daughters. The sons appear to have died without issue, and one of the daughters, Dorothy, married — Cowburn, whilst the other Katherine, became the wife of William Jump, of Hesketh Bank.

RIGBY OF LAYTON HALL.

The Rigbys, of Layton, were descended from Adam Rigby, of Wigan, who married Alice, the daughter of — Middleton, of Leighton, and had issue—John, Alexander, and Ellen. John Rigby, of Wigan, married Joanna, the daughter of Gilbert Molyneux, of Hawkley, and became the founder of the family of Rigby of Middleton. Ellen became the wife of Hugh Forth; and Alexander Rigby, of Burgh Hall, in the township of Duxbury, espoused Joanna, the daughter of William Lathbroke, by whom he had three sons and one daughter—Edward, Roger, Alexander, and Anne. Edward Rigby, of Burgh, who purchased the estate of Woodenshaw from William, earl of Derby, in 1595, was the first of the family, as far as can be ascertained, who held

property in the Fylde, and from his *Inq. post mortem*, dated
1629-30, we find that he possessed Laiton, Great Laiton,
Little Laiton, Warbrecke, Blackepool, and Marton, besides
other estates in Broughton in Furness, Lancaster, Chorley,
etc. This gentleman married Dorothy, the daughter of Hugh
Anderton, of Euxton, and had issue—Alexander, Hugh, Alice,
Jane, and Dorothy. Alexander Rigby, who was born in 1583,
succeeded to Layton Hall, and Burgh, on the death of his father,
and afterwards married Katherine, the daughter of Sir Edward
Brabazon, of Nether Whitacre, in the county of Warwick. In
1641, during the time of Charles I., he was a colonel in the
king's forces, and was, somewhere about that period, removed
from the commission of the peace for this county by command of
Parliament on account of certain charges made against him of
favouring the royal party. In 1646 he compounded for his
sequestrated estates by paying £381 3s. 4d. His offspring were
Edward, of Burgh, and Layton Hall; Thomas, rector of St. Mary's,
Dublin; William, a merchant; Mary, wife of John Moore, of
Bank Hall; Elizabeth, wife of Edward Chisenhall, of Chisenhall;
Jane, the wife of the Rev. Paul Lathome, rector of Standish; and
Alexander, who died in infancy. Edward, the eldest son, who
died before his father, married Mary, the daughter of Edward
Hyde, of Norbury, and left issue—Alexander, William, Hamlet,
Robert, Richard, Mary, and Dorothy. Alexander Rigby, the heir,
who was born in 1634, was also an officer in the royalist army,
and erected a monument to Sir Thomas Tyldesley near the spot
where he was slain at Wigan-lane, at which battle "the grateful
erector" fought as cornet. He was High Sheriff of Lancashire
in 1677 and 1678, and married Alena, the daughter of George
Birch, of Birch Hall, near Manchester. His children were
Edward, Alexander, Mary, Alice, Eleanor, and Elizabeth. Of
Edward we have no account beyond the fact that he was born in
1658, and consequently must conclude that he died young.
Alexander, the second son, succeeded to the estates, and was
knighted for some reason, which cannot be discovered. He was
High Sheriff of the county in 1691-2. Mary, the eldest daughter,
married Thomas Tyldesley, of Fox Hall, and was co-heiress with
Elizabeth, wife, and subsequently, in 1720, widow of — Colley,
to her brother, Sir Alexander Rigby, of Layton Hall and Burgh,

who married Alice, the daughter of Thomas Clifton, of Clifton, Westby, and Lytham, but left no surviving offspring.   Sir Alexander Rigby is reputed to have been a gambler, and to have so impoverished his estates, already seriously injured by the attachment of his family to the fortunes of Charles I. and II., that he was compelled to dispose of his possessions in Poulton and Layton for the benefit of his creditors.   He also appears to have been imprisoned for debt until released by an act of Parliament, passed in the first year of George I., and his property vested in trustees.   His estates in Layton and Poulton were sold for £19,200.   After his liberation he resided in Poulton at his house on the south side of the Market-place, where the family arms, bearing the date 1693, may still be seen fixed on the outer wall.   The pew of the Rigbys is still in existence in the parish church of that town, and has carved on its door the initials A. R., and the date 1636, separated by a goat's head, the crest of the family.

SINGLETON OF STAINING HALL.

There is every reason to suppose that the Singletons who resided at Staining Hall during the greater part of two centuries were a branch of the family founded in the Fylde by Alan de Singleton, of Singleton.   George, the son of Robert Singleton by his wife Helen, the daughter of John Westby, of Mowbreck, purchased the hamlet and manor of Staining from Sir Thomas Holt, of Grislehurst, and was the first of the name to occupy the Hall.   He married Mary Osbaldeston, and left issue at his death, in 1552, William, the eldest; Hugh, who espoused Mary, sister of William Carleton, of Carleton, and left a son, William, who died without issue; Richard; Lawrence; and Margaret, the wife of Lawrence Carleton, heir and subsequently successor to his brother William.   William Singleton, of Staining, became allied to Alice, the daughter and heiress of Thomas ffarington, by whom he had Thomas, John, George, Richard, Helen, and Margaret. On the demise of his father in 1556, Thomas, the heir, came into possession of the estate; he married Alice, the daughter of James Massey, and had one child, a daughter, Ellen, who espoused John Massey, of Layton.   Thomas Singleton died in 1563, and was succeeded by his brother John, who had married Thomasine, the daughter of Robert Anderton, and had issue two daughters, the

elder of whom, Alice, became the wife of Henry Huxley, of
Birkenhead, and the younger, Elizabeth, of James Massey, of
Strangeways. John Singleton died in 1590, and was in his turn
succeeded by the next male representative, his brother George,
who had issue by his wife Mary, the daughter of John Houghton,
of Penwortham or Pendleton, two sons and a daughter—Thomas,
George, and Anne, the wife of Robert Parkinson, of Fairsnape.
Thomas Singleton, the heir, became lord of Staining in 1597,
previously to which he had espoused Cicely, the daughter of
William Gerard, of Ince, and had issue Thomas, John, Mary, Grace,
Alice, the last of whom married John Leckonby, of Great Eccleston,
and Anne, the wife of Richard Bamber, of the Moor, near Poulton.
Thomas Singleton, the eldest son, succeeded to the lordship in
the natural course of events, and formed an alliance with Dorothy,
the daughter of James Anderton, of Clayton, who was left a
widow in 1643, when her husband was slain at Newbury Fight
in command of a company of royalists. The offspring of
Thomas and Dorothy Singleton were John, born in 1635 and
died in 1668, who espoused Jane, the daughter of Edmund
Fleetwood, of Rossall; Thomas, who died childless; George;
James; Anne, of Bardsea, a spinster, living in 1690; Mary, the
wife of John Mayfield; and Dorothy, the wife of Alexander
Butler, of Todderstaff Hall. John Singleton, of Staining, whose
widow married Thomas Cole, of Beaumont, near Lancaster,
justice of the peace, and deputy-lieutanant, had no progeny, and
the manor passed, either at once, or after the death of the next
brother, Thomas, to George Singleton, who had possession in
1679, but was dead in 1690, never having been married. He held
Staining, Hardhorne, Todderstaff, and Carleton manors or estates.
The whole of the property descended to John Mayfield, the son
and heir of his sister Mary, whose husband, John Mayfield, was
dead. John Mayfield, of Staining, etc., ultimately died without
issue, and was succeeded by his nephew and heir-at-law, William
Blackburn, of Great Eccleston, whose offspring were James, and
Gabriel, under age in 1755.

STANLEY OF GREAT ECCLESTON HALL.

The Stanleys, of Great Eccleston, were descended from Henry,
the fourth earl of Derby, who was born in 1531, through Thomas
Stanley, one of his illegitimate children by Jane Halsall, of

Knowsley, the others being Dorothy and Ursula. Thomas
Stanley settled at Great Eccleston Hall, probably acquired by
purchase, and married Mary, the relict of Richard Barton, of
Barton, near Preston, and the daughter of Robert Hesketh, of
Rufford. The offspring of that union were—Richard Stanley;
Fernando Stanley, of Broughton, who died unmarried in 1664;
and Jane Stanley, who was married to Henry Butler, of Rawcliffe
Hall. Richard Stanley, the eldest son, succeeded to Great
Eccleston Hall and estate on the death of his father, and espoused
Mary, the daughter and sole heiress of Lambert Tyldesley, of
Garret, by whom he had one son, Thomas Stanley, who in course
of time inherited the Eccleston property, and married Frances,
the daughter of Major-General Sir Thomas Tyldesley, of
Tyldesley and Myerscough Lodge, the famous royalist officer slain
at the battle of Wigan-lane in 1651. Richard Stanley, the only
child of this marriage, resided at Great Eccleston Hall, and
espoused Anne, the daughter and eventually co-heiress of Thomas
Culcheth, of Culcheth, by whom he had two sons—Thomas and
Henry Stanley. Richard Stanley, who died in 1714, was buried
at St. Michael's church, and the following extract is taken from
the diary of Thomas Tyldesley, of Fox Hall, the grandson of Sir
Thomas Tyldesley, and consequently Richard Stanley's cousin,
who at that time appears to have been in failing health, and
whose death occurred on the 26th of January in the ensuing
year :—

"October 16, 1714.—Wentt in ye morning to the ffuneral off Dick Stanley.
Part^d with Mr. Brandon att Dick Jackson's dor; but fell at Staven's Poole; and
soe wentt home."

It may here be mentioned that for two years the cousins had
not been on very friendly terms, owing to Richard Stanley having
at a meeting of creditors, summoned by Thomas Tyldesley in
1712, when he had fallen too deeply into debt, objected to an
allowance being made to Winefride and Agatha, daughters of
Thomas Tyldesley by a second marriage. We may form some
idea of the strong feeling existing between them from an entry
made on the 7th of May, 1712, by Thomas Tyldesley in his diary:
—" Stanley—Dicke—very bitter against my two poor girlles, and
declared he would bee hanged beffor they had one penny allowed;
yet my honest and never-to-be-forgotten true friend Winckley,

with much art and sence, soe perswaded the othe^r refferys that the slaving puppy was compelled to consent to a small allowance to be sedulled—viz.: £100 each." After the decease of Richard Stanley, Great Eccleston Hall, for some reason we are unable to explain, passed into the possession of Thomas Westby, of Upper Rawcliffe.

TYLDESLEY OF FOX HALL.

The family which inhabited the ancient mansion of Fox Hall in the time of Charles II., and for many subsequent years, sprang originally from the small village of Tyldesley, near Bolton-le-moors. When or how they first became associated with the latter place is impossible to determine, as no authentic documents bearing on the subject can be discovered ; but that they must have been established in or connected with the neighbourhood at an early epoch is shown by the fact that Henry de Tyldesley held the tenth part of a Knight's fee in Tyldesley during the reign of Edward I., 1272-1307. A Richard de Tyldesley was lord of the manor of Tyldesley towards the close of the sovereignty of this monarch, and there is sufficient evidence to warrant the assumption that he was the son and heir of Henry de Tyldesley.

At a later period Thurstan de Tyldesley, a lineal descendant, who is accredited with having done much to improve his native village, and having built Wardley Hall, near Manchester, about 1547, was a justice of the peace for the county of Lancaster, and Receiver-General for the Isle of Man in 1532. He was on intimate and friendly terms with the earl of Derby, and we may safely conjecture that the members of the two houses had for long been familiarly known to each other, as we read that in 1405 Henry IV. granted a letter of protection to William de Stanley, knt., John de Tyldesley, and several more, when they set out to take possession of the Isle of Man and Peel Castle. In 1417, when Sir John de Stanley, lord of the same island, was summoned to England, he left Thurston de Tyldesley, a magistrate, to officiate as governor during his absence. The Tyldesleys held extensive lands in Wardley, Morleys, Myerscough, and Tyldesley, having seats at the three first-named manors. Thurstan de Tyldesley, who erected Wardley Hall, was twice married and had issue by each wife. To the offspring of the first, Parnell,

daughter of Geoffrey Shakerley, of Shakerley, he left Tyldesley
and Wardley; and to those of his second, Jane, daughter of Ralph
Langton, baron of Newton, he bequeathed Myerscough, and some
minor property.   There is nothing calling for special notice
concerning any, except two, of the descendants from the first
marriage—Sir Thomas Tyldesley, a great-grandson, attorney-
general for Lancashire in the reign of James I.; and his son, who
did not survive him many months, and terminated the elder
branch. In consequence of this failure of issue the Tyldesley
estate, but not Wardley, which had been sold, passed to the
representatives of Thurstan's children by his second wife. The
eldest son of the second alliance, Edward, had espoused Anne,
the daughter and heiress of Thomas Leyland, of Morleys, and,
subsequently, inherited the manor and Hall of Morleys. The
grandson and namesake of Edward Tyldesley, of Morleys and
Tyldesley, who was born in 1585, and died in 1618, entertained
James I. for three days at his seat, Myerscough Lodge, in 1617.
Edward Tyldesley, of Myerscough, was the father of Major-
General Sir Thomas Tyldesley, knt., who so greatly distinguished
himself, by his fidelty and valour, in the wars between King and
Parliament. In those sanguinary and calamitous struggles he
served under the standard of royalty. He was slain at the battle
of Wigan-lane in 1651 ; and as a mark of esteem for his many
virtues and gallant deeds a monument was erected, near the spot
where he fell, in 1679, by Alexander Rigby, of Layton Hall, High
Sheriff for the county of Lancaster. The monument was inscribed
as under :—

" An high Act of Gratitude, which conveys the Memory of
SIR THOMAS TYLDESLEY
To posterity,
Who served King Charles the First as Lieutenant-Colonel at Edge-Hill Battle,
After raising regiments of Horse, Foot, and Dragoons,
and for
The desperate storming of Burton on Trent, over a bridge of 36 arches,
RECEIVED THE HONOUR OF KNIGHTHOOD.
He afterwards served in all the wars in great command,
Was Governor of Litchfield,
And followed the fortune of the Crown through the Three Kingdoms,
And never compounded with the Rebels though strongly invested ;
And on the 25th of August, A.D. 1651, was here slain,
Commanding as Major-General under the Earl of Derby,

To whom the grateful erector, Alexander Rigby, Esq., was Cornet ;
And when he was High Sheriff of this county, A.D. 1679,
Placed the high obligation on the whole Family of the Tyldesleys,
To follow the noble example of their Loyal Ancestor."

Sir Thomas Tyldesley married Frances, daughter of Ralph Standish, of Standish, and had issue—Edward, born in 1635 ; Thomas, born in 1642 ; Ralph, born in 1644 ; Bridget, who became the wife of Henry Blundell, of Ince Blundell ; Elizabeth ; Frances, wife of Thomas Stanley, of Great Eccleston ; Anne, who was abbess of the English nuns at Paris in 1721 ; Dorothy; Mary, wife of Richard Crane ; and Margaret.

Edward Tyldesley, the eldest son and heir, followed in the footsteps of his father, and was a staunch supporter of Charles II. When that monarch had been restored to the throne of his ancestors he purposed creating a fresh order of Knighthood, called the Royal Oak,[1] wherewith to reward a number of his faithful adherents, whose social positions were of sufficient standing to render them suitable recipients of the honour. Edward Tyldesley was amongst those selected ; but the design was abandoned by the king under the advice of his ministers, who considered that it was likely to produce jealousy and dis- satisfaction in many quarters, and might prove inimical to the peace of the nation. Under an impression, which afterwards proved erroneous, that Charles II. intended to confer upon him the lands of Layton Hawes, in recognition of the loyal services of his father and himself, Edward Tyldesley erected a residence, called Fox Hall, near its borders, where he lived during certain portions of the year until his death, which occurred between 1685 and 1687. Edward Tyldesley espoused Anne, daughter of Sir Thomas Fleetwood, of Colwich, in Staffordshire, and baron ot Newton, in Lancashire; and after her decease, Elizabeth, daughter of Adam Beaumont, of Whitley, by whom he had only one child, Catherine Tyldesley, of Preston. The offspring of his union with Anne Fleetwood were Thomas, Edward, Frances, and Maria. Thomas Tyldesley succeeded to the estates, on the decease of his father, with the exception of Tyldesley, which had been sold by Edward Tyldesley in 1685, and resided during a considerable part

1. See page 72.

M

of his life at Fox Hall, and occasionally at Myerscough Lodge. Thomas Tyldesley was born in 1657, and at twenty-two years of age married Eleanor, daughter and co-heiress of Thomas Holcroft, of Holcroft, by whom he had Edward, Dorothy, Frances, Elizabeth, Eleanor, and Mary. After the death of his wife Eleanor, Thomas Tyldesley espoused Mary, sister and co-heiress of Sir Alexander Rigby, of Layton Hall, and had issue—Charles, Fleetwood, James, Agatha, and Winefrid. Thomas Tyldesley, whilst living at Fox Hall, employed his time chiefly in field sports, visits amongst the neighbouring gentry, and frequent excursions to his more distant friends, as we learn from his diary, a portion of which is still preserved. The following extracts from it will illustrate what formed the favourite recreations of the numerous well-to-do families peopling the Fylde at that era :—

" May 16, 1712.—In the morning went round the commone a ffowling, and Franke Malley, Jo. Hull, and Ned Malley, shoot 12 times for one poor twewittee ; came home ; after dinner Cos. W : W : went with me to Thornton Marsh, where we had but bad suckses ; tho wee killed ffive or six head of ffowle.

" May 31, 1712.—Went to ye Hays to see a race between Mr. Harper's mare and Sanderson's ; meet a greatt deal of good company, but spent noe thing.

" June 7, 1712.—Pd. Mrs. 2s. 6d., pd. pro ffish 1s., pro meat 3s. ; and affter din^r went with cos Walton to bowle with old Beamont. I spent 10d. att bowling green house with 4 grubcatchers and Tom Walton, and Jo. Styeth.

" June 10, 1713.—Gave Jo^n Malley and Jo. Parkinson 1s. to see ye cock ffeights. Gave Ned Malley 1s. for subsistence. Din^d in the cockpitt with Mr. Clifton and others. Spent in wine 6d., and pro din^r 1s. Gave ye fidler 6d. Spent in the pitt betwixt battles 6d. ; I won near 30s.

" June 17, 1713.—Al day in ye house and gardening; went to beed about 7, and riss at 10, in ord^r to goe a ffox hunting.

" Augt 29, 1713.—Paid 2s. pro servant, &c. ; soe a otter hunting to Wire, but killed none.

" Septr 5, 1713.—In the morning Jos. Tounson and I went to Staining ; * * thence to Layton-heys to see a foot race, where I won 6d. off Jos. Tounson—white against dun ; soe home. Gave white my winings.

" Octr 6, 1713.—We hunted y^{tt} hare ffive hours; but ye ground soe thorrowly drughted by long continewance of ffine wether that we could not kill her.

" Decr 16, 1713.—In the morning went a coursing with S^r W : G :; Law^r Rigby, &c.

" March 16, 1714.—In the morning sent Dick Gorney and 6 more harty lads a ffishing ; I stop^d with a show^r of raine. Two of Rob. Rich his sons came in on my godson, to whom I gave 1s. ; thence followed the ffish^{rs}, where we had very good sport, and tuck 8 brave large growen tenches, and 6 as noble carps as I have seen tuke, severall pearch, some gudgeons, and a large eyell, and 6 great chevens."

The diarist, Thomas Tyldesley, died in 1715, before the outbreak of the rebellion, and was buried at Churchtown, near Garstang. Edward Tyldesley, his eldest son, who succeeded him, had two children by his wife Dorothy—James and Catherine. He was accused, tried, and acquitted of taking part with the rebels of 1715, although the evidence clearly convicted him of having led a body of men against the king's forces. At the death of Edward Tyldesley, in 1725, Myerscough no longer belonged to the family, but Holcroft, acquired by marriage in 1679, passed to his son James, who twenty years later served with the troops of Prince Charles, the younger pretender, and died in 1765. The offspring of James Tyldesley by Sarah, his wife, were Thomas, Charles, James, Henry, and Jane, all of whom with their descendants seem to have sold or mortgaged the remnants of the once large estates, and gradually drifted into poverty and obscurity.

It will not be out of place in concluding the notice of a family connected with the earliest infancy of Blackpool, to state something of the character and habits of Thomas Tyldesley, of Fox Hall, as disclosed by, and deduced from, the entries in his diary, which unfortunately comprises only the last three years of his life. At the present time the appearance of a party of gentlemen in this neighbourhood decorated with curled wigs, surmounted by three-cornered hats, and habited in long-figured waistcoats, plush breeches, and red-heeled boots, would excite no little astonishment, yet in the days of the diarist the sight must have been one of usual occurrence, for such was the style of costume worn by the wealthier classes. The lower classes were clothed in garments made from the undyed wool of the sheep and called hodden gray.

Thomas Tyldesley was a great equestrian, his journeys being so frequent and rapid that it is difficult to be certain of his whereabouts when he finished his day's work and its minute record, with the final "soe to beed." He was on terms of intimacy and friendship with the Rigbys of Layton, the Veales of Whinney Heys, the Westbys of Burn Hall, and all the wealthy families in the neighbourhood. Fishing, hunting, coursing, and shooting were his favourite recreations. Nor was he unmindful in the midst of these amusements of the interests of his farm, as the accompanying remarks amply testify :—"Very bussy all morning in my hay ;" and "Alday in the house and my garden,

bussy transplanting colleflow[r] and cabage plants ;" whilst at other
times we find him in communication with various tenants relative
to some portion or other of the Myerscough property. Unless
confined to bed by gout or rheumatism, and the self-imposed, but
fearful, "Phissickings" he underwent, swallowing doses whose
magnitude alone would appal most men of modern days, he
was ever actively engaged in either business or pleasure. Every
item of disbursement and every circumstance that occurred, even
to the most trivial, has found a place in his diary, and from
it we learn that while evidently anxious to avoid unnecessary
expenditure, he was neither parsimonious nor illiberal, always
recompensing those who had been put to any trouble on his
account, and paying his share of each friendly gathering with a
scrupulous exactness. There is, however, a satisfaction expressed
in the words, "but spent noe thing," after the brief notice of the
horse-race he had attended on the Hawes, which, when we call to
mind his natural generosity, showed that his income required care
in its expenditure, and was barely sufficient to support the position
he held by birth. Many other entries in his diary prove that he
was frequently short of money, and as his mode of living appears
to have been far from extravagant, it seems difficult at first sight
to account for the circumstance. But when we discover that he
had for years been connected, as one of the leading members and
promoters, with a Catholic and Jacobite Society at Walton-le-
dale, having for its object the restoration of the Stuarts, then in
exile, and remember that a scheme of such magnitude and
importance could not possibly be matured or kept in activity
without the purses of its more earnest supporters suffering to a
great extent, we obtain in some measure an explanation of the
matter.

The character of Thomas Tyldesley, as gleaned from his diary,
may be summarised as follows :—He was in every sense a country
gentleman, fond of field sports, happy on his farm, thoughtful of
the condition and comfort of his cattle, although sometimes given
to hard, or at least far, riding ; for the rest, he was active and
intelligent, liberal to his dependants, careful in his household, and
strictly honourable in all his dealings, but above all he had an
earnest and deep reverence for his creed and principles that spared
no sacrifice.

VEALE OF WHINNEY HEYS.

The Veales, of Whinney Heys, who during a time of considerable license and extravagance, were renowned for their piety and frugality, were descended from John Veale, of Mythorp. This gentleman was living during the reign of Elizabeth, and furnished 1 caliver and 1 morion at the military muster which took place in 1574. Francis Veale, the son of John Veale, of Mythorp, is the first of the name we find described as of Whinney Heys.[1] Francis Veale left a son, Edward, who resided at Whinney Heys, and appeared amongst the list of Free-tenants of Amounderness in 1621. According to Sir William Dugdale, he was a justice of the peace for Lancashire in the reigns of James I. and Charles I. Edward Veale married Ellen, the daughter and co-heiress, with her younger sister Alice, of John Massey, of Layton and Carleton, and in that way the Veales acquired much of their property in the neighbourhood of Whinney Heys. The offspring of this union were—John, who was born in 1605 ; Massey; Edward ; Francis ; Singleton ; Ellen, who married Thomas Heardson, of Cambridge ; Juliana ; Dorothy, who married George Sharples, of Freckleton ; Anne, who became the wife of John Austin, of London ; Alice ; and Frances, the wife of William Wombwell, of London. The maiden name of Mrs. Edward Veale's mother was Singleton, she being the daughter of Thomas Singleton, of Staining Hall, and for that reason we find the name borne by one of the sons of Edward Veale. John Veale, the eldest son, succeeded to the Hall and estate, and espoused Dorothy, the daughter of Matthew Jepson, of Hawkswell, in Yorkshire. John Veale was fifty-nine years of age in 1664, and at that date entered the names of his ancestors, etc., before Sir William Dugdale at Preston, who was on his heraldic visitation in Lancashire. The children of John Veale, by Dorothy, his wife, were—John, Edward, Helen, Susan, and Jane. John Veale, who was twenty years old in 1664, became the representative of the family on the decease of his father, some time previous to which he had married Susannah, the daughter of Geoffrey Rishton, of Antley, and by her had issue—Edward, born in 1680 ; Ellen, the wife of Richard Sherdley, of Kirkham, born in 1698 ; and Dorothy, who

1. Dugdale's Visitation.

died unmarried in 1747, aged 76 years. John Veale was a justice of the peace for this county, and died in 1704. After the death of John Veale, whose remains were interred at Bispham church, Edward, his only son, inherited the lands and Hall of Whinney Heys. Edward Veale was living at the same time as Thomas Tyldesley, of Fox Hall, Blackpool, and between the two gentlemen a close friendship seems to have existed, as we glean from the diary of the latter, in which Edward Veale is frequently mentioned, being invariably, for some reason, styled Captain,—perhaps he once held that rank in some temporary or reserve force, for there is no record of his ever having been connected with the regular troops. The following is a short extract from the above diary in 1712 :—

"Aug. 2.—Att my returne I wentt to yᵉ King's Arms, and got my dinʳ with Broʳ. We spent 1s. a pice in whitte wine, and as wee went through yᵉ hall met with Just. Longworth,[1] Capᵗᵗ Veale, Just. Pearson, Franke Nickinson, and small Lᵈ of Roshall.[2] Wee were very merry upon yᵉ small Lord, and spent 1s. a pice in sack and white wine, wʰ elevated yᵉ petite Lᵈ that before he went to bed he tucke yᵉ ffriedom of biting his man Sharocke's thumb off just beyond yᵉ nail. I found cos. W: W: att home."

Edward left issue at his death in 1723, at forty-three years of age—John, Sarah, and Susannah. John Veale, the heir, entered into holy orders, and subsequently died unmarried. Sarah and Susannah Veale, the co-heiresses of their brother, married respectively Edward Fleetwood, of Rossall Hall (the small lord), and John Fayle, of the Holmes, Thornton, who erected Bridge House in Bispham, after the model of the original Hall of Whinney Heys. The lands and residence of Whinney Heys eventually passed into the possession of the Fleetwoods, of Rossall, through the wife of Edward Fleetwood. The Veales were Puritans in religion, and one of the family, named Edward Veale, whose father was the third son of Edward and Ellen Veale mentioned above, and a lay member of the Presbyterian Classis for this district in the time of the Commonwealth, attained considerable eminence, first as a Puritan preacher and afterwards as a Nonconformist minister. Calamy, in his *Nonconformist Memorial*, tells us that "Mr. Edward Veale, of Christ Church, Oxford,

1. Richard Longworth, of St. Michael's Hall, a justice of the peace.
2. The small Lᵈ of Roshall was Edward Fleetwood, of Rossall Hall, who at this time was thirty years of age.

afterwards of Trinity College, Dublin, was ordained at Winwick in Lancashire, August 4th, 1857. When he left Ireland he brought with him a testimonial of his being 'a learned, orthodox minister, of a sober, pious, and peaceable conversation, who during his abode at the college was eminently useful for the instruction of youth, and whose ministry had been often exercised in and about the city of Dublin with great satisfaction to the godly, until he was deprived of his fellowship for nonconformity to the ceremonies imposed in the church, and for joining with other ministers in their endeavours for a reformation ;' signed by Richard Charnock and six other respectable ministers. He became chaplain to Sir William Waller, in Middlesex, and afterwards settled as a Nonconformist pastor in Wapping, where he lived to a good old age. He had several pupils, to whom he read university learning, who were afterwards useful persons ; one of whom was Mr. Nathaniel Taylor. He died June 6th, 1708, aged 76. His funeral sermon was preached by Mr. T. Symonds, who succeeded him."

WESTBY OF MOWBRECK HALL AND BURN HALL.[1]

The family of this name, so long associated with the township of Medlar-with-Wesham, in the parish of Kirkham, is descended from the Westbys of Westby, in the county of York.

William Westby, who was under-sheriff of Lancashire in 1345, is the first of the name, we can find, residing at Mowbreck ; and a great-grandson of his, named William Westby, is recorded as inheriting the Mowbreck and Westby property in the reign of Henry VI., 1422-61. John Westby, the son of the latter William, succeeded to the estates, residing, like his ancestors, at Mowbreck Hall, and was twice married, the offspring of the first union, with Mabill, daughter of Richard Botiler, being two daughters ; and of the second, with Eleanor Kirkby, of Rawcliffe, a son and heir, named William, who succeeded him at his death in 1512. William Westby, although the lawful holder of the estates, did not obtain control over them until after 1517, being a minor at that date. He married Elizabeth Rigmayden, of Wedacer, and

---

1. John Westby, of Mowbreck, was probably the builder or purchaser of Burn Hall about the middle of the sixteenth century. See pedigree above at that date.

had issue—John, Elizabeth, and Helen. John Westby, the heir, had possession of Mowbreck, and Burn in Thornton township, about the year 1556, after the decease of his father; his places of residence were Mowbreck and Burn Halls. He was thrice married, and by his last wife, Ann, daughter of Sir Richard Molyneux, of Sefton and Larbrick, and widow of Thomas Dalton, of Thurnham, had issue—John, Thomas, William, Ellen, and Mary. John Westby succeeded his father in 1591, and dying unmarried in 1604, was in his turn succeeded by his brother, Thomas Westby, who was twice married, and purchased the estate of Whitehall, where the children of his second union established themselves. The offspring of his first wife, Perpetua, daughter of Edward Norris, of Speke, were—John, Thomas, Edward, William, Francis, Margaret, Perpetua, and Anne. John Westby, the heir, came into the Mowbreck estate and Burn Hall some time after 1622, but dying without issue in 1661, was succeeded by his nephew, Thomas, the eldest son of his fourth brother, Francis Westby, Thomas Westby, M.D., slain in the civil wars, and his two other brothers, Edward and William, having died childless. Thomas Westby, the inheritor of Westby, Mowbreck, and Burn, was born in 1641, and espoused Bridget, daughter of Thomas Clifton, of Lytham Hall, his issue being John, Thomas, William, Cuthbert, Robert, Francis, Bridget, Anne, and Dorothy. John Westby, the eldest son, inherited Westby, Mowbreck, and Burn Hall, on the demise of his father in 1700. Thomas Tyldesley, of Fox Hall, was intimate with this gentleman, as observed from the following entry in his diary in the year 1715 :—

"June primo.—Went to Mains to prayers ; thence with Jack Westby to Burn to dinner ; stayed till 4 ; thence to Whinneyheys ; stayed till 9 ; soe home."

John Westby married, in 1688, Jane, daughter of Christopher Parker, of Bradkirk Hall, and had issue four daughters— Catherine, who married Alexander Osbaldeston, of Sunderland ; Bridget, the wife of William Shuttleworth, of Turnover Hall ; Mary, the wife of the Rev. Thomas Alderson ; and Anne, the wife of the Rev. J. Bennison, of London. At the death of John Westby in 1722, Burn Hall and estate passed to the Bennisons, whilst Mowbreck became the property of Thomas Westby, who died childless six years later, and afterwards of Robert Westby, brothers of the deceased John Westby. Margaret Shuttleworth, the daughter of William and Bridget Shuttleworth, of Turnover, married her cousin, Thomas Westby, of Whitehall, in 1744, and had numerous offspring, the eldest of whom, John Westby, succeeded to Mowbreck, as heir-at-law, on the death of his relative, Robert Westby, before mentioned, in 1762. This John Westby died in 1811 unmarried, and was succeeded by his only surviving brother, Thomas Westby. This gentleman also died unmarried, and was succeeded in 1829 in the Turnover Hall estate, by his cousin, Thomas Westby, heir-at-law, to whose eldest son, George Westby, he left Whitehall and Mowbreck. George Westby espoused Mary Pauton, the eldest daughter of Major John Tate, of the 6th West Indian Infantry, and had issue —Mary Virginia Ann ; Matilda Julia, wife of the Rev. Dr. Henry Hayman ; Jocelyn Tate ; Ada Perpetua ; Georgina Blanche ; Ashley George, late captain in the army ; Cuthbert Menzies ; Bernard Hægar, captain 16th regiment ; Basil Clifton, captain 16th regiment. George Westby died at Paris in 1842, and was succeeded by his eldest son, Jocelyn Tate, the present holder, who took by royal license the name and arms of Fazakerley on espousing, in 1862, Matilda Harriette Gillibrand-Fazakerley sister and co-heiress of the late Henry Hawarden Gillibrand-Fazakerly, the son of Henry Hawarden Fazakerley, of Gillibrand Hall, etc., and lord of the manor of Chorley.

Jocelyn Tate Fazakerley-Westby, of Mowbreck Hall, esq., was formerly a cornet in the Scotch Greys, and is now a captain of Lancashire hussars, yeomanry cavalry. He is a justice of the peace and a deputy-lieutenant of the county of Lancaster.

CHAPTER VII.

POULTON.

THE ancient town and port of Poulton occupies the summit of a gentle ascent about one mile removed from the waters of Wyre at Skippool, and three from the Irish Sea at Blackpool. Between 1080 and '86, Poltun, as it was written in the Norman Survey, contained no more than two carucates of land under tillage, or in an arable condition, so that out of the 900 acres composing the township, only 200 were cultivated by the inhabitants. A considerable proportion of the entire area of the township, however, would be covered with lofty trees, and provide excellent forage ground for large herds of swine, which formed the chief live-stock dealt in by our Anglo-Saxon and early Norman ancestors. Taking this into consideration, the comparatively small amount of soil devoted to agriculture, may not, indeed, indicate so meagre a population about the close of the eleventh century as otherwise it would seem to do, but still the evidence adduced is barely sufficient whereon to base the assumption that the antecedents of Poulton had been less under the destructive influence of the Danes than those of its neighbours. Regarding the locality more retrospectively, and turning back, for a brief space, to the era of the Romans, it must be admitted that nothing has as yet been discovered which could be construed into an intimation that the followers of Agricola, or their descendants, ever had a settlement or encampment on the site. It is true that the churchyard has yielded up many specimens of their ancient coinage, whilst others have been found at no great distance, but the character of the relics is in no way suggestive of a sojournment, like that of the fragmentary domestic utensils and urns of Kirkham ; and when it is remembered that the much-used Roman road (Dane's Pad) leading to the most important harbour of the west coast, passed through the vicinity on its way towards the Warren of Rossall, the explanation of the presence of the coins, as of other antiquities along its line, is obvious. The name of the town and district now under examination is of pure Anglo-Saxon origin, and acquired from its proximity to the pool of the Skipton, or Skippool, the signification of the word being, it is scarcely necessary to add, the enclosure or township of the pool. The date at which habitations first became visible on the soil must remain in a great measure a matter of conjecture, as the annals of history are silent respecting this and most other towns of Amounderness, until the arrival of William the Conqueror, but we may safely infer that it was not long after the advent of the Saxons before a situation so convenient both to the stream of Wyre and the frequented pathway just mentioned, attracted a small colony of settlers. Whatever century gave birth to Poulton, it is certain that from such epoch to 1066, the population would be constituted, almost exclusively, of the class known as "Villani," perhaps most appropriately interpreted by our term villagers, and that the occupation of these bondsmen of the soil would be the tillage of the land and the superintendence of swine. Their huts were doubtless of very rude and primitive construction, but somewhere within the boundaries of the township there must have been a dwelling of more pretentious exterior, the residence of the Town-Reve, who received the dues and tolls from the "Villani," on behalf of the large territorial lord, and exercised a general supervision over them. Athelstan appears to have held the lordship of the whole of Amounderness in 936, when he conveyed it to the See of York, and possibly before he ascended the throne it was invested successively in his regal predecessors.

After the Conquest, Poulton passed into the possession of the Norman nobleman, Roger de Poictou, by whom it was granted in 1094, to the priory of St. Mary, at Lancaster. "He gave," says the charter, "Poltun in Agmundernesia, and whatsover belonged

to it, and the church with one carucate of land, and all other
things belonging to it ; moreover he gave the tithe of venison
and of pawnage[1] in all the woods, and the tithe of his fishery."[2]
This extract proves beyond question the existence of a church at
Poulton exactly eight years after the completion of the Domesday
record ; and further, that it was endowed with one carucate of
land, or half the cultivated portion of the township. At the first
glance it seems more probable that the sacred edifice was over-
looked by the investigators in the course of the survey than that
it was erected so shortly afterwards, but a study of other pages of
the register betrays such evident care and minuteness on the part
of those to whom the work of compilation was entrusted, that it
appears impossible for an important building like the church to
have escaped their notice. Roger de Poictou was justly celebrated
for zeal in the cause of his faith ; several monastic institutions
owed their establishment to his liberality, and amongst them was
St. Mary's of Lancaster. It will therefore be but a reasonable
conclusion to arrive at, that he built and endowed the parish
church of Poulton with the intention of presenting it to the
Priory of his own founding, in connection with the abbey of
Sees in Normandy. During the reign of Richard I. (1189-99),
Theobald Walter quitclaimed to the abbot of Sees all his right to
the advowson of Poulton and the church of Bispham, owing to a
suit instituted against him by that ecclesiastic ;[3] and hence it
must be inferred that the donation of Roger de Poictou had
through some cause reverted to him, being subsequently conferred
on Walter in company with other of the confiscated estates of the
rebellious baron. The abbot of Cockersand also had some
interest in the town about the time the last event took place, and
in about 1216 he compounded with the prior of Lancaster for
certain tithes held by him in the parish.[4] In 1246 the mediety of
the church of Poulton and the chapel of Bispham was granted
by the archdeacon of Richmond to the priory of St. Mary, and
half a century later John Romanus, archdeacon of Richmond,
confirmed the gift, bestowing on it in addition the remaining

1. Pawnage, or Pannage, signified the food of swine to be found in woods, such
as acorns and beech-mast, etc.
2. Regist. S. Mariæ de Lanc. MS. fol. 1.
3. Regist. S. Mariæ de Lanc. fol. 77.
4. Regist. of Cockersand Abbey, and S. Mariæ de Lanc.

mediety, to be received when death had removed the present holder. A clause in the document stipulated that immediately the second mediety had been appropriated a vicar should be appointed at a salary of twenty marks (£13 6s. 8d.) per annum.[1] Here again it is clear that some time in the interval between 1199 and 1246 the lands and living of Poulton had once more been forfeited or disposed of by the Lancaster monastery, but in the absence of any records bearing on the subject, the manner and reason of the relinquishment must still continue enveloped in a veil of mystery. From 1246 the vicarage of Poulton remained attached to the Lancaster foundation until the dissolution of alien priories, when it was conveyed to the abbey of Sion, in Middlesex, and retained by that convent up to the time of the Reformation in 1536. Alien priories, it may be explained, were small monastic institutions connected with the abbeys of Normandy, and established on lands which had been granted or bequeathed to the parent houses by William the Conqueror or one of his followers. They were occupied by only a very limited number of brethren and members of the sisterhood. A prior was appointed over each, his chief duty being to collect the rents and other monies due from their estates, etc., and transmit them over to Normandy. Such immense sums were in that way annually exported out of the country, that it was ultimately deemed expedient by the king and his ministers to suppress all priories of this description.

The Banastres were a family long connected with the Fylde through landed property which they held in the neighbourhood ; originally they are stated to have come over from Normandy with William the Conqueror, and to have settled at Newton in the Willows. On their frequent journeys to and from Thornton, Singleton, and Staining, the tenants of the priory of St. Mary were in the habit of crossing over the lands of the Banastres, by whom their intrusions were deeply resented, which led to constant feuds between them and the head of the Lancaster monastery. In 1276, as we learn from the "Regist. S. Mariæ de Lanc.," Sir Adam Banastre with several of his friends and retainers, amongst whom were John Wenne, Richard le

1. Baines's Hist. of Lanc.

Demande (the collector), William de Thorneton, Richard de Brockholes, Geoffrey le Procuratoure (the proctor), and Adam le Reve (the reeve), attacked the prior, Ralph de Truno, and his train of attendants, when on their way to Poulton. They seized and carried off both him and his retinue to Thornton, where, after treating them with great indignity, they chastised and imprisoned them. Edward I., on hearing of the disgraceful outrage, appointed John Travers, William de Tatham, and John de Horneby to investigate the matter and ascertain the cause, if possible ; but no paper is now to be found revealing the result of the examination or hinting at the provocation, although a surmise may be hazarded that it was no new quarrel, but simply the old feud, which had at last culminated in a cowardly assault on a defenseless ecclesiastic.

In 1299, Poulton was held in trust by Thomas, earl of Lancaster, for the prior of St. Mary ; and eight years anterior to that date the abbot of Deulacres, in Staffordshire, drew certain revenues from land in the township, viz., £8 per annum from 16 carucates of land, about 13s. 4d. each year from the sale of meadow land, 10s. from assessed rents, and £5 from the profit of stock, making in all an annual total of £14 3s. 4d. The repeated disputes between Sir Adam Banastre and Adam Conrates, prior of Lancaster, relative to the trespasses of the latter's tenants and the collection of tithes on the domains of the former were peaceably settled in 1330, by an arrangement, in which Sir Adam pledged himself to allow two good roads across his lands—one from Poulton and Thornton to Skippool and thence across the ford of Aldwath, now called Shard, on to Singleton, the other starting from the same localities and running to the ford of Bulk higher up the river, probably the modern Cartford, or in its vicinity, in addition the knight agreed to make good any damage that the prior or his dependants might suffer over that portion of their journeys.[1] Adam Conrates on his side promised to withdraw all actions for trespass, etc., on the fulfilment of these conditions. In 1354 a person named Robert de Pulton held some small possessions in Poulton, but nothing further than that trifling fact is recorded about him, although it is probable from the orthography of his name that his ancestors were at some time closely and honourably

1. Regist S. Mariæ de Lanc.

associated with the town from which their distinctive appellation appears to have been derived. During the time of Elizabeth, James Massey, gentleman, of Carleton and Layton, purchased from the governors of the Savoy Hospital, in London, the tolls in the parish of Poulton, together with all the "chauntry and appurtenances" founded in the parish church of Bricksworth, and all messuages, lands, tenements, etc., situated in the town and parish of Poulton; · the tolls remained subject to an annual rent of £2, to be paid on St. Michael's day to the governors and chaplains of the hospital. Later in the same reign James Massey sold to William Leigh, esq., of High Leigh, in Cheshire, half of these tolls and some pasture fields, called "Angell's Holme," adjoining the Horse-bridge, where in earlier days, when the waters of Wyre made their way along a brook into the interior of this neighbourhood, boats are said to have been built. The Rigbys, of Layton Hall, subsequently became possessed of a great part of Poulton, and at the present day a large number of houses are leased in their name for the remainder of terms of 999 years; the Heskeths, of Mains, and other leading families in the district were also considerable property owners in the town. On one occasion the ruling powers of Kirkham made an unsuccessful attempt to obtain the tolls arising from the cattle fairs held in Poulton and Singleton, but on what plea such claims were urged the record is silent.

In an entry which occurs in the lists of the Norman Roll, an impost consisting of the ninth of corn, fleeces, and lambs, and created in 9 Edward III., 1336, it is stated that in 1291 the vicarage of Poulton was taxed by Pope Nicholas at 10 marks, or £6 13s. 4d. modern coinage, the prior of Norton taking £2 in garbs or wheat sheaves. Afterwards the vicarage was freed from the payments of tenths on account of the smallness of the living. Dr. Whittaker informs us that the priory of Lancaster was granted by Henry V., in 1422, to the chancellor of England, who in that year instituted a vicar to the living of Poulton, but eight years previously, in the same reign, the priory was granted in trust for the abbess and convent of Sion; from which seemingly contradictory statements it may be gathered that the chancellor was the trustee for the property, and in such capacity alone acted as patron of the church of Poulton. In support of this supposition may be cited the fact that the Lancaster house and its belongings were not received by the convent in Middlesex until 1431, during the sovereignty of Henry VI., when the vicarage was endowed by the abbess, and William de Croukeshagh presented to the living. This pastor, the earliest personally mentioned, was succeeded on his death, in 1442, by Richard Brown, appointed by the same convent. " Among the records," writes Baines in his history of Lancashire," in the Augmentation Office is in indenture tripartite in English, bearing the date 11 Henry VIII., 1579, and purporting to be made between the Abbess of Sion on the first part, Thomas Singleton and Henry Singleton on the second part, and William Bretherton, vicar of Poulton, on the third part, by which the tithe-sheaf of Pulton and a tenement are leased to the vicar, that he may better keep and maintain his house in Pulton ; the term to continue during the existence of a lease granted to the persons named Singleton by Sion abbey." At the Reformation the manor and advowson were claimed by the crown, and a few years later became the property of the Fleetwoods. The last royal presentation to the living was made by Edward VI. in 1552, just one year before his death, whilst the first by this family was in 1565, by John Fleetwood, lord of the manor of Penwortham. The Rev. Charles Hesketh, M.A., of North Meols, is now the patron.

The ancient church of Poulton stood on the site now occupied by the existing edifice, and like it, was dedicated to the Saxon St. Chad or Cheadda, bishop of Mercia, and seated at Chester in A.D. 669. The original structure consisted of only a nave and north aisle, the outer walls of which were composed of sandstone, whilst the double roof rested on semicircular arches, extending from the chancel to the font, and supported on four octagonal pillars. These semicircular arches belonged to a very antique style of architecture, and have given rise to the belief that the pillars were at first massive cylinders, being carved into an angular form about the time of Henry VIII. The pulpit had its place towards the south, and at the east end there appears to have been a small gallery. A pipe clay monument *in memoriam* of the Singletons, of Staining, stood inside the church, but was, intentionally or accidentally, destroyed when the building was pulled down. A rude brass crucifix and a chalice, both of which belonged to the church previous to the Reformation, are still preserved, one being in the possession of a late priest at Breck chapel, and the other in the Catholic chapel at Claughton. The upper halves of the windows, including the east one, were semi-circular in form. In 1622 the old chancel was repaired by the Rev. Peter Whyte, the vicar, and a stone, two feet in length and one foot and a half in depth, bearing the name "Peter Whyte," and the date "1622," in raised letters about six inches long, was placed over the east window. This piece of masonry now occupies a situation in the south-west corner of the edifice. The churchyard, which is reported to have been usually in a filthy and disgraceful state, was partly surrounded by a moderately wide ditch, on the brink of which three or four fine sycamore trees flourished, but were cut down when sundry alterations and improvements were effected in the ground. In 1751, after the old church had been standing six centuries and a half, it was determined to demolish it, and erect a more commodious building on the site. The tower, however, was retained, as, being of more recent date, it evinced none of those symptoms of decay which had rendered the body of the edifice dangerous to worshippers. An opinion prevails that the tower was built about the time of Charles I., and such a view is upheld by the discovery on the removal of the pulpit in 1836 of a square stone, having on its face the raised letters TB. WG. in the first line, IH. TG. IH. in the second line, and WG. 1638 in the last line. It is supposed that this stone, which is now fixed in the wall at the south-west corner of the church, was carved in commemoration of the erection of the tower, and the raised letters are the initials of the churchwardens then in office, and the date when the work was accomplished. Between this stone and the one previously referred to, there is a stained-glass memorial window to "Robert Buck, born 1805, died 1862, presented by his sister, C. D. Foxton." Mrs. Catherine Dauntesy Foxton, the lady here indicated, is the representative of the family of Bucks, of Agecroft Hall, Pendle-bury, and inherited considerable property in the neighbourhood of Poulton. During the time the new church was in course of building, divine service was performed in the tithe-barn, and the ceremony of baptism at the residences of the parents. The funds required for carrying out the important undertaking were doubtless chiefly supplied through the munificence of a comparatively small circle of private individuals, whose contributions would probably be in some measure supplemented by minor collections amongst the less opulent agriculturists and peasantry. One person, named Welsh, who resided at Marton, seems to have cherished a bitter antipathy to the levelling of ancient structures in general, and embodied his refusal to assist this particular work in the following rhymes :—

> " While here on earth I do abide,
> I'll keep up walls and pull down pride ;
> To build anew I'll ne'er consent,
> And make the needy poor lament."

It has usually been affirmed that the side galleries were not erected until several years after the new church had been finished, but the annexed extract from an old document discovered in 1875, shows that authority to build them was obtained in 1751, whilst the church was levelled with the ground ; and as the parchment also discloses that a number of seats in these galleries were allotted to certain gentlemen of the parish in the ensuing year, there is ample evidence that the rebuilding of the church and their erection were carried on simultaneously :—" 25 June, 1751. On the Certificate and request of Roger Hesketh, Esq., Patron ; the Rev. Robert Loxham, Clerk, Vicar ; and the Churchwardens of the Parish Church of Poulton ; a Faculty was Granted to John Bird, John Birley, and Richard Tennant, all of Poulton, Gentlemen (for the better uniformity of the Parish Church of Poulton, which was then taken down and rebuilding) to take down the Gallery over the Chancel in the East of the said Church, which was then very irregular and incommodious, and to rebuild the same with a convenient staircase, stairs, and passage leading thereto, of their own expense, in the west end thereof to adjoin to the north side of the gallery there then standing, and to be made uniform therewith, and to make satisfaction to the several owners of the seats in the said Gallery for the damage sustained in removing the same and altering, and lessening the seats therein ; and to erect a Gallery on each side of the said Church, with convenient staircases leading thereto at the north-east and south-east ends of the said Church, if necessary, according to the form of the said Certificate annexed, and also to remove the Pulpit and reading desk from the place where the same then lately stood, near to the place where the Churchwardens' seat was then lately situate, as it would greatly tend to the conformity of the said Church and to the benefit and advantage of the Inhabitants of the said Parish, and also that they might have liberty to sell and dispose of the seats to be contained in the said intended side Galleries, to such persons within the said Parish as should stand most in need thereof, to reimburse themselves the charges and expenses they would be necessarily put to in building the said intended gallaries and making the alterations aforesaid."

The present edifice is of stone, plain but commodious, and comprises a chancel, body, and embattled tower, with buttresses supporting each corner. Formerly a small shed stood on one side of the tower, and was used as a repository for the sculls and other osseous relics of humanity, which were unearthed during the process of making fresh graves ; this house was pulled down some years ago, and its numerous treasures returned to the ground at the south-east corner of the yard. The chancel now standing was erected eight years since, mainly through the exertions of the Rev. Thomas Clarke, M.A., the vicar, who died in 1869. On the exterior of the building, over a door at the south-east corner of the body, is the inscription :—Insignia Rici Fleetwood Ari Hujus Eccliæ Patroni Ann Dni 1699 " ; above which is a circumscribed uneven space formerly occupied by the arms of the Fleetwood family. Within the church the quarterings of the Heskeths and Fleetwoods are hung against the walls in frames. At the west end of the building there is a wooden panel into which the following names have been cut :—

Rich. Dickson.	John Hull.
Rich. Willson.	Rich. Willson.

John Woodhouse, churchwardens, 1730,

From the way in which the holders of similiar offices are arranged at present it is surmised that these gentlemen respectively represented the townships of

Poulton.	Hardhorn.
Carleton.	Thornton.

Marton.

On the south side of the church is a mural tablet to the memory of the Rev. Richard Buck, M.A., of Agecroft Hall, Pendlebury,

born 1761, died 1845, also Margaret, his wife, and Margaret, his
daughter.   Another monument bears the names of Frances Hull,
born 1794, died 1847 ; William Wilson Hull, born 1822, died
1847, in the Queen's service, at Bathurst, St. Mary's Island in the
river Gambia ; Henry Mitchell Hull, M.A., born 1827, died 1853 ;
John Hull, M.D., born 1761, died 1843—"left the eldest of the
three children of John Hull, surgeon ; an orphan at six years of
age, poor, friendless, by the best use of all means of education
within his power, by unwearied industry, by constant self-denial,
he duly qualified himself for the practice of his profession[1] " ;
Sarah Hull, died 1842 ; William Winstanley Hull, M.A,, Fellow
of Brazenose College, Oxford, and Barrister-at-Law, eldest son
of John Hull, M.D., F.L.S., born 1784, died 1873.   Here also was
the old churchwardens' pew, removed in 1876, having a brass
plate inscribed thus :—"Thomas Whiteside, Jno Wilkinson, Jno
Whiteside, Thos. Cornwhite, Jno Hodgson, Churchwardens,
1737 " ; also the old pew formerly belonging to the Rigbys of
Layton Hall, on the door of which are carved the letters " A.R.,"
a goats head, and the date " 1636," being the initials ånd crest of
Sir Alexander Rigby, of Layton Hall.   Until last year, when they
were removed to afford space for more modern seats, the two
family pews of the Fleetwoods and Heskeths stood on this side.
The pews were walled in laterally and in front by a high ornamental railing of oak, and in the larger of the two traces of a
crest were visible on the wall.   Near this spot there are many very
ancient pews, one of which has the date and initals " 17.TW.02 "
carved upon it, whilst on the floor of the aisle close at hand is the
gravestone of "Edward Sherdley, gentleman, dyed 21st September,
1744, aged 71," and almost adjoining lies another stone, surmounting the remains of Geoffrey Hornby, who died in 1732.
On the day of the latter gentleman's funeral the west side of the
market-place was destroyed by fire, and as the procession passed
the scarves of the mourners were scorched by sparks driven by a
high wind in showers from the conflagration.   On the north side

1. John Hull, M.D., F.L.S., commenced his professional education at Blackburn in 1777 ; and in 1791, after graduating in medicine, settled at Manchester,
where he attained to considerable eminence both as a physician and writer on
botanical and medical subjects.   He retired from practice to his native town of
Poulton in 1836, and remained there until his demise.

of the church is a pew bearing the date ' 1662 ' ; and near to are the old pews of Burn Hall, Little Poulton Hall, Mains Hall, and Todderstaff Hall, above which, fastened to the wall and marking the resting place of several members of his family, are the arms of Thomas Fitzherbert Brockholes, esq., of Claughton, the lord of Little Poulton, etc.

The chancel contains a monument in memory of Bold Fleetwood Hesketh died 1819, and his nephew, Edward Thomas Hesketh, died 1820 ; also of Fleetwood Hesketh, of Rossall, who died in 1769, aged 30, and Frances Hesketh, who died in 1809, aged 74, all of whom were interred beneath the Communion. In addition there are two recent tablets, one being to the memory of the late Thomas Clarke, vicar of the parish ; and the other in memory of Francis Wm. Conry, only child of F. A. Macfaddin, surgeon, 47th regt. Within the Communion rails are two antique and elaborately carved oak chairs.

In the south gallery are mural tablets inscribed in remembrance of Edward Hornby, died in 1766, and Margaret, his wife ; Edward Sherdley, died 1744, and Ellen, his wife ; Giles Thornber, J.P., died 1860, and his wife ; Geoffrey Hornby, died in 1732, and Susannah, his wife ; Richard Harrison, vicar of Poulton, died in 1718, aged 65 ; and Christopher Albin, curate of Bispham, died in 1753, aged 56, on a pew door opposite to which is a brass plate engraved :—" Introite et orate, cœlo supinas si tuleris manus sacra feceris, malaque effugies.[1] Christopher and Margery Albin 1752."

At one time a sounding board was suspended over the pulpit. An ancient font, formerly belonging to the church and now the property of the vicar, the Rev. William Richardson, M.A., has carved upon its exterior the date 1649, the letters M.H., a cross, and something, in its damaged state difficult to trace but betraying some resemblance to a crown. The successor to this font was removed several years since to make room for a new one presented by the daughter of the Rev. Canon Hull, of Eaglescliffe, in memory of her sister Frances Mary Hull, who died in 1866, aged 20 years.

---

1. " Enter and pray, if you have raised to heaven your open palms you will have performed sacred duties, and will fly from evil things."

The old church books, extracts from which will be given subsequently, contain many entries of sums paid for rushes to strew the pews and aisles, a custom existing here as late as 1813. In the tower is a peal of six bells, with the inscriptions :—

1st Bell.—" Prosperity to all our Benefactors.	A. R. 1741.
2nd. „ —" Peace and good Neighbourhood.	A. R. 1741.
3rd. „ —" Prosperity to this Parish.	A. R. 1741.
4th. „ —" When us you ring	
We'll sweetly sing.	A. R. 1741.
5th. „ —" Able Rudhall	
Cast us all.	M. T. Gloucester. 1741." [1]

The 6th bell was recast by G. Mears and Company, of London, in 1865, at the sole expense of the Rev. T. Clarke, and is inscribed : —"T. Clarke, M.A., vicar ; W. Gaulter, J. T. Bailey, W. Jolly, J. Whiteside, churchwardens." The original inscription was— "Robert Fishwick, John Wilkinson, William Cookson, James Hull, John Moore, churchwardens."

About thirty years since the roof of the church was altered and renewed. Notwithstanding the fact that the churchyard has been in constant use for so many centuries very few emblems of antiquity, beyond occasional coins of the Roman era, have ever been discovered in it, and at present, unlike most burial grounds of great age, no specimens of raised letters are to be seen amongst the numerous gravestones, the oldest of which still legible, intimates the resting place of Richard Elston, and has the date 1719. At a short distance, and assisting to flag a side pathway to the south of the church, is another stone, covering the grave of "Richard Brown, of Great Marton, who died the third day of April, 1723"; but neither this nor the foregoing one have any interest beyond their antiquity. The ancient practice of tolling the Curfew-bell is still continued in the winter evenings from the 29th of September to the 10th of March, whilst a pancake bell is rung at 12 o'clock on each Shrove Tuesday.[2]

1. Mr. Rudhall, as we learn from the following entry in the registers of the 30 men of Kirkham, was in business at Gloucester :—" 1749, April 14. Paid old Mr. Rudhall for coming from Gloucester to take notes of the bells when the 2nd. was recast, £3 3s. od."
2. The Pancake Bell is usually rung by an apprentice of the town as a signal for his *confreres* to discontinue work for that day, but strange to say on a late occasion not one apprentice could be found in the whole of Poulton, and consequently the duty was performed by the ordinary bell-ringer.

VICARS OF POULTON-LE-FYLDE.

IN THE DEANERY OF AMOUNDERNESS AND ARCHDEACONRY OF LANCASTER.

Date of Institution.	VICARS.	On whose Presentation.	Cause of vacancy.
In 1431	Wm. de Croukeshagh	Abbot and Convent of Sion	
„ 1442	Richard Brown	Ditto	
Before 1519	William Bretherton	Ditto	
In 1552	Ranulph Woodward	Edward VI.	
	Richard Cropper		
„ 1565	Wm. Wrightington	John Fleetwood, of Penwortham	Death of Richard Cropper
„ 1573	Richard Grenhall	Bridget Fleetwood and William, her son	Death of William Wrightington
„ 1582	Peter Whyte	Edward Fleetwood and William Purston	Death of Richard Grenhall
About 1650	John Sumner		
	George Shaw		
In 1674	Richard Harrison	Richard Fleetwood, of Rossall	Death of George Shaw
„ 1718	Timothy Hall	Edward Fleetwood, of Rossall	Death of Richard Harrison
„ 1726	Robert Loxham	Ditto [1]	Death of T. Hall
„ 1749	Robert Loxham	Roger Hesketh, of Rossall	Resignation of R. Loxham
„ 1770	Thomas Turner	Exors. of Fleetwood Hesketh, of Rossall, by consent of his widow	Death of Robert Loxham
„ 1810	Nathaniel Hinde	Bold . Fleetwood Hesketh, of Rossall	Death of Thomas Turner
„ 1820	Chas. Hesketh, M.A.	Peter Hesketh, of Rossall	Cession of N. Hinde
„ 1835	John Hull, M.A.	Rev. C. Hesketh, of North Meols	Resignation of C. Hesketh
„ 1864	Thos. Clarke, M.A.	Ditto	Resignation of J. Hull
„ 1869	William Richardson, M.A.	Ditto	Death of T. Clarke

Of the earlier vicars mentioned above, nothing is known until we come to the Rev. Peter Whyte, of whose immediate

1. In all previously issued lists of vicars, Richard Fleetwood has erroneously been named as patron in this instance. There was no Rich. Fleetwood of Rossall at that time, and Edward, who had been patron at the former institution, was probably still alive as he had no son and but one daughter, who married Roger Hesketh, the next patron in right of his wife.

descendants it is recorded that, after his death, they rapidly drifted into poverty, and that one of them, a granddaughter, regularly attended the fairs of Poulton as the wife of a pedlar or hawker. The Rev. Richard Harrison was cousin to Cuthbert Harrison, the Nonconformist divine who suffered ejection, and belonged to the Bankfield family. Until instituted to Poulton, Richard Harrison was curate at Goosnargh. His son Paul gained some celebrity as a controversial writer on matters of ecclesiastical interest.[1] The Loxhams settled at Dowbridge, near Kirkham, and that estate is still held by the family. The Rev. Thomas Turner purchased the living in 1770, when it was worth no more than £75 per annum, for £200, and held it until his death forty years later. The Rev. C. Hesketh, M.A., brother to the late Sir Peter Hesketh Fleetwood, bart., is rector of North Meols and patron of the living. During a portion of the time when he was vicar of Poulton, the Rev. R. Bowness was curate in charge. The Rev. John Hull, M.A., is honorary canon of Manchester, and and was examining chaplain to the Right Rev. Prince Lee, D.D., the first bishop of this diocese, by whom he was appointed to the rectory of Eaglescliffe, near Yarm, one of the most valuable livings in his gift. The Rev Thomas Clarke, M.A., was originally curate at the Parish Church of Preston, and afterwards became incumbent of Christ Church in the same town, which living he resigned on being presented to the vicarage of Poulton.

Subjoined are a number of extracts selected from the old account books of the churchwardens, and in them will be found much that is both interesting and curious :—

"1764.

"June 4.—To the Ringers, being his Majestie's Birthday, 3s. 0d. ·

July 8.—To a Bottle of Wine to a strange Parson, 2s. 0d.: To ditto to a strange Parson, 2s. 0d.

"1765.

"June 6."—To Mr. Lomas for mending clock, 2s. 2d.

August 18.—To Thomas Parkinson for Rushes, 6s. 8d.: Spent when Rush came, 1s. 7d.

Oct. 20.—To Mr. Loxham for a Prayer, 2d.

---

1. In 1876 a brass plate was found in Poulton church, near the site of the old communion table, inscribed :—"Here lies the body of Anne, wife of Richard Harrison, vicar of Poolton, who dyed the 24th of December, 1679, aged 55 years."

Dec. 25.—Spent Receiving Bassoon, 1s. 6d.: To Clark in full for wages, £4 os. od.: To Ringers Last half y^r Sallary, 18s. od.: To Singers in full, 12s. 6d.

"1766.

" Sept. 15.—Rushes for Church, 6s. 8d.: Candles, Beesoms, &c., 12s. 6d.

"1767.

" May 13.—Court fees at Visitation, 7s. 10d.: Churchwardens' Expenses at Preston, £1 7s. 5d.: Curat's horse hire to D^o, 2s. 6d.

July 20.—To Reed for Bassoon, 4s. 6d.

Nov. 21.—To Hugh Seed for Flaggin, £6 18s. 8½d.: To Thos. Crook for Church steps, 18s. 4d.: Ale at fixing d^o, 1s. od.

"1768.

" Sept. 1.—To Mr. Warbrick for Cloth for Surp^{ce}, 10½d.: To a Sacrament day, 11s. 6d.

"1769.

" Feb. 1.—To A New Prayer Book, £1 1s. 3d.

„   6.—To Cleaning Candlesticks, 2s. od.

Mar. 27.—To Cash wth Marton Parson, 5s. 5d.

Received

By Miss Hesketh's Burial in the Church, 3s. 4d.

"1770.

" Mar. 13.—To Cash allowed Church Wardens for attending sacram^{ent}, 5s. od.

"1771.

" May 29.—To Ringers ale, 3s. od.

Aug. 18.—Spent when Parson Hull preeched, 4s. 6d.

"1772.

Aug. 14.—To cleaning Windows, 7s. ; and lowance of ale 2s. 6d.

"1774.

" July 4.—Spent on Parson Eckleston and another strange Parson, one Red prayrs and the other preached, 3s. 6d.

Dec. 21.—To Expense of a Meeting in sending for boys that had done Mischief at Church, 1s.

"1775.

" May 3.—To 5 Church Wardens attending 7 Sacrament Days, £1 15s. od.

May 6.—To Horse Hire for 5 Church Wardens twice to the Visitation, £1 5s.: To Wm Brown for ale for Richd Rossall whilst he was altering Pulpit, and at settling his acc^t, 3s.

June 30.—Spent on Martin Singers, 10s.

Oct. 4.—Spent on St. Lawrence's Singers, 18s. 4d.

"1781.

" July 14.—It is agreed this Day among the Parishioners of the several Townships of Poulton that all arrears belonging to the said Parish unto the time of Visitation last past shall be paid and discharged by a Tax regularly laid upon the Parish in general, and that all charges of Organ and Organist for the Parish

Church of Poulton shall not be defrayed hereafter by any Tax levied on the Parish in general but by voluntary subscription only. In witness whereof we have hereunto set our hands the Day and Year above written.

THOMAS TURNER, Vicar of Poulton ; EDW^D SMITH, JAMES BISBROWN, PAUL HARRISON.

" 1782.

" Feb. 6.—Rec^d for Mr. Brockhole's Burial in the Church, 3s. 4d.

July 27.—Memorandum : It is agreed at this Vestry Meeting by all the parishioners who have attended here that in future the public ringing days in this parish shall be reduced to two, namely, the King's Birthday and Christmas Day,—the ringers to be allowed Six Shillings on each day ; and further, that the Church Wardens' Expenses on every Visitation shall on no pretence exceed forty shillings.—JOSEPH HARRISON, WILLIAM DICKSON, JAMES STANDEN, EDW. SMITH, THOS. TWISS, RICH. SINGLETON, THOMPSON NICKSON.

" 1788.

" June 7.—Cartage of Rush and allowance, 9s. 0d.: Kirkham Singers, 10s. 6d.

" 1793.

" P^d for ale for Ringers on 29 May, 6s. 0d.

    ,,   ,,   do ,,   do   on the 4 of June, 6s. 0d.

    ,,   ,,   do ,,   do   on the 25 Octob^r, 6s. 0d.

    ,,   ,,   do ,,   do   on the 5 Novemb^r, 7s. 6d.

    ,,   ,,   do ,,   do   on the 25 Decemb^r, 6s. 0d.

    ,,   ,,   do ,,   do   on Easter Tuesday, 7s. 6d.[1]

Dec. 8.—To Cash Rec^d for digging a grave in the Church for Mrs. Buck, 3s. 4d.

Nov. 5.—Spent on Singers, 12s. 0d.: ditto on Ribbons for Girls, 2s. 0d.

" 1798.

" Oct. 4.—To Ringers on Nelson's Victory, 2s. 6d.[2]

" 1805.

" June 9.—To Exp^s to Church Town when John Sauter Clerk convicted himself in getting drunk, and Timothy Swarbrick for making him drunk (when they were each fined 5s.), 1s. 6d.

Oct. 2.—To Rush, 14s. 3d.

" 1806.

Nov. 9.—To Ringers at Lord Nelson's victory of Trafalgar on the 21st, 7s. 0d.

N.B.: No money to be given to the Ringers on account of any Victory in future on the Parish account ; the Victory of Trafalgar was so Extraordinary that 7s. was allowed to the Ringers on that occasion.

" 1811.

" Resolved that in compliance with the request of the inhabitants of Marton one pound shall be allowed for an annual Dinner on Easter Day in future.

1. From these entries it would seem that the regulation of 1782 soon became a dead letter, if indeed it were ever carried into practice.
2. The Battle and Victory of the Nile.

"1817.

" Nov. 20.—To Expenses to Churchtown when Wᵐ Hodkinson, Wᵐ Whiteside, and Wᵐ Butcher was convicted for getting drunk—Wᵐ Hodkinson finde, and the other two acquitted upon the promise of future good behaviour, 3s. od."

The following extracts from the parish registers show the numbers of marriages, baptisms, and burials, which took place during the last and first years of the specified centuries :—

	1600-1601.		1700-1701.		1800-1801.	
Marriages	16	15	22	21	13	13
Baptisms	40	74	73	79	63	57
Burials	52	41	56	57	67	48

Anterior to 1674 the old vicarage was a thatched building of two stories, the upper one being open to the roof and supported on crooks, but about that date the vicar, the Rev. Rich. Harrison, made an addition, abutting the west end, and put the original portion in thorough repair. This house, which was surrounded by venerable trees, was taken down in 1835, and the present vicarage erected on the site.

In 1830, a spacious building, capable of holding three hundred persons, was erected in Sheaf Street by voluntary subscription for the purposes of a Sunday School, previous to which a small cottage in the Green had been used as a meeting place for the scholars connected with the church.

About one hundred and fifty years ago the town of Poulton presented a very different appearance to that it wears in our day. The market-place was surrounded by a number of low thatched houses of very humble exteriors, if we except a few private residences, as those of the Walmsleys and Rigbys, which stood out conspicuously from the rest, not only by their superiority in size, but also by the possession of slated or flagged roofs. The house of the Rigbys was built in 1693 by Sir Alexander Rigby, of Layton Hall, who was High-sheriff of the county in 1691-2, and stands at the south end of the square, the family arms and date of erection being still attached to the front wall. The building is now used as a dwelling and retail shop combined, and contains little of moment beyond the ancient oak balustrade and staircase. It is probable that Sir Alexander Rigby built the house with the intention of using it as a town residence for himself and family during the winter months, for we must remember that Poulton contained several persons of note and distinction at that time, and nothing is more natural than that the knight should prefer the cheerful society to be found amongst them to the long solitudes of the Hall during the dull, inclement season of the year, when country roads were almost impassable. After Sir Alexander Rigby had been released from prison, having satisfied the claims of his creditors, he took up his abode permanently in Poulton until his death, Layton Hall and other property having been sold, but whether his remains were laid in the churchyard here, or removed elsewhere, cannot be ascertained.

At the opposite end of the market-place was the Moot Hall, connected with which were shambles and pent-houses, the latter being continued along the fronts of the dwellings in the square. None of the streets could boast a pavement, and as a consequence intercourse between the inhabitants in rainy weather was a matter of considerable inconvenience and difficulty, visiting under such unfavourable circumstances being usually performed by means of stepping stones. Public lamps were unknown in the streets, and any one whose business or pleasure took him abroad after night-fall or dusk, would have to rely on the feeble glimmer of a horn lantern to guide him along the proper track and protect him from floundering in the mud. Looking on this picture of discomfort, it seems pretty certain to us that our Poultonian forefathers at least, could they but enjoy one week of our modern life and improvements, would be the very last to join in the wish, so often enthusiastically, but rather thoughtlessly, expressed, for a revival of the *good* old times. The market-square still retains its fish-stones, cross, whipping post, and stocks; and although the wooden portion of the last has been recently renewed, we are in a position to inform the curious or alarmed reader that it has not been done with the view of re-introducing the obsolete punishment, but merely to preserve a link, be it ever so painful an one, with the past. The cross surmounts a stone pillar placed on a circular base of similar material, formed in steps and tapering towards the column.

Although Poulton was never the scene of any military encounter during the unsettled eras of our history, still there is ample proof that the inhabitants were far from lethargic or indifferent to the course of events during those times. During the reign of Henry VIII., when James IV. of Scotland succumbed

to the superiority of the English arms, and yielded up his life on
Flodden Field, the yeomanry and husbandmen of this town were
well represented ; and the cheerful alacrity with which they
hastened to join the royal standard under Lord Stanley, in
company with others from the Fylde, between here and Preston,
is lauded in an ancient ballad, written to celebrate the victory,
from which the following lines are extracted :—

> " From Ribchester unto Rachdale,
> From Poulton to Preston with pikes,
> They with yᵉ Stanley howte forthe went."

There is no necessity to recapitulate the stirring incidents of
the Civil Wars, the bivouacking and plundering in the neighbourhood or the frequent demands for recruits by the royal and
parliamentary generals, but it will be sufficiently convincing of
the earnestness and loyalty of the inhabitants to state, that most
of the local families of influence risked their lives and fortunes in
the service of the king, leaving little doubt that those of humbler
sphere would be actuated by a like enthusiasm.

About a century ago it was customary amongst the gentry and
more wealthy yeomanry to hold their interments at night by the
light of lamps or lanterns, and during the passage of the funeral
procession through the town, each householder illuminated his
windows with burning candles. The last person to be buried with
this ceremony was the Rev. Thomas Turner, the vicar, who died
in 1810.

Of the domestic habits of Poulton at that period, and rather
earlier, it need only be said that they presented little variation
from those of other towns or villages similarly situated ; removed
from the enervating and seductive temptations of a city, and
forced, for the most part, to earn their bread under the broad
canopy of heaven, it is not surprising to find that the people were
a long-lived and vigorous race. Their feastings and merry-
makings took place at fair-times, and at such other seasons as
were universally set apart in rural districts for rejoicings and
festivity, notably harvest gatherings and the first of May, the
latter being especially honoured. On that day the causeways
were strewn with flowers, and all things suitable for the festival
were lavishly provided ; wine, ale, and sweetmeats being freely
contributed by the gentry and others. The peasantry were

clothed in sober suits of hodden grey, the productions of the "disty and wharl" or spinning wheel, without which no household was considered complete, whilst their food was of the plainest kind, consisting mostly of barley and rye bread, with boiled parsnips and peas eaten in the pod, wheaten bread being reserved for the consumption of the more wealthy classes. The present station at the Breck, a name of Danish origin, and signifying an acclivity, stands either on, or in close proximity to, the site of the old ducking-pond, or rather brook, where the scolds of Poulton were wont in former days to have the

"Venom of their spleen"

copiously diluted and cooled by frequent immersions.

A native of Poulton thus wrote of the town more than fifty years since, and if the present generation but emulates the virtues of its forefathers as herein stated, there are many places which would form, notwithstanding its protracted inertitia, less agreeable homes than the ancient metropolis of the Fylde :—

"Hail happy place, for health and peace renown'd,
Though not with riches, yet contentment crown'd.
Riches, the grand promoter of each strife,
Content, God's first-best gift in human life.
Here hospitality has fixed her throne,
And discord's jars by name alone are known ;
The stranger here is always entertain'd
With welcome smile and courtesy unfeign'd.
Kind to each other, generous and free,
Plain, yet liberal friends to charity."

Sixty years since Poulton contained a manufactory for sacking, sail-cloth, and sheeting, belonging to a Mr. Harrison, who lived in the house now in the occupation of R. Dunderdale, esq., J.P., and had his weaving shed at the rear of those premises. That gentleman employed from thirty to forty hands regularly during the time he conducted the business—a period of about fifteen years. An establishment connected with flax dressing and twine spinning, and employing several hands, was located in the house erected by Sir Alexander Rigby, of Layton ; and a currier and leather dresser had his works in Church Street. Of other trades and professions in the town at that date, there were four attorneys, two surgeons, seven butchers, nine bakers and flour dealers, three wine and spirit merchants, two maltsters, ten boot and shoe

makers, five linen and woollen drapers, four tailors, three milliners, four grocers, three ironmongers, three joiners, two wheel-
wrights, two coopers, two painters, three plumbers and glaziers,
and two corn-millers. Subsequently Harrison's residence was
used for parochial purposes, and formed the town's workhouse
until the bill of Sir Robert Peel brought about the joint system
of pauper relief and management under the name of Unions ;
and at one time small looms were placed in the old shed behind
the workhouse, for the purpose of providing remunerative occupation for some of the inmates. Three fairs are held annually for
cattle and cloth, and take place on the 3rd of February, the 13th
of April, and the 3rd of November, whilst a general market, but
very indifferently, if at all, attended, is appointed to be held each
Monday. About the year 1840, when the Preston and Wyre
Railway was completed and the Poulton Station erected, a dye-
house of some considerable size, and one that had done a large
business in the Fylde for many years, was taken down, and shortly
afterwards the Royal Oak Hotel built on its site. About the
same time the old brook, over which the cuckstool hung in earlier
days, and whose waters had long been polluted by discharges from
the dye-house, was arched over with brick and earth, and included
in the station premises. The Railway Hotel was erected a little
anterior to the inn just mentioned. The other hotels of Poulton,
situated in the town itself, are ancient, and by their size and number,
considering the smallness of the present population, are indicative
of the former importance of its market and fairs, and intimate
that its position as the centre of a wide district was the means of
exciting and maintaining a large amount of commercial activity,
such as would necessitate the frequent visits of business agents
and others. Several private houses can be pointed out as having
been in earlier days places of public entertainment, amongst
which may be named one now used as a bakery and bread shop
in Queen's Square, and which formerly bore the name of the
Spread Eagle Hotel ; in Sheaf Street, also, there existed about
half a century ago a small but respectable hotel, called the Wheat
Sheaf Inn, with bowling green attached, but like other more
pretentious establishments, it has been converted into a dwelling-
house, whilst a handsome residence occupies the old bowling
green.

The Independents were the first section of the Dissenting community to erect a chapel for their members, which they accomplished in 1808. After being in use twenty or thirty years, this place of worship was closed, and not re-opened until about ten years since. In 1819 a chapel was erected by the Wesleyans in Back Street, and in 1861 the building was enlarged. At the Breck there is a Roman Catholic chapel, which stands back some distance from the road leading to Skippool, and is approached by a long avenue of trees. The chapel is a plain brick building, with three unstained windows on each side ; and above the entrance has been placed a square stone inscribed with a verse from the Psalms—"I have loved, O Lord, the beauty of thy House, and the place where thy Glory dwelleth,"—and the date of erection, "A.D. 1813." Within the edifice the pews are open and arranged in three rows, one running down each side, and a double set occupying the central portion of the body. The solitary gallery at the end opposite the altar is lined with seats, and contains a harmonium, whilst the altar itself is handsomely and suitably decorated. The chapel is dedicated to St. John, and on the east and south sides lies the burial ground, wherein may be seen a stone slab carved by an eccentric character of Poulton, named James Bailey, whose remains are now deposited beneath it. The upper surface of the stone is ornamented with the outlines of two coffins, recording respectively the demises of Margaret Bailey, in 1841, and James Bailey, her father, in 1853. Between the coffins, and severing their upper portions, is a cross, with a few words at the foot, on each side of which are the representations of a scull and cross-bones. Other specimens of the sculptural genius of Bailey are lavishly, if not tastefully, scattered over the remainder of the slab. The residence of the priest is attached to the chapel, and in Breck Road are the elegant Gothic schools connected with it. Until the opening, in 1868, of these schools, which have since been extended by the erection of a wing, a loft over an outbuilding facing the priests' house, received the Catholic children of the parish for educational purposes.

We now come to speak of Poulton as a port, and in this respect our information, it must be acknowledged, is very scanty ; the harbours of Poulton were situated at Skippool and Wardleys, on opposite banks of the Wyre, and it was to the cargoes imported to those places that the custom-house of the town owed its existence. At what date it was first established cannot be discovered, but that it was in being nearly two centuries ago is proved by a paper on "The comparative wages of public servants in the customs," in which the following occurs :—

"We find that William Jennings, collector of the customs at Poulton, in the Fylde, received in 1708, during the reign of Queen Ann, for his yearly services thirty pounds per annum ; and five subordinate officers had seventy-five pounds equally divided amongst them."

The chief traffic of the port was in timber, imported from the Baltic and America; and flax and tallow, which arrived from Russia. In 1825 Poulton was described by Mr. Baines, in his History of Lancashire, as a creek under Preston, and it is probable that such had been its position for a long time anterior to that date. In 1826 Poulton was made a sub-port under Lancaster, and later, when the town of Fleetwood sprang up at the mouth of the Wyre, the customs were removed from Poulton to that new port.

Subjoined are the number of inhabitants of the township at intervals of ten years from 1801, when the first official census was taken :—

1801	769	1841	1,128
1811	926	1851	1,120
1821	1,011	1861	1,141
1831	1,025	1871	1,161

In 1770, during the reign of George III., an act of parliament was obtained by means of which a court was established in this town "for," according to the wording of the deed, "the more easy and speedy recovery of small debts within the parishes of Poulton, Lytham, Kirkham, and Bispham, and the townships of Preesall and Stalmine." A number of gentlemen engaged in commercial pursuits and residing in these several districts were appointed commissioners, any three or more of whom constituted a court of justice, by the name and style of The Court of Requests; they were empowered to hear and determine all such matters of debt as were under forty shillings, further they were authorised and required, "to meet, assemble, and hold the said Court in each of the said Parishes of Poulton and Kirkham, once in every week at least, to wit, on every Monday at Poulton, and on every Thursday at Kirkham, and oftener if there should be occasion, in a Court-house, or some convenient place appointed in each of the said Parishes." Each commissioner on being elected took the following oath :—

" I *   *   do swear That I will faithfully, impartially, and honestly, according to the best of my Judgement, hear and determine all such Matters and Causes as shall be brought before me, by virtue of an Act of Parliament, for the more easy and speedy Recovery of small Debts, within the Parishes etc. ; without Favour or Affection, Prejudice or Malice, to either Party. So help me God."

Edward Whiteside and Simon Russell were elected, respectively, clerk and sergeant of this court, and James Standen, of Poulton, in consideration of having advanced money to pay the expenses of obtaining the act and providing suitable accommodation for its administration, had authority given to him and his heirs to appoint a person to be clerk or sergeant as often as either of those offices should become vacant, until the sum so advanced with lawful interest had been repaid ; after which the appointments were to be filled up by a majority of votes at a special meeting of the commissioners, not less than eleven being present. For the better regulation of the proceedings it was enacted that a majority, amounting to five, of the commissioners assembled in court should have full power and authority to make, as often as occasion required, such rules and orders for the better management of the court as might seem necessary and conducive to the purposes of the act, provided always such rules or orders did not abridge or alter the scale of fees as at first arranged, and were consistent with equity and the true intent of the act. In the event of anyone neglecting to comply with an order from this court for the payment of money owing an execution was awarded against the body or goods of the debtor, if the former, the sergeant was, by a precept under the hand and seal of the clerk, " empowered and required to take and apprehend, or cause to be taken and apprehended, such party or parties, being within any of the parishes or townships aforesaid, and convey him, her, or them, to some common gaol, or house of correction, within the county palatine of Lancaster, there to remain until he, she, or they, had performed and obeyed such order, decree, or judgment, so as no person should remain in confinement upon any such execution, for any longer space of time than three months." In the case of goods the sergeant was similarly empowered " to levy by distress and sale of goods, of such party, being within the parishes or townships aforesaid, such sum and sums of money and costs as should be so ordered and decreed."

One clause of the act stated that if any person or persons affronted, insulted, or abused, all or any of the commissioners, the clerk, or officers of the court, either during the sitting or in going to or returning from the same, or interrupted the proceedings, or obstructed the clerk or sergeant in the lawful execution of their different offices, he, she, or they should be brought before a justice of the peace, who was hereby empowered to inflict on conviction a fine of not more than 40s., and not less than 5s. The jurisdiction of the court did not extend to any debt or rent upon any lease or contract, where the title of any lands, tenements, or hereditaments came in question ; nor to any debt arising from any last will or testament, or matrimony, or anything properly belonging to the ecclesiastical courts ; nor to any debt from any horse-race, cock-match, wager, or any kind of gaming or play ; nor from any forfeiture upon any penal statute or bye-law ; nor did it extend to any debt whatsoever whereof there had not been contract, acknowledgment, undertaking, or promise to pay within six years from the date of the summons, although any of the above mentioned debts should not amount to forty shillings. No attorney or solicitor was allowed to appear before the commissioners as attorney or advocate on behalf of either plaintiff or defendant, or to speak on any cause or matter before the court in which he was not himself a party or witness, under a penalty of five pounds for each offence. It was further enacted "that no action or suit for any debt not amounting to the sum of forty shillings, and recoverable by virtue of this act in the said Court of Requests, should be brought against any person or persons, residing or inhabiting within the jurisdiction thereof, in any of the king's courts at Westminster, or any other court whatsoever, or elsewhere, out of the said Court of Requests, and no suit which had been commenced in the said Court of Requests in pursuance of this act, nor any proceedings therein, should or might be removed to any superior court, but the judgments, decrees, and proceedings of the said court should be final and conclusive to all intents and purposes ; provided always, that nothing in this act should extend, or be construed to extend, to prevent any person from suing for small

debts in any other court, where such suit might have been
instituted before the passing of this act." The various fees to be
paid to the clerk of the court were—for entering every case, 6d. ;
for issuing every summons, 6d. ; for every subpœna, 6d. ; for
calling every plaintiff or defendant before the court, 3d. ; for
every hearing or trial, 6d. ; for swearing every witness, plaintiff
or defendant, 3d. ; for every order, judgment or decree, 6d. ; for
a non-suit, 6d. ; for every search in the books, 3d. ; for paying
money into court, 6d., if by instalments, 6d. in the pound more ;
for every execution, 6d. ; for every warrant of commitment for
misconduct in court, 1s. The fees to the sergeant were—for
every summons, order, or subpœna, and attending court with the
return thereof, 6d.; for calling every plaintiff or defendant before
the court, 1d. ; for executing every attachment, execution, or
warrant, against the body or goods, 1s. ; for carrying every
plaintiff, defendant, or delinquent to prison, 6d. more for every
mile. Although this was purely a lay-court the commissioners
possessed and exercised the power of placing the witnesses on
oath previous to receiving their evidence. In 1847 the Court of
Requests was superseded by a new court, for the recovery of
debts not amounting to twenty pounds, which held its first sitting
on Monday, the 23rd of April in that year, under the presidency
of John Addison, esq., a barrister and the appointed judge, in the
room belonging to the Sunday school. This gentleman wore a
silk gown, as prescribed to the judges of these courts, and Mr.
Elletson, solicitor, the clerk, was also robed. At the first
assemblage the Rev. John Hull, M.A., the vicar, and Giles
Thornber, esq., J.P., were seated on each side of the judge. The
cases for trial or arbitration only numbered seventeen, and were
of little interest, so that the initiative sitting of the court was
but of short duration. The circuits apportioned to the judges
had an average population ranging from 202,713 to 312,220
persons, and the salary paid to each of these officials was £1,200
per annum. In the schedule of fees it was stated that for the
recovery of debts not exceeding 20s. the cost should be 3s. ; under
40s., 5s. ; under £5, 9s. ; under £10, £1 ; under £20, £1 10s. ;
and in jury cases 5s. would be charged for the jurymen, while the
other court charges would be a little increased. The powers of
this court, now designated the County Court, have been con-

siderably enlarged since its first establishment ; the following
gentlemen are the officers at present connected with it :—

Judge ..... William A. Hulton, esq.   Registrar ..... Mr. E. J. Patteson.
High Bailiff .... Mr. J. Whiteside.

Little Poulton is the name given to a district and hamlet lying
on the east of Poulton township, and in it is situated the ancient
manorial residence called Little Poulton Hall, and now used as a
farm-house. The original mansion stood on the land immediately
at the rear of the existing edifice, which was erected about one
hundred and ten or twenty years ago. Until the occupation of
the present tenant, Mr. Singleton, the foundations of the old Hall
remained in the ground, but the indications afforded by them of
its dimensions and appearance were not of any great utility.
In 1570 Little Poulton Hall was occupied by George, the son of
Bartholomew Hesketh, of Aughton, a grandson of Thomas
Hesketh, of Rufford, but only in one of the junior lines. George
Hesketh married Dorothy, the daughter of William Westby, of
Mowbreck, and had issue one son, William, who inherited the
estate and resided at the Hall. William Hesketh was living in
1613, about forty years after the decease of his father, and had
two children, William and Wilfrid, by his wife Elizabeth, the
daughter of John Allen, of Rossall Hall. William, the eldest son,
seems to have removed to Maynes, or Mains, Hall, and settled
there during the lifetime of his father ; it is probable that his
younger brother would remain at Little Poulton Hall, but of this
we have no positive proof, and consequently can advance it
merely as a conjecture. Little Poulton descended in the Heskeths,
of Mains, until about 1750, but the name of that family was ·
changed, after the marriage of William Hesketh, of Mains Hall,
(living in 1714), with Mary, the daughter of John Brockholes, of
Claughton, by Thomas Hesketh, the eldest son of that union, who
inherited the estates af his maternal uncle, and assumed the name
of Brockholes. Thomas Hesketh-Brockholes died without offspring, and the property passed, successively, to his younger and
only surviving brothers, Joseph and James, both of whom adopted
the name and arms of Brockholes, and died childless ; but by the
will of Joseph, Little Poulton and the other estates descended to
William Fitzherbert, the brother of his widow Constantia, the
daughter of Bazil Fitzherbert, of Swinnerton. William Fitzherbert

also assumed the title of Brockholes, and his descendant is the present proprietor.

A family of the name of Barban preceded the Heskeths at the manor house, and Gyles Curwen, a descendant of the Curwens, of Workington, in Cumberland, espoused, about 1550, the daughter and co-heiress of — Barban, of Little Poulton Hall, having issue—Thomas, Elizabeth, Grace, and Winefrid. Thomas Curwen died unmarried ; Elizabeth became the wife of — Camden, by whom she had William Camden, Clarenceux king-at-arms ; Winefrid married and settled in London ; and Grace espoused Gilbert Nicholson, of Poulton, by whom she had issue—Francis, Grace, and Giles. Francis Nicholson had six children—Humphrey, Grace, Bridget, Thomas, Isabell, and Dorothy. Grace Nicholson married Thomas Braithwaite, of Beaumont, and was the mother of nine children in 1613, the eldest, Geoffrey, being fifteen years of age.[1]

On the south side of the Hall is a wood, covering about two acres of land, and freshly planted within the last half century. Until recent years, numerous decaying tree stocks were turned up out of the soil, and their size plainly evidenced the massive nature of the timber formerly growing there. There is a rookery in the modern wood, and it is surmised that there was one also amongst the branches of the ancient trees, and that a large quantity of bullets discovered in a field on its outskirts record the periodical onslaughts on the unfortunate rooks in days when marksmen were not so unerring as long practice and improved firearms have rendered them now. In the hamlet of Little Poulton there are, in addition to the Hall, three antique houses of considerable pretensions, which were erected and occupied by persons of good social standing. One of them, on the opposite side of the road, and a little removed from the old mansion, was built by a gentleman named Fayle, and on an oaken beam over a doorway, now bricked up, in an extensive barn, is the inscription, EF : IF : 1675, the initials of the erector and his wife, with the date when the edifice was completed. This E. Fayle was probably a relative, perhaps grandfather, of Edward Fayle, of the Holmes, Thornton, and afterwards of

1. Visitation of St. George.

Bridge House, Bispham, who married, about 1728, Susannah, the younger daughter of Edward Veale, of Whinney Heys, and co-heiress, with her sister, of the Rev. John Veale, of the same place, her only brother. Another respectable dwelling, but like the few other buildings around, becoming dilapidated through age, bears the initials of Henry Porter, and the date 1723, over the entrance. From sundry documents which have come to light, it seems that Henry Porter was a gentleman of influence and position in the neighbourhood, but beyond that no information can be gained concerning him or his descendants. The tenement he held was purchased by the Brockholes, of Claughton, in 1846. Close by the side of Porter's residence is another of the same model and size, apparently erected by A. Worswick in 1741, but of this person nothing is known. The remainder of the hamlet is made up of a few old thatched cottages.

A free school was established by James Baines, draper, of Poulton, in 1717, shortly before his death ; and by his will, dated that year, he bequeathed to Richard Wilson, Richard Whitehead, sen., Richard Johnson, and Richard Thornton, of Hardhorn-with-Newton, yeomen, to Richard Dickson, woollen draper, and Samuel Bird, yeoman, of Poulton, to Robert Salthouse, of Staining, yeoman, and to their heirs " all that Schoolhouse by me lately erected in Hardhorn-in-Newton, and the parcel of land whereon the same is erected, which is enjoyed therewith, and which by me was lately purchased from Thomas Ords, to remain, continue, and be a Free School for ever for the persons and purposes hereinafter mentioned. Item: I give and devise unto the seven said Trustees and their Heirs, all that messuage and tenement, called Puddle House, with the lands enjoyed therewith, about twenty-two acres, to the special end, intent, and purpose, that the rents and profits over ten shillings a year, (allowed for a dinner to the trustees, and their successors, on their meeting about the affairs of this School on the second of February, on which day they shall yearly meet for that purpose), and after all costs for repairs at the said Schoolhouse and ground it stands on be paid, the balance be given to such person as shall yearly and every year be named, chosen, and appointed, by the said seven Trustees, and their successors, or the major part of them, to act as Schoolmaster, to teach and instruct in writing,

reading, and other school learning, according to the best of his
capacity, all such children of the inhabitants of the townships
of Poulton and Hardhorn-in-Newton as shall be sent to the said
School, and behave themselves with care and good manners,
without any other payment or reward, except what the said
children or their parents shall voluntarily give." The testament
then proceeds to direct that when any two of the seven trustees
died, the five surviving should at the cost of the estate appoint
two other of the "most able, discreet, and sufficient inhabitants
in Poulton and Hardhorn within three months," and that such
a practice should be observed as occasion required "to the end
that the said charity may continue for ever according to the true
intent and meaning of this Will." The Trustees were invested
with power to dismiss any schoolmaster and appoint a successor,
regarding whom there was the following clause :—"All School-
masters on appointment shall give bond with one or more sureties
for good conduct, and be at duty from 7 a.m. to 11 a.m., and 1
p.m. to 5 p.m, except from the 1st November to 1st February, in
which quarter alone shall they attend on all school days from
8 a.m. to 11 a.m., and 1 p.m. to 4 p.m. ; the afternoons of
Thursday and Saturday to be holiday."

The schoolhouse is a whitewashed building, a single story high,
and has four windows in front, with one at each end. It stands
in the township of Hardhorn-with-Newton, about half a mile
from the town of Poulton, and has the annexed inscription fixed
on the wall facing the main road :—"This Charity School was
Founded and Endowed by Mr. James Baines, of Poolton, who
died the 9th January, 1717. Rebuilt 1818." The lands
bequeathed by Mr. Baines have been exchanged for others of
greater value across the river Wyre. The attendance at present
is small.

Mr. Baines also left £800 to six trustees to be laid out in land,
half the annual income or interest from which he directed to be
devoted to the "maintenance, use, and best advantage of the
poorest sort of inhabitants of the township of Poulton, which
receive no relief by the Poor-rate," and "for putting out poor
children of the said township apprentices yearly though their
parents receive relief by the Poor-rate." The other moiety he
directed to be devoted to similar purposes in the townships of

Marton, Hardhorn-with-Newton, Carleton, and Thornton.

Jenkinson's Gift or Charity consists of the rents of a small cottage with garden behind, and two detached crofts at Forton, in Cockerham parish, and amounts to about £5 10s. per annum, which is expended in the purchase of books for the scholars of Baines's school.

Nicholas Nickson, of Compley, in Poulton, by will dated the 12th of April, 1720, charged his estate with the payment, after the decease of his widow, Alice Nickson, of £100 to the church-wardens and overseers of Poulton, in trust, to invest the sum and give half the interest to the vicar for the time being, distributing the remainder amongst the poor house-keepers of the township not in receipt of parish relief. Until the bequest was paid, the heirs of Nickson, after the death of the widow, were ordered to disburse five per cent. interest on the money each year. In 1754 the trustees of this charity released the estate from all charges in consideration of £100, the legacy, paid to them ; and on the 18th of July, 1783, Joseph Harrison and the four other churchwardens of Poulton, together with William Brown and Paul Harrison, the overseers, purchased from James Standen, for £120, a close in Poulton, called Durham's Croft, to hold the same in trust and divide the rents into twelve parts, whereof five were to be given to the vicar, five to indigent inhabitants not receiving relief, and two in aid of the poor's rates.

CHAPTER VIII.

FLEETWOOD-ON-WYRE.

THE site of the present town of Fleetwood was at no very distant period, less than half a century ago, a wild and desolate warren, forming part of the Rossall estate, and belonging to the late Sir Peter Hesketh Fleetwood, bart. At that date the northern side showed unmistakable evidences of having at an earlier epoch been bounded by a broad wall or rampart of star-hills, continuous with the range until recent years visible near Rossall Point, or North Cape, as that portion of the district was locally called, but which has now been destroyed and levelled by the sea. Beyond the warrener's cottage and a small farm-house on the Poulton road, no habitations existed anywhere in the vicinity ; the whole tract of sandhills and sward had been usurped by myriads of rabbits, which were some little time, even after the erection of dwellings, before they entirely deserted the spot where for centuries they had found a home. During the stormy months of winter, and in the breeding season, immense flocks of sea-fowl made their way to these shores, and like the rabbits, were allowed to remain in undisputed and undisturbed possession of the domain they had appropriated.

Whether this district or locality was populated in the earlier eras of history by any of the aboriginal Britons, invading Romans, or piratical Danes, is a question difficult to solve, but the existence of a paved Roman road, discovered some depth beneath the sand when the trench for the sea-wall was being excavated opposite the Mount Terrace, and traced across the warren in the direction of Poulton, proves beyond a doubt that there was traffic of some description, either peaceful or war-like, over the ground at a very remote age. The road is commonly designated the Danes' Pad, from a tradition that these freebooters made use of it during their incursive warfare in the Fylde.[1] Evidence in support of the belief that this part of the coast was visited by the Danes or Northmen, as the inhabitants of Scandinavia were called, is to be found in " Knot End," the name by which the projecting point of land on the opposite side of Wyre has been known from time immemorial. In early days there were both the "Great and Little Knots," or heaps of stones, but the works carried out for the improvement of the harbour involved the destruction of the small, and mutilation of the big " Knot." Now arises the question, why were these round collections of boulder stones called " Knots ?" In answer to which it may be stated that the word " knot " is of pure Scandinavian origin, and in that ancient Northern language always marked a round heap, and we believe also a round heap of stones. This interpretation would be characteristic of what these knots or mounds of stones were before they were despoiled by the Wyre Harbour Company. Such an application of the word to rounded hills of stone is common at no great distance, and must have been applied by the same people to all these rocky elevations, as instance Hard Knot, Arnside Knot, and Farlton Knot, all of which indicate the name by the rotundity of their stony summits, and seem to confirm the opinion that the early inhabitants of Scandinavia visited the coast, suggesting also that they had some settlement in its immediate vicinity.

As regards the Romans, the only traces of their presence which have been discovered in the neighbourhood of the town, consist of the road above mentioned, and a number of ancient coins which were found near Rossall, in 1840, by some labourers engaged in brick-making. These coins, amounting in all to about three hundred, were principally of silver, and bore the impresses of Severus, Sabina, Antonius, Nerva, etc. It is quite possible, however, that other relics belonging to that nation or the Danes, may still exist, hidden by the sand, and more deeply imbedded than it is necessary to sink when preparing for the foundations of

1. For a full description of the direction taken by this road, see page 7.

the houses, whilst many also may have been submerged by the encroaching waves as they have gradually inundated the north and west sides of the district.

Doctor Leigh, in his Natural History of Lancashire, informs us that at the mouth of the river Wyre there was in his time a purging water which sprang up from out of the sand. "This, no doubt," says the Doctor, "is the sea-water which filters through the sand, but by reason of the shortness of its filtration (the spring lying so near the river), or the looseness of the sand, the marine water is not perfectly dulcified, but retains a pleasing brackishness, not unlike that which is observable in the milk of a farrow cow, or one that has conceived."

To the lord of the manor, Sir P. H. Fleetwood, is due the credit of having first conceived the idea of converting the sterile warren into a thriving seaport. Situated at the mouth of a river, the security of whose stream had originated the proverb—"As safe and as easy as Wyre water," and by the side of a natural and commodious harbour, sheltered from ever wind, the illustrious baronet foresaw a prosperous future for the place, could he obtain permission from parliament to construct a railway to its shores from the important town of Preston, thereby creating a communication with the manufacturing and commercial centres of Lancashire and Yorkshire. In 1835, a number of gentlemen, denominated the Preston and Wyre Railway, Harbour, and Dock Company, having obtained the requisite powers, deputed Frederick Kemp, esq., J.P., of Bispham Lodge, then acting as agent to Sir P. H. Fleetwood, to purchase the land along the proposed route. Operations were commenced with little delay, the work progressed with fair rapidity, and on the 15th of July, 1840, the line was declared open and ready for traffic.

In the meantime dwelling-houses, hotels, and a spacious wharf had been springing into existence. In 1836 the earliest foundation was laid at the south-west corner of Preston Street by Robert Banton, of East Warren Farm. This farm was for a short season a licensed house and brewery, and is now, under the title of Warrenhurst, the private residence of J. M. Jameson, esq., C.E. The new erection, which still bears its original name of the Fleetwood Arms Hotel, made no further progress for about a year, when it was completed by Thomas

Parkinson, the head carpenter at Rossall Hall. The first building finished and inhabited in Fleetwood was a beer-house at the south-west corner of Church Street, which was erected in 1836-7, and is now a shop, owned and occupied by Richard Warbrick, outfitter. That small inn or licensed dwelling was in the occupation of a person named Parker, a stonemason, who a little later built the Victoria Hotel, in Dock-street, where he removed and resided for several months, until a sale of the property had been effected.

The streets were marked out by the plough according to the design of Decimus Burton, esq., architect, of London, and so arranged that all the principal thoroughfares, with the exception of the main road of entrance to the town, converged towards the largest star-hill, now known as the Mount, on the highest point of which was placed a small decagon Chinese edifice, surrounded by a raised platform or terrace, whence an extensive view of the broad bay of Morecambe, the lofty ranges of Lancashire, Cumberland, aud Westmoreland, and a wide circuit of the neighbouring country could be obtained. The hollow on the south side of the mound was fashioned into the form of a basin, and a semicircular gravelled walk carried along the ridge of each side, leading with a gentle ascent from the entrance gates on the warren at the end of London Street to the summit, whilst the slopes were tastefully arranged and planted with shrubs, to impart a pleasing and ornamental appearance to the otherwise bare sward. These shrubs, as might have been foreseen, speedily withered and perished, owing to the bleakness of the site, and a lack of that indispensable moisture which the dry sandy soil could neither retain nor supply. In earlier days the Mount was commonly known as Tup, or Top, Hill, and formed a favourite resort for pic-nic parties from Blackpool, or some of the surrounding villages, which visited the place during the summer months, to admire the innumerable sea-fowl and their nests, the latter being scattered over the shore in endless profusion.

Building proceeded with rapid strides ; house after house sprang up in the lines of streets, which had only lately received their first coating of shingle, and in 1841, one year after the opening of the railway, the town had assumed considerable pro-portions. Near the entrance from Poulton road were three or four double rows of cottages for the accommodation of the workpeople, and a Roman Catholic chapel. Preston Street contained but few houses in addition to the Fleetwood Arms Hotel ; thence, travelling eastward were Dock Street, with the Crown Hotel, as far as and including the Victoria Hotel ; the east side of Warren Street, the west side of St. Peter's Place, the church and Sunday school, both sides of Church Street, Custom House Lane, the Lower Queen's Terrace, the North Euston Hotel, and the bath houses. The Upper Queen's Terrace was in process of erection, but was not completed until 1844, after having been allowed, for some reason, to remain in a partially finished state for two years.

The church, standing on a raised plot of ground in the centre of the town and surrounded by an iron palisading, is dedicated to St. Peter, and was first opened for divine service in 1841. It is a stone edifice with a square tower and octagonal spire at the west end, and was erected by voluntary contributions, the site being provided by Sir P. H. Fleetwood, who retained the right of presentation to the living. The interior of the building is neat, and contains sittings for about four hundred persons in the body, with additional accommodation for two hundred more in the gallery, at the end of which are the choir-pew and organ-loft, the latter being occupied by an instrument constructed by Gray, of London. Previous to the alterations, which were made seventeen years since, and consisted of the erection of a gallery and the convertion of some of the private pews into free seats, the family pew of the Fleetwoods stood in front of the organ-loft, and was the only one raised out of the body of the church. The chancel window is of stained glass, large and handsome, representing a central figure of St. Peter bearing the Keys of Heaven, below and on each side of which several scriptural subjects are illustrated. This window, purchased by subscription amongst the parishioners, was inserted in 1860 ; and in the previous year a handsome font of Caen stone was presented by Mrs. G. Y. Osborne. Two upright tablets, the gift of the late vicar, the Rev. G. Y. Osborne, illu-minated with the Ten Commandments, are placed, one on each side of the Communion table. Four other tablets are fixed against the walls of the church, the first of which was erected by a few friends as a tribute of respect to the memory of Dobson Ward,

died 1859, aged 43 years, a humble but zealous worker in the
Sunday school ; another was placed by the Rev. G. Y. Osborne,
in loving memory of his deceased daughter ; the third, a handsome
tablet, was erected at the entrance to the vestry, by parishioners
and friends, to the memory of the Rev. G. Y. Osborne, "for 19
years vicar of this parish, who died 11 November, 1871, aged 53
years,"[1] and the last is to the memory of Charles Stewart, esq.,
died 1873, aged 64 years, late of High Leigh, Cheshire, and
Fleetwood.   The living, endowed with the great tithes of
Thornton and augmented by the pew rents, was originally a
perpetual curacy, but during the ministry of the late Rev. G. Y.
Osborne, a distinct district or parish for all ecclesiastical purposes
was assigned to the church, and the title of vicar accorded to the
incumbent.

PERPETUAL CURATES AND VICARS OF FLEETWOOD.

IN THE DEANERY OF AMOUNDERNESS AND ARCHDEACONRY OF LANCASTER.

Date of Institution.	NAME.	On whose Presentation.	Cause of vacancy.
1841	St. Vincent Beechey, M.A.	Sir P. H. Fleetwod	
1849	G. Yarnold Osborne, M.A.	Ditto	Resignation of St. Vincent Beechey
1868	Saml. Hastings, M.A.	Exrs. of the late Sir P. H. Fleetwood	Resignation of G. Y. Osborne
1871	James Pearson, M.A.	Ditto	Resignation of S. Hastings

The burial ground connected with the church is part of the
general cemetery, situated near the shore in the direction of the
Landmark at Rossall Point, and about one mile distant from the
town.

The small building opposite the Church, now used for infants
only, was for several years, until the erection of the Testimonial
Schools, the ordinary Sunday school under the superintendence
of the incumbent of St. Peter's.

The Market Place, opened on the 7th of November, 1840, is a
spacious, paved area, surrounded by a high wall of sandstone.

1. The Rev. G. Y. Osborne resigned the living of Fleetwood on being
appointed vicar of St. Thomas's, Dudley, which cure he held up to the date of
his decease.

The two entrances are closed by means of large wooden gates, and lead respectively into Adelaide and Victoria Streets. The central portion of the in-walled space is occupied by a square, wooden structure, covered over with a slated roof, in the interior of which are stalls for the goods of the different farmers and traders. Friday is the market day, and the following list comprises the various commodities exposed for sale on Friday, the 10th of July, 1846, the earliest recorded, with their prices :—

Oats, per bushel		3s. 10d.
Meal, per load		36s. 0d.
Beans, per windle		16s. 0d.
Butter, per pound		1s. 1d.
Eggs, fresh	16 to 18 for	1s. 0d.
Peas, per strike		0s. 9d.
Potatoes (new), per score		1s. 10d.
,, (old), per windle		8s. 0d.
Beef, per pound		6d. to 7d.
Lamb ,, ...		0s. 7d.
Mutton ,, ...		0s. 6½d.
Salmon ,, ...		0s. 10d.
Lobsters ,, ...		1s. 0d.

Since the date of the above quotations, Preston has gradually monopolised the chief portion of the grain trade, and consequently transactions in oats and other cereals are not of frequent occurrence at the local markets of the Fylde.

The Roman Catholic chapel, dedicated to the Blessed Virgin, was erected at the north end of Walmsley Street, continuous with the line of houses forming the east side of that street, and opened for divine worship on the 15th of November, 1841. A few years since a more commodious edifice, which will be described hereafter, was erected on another and better site, whilst the old one was dismantled, and subsequently converted into cottages.

The Crown Hotel, a handsome and substantial stone structure facing the Railway Station, was the third hotel erected in Fleetwood, the Fleetwood Arms being the first, and the Victoria the second in point of completion. The original dimensions of the Crown have been considerably increased by the addition in recent years of ample stable accommodation, a large billiard room, and several sleeping apartments.

The North Euston Hotel, which was opened almost

simultaneously with the Crown Hotel, is a superb stone building in the form of a crescent, with a frontage of nearly 300 feet. This edifice was sold to Government in 1859, and subsequently opened as a School of Musketry. The noble portico in front of the main entrance and the spacious hall within are supported by massive stone pillars, whilst a handsome terrace, raised a little above the level of the street, encircles the whole length of the ground floor, and is protected by an ornamental iron railing. On its transfer to Government, quarters were provided for sixty officers and a staff of military instructors. There were three chief courses of instruction held during each year, but in addition to these were two of shorter duration, one being in the month of January for the adjutants of volunteers, and another a little later for the volunteers themselves. The curriculum was similar to that at Hythe. In 1867 the School of Musketry was discontinued, and after a short interval, in which fresh buildings were added, the whole structure was turned into barracks, and as such continues to be occupied. In the early days of the hotel a T-shaped jetty extended out from the steps on the shore opposite the principal entrance to the distance of low-water mark, and was used by the visitors as a short promenade and landing stage, but after standing a few years the erection was removed, being found to interfere with the course of the steamers and other vessels round that section of the channel.

The bath-houses, each of which contained a spacious sea-water swimming bath, were connected with the North Euston Hotel, and therefore became the property of Government on the transfer of the main building itself. Since that date their internal arrangements have undergone material alterations and modifications to suit the requirements of the military, but their handsome stone exteriors and massive porticoes are still intact.

The custom-house on the Lower Queen's Terrace is now a private residence in the occupation of Alexander Carson, esq., who is also the owner, and the offices have for many years been situated in a house of more modest pretensions in the same row.

The two lighthouses, one of which is placed in Pharos Street and the other further north, on the margin of the beach, were also in existence in 1841, having been erected a short time previously. The former is a tall circular column of painted stone, having an altitude of about 90 feet above high-water mark. The base of the column is square, each of the sides being 12 feet high and 20 broad. The focus of the lantern is 104 feet above half-tide level, and outside the reflector is a narrow, circular, stone gallery, guarded by an iron fencing. The cost of the column was £1,480. The other lighthouse is much smaller, and stands on a slightly elevated plot of ground. Each side of its base forms a recess, furnished with seats, and supported above by round stone pillars. The centre of the lantern is 44 feet above half-tide level. The whole fabric, which is built throughout of finely cut stone, was erected at a cost of £1,375.

We have now reviewed the general appearance of the town in 1841, including brief accounts of all the more important buildings, but accidentally omitting to state that gas works were amongst the early erections, and before proceeding with the history of its further progress and increase, it will be convenient to revert for a moment to the railway and matters connected with it, leaving, however, the harbour, wharf, and shipping for separate examination towards the later pages of the chapter. The railway, consisting of a single line throughout the whole extent, was carried over a portion of the estuary of the Wyre, along an embankment and viaduct of huge wooden piles, running from Burn Naze to the west extremity of the wharf at Fleetwood, near to which the station is situated. In 1846 the traffic, both in passengers and goods, had increased so rapidly that the directors determined to have a double line without delay. Instructions for that purpose were accordingly issued to the engineer of the company, and at the same time he was directed that, in order to afford space and facilities for the construction of the proposed docks to the westward of the existing railway piling, the double line should diverge at Burn Naze, run round the Cops, and terminate as before. The programme here stated was not fully carried out, and the double line extended only as far as Burn Naze, from which point a single line ran along a semicircular embankment, lying west of the old one, to the terminus at Fleetwood.[1] This embankment was the means of rescuing from

1. A second line was laid on this length in 1875 for the first time.

the incursions of the tide about 400 acres of marsh land, which has since by drainage and cultivation been converted into excellent pastures and productive fields. The entire line was leased, under acts of 1846, to the Lancashire and Yorkshire and London and North Western Railway companies, the former taking two thirds and the latter one third of the profits or losses. The terms agreed upon were a rent of £7 1s. 6d. per cent., and £1 15s. 4½d. per share on a total capital of £668,000, until the close of 1854, when the payments were raised to £7 17s. 6d. per cent., and £1 19s. 3½d. per share in perpetuity. In the month of July, 1846, the electric telegraph in connection with the Preston and Wyre Railway was introduced into the town, and as its first public act was the interception, at Kirkham, of a defaulting steamship passenger, who had neglected to pay her fare, it may be concluded that the inhabitants welcomed the ingenious invention as a valuable ally in the protection of their commercial interests, as well as a rapid and convenient mode of friendly intercommunion in cases of urgency.

The Improvement Act, for "paving, lighting, cleansing, and otherwise improving the town of Fleetwood and the neighbourhood thereof, and for establishing a market therein," came into operation on the 18th of June, 1842. Meetings were appointed to be held on the first Monday in every month, at which any male person was empowered to sit as a commissioner on producing evidence that he was either a resident within the limits prescribed by the act, and rated to the poor-rates of the township of Thornton for a local tenement of the annual value of £15, or possessed as owner or lessee or in the enjoyment of the rents and profits of a messuage, lands, or hereditaments, similarly situated and rated, for a term of not less than fifty years. In 1869 authority was obtained to repeal certain sections of the old act and adopt others from the Public Health Act of 1848, and the Local Government Act of 1858, the most important being that in future the Board of Commissioners should consist of twelve members only, having personally the same qualifications as before, but being elected by the ratepayers. The new regulations also ordained that one third of the commissioners should retire each year, and the vacancies be filled up by a general election. This act is still in force.

It was not possible that the claims of a place so happily situated as Fleetwood for a summer residence could long remain unrecognised by the inhabitants of the inland towns. No sooner was free access given to its shores by the opening of the railway in 1840, than the hotels and lodging-houses were inundated with visitors, whose annual return testified to their high appreciation of its mild climate, firm sands, excellent boating accommodation, and lastly, the diversified and beautiful scenery of the broad bay of Morecambe. A number of bathing vans were stationed on the shore opposite the Mount, but were little patronised during the first two or three seasons owing to the proprietors demanding 1s. from each person using them, a sum exactly double that required at other watering-places. The injurious effects of this exhorbitant charge were speedily experienced, not only by the van owners, whose receipts were reduced to a minimum, but generally throughout the town, as visitors who greatly preferred Fleetwood were driven to other places on that account, and each year many who came with the intention of remaining during the summer left because their families were debarred from bathing, except at an excessive cost. The error of so grasping a policy being at last demonstrated to the proprietors by the small and diminishing patronage extended to their vans, it was resolved, in 1844, to reduce the charge to 6d. That year several newly-erected houses in Kemp Street were furnished and tenanted, whilst the hitherto unoccupied stone residences comprised in the Upper Queen's Terrace were fitted up with elegance and convenience for the wealthier class of sojourners, to whom they were let for periods varying from a few weeks to three or four months. The terrace of houses situated between the North Euston Hotel and the Mount, and bearing the latter name, was also completed that year. The prices at the North Euston Hotel were arranged as under :—

Sitting-room	...	...	...	3s. 4d. per day.
Bed-room	...	...	...	2s. 3d. and 4s. 0d. per day.
Table d'Hote	...	...	...	4s. per head.
Breakfast or Tea	...	...	2s. 0d. and 2s. 6d. per head.

During the Whit-week of 1844 the place was crowded with excursionists, many of whom, amounting to 1,000 daily, were carried at half fare by the Preston and Wyre Railway, and came from the neighbouring towns and villages, whilst others arrived by sea in excursion boats from Dublin, the Isle of Man, Ulverstone, Blackpool, and Southport. Festivities were entered into on the warren and slopes of the Mount, lasting three days and consisting of horse, pony, donkey, foot, sack, and wheelbarrow races, a cricket match, foot steeplechases, wrestling, and gingling matches.

In 1844 Fleetwood was reduced from a distinct port to a creek under Preston, and during the month of July the mayor of the latter town paid a state visit to the watering-place, arriving by sea in the small steamer " Lily." A series of misfortunes rather tended to upset the dignity and imposing aspect of the official cortege. A somewhat rough sea retarded their passage and rapidly converted the ship into a temporary hospital for that, perhaps, most distressing of all sicknesses ; nearing, at last, the lighthouse at the foot of Wyre, a large portion of the larboard gunwale was carried away by the bowsprit of the steamer " Express," which had been sent out to meet and tow them into harbour, if necessary ; and finally the unfortunate " Lily " stranded on a bank opposite the beach at Fleetwood, and the mayoral party, now pallid and dejected, in their gorgeous robes and liveries, were brought to land in small open boats, and having formed the following order, marched to the North Euston Hotel, where a banquet was prepared :—

Three Policemen.
Two Sergeants-at-Mace.
Mace Bearer.
The Mayor in his Robes of Office.
The Corporation Steward.   Recorder of the Borough.
The Aldermen of the Borough.
The Members of the Common Council.
Military Officers and Private Gentlemen.
Town Crier and Beadle.

This year the Preston and Wyre Railway Company, in conjunction with the line from Manchester and Bolton, commenced to run Sunday excursion trains to Fleetwood at reduced fares during the genial months of summer, and in August upwards of ten thousand pleasure-seekers were estimated to have been brought into the town by their means alone. These lines were amongst the first to try the experiment of cheap trains, and the immense success which attended their efforts on the above occasions soon induced them to extend the privileges to other days besides the Sabbath. The promoters of private excursions, also, were offered facilities to direct their course to this watering-place. During the summer of 1844 no less than 60,000 people in all, that is including both day excursionists and those who remained for longer periods, arrived, being considerably more than in any previous season. In July, 1846, the whole of the workpeople of Richard Cobden, esq., M.P., the great free-trade statesman, visited the town to celebrate the triumph of free-trade principles in parliament, the entire expense of the trip being defrayed by that gentleman. Each of the operatives and others, numbering about 1,300, had a free-trade medal suspended by a ribbon from the neck; and, having formed in procession, the large assembly paraded through the streets of Fleetwood, carrying banners adorned with such appropriate mottoes and inscriptions as "Free Trade with all the World," "Peel, Bright, and Cobden," etc. In the same year an immense Sunday school trip, bringing no less than 4,200 children and adults, arrived; and after amusing themselves by rambling about the shore for a time, the youthful multitude formed a huge pic-nic party on the warren. This was without doubt the largest single excursion which ever visited these shores, and on its return, the enormous train of two engines and fifty-six carriages, many of which were cattle trucks provided with forms and covered in with canvas, was divided, each engine taking half, for fear of accidents and delays. In later times it was no uncommon circumstance to see the spacious wharf opposite the Upper and Lower Queen's Terraces, crowded with cheap trains during Easter and Whit-weeks. Hourly trips in the small steam tug-boats or pleasure yachts, pony and donkey rides, bathing, and mussel gathering on the bank opposite the Mount Terrace were the chief amusements of the day visitors, and innumerable were the exclamations of wonder and delight uttered by thousands, who for the first time beheld

" The broad and bursting wave "

at Fleetwood, for our readers may be reminded that at the date of which we are writing, railway fares, except on special occasions, were beyond the compass of the labouring populations of our manufacturing and agricultural districts, and consequently a visit to the, in many cases unknown, sea, was an event eagerly anticipated and long remembered.

In January, 1845, a general meeting of those who were interested in Fleetwood, or wished to testify their respect and admiration for the noble efforts of the founder of the town, was held at the North Euston Hotel, to determine upon the most suitable public testimonial to be erected in honour of Sir Peter Hesketh Fleetwood. Doctor Ramsay proposed that day schools for 200 children of the labouring classes, with a house for a master and mistress, having the name of the "Fleetwood Testimonial Schools," open to all denominations of Christians and connected with the National Society, should be erected. This resolution was carried without a dissentient ; subscription lists were opened ; and on Wednesday, the 26th of August, 1846, the foundation stone of the building was laid by Charles Swainson, esq., of Preston. Large numbers arrived early in the morning to be present at the ceremony. The town, shipping, and river craft, decked out in bunting, presented quite a gala appearance as the officials and guests proceeded to the site in West Street. The procession marched as stated below:—

The Beadle.
Band.
The Wesleyan Sunday School Children.
The Independent Sunday School Children.
The Church Sunday School Children.
The Architect holding the Mallet and Trowel.
The Contractors.
The Clergy.
Charles Swainson, esq.
The Treasurer and Mr. Swainson's Friends.
Rossall School.
. The Gentry and Visitors.
The Tradesmen.
Independent Order of Oddfellows.
The Rechabites.

In the cavity beneath the foundation stone were enclosed a bottle containing coins of the present reign, a copy of the *Fleetwood Chronicle* of that date, printed on parchment, and another sheet of parchment inscribed thus :—

"The first stone of these schools, which are to be erected as the fittest Testimonial to the benevolent founder of this town, Sir P. H. Fleetwood, Bart., M.P., was laid by Charles Swainson, Esq., of Preston, this 26th day of August, 1846.

THE REV. ST. VINCENT BEECHEY, M.A., Incumbent;
THE REV. W. LAIDLAY, B.A., Curate;
B. WALMSLEY,
FREDERICK KEMP, } Churchwardens;
THE REV. JOHN HULL, Vicar of Poulton, Chairman of the Committee.
JOHN LAIDLAY, Esq., Treasurer of the Committee;
R. B. RAMPLING, Esq., Architect;
H. B. JONES, Esq., Secretary.
Non nobis, Domine, sed nomini tuo da gloriam."

This scholastic institution is in the Gothic style of architecture, and the principal front, facing into West Street, extends over a distance of seventy-one feet. The interior of the building contains separate school accommodation for boys and girls; and at the east end there is a comfortable residence for the mistress. The school is surrounded by an extensive play-ground, and enclosed by a brick wall, surmounted anteriorly by ornamental iron railings. Since the building was completed the provision for the reception of boys has been greatly increased by the erection of a new wing, by private munificence, abutting at right angles with the east end of the original structure.

In the spring of 1845 a handsome promenade and carriage drive was completed along the border of the shore from the North Euston Hotel to the west extremity of the Mount Terrace. The pathway, which ran on the inner side of the drive, was flagged throughout its entire length, whilst the outer margin of the road was connected with a substantial sea-wall of square-cut stone by a broad and well-kept grass plat. Subsequently this elegant walk was extended round the south side of the Mount, along Abbots' Walk, and so on by the side of the shore to the Cemetery Road. Very little of the portion first constructed is now to be seen, and that remnant is in such a dilapidated condition as almost to be impassable. Huge stones which formerly protected the green sward and road from the waves are now lying scattered and buried about the beach; whilst the westerly end of the promenade has not only suffered utter annihilation itself, but serious inroads have been made by the water into the ornamental gardens fronting the houses of the Mount Terrace.

Strenuous efforts were put forth during the autumn of 1845 to prevent the visitors forsaking the town immediately the long evenings had commenced; pyrotechnic displays took place each week on the plot of land lying to the north of the Upper Queen's Terrace, and designated the Archery Ground. Sea excursions to Blackpool, Southport, and Piel Harbour were liberally provided for by the steamers of the port; a military band was hired for several weeks, and played daily either on one of the pleasure craft or near the new promenade; foot races, wrestling, and cricket matches were arranged and contested at short intervals. But all in vain, for towards the end of August the reflux of visitors had thoroughly set in, and by the middle of September the shores were almost deserted. During that brief period of excitement it was proposed amongst the inhabitants to erect a large public building to be ready for the ensuing season, which should combine all the advantages of a reading and news room, public library, bazaar, ball room, and theatre; but either the ardour of the people cooled during the winter months or they failed to discern a fair prospect of dividends from the investment, for the summer of 1846 discovered that the idea had vanished with the closing year, and

> " Like the baseless fabric of a vision,
> Left not a wreck behind."

Perhaps, however, it is going too far to assert that no trace or vestige of the comprehensive project remained after the first ebullition of enthusiasm had passed from the popular mind, for we find that, although no noble hall graced the town, a Mechanics' Institution was modestly established on the 18th of May, 1846, by the opening of a reading room in one portion of the Estate Office. This office formerly occupied the site of the present Whitworth Institute, and was a small, lightly constructed, Gothic edifice. Subsequently a larger and more convenient place for the purposes of the Institution was engaged in Dock Street; a library was provided and arrangements made for lectures and classes to be held on the premises. In the report of the establishment, issued twelve months after its foundation, it was stated that the members at that date amounted to 184, being 138 full members, 20 females, and 26 youths and apprentices; and that since its organisation 213 persons had availed themselves of the privileges offered by the society. A considerable number of cottage houses were erected in different parts of the town, and not only were these tenanted directly they were completed, but the demand for further building was still on the increase. A public abattoir, or slaughter-house, was constructed in 1846 on the outskirts of the town, and a notice issued, prohibiting the slaying of any cattle, sheep, or swine anywhere except within its walls, under a penalty of £5 for every offence. A Wesleyan chapel was also in course of erection in North Church Street, then open warren, and finished the following year, divine service being first conducted in it on Monday, the 24th of May, by the Rev. George Osborne, of Liverpool. As the town gradually developed in size and population, the attendants at this place of worship outgrew the space provided for them, and lately, in 1875, it became necessary to enlarge the edifice. The west gable-end was taken out and the main building extended in that direction. Galleries were placed along the two sides and across the east wall; the old-fashioned pulpit was superseded by a platform situated at the centre of the west end, and extending to within six feet of the galleries at either side. The new sittings resemble the old ones in being closed pews, and not open benches. The chapel is now capable of containing double the congregation it could have held previous to the recent alterations.

In the month of February, 1847, an extraordinary high tide, rendered more formidable by strong westerly winds, did great damage on the coast from here to Rossall; the Landmark was so far undermined that its fall was hourly expected; an embankment raised on the shore from that point to Rossall suffered severely, large portions being completely washed away; and the out-buildings of a farm called "Fenny" were overthrown and destroyed, serious injury being done also to the land in the neighbourhood. The more immediate vicinities of the town escaped with comparatively little loss, the most important being that resulting from the inundation of several fields and gardens near the Cops, and the levelling of a few wooden sheds for labourers' tools and other outbuildings.

A failure in the potatoe and grain harvests of 1846 spread fearful distress and famine throughout the United Kingdom; bread riots and disturbances amongst the starving poor of Ireland were of frequent occurrence, and it was to assist in alleviating the sufferings of those unfortunate people that a subscription was started in Fleetwood during the latter months of that year. Donations purely from the inhabitants of the town were collected, and in January, 1847, the sum of £105 was forwarded to the sister country. In consequence of the severe national affliction, Her Majesty ordained that Wednesday, the 24th of the following March, should be observed as a general fast-day. On that date all the shops in the watering place, with one or two exceptions, were closed ; the public-houses and streets were quiet ; and stillness and solemnity everywhere apparent. The church was crowded to overflowing ; every seat was packed, and forms were brought in from the Sunday school and placed in the aisles to create extra accommodation, so excessive was the congregation which assembled to join in the special service for divine intervention.

On Monday, the 20th of September, 1847, Her Majesty, Queen Victoria, accompanied by their Royal Highnesses, the Prince Consort, the Prince of Wales, and the Princess Royal, landed at Fleetwood *en route* from Scotland to London. The spot fixed for the debarkation of the royal party was near the north end of the covered pier, upwards of 100 feet of which were boarded off and converted into a saloon, a covered gallery being erected leading from it to the railway, where the special train was stationed. The floors of the saloon and gallery were covered with crimson drugget and at the entrance to the former a beautiful triumphal arch was formed of various coloured draperies, and adorned with the national flag and other emblems of loyalty. The walls of the saloon were hung with white and coloured draperies, festooned with evergreens, and British ensigns were suspended from the roof. This elegant apartment contained a gallery for ladies at the north end, and near to the entrance was a small octagonal throne, having an ascent of three steps, upon which a handsome gilded chair of state and a footstool were placed. Behind the two latter, draperies of crimson cloth were suspended, surmounted by the Arms of Her Majesty. On Sunday, the 19th of September, the High-sheriff of the county of Lancaster, William Gale, esq., of Lightburne House, near Ulverston, who had arrived in order to receive Her Majesty on the following day, attended divine worship at St. Peter's Church, being driven there in his state carriage, drawn by four splendid greys and preceded by his trumpeters and twenty-four javelin men with halberds. Monday was ushered in with boisterous winds, a cloudy sky, and other indications of unpropitious weather, which fortunately for the thousands who crowded into the place from Yorkshire, Manchester, and intermediate localities, considerably improved as the day advanced. The ships in the harbour were draped with flags, and similar decorations floated from the windows of almost every house. A little after three o'clock in the afternoon the report of a signal gun announced that the royal squadron, consisting of the Victoria and Albert, the Black Eagle, the Fairy, the Garland, and the Undine, was in sight, and as the noble vessels steamed up the channel the North Euston Hotel and the Pier burst out into brilliant illuminations. As soon as the royal yacht, Victoria and Albert, had been safely moored to the quay opposite the triumphal arch, and the gangways adjusted, the High-sheriff, W. Gale, esq.; Lieut.-General Sir Thomas Arbuthnot, K.C.B.; Sir P. H. Fleetwood, bart.; Major-General Sir William Warre; John Wilson Patten, esq., M.P.; the Rev. St. Vincent Beechey, incumbent of Fleetwood; Henry Houldsworth, esq., chairman of the Lancashire and Yorkshire Railway Company; George Wilson, esq., deputy-chairman; and Thomas H. Higgin, esq., managing director of the Preston and Wyre district; presented their cards, and explained to Captain Beechey the several arrangements which had been made for Her Majesty's conveyance to London. Afterwards Sir P. H. Fleetwood, the Rev. St. Vincent Beechey, Frederick Kemp, and James Crombleholme, esqrs., of Fleetwood; and Daniel Elletson, esq., of Parrox Hall, were admitted to an interview with Lord Palmerston, who, on behalf of Her Majesty, received the subjoined address from the inhabitants of Fleetwood, printed in gold on white satin, and promised that it should be laid before the Queen :—

"THE LOYAL AND DUTIFUL
"ADDRESS
"OF THE
"INHABITANTS OF FLEETWOOD,
"TO HER MOST GRACIOUS MAJESTY THE QUEEN.

"*May it Please your Majesty,*

"We, the Inhabitants of the Town of Fleetwood, in the county of Lancaster, desire to approach your Majesty on this auspicious occasion, with the most sincere expression of our devoted loyalty and attachment to your Majesty, of our deep respect and esteem for your Majesty's august Consort, for his Royal Highness the Prince of Wales, and the other members of the Royal Family.

"We beg to assure your Majesty that it is with feelings of the liveliest gratitude that we hail this Royal visit to our humble shores, now for the first time pressed by the foot of Sovereignty.

" We rejoice to think that it has fallen to our happy lot to be the first to welcome the Queen of England to her own Royal Patrimony in the Duchy of Lancaster.

"We hasten to lay at your Majesty's feet the dutiful allegiance of the inhabitants of the youngest Town and Port in all your Majesty's dominions, which dates its existence from the very year in which your Majesty first ascended the Throne of these realms ; and which, from the barren and uninhabited sands of the Fylde of Lancashire, has already obtained some importance for its town of 3,000 inhabitants, its Watering-place, Harbour, and Railway, together with its College for the sons of clergymen and other gentlemen.

" We sincerely trust, that the natural facilities and local arrangements of this Port may be found such as shall conduce to the safety, comfort, and convenience of your Majesty in your royal progress. And we beseech your Majesty to receive our united and solemn assurance, that whatever progress our Harbour and Town may make in wealth and importance, it shall ever be our firmest determination and most earnest prayer, that we may never cease to boast of a loyal population, entertaining the same feeling of devoted duty and attachment to your Majesty and the Royal Family, which we experience at this moment, and which the grateful remembrance of this Royal visit must ever tend to keep alive in our bosoms.

" Signed on behalf of the Inhabitants,

" ST. VINCENT BEECHEY, M.A.,

" Incumbent of Fleetwood."

To the foregoing address the annexed reply was received from London in the course of a few days :—

" Whitehall, 25th September, 1847.

" SIR,—I am directed by the Secretary, Sir George Grey, to inform you, that the Loyal and Dutiful Address of the Inhabitants of Fleetwood, on the occasion of Her Majesty's late visit, has been laid before the Queen, and that the same was very graciously received by Her Majesty.

" I have the honour to be, Sir, your obedient servant,

(Signed)

" DENNIS LE MERCHANT.

" Rev. St. Vincent Beechey, Incumbent of Fleetwood."

Early next morning the handsome saloon was occupied by the High-sheriff, the Under-sheriff, and a select number of gentlemen, and shortly after ten o'clock Her Majesty and the royal party proceeded from the yacht to the special train amid joyful acclamations which resounded from all parts of the shore. The moment Her Majesty set foot, for the first time, on her Duchy of

Lancaster, the royal standard was lowered from the mast-head of the yacht, and instantly raised on the flag-staff at the custom-house of Fleetwood, where it received a salute of twenty-one guns. After another salute of a similar number of guns, as Her Majesty reached the end of the gallery, the royal party entered their saloon carriage, Mr., now Sir John, Hawkshaw, engineer to the Lancashire and Yorkshire Railway Company, took his station on the engine, and the train moved slowly off, followed by the ringing cheers of at least ten thousand spectators.

It should be mentioned that a loyal address, written in Latin, from the students of the Northern Church of England School, at Rossall, arrived too late for presentation, and was afterwards forwarded to London.

In the month of July, 1847, Mr. Thomas Drummond, contractor, commenced the erection of the present Independent Chapel in West Street, and notwithstanding a serious delay through the destruction of the north gable and roof-framing by a heavy gale in September, the building was completed the same year. The edifice, which will contain about 600 persons, is a neat brick structure with side buttresses, and adorned with a castellated tower. Beneath the chapel are spacious school-rooms for boys and girls. The site was granted by Sir P. H. Fleetwood, and conveyed in trust for the use of the church and congregation.

For two or three years little of special interest occurred in the progress or condition of the town. Each summer brought its assembly of regular visitors, upon whom many of the inhabitants depended for support, whilst Whit-week annually inundated the warren, streets, and shores with crowds of day-excursionists, for whose benefit sports, resembling those to which allusion has already been made, were instituted. Regattas also were added to the other attractions of the watering-place, but after existing for some little time they gradually died out, either because they failed to excite their former interest amongst the visitors, or the public spirit of the inhabitants was tardy in providing the funds necessary for their continuance. Houses in Albert Street, and in other parts of the town, were slowly increasing in number, but no large demand for dwellings bespoke a rapid rise in the prosperity or popularity of the place, like that to which we referred a little earlier. Trade, although comparatively steady, evinced no signs of enlargement at present, and as a consequence fresh families hesitated to venture their fortunes in the new land, until some more regular and reliable means of gaining a livelihood were offered them than the precarious patronage of uncertain visitors, many of whom, now that free access had been given to Blackpool and Lytham through the opening of branch lines, were already being seduced from their old allegiance to Fleetwood, and attracted to the gayer promenades of those rival resorts.

In the month of December, 1852, and just at the Christmas season, a fearful hurricane swept over Fleetwood; slates, chimney tops, and boardings were torn from their fastenings, and hurled about the streets; indeed so terrific was the violence of this gale that at its height it was difficult for the pedestrian to avoid being forced along by its fury in whatsoever direction the huge gusts willed. During the storm a singular accident occurred in the harbour. The barque "Hope," which had arrived shortly before from America with timber, was lying in the river attached to one of the buoys, and by some carelessness the men employed in unloading her had neglected, on leaving their work, to close up the large square hole near the stem of the ship, through which the baulks of wood were discharged. The hurricane came on fiercely and suddenly from the west, and, to the dismay of the solitary watchman who had been left in charge of the vessel, heeled over her lightened hull so that the swollen and boisterous tide poured wave after wave through the unprotected aperture at her bows; a few minutes only were needed to complete the catastrophe, for as the vessel settled in the deep, no longer waves but continuous volumes of water rushed into her, and with a heavy lurch she rolled over on her side, the masts and more than half her hull being submerged. Fortunately, however, the remnant of the cargo was sufficiently buoyant to prevent her from vanishing bodily beneath the surface. The luckless guardian, whose feelings must have been far from enviable, was quickly rescued from the perilous position he occupied on the floating portion of the ship; but it was not until some weeks afterwards that they were able, in the words of the poet Cowper,

"To weigh the vessel up."

The "Hope," 415 tons register, was built up the river at the old port of Wardleys, being the only vessel of such dimensions constructed in the shipyard there. Ten years later, on the 27th of February, 1862, this ill-fated barque was abandoned on the high seas in a sinking condition.

In 1854 sundry improvements were effected in the extent and condition of the place, and consisted in part of the erection of a row of model cottages in Poulton Road, near the entrance to the town, as well as a new police Station in West Street, comprising two dwellings for the constables and cells for prisoners. The streets were also put in better order, and efforts made to render the aspect of Fleetwood more finished and pleasing than it had been during the two or three previous seasons. A scheme for the partial drainage of the town was proposed at the assembly of commissioners, and arrangements were entered into for the work to be promptly carried out at an estimated cost of £1,200. Altogether a sudden spirit of activity seemed to have superseded the lethargy or indifference which lately had been too much visible amongst the inhabitants in all matters of public interest, and which had already exercised a serious and baneful influence upon the prospects of the place as a sea-side resort. In the ensuing year the body of Primitive Methodists, which had now become rather numerous, chiefly owing to the prosperity of the fishing trade attracting many followers of that calling to the port, most of whom were members of this sect, commenced and completed a chapel in West Street. Recently it has been found necessary considerably to enlarge the edifice, in order to furnish more accommodation for the increasing congregation. Although the erection of this chapel and of the other buildings mentioned above mark undoubtedly an era of progress in the history of the town, still we are constrained to admit that the wants they supplied were not brought about by the spread of Fleetwood's reputation as a watering-place. From the first little had been done to supplement its natural attractions by laying out elegant promenades, or improving the state of the Cops or Poulton Road, so as to render them agreeable rural walks for many who, after a time, grew weary of watching the eddies and dimples of the river's current

> " Play round the bows of ships,
> That steadily at anchor rode ;"

or of daily rambling where the receding waves left a broad floor

of firm, unbroken sands.   True, a carriage-drive and foot-way of
some pretensions to beauty had been constructed along the north
shore in 1845, but the storms we have described, and other
heavy seas, had torn breaches in its wall, and made sad havoc
amongst its light sandy material, completely ruining the fair
appearance of the shoreward grass-plat, and threatening the
road with that very destruction which has since overtaken it
through the continued negligence of the residents or governing
powers. There was no public hall, such as that once contemplated,
where a feeling of fellowship might be engendered amongst the
visitors. The regattas instituted for the interest and amusement
it was hoped they would excite amongst the spectators were, as
previously stated, conducted in a desultory manner for a few
years, and then abandoned ; whilst the land sports during the
week of high festival were discontinued as the Whit-week
excursion trains found other outlets more attractive than Fleetwood for their pleasure-seeking thousands ; but it was not until
the North Euston Hotel was opened for military purposes, that all
hope of·reviving the fading reputation of the town as a summer
resort was finally relinquished. For some little time after the foregoing transfer, the bathing vans, as if to keep up the fiction of the
season, re-appeared with uninterrupted regularity each year upon
the beach, but even that last connecting link between the deserted
town, as far as visitors were concerned, and its former popularity,
was doomed shortly to be broken, for the ancient machines, never
renewed, and seldom repaired, were at length unequal to the
rough journey over the cobble stones, and crumbled to pieces on
the way, expiring miserably in the cause of duty, from old age
and unmerited neglect.

In the early part of 1859, a lifeboat, thirty feet in length, was
stationed here by the National Lifeboat Institution, and in the
month of September in the same year, a neat and substantial
house was built for it on the beach opposite the North Euston
Hotel. After doing good service along the coast, in rescuing
several crews whose vessels had stranded amidst the breakers on
the outlying sand-banks, this boat was superseded, in 1862, by
one of larger dimensions. In January, 1863, the erection on the
beach was swept away by the billows during a heavy gale, and in
the course of a few months the present structure in Pharos Street,

Q

far removed from the reach of the destructive element, was raised, and the lifeboat transferred to its safer keeping.

The census of the residents taken in 1861 showed a total of 4,061 persons, being an increase of 940 over the number in 1851, and of 1,228 over that in 1841. Hence it is seen that during the long period of twenty years, almost from its commencement to the date now under consideration, through fluctuating seasons of prosperous and depressed trade, the town had succeeded in adding no more than 1,228 individuals to the roll of its inhabitants, many of whom would be the offspring of the original settlers. Truly the foregoing picture is not a very satisfactory one to review when we call to mind the bright auspices under which the place was started,—the early and ample railway accommodation, the short and well-beaconed channel, and the safe and spacious harbour; but could we only add the extensive area of docks, the Fleetwood of 1871 would doubtless have presented a widely different aspect to that we are here called upon to portray. It is scarcely just, however, to lay all the burden of this slow rate of progress on the want of suitable berth provision for heavily-laden vessels coming to the harbour. Fleetwood had other means of extending its circle besides those derived from its happy situation for shipping trade. Its merits as a watering-place were allowed on every hand; eulogistic versions of its special charms were circulated through the public prints; strangers flocked each summer to its shores, and were enchanted with their visits; but after a while the refreshing novelty wore off, and the puny efforts made by those whose interests in the prosperity of the town were greatest, failed to fill the inevitable void the waning newness left in its train. In the meantime other season places, urged on by emulation, enhanced the beauties of nature by works of art; promenades, walks, drives, and, at no distant period, piers, were constructed to meet the popular demands, and in that way the tide of visitors was turned from the non-progressive and now over familiar attractions of Fleetwood to swell the annually increasing streams which overflowed the rising towns of Blackpool and Lytham. The year 1861 will ever be remarkable in the history of Fleetwood as being the date at which the town was for the first time practically diverted from that line of progress which its founder, in too sanguine expectancy, had early marked out for it. Its decadence as a summer resort had been too pronounced to allow of any hope being entertained that a revulsion was probable, or even possible, in the feelings and tastes of the multitude, which would again people its shores, during the warm months, with a heterogeneous crowd of valetudinarians and pleasure-seekers. The noble hotel which had been erected by Sir P. H. Fleetwood on the northern margin of the shore, in a style of architecture and at an expense which bore witness to the firm confidence of the baronet in the brilliant future awaiting the infant town, had been sold to Government, as previously stated, in 1859, but it was not until two years afterwards that the first detachment of officers took up their quarters in the newly-established School of Musketry, and Fleetwood awoke to the novel sound of martial music and the reputation of being a military centre. Rumour, also, had for several months been active in circulating a report that the sward lying between the Landmark and the cemetery, and a field at the corner of Cemetery Road, had attracted the eye of Government as a suitable locality whereon to place barracks and lay out a rifle-practice ground ; and in February, 1861, doubt on the subject was no longer admissible, for the contract to carry out the fresh project was let during that month to the gentleman who had been engaged in the necessary alterations at the North Euston Hotel. The scheme involved the creation of residential accommodation in the field just indicated for a small force of 220 men and 12 officers, some of the quarters being specially designed for married soldiers, in addition to which lavatories, a canteen, mess-room, magazine, and guard-house, were to be erected. The work was entered on without delay, and at no long interval, about ten months, or rather more, the whole of the buildings were completed, and soon afterwards occupied. The practice-ground was marked out for range firing, and butts provided, where the targets were shortly stationed. A spacious hospital, it should be mentioned, was constructed almost contemporaneously with the main portion of the barrack buildings.

On Monday, the 20th of May, 1861, a mass meeting was convened to ascertain the opinion of the inhabitants with regard to a claim of exclusive use of the road over the Mount-hill, which had recently been set up by Sir Peter Hesketh Fleetwood, who in order to establish his right had caused a cobble wall to be erected round that portion of the estate. The meeting, consisting of about three hundred persons, was held on the pathway in dispute, which crosses the highest point of the elevation. A platform was raised, and a chairman, elected by the unanimous voice of the company, ascended the rostrum, being accompanied by several of the more enthusiastic advocates of free-road, who in the course of earnest addresses declared that for twenty years the Mount had been dedicated to the public service, in consideration of certain sums paid annually to the lord of the manor out of the town's rates, and that having been so long the property of the people, Sir P. H. Fleetwood had now no moral or legal title to wrest it from them. The ardent language of the speakers aroused a sympathetic feeling in the breasts of the small multitude, and murmurs of discontent at the attempted deprivation of their privileges had already assumed a threatening tone, when a gentleman who happened to be visiting the neighbourhood, appeared upon the scene, and in a few spirited words urged the excited listeners to some speedy manifestation of their disapproval. Uttering a shout of indignation and defiance the crowd rushed at the enclosure wall, tore down the masonry, and quickly opened out a wide breach through the offending structure, after which they filled the air with triumphant cheers and shortly retired homewards in a comparatively orderly manner. In the course of a few months the vexatious question was settled between the representatives of the town and Sir P. H. Fleetwood, who on his part agreed only to retain to himself a plot of land fifty yards square, lying on the west side of the hill ; another piece one hundred yards square, extending from the base of the elevation to the sea ; the wooden edifice on the summit of the mound ; six square yards whereon to erect a look-out house for the Coast-guards ; and the gardens and cottage-lodges at the entrance. The remainder of the Mount, amounting to about three-fourths, was given up to the public, together with the right of footway through the cottages just mentioned, and over the east and west plots ; the commissioners engaging, on their side, to erect and maintain a suitable fence round the Mount, and to keep the hill itself in a proper manner for the benefit of the inhabitants or visitors, as well as binding themselves upon no account to raise any building on the site. The entire ground, with the buildings, has since been given, on much the same conditions, to the town.

During the year 1862 the town, which for some time had lain dormant in a commercial point of view, evinced unmistakable signs of returning animation ; trade was more active, rumour once more hinted at the probable commencement of docks at an early date, and ninety-five houses of moderate size were erected. In the earlier half of the following twelve months no less than thirty-seven more dwellings were added to the town, the foundations of several others being in course of preparation. A branch of the Preston Banking Company was also opened for a few hours once in each week; and during later years has transacted business daily.

On Tuesday, the 20th of January, 1863, a storm and flood, such as has seldom been witnessed on this coast, arose suddenly and raged with fury for about twenty hours. The whole of the wall under the Mount, which had been brought to light by some gales in the previous November, after having been buried in the sand for long, was uttterly demolished, not one stone being left upon another. In addition, the breakers penetrated with destructive violence, several yards inland beyond the line of that barrier throughout its whole length, from the west end of the Euston Barracks to the further extremity of Abbot's Walk. A wooden battery of two 32-pound guns at the foot of the Mount, belonging to the Coastguards,[1] and used for training the Naval Volunteer Reserve, was undermined and so tilted that its removal became a necessity. The marine fence, which had been constructed at an immense cost, between the Landmark and Cleveleys, was almost entirely swept away, leaving the adjacent country open to the inundations of the sea, which rushed over and flooded all the land between the points just named, extending eastward even to the embankment of the Preston and Wyre Railway. Several of the streets at the west side of Fleetwood were under water, as also were the fields about Poulton road and the highway itself. The proprietor of the "Strawberry Garden," off the same road, and his family, were compelled to take refuge in an upper storey of their

---

1. Coastguards were first located at Fleetwood in 1858, and consisted of six men and an officer. Their present station in Abbot's Walk was erected in 1864, and comprises cottage accommodation for six men, and another residence for the officer in command.

dwelling until rescued in a boat, the following day, from their unpleasant, if not perilous, position. It was in this hurricane that the house erected on the shore for the reception of the life-boat suffered annihilation, and the boat itself narrowly escaped serious damage. Tuesday, the 10th of March, in the same year was observed by the residents as a general holiday and gala day, in honour of the marriage of Albert Edward, Prince of Wales, with the Danish Princess, Alexandra. Flags and banners floated from the windows of nearly every habitation, as well as from the roofs of many, while the steamships and other vessels in the harbour were gaily decorated with bunting, which waved in rich and varied tints from their masts, spars, and rigging. Triumphal arches of the "colours of all nations" were suspended across the streets at several points. A large procession of schools and friendly societies in full regalia, with their banners and devices, paraded the different thoroughfares, and were afterwards sumptuously entertained, the latter at their various lodges, and the former in the large area of a cotton warehouse, recently built on the quay by Messrs. B. Whitworth and Bros., of Manchester. The military stationed at the School of Musketry evinced their loyalty by discharging a *feu de joie* on the warren. In the following November a scheme was proposed for the construction of a coast railway between Fleetwood and Blackpool, to pass through Rossall and Bispham. A survey was made of the route, and according to the plans drawn out, the projected line was intended to have its Fleetwood terminus at the south extremity of Poulton Terrace, opposite the end of West Street, whence it was to run towards the new barracks, near the cemetery, then diverge to the south in the direction of Rossall. From Rossall its course lay towards Bispham and thence onwards to the Blackpool terminus, which would be located in Queen's street, adjoining the station already standing there. The stations, besides those at the two termini, were to be placed at the barracks, Rossall, and Bispham. At Fleetwood the promoters proposed to form a junction with the Preston and Wyre Railway near the old timber pond, for the purpose of passing carriages from one line to the other, whilst at Blackpool a similar object would be effected with the Lytham and Blackpool Railway by deviating eastward from Queen Street, so as to avoid the town, and establishing a junction with the latter line near Chapel Street.

On an application being made to parliament for powers to carry out the design, strenuous opposition was offered by the representatives of the Preston and Wyre Railway, who pledged themselves to erect additional stations along their track to accommodate the people residing at Rossall, Cleveleys, and Bispham, in consequence of which the bill for a coast-line was thrown out and the project abandoned.

On the 4th of December, 1863, the Lancaster Banking Company established a branch here ; and on the 15th of that month the Whitworth Institute in Dock Street was publicly opened. This handsome Hall was erected through the munificence of Benjamin Whitworth, esq., M.P., of London, who for long resided at Fleetwood, and during that period, and afterwards, was instrumental in giving a marked stimulus to the foreign trade of the port by shipping each year, on behalf of the large firm of which he is the head at Manchester, numerous cargoes of cotton from America *via* Fleetwood. The buiding is in the Gothic style of architecture. The walls are built of bricks with stone dressings, the principal features being the ten arcaded windows, with the stone balcony beneath running across the entire width of the front, and the elegant entrance. The interior comprises a spacious reading room and library, a smoking and coffee room, provided with chess and draughts, an assembly room, capable of containing 400 persons, and two billiard rooms. At the time of its presentation to the inhabitants the donor generously provided tea urns and other appliances necessary for holding soirees, in addition to having liberally furnished the whole of the building, including the gift of a choice and extensive selection of books, chess and draught-men, a bagatelle-board, and a billiard-table. The second billiard-table was added out of the surplus funds in 1875. The Institute is vested in trustees for the use of the town, and governed by a committee chosen from amongst the subscribers.

During 1864-5 building continued to progress, but not with that great rapidity which had characterised its advance in 1862 and the earlier months of the following year. An act of parliament was granted in 1864 to certain gentlemen for the formation of a dock in connection with the harbour, confirming the rumour which had now agitated the place for the last two years, and bringing conviction to the hearts of many of the older

inhabitants, whose past experience had taught them to look with
eyes of distrust on all reports which pointed to such a happy
realisation of their youthful dreams. The inaugural ceremony of
breaking the turf did not, however, take place for some time, and
will be noticed shortly. On the 17th of May, 1866, the foundation
stone of the present Roman Catholic church in East Street was
laid by Doctor Goss, bishop of Liverpool, who performed the
ceremony, attired in full ecclesiastical robes, and attended by a
numerous retinue of priests and choristers. The sacred edifice
was opened on Sunday, the 24th of November in the ensuing year.
Its general style is early English of the 13th century. The
building consists of a nave and two aisles, with an apsidal
sanctuary at the east end; it is about one hundred feet long,
thirty-five feet wide, and fifty feet in height. The exterior is
built of stone, the body of the walls being Yorkshire parpoints,
whilst the dressings are of Longridge stone. Mr. T. A.
Drummond, of Fleetwood, was the builder, and the design
was drawn by E. Welby Pugin, esq., architect, the total cost
being about £4,000.

For many years, in fact ever since steamship communication
had been established between this port and Belfast, large quantities of young cattle from Ireland were landed each season at
Fleetwood, and carried forward by rail to the markets of Preston
and elsewhere. For the benefit of the dealers, who would thus
escape the railway charges, as well as for the convenience of the
graziers and other purchasers residing in the neighbourhood, it
was determined to open a place for the public sale of such live
stock at Fleetwood; the necessary authority was obtained from
the Privy Council, and on the 2nd of April, 1868, the Cattle
Market, lying on the east side of that for general produce, and
consisting of sixteen large strong pens, arranged in two rows with
a road between them, was used for its earliest transactions and
much appreciated by those who were concerned in the traffic.

Wednesday, the 2nd of June, 1869, will not readily be obliterated
from the memories of the people of Fleetwood. On that day the
first sod of the long expected dock was cut by H. S. Styan, esq.,
of London, the surviving trustee of the estate under the will of
the late Sir P. H. Fleetwood, who died in 1866. The auspicious
event was celebrated with universal rejoicing, in which many-

coloured bunting played its usual conspicuous part. A large procession of the clergy, gentry, schools, and friendly societies,
enlivened by the band of the 80th regiment of Infantry from the
Euston Barracks, and gay with waving banners, accompanied
Mr. Styan to the site where the important ceremony was
performed, and sent forth hearty congratulatory cheers when the
piece of turf had been duly dissected from the ground. With all
apparent earnestness and eagerness, operations were at once
commenced, and for two or three months the undertaking, under
the busy hands of the excavators, made satisfactory progress, when
suddenly several gangs of labourers were discharged, and the
works partially stopped—

"While all the town wondered."

Wonderment, however, was turned to a feeling of disappointment
and chagrin, when it was discovered, a little later, that the closing
year would put a period to the labours at the dock as well as to
its own epoch of time, and that its last shadows would fall on
deserted works and idle machinery. For some reason, which
may fairly be conjectured to have been an incompleted list of
shareholders, the Fleetwood Dock Company determined to
suspend all operations barely six months after they had been
begun, and it is scarcely necessary to inform our readers that the
work was never resumed under the same proprietorship. Two
years subsequently, in 1871, the Lancashire and Yorkshire Railway Company obtained an act of parliament to carry out, on a
larger scale, the undertaking which their predecessors had
abandoned almost in its birth. The dock, which embraces an
area of nearly ten acres, being one thousand feet long, by four
hundred feet wide, has already been in course of formation for
more than two years, and although the labour is being pushed
forward by the contractors, Messrs. John Aird and Sons, of
Lambeth, with as much expedition as is consistent with good
workmanship, the completion of this much-needed accommodation
is not expected until some time in 1877. The dock walls are built
with square blocks of stone, surmounted by a broad and massive
coping of Cornish granite, and filled in behind with concrete, the
whole having an altitude of thirty-one feet, and being placed on a
solid concrete foundation fourteen feet wide. The walls themselves vary in width as they approach the surface, being in the

lower half of their distance $12\frac{1}{2}$ feet, then $10\frac{1}{2}$ feet, and in the highest section $8\frac{1}{2}$ feet wide. The lock entrance communicates with the north extremity of the dock, and is two hundred and fifty feet long by fifty feet wide, being protected at each end by gates, opening, respectively, into the dock and the channel now in process of excavation to the bed of the river Wyre. Lying to the south of the dock is the recently-constructed timber pond, covering an area of $14\frac{1}{2}$ or 15 acres, and having a depth of 15 feet. The pond is connected with the dock by means of a gateway, so arranged in the southern wall of the latter that two feet of water will always remain in the former after the tide has ebbed below the level of its floor. The timber pond has no other entrance beyond the one alluded to. Sir John Hawkshaw, previously mentioned in connection with the visit of Queen Victoria to Fleetwood, is the eminent engineer from whose designs the dock is being constructed.

The prospect, or indeed certainty, of materially increased trade when the dock is thrown open has not been without effect upon the town generally, but its stimulating influence is most remarkable in the large number of houses which, during the last few years, have sprung into being. Streets have been lined with habitations where recently not a dwelling existed, and others have had their vacant spaces filled in with buildings. Handsome shops have been erected in Dock Street, East and West Streets, and other localities, whilst many of the residences in Church Street have been remodeled and converted into similar retail establishments. Everywhere there is a spirit of activity visible, contrasting most pleasingly and favourably with the passive inertitia which pervaded the place for a considerable period previous to the commencement of the dock operations. In 1875 the commissioners determined to do something towards protecting the northern aspect of the Mount from the devastations of the waves, whose boisterous familiarity had already inflicted serious injury on its feeble sandy sides, and seemed disposed, if much longer unchecked, to reduce the venerable pile to a mere matter of history. A public promenade, fenced with a substantial wall of concrete, was laid out at the base of the hill, extending from near the west extremity of the Mount Terrace to the commencement of Abbot's Walk. The damaged side of the mound itself has been levelled and sown with grass-seed, so that in course of time the marine walk will have a lofty sloping background of green sward, and form the prettiest, as it was doubtless the most needed, object in the neighbourhood.

On the 1st of January, 1875, a number of gentlemen, denominated the Fleetwood Estate Company, Limited, and consisting of Sir Jno. Hawkshaw, knt., of Westminster ; Thos. H. Carr, J. M. Jameson, C.E., and Philip Turner, esqrs., of Fleetwood ; Capt. Henry Turner and Sturges Meek, esq., C.E., of Manchester ; Thomas Barnes, esq., of Farnworth ; James Whitehead, esq., of Preston ; Joshua Radcliffe, esq., of Rochdale ; Samuel Burgess, esq., of Altringham ; William Barber Buddicom, esq., C.E., of Penbedw, Mold ; and Samuel Fielden, esq., of Todmorden ; purchased the lands, buildings, manorial rights and privileges (including wreckage, market-tolls, and advowson of the church), of the late Sir P. H. Fleetwood, in and near this town, from the trustees of his property, for £120,000, subscribed in equal shares. Although negotiations were satisfactorily concluded in 1874, it was not until the month just stated that the actual transfer was effected, and the gentlemen enumerated became lords of the soil. We must not omit to name that portion a of the Fleetwood estate, amounting to about 600 acres, lying between the old and present railway embankments, had been acquired in a similar manner, for £25,000, in 1871, by the Lancashire and Yorkshire Railway Company. Under the new proprietorship leases for building purposes are sold or let, as formerly, for terms of 999 years.

In closing this account of Fleetwood as a watering-place and town, and before delineating its career as a seaport, it should be stated that the census of the inhabitants taken in 1871 yielded a total of 4,428 persons, of whom 2,310 were males, and 2,118 females ; but in the limited period which has elapsed since that result was obtained the population has grown considerably, and the increase during a similar interval after any of the previous official returns cannot be taken as a criterion of the present numerical strength of the residents.

Fleetwood was started in 1839 as a distinct port with customs established by an order of the Treasury ; subsequently in 1844 it was reduced to a creek under Preston ; then two years later elevated to a sub-port ; and finally in 1849 reinstated in its first position of independence. The iron wharf was completed in 1841, and is constructed of iron piles, each of which weighs two and three quarter tons, driven seventeen feet below low water mark, and faced with plates of the same metal, seven or eight inches thick, which are rivetted to the flanges of the piles, and filled in at the back with concrete. The wooden pier, about 400 feet in length, and abutting on the north extremity of this massive structure, was finished in 1845, and roofed over shortly afterwards. On the 22nd of July in the ensuing year, the last stone of the wharf wall, erected by Mr. Julian A. Tarner, of Fleetwood, and extending fourteen hundred feet from the south end of the iron wharf in the direction of the railway, was laid ; and at the same time the coal-shoots connected with the new portion of the quay were approaching completion.

The improvement of the harbour was entrusted to Captain Denham, R.N., F.R.S., under whose superintendence the seaward channel of the river was buoyed and beaconed, being rendered safe for night navigation by the erection of a marine lighthouse, in 1840, at the foot of Wyre, nearly two miles from the mouth of the river at Fleetwood. This lighthouse was the first one erected on Mitchell's screw-pile principle. The house in which the light-keepers lived was hexagonal in form, and measured 22 feet in diameter, from angle to angle, and nine feet in height. It was furnished with an outside door and three windows ; and divided within into two compartments, one of which was supplied with a fireplace and other necessaries, whilst the second was used purely as a dormitory. The lantern was twelve-sided, 10 feet in diameter and 8 feet in height to the top of the window, the illumination it produced being raised about 31 feet above the level of the highest spring-tide, and $44\frac{1}{2}$ feet above that of half-tide. A few years since, in 1870, this lighthouse was carried away by a vessel, and for some time a light-ship occupied the station, but subsequently another edifice, similar in appearance and construction to the original one, was raised about two hundred yards south of the same site.

Captain Denham, having accomplished his survey of the river and harbour, issued the following report in 1840 :—

"The river Wyre assumes a river character near Bleasdale Forest, in Lancashire, and after crossing the line of road between Preston and Lancaster, at

Garstang, descends as a tortuous stream for five miles westward ; then, in another five mile reach of one-third of a mile wide, north-westward, sweeping the light of Skippool, near Poulton-le-Fylde, on its way, and bursting forth from the narrows at Wardleys, upon a north trend, into the tidal estuary which embraces an area of three miles by two, producing a combined reflux of back-water, equal to fifty million cubical yards, and dipping with such a powerful *under-scour* during the first half-ebb, as to preserve a natural basin just within its coast-line orifice, capable of riding ships of eighteen or twenty feet draft, at *low water spring tides ;* perfectly sheltered from all winds, and within a cable's length of the railway terminus, nineteen miles from Preston, and in connection with Manchester, Lancaster, Liverpool, and London. It is on the western margin of this natural dock that the town, wharfs, and warehouses are rising into notice, under the privilege of a distinct port, and abreast of which, the shores aptly narrow the *back-water escape* into a bottle-neck strait of but one-sixth the width of the estuary, so impelling it down a two-mile channel as scarcely to permit diminishment of its three and four-mile velocity until actually blended with the *cross-set* of the Lune and Morecambe Bay ebb waters. Thus, the original short course of Wyre to the open sea, is freed from the usual river deposit, its silting matter being kept in suspension until transferred and hurried forth at right angles by the ocean stream. It is, therefore, the peculiar feature and fortune of Wyre that, instead of a *bar* intervening between its bed or exit trough and the open sea, a precipitous river shelf, equal to a fall of forty-seven feet in one-third of a mile, exists."

The first steam dredger, of 20 horse power, was launched on the 21st of January, 1840, and the important work of deepening and clearing the channel at once commenced.

At a meeting of the Tidal Harbour Commissioners held at the port on the 21st October, 1845, it was stated that the harbour dues were—for coasting vessels, 1d. per ton, and for foreign ships, 3d. per ton ; whilst the light charges were in all cases 3d. per ton. At the same time it was observed that the whole of the dues amounted in 1835 to £36 2s. od., and in 1845 to £528 9s. 5d. (In 1855 the dues on similar accounts reached £1,520 ; and in 1875, £2,427.) The Walney light was reported to be a great tax on vessels coming to Fleetwood, as they were charged 3d. a ton per year, commencing on the 1st of January ; so that if a vessel arrived at the port on the 28th of December, a charge was made for the year just closing, and a further sum demanded from the craft on going out in the month of January. This was not the case with regard to similar taxes in other localities, where one payment exempted a ship for twelve months ; and consequently the regulation acted in some degree as a deterrent to traders, who might under a more liberal arrangement have been induced to have availed themselves in larger numbers of the facilities offered by the new haven. The total length of useful wharfage in 1845 extended over 1,000 feet, being well supplied with posts and rings, and possessing no less than sixteen hand cranes, thirteen of which were for the purpose of unloading vessels at the quay. There was a depth of five feet at low-water spring tides from the marine lighthouse, at the foot of Wyre, to the wharf, and it was proposed to dredge until ten feet had been obtained.

On examining the state of the shipping trade of the harbour during the year 1845, it is discovered that the imports and exports of foreign produce and home manufacture, respectively, far out-stripped those of any of the few preceding years. There had been vessels laden with guano from Ichaboe, sugar from the West Indies, flax from Russia, and timber from both the Baltic and Canada, making in all twenty-three ships of large tonnage, only two of which returned with cargoes, in far from complete stages of fulness, from the warehouses of Manchester, Preston, or other adjacent commer-cial towns. The coasting trade had also given earnest of its pro-gressive tendencies by a remarkable increase in the number of discharges and loadings over those of the previous twelve months, and notwithstanding the four hundred feet of extra wharfage, forming the wooden pier, just opened, the demands for quay berths could not always be supplied.

New bonding warehouses were erected towards the close of 1845 at the corner of Adelaide and Dock Streets, the temporary ones previously in use being abandoned, and comprised three stories capable of providing accommodation for 400 hogsheads of sugar at one time, as well as spacious vaults and other con-veniences for duty-bearing articles. The goods allowed to be warehoused were wine, spirits, tea, tobacco, East India goods, and goods in general.

In 1846 prosperity continued to reward the efforts put forth by the authorities of the young haven. Twelve vessels arrived from America with timber, and nine similarly laden from the Baltic ; tobacco, sugar, and other commodities were imported in two ships from the Indies ; but the event which kindled the brightest anticipations in the breasts of the inhabitants and others interested in the success of the port was the arrival of the barque "Diogenes," chartered by Mr. Evans, of Chipping, with the first cargo of cotton ever landed at Fleetwood. In it was welcomed an introduction to the chief trade of the county, and a happy augury of future activity in an import which would not only of itself materially assist the financial condition of the harbour, but would also be the means of spreading its reputation throughout the commercial world, and extending its field of action to a degree which could scarcely be foretold. How these pleasant visions have been fulfilled the reader is perhaps aware, but if not a glance at the tables of coasting and foreign trade, given a little later, will furnish the necessary information. On the 12th of February, immediately the novel consignment just referred to, which "afforded a suitable opportunity," had come to hand, a public dinner was given by their fellow-townsmen to Frederick Kemp and John Laidlay, esqrs., as a mark of respect for their assiduous efforts to develope the mercantile resources of the place. During the evening Mr. Laidlay remarked that "within a short period the trading intercourse of the port had extended to various and distant portions of the world, the products of Africa, the West Indies, and North America having been imported ; and stretching our arm still further, a cargo from the East Indies may be stated as almost within our grasp." Mr. Evans, in alluding to his transatlantic shipment, affirmed that in bringing it by way of Fleetwood, he had effected a saving of at least a farthing per pound ; and continued,—"When the order was given, it could not have been imported into Liverpool without loss."

In the latter part of the year a testimonial was presented by the inhabitants of the town to Henry Smith, esq., of Fleetwood, manager of the North Lancashire Steam Navigation Company, as a tribute to his untiring and successful attempts to promote steamship traffic and advance the interests of the place, and in the course of a speech made on the occasion, Mr. Smith said :— "In 1842 I first visited Fleetwood at the request of the London board of directors, it then presented a most gloomy aspect—a splendid modern ruin, no shipping, no steamers, no passengers for the trains, and yet it required no very keen discernment to learn that all the facilities for trade and commerce existed here, but life was wanting ; here was one of the finest and safest harbours, certainly the best lighted and marked port on the west coast, being as easily made by night as by day, with that wonderful natural phenomenon, the Lune Deep, making it a safety port to take in fog by sounding—a thing having no parellel in England. * * * * * * What changes have we witnessed here since 1842? I have seen your population without employment, and now there is more work than there are hands to perform—the wages from one shilling a day have advanced to two shillings and sixpence and three shillings ; then indeed was your port without a ship, now there is a general demand for more quay room, although since then upwards of 1,000 feet have been added to the wharfage; then your railway receipts were £100, this year they have attained £1,500 per week." This unfortunate gentleman was killed in the June following, through a collison on the London and North Western Railway ; and there can be no hesitation in affirming that, had his career of usefulness and activity not been thus prematurely cut short, the trade of Fleetwood would have developed, in the long period which has elapsed since his death, into something more important than it presents to day.

The following authentic returns of the whole business of the port in 1846 forms a favourable comparison with those of 1840, the year in which the railway was opened, when they amounted to 57,051 tons of imports, the exports being proportionately small:—

COASTING.

		IMPORTS.			EXPORTS.		
1846.	January	... 59 ships	...... 11,564 tons.	59 ships	...... 11,875 tons.
„	February	... 60 „	...... 11,251 „	62 „	...... 11,208 „
„	March	.... 72 „	...... 11,252 „	70 „	...... 11,289 „
„	April	.... 63 „	...... 10,971 „	66 „	...... 11,098 „
„	May	.... 61 „	...... 11,539 „	121 „	...... 11,790 „
„	June	.... 61 „	...... 10,637 „	97 „	...... 14,715 „
„	July	.... 81 „	...... 13,413 „	94 „	...... 14,274 „
„	August	...... 80 „	...... 13,194 „	93 „	...... 16,042 „
„	September	... 94 „	...... 13,515 „	65 „	...... 11,609 „
„	October	...... 64 „	...... 11,472 „	71 „	...... 13,158 „
„	November	... 63 „	...... 11,094 „	51 „	...... 8,619 „
„	December	... 41 „	...... 7,785 „	not obtained.	

	799 ships	......137,687 tons.	849 ships	......135,677 tons.
Foreign	.... 24 „	...... 6,935 „	13 „	...... 2,703 „

Total................823 ships ......144,622 tons.   862 ships ..... 138,380 tons.

The animated appearance of the harbour was described in 1846 by a gentleman connected with the town, as here quoted :—

"With two Indiamen at their berths, the splendid steamers alongside, schooners, small craft innumerable dotting the river, wharfmen, porters, etc., removing merchandise from vessel to wagon, and *vice versa*, the cranes in constant operation, goods-trains arriving and preparing for departure, give the pier-head and harbour an air of bustle and activity, and are themselves a pleasing indication of what our commerce may become ; of the trade which vigilance, patience, and effort, may secure to the harbour and railway."

The twelve months of 1847 proved anything but a re-assuring time. The foreign imports suddenly fell off to six cargoes, four of which were timber from America, the two remaining being guano and timber from Hamburg. One left for Mexico and Hong Kong, laden with British goods, silk, wine, and spirits from the bonding warehouses. The coasting returns also showed a diminution of almost fifty discharges at the quay, as compared with the previous year, and a corresponding decrease in the exports ; but in spite of the sudden dispiriting experience, we find from the annexed extract out of the annual official report concerning the harbour, that the future was regarded hopefully :—"There is every probability of the business increasing at this Port, as an extensive trade with the Baltic is expected, and most of the goods now in warehouse under bond will no doubt be taken out for home consumption during the present year." 1848 was marked by an increase of nine in the number of foreign importations ; and of the fifteen large vessels which arrived, one was from France with wines and spirits for re-exportation to Mexico, two were from the Baltic and Hamburg with timber, eleven from Canada with timber, and one from Russia with flax. The importers of timber carried on, and used sedulous efforts to extend, a healthy retail trade in the adjoining districts and in the west of Yorkshire. The export trade was still inconsiderable, although gradually increasing, but it was expected, from the convenient situation of the harbour to the manufacturing towns, and the local dues upon vessels and goods being much lower than at other ports, that both it and the imports would, before many years had passed over, become very extensive, more especially as the Lancashire and Yorkshire Railway Company had recently acquired a right to the line between Fleetwood and Preston, and were offering every facility and inducement to

R

shippers and manufacturers, with the view of making this haven the inlet and outlet for goods to and from the towns and villages on their several lines. During the twelve months eighteen small importations of paper from the Isle of Man took place, and it was necessary for the officers connected with the customs to keep a strict guard upon the wharf to prevent the smuggling of that and other dutiable articles by the numerous passenger and coasting vessels from the above island, as well as from Scotland and Ireland.

In 1849 the foreign imports were more than doubled, the excess being chiefly due to the increase of timber-laden vessels. Six of the total number sailed outwards with cargoes of warehoused goods, and nine with coal and salt. The coasting trade underwent a most remarkable rise of about four hundred cargoes inwards, and two hundred outwards, the principal of the former being iron ore, pig iron, and, more occasionally, grain ; and of the latter, coal. The barque " Isabella " discharged 609 bales of cotton at Fleetwood from America in July, 1850, being the second cargo landed here, and later in the year another consignment of 400 bales was brought by the same vessel. In 1851 the only novel feature was the arrival of a large shipload of currants ; the value of British goods exported amounted to £90,000, besides which there were considerable quantities of merchandise sent outwards from bond. The main foreign business in 1852 was in timber and dried fruits, but such importations were seriously diminished during the ensuing year by the high price of the latter and by a temporary misunderstanding between the railway company and one of the chief timber merchants, through which several consignments intended for the Wyre were diverted elsewhere ; in addition five large cargoes were lost at sea and not replaced. The coasting trade continued to expand until 1856, when its zenith was reached, since when it has been characterised by a gradual decline, and the last report, that of 1875, is as little encouraging as any, with one exception, of its degenerate predecessors. The fourth freight of cotton, consisting of 1,327 bales, made its appearance in the ship " Cleopatra," in the spring of 1857, and was consigned to Messrs. Benjamin Whitworth and Brothers, of Manchester, etc. Shortly afterwards, barely two weeks, the " Favourite " arrived with a further consignment for the same firm, and gave the signal for the real commencement of a prosperous trade in that commodity with America, which rapidly developed until the outbreak of civil war in the transatlantic continent brought it somewhat abruptly to a close in 1862. In a comparative statement of charges between Liverpool and Fleetwood, issued during that flourishing time, it was demonstrated that on a vessel of 500 tons, cotton in and coals out, the following saving in favour of this port could be effected :—

	£	s.	d.
Charges on Ship	66	0	0
„ on Cargo inwards	96	8	4
„ on Cargo outwards	8	6	8
Total saving	£170	15	0

Supposing the cargo to have been consigned to parties in Preston, a further advantage, amounted to £230 0s. 0d. in carriage would be gained, raising the entire saving to £400 15s. 0d.

During late years, the business firm just alluded to, whose interests in, and efforts for, the welfare of the port have so long been unflagging, has made a vigorous attempt to revive the American cotton importations. For the last few seasons several of their shipments, about ten, have annually arrived, and there is every prospect that when the dock is completed many more vessels will be chartered. A large shed for the reception of cotton was erected in 1875, in Adelaide Street, by Messrs. B. Whitworth and Bros., who have also established a permanent office in the town.

In 1859 the trade between Fleetwood and Belfast had developed to such an extent that a larger covered area for the temporary warehousing, loading, and discharging of goods was urgently called for, and towards the close of that year a space of about 190 feet in length, by 30 feet wide, was walled in and roofed over on the quay, adjoining the building then in use for the same purposes. Four years later, in 1863, two steam cranes were placed on the wharf by the North Lancashire Steam Navigation Company. Subsequently other cranes, working on a similar principle, have been added to those experimental ones, and gradually the old system of hand-labour at the quay-side has been superseded by the adoption of this more expeditious and economical plan. Shortly before the last-named facilities had augmented the conveniences of the wharf, a fresh description of mooring appliance was laid down in the harbour, and consisted of two longitudinal ground chains of 1,000 feet each, attached at intervals of 50 feet to two sets of Mitchell's screws, which were worked into the clay in the bed of the stream. The bridle chains, shackled above to the mooring buoys, were secured below to the ground links between the attachments of the screws, the buoys being so arranged that each vessel was held stem and stern, instead of swinging round with the tide, or stranding with one end on the large central sandbank, as heretofore.

From 1862 to the present date, the story of the haven, with the exceptions of the trawling fleet and the Belfast line, which will be treated of directly, is not one which will awaken envy in the breasts of those whose interests are bound up in rival ports, nor indeed can it be a source of congratulation to those whose interests might ordinarily be supposed to be best promoted by its prosperity. It is true that the foreign trade for seven years after 1862 was in a state of fluctuation rather than actual decline, but the three succeeding years were stationary at the low figure of 21 imports each, after which there was a slight improvement, raising the annual numbers to 24, 32, and, in 1875, 33, due more to the staunch allegiance of Messrs. B. Whitworth and Bros., whose cotton again appeared on the wharf, than to any inducements offered to them or others by increased facilities or more appropriate accommodation. The coasting trade has already been referred to, so that there is no necessity to recapitulate facts but just laid before our readers. It is proper, however, to mention a few statistics respecting the trade in exports of coal, the chief business, and below are given the numbers of tons shipped, mostly to Ireland, in each of the specified years :—

1855	31,490	1869	24,741
1860	23,652	1870	43,653
1865	16,225	1871	51,473
1866	12,315	1872	54,794
1867	10,912	1873	55,447
1868	6,809	1874	56,939
	1875	71,353.	

The large and sudden increase from 1869 is mainly owing to several screw steamships having been extensively engaged in the traffic, and there is every probability, from the addition within the last few months of a new and handsome coal-screw, and

other indications, that this branch of commerce will continue
to develope with equal, if not greater, rapidity. Again, it
should be remembered, when considering the falling off in the
numerical strength of the coasting vessels trading here, that
those now plying are of much greater carrying capacity than
formerly, and consequently the actual exports and imports have
not suffered diminution in anything like the same proportion
as the ships themselves. A series of tabular statements of all
the most important and interesting matters connected with the
harbour from the earliest obtainable dates has been prepared
from the official returns made to the custom-house during each
twelve months, and subjoined will be found a list of the vessels
retained on the register as belonging to the port at the end of the
years indicated, with their tonnages and the number of hands
forming the crews :—

Year.	Steam Vessels.	Tonnage.	Hands.	Sailing Vessels.	Tonnage.	Hands.
1850	3	739	49	15	560	54
1851	3	739	49	21	856	77
1852	3	739	49	24	1495	104
1853	4	806	54	31	4002	196
1854	2	560	32	41	5337	261
1855	3	586	35	49	4933	267
1856	4	978	52	51	5458	280
1857	3	952	49	71	7839	391
1858	4	968	54	79	8168	427
1859	4	968	54	76	6930	392
1860	4	968	54	84	12075	570
1861	5	1508	74	93	14760	640
1862	4	1249	62	89	13957	602
1863	4	1249	62	85	12147	567
1864	5	1355	71	81	10338	513
1865	6	1372	74	83	9757	479
1866	6	1372	74	80	8831	454
1867	6	1779	90	77	9265	451
1868	6	1779	90	85	11226	515
1869	5	1239	70	99	12601	587
1870	7	1797	93	104	12546	609
1871	7	1571	81	115	13642	690
1872	7	1571	81	133	15161	789
1873	7	1994	92	150	19379	947
1874	7	1994	122	162	22598	1045
1875	9	2671	160	165	22655	1061

The foregoing tables, taken by themselves, would seem to

imply that from the year 1868, the business of the place had
been characterised by a rapid and most satisfactory increase, but
unfortunately for such a deduction, the ships registered as
belonging to any port afford no clue to the number actually
engaged in traffic there, hence it happens that many vessels
hailing from Fleetwood, as their maternal port, are seldom to be
observed in its waters.

The following are the annual records of the foreign and coasting
trade of the harbour, in which the Belfast and all other steamships
are included under the latter heading:—

VESSELS WITH CARGOES.

Year.	FOREIGN TRADE. Inwards.	Outwards.	COASTING TRADE. Inwards.	Outwards.
1844	8	1	436	327
1845	23	2	580	473
1846	24	13	799	927
1847	6	1	752	913
1848	15	5	873	857
1849	36	15	1247	1059
1850	38	14	986	1014
1851	35	13	943	932
1852	32	12	951	823
1853	22	7	1093	919
1854	23	6	1119	983
1855	21	4	1101	971
1856	10	4	1181	1120
1857	18	7	1130	1150
1858	26	13	1020	986
1859	38	20	1023	865
1860	71	30	1123	813
1861	68	28	953	713
1862	41	7	884	560
1863	27	10	795	615
1864	35	6	783	610
1865	29	2	868	623
1866	39	2	762	612
1867	37	4	737	573
1868	26	3	689	512
1869	28	3	730	512
1870	21	4	694	573
1871	20	6	545	526
1872	21	3	697	621
1873	24	3	696	670
1874	32	6	703	587
1875	33	2	659	589

The particulars given below, concerning the vessels belonging to Fleetwood, will form an interesting and useful accompaniment to the foregoing :—

Year.	New Vessels[1] Registered.		Lost at Sea.		Broken-up (condemned).		Transferred to other Ports.	
	No.	Tons.	No.	Tons.	No.	Tons.	No.	Tons.
1850	—	—	—	—	—	—	—	—
1851	—	—	1	83	—	—	1	27
1852	—	—	—	—	—	—	—	—
1853	3	199	2	62	—	—	1	44
1854	1	128	—	—	—	—	8	1003
1855	2	104	1	595	—	—	5	562
1856	3	484	1	23	—	—	4	294
1857	8	364	1	26	—	—	—	—
1858	5	239	4	1050	—	—	1	54
1859	3	97	5	739	—	—	3	726
1860	3	865	—	—	1	29	2	74
1861	8	1012	—	—	—	—	7	518
1862	5	534	1	416	—	—	12	1844
1863	2	226	4	1308	—	—	4	318
1864	2	201	9	3363	—	—	3	666
1865	2	273	1	538	—	—	2	517
1866	4	520	5	1449	1	16	2	64
1867	3	439	6	605	—	—	2	214
1868	5	588	—	—	—	—	—	—
1869	6	512	1	518	—	—	—	—
1870	8	1610	2	683	2	65	1	424
1871	10	991	—	—	—	—	2	339
1872	15	1588	3	427	—	—	1	42
1873	19	2921	6	1966	—	—	2	120
1874	15	2928	5	2304	1	32	—	—
1875	9	2410	4	2021	1	16	4	300

Now that the dock is no longer a mere word and promise, but has at length a definite signification and a material existence, there is every appearance that those into whose hands the fortunes of the port may be said to have been entrusted have no intention of any dilatory action in furthering the interests of their charge. Already, in 1875, a powerful steam dredger has been purchased at a cost of £12,000 and set to its labours in the channel and harbour. This dredger, which has superseded the older and much smaller one, launched in 1840 and

1. Newly-built vessels registered for the first time, the other vessels belonging to the harbour being transferred from other parts and re-registered here.

used until recently, was built by Simonds and Company, of Renfrew, on the Clyde, and is of 100-horse power, being capable of raising 250 tons of sand, shingle, etc., in an hour. In addition it is able to work in twenty-six feet of water, whereas the original one was obliged to wait until the tide had ebbed to fourteen feet before operations could be commenced, so that really the work which can be accomplished by the new machine is out of all proportion to that which its predecessor could effect. Several iron pontoons, or lighters, furnished with false bottoms to expedite the business of discharging them, formerly performed by hand and spade, have also been obtained ; and the bed of the river seaward from Fleetwood is rapidly being relieved of its super-abundance of tidal deposits and scourings, which is carried by the lighters beyond the marine lighthouse at the foot of the Wyre and deposited in the Lune.

Steamboat traffic was, and is, the most important branch of shipping connected with the port, but notwithstanding the support and encouragement which has been so freely extended to the Belfast line, sundry attempts by the same company to establish sea-communications between Fleetwood and other places have invariably ended in complete failures. In the context we have endeavoured to trace a brief outline of the steamship trade of the harbour from its earliest days up to our time. The North Lancashire Steam Navigation Company was established in 1843, and commenced operations by running the " Prince of Wales" and the " Princess Alice," two large and fast iron steamships for that date, between this port and Belfast on each Wednesday and Saturday evening, the return trips being made on the Monday and Friday. In that year, however, the number of trips was increased to three per week, the fares for the single journey being, saloon, 15s. ; and deck, 3s. Another steamship the " Robert Napier," of 220 horse-power, sailed also from Fleetwood in 1843, every Friday morning, at 10 a.m. for Londonderry, calling at Portrush, and returned on Tuesday, the fares being, cabin, 20s. ; and deck, 5s. In 1844 we find that communications, through the exertion and enterprise of the above company, were open between Fleetwood and Belfast, Londonderry, Ardrossan, and Dublin, respectively. The Ardrossan line consisted of two new iron steamboats, "Her Majesty," and the "Royal

Consort," each of which was 300 tons register, and 350 horse-power, the fares being, cabin, 17s.; and deck, 4s. The Dublin trip was performed once, and afterwards twice, a week each way, by the iron steamship "Hibernia," which called off Douglas, Isle of Man, to land passengers, but after a year's trial this communication was closed. In the summer of 1845, an Isle of Man line was opened by the steamship "Orion," which ran daily, except Sundays; and at the same season the Belfast boats commenced to make the double journey four days a week, whilst the London-derry route was abandoned. As early as 1840, on the completion of the Preston and Wyre Railway, a daily steam communication had been established to Bardsea, as the nearest point to Ulverston and the Lakes; and in the month of September, 1846, on the completion of Piel Pier, it was transferred to that harbour, and continued by the steamship "Ayrshire Lassie," of 100 horse-power, the fares being, saloon, 2s.; and deck, 1s. In the following year this boat was superseded by a new steamer, the "Helvellyn," of 50 tons register and 75 horse-power, which continued to ply for many years, in fact, almost until this summer line was closed, at a comparatively recent date, about eight or ten years ago. The Fleetwood and Ardrossan steamers discontinued running in 1847, and at the same time an extra boat, the "Fenella," was placed on the Isle of Man route, whilst the Belfast trips were reduced to three double journeys per week. After a few years experience the Isle of Man line, a season one only, was given up; but the Belfast trade, continually growing, soon obliged the company to increase the number of trips, and step by step to enlarge and improve the boat accommodation. We need not trace through its different stages the gradual and satisfactory progress of this line, but our object will be sufficiently attained by stating that the two steamships were shortly increased to three. Afterwards larger and finer boats, having greater power, took the places of the original ones, and at the present day the fleet consists of four fine steamers of fully double the capacity of the original ones, which cross the channel from each port every evening except Sunday.

In the year 1874 the whole of the interests of Frederick Kemp, esq., J.P., of Bispham Lodge, in the Fleetwood and Belfast steam line were acquired by the Lancashire and Yorkshire and

London and North Western Railway Companies, at that time owners of the larger share, and now practically sole proprietors. Up to the date of this transaction the vendor had been intimately and personally associated with the traffic as managing-owner from its first institution, in addition to which he was the chief promoter of the Ardrossan and Isle of Man routes.

With the solitary exception of the service whose progress has just been briefly traced out, there is perhaps no single branch of industry which has assisted so ably in maintaining and stimulating such prosperity as the town of Fleetwood has enjoyed, throughout its chequered career, as the fishing traffic. In the earliest years of the seaport, shortly before the Belfast steamer communication was established, a second pilot boat, named the " Pursuit," arrived in the river from Cowes, but finding little occupation the crew provided themselves with a trawl-net and turned their long periods of vigil to profitable account by its use. This sensible plan of launching out into another field of labour when opportunities of prosecuting their more legitimate avocation failed them was not of long duration, probably no more than a few months, for on the Irish line of steamships commencing to ply the pilots secured berths as second officers, and their boat was laid up. The "Pursuit" soon became a tender to a government ship engaged in surveying ; and about ten or twelve months later was purchased by some gentlemen, denominated the Fleetwood Fishing Company, and, together with four more boats, hired from North Meols, Southport, sent out on fishing excursions. At the end of one year the hired sloops were discharged, and five similar craft bought by the company, thus making a fleet of six smacks belonging to the place, connected with the trawling trade. In the course of three or four years the whole of the boats were sold, as the traffic had not proved so remunerative a venture as at first anticipated ; and one only remained in the harbour, being purchased by Mr. Robert Roskell, of this place. Shortly afterwards a Scotch smack arrived from Kirkcudbright, and in about twelve months the two boats were joined by three or four from North Meols, owned for the most part by a family named Leadbetter, which settled here. Almost simultaneously another batch of fishing craft made its appearance from the east coast and took up a permanent station at Fleetwood. The success which attended the expeditions of the deep-sea trawlers was not long in being rumoured abroad and attracting others, who were anxious to participate in an undertaking capable of producing such satisfactory results. Year by year the dimensions of the originally small fleet were developed as new-comers appeared upon the scene, and added their boats to those already actively prosecuting the trade. To trace minutely each gradation in the prosperous progress of this line of commerce would be wearisome to the reader, and is in no way necessary to the object we have in view. It will be sufficient for the purpose to state that in 1860 the number of fishing smacks on the Fleetwood station amounted to thirty-two, varying in tonnage from 25 to 50 tons each and built at an average cost of £500 each, the lowest being £400 and the highest £1,000. The following will illustrate the plan by which men in the humble sphere of fishermen were enabled to become the proprietors of their own craft: A shipmaster supplied the vessel on the understanding that £100 was deposited at once, and the remainder paid by quarterly instalments, no insurance being asked for or proffered regarding risk. The arrangement entered into by the smack-owners for the conveyance of fish to shore, when they were engaged out at sea in their calling was most simple and business-like. The boats kept company during fishing, and on a certain signal being given one of the number, according to a previous agreement, received the whole of the fish so far caught by her fellow craft and returned home, for which service her men were paid 2s. each by the other crews, who continued their occupation and arrived in harbour generally on Friday. For the next week another smack was selected, and thus all in turn performed the mid-week journey. At present there are no less than eighty-four sloops belonging to this port, pursuing the business of fishing, and the arrangements both for their purchase and the landing of the captured fish have undergone a revolution. All boats are now paid for when they leave the shipbuilder's yard, and the former custom of a mid-week relief, has been relinquished, each sloop returning and discharging as occasion requires. A fishing boat's crew usually consists of four men and a boy. In conclusion it should be noticed that a special warehouse, about 90 feet long, was erected in 1859, solely for the use of the fishermen and agents, or dealers, connected with the trade.

CHAPTER IX.

THORNTON, CARLETON, MARTON, AND HARDON-WITH-NEWTON.

TORENTUM, or Thornton, was estimated in the time of William the Conqueror to contain six carucates of land fit for the plough, but this computation was exclusive of Rossall and Burn, which were valued at two carucates respectively, so that the whole townships held ten carucates, about one thousand acres of arable soil, or farming land, a large amount for those days, but insignificant indeed when we recall the nine thousand seven hundred and thirty acres embraced by the township at present, either in use for grazing and agricultural purposes, or forming the sites of town and village buildings.

Thornton was held immediately after the Conquest by Roger de Poictou, and subsequently by Theobald Walter, after whose death it passed to the crown.

During the reign of King John, Margaret Wynewick held two of the six carucates of Torentum, or Thornton, in chief from that monarch, and her marriage was in his gift. In 1214-15 Baldewinus Blundus paid twenty marks to John for permission to espouse the lady and gain possession of her estate.[1] The request was granted conditionally on Blundus obtaining the consent of her friends; and in this he appears to have been successful, for we learn from a writ to the warden of the Honor of Lancaster in 1221, that Michael de Carleton paid a fine of ten

1. Rot. Lit. Claus. 16 John, m. 7.

marks to Henry III. at that date for having married Margaret, the daughter and heiress of William de Winewick, without the royal assent, and for marrying whom Baldewinus Blundus had formerly paid twenty marks to King John.[1]

In 1258, Margaret de Carleton still retained her lands in Thornton in her maiden name of Winewick,[2] and it is probable from that circumstance that her second husband was then dead, for the writ cited above expressly commanded that her inheritance should be handed over to Michael de Carleton, the penalty of ten marks for his disobedience having been received.

According to the *Testa de Nevil*, Matilda de Thorneton, a spinster, whose marriage also lay in the king's gift, held lands in Thornton, of the annual value of twenty shillings ; and later, about 1323, a moiety of Thornton was held by Lawrence, the son of Robert de Thorneton, a member of the same family. In 1346, John, son of Lawrence de Thorneton, held one carucate of land in Thornton and Staynolfe, lately of Robert Windewike, in thanage, paying yearly at four terms thirteen shillings relief, and suit to the county and wapentake.[3] In 1421 John de Thornton died, possessed of half the manor of Thornton and the Holmes, which descended to his son, William de Thornton, who died in 1429, aged thirty years, leaving four daughters—Agnes, afterwards the wife of William Wodey ; Katherine, who married William Carleton ; Elizabeth, the wife of Robert Adlington ; and Johanna, who espoused Christopher Worthington.[4] Much as it is to be regretted, no more than the scanty information here given can be discovered concerning the Thorntons, of Thornton ; even tradition is silent on the matter of their residence or local associations, although it is very likely they occupied Thornton Hall, a mansion long since converted into a farm house, and consequently we are obliged to dismiss with this brief notice what under more favourable auspices would probably have proved one of the most interesting subjects in the township, In 1292 the king's attorney sued Thomas de Singleton for the manor of Thornton, etc., but the defendant pleaded successfully, that he only held a portion of the manor, Thomas de Clifton and Katherine, his wife, holding the third of two parts of twelve

1. Rot. Finium 5 Henry III. m. 8.   2. Escaet. 42 Henry III. n. 11.
  3. Survey of Lancashire ending in 1346.   4. Visitation of St. George.

bovates of the soil.[1] In the seventeenth year of the reign of
Edward II., William, father of Adam Banastre, who granted
certain concessions to the prior of Lancaster, held, half the vill of
of Thornton, the other half being held, as before shown, by
Lawrence de Thorneton.

In an ancient survey of the Hundred of Amounderness, completed in the year 1346, it is stated that the following gentlemen
had possessions in the place called Stena, or Stainall, in Thornton,
at the rentals specified :—John de Staynolfe held four oxgangs of
land, at four shillings and sixpence ;[2] Roger de Northcrope, one
messuage and one oxgang, at sevenpence halfpenny ; Sir Adam
Banastre, knt., five acres, at fourpence ; Thomas, the son of Robert
Staynolfe, one messuage and one oxgang, at sevenpence halfpenny ; William Lawrence, a fourth part of an oxgang, at sixteen
pence ; Thomas Travers, a fourth part of an oxgang, at sixteen
pence ; John Botiler, a fourth part of an oxgang, at sixteen
pence ; and Richard Doggeson, five acres, at sixpence. William
de Heton held one carucate of land at Burn, in Thornton township, for which he paid yearly at two terms, Annunciation and
Michaelmas, ten shillings relief, and suit to the county and
wapentake.[3]

In 1521, during the sovereignty of Henry VIII., Thomas, earl
of Derby, was lord of the manor of Thornton, which subsequently passed into the hands of the Fleetwoods, of Rossall, who
retained it until the lifetime of the late Sir Peter Hesketh Fleetwood, bart., when it was sold. Thornton has for long been
regarded only as a reputed manor. The largest land proprietors
at present are the Fleetwood Estate Company, Limited, and the
trustees of the late John Horrocks, esq., of Preston, but in
addition there is a number of smaller soil-owners and resident
yeomen. Burn Hall is a building of the fifteenth century, and
was occupied in 1556 by John Westby, of Mowbreck, the owner.[4]
In 1323 the land of Burn was held by William Banastre at a
rental of ten shillings per annum, and about 1346 one carucate of
the same land was held, as already stated, by William de Heton

1. Placit de Quo Warr. 20 Edw. I. Lanc. Rot. 13d.
2. An oxgang is as much land as an ox can plough in a year, something considerably less than a carucate, which is estimated at one hundred acres.
3. Chethem Soc. Series, No. lxxiv. p. 57.
4.—For " Westby of Burn Hall" see Chapter VI.

for a similar yearly payment. Within the residence of Burn was a domestic chapel, over the doorway of which stood a polished oaken slab or board inscribed—"Elegi abjectus esse in domo Dei mei, magis quam habitari in tabernaculis peccatorum."[1] The walls were panelled with oak and carved with shields and foliage, whilst the ceiling was embellished with representations of vine leaves and clusters of grapes. Modern alterations have destroyed most, if not all, interesting relics of past ages. After the death of John Westby, of Burn Hall, a descendant of the John Westby before mentioned, in 1722, Burn passed to the Rev. J. Bennison, of London, who had married Anne, his fourth daughter. It is said that Mr. Bennison utterly ruined his property, by attempting a style of agriculture similar to that described by Virgil in his Georgics. Burn Hall is now, and has been for many years a farm-house, and the estate forms part of the large tract held by the representatives of the late John Horrocks, esq. The land lying towards the coast was formerly subject to occasional inundations of the sea, but an effectual barrier has been put by raising a mound round such exposed localities.

The extensive area known as Thornton Marsh, was a free open common, used as a pasture by the poor cottagers of the township until 1800, when it was enclosed, together with Carleton Marsh, and has since by cultivation been converted into valuable and productive fields.

A church and parsonage house were erected at Thornton in 1835, the former being a neat whitewashed building in the early English style of architecture, with a low square tower, but presenting externally no special features of attraction beyond its profuse covering of ivy, which renders it a most picturesque object in the surrounding landscape. The churchyard also is well worthy of notice, if only for the luxuriance of its foliage, the beauty of its flowers, and the taste and elegance exhibited in several of the monuments. This, like the church and parsonage, is embosomed in trees. The sacred edifice has been named Christ Church, and a separate parochial district was assigned to it in 1862, the title of vicar being accorded to the incumbent.

1.—" I had rather be a doorkeeper in the house of my God, than to dwell in the tents of wickedness."

CURATES AND VICARS OF THORNTON.

Date of Institution.	NAME.	Cause of vacancy.
1835	David H. Leighton.	
1837	Edward Thurtell.	Resignation of D. H. Leighton.
1841	St. Vincent Beechey, M.A.	„ „ E. Thurtell.
1846	Robert W. Russell.	„ „ St. V. Beechey.
1853	Isaac Durant, M.A.	„ „ W. Russell.
1869	Samuel Clark.	„ „ I. Durrant.
1870	Thomas Meadows, M.A.	„ „ S. Clark.

Within the building there is a small gallery at the west end, and the private pews are arranged in two rows, one being placed along each side of the body of the church, whilst the central portion is filled with open benches, or forms, free to all worshippers. A marble tablet " To the memory of Jacob Morris, a faithful warden for 20 years, who died Oct., 1871," is fixed against the south wall, and over the mantel-piece in the vestry is a white-lettered black board stating that—" This Church was erected in the year 1835, containing 323 sittings; and, in consequence of a grant from the Incorporated Society for promoting the enlargement, building, and repairing of churches and chapels, 193 of that number are hereby declared to be free and unappropriated for ever.—David Hilcock Leighton, minister ; James Smith and Richard Wright, church-wardens." On the font is the following inscription :—" Presented to Thornton Church by Elizabeth Nutter, of Rough Hall, Accrington, July 13th, 1874."

Mr. James Baines, of Poulton, by will dated 6th of January, 1717, devised to Peter Woodhouse, of Thornton, and six others, and their heirs, the school-house lately erected by him on Thornton Marsh, and the land whereon it stood, to be used for ever as a free school for the children of the township ; in addition he bequeathed to the same trustees several closes in Carleton, called the Far Hall Field, the Middle Hall Field, and the Vicar's Hey, amounting to about twenty-one acres, to the intent, that the annual revenue therefrom, less 10s. to be expended each year in a dinner for the trustees, should be devoted to the payment of a suitable master. In 1806, Richard Gaskell, the sole surviving trustee, conveyed by indenture to John Silcock, John Hull,

Thomas Barton, of Thornton, Charles Woodhouse of Great Carleton, Bickerstaff Hull, and Thomas Hull, and the said Richard Gaskell, their heirs and assigns, the premises above-mentioned, for the purposes set forth in the will of the founder.[1] A further endowment of £500 was left by Mr. Simpson, with a portion of which farm buildings have been erected on the school estate. The school-house is situated on the east side of Cleveleys Station, and consists of a small single-storey building, having two windows and a central doorway in front. To the west end is attached a two-storey teacher's residence. The double erection was built some years ago, by subscription amongst the inhabitants, on the site of the original fabric at a cost of rather more than £100. The master is elected and, when necessary, dismissed by the trustees, who forego their claim on the 10s. left for an annual dinner. In 1867 the number of scholars amounted to eighty-eight, fifty-nine of whom were boys, and twenty-nine girls, presenting about an average attendance since that date.

The small village of Thornton comprises only a limited cluster of dwellings and the old windmill. The Wesleyan Methodists had established a place of worship in the township as early as 1812, and about ten years later the Society of Friends opened a meeting-house here.

The arable land of Rossall, in Thornton township, or Rushale, as it was written, is estimated in the Domesday volume at two carucates. At that time Rossall was included amongst the princely possessions of the Norman baron, Roger de Poictou, after whose banishment it passed, by gift of Richard I., to Theobold Walter, and again reverted to the crown in 1206, on his demise. King John, at the instigation of Ranulph de Blundeville, earl of Chester and Lincoln, presented the grange of Rossall to the Staffordshire convent of Deulacres, a monastic house founded by that nobleman ; and in 1220-1 Henry III. issued a writ to the sheriff of this county, directing him to institute inquiries by discreet and lawful men, into the extent of several specified places, one of which was the pasture of Rossall, recently, "granted by my father, King John, to the abbot of Deulacres."[2] In 1227-8 a deed was drawn up between Henry III. and the abbot whereby

1. Charity Commissioners' Report.   2. Rot. Lit. Clause 5 Henry III., p. 474.

the grange was conveyed, or confirmed, to the latter[1] ; and twenty
years subsequently a fresh charter appears to have been framed
and to have received the royal signature, for in the following reign
of Edward I., when that monarch laid claim to the land as a
descendant of King John, the head of the Staffordshire convent
produced a document of 31 Henry III. (1247), at the trial, granting
"to God, the church of St. Mary, and the abbot of Deulacres and
his successors for ever, the manor of Rossall with its appurtenances
and with the wreck of the sea."[2] Sir Robert de Lathum, Sir
Robert de Holaund, Sir John de Burun, Sir Roger de Burton,
Sir John de Cornwall, Sir John de Elyas, and Sir Alan de
Penyngton, knights; Alan de Storeys, Robert de Eccleston,
William du Lee, Hugh de Clyderhou, and Roger de Middleton,
esquires, who composed the jury in the above suit, decided in
favour of the abbot's title, but at the request of the king's
attorney, judgment was arrested, and it was pleaded on behalf of
the regal claimant that the abbot's allegations seemed to imply
that the manor of Rossall was formerly held by the monks of
Deulacres in bailiwick of Kings, John and Henry ; that thirty
years at least of the reign of Henry had elapsed before the
predecessors of the present abbot held any fee or free tenement
in the manor, which was worth 100 marks per annum ; and
that this rent had been in arrears during the whole of the time ;
wherefore the king's attorney demanded that the accumulation
of these arrears, amounting to 3,000 marks, or £2,000, should
be paid by the abbey to Edward I. The jury stated in their
verdict that the manor had been held by the abbot's predecessors
as pleaded by the king's attorney, but that during the last seven
years of King John, and the first twenty-four years of Henry III.,
the manor was only worth 30 marks per annum, and in the
remaining six years before the date of the charter put in as
evidence by the abbot in the first trial, they valued the manor
at 40 marks per annum, on which scales the abbey of Deulacres
was condemned to pay the accumulated arrearages. In 1539,
during the reign of Henry VIII., the grange was valued in the
Compotus of the king's ministers at £13 6s. 3d. per annum.

The site of the original Hall has long since been washed away

1. Rot. Chart. 12 Henry III., m. 3.   2. Placit de Quo. Warr. 20 Edward I.

by the waves, but in earlier years, before the sea had made such encroachments on the land, the foundations of red sandstone and the remnant of an old ivied wall were visible near the edge of the cliff, all being sufficiently traceable to indicate that the mansion had been one of no mean dimensions. A coat of arms of the Fleetwood family, rudely engraven on a flat stone, some ornamental pinnacles, and other relics of the ancient edifice, have also been discovered at different times. Numerous foundations of large buildings were once scattered about the sandy soil of the grange, but most of them were removed eighty years since as impediments to the course of the plough. In a plot of ground, known by the title of "Churchyard field," remains of a structure, running east and west, in length thirty and in breadth twelve yards, were taken up about half a century or more ago by a farmer named John Ball, who whilst removing them came upon some human bones. The fabric once standing there was conjectured to have been a chapel or oratory, and the bones to have been those of priests or others buried within its precincts. Harrison, in describing the course of the Wyre, says "that at the Chapell of Allhallowes tenne myles from Garstone it goeth into the sea," and Mr. Thornber suggests, in his History of Blackpool and Neighbourhood, that the foundations disturbed by Mr. Ball may have been the remains of the oratory alluded to by the ancient topographer ; but whilst admitting that the character of the relics discovered points to there having been at one time a religious edifice on the site, we cannot think that its claims to be the missing chapel are nearly so great as those of Bispham, which is now known, by an inscription on an old communion goblet, to have been actually dedicated to All-Hallows, or at least to have been commonly designated by that name in the seventeenth century.

The Allens appear to have held Rossall on lease from the abbot of Deulacres about a century after the dispute between that monastery and Edward I. had been decided, for in 1397, during the reign of Richard II., the name of "Allen of Ross-hall" was entered in the list of donors to the fraternities of the Preston Guild of that year. George Allen, of Brookhouse, Staffordshire, who held Rossall at the date of the Reformation, by virtue of a long lease granted to his ancestors by an abbot of Deulacres, is the earliest of this family to whom these tenants of the grange can be traced genealogically. The widow and daughters of the grandson of George Allen were ejected from Rossall in 1853, before the expiration of their lease, and despoiled of valuable documents and propety by Edmund Fleetwood, whose father had purchased the reversion from Henry VIII., at the time of the dissolution of monasteries. On that occasion a neighbour, Anion, seized and appropriated £500 belonging to the Allens on pretence of remitting it to Dr. William Allen, at Rheims. Mrs. Allen made an attempt to recover possession of the grange, and a trial for that purpose took place at Manchester, but her case broke down through inability to produce the original deeds and papers, all of which had been either stolen or destroyed when the Hall was plundered during the ejection.[1] The estate, or grange, of Rossall, remained in the hands of the Fleetwoods until the death of Edward Fleetwood, when it passed to Roger Hesketh, of North Meols, who married Margaret, the only child and heiress of that gentleman in 1733.[2] The Heskeths, of Rossall, were descended from the Heskeths of Rufford, through Hugh Hesketh, an offspring of Sir Thomas Hesketh, of Rufford. Hugh Hesketh married the eldest daughter and co-heiress of Barneby Kytichene, or Kitchen, and thus acquired a moiety of the manor of North Meols. At the decease of Hugh Hesketh, in 1625, the the lands of North Meols descended to his son, Thomas Hesketh, then 56 years of age, whose son and heir, Robert Hesketh, was already married to the daughter of — Formby, of Formby. The only child of Robert Hesketh was the Roger Hesketh, mentioned above, who also held Tulketh Hall and estate. The Heskeths continued to reside at Rossall until the lifetime of the late Sir Peter Hesketh Fleetwood, bart.; and under their proprietorship, at an early period, or in the latest years of their predecessors, the ancient Hall was pulled or washed down and another mansion erected more removed from the shore.

In 1843 the design of establishing a school for the education of the sons of clergymen and other gentlemen, under the direct superintendence of the Church of England, but at a less cost than incurred at the public schools then in existence, was first

1. See "Allen of Rossall" in Chapter VI.
2. See "Fleetwood of Rossall" in ditto.

promulgated by the Rev. St. Vincent Beechey, incumbent of Thornton and Fleetwood ; and mainly through the exertions of that gentleman a provisional committee for arranging details and furthering the object in view, was formed in the first month of the ensuing year. This committee consisted, amongst others, of the Rev. J. Owen Parr, vicar of Preston, chairman ; the Revs. Charles Hesketh, vicar of North Meols ; William Hornby, vicar of St. Michael's-on-Wyre ; John Hull, vicar of Poulton ; R. B. Robinson, incumbent of Lytham ; St. Vincent Beechey, incumbent of Thornton and Fleetwood, hon. sec. *pro. tem.;* and Messrs. Thomas Clifton, of Lytham Hall ; Daniel Elletson, of Parrox Hall, and T. R. Wilson-ffrance, of Rawcliffe Hall. At their first meeting it was decided that the management of the school should be placed in the hands of a committee of twenty-four of the principal clergy and laity in the neighbourhood, of whom fourteen should be clergymen and ten laymen, with power to fill up vacancies ; that the bishop of the diocese should always be the visitor ; that the provisional committee should be the first members of the council, with which should rest the appointment of the principal, who must be in holy orders, at such a liberal salary as would insure the services of one eminently qualified for so important a post ; that the council should have power to dismiss the principal ; that the internal management, subject to certain regulations, should be committed to the principal, who should have the appointment and dismissal of all the inferior or subordinate masters ; and that the system of education should resemble that in the school connected with King's College, London, and in Marlborough school, consisting of systematic religious instruction, sacred literature, classics, mathematics, modern languages, drawing, music, etc.

With regard to the admission of pupils it was resolved that the school should consist of not less than two hundred boys ; that no child should be admitted under eight years of age ; that the mode of admission should be by annual payment, nomination, or insurance ; that any pupil should be admitted on the payment, half-yearly in advance, of £50 per annum for the sons of laymen, and £40 for the sons of clergymen ; that nominations might be procured, at the first opening of the school, in order to raise the required capital, whereby pupils could be admitted on the

yearly payment of £40 for the sons of laymen, and £30 for the
sons and wards of clergymen ; that a donation of £25, or the
holding of two £25 shares, fully paid up, should entitle the donor
or holder, to one nomination, and a donation of £50, or the
holding of four shares of £25 each, should constitute the donor,
or holder, a life-governor, entitled to have always one pupil in the
school on his nomination ; that the shares should be limited to an
annual interest of 5 per cent., and be paid off as soon as possible,
the return of such capital, however, not to destroy the right of
nomination during the life of a governor ; that clergymen should
be able to provide for the admission of their children to the
school at a reduced charge of £25 per annum, by paying, on the
principle of life-insurance, small sums for several years previous
to, or one large sum at, the date of entry of each child into the
establishment, such payments to be regulated according to certain
tables, and, of course, forfeited in case the child died.

The committee stated that the outlay of capital required to
erect a building expressly for the purposes of the school would be
greater than they were likely to be able to meet at the low rate of
nomination which it had been deemed expedient to adopt, and,
therefore, it had been determined to take advantage of the offer
of Rossall Hall by Sir P. H. Fleetwood, bart., the mansion being
eminently adapted to the purpose, on account of its size and
situation. It contained many suites of rooms, and an organ
chamber, well suited for a chapel, and furnished with a fine
instrument; and surrounding the Hall were meadows convenient
for play-grounds, and very productive gardens.

The title of the Northern Church of England School was given
to the institution, and on Thursday, the 22nd of August, 1844, it
was formally opened by the Head Master, Dr. Woolley, in the
presence of the junior masters and from forty to fifty pupils, with
their parents. At that date the school-buildings consisted of
apartments in the old Hall for the principal, junior masters, and
lady superintendent ; a dining room, 44 feet long and 20 feet wide,
fitted with a general and masters' tables ; four dormitories, able to
accommodate 100 boys ; and a chapel, formerly the organ-room
above mentioned, having benches for the scholars and stalls for
the masters, the school-house itself consisting of four lofty rooms,
each about 34 feet long by 20 feet wide, being detached from the

Hall, and fitted up with handsome oak desks and benches, fixed upon bronzed cast-iron standards. The play-ground comprised many acres, and in addition there were convenient covered areas for the recreation of the boys in wet weather.

The school was opened with only 70 pupils, but at the beginning of the second six months the number had increased to 115, and the establishment was self-supporting.

The rules of the school have undergone some slight modifications and additions since they were first framed by the provisional committee, and no pupils are now admitted under ten or over fifteen years of age, whilst the annual payments of all pupils have been raised £20 in each case. The insurance plan of entrance was never adopted. A donation of 50 guineas now entitles the donor to a single nomination, and one of 100 guineas constitutes him a life-governor, with power to vote at all general meetings, and to have always one pupil in the school on his nomination. Other rules for the internal management and government of the school have been framed as the number of scholars has increased and their requirements become greater.

There are three exhibitions connected with this institution, of £50 a year each, called respectively the Council, Beechey, and Osborne exhibitions, (the last two being named after the late Honorary Secretary and the late Head Master, through whose exertions the funds were mainly contributed,) tenable for three years at any of the colleges of Oxford or Cambridge; and one of £10 a year, in books, tenable for three years, and founded by Lord Egerton, of Tatton. Besides these there are about eight or ten entrance scholarships offered for competition every year, ranging in value from £10 to £20 each. Of these seven were founded by George Swainson, esq., and one by the Bishop of Rupertsland. A number of other special prizes have been instituted by the present Head Master, the Rev. H. A. James, B.D.

In 1850 the estate was purchased, and since then fresh buildings have been erected to provide accommodation for 400 boys. The old chapel, which was built to supersede the one in the organ-room, has of late years been converted into a library and class-room. A dining hall, schools, class-rooms for different branches of study, spacious dormitories, and a swimming bath have all been added ; whilst extensive enlargements and improvements have taken place in the sanatorium, kitchens, laundries, etc. The old school has been arranged and fitted up as a lecture-room and laboratory. The new chapel is a handsome edifice, containing stained glass windows and a richly decorated chancel; it is dedicated to the Holy Trinity. It should be added that the original name,—The Northern Church of England School,—has been discontinued, and that of Rossall School, substituted, as a more comprehensive title for a great public school.

HEAD MASTERS OF ROSSALL SCHOOL.

Date of Appointment.	NAME.	Cause of vacancy.
1844	Rev. John Woolley, D.C.L.	
1849	Rev. William A. Osborne, M.A.	Resignation of John Woolley.
1869	Rev. Robert Henniker, M.A.	„ „ W. A. Osborne.
1875	Rev. Herbert A. James, B.D.	„ „ R. Henniker.

A preparatory school in connection with this college was successfully established during the reign of Mr. Osborne, about one mile distant along the shore, in a southerly direction, to which pupils are admitted at seven years of age, but not younger, and subsequently drafted into the higher institution.

POPULATION OF THORNTON TOWNSHIP, EXCLUSIVE OF FLEETWOOD.

1801.   1811.   1821.   1831.   1841.   1851.   1861.   1871.

617 ... 739 ... 875 ... 842 ... 1,014 ... 1,013 ... 1,023 ... 934

CARLETON, anciently written Carlentun, is named in the Domesday Book as comprising four carucates of land; and in the Black Book of the Exchequer, it is stated that during the reign of Henry II., 1154—89, Gilbert Fitz Reinfred held four carucates in Carlinton and another place. In 1254 the manor of Carleton in Lancashire belonged to Emma de St. John, and at that date there appears to have been some litigation concerning her right of proprietorship, but how settled we have no means of discovering.[1] In the *Testa de Nevill* it is recorded that Roger Gernet had the 24th part, and Robert de Stokeport the 48th, of a knights' fee in Little Carleton of William de Lancaster's fee.

The earliest allusion to the local territorial family occurs in 1221, when Michael de Carleton, as before stated under "Thornton,"

1. Placit. coram Consil. in Octab. S. Hyll. 38 Hen. III. Lanc. Ror. 5, in dorso.

paid a fine to Henry III. for having espoused Margaret Wynewick, or Winwick, a royal ward, without first obtaining permission from the king. It has been conjectured that Much Carleton received its peculiar title from this member of the family, and amongst the records of some ancient pleadings is one of 1557 concerning certain lands in *Miche Carlton*, a mode of writing the name which lends considerable support to the theory. Alyce Hull, widow, was the plaintive in the dispute. The Carletons, of Carleton, were connected with the neighbourhood for a very long period as holders of the manor; Alicia, the daughter of William de Carleton married Sir Richard Butler, of Rawcliffe Hall, in 1281, and received the manor of Inskip as her dowry; and in 1346 H. de Carleton possessed four carucates and a half in Carleton.[1] Thomas de Carleton held the manor of Carleton up to the time of his death in 1500, when he was succeeded by his son and heir George Carleton, aged 22,[2] who died in 1516, leaving an only child, William, then eleven years of age.[3] William de Carleton came into possession of the property on attaining his legal majority,[4] and died in 1557, being succeeded by Lawrence Carleton, probably his brother. Lawrence Carleton, who had married Margaret, the daughter of George Singleton, of Staining, held the estate for barely twelve months, as he died in 1558 without issue, leaving his lands and tenements in Carleton, amounting to several extensive messuages and Carleton Hall, to his only surviving sister, Margaret, the wife of Thomas Almond.[5] Thus Lawrence Carleton was the last of the manorial family of that name connected with the township. Of the ancient Hall of Carlton, the seat of the Carletons for over three centuries, nothing can be learnt beyond the fact that it stood opposite the Gezzerts farm, and that almost, if not quite, within the recollection of the present generation some ruins of the once noble mansion were visible on its former site, long since enclosed and used for purposes of agriculture. In 1261 the abbey of Cockersand held some property in Carleton, as appears from an agreement entered into at that date between the abbot of Cockersand and H. de Singleton Parva, by which the latter transferred a messuage in Carleton, by the side of other

1. Duc. Lanc. vol. iii. n. 49. 2. Dr. Kuerden's MSS. vol. iv. c. 1 b.
3. Duc. Lanc. vol. iv. n. 71. 4. Harl. MSS. cod 607, fol. 101 b.
5. Dr. Kuerden's MSS. ibid.

messuages already belonging to the abbey, to the abbot, in exchange for messuages and an acre of ground in the vicinity of Stanlawe abbey in Cheshire.[1] Stanlawe abbey itself had sundry possessions in Carleton shortly after its foundation in 1175,[2] all of which were conveyed to the abbey of Whalley in 1296, when the two monastic houses were united, and thus it happened that this township was included amongst the localities in which Whalley abbey held lands at the time of its dissolution.

Sometime during the reign of Henry VIII. the Sherburnes, of Stonyhurst, Hambledon, etc., became holders of soil in Carleton, and at a later period had acquired the manorial rights and privileges. In 1717 Sir Nicholas Sherburne, bart., bequeathed the manor of Carleton, amongst numerous other estates, to his only child and heiress, Maria Winifreda Francisca, the duchess of Norfolk, and two years later the duke of Norfolk had obtained a settlement by which he held a life interest in Carleton, Stonyhurst, and other places, the duchess, however, having reserved to herself the power to dispose of the reversion or inheritance by will or deed, executed in the duke's lifetime. The duchess of Norfolk bequeathed her real estate, including Carleton, on her death in 1745, to her cousin Edward Weld, esq., grandson of Sir John Weld, of Lulworth Castle, Dorsetshire, whose descendant Edward Joseph Weld, esq., has disposed of most of his inheritance in the township to various purchasers, chiefly amongst the local yeomanry and gentry.

The Bambers, of the Moor, in Carleton, were people of position in the township. Richard Bamber, during the latter half of the sixteenth century, married Anne, the daughter of Thomas Singleton, of Staining Hall, and consequently was the brother-in-law of John Leckonby, of Leckonby House, Great Eccleston, who had espoused Alice, another daughter of the same gentleman. It is impossible to affirm with certainty what children sprang from the union of Richard Bamber and Ann Singleton, but of one of them, Edward, who entered the Romish priesthood, we subjoin an interesting and tragic account, extracted from the " Memoirs of Missionary Priests, by the Right Rev. Richard Challoner, D.D.":—

"Edward Bamber, commonly known upon the commission by the name of Reding, was the son of Mr. Richard Bamber, and born at a place called the Moor,

1. Dr. Kuerden's MSS.　　　2. Whittaker's History of Whalley.

the ancient mansion-house of the family, lying not far from Poulton, in that part of Lancashire called the Fylde. Having made good progress with his grammar studies at home, he was sent abroad into Spain, to the English college at Valladolid, where he learnt his philosophy and divinity, and was ordained priest. My short memoirs leave us much in the dark as to many passages and particulars relating to the life and labours of this good priest, as well as to the history of his trial ; but then short as they are they are very expressive of his zeal and indefatigable labours, his unwearied diligence in instructing the catholics under his charge, disputing with protestants, and going about doing good everywhere, with a courage and firmness of mind almost above the power and strength of man. When, how, or where, he was apprehended, I have not found, but only this, that he had lain three whole years a close prisoner at Lancaster castle, before he was brought to the bar, where he stood with an air of fortitude and resolution of suffering in defence of truth. Two fallen catholics, Malden and Osbaldeston, made oath that they had seen him administer baptism and perform the ceremonies of marriage ; and upon these slender proofs of his priesthood, the jury, by the judge's direction, found him guilty of the indictment. Whereupon the judge sentenced him to be hanged, cut down alive, drawn, quartered, etc., as in cases of high treason. It was on the 7th of August, 1646, that he, with two fellow priests, and a poor wretch, named Croft, condemned to death for felony, were drawn upon sledges to the place of execution at Lancaster. There Mr. Bamber exhorted Croft to repentance, and besought him to declare himself a Catholic, confess some of his more public sins, and be truly contrite and sorry for all—'and I, a priest and minister of Jesus Christ, will instantly in his name, and by his authority, absolve thee.' On hearing this the officers of Justice began to storm but Mr. Bamber held his ground, and finally absolved the man in sight and hearing of the crowd. As Mr. Bamber mounted up the ladder, he paused after ascending a few steps, and taking a handful of money from his pocket, threw it amongst the people, saying, with a smiling countenance, that 'God loveth a cheerful giver.' Mr. Bamber was encouring Mr. Whitaker, one of the other two priests about to suffer, who appeared not a little terrified at the approach of death, to be on his guard against the temptation to save his life by renouncing his creed, when the sheriff called out hastily to the executioner to dispatch him (Bamber) ; and so he was that moment turned off the ladder, and permitted to hang but a very short time, before the rope was cut, the confessor being still alive; and thus he was butchered in a most cruel and savage manner."

The two following verses, relating to his death, form part of a long ode or sonnet written at the time :—

" Few words he spoke—they stopp'd his mouth,
   And chok'd him with a cord ;
 And lest he should be dead too soon,
   No mercy they afford.
" But quick and live they cut him down,
   And butcher him full soon ;
 Behead, tear, and dismember straight,
   And laugh when all was done."

The free school of Carleton was founded towards the close of
the seventeenth century. On the 17th of May, 1697, Richard
Singleton, John Wilson, John Davy, and six others recited in an
indenture between them, that Elizabeth Wilson, of Whiteholme,
by her verbal will of the 22nd of September, 1680, declare it to
be her wish that the interest of a fourth of her goods, which
amounted to £59 2s. od., should be used by the overseers of
Carleton for the purpose of procuring instruction for so many of
the poorest children of the town of Carleton as they should think
proper ; and that one-quarter of her estate had been invested in
land, and the annual revenue therefrom employed according to
her last directions and desire. William Bamber, by will dated
13th of October, 1688, bequeathed £40 to his wife Margaret
Bamber, and Richard Harrison, vicar of Poulton, to the intent
that they should lay out the sum in land or other safe investment,
not to yield less than 40s. per annum, half of which was to be
given, at their discretion, amongst the most needful of the poor
of Great Carleton, and the other moiety to be expended in
purchasing books, or obtaining tuition for such poor children of
the same place as they might select. After the deaths of the two
original trustees, the will directed that the bequest should pass
under the management of the vicar of Poulton, for the time
being, and the churchwarden of Carleton. The money was
invested on the 11th of May, 1689, in a messuage and appurtenances, a barn, and several closes, called the Old Yard, the Great
Field, the Croft, the New Hey, the Two Carrs, and the third part
of a meadow, named the Great Meadow, all being situated in
Blackpool, and containing by estimation six acres and a half.
The property was immediately leased to the vendor, John Gualter,
at a rental of 40s. a year. By an indenture, dated the 31st of
December, 1607, between Sir Nicholas Sherburne, of Carleton,
Hambleton, and Stonyhurst, and John Wilson, with three others,
of Carleton, it appears that Sir Nicholas leased to the latter, and
their assigns, the school-house, newly erected at a place called
the Four Lane Ends, in Great Carleton, and the site thereof, for a
term of 500 years from the foregoing date, at the nominal rent of
1s. per annum ; and John Wilson, with his co-trustees, covenanted
that the same should be used for no other purpose but that of a
school, excepting that Sir Nicholas Sherburne and his heirs

should have free liberty to hold the courts for the manor of Carleton within the building. Margaret Bickerstaffe, by her will of the 19th of April, 1716, left £20, the interest of which she directed to be employed by her executors in educating some of the poor children of Carleton. On the 2nd of February, 1737, Richard Butler and Richard Dickson, trustees for the sale of certain estates for paying the debts of James Addinson, conveyed to George Hull, John Sanderson, and others, and their heirs, in consideration of £42, a close in Thornton, formerly called Rushey Full Long Meadow, and now Wheatcake, comprising one acre, in trust, to hold the same and pay the annual proceeds to the master of the Four Lane Ends school "for his care and pains in teaching such poor children of Carleton as should be appointed each year by the chief inhabitants or officers of the township." The money seems to have been given by some persons not wishing to disclose their names, and who selected George Hull, John Sanderson, and five more, as their agents in the matter, and as first trustees of the charity. When five of the trustees had died, it was ordained that seven fresh ones should be elected, and the two remaining be relieved of their trust. John Addinson, in return for £20, given by some person, to the inhabitants of Carleton, conveyed to the same parties a close called the Rough Hey, in Thornton, containing half an acre, to be dealt with and used as in the previous case. It is very likely that the £20 here concerned was the sum before mentioned as the legacy of Margaret Bickerstaffe. All the premises belonging to the school were vested in six new trustees by a deed, dated 3rd of June, 1777 ; and at the visit of the school commissioners in 1867, the attendance of boys was 50, and of girls 20, being somewhere about the usual average of later years. The trustees manage the school property, and appoint or dismiss the master.

POPULATION OF GREAT AND LITTLE CARLETON.

1801.	1811.	1821.	1831.	1841.	1851.	1861.	1871.
269	308	356	319	378	400	363	433

The area of the township embraces 1,979 statute acres.

MERETUN, or the town of the Mere, was estimated by the surveyors of William the Conqueror to comprise six carucates of arable land, and shortly afterwards Sir Adam de Merton held half of it, on condition that he performed military service

when required.[1]   Somewhere about 1200 William de Merton, a
descendant of Sir Adam, was one of the witnesses to a charter,
concerning a local marsh, between Cecilia de Laton and the abbot
of Stanlawe.[2]   In 1207-8 the sheriff of Lancashire received orders
to give Matilda, widow of Theobald Walter, her third of the lands
at Mereton, which her late husband had held up to the time of
his death in 1206, at first for 12s. per annum, and subsequently
for one hawk each year.[3]   According to the *Testa de Nevill*,
Henry III. held three carucates of the soil of Mereton for a few
years, as guardian of the heir of Theobald Walter, and in 1249,
during the thirty-third year of the reign of that monarch, Merton
cum Linholme was in the possession of Theobald Walter, or
le Botiler as he was afterwards called, the heir here mentioned.[4]
Marton descended in the Botiler, or Butler, family until the time
of Henry VIII., when it was sold by Sir Thomas Butler to John
Brown, a merchant of London, in company with Great Layton,
of which manor it had for long been regarded as a parcel, although
in 1323, Great Marton was alluded to as a distinct and separate
manor held by Richard le Botiler.[5]   Marton was purchased from
John Brown by Thomas Fleetwood, esq., of Vach, in the county
of Buckingham, whose descendants and heirs resided at Rossall
Hall ; and after remaining in the Fleetwood family for many
generations the manor of Layton, with its dependency Marton,
was again sold, and this time became the property of Thomas
Clifton, esq., of Lytham Hall, Sir P. H. Fleetwood, bart., being
the vendor.

Little Marton was held in trust by William de Cokerham,
in 1330, for the abbot and convent of Furness,[6] but eight years
afterwards, the manor of Weeton and Little Marton, were held by
James, the son of Edmund le Botiler, earl of Ormond.[7]   What
claim James Botiler had to include Little Marton amongst his
possessions in 1338, cannot now be ascertained, but it is certain
that later, at the dissolution of monasteries, it passed to the crown
as part of the fortified lands of Furness Abbey.   Subsequently
Little Marton passed to the Holcrofts, and from them, in 1505, to

1. Testa de Nevill, fol. 403.   2. Coucher Book of Whalley Abbey.
3. Rot. Lit. Clause 9 John, m. 16.   4. Escaet. 33 Henry III., n. 49.
    5. Escaet. 16 Edward II., n. 59.   6. Escaet. 4 Edward III., n. 100.
                7. Lansd. MSS. 559, fol. 36.

Sir Cuthbert Clifton, of Lytham Hall, by exchange. John Talbot Clifton, esq., of Lytham Hall, a descendant of Sir Cuthbert, and the son of the late Thomas Clifton, esq., of Lytham, is the present owner of Great and Little Marton. As the moss and mere of Marton, perhaps the most interesting objects in the township, have been fully described in an earlier chapter, devoted to the country, rivers, etc., of the Fylde, we refer our readers to that portion of the volume for more detailed information concerning them. In this place we must content ourselves by stating that the mere was at one time a lake of no inconsiderable dimensions, having a fishery of some value attached to it, and that from the number of trunks of trees, discovered on the clayey soil beneath the original moss, which extended six miles by one and a half, there is conclusive evidence that in ancient times the whole of the wide tract was covered by a dense forest, composed chiefly of oak, yew, and fir trees. So enormous were some of the trunks discovered that it was impossible for one labourer to grasp the hand of another over them. The hamlet of Peel, situated within, but close to the Lytham border of the township, contains in a field called Hall-stede, traces of the ancient turreted manorial mansion of the Holcrofts, of Winwick and Marton,[1] and the remains of a moat out of which about sixty years ago a drawbridge and two gold rings were taken. The old lake of Curridmere, mentioned in the foundation charter of Lytham priory in the reign of Richard I., was also located in this neighbourhood, the site being indicated by the soil it once covered bearing the name of the *tarns*. A little more than half a century since the *tarns* formed nothing but a trackless bog, and beneath its surface a husbandman discovered the remains of a small open boat, which had doubtless been used in earlier days on the waters of Curridmere.

About 1625 the inhabitants of Marton petitioned, that in conjunction with "Layton, Layton Rakes, and Blackpool,"[2] the township might be constituted a separate parish, stating in support of their prayer that the parish church of Poulton was five miles distant, and during the winter they were debarred by inundations

1. Dodsworth's MSS., c. xiii., p. 161. These traces which were fairly evident forty years ago, have been in a great measure obliterated in more recent days.
2. Parl. Ing. Lamb. Libr. vol. ii.

from attending that place of worship. This reasonable request does not appear to have evoked a favourable response from the parliamentary commissioners, and it was not until more than a century and a half later that the district had its claims to the privilege desired practically acknowledged. The church of St. Paul, in Great Marton was erected by subscription in 1800, and opened by license the same year, but was not consecrated until 1804. It was a plain, unpretending structure with front and side galleries, but having neither chancel nor tower, and capable of holding upwards of 400 worshippers. In 1857 the increase of the population rendered it necessary to lengthen the church at the east end, and at the same time a neat and simple tower was added. Within the tower is the vestry, above which a number of seats were raised for the Sunday school children, many of whom had previously, for want of space, occupied forms in the aisles. A porch was built over the entrance of the church about 1848, and in 1871 a chancel was erected. Three bells were purchased by the parishioners, and placed in the tower in 1868, whilst the present reading desk and pulpit, were the gift of Miss Heywood, the daughter of Sir Benjamin Heywood, bart., who formerly had a handsome marine residence at Blackpool. Previous to 1845 the musical portion of the service was accompanied by two bassoons and another wind instrument, but about that date they were abolished, and a barrel organ substituted, which continued in force until a few years ago, when it was succeeded by the more modern key organ at present in use. The church of Marton has now an ecclesiastical district of its own, but was originally a chapelry under Poulton. A little anterior to the erection of the church divine service was conducted in the school-house of Baines's Charity, Mr. Sawyer being the first appointed minister.

CURATES AND VICARS OF MARTON.

Date of Institution.	NAME.	Cause of Vacancy.
About 1762	— Sawyer.	
,, 1772	George Hall.	
In 1814	Thomas Bryer.	Death of G. Hall.
,, 1843	James Cookson, M.A.	Resignation of T. Bryer.

The old parsonage stood on the same site as the present one, and consisted simply of two cottages united to form one small residence. In 1846 this house was pulled down, and another, elegant and commodious, erected in its place, being completed the following year. Attached to the parsonage are eleven acres of glebe land.

James Baines, of Poulton, by will dated 6th of January, 1717, devised unto John Hull and six others, of Marton, their heirs and assigns, the school-house lately erected by him in Marton, the land whereon it stood, a messuage or tenement in Warbreck, containing about six acres, a messuage or dwelling-house in Hardhorn-with-Newton, with the smithy and two shippons thereto belonging, and several closes of land in the same township, called the Sheep Field, the Croft, the Garden, being about three acres ; also the Many Pits, the Debdale, the Cross Butts, the Wradle Meadow, and the field adjoining its north-west end, and the Carr, containing twelve and a half acres, to the intent that the rents arising from the foregoing should after the deduction of 10s. for an annual dinner to the trustees, be directed to the maintenance of a master to instruct the children of the township in the above-mentioned building. The revenue of the school was greatly impoverished for many years by the expenses of a chancery suit about 1850, which arose on the question whether the school should be continued as formerly or be divided, and part of its income be devoted to the establishment and support of a similar institution in the adjoining district of Little Marton. The whole of the funds were defrayed out of the funds of the charity. A scheme for its regulation was framed in 1863 by the Master of the Rolls, providing amongst other matters that the school should be open to Government inspection, but in no way interfering with its gratuitous character. The commissioner of 1869 reports :— "Sixty-three children were present on the day of my visit, of whom fifty-two were girls, who are taught in the same classes as the boys, and are with them in play hours. The school being free, no register of attendance is kept. In arithmetic, six boys (average age 11), and four girls (average age 10½), did fair papers ; the questions of course were simple ones. Grammar and geography, in which subjects I examined the highest class, were tolerably good. The girls read well ; the boys (as usual) less so ;

spelling was up to the average. The girls are taught to write a bad angular hand; the master says that it is to please the parents. He has been in his present position five years, and receives a salary of £50 a year." The school property consists of forty acres of land, producing a gross annual income of about £130. Both a playground and gymnasium are attached to the school. There are now two masters. The vicar of Poulton and the vicar of Marton, *ex officio*, and five other trustees self-electing, residing within the township, appoint and dismiss the masters, admit and expel scholars, appoint an examiner, and regulate the studies. The chief master must be a member of the Church of England, and is not permitted to take boarders.

Margaret Whittam, widow, by will dated 26th of July, 1814, bequeathed to Edward Hull, Richard Sherson, and John Fair, of Marton, and her brothers, their executors and administrators, the sum of £40, duty free, in trust, the interest to be applied to the benefit of the Sunday school in Marton so long as it should continue to be taught, and in the event of its being abolished, to use the same income for the relief of such necessitous persons of the township as received no alms from the poor rate. The Sunday school established in 1814 is still kept at Marton, and the master paid, in part from the interest of the legacy, and the remainder from subscriptions. About twenty years ago between £200 and £300 were obtained by means of a bazaar, and expended in the erection of a school building on a piece of waste land in Marton, for the purpose of providing for the education of children, both male and female, under the superintendence of a mistress. At Marton Moss there is another school, used also as a church, being served from South Shore, which was built a few years since through the munificence of Lady Eleanor Cicily Clifton, of Lytham Hall; and at Moss Side, a small Wesleyan Chapel was erected by subscription about 1871.

Edward Whiteside, of Little Marton, sailor, bequeathed by will, dated 22nd December, 1721, as follows:—"It is my will, that my ground be kept in lease, according as my executors shall see fit, and what spares it is my will that they buy cloth and give it to poor people that has nothing out of the town; it is my will that it be given in Little Marton, and if there be a minister that preaches in Marton, that they give him something what they shall see fit : It is my will, that if they can buy land, that they sell my personal estate, and buy as much as it will purchase : It is my will, that two acres, which my father hath now in possession, that when it falls into my hands and possession, that it go the way above named : It is my mind and will, that my executors give it when they shall see fit, and I hope they will choose faithful men, who will act according to themselves ; and I make my well-beloved friends, Anthony Sherson and Thomas Grimbalson, executors of my last will."

William Whiteside left by will, dated 1742, £100 to be invested, and the annual proceeds to be spent in furnishing clothing to the poor of Marton, not in receipt of parish relief. John Hull, Thomas Webster, and Robert Bickerstaffe, were the original trustees of this charity.

John Hodgson, by will dated 25th of September, 1761, devised his messuage and lands in Marton, and his personal estate, to John Hull and Richard Whittam, their heirs and assigns, in trust, to dispose of the same, and after paying his debts and funeral expenses, to lay out at interest the remainder of the money so acquired, and devote the yearly income therefrom to the purchase of meal for poor housekeepers of Great Marton, not relieved from the town's rate. The meal to be distributed annually on the 25th of December. The net amount of the legacy was £100.

Edward Jolly, of Mythorp, by indenture, dated 13th of February, 1784, conveyed to James Jolly, James Sherson, and Thomas Fair, their executors and assigns, the sum of £60, to the intent that it should be placed on good security, and one shilling of the yearly income derived be expended weekly in bread, to be distributed each Sunday to those poor persons who had attended divine service in the morning at the chapel of Great Marton. The deed directed that the dole should be given at the door of the chapel immediately after morning service, by the clerk or some other authorised person, and that in the event of Marton Chapel, which was then unconsecrated and supported by subscription, being closed for four successive Sundays, or converted into a Dissenting place of worship, the bread money should be transferred to the townships of Great and Little Singleton, and Weeton-cum-Preese ; and the weekly allowance of food be distributed as above at the parochial chapel of Great and Little Singleton. The dole, however, had to return to Marton chapel as soon as service, according to the Church of England, was again conducted there. The chapel alluded to was Baines's school-house, where it had been the custom of Edward Jolly to distribute bread each Sunday for several years previously, and it was with the intention of rendering this practice perpetual, that the indenture was made. No re-investment of the money can be legally made without the approval of the minister of Marton church.

POPULATION OF GREAT AND LITTLE MARTON.

1801.	1811.	1821.	1831.	1841.	1851.	1861.	1871.
972	1,093	1,397	1,487	1,562	1,650	1,691	1,982

The area of the township amounts to 5,452 statute acres, inclusive of the sheet of water called Marton mere.

HARDHORN-WITH-NEWTON contains within the limits of its township the three hamlets or villages of Hardhorn, Newton, and Staining, of which the last only is alluded to in the Domesday Survey, where Staininghe is mentioned as comprising six curucates of land in service. The Coucher Book of Whalley Abbey furnishes much valuable and interesting information relating to the district of Staining, and from it we find that sometime between 1175 and 1296 John de Lascy, constable of Chester, "gave and by this charter confirms to God and the Blessed Mary, and to the abbot and monks of the Benedictine Monastery (Locus) of Stanlawe the *vill* of Steyninges, with all things belonging to it, in the *vill* itself, in the field, in roads, in footpaths, in meadows, in pastures, in waters, in mills, and in all other easements which are or can be there, for the safety of my soul and those of my antecessors and successors. To be held and possessed in pure and perpetual gift without any duty or exaction pertaining to me or my heirs, the monks themselves performing the service which the *vill* owes to the lord King." The monks of Stanlawe retained possession until 1296, when their monastic instition, with all its property, including Staining, was united to, or appropriated by, the abbey of Whalley, shortly after which, in 1298, an agreement was arrived at between the prior of Lancaster, who held Poulton church, and the abbot of Whalley, concerning the tithes of Staining, Hardhorn, and Newton. "At length," says the record, "by the advice of common friends they submitted the matter to the arbitration of Robert de Pikeringe, Elbor. Official," who decided that the abbot and convent of Whalley, formerly of Stanlawe, should receive in perpetuity the major tithes of every and all their lands within the boundaries of Staining, Hardhorn, and Newton, whether the harvests were cultivated by the monks themselves or by their tenants ; but the minor tithes, personal and obligatory, whether of the abbey tenants or of the secular servants, were adjudged to the vicar of the church of Poulton and the prior and monks of Lancaster. The abbot of Whalley was also directed to pay to the prior of Lancaster at the parish church of Poulton an annual sum of eighteen marks, as an acknowledgment, half at the festival of St. Martin and the remainder at Pentecost. The Coucher Book contains several deeds of arrangement touching marsh-land in the vicinity of Staining. Cecilia de Laton, widow, gave to the abbot and convent of Stanlawe, all her marsh between certain land of Staining and a long ditch, so that the latter might mark the division between Staining and Little Layton, the witnesses to the transfer being William de Carleton, William de Syngleton, and Alan, his son, William de Merton, and Richard de Thornton ; Cecilia de Laton also quitclaimed to the same monastery all her right to the mediety of a marsh between "Mattainsmure" and Little Carleton. William le Boteler exchanged with the Stanlawe brotherhood all the marsh between the ditch above mentioned and the land of Staining for a similar tract beyond the trench towards Great Layton, stipulating that if at any time a fishery should be established in the ditch, which was doubtless both wide and deep, the monks and he, or his heirs, should participate equally in the benefits accruing from it. Theobald Walter granted power to the abbot of Stanlawe to make use of his mere of Marton for the purpose of conducting therefrom a stream to turn the mill at Staining, belonging to the monastery, care being taken that the fish in the said mere were not injured or diminished. Within the grange of Staining a chantry was in existence, and its services were presided over by two resident priests, whose duty it also was to superintend the property held by the convent of Stanlawe, and subsequently by the abbey of Whalley, in the neighbourhood.

The following is a list of the conventual possessions and rentals in Staining at the date of the Reformation :—The house of

Staining 6s. od. ;   Scotfolde close, held by Lawrence Richardson,
5s. od., also Cach Meadow, of one acre, 1s. 8d.; a messuage, 30 acres
of land, held by Lawrence Archer, £1 10s. 4d; a messuage, 16 acres,
held by Thomas Salthouse, 16s. od. ;   a messuage, 15 acres, held
by John Johnson, 18s. 2d. ; a fishery, held by Richard Whiteside,
18s. 4d. ;   a messuage, 15 acres, held by Richard Harrison, 18s.
10d. ;   a messuage, 18 acres, held by William Salfer, 18s. 2d. ;   a
messuage, 8 acres, held by William Hall, 10s. 4d. ;   a house and a
windmill, held by Lawrence Rigson, £2 os. od. ;   a messuage, 18
acres, held by Robert Gaster, 18s. 2d. ;   a messuage, 30 acres, held
by Constance Singleton, widow, £1 13s. od. ;   a messuage, 20 acres,
held by Thomas Wilkinson, £1 os. od. ;   a messuage, 10 acres,
held by John Pearson, 10s. od. ;   a messuage, 10 acres, held by the
wife of William Pearson, 10s. od. ;   a messuage, 6 acres, held by
Robert Walsh, 6s. 8d. ;   a messuage, 13 acres, held by Thomas
Dickson, 13s. 4d., and 4 hens ; a messuage, 20 acres, held by John
Sander, £1 os. od. and 6 hens ;   a messuage, 10 acres, held by
William Hey, 10s. od. and 3 hens ; a messuage, 6 acres, held by
Ralph Dape, 7s. 6d. and 3 hens ;   a messuage, 8½ acres, held by
the wife of Richard Dane, 7s. 6d. and three hens.   In Hardhorn
the abbey possessed a messuage, 10 acres, held by William
Lethum, at 10s. per annum ; a messuage, 20 acres, held by Robert
Lethum, £1 os. od. ;   a messuage, 10 acres, held by Henry ffisher,
10s. ;   a messuage, 10 acres, held by William Pearson, 10s. od.
and 3 hens ; a messuage, 10 acres, held by John ffisher, 10s. od.
and 3 hens : a messuage, 10 acres, held by William Silcocke, 10s.
od. and 3 hens ;   a messuage, 10 acres, held by Richard Hardman
until " ye time that Richard Hardman, son of William Hardman,
come to ye age of 21 yeares," 10s. od. ;   a messuage, 10 acres, held
by Richard Hardman, junior, 10s. od. and 3 hens ; a messuage, 10
acres, held by Robert Silcocke, 10s. od. ;   a messuage, 12 acres,
held by Robert Whiteside, 12s. 6d. and 3 hens ;   a messuage, 12
acres, held by Richard Bale, 12s. 6d. and 3 hens ;   a messuage, 7
acres, held by Henry ffisher, junior, 7s. 6d. and 2 hens ; a messuage,
2 acres, held by John Allards, 2s. od. and 2 hens ;   a messuage, 10
acres, held by John Walch, 10s. od. and three hens ;   a messuage,
10 acres, held by Robert Crow, 10s. od. and 2 hens ;   a messuage,
20 acres, held by Richard Garlick, £1 os. od. and 6 hens ;   a
messuage, 10 acres, held by John Ralke, 10s. od. and 3 hens ;   a

messuage, 10 acres, held by Edmund Holle, 10s. od. In Carleton the abbey owned a close named Whitbent, which William Carleton rented at 1s. 6d., a year ; and in Elswick, a barn and 3 acres of land, held by Christopher Hennett, for an annual payment of 3s. 4d. In the Coucher Book of Whalley Abbey, from which the foregoing information has been obtained there occurs the following notice, relating to the Hall, apparently written when the above survey was made :—" The house of Stayning is in length xxvii. yards, and lofted ou'r and slated ; ye close called ye little hey contains by estimation halfe an acre, and ye said house payeth yearly, 6s." Sir Thomas Holt, of Grizlehurst, appears to have been the first proprietor of the conventual lands of Staining after they had been confiscated to the crown at the dissolution of monasteries ; and from him they were purchased, either towards the end of the reign of Henry VIII., or at the commencement of that of Edward VI., by George the son of Robert Singleton, by his wife Helen, daughter of John Westby, of Mowbreck. The Singletons, of Staining, resided at the Hall until the close of the seventeenth century, and during that long period formed alliances with several of the local families of gentry, as the Carletons of Carleton, the Fleetwoods of Rossall, the Bambers of Carleton, and the Masseys of Layton. On the death of George Singleton, the last of the male representatives of the Singletons of Staining, somewhere about 1790, the estates descended to John Mayfield, the son of his sister Mary, and subsequently, on his decease without issue, to his nephew and heir-at-law, William Blackburne. Staining Hall, now the property of W. H. Hornby, esq., of Blackburn, is a small and comparatively modern residence, presenting in itself nothing calling for special notice or comment from an antiquarian point of view. Remains of the old moat, however, are still in existence round the building, but beyond this there is no indication of the important station the Hall must have formerly held in the surrounding country, both as the abode of some of its priestly proprietors, of Stanlawe and Whalley, and the seat of a family of wealth and position, like the Singletons would seem to have been.

The township of Hardhorn-with-Newton contains the free school erected and endowed by Mr. James Baines, which has already been fully noticed in the chapter devoted to Poulton.

In the hamlet of Staining a chapel and school combined was erected by private munificence in 1865, the former building used for such purposes being both inadequate and inappropriate. The foundation stone was laid by Mrs. Clark, the wife of the late vicar of Poulton, on a site given by W. H. Hornby, esq., of Blackburn and Staining. The ceremony took place on the 26th of May, 1865, and on the 3rd of December in that year service was first performed in the edifice by the Rev. Richard Tonge, of Manchester. The building is of brick, with stone dressings, and comprises a nave, apsis, and tower of considerable altitude, containing a fine toned bell.

On the 1st of February, 1748, Thomas Riding re-leased to John Hornby and Thomas Whiteside, a dwelling-house and certain premises for the remainder of a term of 1,000 years, to be held in trust by them and their heirs for the use and benefit of the poor housekeepers in Hardhorn-with-Newton township, in such manner as directed by the will of Ellen Whitehead. The property of this charity in 1817 consisted of half an acre of ground, and three cottages and a weaving shed standing upon it, together with £40 in money, out at interest. It cannot be ascertained either who Ellen Whitehead was or when she died.

POPULATION OF HARDHORN-WITH-NEWTON.

1801.	1811.	1821.	1831.	1841.	1851.	1861.	1871.
311	324	392	409	358	386	389	436

The area of the township extends over 2,605 statute acres.

CHAPTER X.

THE PARISH OF BISPHAM.

ISCOPHAM was the appellation bestowed on the district now called Bispham at and before the era of William the Conqueror, in whose survey it appears as embracing within its boundaries eight carucates of arable land. The original name is simply a compound of the two Anglo-Saxon words *Biscop*, a bishop, and *Ham*, a habitation or settlement, the signification of the whole being obviously the 'Bishop's town,' or 'residence.' Hence it is clear that some episcopal source must be looked to as having been the means of conferring the peculiar title on the place, and fortunately for the investigator, the annals of history furnish a ready clue to what otherwise might have proved a question difficult, or perhaps impossible, of satisfactory solution. In a previous chapter it has been noted that for long after the reign of Athelstan Amounderness was held by the See of York, and nothing can be more natural than to suppose, when regarding that circumstance in conjunction with the significance of the name under discussion, that the archbishops of the diocese had some residence on the soil of Bispham. It is quite possible, however, that there may have been merely a station of ecclesiastics who collected the rents and tithes of the Hundred on behalf of the bishopric, acting in fact as stewards and representatives of the archbishop for the time being, but in either case it is evident that the name and, consequently, the town, are of diocesan origin, doubtless associated with the proprietorship above mentioned. The presence of priests in residence within the manor of Bispham would necessarily lead to the establishment there of some chapel or oratory, and the absence

of any allusion to such a structure by the investigators of William
I. seems, at the first glance, a serious obstacle to the episcopal
theory, but Bispham was located between the two Danish colonies
of Norbreck and Warbreck, a people whose hostility to all religious
houses was almost proverbial, and hence it is scarcely likely that
a church so conveniently situated, as that of Bispham would be,
could long escape spoliation and destruction after the prelates of
York had removed their protection from the neighbourhood, at
some date anterior to the arrival of the Normans in England.
The ravages of the Danes indeed, throughout the Hundred of
Amounderness are usually the reasons assigned why the district
was relinquished by the See of York, so that the non-existence of
a sacred pile of any description at the period of the Domesday
Survey, is in no way contradictory of such a building having been
there, at an earlier epoch. At the close of the Saxon dynasty the
number of acres in cultivation in the manor of Bispham exceeded
those of the five next largest manors in the Fylde by two hundred,
thus Staining, Layton, Singleton, Marton, and Thornton, each
contained six hundred acres of arable soil, whilst Bispham had
eight hundred in a similar condition. About thirty years after
the Norman Survey, Geoffrey, the sheriff, bestowed the tithes of
Biscopham, upon the newly founded priory of St. Mary, in
Lancaster, being incited thereto by the munificent example of
Roger de Poictou. In this grant no allusion is made to any
church, an omission which we should barely be justified in
considering accidental, but which would rather seem to indicate
that the edifice was not erected until later. The earliest allusion
to it is found in the reign of Richard I., 1189—1199, when
Theobald Walter quitclaimed to the abbot of Sees, in Normandy,
all his right in the advowson of Pulton and the church of
Biscopham, pledging himself to pay to the abbey ten marks a year
during the period that any minister presented by him or his heirs
held the living.[1] In 1246 the mediety of Pulton and Biscopham
churches was conveyed to the priory of St. Mary, in Lancaster, an
offshoot from the abbey of Sees, by the archdeacon of Richmond ;
and in 1296 the grant was confirmed to the monastery by John
Romanus, then archdeacon of Richmond, who supplemented the

---

1. Regist. S. Mariæ de Lanc. MSS. fol. 77.

donation of his predecessor with a gift of the other mediety, to be appropriated after the decease of the person in possession, stipulating only that when the proprietorship became complete the conventual superiors should appoint a vicar at an annual salary of twenty marks. At the suppression of alien priories the church of Bispham was conveyed to the abbey of Syon, and remained attached to that foundation until the Reformation of Henry VIII.

The original church of Bispham, subsequently to the Norman invasion, was built of red sandstone, and comprised a low tower, a nave, and one aisle. A row of semicircular arches, resting on round, unornamented pillars, supported the double-gabled roof, which was raised to no great altitude from the ground; whilst the walls were penetrated by narrow lancet windows, three of which were placed at the east end. The pews were substantial benches of black oak. In 1773 this venerable structure was deprived of its flag roof and a slate one substituted, the walls at the same time being raised to their present height. During the alterations the pillars were removed and the interior thoroughly renovated, more modern windows being inserted a little later. There is a traditional statement that the church was erected by the monks of Furness, but beyond the sandstone of which it was built having in all probability come from that locality, there appears to be nothing to uphold such an idea. Over the main entrance may still be seen an unmistakable specimen of the Norman arch, until recent years covered with plaster, and in that way retained in a very fair state of preservation.

In 1553 a commission, whose object was to investigate "whether ye belles belongynge to certayne chapelles which be specified in a certayne shedule be now remaynyng at ye said chapelles, or in whose hands or custodie the same belles now be," visited Bispham, and issued the following report :—" William Thompson and Robert Anyan, of ye chapell of Byspham, sworne and examyned, deposen that one belle mentioned in ye said shedule was solde by Edwarde Parker, named in ye former commission, unto James Massie, gent., for ye some of xxiiis. ivd." Nothing is known respecting the number or ultimate destination of the peal alluded to. The belfry can now only boast a pair of bells.

Formerly there were many and various opinions as to the
dedication of the church, Holy Trinity and All Saints having
both been suggested, but the question is finally set at rest by a
part, in fact the sole remnant, of the ancient communion service,
the chalice, which is of silver gilt, and bears the inscription :—
"The gift of Ann, Daughter to John Bamber, to ye Church of
Allhallows, in Bispham ; Delivered by John Corritt, 1704."
Within the building, fastened to the east wall, and immediately to
the right of the pulpit, are four monumental brasses inscribed as
under :—

" Here lyes the body of John Veale, late of Whinney Heys, Esq., who dyed the
20th Jan., 1704, aged sixty."

" Here lyes the body of Susannah, wife of the late John Veale, Esq., of
Whinney Heys, Esq., who departed this life the 20th of May, 1718, aged 67
years."

" Here lyes the body of Edward Veale, late of Whinney Heys, Esq., who
departed this life the 11th of August, 1723, aged 43 years."

" Here lyes the body of Dorothy Veale, eldest daughter of John Veale, late of
Whinney Heys, Esq., who departed this life the 9th day of January, in the year of
our Lord, 1747, and in the 77th year of her age."

Beneath these tablets, the only ones in the church, was the
family vault of the Veales, of Whinney Heys, now covered over
by pews. During the year 1875 the nave was re-seated, and at the
time when the flooring was taken up numerous skulls and bones
were found in different parts of the building, barely covered with
earth, plainly indicating that interments had once been very
frequent within the walls, and causing us to wonder that no mural
or other monuments, beyond those just given, are now visible, or,
indeed, remembered by any of the old parishioners. None of the
stones in the graveyard are of great antiquity, and the most
interesting object on that score is a portion of an ancient stone
cross, having the letters I.H.S. carved upon it, on the broken summit
of which a sun-dial has been mounted. Tradition has long affirmed
that Beatrice, or Bridget, the daughter of Oliver Cromwell, who
espoused General Ireton, and after his death General Fleetwood,
lies buried here, but this is a mistake, probably arising from the
proximity of the Rossall family, having the same name as her second
husband ; the lady was interred at Stoke Newington on the 5th
of September, 1681. There are no stained glass windows, and the
walls of the church are whitewashed externally.

PERPETUAL CURATES AND VICARS OF BISPHAM.

Date of Institution.	NAME.	On whose Presentation.	Cause of Vacancy.
Before 1559	Jerome Allen	Abbey of Syon	
About 1649	John Fisher		
In 1650	John Cavelay		Resignation of J. Fisher
Before 1674	Robert Brodbelt		Death of J. Cavelay
„ 1689	Robert Wayte		
„ 1691	Thomas Rikay		Death of R. Wayte
In 1692	Thomas Sellom	Richard Fleetwood	Death of T. Rikay
About 1715	Jonathan Hayton		
Before 1753	Christopher Albin	Edward Fleetwood	
In 1753	Roger Freckleton	Roger Hesketh	Death of C. Albin
„ 1760	Ashton Werden	Roger Hesketh	Death of Roger Freckleton
„ 1767	John Armetriding	Roger Hesketh	Death of A. Werden
„ 1791	William Elston	Thomas Elston	Death of John Armetriding
„ 1831	Charles Hesketh, M.A.	Sir P. H. Fleetwood	Death of W. Elston
„ 1837	Bennett Williams, M.A.	Rev. C. Hesketh	Resignation of C. Hesketh
„ 1850	Henry Powell, M.A.	Ditto	Resignation of B. Williams
„ 1857	W. A. Mocatta, M.A.	Ditto	Resignation of H. Powell
„ 1861	James Leighton, M.A.	Ditto	Resignation of W. A. Mocatta
„ 1874	C. S. Hope, M.A.	Ditto	Resignation of J. Leighton
„ 1876	Francis John Dickson	Ditto	Resignation of C. S. Hope

The living was a perpetual curacy until lately, when it was raised to the rank of a vicarage. The Rev. Charles Hesketh, M.A., of North Meols, has been the patron for almost half a century. Divine worship, according to the ritual of the Roman Catholics, was last celebrated in Bispham church during March, 1559, immediately after the death of Queen Mary, when her protestant successor, Elizabeth, ascended the throne. The pastor, Jerome Allen, a member of the Benedictine brotherhood, assembled his flock at nine in the morning of the 25th of that month, and previous to administering the holy sacrament, addressed a few words of farewell and advice to his congregation. "Suffused in tears," records the diary of Rishton, "this holy and good man admonished his people to obey the new queen, who had succeeded Mary, the late one, and besought them to love God above all things, and their neighbours as themselves." It is said that after vacating his cure at Bispham, the Rev. Jerome Allen, retired to Lambspring, in Germany, where he spent the remainder of his life in the strictest religious observances enjoined by his creed. In 1650 the following remarks concerning Bispham were recorded by the ecclesiastical commissioners of the Commonwealth :—"Bispham hath formerly been a parish church, containing two townships, Bispham-cum-Norbreck and Layton-cum-Warbreck, and consisting of three hundred families ; the inhabitants of the said towns desire that they may be made a parish." In the survey of the Right Rev. Francis Gastrell, D.D., bishop of Chester, the annexed notice occurs :—"Bispham. Certif. £8 os. od., viz., a parcell of ground, given by Mr. R. Fleetwood, worth, taxes deducted, £5 per year ; Easter Reckonings, £3. Richard Fleetwood, esq., of Rossall Hall, settled upon the church in 1687 a Rent Charge of £10 per ann. for ever. Bispham-cum-Norbreck, and Layton-cum Warbreck, for which places serve four Churchwardens, two chosen by the ministers and two by the parish." In 1725 Edward Veale, of Whinney Heys, gave £200 to augment the living, and a similar amount was granted from Queen Anne's Bounty for a like purpose. Three years later £400 more were acquired, half from the fund just named, and half from Mr. S. Walter. The parish registers commence in 1599.

William le Botiler, or Butler, held the manors of Layton, Bispham, and Warbreck, according to the Duchy Feordary, in the early part of the fourteenth century, and in 1365 his son, Sir John Botiler, granted the manors of Great and Little Layton and Bispham, to Henry de Bispham and Richard de Carleton, chaplains. Great Bispham probably remained in the possession of the church until the dissolution of the monasteries. Norbreck and Little Bispham appear to have belonged to the convent of Salop, and were leased by William, abbot of that house, together with certain tithes in Layton, to the abbot and convent of Deulacres, by an undated deed, for eight marks per annum, due at Martinmas.[1] In 1539 the brotherhood of Deulacres paid rent for lands

---

1. Dugd. Monast. vol. v. p. 630.

in Little Bispham and Norbreck, and an additional sum of 2s. to Sir Thomas Butler, for lands in Great Bispham.[1] After the Reformation, Bispham was granted by Edward VI., in the sixth year of his reign, to Sir Ralph Bagnell, by whom it was sold to John Fleetwood, of Rossall; and in 1571, Thomas Fleetwood, the descendant of the last-named gentleman, held Great and Little Bispham and Layton.[2] The manors remained invested in the Rossall family until the lifetime of the late Sir P. H. Fleetwood, by whom they were sold to the Cliftons, of Lytham, John Talbot Clifton, esq., of Lytham Hall, being the present lord.

The subjoined account of a shipwreck on this coast is taken from the journal of William Stout, of Lancaster, and illustrates the uses to which the church was occasionally put in similar cases of emergency :—

"Our ship, Employment, met with a French ship of some force, bound to Newfoundland, who made a prize of her. The French were determined to send her directly to St. Malo ; when John Gardner, the master, treated to ransome her, and agreed with the captors for £1,000 sterling. The French did strip the sailors of most of their clothes and provisions ; and coming out of a hot climate to cold, before they got home they were so weak that they were scarce able to work the ship, and the mate being not an experienced pilot, spent time in making the land, and was embayed on the coast of Wales, but with difficulty got off, and then made the Isle of Man, and stood for Peel Fouldrey, but missed his course, so that he made Rossall Mill for Walna Mill, and run in that mistake till he was embayed under the Red Banks, behind Rossall, so as he could not get off ; and it blowing hard, and fearing she would beat, they endeavoured to launch their boat ; but were so weak that they could not do it, but came to an anchor. She struck off her rudder, and at the high water mark she slipped her cables and run on shore, in a very foul strong place, where she beat till she was full of water, but the men got well to land. But it was believed if they had been able to launch the boat and attempted to land in her, the sea was so high and the shore so foul, that they might have all perished. This happened on the 8th month, 1702, and we had early notice of it to Lancaster, and got horses and carts with empty casks to put the damaged sugars in, and to get on shore what could be saved, which was done with much expedition. We got the sugar into Esquire Fleetwood's barn, at Rossall, and the cotton wool into Bispham chapel, and in the neap tides got the carpenters at work, but a storm came with the rising tides and beat the ship to pieces. The cotton wool was sent to Manchester and sold for £200."

In the early years of this century Bispham contained a manufactory for the production of linsey-woolsey. The building was three stories in height, and employed a considerable number

1. Monast. Anglic. vol. v. p. 530.   2. Duc. Lanc. vol. xii., Inq. n. 2.

of hands. Subsequently it was converted into a ladies' school, and afterwards pulled down. Two or three residences in the township near the site of the old manufactory still retain the names of 'factory houses,' from their association with it. There is a small Nonconformist place of worship in the village, surrounded by a wall, being partially covered with ivy and overshadowed by trees. This edifice is called Bethel Chapel, and a date over the doorway fixes its origin at 1834. In 1868 a Temperance Hall, comprising a reading room, library, and spacious lecture and assembly room, was erected here by subscription, and forms one of the most striking objects in the village. The Sunday school connected with the parish church, and situated by its side, was erected also by subscription, in 1840, and rebuilt on a larger scale in 1873.

The hamlet of Norbreck is situated on the edge of the cliffs overhanging the shore of the Irish Sea, and consists of several elegant residences tenanted by Messrs. Swain, Burton, Harrison, Wilson, and Richards. None of the houses present any features calling for special comment, but appear, like others at no great distance, as Bispham Lodge, the seat of Frederick Kemp, esq., J.P., to have been built within comparatively recent years as marine retreats for the gentry of neighbouring towns, or others more intimately associated with the locality.

POPULATION OF BISPHAM-WITH-NORBRECK.

1801.	1811.	1821.	1831.	1841.	1851.	1861.	1871.
254	297	323	313	371	394	437	556

The area of the township includes 2,624 statute acres.

The Free Grammar School was established in 1659, when Richard Higginson, of St. Faith's, London, bequeathed unto the parish of Bispham sundry annual gifts in perpetuity, and especially the yearly payment of £30 for and towards the support of a school-master and usher at the school of Bispham, lately erected by him. From a subsequent deed it appears that the annual sums were made chargeable on two messuages in Paternoster Row, London, belonging to the dean and chapter of St. Pauls, but as the interest Higginson possessed in such property was acquired at the sale of the dean and chapter lands during the Commonwealth, it followed that on the restoration of Charles II., the rentals forming his bequest were not forthcoming. Further, the document recites that John Amburst,

of Gray's-inn, esq., and Elizabeth, his wife, who was the widow
and sole executrix of Richard Higginson, being desirous that
the object of the founder should be carried out, paid to John
Bonny and others in trust £200, to be invested in land and the
annual income thereof devoted to the maintenance of an able and
learned schoolmaster at the before-mentioned school of Bispham.
The costs of a chancery suit in 1686 reduced the donation to £180,
but the trustees made up the sum to the original amount and
reimbursed themselves by deducting £5 per annum from the salary
of the master for four years. In 1687, Henry Warbreck conveyed
in consideration of £200, to James Bailey and five other trustees
of the charity, elected by a majority of the inhabitants, the closes
known as the Two Tormer Carrs, the Two New Heys, the Great
Hey, the Pasture, the Boon Low Side, the Little Field, and 35
falls of ground on the west of the Meadow Shoot close, amounting
to about 14 acres, and situated in Layton, "for the above-named
pious use ; and it was agreed, that when any three of the five
trustees, or six of any eight which should hereafter be chosen,
should happen to die, the survivors should convey the premises to
eight new trustees to be chosen, two out of each of the respective
townships of Layton, Warbreck, Bispham, and Norbreck, by the
consent of the major part of the inhabitants of those townships,
and that the said trustees should from time to time employ the
rents for and towards the maintenance and benefit of an able and
learned schoolmaster, to teach at the school at Bispham."[1] In
1817, Thomas Elston, and George Hodgson, of Layton, Robert
Bonny, and William Bonny, of Warbreck, William Butcher,
junior, and James Tinkler, of Bispham, and Thomas Wilson, and
Joseph Hornby, of Norbreck, were appointed trustees at a public
meeting convened by William Bamber and William Butcher, the
two surviving trustees. The newly elected governors were directed
" to permit the dwelling-house and school to be used as a residence
for the schoolmaster and a public school for the instruction of the
children of the parish of Bispham-with-Norbreck, in reading,
writing, arithmetic, English grammar, and the principles of the
English religion, gratuitously, as had been heretofore done, and to
hold the residue of the premises upon the trust mentioned in the

1. Charity Commissioners' Report.

last deed."[1]   The commissioner who visited the school in 1868 remarked :—" The building is an old house, through whose thatched roof the rain penetrates in winter, dropping all over the desks, and gathering in pools upon the floor ; the room is very small, 30½ by 14½ feet and 7½ feet high to the spring of the roof, and the air being so foul that I was obliged to keep the door open while examining the children."   The use of the dilapidated structure here alluded to has been discontinued, and the scholars assemble in a room in the Temperance Hall until a fresh school-house has been erected.

LAYTON-WITH-WARBRECK is the second of the two townships comprised in the ancient parish of Biscopham or Bispham. The Butlers, barons of Warrington, were the earliest lords of Layton.   In 1251, Robert Botiler, or Butler, obtained a charter for a market and fair to be held in " his manor of Latton."   The estate descended in the same family with some interruptions, until the reign of Henry VIII., when it was sold by Sir Thomas Butler to John Brown, of London, who on his part disposed of it, in 1553, to Thomas Fleetwood.   The manor was retained by the Fleetwoods up to the time of the late Sir. P. Hesketh Fleetwood, of Rossall, by whom it was conveyed, through purchase, to the Cliftons, of Lytham.   The following abstract from the title deed touching the transfer of the property from John Brown to Thomas Fleetwood will not be without interest to the reader :—

" By Letters Patent under the Great Seal of England, bearing date the 19th day of March, in the first year of the reign of Queen Mary. After reciting that Sir Thomas Butler, Knight, was seized in fee of the Mannour of Layton, otherwise Great Layton, with the Appurtenances, in the county of Lancaster, and that his estate, title, and interest therein by due course of Law, came to King Henry the Eighth, who entered thereon and was seized in fee thereof, and being so seized did by his letters patents under the seal of his Duchy at Lancaster, bearing date the 5th day of April, in the thirty-fourth year of his Reign, (amongst other things) give, grant, and restore unto the said Sir Thomas Butler, his heirs, and Assigns, the said Mannour and its Appurtenances, by virtue whereof the said Sir Thomas Butler entered and was seized in fee thereof, and granted the same to John Brown, Citizen and Mercer of London, his heirs and assigns, and that Brown entered and was seized thereof in fee, and granted and sold the same to Thomas Fleetwood, Esq., his heirs and Assigns, and that the said Thomas Fleetwood entered thereon and was at that time seized in fee thereof. And further reciting that the said Sir Thomas Butler held and enjoyed the said Mannour, with its Appurtenances, from

1. Charity Commissioners' Report.

the time of making said Grant until he sold and conveyed the same to the said
Brown without disturbance, and that the said Brown held the same until he sold
and conveyed to the said Thomas Fleetwood without disturbance, and that the said
Thomes Fleetwood had held and enjoyed the same for near four years without
disturbance, and was then seized in fee thereof. But because it had been doubted
whether the said Letters Patent and Grant made by King Henry the Eighth to
Sir Thomas Butler were good and valid in the Law, because they were under the
Seal of the Duchy of Lancaster, and not under the Great Seal, and because it
appeared unto her said Majesty, that the said King Henry the Eighth, her Father,
had promised that the said Sir Thomas Butler, should have the said Grant either
under the Great Seal or the seal of the Duchy of Lancaster, She willing to perform
her Father's promise and to remove all doubts, and for greater security of the said
Mannour, unto the said Thomas Fleetwood and his heirs, and in consideration of
the faithful services done by the said Thomas Fleetwood to her said Father, and
to her Brother King Edward the Sixth, and to her, did give, grant, and confirm
unto the said Thomas Fleetwood, his heirs and assigns, the Mannour of Layton,
otherwise Great Layton, with its rights, members, and Appurtenances, in the said
county of Lancaster, and all and singular the Messuages, Houses, Buildings, Tofts,
Cottages, Lands, Tenements, Meadows, Feedings, Pastures, &c. &c. &c., Fishing,
Wrecks of the Sea, Woods, Underwoods, &c. &c. &c., commodities, emoluments and
Hereditaments whatsoever, with their Appurtenances, situate, lying, and being in
the Vill, Fields, or Hamlets of Layton, otherwise Great Layton, aforesaid, which
were of the said Thomas Butler, and which the said John Brown afterwards sold
to the said Thomas Fleetwood as aforesaid, To hold the same unto the said
Thomas Fleetwood his heirs and assigns for ever."

Reverting to the market and fair above-mentioned we find that
in 1292 Sir William le Botiler was called upon to show upon what
right he laid claim to free warren in Layton, and two other places.
In proving his case, the knight stated that his privileges extended
to markets, fairs, and assize of bread and beer, in addition to which
he affirmed that wreck of the sea had been the hereditary rights of
his ancestors from the accession of William the Conqueror. The
jury acknowledged the title of Sir William in each instance,
ordaining that the same markets, fairs, etc., should continue to be
held or exercised as aforetime. It would appear that the market
took place each week on Wednesday, the chief merchandise offered
for sale being most likely cattle and smallware. There are now
no remnants of the market, which must at one era have been an
assembly of no mean importance, beyond the names of the market-
house and the market-field. The cross and stocks have also
succumbed to the lapse of years, the latter being a matter of
tradition only, with all, even to the oldest inhabitant.

In 1767 a petition was presented to the House of Parliament, setting forth that within the manor of Layton and parishes of Poulton and Bispham there was situated an extensive tract of land containing about 2,000 acres, called Layton Hawes, and begging on the part of those concerned, for permission to enclose the whole of the common. The document states " that Fleetwood Hesketh, Esquire, is Lord of the Manor of Layton aforesaid ; and Edmund Starkie, Esquire, is Impropriator of the Great Tythes arising within that part of the Township of Marton called Great Marton, within the said Manor of Layton and Parish of Poulton, and of One Moiety of the Great Tythes arising in that part of the Township of Bispham called Great Bispham, within the said Manor and Parish of Bispham ; and Thomas Cross, Esquire, and others, his partners, are proprietors of the other Moiety of the Great Tythes arising within Great Bispham aforesaid ; and Ashton Werden, Clerk, present Incumbent of the Parish Church of Bispham afore- said, and his Successors for the time being, of the Great Tythes, arising within the Township of Layton-with-Warbreck, within the said Manor and Parish of Bispham. Also that the said Fleetwood Hesketh, Thomas Clifton, and other Owners and Proprietors of divers ancient Farms, situate within the Manor of Layton, and the towns of Great Marton, Little Marton, Black Pool, and Bispham, have an exclusive Right to turn and depasture their Beasts, Sheep, and other Commovable Cattle, in and upon the said Waste or Common, called Layton Hawes, at all Times of the Year ; and the Parties interested are willing and desirous that the said Waste or Common should be inclosed, allotted and divided, and therefore pray that the said Waste or Common called Layton Hawes, lying within the Manor of Layton, may be divided, set out, and allotted by Commissioners, to be appointed for that purpose and their Successors, in such manner, and subject to such rules, orders, regulations, and directions, as may be thought necessary." Leave to carry out the object contained in the prayer was granted to the petitioners, and within a comparatively short time the work of dividing and apportioning the soil accomplished.

The greater part of the township of Layton-with-Warbreck being now absorbed in the borough of Blackpool, to which the ensuing chapter will be devoted, there is little further to notice beyond the ancient seats of the families of Rigby and Veale. Layton Hall was probably the residence of the Butlers, of Layton, previous to the opening of the seventeenth century, when it was sold to Edward Rigby, of Burgh ; at least that gentleman was the first of the Rigbys whose *Inq. post mortem* disclosed that he held possessions in Layton. The Hall remained in the ownership and tenancy of the Rigbys until the lifetime of Sir Alexander Rigby, who married Alice, the daughter of Thomas Clifton, of Lytham, and died about 1700.[1] The original edifice, which was taken down and a farm-house erected on the site about one century ago, was a massive gabled building. At the bottom of the main staircase was a gate, or grating, of iron, the whole of the interior of the Hall being fitted with oak panels, etc., in a very antique style.

Whinney Heys was held by the Veales from the time of Francis Veale, living in 1570, until the death of John Veale, about two hundred years later, when it passed to Edward Fleetwood, of Rossall Hall, who had married the sister and heiress of John Veale.[2] The Hall of Whinney Heys was embosomed in trees and presented nothing of special moment to the eye, being simply a large rough-cast country building of an early type. It was partially taken down many years since and converted to farming uses.

"The village affords," says Mr. Thornber,[3] "an example of covetousness seldom equalled. John Bailey, better known by the name of the Layton miser, resided in a cottage near the market-house. His habits were most frugal, enduring hunger and privation to hoard up his beloved pelf. Once, during every summer, his store was exposed to the beams of the sun, to undergo purification, and he might be seen, on that occasion, with a loaded gun, seated in the midst of his treasure, guarding it with the eyes of Argus, from the passing intruder. Notwithstanding all this vigilance, upwards of £700 was stolen from his hoard ; and this ignorant old man journeyed to some distance to consult the wise man in order to regain it ; his manœuvre to avoid the income-tax also failed, for although he converted his landed property into guineas, concealing them in his house, and then pleaded that he possessed no *income*, but a *capital* only, the law compelled him to pay his due proportion. In the midst of his savings, death smote

1. See ' Rigby of Layton Hall,' in Chapter vi.
2. See ' Veale of Whinney Heys,' in Chapter vi.
3. History of Blackpool and Neighbourhood.

this wretched being, and even then his ruling passion was strong in the very agony of departing nature. His gold watch, the only portion of his property which remained unbequeathed, hung within his reach ; his greedy eye was riveted upon it ; no he could not part with that dear treasure—and, with an expiring effort, he snatched it from the head of his bed, and it remained clenched in his hand and convulsed fingers long after warmth had forsaken his frame. Alas ! His hidden store, all in gold, weighing 65℔, was discovered at the close of a tedious search, in a walled up window, to which the miser had had access from without, and was carried home in a malt sack, a purse not often used for such a purpose."

CHAPTER XI.

BLACKPOOL.

BLACKPOOL is situated in the township of Layton-with-Warbreck, and occupies a station on the west coast, about midway between the estuaries of the rivers Ribble and Wyre. The watering-place of to-day with its noble promenade, elegant piers, handsome hotels, and princely terraces, forms a wonderful and pleasing contrast to the meagre group of thatched cabins which once reared their lowly heads near the peaty pool, whose dark waters gave rise to the name of the town. This pool, which was located at the south end of Blackpool, is stated to have been half a mile in breadth, and was due to the accumulation of black, or more correctly speaking, chocolate-coloured waters,[1] from Marton Mere and the turf fields composing the swampy region usually designated the "Moss." It remained until the supplies were cut off by diverting their currents towards other and more convenient outlets, when its contents gradually decreased, finally leaving no trace of their former site beyond a small streamlet, which now discharges itself with the flows of Spendike into the sea, opposite the point where the Lytham Road branches from the promenade. The principal portion of the town stands a little removed from the edge of a long line of cliffs, whose altitude, trifling at first, considerably increases as they travel northwards ; and from that broad range of frontage streets and houses in compact masses

---

1. The following is extracted from a paper, written by Mr. Henry Moon, of Kirkham, about 1783, and refers to this pool :—"The liquid is of a chocolate or liver colour, as all water must be which passes through a peaty soil, so that the place might, with as much propriety, bear the name of Liver-pool, as Black-pool.'

run backwards towards the country, covering an annually extending area.

One of the oldest and most interesting relics of antiquity is still preserved in the Fox Hall Hotel, or Vaux Hall, as it is sometimes, but we opine, for reasons stated hereafter, incorrectly written, although its name, site, and long cobble wall are nearly the only mementoes that time and change have failed to remove. It was here in the reign of Charles II. that Edward, the son of the gallant and loyal Sir Thomas Tyldesley who was slain at the battle of Wigan-lane in 1651, having been led to expect a grant of the lands of Layton Hawes, or Heys Side, from the king, after the restoration, in return for his own and his father's staunch adherence to the royal cause, built a small sequestered residence as a summer retreat for his family. Modest and unpretending as the dimensions appear to have been, no doubt at that time it was regarded as a stately mansion, and looked upon with becoming respect and admiration by the inhabitants of the few clay-built and rush-roofed huts which were scattered around it. The house itself was a three gabled structure with a species of tower, affording an extensive survey over the neighbouring country; there were four or five rooms on each story, and one wing of the building was fitted up and used as a chapel, the officiating priest being most probably the Rev. W. Westby, the "W. W." of the diary kept by Thomas Tyldesley during the years he resided there. The chapel portion of the old house was at a later period, when the remainder, after experiencing various fortunes, had fallen into decay, converted into a cottage. Over the chief entrance Edward had inscribed the words—"Seris factura Nepotibus," the motto of an order of Knighthood, called the Royal Oak, which Charles II. contemplated establishing when first he regained his throne, but afterwards for certain reasons[1] altered his mind, as he also appears to have done in regard to the Hawes property, for it never passed into the possession of the Tyldesleys by royal favour, or in any other way. A fox secured by a chain was allowed to ramble for a short distance in front of the doorway, and whether the presence of that animal, together with the use of the Hall as a hunting seat, as well as a summer retreat, originated its name, or its first title was Vaux,

1. For a list of the Knights of the Royal Oak, and other matters concerning that Order see page 72.

and by an easy and simple process of change became altered to Fox, the reader must decide for himself ; but after he has perused the following extract from the Tyldesley Diary, in which the priest already mentioned is alluded to as "W : W.," he will, we venture to think, have little difficulty in concluding that the cognomen Vaux is merely a modern adaptation when applied to this Hall :—

" May 14, 1712.—Left Lan^r about ffive ; p^d 3d. ffor a shooe at Thurnham Cocking, having lost one. Thence to Great Singleton to prayers, and ffrom thence to Litham to din ^{r}, ffound Mr. Blackborne, of Orford ; stayed there 11 at night. Soe to ffox hall. Gave W : W : 1s."

Edward Tyldesley surrounded the Hall with a high and massive wall of cobble stones, strongly cemented together, as a protection very needful in those times of turmoil and persecution. A large portion of the wall still exists in an almost perfect state of preservation, notwithstanding the fierce gales and boisterous tides that have, at intervals, battered against it for more than two centuries. This, with the additional safeguards that nature had provided by means of the broad sea to the front, a small stream running over swampy, almost impassable, ground to the south, and a pool[1] under its east side, rendered the house a secure asylum for those who were constrained to practise

"The better part of valour,"

and remove themselves for a season from the eyes of the world and their enemies. Over the high gateway at the south end of the enclosure he placed a stone carved with the crest of the Tyldesley family—a pelican feeding its young—encircled by the loyal and patriotic motto—"Tantum valet amor regis et patriæ" : for long the roughly finished piece of carving was visible in the wall of an outbuilding, from which, however, it has recently been removed. Fox Hall was not without its plot of garden ground, a considerable space, being devoted to the useful products, was known as the kitchen garden, whilst another space was devoted to an apiary, and flowers must be supposed to have been an accompanyment of bees. It also boasted a bowling green and an ancient fig tree.

Thomas, the son of Edward Tyldesley, born in 1657, succeeded to the family estates on the death of his father, and later married, as his second wife, Mary, sister and co-heiress, with Elizabeth

1. Black-pool.

Colley, of Sir Alexander Rigby, knt., of Layton Hall, High-sheriff
of the county of Lancashire in 1691, whose father had erected a
monument to the memory of Sir Thomas Tyldesley near the spot
where he was slain.

During the year 1690, when the dethroned monarch James
II. invaded Ireland in the hope of regaining his crown,
Thomas Tyldesley prepared a secret chamber for his reception
in the interior of the Hall.   The closet or hiding-place was
afterwards known as the King's Cupboard.   The Pretender,
also, was reported to have been concealed for some time within
Fox Hall, and although it is certain that this aspirant to the
British throne was never within its friendly walls, still the secret
recesses, called " priests' holes," with which it appears to have
been liberally provided, formed excellent refuges for the clergy
and other members of the Romish Church, who on the slightest
alarm were enclosed therein, and so secluded from the prying eyes
of their hostile countrymen until the danger had passed.   These
latter incidents did not take place until after the decease of
Thomas Tyldesley, who died in 1715, shortly before the outbreak
of the rebellion, and was buried at Churchtown, near Garstang.
His son Edward, who succeeded him, was arrested for taking part
with the rebels, and escaped conviction and punishment only by
the mercy or sympathy of the jury, who after returning their
verdict of acquittal were severely censured by the presiding judge
for their incompetency and disaffection.   Edward Tyldesley died
in 1725.[1]   At what date Fox Hall passed out of the hands of the
Tyldesleys, it is impossible to trace, but it is doubtful whether the
Edward here named ever resided there, as he is always described
as of Myerscough Lodge, another seat of the family.   Mary
Tyldesley, the widow of his father, whom it will be remembered
he married as his second wife, was living there as owner in 1720,
and from that circumstance we must infer that the Blackpool
house was bequeathed to her by her husband Thomas Tyldesley,
and that the other portion only of the estates fell to Edward, the
son of his first marriage and his heir.   Poverty seems to have
overtaken the family with rapid strides ; their different lands and
residences were either mortgaged or sold, and whether Fox Hall

1. See ' Tyldesley of Fox Hall' in Chapter VI.

descended to the children of Mary Tyldesley, or returned again into the more direct line, it is certain that not many years after the death of Thomas Tyldesley it had ceased to be one of their possessions.

Thus, the annals of the founders of this solitary mansion carry us back to the period between 1660 and 1685, that is from the restoration to the death of Charles II., but certain entries in the register of Bispham church show that there must have been dwellings and a population, however thinly scattered, on the soil anterior to that period, sometime during the sixteenth century, and it was doubtless the descendants of these people who inhabited the neighbourhood when Edward Tyldesley appeared upon the scene and erected Fox Hall. The primitive structures forming the habitations of these aborigines were built of clay, roughly plastered on to wattles, and thatched with rushes more frequently than straw, the whole fabric being supported on crooks driven into the ground. About the epoch of Thomas Tyldesley drainage and cultivation began to render the aspect of the country more inviting, and fresh families were tempted to come down to the coast and rear their humble abodes under the wing of the great mansion, so that after a while a small hamlet of clustering huts was formed. It is more than probable that the morals and conduct of the dwellers in these huts were influenced in some way or other by the sojourners at the Hall, but whether for good or evil we are unable to say, as the time is now so hopelessly remote and no records of their habits and doings are extant, so that in the absence of any proof to the contrary, it is only fair and charitable to surmise that their lives were as simple as their surroundings

Whether the Tyldesleys were induced to locate themselves on this spot solely by a prospect of possessing some of the territory around, or were actuated also by a desire to have a retreat far removed from the scenes of disturbance with which the different factions were constantly vexing the land, is a matter of little importance, but to their presence it was due that the natural beauties of Blackpool were brought before the people at an early date. There can be no doubt that the priests and others, who had fled to the Hall as a harbour of refuge, would, on returning to their own districts, circulate glowing and eulogistic accounts of

the place they had been visiting—of the glorious beauty of the
sea, the endless stretch of level sands, and the bracing purity of
the breeze. In such manner a desire would readily be implanted
in the bosoms of their auditory to become personally acquainted
with the new land, which had created such a deep and favourable
impression on the minds of men, whose positions and education
warranted the genuineness of their statements and enhanced the
value of their opinions. There is one other circumstance worthy
to be mentioned as having in all likelihood aided considerably in
bringing the place into notice, and that is an annual race meeting,
held for long on Layton Hawes. The proximity of the site to the
residences of so many families of wealth and distinction, as the
Allens of Rossall, the Westbys of Burn Hall, the Rigbys of Layton
Hall, the Veales of Whinney Heys, the Heskeths of Mains, the
Cliftons of Lytham, and the Tyldesleys of Blackpool, must have
rendered the assembly one of no mean importance, and we may
picture in our minds the gay and brilliant scene presented each
year on the outskirts of the present town, when our ancestors in
their antique and many-hued costumes congregated to witness the
contests of their favourite steeds, and the level turf echoed to the
fleet hoofs of the horses as the varied colours of their riders flashed
round the course.

Although these incidents must have greatly tended to give
publicity to Blackpool, its early advances towards popularity were
dilatory, but this is to be attributed rather to the unsettled state
of the times than to a tardy appreciation of its advantages by
those who had enjoyed them or heard them described. During
the reign of George I., 1714-1727, a mere sprinkling of visitors
seems to have been attracted each summer to the hamlet, but a
few years later, about 1735, they had become sufficiently numerous
to induce one Ethart à Whiteside to prepare a cottage specially
for their reception and entertainment. Common report whispers
that he was further prompted to the venture by being the
fortunate possessor of a wife whose skill in cookery far excelled
that of any of her neighbours, but be that as it may, whether he
espoused the Welsh maiden because her culinary accomplishments
were an additional recommendation to him in the sphere in which
he had embarked, or whether the lodging house was a cherished
dream only converted into a reality on their discovery after

marriage, one thing is certain, his speculation prospered, and at
the end of fifty years he retired on what at that era was considered
a fortune.   The house in which he had laboured for half a century
was situated in the fields now occupied by General Street and the
neighbouring houses, on the site of what not long ago was a ladies'
school ; in appearance, it was a very ordinary cottage with the
usual straw thatch, somewhat oblong in form and possessing few
attractions to tempt the stranger to prolong his stay, but in spite
of all its disadvantages, the fascination of the sea and the novelty
of the surroundings filled it with guests summer after summer.
This dwelling claims the honour of having been the first ever fitted
up and arranged as a lodging house in Blackpool. On the retirement
of Whiteside, who a few years afterwards died at Layton, it passed
into the hands of a noted aboriginal, called Tom the Cobbler,
who appears to have held more ambitious views than his
predecessor, and converted the cottage into an inn, or at least
embellished its exterior with a rude lettered sign, and procured a
license to supply exciseable commodities within.   Those who had
been accustomed to the scrupulous care and cleanliness of
Whiteside and his thrifty wife, must have experienced a considerable shock from the eccentricities of the new proprietor ; each day
at the dinner hour he entered in working costume amongst the
assembled guests, and with grimy fingers produced from the depths
of his well rosined apron the allotted portion of bread for each.
How this peculiarity was appreciated by his visitors there are no
means of ascertaining, but as his dwelling did not develope in the
course of years into a modern and commodious hotel like the
other licensed houses which sprang up about that time and a little
later, we are inclined to fear that some internal mismanagement
caused its collapse.

In 1769 the whole hamlet comprised no more than twenty-eight
houses, or more correctly speaking hovels, for, with the exception
of four that had been raised to the dignity of slate roofs and a small
inn on the site of the present Clifton Arms Hotel, they were little
if any better.   These were scattered widely apart along the beach,
and one of them standing on the ground now occupied by the
Lane Ends Hotel, and adjoining a small blacksmith's shed, was
a favourite resort of visitors in search of refreshment.   Turf stacks
fronted almost every door, and the refuse of the household was

either carelessly thrown forth or else accumulated in putrifying heaps by the sides of the huts, so that nothing but their isolated situations and the constant currents of pure air from the sea sweeping over and around them could possibly have prevented the outbreak of some infectious and fatal disorder.

Bonny's Hotel, then known as old Margery's, and standing in the fields to the south, some distance from the sea, sprang up a little anterior to this time and received its share of patronage ; later it was converted into a boys' school and during recent years has been divided into cottages, etc. The Gynn House, erected northwards near the extremity or apex of a deep and wide fissure in the cliffs, formed another popular haunt during the season; the landlord at that hostel created much amusement by his oddities, and especially by his quaint method of casting up the reckoning on a horse-block in front of the door and speeding the "parting guest" with—" and Sir, remember the servants." A true and remarkable anecdote is related about the old inn ; sometime during the summer of 1833 a sudden and terrific storm burst over the western coast of this island, many vessels were lost and the shore off Blackpool was strewn with the battered fragments of unfortunate ships, which had either foundered in the deep or been dashed to pieces as they lay helplessly stranded on the outlying sandbanks. In the night as the gale raged with its utmost fury, a Scotch sloop was beating off the coast, vainly endeavouring to battle with the hurricane, and driven by the force of wind and wave nearer and nearer to the precipitous cliffs. When all hope had been abandoned and destruction seemed inevitable, some thoughtful person placed a lighted candle in the window of the Gynn House ; guided by this faint glimmer, the vessel passed safely up the creek, and the exhausted sailors were rescued from a dreadful death. Next morning a sad and harrowing scene presented itself along the coast ; no less than eleven vessels were lying within a short distance of each other, with their torn rigging and shattered spars hanging from their sides ; brigs, sloops, and schooners, the short but fearful gale had left little of them beyond their damaged hulls. Nor were these the only victims of the storm, for as the tide receded to its lowest the masts of two others rose above the surface of the water ; and during the next few days three large ships drifted past the town in an apparently waterlogged condition.

About that date, 1769, several heaps of mortar and other building materials, lying on the road which separated the front of the village from the edge of the cliffs, showed that more were anxious to follow in the footsteps of Whiteside and his earlier imitators.

Some idea may be formed of the class of people who visited Blackpool at that period from the charges made at Bonny's Hotel and the Gynn, the two principal inns, for board and lodging ; at the latter eightpence per day satisfied the modest demands of the host, while at the former the sum of tenpence was exacted, with a view no doubt of upholding its superior claims to respectability. In drawing our conclusions from these facts we must bear in mind that a shilling in those days represented much greater value than it does at present, so that the charges may not have been really so inadequate as they now appear. The village contained neither shop nor store where the necessaries or luxuries of life, if such things were ever dreamt of by the people, could be purchased, and large quantities of provisions had to be laid in at one time. Occasionally a sudden and unexpected influx of visitors occurred inopportunely, when the larder was low, and as a consequence the hungry guests were forced to wait, temporising with their appetites as best they could, until a journey had been made to Poulton and fresh supplies procured.

Ten years later the hamlet had grown somewhat in size, and the annually increasing numbers who flocked to its shores showed that its popularity was steadily gaining ground. Intercourse with the world beyond their own limited circle seems, however, to have had anything but an elevating or civilising effect upon the inhabitants, for we find amongst them at that time a band of professed atheists, whose blasphemous conduct called forth no rebuke or opposition from the rest, but was quietly tolerated, if not indeed approved. Each fortnight during the summer fairs were held on the Sabbath to provide refreshment and amusement for the visitors, who came in crowds to witness the magnificence of the highest spring tides. These gatherings usually terminated in disgraceful scenes of revelry and debauchery. Smuggling was carried on between the coast opposite the Star-hills and the Isle of Man, but never to a great extent or for any lengthened period.

These huge mounds of sand, much more numerous than in our day, formed excellent store-houses for the contraband goods, generally spirits, which were packed in hampers, and so overlaid with fish that their presence was never even suspected. The illicit cargoes were brought across the channel in trading vessels, from which they were landed by means of light open boats, and at once secreted in the manner just indicated, until a suitable opportunity occurred for their removal to one of the neighbouring towns. The success attending these ventures induced the smugglers to construct a sloop of their own, with the intention of prosecuting so profitable a trade on a larger scale, but information of their proceedings having been conveyed by some one to official quarters, a detachment of soldiers was promptly despatched to put an end to the nefarious practices. So thoroughly did these men effect their purpose, that, although no capture is recorded as having taken place, the whole band was dispersed, and from that date no more offences of this character have been known on the coast.

In 1788 the houses of Blackpool had increased to about thirty-five, and these were arranged in an irregular line along the edge of the cliffs; the intervals between the habitations being with few exceptions so wide that this small number stretched out from north to south, over a distance of quite a mile. One group of six was especially remarkable as presenting a more respectable and modern exterior than any of the others, most of which still retained a great deal of their original defective appearances, as though their owners were unwilling or unable to adapt themselves and their abodes to the improved state of things springing up around them. The company during the busiest part of the season amounted to about four hundred persons, and a news-room had been established for their use in the small cottage, before mentioned, on the site of the Lane Ends Hotel, the smith's shop adjoining having been converted into a coffee-room and kitchen, at which a public dinner was prepared each day during the summer, and served at a dining-room erected across the way. There were now four additional inns in the village, named respectively, Bailey's, Forshaw's, Hull's, and the Yorkshire House. The first of these had sprung up on the cliffs towards the north, and was kept by an ancestor of its present proprietor; the second was the nucleus from which has grown the Clifton Arms Hotel, whilst the third stood on the site of the Royal Hotel. The roads leading to the hamlet were in such an unfinished state that after heavy falls of rain they could be travelled only with the greatest difficulty, and often with considerable danger both to the vehicle and its occupants ; so that under these circumstances most people deemed it more prudent and expedient to perform the journey on horseback, some of them in the pillion fashion usual at that era. In an earlier part of this chapter we spoke of the troubled state of the times and the unsettled and harassed condition of the people as being the most probable causes why Blackpool was so long neglected by many who must have been well cognisant of its beauties in the days of the Tyldesleys, and with equal probability may we now conjecture that the dilapidated and frequently unsafe state of the highways had a serious effect in preventing numbers from visiting the place at this period. Regarding the matter from another point of view, we are led to infer that the four hundred composing the company of 1788, were people who, either in search of health or recreation, had willingly undergone the discomforts of a dreary and sometimes hazardous journey in order to make but a brief sojourn by the shores of Blackpool. Here, then, there is evidence of the great estimation in which the place was held at that early date by the dwellers in the inland towns, and of the rapidity with which its good fame was increasing and extending throughout a large section of the county. As may be naturally supposed, the large influxes of visitors and their turn-outs during the height of the season very much overtaxed the accommodation provided for them by the inhabitants, but that difficulty was easily surmounted by turning the horses loose into a field until their services were again required, whilst the surplus health or pleasure-seekers were lodged in barns or any outbuildings sufficiently protected from the weather. The village possessed two bowling greens of diminutive size, one of which occupied the land at the south-west corner of Lytham Street, whilst the other was in connection with the Yorkshire House, afterwards the York Hotel, and since purchased by a company of gentlemen, who razed it to the ground in order to erect more suitable buildings on the site. There was also a theatre, if that will bear the name which during nine months of the year existed under the more modest title of a barn ; rows of benches were placed one behind another, and separated into a front and back division, designated respectively pit and gallery. This house is said to have been capable of holding six pounds, the prices of admission being one and two shillings. At that period bathing vans were scarce, the majority of bathers making use of boxes, which were placed for their convenience along the shore, and as the mode in which they secured privacy and a proper separation of the sexes during indulgence in this pastime was both ingenious and entertaining, we will give a brief sketch of their arrangements. At a certain hour each day, varying according to the changes of the tide, a bell was rung when the water had risen almost to its highest. On hearing the signal, the whole of the gentlemen, however agreeably occupied, were compelled, under a penalty of one bottle of wine for each offence, to vacate the shore and betake themselves to their several hotels or apartments, whilst the ladies, after sufficient time had elapsed for any stray member of the sterner sex to get safely and securely housed, emerged singly or in small groups from the different doorways, and, hurrying down to the edge of the sea, quickly threw off their loose bathing robes, and in a moment were sporting amid the waves like a colony of nereids or mermaids. When these had finished their revels and duly retired to their homes, the bell rang a second time, and the males, released from *durance vile*, made their way to the beach, and were not long in following the example of their fair predecessors.

Mr. Hutton, in his small pamphlet descriptive of Blackpool in 1788, says :—" The tables here are well supplied ; if I say too well for the price I may please the innkeepers, but not their guests. Shrimps are plentiful ; five or six people make it their business to catch them at low water, and produce several gallons a day, which satisfy all but the catchers. They excel in cooking, nor is it surprising, for forty pounds and her maintenance is given to a cook for the season only. Though salt water is brought in plenty to their very doors, yet this is not the case with fresh. The place yields only one spring for family use ; and the water is carried by some half a mile, but is well worth carrying, for I thought it the most pleasant I ever tasted."

The prices at the inns and boarding-houses had risen as the

accommodation they offered had improved in quality and increased in extent, so that it was no longer possible to subsist on the daily expenditure of a few pence as in former times. In hotels of the first class 3s. 4d. per day, exclusive of liquors, was the charge for board and lodging ; dinner and supper being charged 1s. each to the casual visitor, and tea or breakfast 8d. In those of the second-class and some of the lodging-houses, 2s. 6d. per day covered everything with the exception of tea, coffee, sugar, and liquors ; whilst the smaller lodging-houses, generally crowded with visitors who were either willing or compelled to content themselves with the more frugal fare provided, charged only 1s. 6d. per day for each guest.

A promenade, six yards wide, carpeted with grass and separated from the road by white wooden railings, ran along the verge of the sea bank for a distance of two hundred yards, and was ornamented at one end with an alcove, whilst the other terminated abruptly at a rough clayey excavation, afterwards used as a brick croft. "Here," says the topographer already quoted, "is a full display of beauty and of fashion. Here the eye faithful to its trust, conveys intelligence from the heart of one sex to that of the other ; gentle tumults rise in the breast ; intercourse opens in tender language ; the softer passions are called into action ; Hymen approaches, kindles his torch, and cements that union which continues for life. Here may be seen folly flushed with money, shoe-strings, and a phæton and four. Keen envy sparkles in the eye at the display of a new bonnet. The heiress of eighteen trimmed in black, and a hundred thousand pounds, plentifully squanders her looks of disdain, or the stale *Belle*, who has outstood her market, offers her fading charms upon easy terms."

This parade was extended some years later by means of a bridge thrown from its south extremity over the road leading down to the shore, and on to the cliffs of the opposite side. Riding or walking, for those who were not fortunate enough to possess a horse or equipage, on the sands or promenade, and excursions into the country as far as the "Number 3 Hotel," where many of the company amused themselves with drinking "fine ale," were the favourite pastimes during the day, varied, however, with an occasional practice at the butts for bow and arrow shooting, the diurnal bathe, and contests on the bowling greens, to which we

have already alluded; in the evening or during unfavourable
weather cards and backgammon, or the theatre, were the means
with which the visitors beguiled the wearisomeness of the quiet
hours. The "Number 3 Hotel" above-mentioned stood behind
the present building bearing that name, at the corner of the
Layton and Marton roads.

Mr. Hutton relates several somewhat startling instances of the
curative properties of the sea at Blackpool; amongst them that of
a man, by trade a shoemaker and a resident of Lancaster, who
having become, through some unexplained cause, totally blind,
visited this watering-place for six weeks, during which he drank
large quantities of the marine element, daily bathing his eyes in the
same, and at the end of that time had so far recovered his sight
that he could readily distinguish objects at a distance of two miles.
Another case was that of a gentleman, who, having been seized
with a paralytic attack, which deprived him of the use of one
side, was ordered by his physican to Bath, but finding, after a fair
trial, that he derived no benefit from the combined action of its
climate and waters, he determined to travel northwards and make
a short sojourn at Blackpool. Whilst there the invalid was daily
carried into and out of the sea, and even after this process had been
only twice repeated he had lost the violent pains in his joints,
recovered his sleep, and in some considerable degree the muscular
power of the affected side, but of his further progress there is
no account.

The following lines, written by a visitor a few years after the
incidents we have just narrated, also show in what great estimation
the climate and sea of the village were held as remedial and
invigorating agents :—

> "Of all the gay places of public resort,
>   At Chatham, or Scarbro', at Bath, or at Court,
>   There's none like sweet Blackpool, of which I can boast,
>   So charming the sands, so healthful the coast ;—
>   Rheumatics, scorbutics, and scrofulous kind,
>   Hysterics and vapours, disorders of mind,
>   By drinking and bathing you're made quite anew,
>   As thousands have proved and know to be true."
>   *   *   *   *   *   *

At this time Blackpool was not only without a church, but in
the whole place there was no room where the inhabitants or

visitors were accustomed to assemble together for divine worship, and it was not until 1821 that the sacred edifice of St. John was completed and opened. In 1789 a subscription was started for the purpose of erecting a church, but was soon closed for want of support, barely one hundred pounds having been promised. Some years later a large room at one of the hotels was used as a meeting house on each Sabbath, the officiating ministers being obtained alternately from Bispham and Poulton, and occasionally from amongst the visitors themselves.

In 1799, the poorer inhabitants of Blackpool and its neighbourhood suffered severely, in common with others, from a failure in the grain and potato harvests. They, like most members of the working classes at that date, relied almost entirely upon good and plentiful crops of these important articles of diet, to furnish them with the means of sustenance throughout the year, so that a small yield, raising the prices exorbitantly, became a matter of serious moment to them, and in most instances, meant little less than ruin or starvation. After the cold and inclement approach of winter had banished the last stranger from their midst, the sums demanded for their accustomed provisions soon swallowed up the little these people had saved during the summer, and such occasional trifles as could be earned on the farm lands around whenever extra services were required. Their condition, deplorable from the first, gradually grew worse, until, reduced to the deepest distress, they became dependent for the bare necessaries of existence upon the charity of those whose positions, although seriously affected by the failure, were not placed in such great jeopardy as their own. After this precarious and pitiable state of things had lasted some time without any signs of amelioration, and it seemed difficult, if not impossible, to conjecture how the remaining months were to be provided for until the returning season brought fresh assistance to their homes, an unexpected, and, to them, providential occurrence relieved their sufferings. A large vessel laden with peas was wrecked upon the coast, and the cargo, washing out of the hold, was strewn upon the beach, supplying them with abundance of food until better days shone upon the impoverished village once more.

Reviewing the appearance of Blackpool at the opening of the nineteenth century we find that the whole hamlet was comprised between the Gynn to the north, and the ruins of the once aristocratic mansion of Fox Hall to the south. The houses with the exception of Bonny's Hotel and a few scattered cottages, had all been erected along the sea bank, the great bulk lying to the south of Forshaw's Hotel, and amounting to about thirty, whilst the space north of that spot as far as Bailey's Hotel was only occupied by one or two dwellings of very humble dimensions. These with the Gynn and a few habitations standing south of it on Fumbler's Hill, made up the number of houses to about forty. A detailed description of the different erections at that epoch is impossible, but we may state generally that those of modern origin, especially the hotels, although unpretending externally, were so arranged and provided that the comforts of the guests were fully insured, and in every way the accommodation they offered was immensely superior to any that could have been obtained thirty years before. The few old buildings that still remained had for the most part undergone considerable alterations, and been rendered more suitable for the purposes to which they were now devoted.

In 1801 the first official census of the inhabitants of the township of Layton-cum-Warbreck, in which Blackpool is situated, was taken, and furnished a total of 473 persons.

At that period many people attracted by the rising reputation of the watering-place were anxious to invest their capital in the purchase of land by its shores, and in the erection of houses adapted for the reception of visitors, but the proprietors of the hotels were the owners of a large portion of the soil, and fearing that the introduction of substantial and commodious apartments would interfere with the patronage of their inns, refused to dispose of any part of their lands, or at least placed such obstacles in the way of the would-be purchasers that bargains were seldom concluded. Had it not been for the energy and foresight displayed by one resident, Mr. H. Banks, who built several cottages and fitted them up with every convenience and requisite for summer dwellings, the prosperity of the village would have received a sudden check and doubtless a serious injury, for the provision made would have fallen far short of the requirements of an ever-increasing throng of visitors, and thus repeated disappointments would in the end have led to disgust and the absence of many when the following seasons rolled round. The probability of such a disastrous result seems at length to have been realised by the landlords themselves, who discovered that the plan to enlarge their own business was not to drive visitors away from the place by limiting the accommodation, but to offer them every inducement to come, and to have a sufficiency of houses ready to receive them when they had arrived. Under this new and more liberal impression greater facilities were offered both to purchasers of land and builders, so that the early error into which they had fallen was rectified before any great amount of harm had been done.

During the summer of 1808 the Preston volunteers were on duty at Blackpool for two weeks, and on the 4th of June celebrated the seventieth birthday of His Majesty George III. with many demonstrations of loyalty and rejoicing.

The small town now boasted five good class hotels, which, in their order from north to south, were named Dickson's, Forshaw's, Bank's, Simpson's, and the Yorkshire House. Simpson's, formerly Hull's, is now the Royal Hotel ; Bank's the Land Ends Hotel, and Dickson's was the one already mentioned as Bailey's Hotel. "Adjoining Forshaw's Hotel," writes a gentleman who visited Blackpool about that date ; "there are two or three houses of genteel appearance, compared with the many small cottages leading thence to the street, which is the principal entrance from Preston. There is a promenade with an arbour at the end of it, and beyond it nearer to Dixon's Hotel stands a cottage used as a warm bath. Beyond Dixon's there is a public road where two four-wheeled vehicles can pass each other." At a later period both the road and cottage alluded to had succumbed to the unchecked power of the advancing sea ; and here it will be convenient to mention other and much more serious encroachments made by the same element in the course of years now long gone by. We can scarcely conceive, when gazing on the indolent deep in its placid mood, that at any time it could have been possessed with such a demon of fury and destruction as to swallow up broad fields, acres upon acres, of the foreland of the Fylde, and in its blind anger sweep away whole villages, levelling the house walls and uprooting the very foundations, so that no trace or vestige of their former existence should remain. History, however, points to a hamlet called Waddum Thorp, which once stood off the coast of Lytham, fenced from the sea by a broad area of green pasture-land, now known as the Horse-bank ; and in more recent years a long range of star-hills ran southward from opposite the Royal Hotel, protecting a highway, fields, and four or five cottages from the waves, whilst a little further north a boat-house afterwards a shoemaker's shop, stood in the centre of a grassy plot, all of which have vanished, and their sites are now covered and obliterated by the sand and pebbles of the beach. The several roads, which had been formed at different seasons, leading over the cliffs to Bispham, were sapped away and destroyed so rapidly by the incursions of the tide that one more inland and circuitous was obliged to be made. On the sands, about three miles to the north of Blackpool, and so far distant from the shore that it is only visible when the water has receded to its lowest ebb, stands the famous Penny-stone. Near the spot marked by the huge boulder, tradition affirms that in days of yore there existed a small road-side inn, celebrated far and wide for its strong ale, which was retailed at one penny per pot, and that whilst the thirsty traveller was refreshing himself within, and listening to the gossip of "mine host," his horse was tethered to an iron ring fixed in this stone. It is stated that documents relating to the ancient hostelry are still preserved, but as the assertion is unsupported by any evidence of its veracity, we are prohibited from accepting it as conclusive proof that the inn owes its reputed existence to something more substantial than the lively imaginations of our ancestors. There is, certainly, one thing which gives some colouring of possibility, or perhaps, out of veneration for the antiquity of the tradition, we may advance a step and say, reasonable probability, to the story, and that is the historic fact, that at no very great distance from the locality there stood a village called Singleton Thorp until 1555, when it was submerged and annihilated by a sudden and fearful irruption of the sea. Several other boulders of various sizes are lying about in the neighbourhood of Penny-stone, bearing the names of Old Mother's Head, Bear and Staff, Carlin and its Colts, Higher and Lower Jingle, each of which is covered in a greater or less degree with shells, corallines, anemonies, and other treasures of the deep.

In 1811 the census of the persons residing in the township before specified, was again taken, and amounted to 580, showing an increase of 107 in the number of inhabitants during the preceding ten years.

The year 1816 is remarkable as being the first in which public coaches ran regularly between Preston and Blackpool. Previously the chief communication between the village and outlying places had been by means of pack-horses, carts, and private vehicles, with only occasional coaches.

The following description of Blackpool about the year 1816 was furnished by one of its oldest inhabitants, and, although unavoidably entailing some repitition of what has been mentioned before, will, we trust, be interesting in itself, as well as useful in confirming the earlier parts of this history, which have necessarily been compiled from previous writings on the subject, and not from the evidence of living witnesses. The Gynn House formed the most northerly boundary of the village, and, passing from that hostelry in a southerly direction, the next dwelling arrived at was Hill-farm, which still exists, and is at present used as a laundry for the Imperial Hotel. A few gabled cottages stood on the eminence called Fumbler's Hill, near the site of Carleton Terrace :—

> "Old Ned, and Old Nanny, at Fumbler's hill,
> Will board you and lodge you e'en just as you will."[1]

These cottages faced the south, as indeed did all the other dwellings at that time, with the exception of two or three of the hotels and a few of the more recent buildings. Bailey's, or rather Dickson's, Hotel was built in blocks of two and three stories, and possessed one bay window. It must be remembered that the stories of that day were much lower than those with which modern improvements have made us familiar. The next hotel was Forshaw's, similar in its construction, but unadorned with even one bay window ; between these two large inns were two or three small thatched cottages. Continuing our survey southwards were Dobson's Row, consisting of several slated cottages, with a circulating library and billiard room ; and the Lane Ends Hotel, containing three bay-windows, built, like the others, in parts of two and three stories each. In Lane Ends Street there

---

1. A couplet extracted from some lines descriptive of Blackpool and its accommodation, etc., in 1790, written by a visitor about that date.

was a general shop and lodging house combined, tenanted by a person named Nickson. The Royal, then commonly called the Houndhill Hotel, comes next in order, and a little distance behind it on the rising ground was a small thatched cottage for the reception of visitors. South Beach contained only a few thatched cottages, and on the site of the present Wellington Hotel stood a circular pinfold, built of cobble stone. Considerably west of the present line of frontage, and south of the pinfold, stood two rows of cottages almost on the edge of the shore; the last of these habitations was washed away or pulled down in 1827. Beyond the Yorkshire House and its bowling green was the dilapidated remains of Fox Hall, part of which had been converted into a small farm-cottage, in the occupation of a person named Wignall. Between Fox Hall and the Yorkshire House, but further removed from the beach, was a thatched cottage adjoining a stable, in which Mr. Butcher, of Raikes Hall, kept two or three racehorses, the field now occupied by the Manchester Hotel being used as an exercise ground for them. Chapel Street contained a small farm-house and several cottages, in addition to Bonny's Hotel, which was situated in a field at the lower end of this lane. In Church Street there were only three or four cottages, two of which, standing at the south-west corner, were slated and used as shops. A few other cottages, whose exact sites could not be recalled with accuracy, were scattered here and there, but the above will furnish the reader with a fairly correct idea of the extent and appearance of Blackpool about the year 1816.

The National Schools, at Raikes Hill, were the first provision made for the education of the young, and were built in 1817, chiefly through the exertions of Mr. Gisborne, then a temporary resident. They consist of two schools, for boys and girls respectively, with a teachers' home between. The accommodation has since been considerably enlarged and the institution is now under government inspection.

The parish church of St. John, in course of erection in 1820, was built with bricks from a croft situated on the cliffs between Dickson's Hotel and the promenade. This place of worship, originally an episcopal chapel under Bispham, with a perpetual curacy attached, was consecrated to St. John on July 6th, 1821, by Doctor Law, bishop of Chester. In 1860 a special district was assigned by order of Council to St. John's, which in that manner became, under Lord Blanford's Act, the parish church of Blackpool. The district thus cut off from the wide parochial area of Bispham, and constituted a distinct parish for all ecclesiastical purposes, was included between the Spen Dyke to the south and the central line of Talbot road to the north. The cost of the sacred edifice, which consisted, externally, of a plain brick structure, having a low embattled tower with pinnacles at the angles, amounted to £1,072, the whole of which was defrayed by voluntary subscriptons, the following individuals being the principal contributors :—

Mrs. Dickson	£100	Mr. John Forshaw	£100
Mr. Robert Banks	100	„ Robert Hesketh	50
„ H. Banks	100	„ Fielding	50
„ John Hornby	100	„ Jonathan Peel	50 10s.
A Friend	100	„ Bonny	50

The interior of the church, plain and neat, was lighted by small lamps for evening service during the winter, and contained a font which had once belonged to the old Roman Catholic chapel of Singleton ; and, a few years later, an organ built by Wren, of Manchester. In 1832 this building was enlarged by drawing out the east end, into which a plain window was inserted. The still increasing popularity of the watering place demanded another enlargement, which took place in 1847 ; but it was not until 1851 that the present chancel, containing a handsome stained glass memorial window to H. Banks, esq., who died in 1847, was added. The window embraces representations of Christ, the four evangelists, and the infant Jesus, with Joseph and his mother, etc., below which is the following inscription, surmounted by a coat of arms and motto :—"In memoriam Henrii Banks de Blackpool patris, et unius ex hujus Ædis patronis, tres sui liberi hanc fenestram fieri fecerunt." In 1862 it was thought desirable that further improvements should be made, and an open domed roof of pitch-pine was substituted for the old ceiling ; the floors of the pews, previously covered with asphalt, were boarded ; new windows of ground glass, and a fresh pulpit and reading desk were added to the church ; whilst a substantial iron railing was erected round the yard in place of the cobble wall, which had stood since the opening of the edifice, and in the same year the burial space was increased by including the plot of land lying to the west of the church, and now abutting on the houses of Abingdon Street. Four years later, in 1866, a new and larger tower, furnished with a clock and a peal of eight bells, was completed on the site of original one, which had been pulled down for this purpose. The interior of the church contains, in addition to the memorial window already alluded to, mural tablets *in memoriam* of Robert Banks, gent., died May 27th, 1838, aged 76 years,—" Ever mindful of the calls of general duty, he was also a liberal promoter of the erection and endowment of this church, and by will bequeathed the sum of £100, for the perpetual support of the national school"; Edward, the son of Henry and Margaret Banks, died August 8th, 1845, aged 35 years; the Rev. Thomas Banks, "who was for thirty-five years incumbent of Singleton church, and an eminent instructor of youth," died 1842, aged 73 years.

PERPETUAL CURATES AND VICARS OF ST. JOHN'S.

Date of Institution.	NAME.	On whose Preesentation.	Cause of Vacancy.
1821	James Formby, B.A.	Trustees.	
1826	G. L. Foxton, B.A.	Ditto.	Resignation of J. Formby.
1829	Wm. Thornber, B.A.	Ditto.	Resignation of G. L. Foxton.
1846	W. T. Preedy, B.A.	Ditto.	Resignation of W. Thornber.
1853	Alfred Jenour, M. A.	Ditto.	Resignation of W. T. Preedy.
1869	Norman S. Jeffreys, M.A.	Ditto.	Death of A. Jenour.

The present patrons of St. John's church are the Rev. C. Hesketh, of North Meols; the Vicar of Bispham; J. Talbot Clifton, esq., of Lytham Hall; and the Raikes Hall Park, Gardens, and Aquarium Company.

In 1821 the census returns of the population of Layton-with-Warbreck showed a total of 749 persons. On the 19th of July in that year the coronation of George IV. was celebrated by the inhabitants and visitors of Blackpool "in a manner most grateful to every benevolent heart." A handsome subcription, we are told by the gentleman whose words have just been quoted and who was present on the occasion, was expended in procuring one day's festivity for the poor and needy, the aged and the young. About ten in the morning, the children of the township, amounting to one hundred and thirty-nine, assembled at the national school, erected near the church, where they were each presented with a coronation medal. Afterwards they paraded the beach, headed by two musicians, and sang the national anthem at all the principal houses, followed by ringing cheers; returning to the school-house, each child was regaled with a large bun, and spiced ale and coppers were distributed amongst them. When these had been dismissed to their homes, upwards of thirty old people met in the same room, where they sat down to an ample and excellent dinner, at the conclusion of which they each drank the king's health in a pint of strong ale. The same kind-hearted ladies who had superintended the children in the procession, waited on this venerable company, and had their generosity rewarded by witnessing the amusing spectacle of three old women, upwards of seventy, who had probably danced at the coronation of George III., go through a Scotch reel, which they accomplished in excellent style.

On the 21st of March, 1825, the first stone of a small Independent chapel, situated at the lower end of Chapel Street, and lying on the south extremity of the village, was laid by the Rev. D. T. Carnson, and on the 6th of the ensuing July it was opened for public worship by the Rev. Dr. Raffles.

The summer of 1827 is remarkable as having been an exceptionally prosperous season for Blackpool; vast numbers of carts and other vehicles laden with their living freights arrived from Blackburn, Burnley, Colne, Padiham, and the borders of Yorkshire, and during the month of August so crowded was the place that many were lodged in stables and barns, whilst others sought refuge at Poulton. The following year a fine gravel promenade was tastefully laid out on the sea bank to a considerable distance, occupying a large portion of the site of the old road. A beautiful green turf walk was constructed from the beach to the church, leading through pleasant fields, and furnished at intervals with covered seats. The Albion Hotel was also erected at the north-west corner of Lane Ends Street.

Mr. Whittle, in his publication descriptive, amongst other resorts, of Blackpool in 1830, and entitled "Marina," says :— "Blackpool is furnished with excellent accommodation, although it is a pity but what there had been some kind of uniformity observed, as all sea-bathing stations ought to have their houses built upon a plan entirely unique. Four assemblies have been known to take place in one week during the bathing season, extending from July to October. In fact the rooms at the hotels are very extensive. Bank's is the most commodious. The inhabitants seem to have no taste for ornamenting their door-ways or windows with trellis work or verandahs, or with jessa-mines, woodbines, or hollyhocks, similar to those at Southport, and many of the sea-bathing situations in the south. It is not to be wondered at that there are here frequently at the flux of the season, from eight hundred to a thousand visitors. Blackpool has most certainly been honoured since its commencement as a watering-place by persons of distinction and fashion. The hotels and other houses of reception are scattered along the beach with an aspect towards the Irish Sea ; and in the rear are the dwellings of the villagers. The cottages on the beach have of late years considerably increased, and they serve, with the hotels in the centre, to give the place, when viewed from the sea, a large and imposing appearance."

The ball and dining-room at Nickson's Hotel, (the Clifton Arms,) was of large dimensions, and contained a neat orchestra at one end, whilst the following notice was suspended in a prominent position against the inner wall :—

" The friends of Cuthbert Nickson will please to observe that the senior person at the hotel is entitled to the president's chair ; and the junior to the vice-presi-dent's. Also the ladies to have the preference of the bathing machines."

Placards, similar in their import to this one, were to be seen in both Dickson's and Bank's Hotels.

The new promenade was improved in 1830 by the addition of a wooden hand-rail along its entire length, whilst comfortable seats were placed opposite the hotels of Banks and Nickson. The fairs, to which we have already alluded, continued to be held every second Sunday during the season, but a few years later they were abolished by the action of the more respectable portion of the residents. Letters arrived at half-past eleven in the morning, and were despatched at noon, daily in the summer months, but only three times a week during winter. Mr. Cook, an American, was the originator of the post, which he commenced some time before by having the letters carried to Kirkham three times a week during the season. At that day the arrival of the letter-bag was made known to the anxious public by exposing a board on which was written or painted, "The post is arrived." This ingenious device proclaimed, on reversing the board, "The post is not yet arrived;" so that by a proper use of the signal the postmaster was enabled to save himself much trouble in answering the frequent inquiries of expectant visitors. Mr. Cook, who is described as having been the "Beau Nash" of Blackpool, died in 1820, and was buried at Bispham. The charges at the best hotels were 6s. per day in private and 5s. in public, with an addition of 1s. each night for a front, or 6d. for a back, bedroom. At Bonny's the price was 4s. 6d. per day ; and at Nickson's and the Yorkshire House 3s. 6d. per day at the first table, and 2s. 6d. at the second, subject to an additional charge for extra attendance if required.

The census returns of 1831 showed that the population of the township had increased to 943 persons since 1821, when, the reader may be reminded, the total amounted to 749.

In 1835, a Wesleyan chapel, calculated to hold between 250 and 300 persons, was erected and opened in Bank Hey Street. This building, having in the course of time become inadequate for the accommodation of its increasing congregation, was pulled down, and the corner stone of the present edifice laid by W. Heap, esq., of Halifax, on Friday, November 1st., 1861. The chapel, which occupies a site near the old one, was opened for service on the 4th of July, 1862, and is capable of seating 760 persons. The total expenditure for the erection and other incidental expenses connected with it, amounted to £3,500. An organ, built by Mr. E. Wadsworth, of Manchester, at a cost of £320, was obtained in 1872.

During 1836 great improvements were made in the appearance of the town ; shops were beautified and increased in number ; many of the cottages were rendered more ornamental, whilst others were constructed on modern principles, and on a moderate calculation it may be estimated that two hundred beds were added to the existing accommodation. Sir Benjamin

Heywood, bart., of Claremont, purchased an extensive plot of land, now occupied by the Prince of Wales's Market and Aquarium Buildings, on which he shortly afterwards raised a handsome marine family residence, called West Hey. Numerous and copious springs of fine fresh water were found at a depth of fifteen yards from the surface ; until which fortunate discovery, water for drinking purposes had been collected in cisterns dug out of the marl. Public Baths were also erected on the beach adjoining the Lane Ends Hotel.

The following year, 1837, the Victoria Terrace and Promenade, erected at the north-west corner of Victoria Street, were completed. This block of buildings was formed of seven shops, above them being the Promenade, a room thirty-two yards long, which opened through folding windows upon a balcony six feet wide ; attached to it were a news-room, library, and billiard table. The Promenade acquired its distinctive title from being first used on the 24th of May, 1837, when the Princess Victoria, the present Queen, attained her legal majority ; on that day the principal inhabitants of Blackpool assembled there to celebrate the important event with a sumptuous dinner, and from the subjoined extract, taken from an account of the gathering in a public print, we learn the great estimation in which the saloon was then held :—

" * * * * dinner and excellent wine provided by Mr. C. Nickson, to which fifty-two gentlemen sat down, in the splendid Promenade Room newly erected by Doctor Cocker, who was highly extolled for his taste in the architectural design and decorations of the building, which is of the chaste Doric order, and for his spirited liberality in providing the visitors of this celebrated resort with so spacious and magnificent a saloon, where, as in a common centre, they may meet each other and enjoy the social pleasures of a *conversatione* whenever they please ; thus evincing his wish to promote a more friendly intercourse amongst the strangers collected here from all quarters of the kingdom during the summer season—this has hitherto been a *desideratum* at Blackpool."

For long afterwards balls and all public meetings were held in this assembly room, which still exists in its original condition, although the other parts of the block, especially the shops, have recently been improved and beautified.

From 1837 to 1840 the progress of the place was steady, but not rapid, as compared with more recent times. In the latter year the opening of the Preston and Wyre Railway to Poulton, initiated a mode of travelling until then unknown in the Fylde

district, and by its means Blackpool became nearer in point of
time to Preston, Manchester, and many other large towns already
possessing railway accommodation, a great accession of company
being the immediate result. Omnibuses, coaches, and other
carriages met every train at Poulton station, and the four miles of
road were scampered over by splendid teams in less than half an
hour. Then it was that the jolting, homely vehicles, and the
through coaches, which had for long been the dashing wonders of
the country roads, were driven off, and a greatly multiplied
number of visitors brought into the town daily by the more
expeditious route, at a less cost and with greater personal convenience than had been possible in earlier days. More accommodation was soon called for and as readily supplied by the
spirited inhabitants, who erected numerous houses at several
points, which served, at no distant period, as the nucleus for new
streets and terraces. The census of the township in 1841 had
risen to 2,168. In 1844 the erection and opening of a Market House,
evinced the growing importance and prosperity of the watering-
place ; this building has lately, since 1872, been enlarged by lateral
extension to quite double its original capacity, whilst the extensive
unprotected area opposite, used for similar trading purposes and
occupied by stalls, has been covered over with a transparent roof.
Talbot Road was opened out and the lower end formed into a
spacious square, (furnished with an elegant drinking fountain in 1870)
by the removal of a house from its centre. These improvements
were effected at the sole cost of John Talbot Clifton, esq., of
Lytham, the owner of the soil. The Adelphi and Victoria Hotels,
which had sprung into being, were altered and enlarged ; the
former by raising it a story, and the latter by the addition of a
commodious dining room, two sitting rooms, and sundry bedrooms.
Several spacious residences were finished on South Beach, and
a handsome terrace of habitations stretching south from Dickson's
Hotel, was also erected about that time.

In 1845, several houses on a larger scale, including the Talbot
Hotel, were built, and great improvements and additions made to
many former establishments.

The opening of the branch line from Blackpool to join the main
railroad at Poulton, on the 29th of April, 1846, gave another marked
impetus to the progress of the town ; by its formation direct steam

communication was completed with the populous centres of Lancashire and Yorkshire, and many, who had previously been deterred from visiting Blackpool by its comparative inaccessibility, now flocked down to its shores in great numbers ; building increased, and dwellings arose, chiefly on the front, and in Church and Victoria Streets.

During the ensuing year the first meeting of the Blackpool Agricultural Society was held on the grounds of a recently built inn, the Manchester Hotel, at South Shore ; the attendance was both numerous and respectable, including many of the most influential gentlemen, yeomen, and farmers of the neighbourhood, and several from the remoter localities of the Fylde. Cows, horses, and pigs appear to have been the only stocks to which prizes were awarded. The first Lodge of Freemasons held their initiatory meeting in that year at the Beach Hotel, another house of entertainment which had risen shortly before, on the site of some furnished cottage facing the beach.

A new Independent Chapel was commenced in Victoria Street, to supersede the small one erected in Chapel Street in 1825 ; the edifice was finished and used for divine service in 1849. Serious differences seem to have arisen a few years later between the pastor of that date, the Rev. J. Noall, and a limited section of his congregation, who were anxious to deprive him of his charge, and even went so far, in 1860, as to publicly read in the chapel, after morning service, a notice convening a meeting for that purpose. This act, being repeated on the ensuing Sabbath, led to retaliation on the part of the partizans of the minister, who, unknown to that gentleman, paraded three figures, intended to represent the three principal opponents to the continuance of his pastorate, suspended from a gibbet, which had been erected in a cart, through the streets of the town, and afterwards gave them up to the flames on the sands. The Rev. J. Noall was shortly afterwards presented with a testimonial of esteem by a number of sympathisers. Schools, in connection with the chapel, were built in 1870.

Two years subsequently, the watering-place had grown, without the fostering care of a public governing body, into a large and prosperous town, boasting a resident population of over two thousand persons, but this very increase and popularity had rendered it impossible for private enterprise to provide the requisite comforts and conveniences for such a mixture of classes as visited it during the summer. Acting under this necessity and for the welfare of the resort a Local Board was formed, composed of gentlemen elected from amongst inhabitants, into whose hands was entrusted the government and regulation of all matters connected with the place. An accession of power was sought in 1853, and on Tuesday, the 14th of June, the Blackpool Improvement Act received the royal assent. The Board originally consisted of nine members, but in 1871 the number was increased to eighteen.

One of the earliest acts of the new commissioners of 1853 was to provide for the proper lighting of the town by the erection of Gas Works, which they accomplished in their first year of office; for some time it had been evident that the season was seriously curtailed by the absence of any illumination along the promenade and thoroughfares during the autumn evenings, but private speculation had for some reason held aloof from so important an undertaking, although the question had been much discussed amongst the inhabitants. Here it may be stated, in order to avoid reverting to the subject again, that in 1863 there were 650 consumers of gas; in 1869, 1270; and in 1875, no less than 2,000; the miles of mains in those years being respectively 5, 7, and 12.

In 1856, the promenade, which had suffered much injury from frequent attacks of the sea, and perhaps from some amount of negligence in not bestowing due attention to its proper maintenance, was put in better order and extended from its northern extremity, opposite Talbot Square, along the front of Albert Terrace as far as Rossall's, formerly Dickson's Hotel. Four years later a portion of this walk opposite Central Beach was asphalted and sprinkled over with fine white spar. The Infant School-house in Bank Hey Street, was opened in 1856.

The Roman Catholic Church, situated in Talbot Road, was erected in 1857, from the design of Edwin W. Pugin, Esq., and at the sole expense of Miss M. Tempest, sister to Sir Charles Tempest, Bart., of Broughton Hall, Yorkshire. It is in the Gothic style, the exterior being built with Yorkshire flag in narrow courses, hammer dressed and tuck pointed. The church comprises a chancel, north and south transepts, two sacristies, confessionals, nave, aisles, south porch, and central western tower. The chancel, which is separated from the nave and transepts by a richly decorated and moulded arch, contains four side windows in addition to a large one at the east end. The nave is divided into five bays of fifteen feet each, with massive arches ornamented with deeply cut mouldings. The tower is of great solidity, and rises to a height of one hundred and twenty-four feet. Almost the whole of the windows are filled with richly stained glass ; and the altar within the chancel is beautified with elaborately carved groups, designed by J. H. Powell, of Birmingham, of the " Agony in the Garden," and the " Last Supper ;" whilst that in the lady chapel is adorned, from the pencil of the same artist, with illustrations of the " Assumption of the Virgin," and the " Annunciation," all of which are exquisitely carved by Lane. This church is dedicated to the Sacred Hearts of Jesus and Mary, and was the first one ever erected in Blackpool for members of the Roman Catholic Faith, service having been previously celebrated in a room in Talbot Road. In 1866 an excellent peal of cast steel bells was added to the tower ; and ten years afterwards a magnificent organ was opened in the main building. Attached to the church, and within the same enclosure, were placed day and Sunday schools, as well as a residence for the officiating priests. The cost of this magnificent pile, without the internal decorations, amounted to £5,500.

The foundation stone of the Union Baptist Chapel, in Abingdon Street, was laid on the 9th of April, 1860, and on Good Friday in the following year it was opened for divine worship by the Rev. Dr. Raffles. The main building, 80 feet long by 49 feet wide, is of brick, and finished with moulded and polished stone dressings in the Grecian style of architecture. The principal or west front is surmounted by a bold cornice and pediment, and contains the two chief entrances, which are approached by a long range of steps and a spacious landing. The interior is fitted with substantial open pews of red pine in the body, and similar seats are placed in the two end galleries, the whole being capable of providing accommodation for about 650 persons. The communion floor, under a portion of which is the Baptistry, is enclosed with an ornamental balustrade. The edifice is well supplied with light through plain circular-headed windows. A Sunday school was added in 1874, and an organ also purchased during that year.

From 1858 to the completion of the chapel the Baptists worshipped in the room formerly used by the Roman Catholics in Talbot Road.

In 1861, the progress and improvement of the town was well shown by three events which occurred at that date—the first sod of the Lytham and Blackpool coast line was cut at Lytham Park, on the 4th of September ; a large Market Hall, raised on South Beach, by Mr. W. Read, for the sale of useful and fancy articles was completed ; and the original Christ Church was opened on Sunday the 23rd of June, by the Rev. C. H. Wainwright, M.A. This church, which stood until the erection of the present one, was built of iron by Mr. Hemming, of London, at a cost of £1,000, which was advanced by eight gentlemen, who were subsequently reimbursed by contributions from the public and collections from the congregation at various times.

The population of Layton-with-Warbreck in 1861 amounted to 3,907 persons, of which number Blackpool contributed 3,506.

The passenger traffic on the Blackpool and Lytham Railway commenced on the 6th of April, 1862, and between that date and the 30th of June over 35,000 persons had taken advantage of the line and been conveyed between the two watering-places. In 1862 a handsome Police Station and Court-House sprang into being in Abingdon street, including residences, lock-ups, offices, magistrates' room, etc.

The streets of Blackpool no longer presented the meagre and broken lines of earlier days, but were in most instances well filled on each side with compact blocks of houses. In December, 1861, a few of the townpeople assembled at the Clifton Arms Hotel to consider the advisability of erecting a pier, to extend westward from the promenade opposite Talbot square ; and on the 22nd of January, 1862, the memorandum of association was signed with a capital of £12,000, being immediately registered. Plans were examined on the 10th of February, and the design of E. Birch, esq., C.E., selected, that gentleman being also appointed engineer. In April, the tender of Messrs. Laidlaw, of Glasgow, to construct the pier for £11,540 was accepted ; and a grant of the foreshore required for the undertaking having been obtained from the Duchy of Lancaster for £120, and £7 paid to the Crown for the portion beyond low-water mark, the first pile of the North Pier was screwed into the marl on the 27th of June, 1862, by Captain Francis Preston, the chairman of the company. A violent storm in the ensuing October damaged the works to some extent, and induced the company to raise the deck of the pier three feet above the altitude originally proposed, at an expense of £2,000. On the 21st of May, 1863, the pier was formally opened by Captain Preston, the auspicious event being celebrated by general rejoicings throughout the town and a procession of the different schools and friendly societies. The dimensions of the erection at that date were :—Approach, 80 feet long ; abutment, 120 feet long and 45 feet wide ; main portion, 1,070 feet long and 28 feet wide ; and the head, 135 feet long and 55 feet wide, giving a total length of 1,405 feet available as a promenade. The entire superstructure was placed upon clusters of iron piles, fixed vertically into the ground by means of screws, those at the abutment and main body being wholly of cast, and those at the head partly of cast and partly of wrought iron. The largest of the cast-iron columns measured 12 inches in diameter, and $1\frac{1}{3}$ inch in thickness, each column being filled in with concrete. The piles were arranged in clusters at intervals of 60 feet, and firmly secured together longitudinally, transversely, and diagonally, by rods and braces. The main girders, of the sort known as plated, were rivetted on the clusters in lengths of 70 feet, and formed parapets, presenting a pleasing appearance and constituting a most efficient wind guard to the pier. The tops of the girders were turned to useful account by converting them into a continuous line of seats. Next to the chief girders were fixed transverse wrought iron girders, upon the top of which the planking of the deck was laid, being arranged in longitudinal and transverse layers, so that no open spaces were left to admit the passage of wind or spray. The head of the pier, rectangular in form, was raised 50 feet above low-water mark, and leading from it to ample landing stages below, was a flight of steps 10 feet wide. The limits of the pier shore-wards were defined by ornamental iron gates with lamps, immediately inside which were the toll houses. Upon the main portion of the pier were erected several ornamental shelter and refreshment houses of an octagonal shape, and standing on side projections. Another ornamental shelter house of much larger dimensions was placed, within a few months, on the head. Lamps were provided along the entire length of the pier. In 1867 the directors determined to erect an iron extension or jetty, and in less than two years the work was accomplished at a cost of £6,000. During the month of May, 1869, a tender for the formation of the present entrance for £2,700 was accepted, and the agreement promptly carried out by Messrs. Laidlaw, of Glasgow. In October, 1874, the company arranged with the same contractors to enlarge the pierhead by putting out two wings, from the designs of E. Birch, esq., C.E., at an expenditure of £14,000. On the north wing it is intended to build a pavilion, 130 feet long by 90 feet wide, in an eastern style of architecture, and estimated to hold 1,200 persons seated. The edifice, around which there will be a promenade, is to be supplied with an orchestra, refreshment rooms, etc., and used as a concert room and fashionable marine lounge. The south wing, which is about 130 feet long, contains a bandstand, capable of holding 30 performers, at the further end, and on the east and west side two other buildings 62 feet by 27 feet each, the former being designed for the purposes of a restaurant, and the latter for the sale of fancy goods and other commodities. The unoccupied space, nearly 100 feet by 80 feet, will be provided with seats in the centre, the remainder serving as a promenade. The contract for the foregoing erections was let in 1875, to Messrs. Robert Neill and Sons, of Manchester, for nearly £12,000. In 1863, the capital of the company was raised to £15,000 ; in 1864, to £20,000 ; in 1865, to £25,000 ; in 1874, to £40,000 ; and in 1875, to £50,000.

About the period when the North Pier was constructed, and for years previously, the visitors to Blackpool could certainly complain of no lack of ordinary amusements during their brief residence by the sea. Horses, donkeys, and vehicles were ever in readiness to administer to their entertainment, either by conveying them for short drives to explore such objects of interest as the country afforded, or translating them for the day to the seaport of Fleetwood, or the neighbouring resort of Lytham. Bathing machines abounded on the sands, and during suitable states of the tide were busily engaged in affording ready access to the briny element to numbers, who were anxious to experience the invigorating effects of a bath in Neptune's domain. In the evenings theatrical representations were frequently held,

since 1861, in the spacious room of Read's Market. The Crystal
Palace, formerly the Victoria Promenade, was also devoted to
similar purposes, having long been diverted from the use for
which it was first intended. The Number 3 Hotel, under its old
name, but in a more modern building than that described by Mr.
Hutton at the close of last century, still flourished, and proved
equally attractive, not so much, however, on account of its "fine
ale" as the wealth of strawberries and floral beauties adorning its
gardens. Carleton Terrace was built in 1863; and on the 10th of
March in that year the marriage of the Prince of Wales and the
Princess Alexandra of Denmark, was celebrated with many
manifestations of loyalty and joy. Flags, banners, and ensigns
were suspended from the windows of almost every house, whilst
sports of various kinds were held on the sands during the
morning, after which the school children, belonging to the
different denominations, and a body of Oddfellows, amounting in
all to 900 persons, assembled in Talbot Square, and sang the
national anthem, previous to forming a procession and parading
the streets of the town. Subsequently the children were regaled
with tea, buns, etc. The Preston Banking Company established
a branch at Blackpool during 1863; and in the month of January
a party of gentlemen purchased the whole of the land lying
between the site of Carleton terrace and the Gynn, for the
purpose of laying it out in building plots and promenades, the
main feature to be a large central hotel standing in its own
grounds. The contracts were let by the company in October, 1863,
for embanking, sewering, and forming the necessary roads and
promenades on their estate, and shortly afterwards an agreement
was entered into for preparing the foundation of the hotel, the
work in both instances being promptly commenced. The
magnitude of the scheme far exceeded that of any undertaking
which had ever yet been attempted in Blackpool, but undisturbed
by the speculative character of their venture the proprietors
carried the enterprise through its various phases with a liberal
and vigorous hand, succeeding in the course of time in creating
an acquisition of incalculable beauty and benefit to the town.
The Imperial Hotel has its station on the highest point of the
land, now called Claremont Park, and is a palatial edifice,
surrounded by elegant lawns and walks, walled off from the park

outside. In 1876 an extensive enlargement, consisting of a south wing, containing 39 bedrooms and 6 sitting-rooms, was made to the establishment. The cliffs fronting the estate, formerly rugged and uneven, were sloped and pitched to form a protection from the inroads of the tide, whilst a broad marine promenade was made along the whole length of the park, about a mile, and fenced with an iron railing on its open aspect. The main promenade of the town was continued round the west side of the park as far as the Gynn, but on a lower level than the walk just indicated. Shrubs were planted and toll houses, with gates, fixed at the entrances to the estate, all of which was enclosed with railings. The splendid residences denominated Stanley Villas, Wilton Parade, Imperial Terrace, and Lansdowne Crescent were not dilatory in rearing their several heads in a locality so congenial to their aristocratic proclivities, the foundations of the last being prepared in 1864.

In 1864 the Lane Ends Hotel was levelled to the ground, and the present handsome structure, in the Italian style of architecture, raised on the site, being re-opened again two years later. The foundation stone of the United Methodist Free Church was laid in Adelaide Street on the 30th of March, in the year specified, by James Sidebottom, esq., of Manchester, service being held in the building in the course of a few months ; whilst the newly-arrived lifeboat was launched, and the first supply of the Fylde Waterworks Company passed through their pipes to Blackpool on the 20th of July. The station of the lifeboat, named the "Robert William," is situated near the beach at South Shore, close to the Manchester Hotel ; and here we may mention that this boat, under the skilful and intrepid management of its crew and coxswain, has been instrumental on several occasions in affording aid in time of shipwreck. Amongst these instances may be noted the rescue of a crew of fourteen persons belonging to the barque "Susan L. Campbell," wrecked on Salthouse Bank on the 11th April, 1867, assistance being rendered also to the barque "A. L. Routh "; and the rescue of the crew of the schooner "Glyde," stranded on the South Beach on the same eventful morning. The annual expense incurred in the support of this valuable institution is defrayed by voluntary contributions.

The unflagging efforts of the inhabitants to promote the comfort of their visitors in matters of household convenience and accommodation, and to render their sojourns by the shore productive of pleasurable, as well as healthful, sensations, were manifestly well appreciated by those for whose benefit they were intended. The daily crowds parading the recently-erected pier were satisfactory evidence of the high estimation in which that elegant addition to the attractions of the place was held, whilst the thronged thoroughfares during the heat of summer bore witness to the growing affection which Blackpool was gaining for itself in the hearts of the million. Active exertions were necessary on the part of the builders to keep pace with the ever-increasing demand for more extended residential provision, houses being scarcely completed before the eager tenants had established themselves in their new domiciles. The greater portion of the Clifton Arms Hotel was pulled down in the autumn of 1865, and rebuilt on an enlarged and improved scale, being finished and ready for occupation in the ensuing spring. On the 20th of June, 1865, the first members of the Blackpool Volunteer Artillery Corps, amounting to about 60 men, took the oath customary on enrolment, and at the same meeting appointed their officers. Ten years later a commodious drill-shed was erected for their use.

In 1866 the temporary iron church, to which allusion has been made in a late page, was superseded by the existing substantial one in Queen Street, bearing the name of its predecessor. The edifice was opened for divine service on Thursday, the 3rd of May, by the Rev. E. B. Chalmers, M.A., of Salford, but was not consecrated until 1870. The architecture is an early and simple style of decorated Gothic, with thick walls and prominently projecting buttresses. The east and west ends are lighted respectively by four and five-light traceried windows and lancets. The steeple, which is well buttressed, has in its upper stage a belfry for six bells, and is surmounted by a vane. Until recent additions were made, the church contained sittings for 1,000 persons. The building originally comprised a broad nave, with a central aisle and two side passages giving access to the seats, all of which were open benches with sloping backs; north and south transepts with galleries, lighted by bay windows; a spacious chancel, with north and south aisles, the former being fitted up as a vestry, and the latter used as the organ-chamber; a spacious porch at the west end, with a wide double door ; a west gallery extending over the porch, and approached by a stiarcase along the basement of the tower ; and a baptistry covered with a separate hipped roof. The alterations just alluded to were carried out in 1874, and consisted of the erection of north and south aisles to the nave, providing accommodation for about 300 more worshippers. The district assigned to Christ Church in 1872 was converted into a parish in 1874, and the title of vicar given to the incumbent. The Rev. C. H. Wainwright, M.A., to whose exertions the new structure mainly owes its existence, was the first incumbent, and is the present vicar. The schools connected with the church are situated in Queen Street, and were built in 1872.

During the year 1866 the Lancaster Banking Company and the Manchester and County Banking Company each opened a branch in Blackpool, and like the Preston Bank, previously referred to, now transact business daily.

In July, 1867, the Prince of Wales Arcade on Central Beach was finished and opened, comprising a block of building, with extensive market accommodation, assembly rooms, etc., erected on the site between the Beach and Royal Hotels in an imposing and ornamental style of architecture ; and on the 19th of December, the corner stone of the Temperance Hall in Coronation Street was laid by the Rev. R. Crook, and in the following July the erection was completed and opened. The temperance movement had been commenced in Blackpool four years anterior to that date, when a Band of Hope in connection with the United Methodist Free Church was formed, and the number of its members increased so rapidly in the intervening time that it was considered advisable to build the present Hall for their meetings, and for those of others who were interested in the same cause.

The marked success which had attended the construction of the North Pier induced a company of gentlemen to erect a similar one, running seaward from the margin of the promenade at the south of Blackpool. The first pile was screwed in July, 1867, and on the 30th of May, 1868, the South Pier and Jetty were thrown open to the public without any inaugural ceremony. It is built of wrought iron and timber, and has the following dimensions :—Total length 1,518 feet, the main promenade being 1,118 feet, and the lower promenade or jetty 400 feet ; the entrance is on an abutment 60 feet wide, where there are gates, toll-houses, waiting and retiring-rooms ; the pier head is rectangular in form, and composed of strong timber, containing an area of 8,120 superficial feet. The chief promenade is furnished with seats on each side throughout its whole length, together with twelve recesses, on which are shops for the sale of fancy articles and refreshments. On the head of the pier are placed two large waiting and refreshment rooms, as well as a commodious shelter and wind guard. At the extremity of the jetty is a beacon and light as required by the authorities at Trinity House.

In 1868 a magnificent pile of buildings, erected in Talbot Square, and called the Arcade and Assembly Rooms, was completed. This structure contains a basement and arcade of very elegant shops, a restaurant, refreshment and billiard rooms, together with a handsome and spacious saloon, surrounded within by a gallery, and furnished with a neat stage for theatrical representations and other entertainments. Several sleeping apartments were added in 1874, and a certain section of the edifice arranged as a private hotel.

The promenade had always been esteemed so much the property of the house and land owners on the front of the beach that to them was delegated the onerous duty of maintaining in repair such portions of the hulking as ran before each of their possessions, the walk itself being kept in order and supported by subscriptions amongst the visitors and residents generally. Under this arrangement although the embankment was ensured from being carried away by the waves, there was no certainty that its upper surface would invariably present that neat and finished appearance so necessary to the success of a marine promenade. Voluntary contributions are in most instances but a precarious support on which to rely exclusively, and at Blackpool their unfortunate characteristic was prominently exemplified, more particularly during the earlier years of the watering-place, when visitors, whom the summer had drawn to the coast, too frequently discovered their favourite lounge in a state far from attractive to the pedestrian. Recently there had been comparatively little cause for complaint as to the condition in which each opening season found the promenade, but it was felt on all sides that the day had arrived when a new and much more extensive walk should be laid out, and that the responsibility of maintaining both it and the fence in proper order should devolve upon the town, from the funds, or rather borrowing powers, of which it was proposed to carry out the undertaking. In 1865 a special act of parliament had been obtained with this object by the Local Board of Health, at a cost of £2,159, by which permission to borrow up to £30,000 was granted, but no active steps were then taken, and three years later a supplemental act was procured to borrow up to an amount which, when added to the amount already in hand under the former act, would not exceed altogether two years' assessable value, the whole to be repaid within a period of fifty years from the date of receiving the loan. There were other difficulties to encounter, notwithstanding that the Board had the power .of compulsory purchased granted, in the buying of land to prosecute the purpose of the act. These were ultimately overcome by arbitration in cases where disputes had arisen. A supplemental act in 1867 allowed the board to amend and curtail several clauses in the original act, the first of which was to abridge the dimensions of the proposed work, the second to empower the levying of rates according to the act of 1865 on the completion of each section of the undertaking, and the third to extend the time for the compulsory purchase of land from three to five years. According to the act the commissioners gained a right to collect tolls for the usage of the promenade from all persons not assessed or liable to be assessed by any rate leviable by the Local Board of Health, with the exception of those crossing to the piers. This power, it may be stated, was not intended to be, and never has been, put in force. The promenade proposed to be made would reach from Carleton Terrace to the further end of South Shore, a distance of about two miles ; and the work was divided into three sections, the first of which, begun in 1868, was let to Mr. Robert Carlisle, contractor, for £16,043, and extended from South Shore to the Fox Hall Hotel. The storm which occurred on January 31st, 1869, washed away 350 yards of the newly-constructed sea fence and carriage-drive, with about 16,000 cubic yards of embankment, and about 6,000 square yards of pitching. Another storm which took place on the 28th of February, added considerably to the damage just stated, by tearing down a length of 250 yards, which was entirely completed, so that the total injury inflicted by the waves during the gale represented 600 lineal yards of sea fence, carriage-drive, and promenade, comprising 21,000 cubic yards of embankment, all of which had to be replaced from the shore at a considerable expense, in addition to 9,500 square yards of pitching, etc., connected therewith. No. 2 section, running from the Fox Hall Hotel to the New Inn, was contracted for by a Manchester gentleman at £3,964, but in consequence of his not not being able to carry out the work, it was re-let, and Mr. Chatburn succeeded him on the increased terms of £4,942. No. 3 section, stretching from the New Inn to the southern extremity of Carleton Terrace, was also constructed by Mr. Robert Carlisle, at a cost of £10,356. The whole of the ironwork was supplied by Mr. Clayton, of Preston, and necessitated an expenditure of £3,275. The sea fence consists of a sloping breastwork, pitched with stones on a thick bed of clay puddle, the interstices between the stones having been filled in with asphalt or cement concrete. The slope is curvilinear, and one in four on an average. Next to the breast is the promenade and carriage-drive. The promenade is seven yards wide, and has an even surface of asphalting, being separated from the carriage-drive by a line of side stones. In order to obtain space between the houses and the sea for the promenade and carriage-drive, a part of the shore was regained by an embankment along South Shore, and along the northern district by an iron viaduct, which projects considerably over the sea fence, and encircles the marine aspect of Bailey's Hotel. The floor of the viaduct is formed with patent buckled plates, filled in with concrete, and finished with asphalt. The plates are fixed to rolled joists, and supported on neat cast-iron columns, screwed down into the solid. The west front of the promenade is guarded by an iron railing, and furnished at intervals with seats of the same material, situated on the embankment to the south, and on projecting ledges of the viaduct along the northern length. The carriage-drive, twelve yards wide, runs parallel with the promenade throughout the entire extent, and is formed of shingle, clay, and macadam. It has a footway along the frontages of the adjoining property, the whole being well drained and lighted with gas. The complete structure was finished and formally opened to the public on Easter Monday, 18th of April, 1870, by Colonel Wilson-Patten, M.P., the present Lord Winmarleigh. The town was profusely decorated with bunting of every hue ; triumphal arches of evergreens and ensigns spanned many of the thoroughfares, notably Talbot Road and along the front ; whilst an immense procession, consisting of the Artillery Volunteers, Yeomanry in uniform, trades with their emblems, friendly societies, schools, etc., headed by a band, and comprising in its ranks no less than twelve mayors from important towns of Lancashire, conducted Colonel Wilson-Patten to that portion of the promenade opposite Talbot Square, where the ceremony of declaring the walk accessible for public traffic was gone through. During the evening the watering-place was illuminated, and the eventful day closed with a large ball, held in honour of the occasion.

The wisdom of the authorities in having Blackpool provided with a marine promenade and a frontage unrivalled by any on the coasts of England was soon evinced by the increase in the stream of visitors poured into the place during the summer months. Fresh houses for their accommodation were being rapidly erected in many parts of the town, and everywhere there were ample evidences that prosperity was dealing liberally with the town. The wooden railings, which heretofore had been deemed sufficiently ornamental fences for the residences facing the sea, were removed, and elegant iron ones substituted, apportioning to each habitation its own plot of sward or garden. The proprietor of Bailey's Hotel hastened to follow the example which had been set by those who were interested in the Clifton Arms and Lane Ends Hotels, and commenced a series of levellings and rebuildings, under the superintendence and according to the designs of Messrs. Speakman and Charlesworth, architects, of Manchester, which extended over several years, and have now rendered the hotel one of the most imposing and handsome edifices in the watering-place. Further alterations, consisting in the erection of shops on a vacant piece of land lying on the north side of the hotel, in the same style of architecture, and continuous with it, were carried out in 1876.

In 1871 a project was launched for purchasing Raikes Hall with the estate belonging thereto, situated on the east aspect of Blackpool, and converting the latter into a park and pleasure gardens. In that year a company was formed, entitled the Raikes Hall Park, Gardens, and Aquarium Company, and the land obtained without delay. Vigorous operations were at once commenced to render the grounds of the old mansion suitable for the purposes held in view, whilst the building itself speedily underwent sundry alterations and additions in its transformation into a refreshment house on a large scale. A spacious terrace, walks, promenades, and flower beds were laid out, and an extensive conservatory constructed with all haste, and in the summer after gaining possession of the estate, the works had so far progressed that the public were admitted at a small charge per head. Since that date a dancing platform has been put down, an immense pavillion erected, and many other changes effected in the wide enclosure. Pyrotechnic displays, acrobatic performances, etc., are held in the gardens, which comprise about 40 statute acres, during the season, whilst agricultural shows and other meetings occasionally take place within its boundaries. An extensive lake was formed in 1875, and an excellent race-course marked out. Raikes Hall has a brief history of its own, and was erected about the middle of the eighteenth century by a Mr. Butcher, who resided there. Tradition affirms that this gentleman sprang suddenly into an ample fortune from a station of obscurity and poverty, giving rise to a supposition that he had appropriated to his own uses a large mass of wealth asserted to have been lost at that time in a vessel wrecked on the coast. It is probable, however, that the foregoing is merely an idle tale, utterly unworthy of credence. Mr. Butcher, who was succeded by his son, died in 1769, at the ripe age of 80, and was interred in Bispham churchyard, the following words being inscribed on his tombstone :—

> " His pleasure was to give or lend,
> He always stood a poor man's friend."

The mansion and estate were purchased by William Hornby, esq., of Kirkham, shortly before his death in 1824, and by him bequeathed to his brother John Hornby, esq., of Blackburn, who married Alice Kendall, a widow, and the daughter of Daniel Backhouse, esq., of Liverpool. Daniel Hornby, esq., the eldest son of that union, inherited the property on the decease of his father in 1841, and took up his abode at the Hall until the early part of 1860, when he left the neighbourhood. Raikes Hall then became the seat of a Roman Catholic Convent School, which continued in possession for several years, until the new and handsome edifice standing on a rising ground in Little Layton was erected and ready for its reception. Shortly after the removal of the school the land and residence were purchased by the company above named, and their aspects began to undergo the changes already indicated. The census returns of the township collected in 1871, furnished a total of 7,902 persons, all of whom, with the exception of an insignificant proportion, were resident in Blackpool.

In consequence of a letter from the Secretary of State, giving notice that the burial ground in connection with St. John's Church must be closed after the 31st of December, 1871, the responsibility of providing a suitable place for interments was thrown upon the authorities, and the members of the Local Board of Health formed themselves into a Burial Board, their first meeting being held on the 20th of June in the year just specified. A committee was appointed, and in the ensuing August purchased for £1,759 an eligible site of 8½ acres, lying by the side of the New Road, into which the entrance gates of the cemetery now open. The plans for the requisite erections were prepared by Messrs. Garlick, Park, and Sykes, architects, of Preston, and the work of preparing the ground commenced in October, the contract for the chapels and lodge being let in December. As such a brief interval had to elapse before the order for closing the churchyard would be put in force, the Board applied, successfully, for permission to keep it open six months longer. The cemetery, however, progressed so tardily that it was necessary to renew the application on two future occasions, and the churchyard continued in use until the 31st of May, 1873. Five acres of the land were laid out from plans supplied by Mr. Gorst, surveyor to the board, and were divided into nine sections, four of which were apportioned to the Church of England, three to the Nonconformists, and two to the Roman Catholics. The cemetery was enclosed from the highway by stone palisadings and boundary walls, having massive iron railings. The approach to the grounds is through a spacious entrance, with a double iron gate in the centre, and a single gate on either side, hung to stone pillars. Inside the gate is the lodge, built of stone and comprising a residence for the keeper, offices,. etc. The mortuary chapels, which are all of stone, have an elegant appearance, that of the Church of England being stationed in the middle, with the Nonconformists' and Roman Catholics' edifices lying respectively west and east of it. The style of the buildings is Gothic of the first pointed period. The roofs are open-timbered, high-pitched, and covered with Welsh slates in bands of different colours, being also crested with tiles. Entrance to the chapels is gained by a porch, and there is a vestry attached to each. The floors are laid with plain tiles of various tints. Evergreens, shrubs, and forest trees have been planted on the borders of the grounds, whilst the walks are wide and well cared for. The Nonconformists were the first to take possession of their portion, which was dedicated to its solemn uses by a service held on the 7th of February, 1873, exactly one week after which an interment took place, being the earliest not only in their land but in the whole ground. On the 2nd of August in the same year the Right Rev. Dr. Fraser, bishop of Manchester, consecrated the division set apart for the Church of England, which had been licensed for burials in the previous May. The Roman Catholics deferred their ceremonial until the month of June, 1874, acting under license during the interval.

On the 26th of August, 1872, the Blackpool Sea Water Company was registered under the limited liability act, with a capital of £10,000, in shares of £10 each, for the purpose of supplying water from the deep, together with the requisite appliances for conducting it to the houses and elsewhere, to the inhabitants of Blackpool ; and rather more than two years later a main of pipes had been laid along the front from the Merchants' College in South Shore as far as their steam pumping works in Upper Braithwaite Street.

In 1874 the watering-place had developed so rapidly during past years that the members of the Local Board of Health felt that the powers appertaining to a body of that description were no longer adequate to the proper government of the town, and a public meeting to ascertain the opinion of the ratepayers on the subject of incorporation was called on Tuesday, the 6th of November, 1874. After considerable discussion, it was proposed by the Rev. N. S. Jeffreys : "That a petition be drawn up and signed by the chairman on behalf of the meeting, praying that a Charter of Incorporation be granted for the town of Blackpool, and that the same be forwarded to the proper authorities; and that the necessary steps be taken to obtain such Charter." The proposition was adopted without a dissentient; and at the ensuing assembly of the Local Board of Health on Tuesday, the 10th of November, a similar motion was brought forward by W. H. Cocker, esq., J.P., with an equally successful result. The prayers were forwarded to the appropriate official quarters in London, and on the 26th of May, 1875, Major Donnelly, R.E., the commissioner appointed by Her Majesty's Privy Council, attended at the Board-room to hold an inquiry as to whether the importance and necessities of the place warranted a favourable answer to the request. In the course of the examination, it was stated, amongst other things, that the rateable value of the proposed borough was in 1863, £17,489; 1866, £35,175; 1869, £45,755; 1872, £55,653; 1874, 63,848; and in 1875, £73,035. Also that the town contained three churches, seven chapels, three rooms used for religious services, two markets under the Local Board, other markets owned by private individuals, four public sea-water baths, three banks, an aquarium, public gardens, etc. On the 16th of the following July information was officially conveyed to W. M. Charnley, esq., the law-clerk of the board, that the lords of the Privy Council had determined to accede to the prayer of the town, and that the borough should consist of six wards, with one alderman and three councillors for each. A draft of the scheme of incorporation was prepared by the law-clerk, and forwarded to London. On the 22nd January, 1876, the charter, having passed through the necessary forms, obtained the royal assent, being received by W. M. Charnley, esq., two days later. The document, after quoting several acts of parliament, proceeds to "grant and declare that the inhabitants of the town of Blackpool and their successors, shall be for ever hereafter one body politic and corporate in deed, fact, and name, and that the said body corporate shall be called the Mayor, Aldermen, and Burgesses of the Borough of Blackpool, who shall have and exercise all the acts, powers, authorities, immunities, and privileges which are now held and exercised by the bodies corporate of the several boroughs" similarly created. Further, the deed "grants and declares that the said Mayor, Aldermen, and Burgesses and their successors shall and may for ever hereafter use a common seal to serve them in transacting their business, and also have armorial bearings and devices, which shall be duly entered and enrolled in the Herald's College;" also shall they have power "to purchase, take, and acquire such lands, tenements, and heriditaments, whatsoever, situate, lying, and being within the borough, as shall be necessary for the site of the buildings and premises required for the official purposes of the corporation." The Council was ordained to consist of "a Mayor, six Aldermen, and eighteen Councillors, to be respectively elected at such times and places, and in such manner" as those of other boroughs existing under the same acts, in common with which they "shall have, exercise, and enjoy all the powers, immunities, and privileges, and be subject to the same duties, penalties, liabilities, and disqualifications" appertaining to such positions. The first election of councillors was directed to be held on the eleventh day of April, 1876, followed by another on the 1st of November, at which latter date one-third part of the councillors should go out of office each year, and the vacant seats be refilled as specified; the councillors to retire in the November, 1876, being those who had obtained the smallest number of votes, and in November, 1877, those with the next smallest number of votes. The first aldermen of the borough "shall be elected and assigned to their respective wards on the 19th day of April, 1876, and the councillors immediately afterwards shall appoint who shall be the aldermen to go out of office upon the 9th day of November ensuing," and in subsequent years those so retiring to be aldermen who have retained their seats for the longest period without re-election. The first mayor of the borough "shall be elected from and out of the aldermen and councillors of the said borough, on the 19th day of April, 1876," the earliest appointment of auditors and assessors being made on the 19th day of the following month. The subjoined extent and names of the wards are also taken from the charter :—

CLAREMONT WARD.

"Commencing at the Sea beyond the Gynn, at the junction of the old existing township boundary, thence running inland along the same boundary across the fields, across Knowle-road, behind Warbrick and Mill Inn, across Poulton-road to the centre of the Dyke at Little Layton, thence along the Dyke to the centre of

Little Layton Bridge, thence westward along and including the north side of Little Layton-road, north side of New-road, north side of Talbot-road, to Station-road, thence along and including the east side of Station-road to Queen-street, thence along and including the north side of Queen-street, Queen's-square, across the Promenade to the sea.

TALBOT WARD.

"Commencing at the Sea opposite the centre of Queen's-square, thence along and including the south side of Queen's-square, south side of Queen-street to Station-road, thence running along and including the west side of Station-road to Talbot-road, thence along and including the south side of the upper portion of Talbot-road, south side of New-road, the south side of Little Layton-road to the centre of Little Layton Bridge, thence along the Dyke to the old township boundary, thence south-east by the township boundary to the centre of Dykes-lane, thence westward along and including the north side of Dykes-lane, the north side of Layton-road, the north side of Raikes-road, the north side of Raikes Hill, the north side of Church-street to Abingdon-street, thence along and including the east side of Abingdon-street to Birley-street, thence along and including the north side of Birley-street, the north side of West-street, across the Promenade to the Sea.

BANK HEY WARD.

"Commencing at the Sea opposite the centre of West-street, thence along and including the south side of West-street, the south side of Birley-street to Abingdon-street, thence along and including the west side of Abingdon-street to Church-street, thence along and including the south side of Church-street to Lower King-street, thence along and including the west side of Lower King-street to Adelaide-street, thence along and including the north side of Adelaide-street, the north side of Adelaide-place, across the Promenade to the Sea.

BRUNSWICK WARD.

"Commencing at the Sea opposite the centre of Adelaide-place, thence along and including the south side of Adelaide-place, the south side of Adelaide-street to Lower King-street, thence along and including the east side of Lower King-street to Church-street, thence along and including the south side of Church-street, the south side of Raikes Hill, the south side of Raikes-road, the south side of Layton-road, the south side of Dykes-lane to the existing township boundary, thence along the same boundary beyond the Whinney Heys, around the Belle Vue Gardens, southward of Raikes Hall Gardens to the centre of Revoe-road, thence along and including the north side of Revoe-road, the north side of Chapel-street, across the Promenade to the Sea.

FOXHALL WARD.

"Commencing at the Sea opposite to the end of Chapel-street, thence along and including the south side of Chapel-street, the south side of Revoe-road to the existing township boundary, thence south-westerly, and thence south-easterly along the same boundary to the centre of Cow Gap-lane, thence west along and including the north side of Cow Gap-lane to Lytham-road, thence along and including the east side of Lytham-road to Alexandra-road, thence along and including the north side of Alexandra-road, across the Promenade to the Sea.

WATERLOO WARD.

" Commencing at the Sea opposite the centre of Alexandra-road, thence along and including the south side of Alexandra-road to Lytham-road, thence along and including the west side of Lytham-road to Cow Gap-lane, thence eastward, along and including the south side of Cow Gap-lane to the existing township boundary, thence south-easterly, along the same boundary on the easterly side of Hawes Side-road, the north side of Layton-lane, across the Blackpool and Lytham Railway to the Sea at Star Hills.

The election of councillors took place at the date specified in the charter, under the superintendence of Mr. William Porter, of Fleetwood and Blackpool, who had been nominated by the authorities of the town as returning officer. On the 19th of April the gentlemen elected assembled in the old board-room and appointed aldermen and a mayor from amongst themselves, the vacancies thus created being supplied by another appeal to the burgesses of those wards whose representatives had been elevated to the aldermanic bench. The first completed town council of Blackpool consisted of—

Alderman	William Henry Cocker (the mayor)	Bank Hey Ward.
„	Thomas McNaughtan, M.D.	Claremont „
„	Thomas Lambert Masheter	Talbot „
„	John Hardman	Foxhall „
„	Francis Parnell	Waterloo „
„	J. E. B. Cocker	Brunswick „
Councillor	John Braithwaite	
„	William Bailey	} Claremont „
„	Leslie Jones, M.D.	
„	T. Challinor	
„	R. Marshall	} Talbot „
„	John Fisher	
„	John Coulson	
„	George Ormrod	} Bank Hey „
„	Henry Fisher	
„	George Bonny	
„	Robert Mather	} Brunswick „
„	John William Mycock	
„	James Blundell Fisher	
„	Alfred Anderson	} Foxhall „
„	Robert Bickerstaffe, jun.	
„	Francis Parnell	
„	Richard Gorst	} Waterloo „
„	Lawrence Hall	

William Mawdsley Charnley, esq., solicitor, town-clerk.

From the time when the subject of incorporation was first beginning to dawn upon the inhabitants as something to which the rapid extension and growing importance of their town was tending with no tardy pace, up to the present year of 1876, buildings have increased at a rate unparalleled in any former period of Blackpool's history. No longer solitary erections, or even small groups, but whole streets have been added to the expanding area of the place, consisting of handsome and spacious edifices, of, indeed, notwithstanding their being situated to the rear, exteriors which would, not many years ago, have been deemed highly ornamental to the beach itself. In 1874 the south section of the noble market-hall, on Hygiene Terrace, was being arranged and fitted up with roomy tanks to form an aquarium on a fairly large scale by W. H. Cocker, Esq., J.P., who had recently acquired the proprietorship of the entire pile. The open space in front of the building was fenced in, and furnished with three tanks for seals, and other novel features to render it attractive and pleasing. The walls of the interior were adorned with landscapes in the spacious saloon, where the main tank, divided into numerous compartments, each being supplied with a variety of fish differing from its neighbours, occupies a central position. Subsidiary tanks, filled with curious specimens of animated nature from the "vasty deep," stand in the entrance hall and recesses. The aquarium was opened to the public on the 17th of May, in the ensuing year.

On the 22nd of May, 1875, the foundation stone of a Primitive Methodist chapel was laid in Chapel Street by Mr. J. Fairhurst, of Wigan. Heretofore the members of that sect had met for religious purposes in a mission room located in Foxhall Road. The earliest service in the new chapel was conducted by the resident minister, the Rev. E. Newsome, on Sunday, the 29th of the following August. The Unitarians have a chapel in Bank Street, which was formally opened by the Rev. J. R. Smith, of Hyde, also in August, 1875. During the same month a number of influential gentlemen purchased the estate of Bank Hey from W. H. Cocker, esq., J.P., for £23,000, with the intention of converting it into Winter Gardens. Possession was gained, according to agreement, on the 1st of October. The design of the company is to place on the land a concert room, promenades, conservatories, and other accessories calculated to convert the estate into a pleasant lounge, especially desirous during inclement days.

Although South Shore is now intimately connected and associated with Blackpool as one town, there was a period, and not a very remote one, when it flourished as a separate and distinct hamlet, widely divided from its more imposing neighbour. The first house of South Shore was erected in 1819 by Mr. Thomas Moore, who speedily added about ten more to the solitary edifice. The growth of the village in earlier years was not characterised by any great rapidity, and in 1830 the whole of the buildings comprised no more than a thin row of respectable cottages overlooking the sea, with a lawn or promenade in front. In 1836 a church was built, partly by subscription and partly from Queen Anne's Bounty, and dedicated to the Holy Trinity. Twenty-two years afterwards, owing to the development of South Shore through the number of regular visitants who preferred the quietude of its beach to the greater animation which prevailed at Blackpool, the building was enlarged by the erection of transepts and a new chancel, alterations which supplied further sitting room for about 380 worshippers. The church is of brick, and contains a handsome stained-glass east window, representing the baptism of Christ by St. John the Baptist, another ornamental window being inserted in the south wall. The mural tablets are in memory of William Wilkinson, "who for twenty-five years was an indefatigable teacher in the Sunday Schools of Marton and South Shore,—he served his country in the battles of Talavera, Busaco, Albuera, Vittoria, Pyrenees, Nive, Nivelle, and Toulouse," died 11th September, 1853, aged 66 years ; and of James Metcalf, "curate of South Shore, who departed this life July 24th, 1875, aged 42 years, and was interred at the Parish Church of Bolton-le-Sands." The font is of grey stone, massive and carved. The first organ obtained by the congregation was purchased in 1847. In 1872 a tasteful lectern was forwarded to the church by the Rev. J. B. Wakefield, to whom it had been presented by his parishioners, as a token of esteem, about the close of his ministry amongst them in 1870. The burial ground encircling the church of Holy Trinity contains no monuments of special interest, if we except a stone pedestal, surmounted by a broken column, erected by public subscription to the memories of three fishermen, drowned off Cross-slack, whilst following their avocation on the 11th of October, 1860.

PERPETUAL CURATES AND VICARS OF HOLY TRINITY.

Date of Institution.	NAME.	On whose Presentation.	Cause of Vacancy.
1837	G. F. Greene, M.A.	J. Talbot Clifton, esq.	
1841	John Edwards	Ditto.	Resignation of G. F. Greene
1845	C. K. Dean	Ditto.	Resignation of J. Edwards
1848	T. B. Banner, M.A.	Ditto.	Resignation of C. K. Dean
1853	J. B. Wakefield	Ditto.	Resignation of T. B. Banner
1870	J. Ford Simmons, M.A.	Ditto.	Resignation of J. B. Wakefield

There is now an ecclesiastical parochial district attached to the church, of which the incumbent is the vicar.

On Thursday, the 24th of March, 1869, the corner stone of a Wesleyan chapel in Rawcliffe Street, built at the sole expense of Francis Parnell, esq., of South Shore, who subsequently added the schools, was laid by Mrs. Parnell, wife of the donor. For four or five years the members of this denomination had met on the Sabbath in a small room in Bolton Street, originally designed for a coach-house, and the necessity for more suitable and extended accommodation through growing numbers had of late pressed urgently upon the limited and not over wealthy assembly, so that the generous offer of their townsman was gratefully appreciated. The structure is in the Gothic style of architecture, about fifty feet in length and forty feet in width, with brick walls and stone facings, and will contain upwards of three hundred persons. Service was first held in the new place of worship, styled the Ebenezer Wesleyan Chapel, on Thursday, the 2nd of September, 1869, the officiating minister being the Rev. W. H. Taylor, of Manchester. The room in Bolton Street was subsequently converted into a Temperance Hall, and remained in that capacity until the 30th of March, 1873, when it was appropriated as a meeting-house by the Baptist sect. The progress of South Shore has not until the last two or three years been marked by that wonderful rapidity which has already been noticed whilst delineating the prosperous career of Blackpool. Nevertheless a steadily-increasing patronage was always extended to the milder climate of the village under consideration, from its earliest existence. Terraces of pretty and commodious residences arose at intervals along the marine frontage, whilst elegant villas have been erected both opposite the sea and nearer to the Lytham Road. Building is at present (1876) being pushed forward with great activity, houses springing up in endless succession along the sides of thoroughfares but recently mapped out.

CHAPTER XII.

THE PARISH OF KIRKHAM.

KIRKHAM.

THE township of Kirkham was probably the earliest inhabited locality in the Fylde district; and although it is impossible to assert that the very site of the present town was a spot fixed upon by the Romans for erecting their habitations, still as the road formed by those people passed over it, and many remnants of their domestic utensils, funereal urns, and other relics have been discovered in the surrounding soil, there is strong presumptive evidence that an ancient settlement was at least close at hand. Amongst the traces of the old warriors disinterred in this neighbourhood may be mentioned a large quantity of stones prepared for building purposes, and numerous fragments of urns, ploughed up about half a mile from Kirkham. The Mill Hill Field has also disclosed frequent witnesses to the former presence of the Romans, notably abundant specimens of their pottery and coinage, but perhaps the greatest curiosity found in the vicinity is the boss or umbo of a shield, wrought in brass, which was removed from a brook in the field specified during the year 1792. In form the shield is somewhat oval, having its central portion semi-globular, whilst the outer rim is flat. The entire diameter is about eight inches, of which the embossment supplies five. The horizontal and encircling part is perforated in four separate places, apparently for the passage of thongs or rivets. The highest surface of the boss holds the representation of a human figure seated, with an eagle to the left, the sides being adorned with an athlete respectively. Birds, swords, diminutive shields, etc., complete the decorations.

From the year 418, when the Romans vacated the island, up to the compilation of the Domesday Book by William the Conqueror in 1080-86, a period of over six and a half centuries, history preserves no record of any matter or event directly connected with the town, as distinct from the Hundred in which it is situated. Nevertheless it is obvious that Kirkham must have sprung into being some time during that protracted era, insomuch as it appears amongst the places existing in Amounderness in the Norman survey just indicated. The name is a compound derived from the Anglo-Saxons and Danes, and although the syllable "Kirk," coming from the latter, and signifying a church, could not have been in use until those pirates first invaded the land in 787, and probably was not applied until the mistaken policy of Alfred the Great allowed them to colonise this and other parts of Northumbria, one hundred years later, still it would scarcely be justifiable to conclude that there was no dwelling or village here, as the Anglo-Saxon "ham" implies, anterior to that date. The location of the place on the margin of an open thoroughfare, and the former establishment of the Romans within or near to its boundaries, incline us rather to the opinion that from the earliest arrival of the Anglo-Saxons they had selected this site for the foundation of a small settlement, and that the "ham" or hamlet so created bore a purely Saxon title until the advent of the Danes, under whose influence the orthography became altered by the substitution from their vocabulary of the word "kirk" for the one originally bestowed upon it.

Some idea of the condition of Kirkham at the Norman Conquest may be gleaned from the report concerning the Fylde in the Domesday Book, in which it is stated that of the 840 statute acres comprised in the township, only 400 (four carucates) were under cultivation, the rest being waste, that is, untilled, but very possibly in service as forage ground for swine. At that period the town undoubtedly possessed a church, one of the three mentioned in the record above-named, as standing in Amounderness, but the era of its erection is conjectural merely. The name of Kirkham, however, — the church hamlet, — is manifestly of ecclesiastical origin, and the Danish derivation of "kirk" implies that some religious building existed there, very likely about the year 900, when that nation colonised the district, but that a sacred edifice of some description had been constructed long before may be deduced from the fact that Christianity had been pretty generally embraced by the Anglo-Saxons dwelling in this locality about the middle of the seventh century.

From the commencement of the Norman dominion the history of Kirkham rises out of the mist which has obscured its earlier ages, and we are enabled from the disclosures of ancient documents, to follow out its career in a more satisfactory manner. The church and tithes of Kirkham were presented amongst other possessions, as a portion of the Hundred of Amounderness, by William the Conqueror to the baron Roger de Poictou, and were conferred by that nobleman about the year 1100, on the priory of St. Mary's, Lancaster,[1]—a monastic institution founded by him from the Abbey of Sees in Normandy. This priory retained possession of the church for only a few years, when it reverted to its former owner, and was bestowed by him on the convent of Shrewsbury, as shown by the charter of William, archbishop of York, as follows :—

" The monks of Salop in the day of my ancestors were often making complaints that their church was unjustly robbed of the church of Kirckaham, because it had been legally bestowed upon it by Roger, count of Poictou, and confirmed by Thomas, archbishop, by authority of grants under seal. At length they have come before us to state their complaints; and we, thus constrained and by the command of lord Henry, legate of the apostolical see, committed their cause to be laid before the synod of York."

The archbishop Thomas here mentioned died either in 1100 or 1113, whilst William, the writer of the charter, died in 1154. The York tribunal decided, after seeing the writings touching the confirmation of the grant of the church of Kirkham to the Shrewsbury convent, which the monks of Salop had sealed with the seal of Thomas, the archbishop, that " the aforesaid church should be restored to the church of Peter of Salop."

In 1195 "a great controversy arose between Theobald Walter, on the one part, and the abbot of Shrewsbury, on the other, concerning the right of patronage of the church, which was thus settled : a certain fine was levied in the king's court that the abbot and his

1. Regist. S. Mariæ Lanc. MS.

successors should receive from the church of Kirkham a pension of twelve marks a year, and Theobald himself should for ever remain the true Patron of the said church."[1]

After the death of Theobald Walter, king John, who had the guardianship of that nobleman's heir, gave two parts of the church to Simon Blund,[2] and later, in 1213, he bestowed the church upon W. Gray, chancellor, for life.[3] Edward I. conferred the advowson of the church of Kirkham upon the abbey of Vale Royal, a monastic house founded by him in Cheshire; but the grant was not made without strenuous opposition on the part of Sir Theobald Walter or le Botiler,[4] a descendant of the Theobald specified above, who maintained that the king had no legal right to the advowson, which belonged to him as heir-at-law and descendant of Theobald Walter, the first. A council assembled to investigate the rival claims, and Edward, having asserted that his father, Henry III., had granted the advowson to his clerk by right of his crown, and not through any temporary power he had as guardian of Theobald Walter's heir, a statement which Le Botiler's attorney either could not or would not gainsay, the advowson was adjudged to him, and Sir Theobald lay under mercy.[5] This dispute probably occurred in the 8th year of Edward's sovereignty, 1280, for we find from the Rot. Chart. that at that date the advowson was granted by the monarch to the abbey of Vale Royal.

In 1286 Sir Otto de Grandison, who was ambassador at the apostolic see, obtained a bull from the pope, Honorius IV., by which the advowson of Kirkham was conferred upon the abbey of Vale Royal for ever,[6] and on the 27th of January in the ensuing year, Edward I. confirmed his former grant.[7]

In the fifty-fourth year of the reign of Henry III., 1269, power was granted by royal charter to the manorial lord of Kirkham to

---

1. Harl. MSS., No. 2064, f. 27. 2. Testa de Nevill, fol. 371.
3. Rot. Chart. 15 John. m. 3, n. 15.
4. Theobald Walter, the 2nd, adopted the surname of Botiler, or Butler, on being appointed chief Butler of Ireland; this titular surname was retained by his descendants.
5. This account occurs in the Register of Vale Royal, and is endorsed—" Of the church of Kyrkham, how the king had conferred it upon this monasterie," etc.
6. Monast. Anglic. vol. II. p. 925. Ellis' edit. Harl. MSS. No. 2064. f. 27.
7. Rot. Chart., 15 Edw. I., No. 8, m. 3.

hold a market and fair,[1] and as such privileges were allowed at
that time to only a few other towns in the whole county of
Lancashire, we must conclude that even at such an early date
Kirkham possessed some special advantages or interest to be able
so successfully to press its claims to this signal favour. That such
important powers as the holding of markets and fairs were not
allowed to be exercised without due and proper authority
is proved by a warrant which was issued twenty-three years
later, in the reign of Edward I., against the abbot of Vale
Royal, to which convent the manor of Kirkham belonged, to
appear before a judicial court to show by what authority he held
those periodical assemblies of the inhabitants. He pleaded that
the right had been first conceded to his predecessors by Henry III.,
and that subsequently the grant had been confirmed by the
present monarch, Edward I., in the fifteenth year of his dominion.
These assertions having been verified, the abbot was exculpated
from all blame, and orders were issued to the justices itinerant in
this county to the effect that they were in no way to interfere
with the exercise of those privileges, which were to be continued
exactly as they had been heretofore.[2] From a copy of a document[3]
framed four years later, in 1296, in which the whole of these rights
are embodied amongst other interesting matters, we learn that the
manor of Kirkham was granted to the abbot and convent of Vale
Royal in *frank-al-moigne*, that is, a tenure by which a religious
corporation holds lands for themselves and their successors for ever,
on condition of praying for the soul of the donor ; that power was
given or confirmed to hold a fair of five days duration at the
Nativity of St. John the Baptist ; that the borough of Kirkham,
which had been incorporated by the name of the burgesses of
Kirkham in the year 1282, the tenth of the reign of Edward I.,
was to be a free borough ; that the burgesses and their heirs were
to have a free guild, with all the liberties which belonged to a free
borough ; that there was to be in the borough a pillory, a prison,
and a ducking stool, and other instruments for the punishment of
evil doers ; and that there were to be assizes of bread and ale,
and weights and measures. Continuing the perusal of this
document we find that the abbot of Vale Royal consented that

---

1. Placito de Quo Warranto, Lanc. Rot., 10d.   2. Ibid.
3. Discovered in the old chest at Kirkham amongst the archives of the bailiffs.

the burgesses should elect two bailiffs from amongst themselves annually, and that these should be presented and sworn ; on the other hand, however, the convent reserved to itself the perquisites arising from the courts, stallage, assizes of bread and ale, etc., and annual rents due at the period of festival legally appointed as above. The names of the following gentlemen are appended to the deed as witnesses :—Radulphus de Mouroyd, William le Botyler, Robert de Holonde, Henry de Kytheleye, John Venyal, William de Clifton, Thomas Travers, and others.

In 1327 an edict was published by the dean of Amounderness in the church of Kirkham on behalf of the archbishop of York, which commanded that the abbot or some one connected with the convent of Vale Royal, should appear before that prelate at the cathedral of his see on " the third lawful day after the Sunday on which is sung *Quasi modo genite vira et munimenta*,"[1] to show by what right and authority the Cheshire convent held the church just mentioned. In answer to this summons a monk, named Walter Wallensis, from Vale Royal, appeared before the archbishop on the day named, in 1328, and produced in proof of the title of his monastery to the church, the charter of Edward I., the bull of the pope, and letters from several archdeacons, recognising the proprietorship of the convent. In addition he brought four witnesses, viz., William de Cotton, advocate in the court of York, who stated that for eighteen years the abbot and convent of Vale Royal had supplied the rectors to the church of Kirkham ; John de Bradkirk, who said that he had known the church for forty years as a parishioner, and had on many occasions seen the charter confirming the grant of the advowson, etc., to Vale Royal, as for fifteen years he had been in the service of that monastery, and at the time when the present archbishop of York farmed the church of Kirkham, twelve years ago, from the convent of Vale Royal, had been the bearer of the money raised from this church to that dignitary at York ; Robert de Staneford, of Kirkham, who gave similar evidence, and bore witness to the existence of the charter of Edward I., which he had seen ; and Robert de Blundeston, of Vale Royal, who gave evidence as to the genuineness of the documents produced having been admitted by

1. That is, the Sunday after Easter.

Roger de Nasynton, public notary, etc. The result of these attestations was that the case was dismissed against the abbot of Vale Royal, and his right to the church of Kirkham, with all its chapels, fruits, rents, etc., allowed to have been fully proved.[1]

In 1334 a mandamus was issued by Edward III., at York, to Robert Foucher, the sheriff of Lancashire, stating that, contrary to a charter of Edward I., which prohibited the sheriffs from making distraints on the rectors of churches or on estates with which the churches had been endowed, he had " under pretext of his office lately entered into the lands and tenements near Kirkham, which are of the endowment of that church, and had heavily distrained the abbot of Vale Royal, parson of that church"; and ordering the said sheriff to abandon the claim, and to make restitution of anything he might thus have illegally obtained, and "by no means to attempt to make any distraint in the lands and tenements which are of the endowment of the aforesaid church," at any future time.[2]

Somewhere about the year 1332 a monk, named Adam de Clebury, who held the temporalities of Shrewsbury Abbey, sued Peter, the abbot of Vale Royal, for five hundred marks, which he declared were the accumulated arrears of twelve marks, ordered to be paid annually by Theobald Walter, to the former monastery, out of the funds of the church of Kirkham, according to the issue of a trial in the king's court, between Theobald and the convent of Shrewsbury, respecting the advowson, etc., of that church in 1195. Peter is said, in the Harleian manuscript, from which this account is taken, to have "redeemed that writ and many others from the sheriff of Lancashire," from which it may be understood that he had paid the sum demanded, or in some conciliatory way settled the case during his lifetime, for we hear no more of the matter until shortly after his death in 1342, when an action to enforce a similar payment was brought against his successor, Robert de Cheyneston. This ecclesiastic, however, is said to "have manfully opposed the abbot of Shrewsbury," and to have journied up to London to hold an interview with him on the subject, at which, after "many allegations on each side, he gave to the abbot of Shrewsbury £100 to pay his labours and

---

1. Harl. MSS., No. 2064, f. 25 and 25b.   2. Harl. MSS., No. 2064, f. 27.

expenses," and in that manner the dispute was brought to a termination about the year 1343.

In 1337 Sir William de Clifton, of Westby, made an offer to the abbot of Vale Royal to purchase certain tithes from him for twenty marks, and on the ecclesiastic refusing to entertain this proposition, the indignant knight became most unruly and outrageous in his conduct, as shown by the following charge which was that year preferred against him by the abbot, who stated :—

" That he had thrust with a lance at a brother of the monastery in the presence of the abbot and convent ; that he had retained twenty marks which he was pledged and bound to pay to the abbot, in order to weary him with expenses and labours ; that it was the custom, from time immemorial, for the parishioners of Kirkham to convey their tithe-corn to their barns, and there keep it until the ministers of the rector came for it ; but that he (Sir William Clifton), in contempt of the church, had allowed his tithes and those of his tenants to waste and rot in the fields, and very often by force and arms had driven away the tithe-collectors ; he also had compelled a cart of the rector, laden with hay, to remain on his land for upwards of a month, and in derision had made the rector's mare into a hunting palfrey ; he also had neglected to keep the tithes of his calves, pigeons, orchards, huntings, and hawkings, and would not allow the procurator, under threat of death, to enter his estate, but he and his satellites had irreverently burst into the sanctuary of God, where they had assailed the priests and clerks, and impeded them in the discharge of their duties. Moreover the aforesaid knight would not permit any of his tenants who were living in flagrant sin, to be corrected or punished by the ordinaries."[1]

In concluding the above list of misdemeanours, the abbot complained that Sir William had ordered a severe flagellation " even to the effusion of blood," to be inflicted on Thomas, the clerk, in the town of Preston, and that this scourging had taken place as directed, in the presence of the under-mentioned gentlemen, who seemed to have been well pleased with the vigorous measures adopted by the knight, and to have rendered him willing assistance when called upon :—

Richard de Plumpton,	Richard de Tresale,
Nicholas Catford,	Henry de Tresale,
William the provost,	William Sictore,
William Jordan, junr.,	William Sictore, junr.,
John Dence,	Adam de Scales,
Robert Carter,	Richard Walker,
John Garleigh,	John Mydelar,

1. Fishwick's History of Kirkham—from the Harl. MSS.

Henry Thillon,	Thomas Adekoe,
William Randell,	Adam del Wodes,
John de Reste,	William de Mydelar,
William de Morhouse,	Thomas de Wytacres,

And several others, including Adam, the harper.

This charge was laid before the lord abbot of Westminster by the abbot of Vale Royal, and the former, after hearing the statement of offences, commanded that Sir William de Clifton and others enumerated therein, should appear before him to answer for their misdeeds; but as neither Sir William nor any of his friends and abettors took the least notice of the summons, it was decided that an endeavour should be made to arrange the quarrel by arbitration. To this the knight seems to have been favourable, and nominated William Laurence, John de Crofton, and Robert Mareys to act as his arbitrators; whilst those of the abbot were William Baldreston, rector of St. Michael's-on-Wyre; Robert Baldreston, his brother, and a rector also; and Richard de Ewyas, a monk of Deulacres. The decision of the court thus constituted was that Sir William de Clifton should acknowledge his guilt, and ask pardon and absolution for the same from the abbot, unto whose will and grace he should submit himself; in addition the knight was ordered to pay a fine of twenty marks, and make good to the abbot the tithes which he had destroyed or refused to pay. Sir William accepted the verdict, and bound himself to fulfil its conditions by oath; the rest were required to enter into a promise to abstain in future from making any attempt to injure the church of Kirkham, or anything connected with it, and to provide a large wax candle, which was paraded round that church on the feast of palms, and afterwards presented as a peace-offering to St. Michael.[1]

In 1357 Cardinal John Thoresby, archbishop of York, made a new ordination of the vicarage of Kirkham, by which it was decreed that, instead of the secular vicar appointed aforetime, the abbot and convent of Vale Royal should select some one from their own monastery to fill the office whenever a vacancy occurred. By this fresh regulation the abbot and convent of Vale Royal were bound to pay to the vicar forty marks per annum, and he on his part was pledged to keep the parsonage house in proper repair and

1. Vale Royal ledger.

perform all ecclesiastical duties. Three years afterwards a vicar of Kirkham was charged and convicted of having been guilty of maladministration in his position as dean of Amounderness, but subsequently he received a full pardon from King Edward III.

In the year 1401, during the reign of Henry IV., the right to hold a market and fair was again confirmed to the abbot and convent of Vale Royal ; subjoined is a translated copy of the grant, which bore the date of the 2nd of July :—

"The king to all men greeting : We have inspected a charter made by our progenitor, Lord Edward, formerly king of England, in these words :—' Edward, by the grace of God king of England, lord of Ireland, and duke of Aquitaine, to the archbishops, bishops, abbots, priors, earls, barons, justices, sheriffs, provosts, ministers, and to all his bailiffs and subjects, health. Know that we have granted and by this our present charter confirm to our beloved in Christ the Abbot and Convent of Vale Royal, that they and their successors for ever shall have a market in each week on Thursday at their manor at Kirkham in the county of Lancaster, and also in each year a fair at the same town of five days duration, that is on the vigil, on the Day, and on the morrow of the Nativity of St. John the Baptist, and on the two days succeeding ; unless the market and fair be found injurious to neighbouring markets and fairs. Therefore we desire and firmly enjoin, both for ourselves and our heirs, that the aforesaid Abbot and Convent and their successors for ever shall have the aforesaid market and fair at the aforesaid manor with all the liberties and free customs appertaining to similar institutions, unless such market and fair be detrimental to neighbouring interests as aforesaid.

"'These being witnesses :—The venerable fathers Robert Bath and Wells, John Winchester, and Anthony Durham, bishops ; William de Valence, our uncle ; Henry de Lacy, earl of Lincoln ; master Henry de Newark, archdeacon of Richmond ; master William de Luda, archdeacon of Durham ; master William de Cornere, dean of Wymburne ; John de St. John ; William de Latymer ; and others.

"'Given under our hand at Bourdeaux on the 21st of January, in the 15th year of our reign.'

"Holding the aforesaid charter and all matters contained in it as authentic and acceptable both for ourselves and our heirs, as far as our power extends, we accept, approve, grant, and confirm to our beloved in Christ, the present Abbot and Convent of the aforesaid place and their successors that the aforesaid charter be considered just, also we affirm that the same Abbot and Convent and their predecessors legally had and held the said market and fair before this date.

"In testimony thereof, etc. Witness the king at Westminster on the 2nd of July."[1]

At the dissolution of monasteries the manor of Kirkham, together with the advowson of the church, was transferred by

---

1. Pat. Rolls. 2. Hen. iv., p. 3, m. 5 n. (Duchy Office.)

Henry VIII. from the abbot and convent of Vale Royal to the dean and chapter of Christ Church, Oxford.

In 1560 Queen Elizabeth ratified and confirmed by letters patent all former charters concerning Kirkham by a deed bearing the date of July 2nd; and later, in 1619, the 17th year of the reign of James I., a record of the Duchy Court of Lancaster states that the bailiffs and burgesses of Kirkham presented a petition praying that they might elect into their government some men of account dwelling near the town, and that it might be declared that the bailiffs had lawful power and authority to correct all malefactors and offenders according to the laws and liberties of the town, and to do and perform all other duties appertaining to their office. They prefaced their prayer by asserting that "the town of Kirkham had been used as an ancient market town and that the inhabitants thereof had time out of mind been accounted a Corporation, incorporated by the name of Bailiffs and Burgesses, and that of late owing to some of the bailiffs being but simple and weak men, and the inhabitants but poor and numerous, it had been found impossible to govern in a proper and satisfactory manner the large confluences of people at fair and market seasons," for which reason they were desirous of gaining an extension of their existing powers as set forth in the plea. The court decreed that "the then Bailiffs of Kirkham and the Burgesses of the same, and their successors, for ever, should and might from thenceforth have and enjoy their ancient usages and liberties by the name of the Bailiffs and Burgesses of the Town of Kirkham, and that the Bailiffs should yearly be chosen out of the Burgesses according to the said usages, or as they in their discretion should think meet, for the better government of the said Town and the people thereunto resorting, also that the Bailiffs, Burgesses, and Inhabitants should be guildable, and have in the said Town a prison, etc., as had been heretofore, and that the Dean and Chapter and their successors, farmers, and tenants, should and might from henceforth have all their fairs, markets, liberties, privileges, jurisdictions, Court Leets, Court Barons, Courts of Pleas, and the Fair Court, as heretofore had been." The foregoing was ordered to be read in the parish church on the ensuing sabbath, and also in the market place.

From the following ancient and somewhat lengthy document

or lease, much interesting matter may be gleaned, and for that reason it was deemed better to give it unabridged :—

"To all Christian people to whom this present writing shall come the Dean and Chapter of the Cathedral Church of Christ of King Henry the eighth's foundation do send greeting in our Lord God everlasting : Whereas we the said Dean and Chapter by our Indenture of Lease, sealed with our common Seal, bearing date the sixteenth day of July, in the three and fortieth year of the reign of our sovereign lady Elizabeth (1601), late Queen of England, &c., did, as much as in us was, demise, grant, and to farm, lett unto Thomas ffleetwood, of Caldwich, in the County of Stafford, esquire, all our Court Leets and view of franchpledge within our parsonage and manor of Kirkham, in the County of Lancaster, or in either of them, or to, or with them, or either of them used, occupied, incident, or belonging appertaining, with all and every thing (singular) there appertaining. also the keeping of the Court Barons there, and all waifs, strays, treasure trove, deodands, felons' and outlaws' goods, forfeitures, fines, amercements, serving and executing of writs and processes, and all royalties, liberties, perquisites and profits of Court Leets, all commodities and advantages whatsoever to the same Court Leets incident, due, or in any wise belonging, or which heretofore have been, or of right ought to have been, had and enjoyed by us, the said Dean and Chapter, or any of our predecessors, or any other person or persons by or by means of our estate, right, or title to the same or any part thereof, in as large and ample manner as we, the said Dean and Chapter, or our successors, may or ought to have or enjoy, together also with the Stewardship, office of Steward, or authority for appointing the Steward for the keeping of the said Courts ; And also the profits of all and each of our fairs and markets to be kept at or within the said manor and parsonage of Kirkham ; The Courts of Pipowder ; And all manner of Toll and Stallage—That is to say, Turne-toll, Traverse-Toll, and Through-Toll, and all manner of payments, fines, forfeitures, fees, sums of money, with all other kind of profits and commodities whatsoever, which do or may lawfully accrue, arise, come, or be due, unto us, the said Dean and Chapter, our successors, or assignees, by reason of any fair or market, or fairs or markets, which hereafter shall be kept within the manor or parish of Kirkham aforesaid; And half an Oxgang of Land, called by the name of the old Eworth, with so much of the late improved Common in Kirkham aforesaid as was allotted, used, or occupied, or ought to be used, allotted, or occupied to or with the said half Oxgang ; One Burgage house with the appurtenances in Kirkham aforesaid, now in the tenure, holding, or occupation of one Thomas Singleton and William Kitchen, or the one of them ; One Croft called the hemp garden, certain grounds, called the Vicar's Carrs, set, lying, and being in Kirkham aforesaid ; One house built upon the waste in Kirkham aforesaid, commonly called or known by the name of the moote hall, with all shops underneath the said moote hall, and all the tythes of the new improvements not formerly demised within the said manor or parish of Kirkham, or within the liberties thereof ; And all encroachments within the same manor—That is to say, all such arable lands, meadow, pasture, woodlands, furzeland, heath, and marsh-land, and all other such vacant and waste land, as is or hath been heretofore by any man encroached or taken to his own use by the making of any hedge, pale, wall, ditch, or other mound, out of the lands belonging to the manor of Kirkham aforesaid, without the special license of the said Dean and Chapter, with all and every ways, booth-places, stall-places, liberties, easements, profits, commodities, and advantages to the said messuages, lands, tenements, houses, grounds, encroachments, tythes, hereditaments, and also the premises or any of them belonging or in any wise appertaining (except as in our said Indenture of Lease is excepted and reserved). To have and to hold the said Court Leets and the keeping of the Court Barons, profits of fairs and markets, messuages, lands, tythes, and all and every other the before-recited premises by that our said recited Indenture of Lease demised, or mentioned, or intended to be demised, with their and every of their appurtenances (except as is aforesaid) from the feast day of the Annunciation of the Blessed Virgin Mary last past before the date thereof, for and during the tenure and unto the end and term of one and twenty years then next following, fully to be completed and ended. In our said Indenture of Lease (amongst other things therein contained) it is provided always that it shall not be lawful to nor for the said Thomas ffleetwood, his executors, administrators, or assignees, to lett, set, or assign over to any person or persons the demised premises herein contained and specified, or any part or parcel of them without the special license of us, the said Dean and Chapter, or our Successors, in writing under our common Seal thereunto first had and obtained. The estate, right, tythe, interest, and term of years yet in being of the said Thomas ffleetwood, are now lawfully come unto the hands and possession of S*r* Richard ffleetwood, of Caldwich, knight baronet, and baron of Newton, within the said County of Lancaster, son and heir, and also executor of the last will and testament of the said Thomas ffleetwood, lately deceased. Know ye now that we, the said Dean and Chapter, of our common assent and consent have licensed and granted, and by these presents for us and our Successors do license and grant that from henceforth it shall and may be lawful to and for the said S*r* Richard ffleetwood, knight baronet, his executors, administrators, or assignees, or any of them, to lett, set, or assign over the said demised premises and every one of them and any or every part or parcel of them with the appurtenances unto John Clayton, James Parker, and John Wilding, of Kirkham, in the County of Lancaster, yeomen, their executors, administrators, or assignees for and during all the residue of the said term of years yet in being, to come, and unexpired, the said proviso, or anything else, in our recited Indenture of Lease contained to the contrary, Provided always that all and every other covenant, clause, article, exception, reservation of rent, payment, condition, and proviso, in that our recited Indenture of Lease comprised shall stand, remain, continue, and be in its, and their, full power, force, and effect, as if this our present license or deed in writing had never been, had, nor made. In Witness whereof we, the said Dean and Chapter, have hereunto put our common Seal. Proven in our Chapter house at Oxford the fourth day of December in the years of the reign of our sovereign lord James, by the Grace of God king of England, Scotland, ffrance, and Ireland, Defender of the Faith, &c.— That is to say, of England, ffrance, and Ireland the eleventh, and of Scotland the seven and fortieth."[1]

1. Original lease in Bailiffs' Chest.

There is an old deed in the bailiffs' chest, bearing the date 1725, and evidently a summary of charters, powers, etc., drawn up in order to be submitted to the inspection of some legal authority, whose opinions on different points are appended, from which it appears that from the earliest incorporation of the town it had been governed by two bailiffs and twelve burgesses in common council assembled, who were annually chosen within the borough, and that they "usually assessed such persons, not being free burgesses in the same borough, as had come into and exercised trades within the borough (whether they had served apprenticeships to such trades or not), in and with such reasonable annual payments to the Corporation as the bailiffs and burgesses thought fit "; persons born in the borough were treated in a similar manner. The bailiffs inflicted penalties on all breakers of the peace, the amount of fine imposed being regulated according to the condition of the offender, thus an esquire was mulcted in 40s., a gentleman 10s., and anyone of an inferior grade 5s. Profane cursing and swearing also came under their jurisdiction. The collection of freedom money from traders commencing business in Kirkham was a somewhat questionable act on the part of the local rulers, and indeed they themselves were evidently troubled with doubts as to their right to levy the tax, for the muniment chest contains several opinions of eminent counsel as to the validity of such a course. In 1738 a person named William Marsden started as a tanner in Kirkham, and obstinately refused to purchase his freedom or close his premises, but, at the end of twelve months, the assembled bailiffs and burgesses instructed and authorised the town or borough serjeant to collect and levy the sum of two shillings and sixpence upon the goods and chattels of William Marsden, by distress and sale. This impost was abolished during the latter half of the eighteenth century. The bailiffs formed part of the Court Leet held annually in the seventeenth century and were elected from amongst the jurors. Subjoined are a few extracts from the minute book of the "Court leet of frank pledge of yᵉ foundation of Henry VIII.," as it is styled in one place :—

"Oct. 1681.

The court leet houlden at Kirkham yᵉ day above written by Tho. Hodgkinson Stuart.

" Juriars

James Smith, junior.	John Hanson.	Geffery Wood.
James Lawson.	Tho. Tomlinson.	Alex. Lawder.
John Dickson.	Henry Smith.	Charles Fale.
Will. Butler.	James Hull.	Will. Hornby.
James Clayton.	George Whiteside.	Tho. Shardley.

" Bayliffes

Geffrey Wood.
Tho. Tomlinson. } John Colly, serjeant.

James Hull, constable.

(Here follow the 'Gauldlayers,' 'Barleymen,' 'Prizards,' 'Leather searchards,' and 'Flesh and Fish viewards')

" Wm Hunt fined 1s. for keeping his geese in the loanes "

" John Wilding for keeping a greyhound not being qualified "   (Punishment ?)

1682.

" Presented that the earl of Derby, Mr. Westby, of Mowbrick, Mr. Hesketh, of Mains, were constantly called at the court leet for the borough of Kirkham and anciently did either appear or some assign for them, but now of late they do not appear nor any assign for them."

"4 May. 1683.

" Recd of Richard Riley for his fredom within the borow of Kirkham 16s.

" May the 4th day Recd of Rodger Taylor for his freedom in Kirkham £1.

" Oct. 19th. Recd of Thomas Sherdley for his freedom 2s.

" Ordered that no person shall set or let any house or shop to Richarde Blackburne or his wife that stands within the liberties in Kirkham in pain of £2 0s. 0d."

1685.

" Ralph Rishton paid to John Wilding and Thomas Hankinson, the bailiffs, for his freedom to trade in Kirkham £4."

12 Oct. 1686.

" Prudence Cardwell, presented for not making her bread sufficient in goodness and weight, and fined in 12d."

Nov. 17. " It is ordered that Nicholas Wilkinson shall pay unto the bailiffs 13s. 4d. for one year's trading in the town."

30 April 1692.

" Ordered that if any hereafter suffer their swine to ly out in the night time they shall forfeit for every night 3s. 4d."

26 April 1699.

" Ordered that neither Wm Boone nor Rowland Roberts maltmakers nor any as they employ shall dry any malt or weete upon the Sabbath day for the time to come in the pain of 20s."

13 Oct. " We present these persons for want of their appearance at court & so fine every one of them 12d.

" Will. George Ric. Earl of Derby.

" Tho. Westby, esq.   Thos. Hesketh, esq.

" John Walker, esq.   Jennet Thompson, widow.

and Thomas Dickson."

22 Aprill 1707.

" Every person that shall carry away any fire thro' the street to cover the same close on penalty of 10s.

April 1713.

" No person to water any sort of cattle at the bucket belonging to the town well nor wash any skins at the trough."

10 May 1715.

" We find Charles Hardy for harbouring and lodging of vagrants and beggars in this town in 13s. 4d."

22 May 1726.

" Mem. That the town of Kirkham was summonsed from house to house and the inhabitants unanimously agreed to the setting up of a workhouse."

30 Nov. 1728.

" Ordered that a lamp should be fixed up in the middle of the borough of Kirkham in some convenient place, and that the charge of it together with oyl necessary for it be paid out of the town's stock."

" All persons refusing to clean or cow (rake) the streets opposite their respective houses to be fined 6d. after notice from the serjeant with his bell."

The official notice concerning the last resolution is still preserved, and ran as under :—

" To the Inhabitants of the Burrough of Kirkham.

" You are hereby required forthwith to cleanse the Streets over against your Dwelling Houses, Outhouses, and all other Buildings, together with all Front-steads whatsoever, on Penalty of Sixpence for each default.

" You have also hereby notice to remove all the Dung-hills out of the Streets in a month's time or otherwise they will be removed for the use of the Burrough.

" Likewise all the Rubbish out of the Streets on such Penalties as the Bayliffs and Common Council shall think fit to inflict. Given under our Common Seal of the Towne this first Day of December, 1728."

At a later period the burgesses neglected to choose and appoint bailiffs for many years, or to use their privileges; and apprehensive at length that such remissions were tantamount to a forfeiture of their charter by their own act, they determined to take legal advice as to the most expeditious way to resume their powers. It was given as follows :—

" If any of those acting Burgesses are alive I would advise them to assemble at their former Gild or usual Place of meeting, and then and there choose other Burgesses, after which they may elect from among them Two Bailiffs and make an entry of such choice in one of the Old Books, and then proceed as formerly to act in their corporate capacity ; and let their first Punishment be inflicted on some person unlikely to dispute their authority, for instance a woman drunkard may be set in the stocks.

" Having done as above directed they may for the better Government of the town make some Byelaws, and enter them ffair into a Book to be kept for that purpose, but let none of these new Laws be put in Execution till they are confirmed by the Chancelour, and that will be some foundation ffor a petition to that Court.

"But if all the Burgesses are dead I can see no Remedy whatsoever but by obtaining a new Charter, which will be very Difficult if not Impracticable."

A statement as to manorial extent of Kirkham at the latter part of the seventeenth century is preserved amongst the records of a court, further reference to which will be made anon, and reads as here given :—"The lands lying within the manor of Kirkham, belonging to the Dean and Chapter of Christ Church, in Oxford, and to the burgesses inhabitants of the borough of Kirkham, are bounded east by the lands of Edward Robinson and George Brown, lying within Newton and Scales ; westward by the lands of Sir Thomas Clifton, within Westby, and the lands of Christopher Parker, esq., lying in Ribby with Wrea ; northwards by the lands of Mrs. Dor^y· Westby, of Mowbreck, and the lands of Mr. Edward Fleetwood, of Wesham ; and southwards by the lands of Mr. George Sharples, of Freckleton."

It has already been shown that the manor was conveyed by the authorities at Oxford to Thomas Fleetwood as fee-famer in 1601, and that the lease was subsequently renewed or confirmed to his son and heir Sir Richard Fleetwood. Before 1700, however, probably about 1650, from the contents of a petition presented by the inhabitants to the dean and chapter in 1705, the Cliftons, of Lytham, had the manor in a tenure similar to that of their predecessors, and held each year, in the month of June, a court leet, at which the two bailiffs were elected. The late Thomas Langton Birley, esq., of Carr Hill, Kirkham, acquired the lordship by purchase a short time previous to his death in 1874, when it descended to his son and heir, Henry Langton Birley, esq. Bailiffs still continue to be annually appointed, and have in their hands several charitable bequests, the interest arising therefrom being devoted to the service of the poor of the township, either in the form of alms, or in maintaining some useful convenience, as the parish pump, for their benefit. The property at present belonging to the bailiffs consists of one meadow, situated behind the Roman Catholic church; a garden in front of the same edifice; a plot in the field called the "Iron Latch" ; and a pew in the parish church of Kirkham. In 1676 the bishop of Chester acceded to a petition from the minister and churchwardens that a wainscot might be placed so as to enclose the bailiffs' pew, "which seat, for want thereof, was pressed into and thronged by others to the disturbance of the said officers."[1]

The Moot Hall, in which all business relating to the town was transacted, stood in the Market-place until about the year 1790, when it was accidentally burnt down. This building was erected in two stories, the upper of which was divided into a small room, used for flax dressing at the time the Hall was destroyed, and a larger one, devoted to court meetings and other public matters, which was separated from the remainder of the edifice insomuch as it could only be entered from the outside by means of a flight of stone steps. The ground floor or lower story was converted into shops in the occupation of tradesmen of the town. The original borough seal, which still exists, although somewhat defective, represents a dove bearing an olive branch in its beak. Notwithstanding that Kirkham was made a borough, during the last years of the thirteenth century, it never appears upon any occasion to have returned a Member of Parliament, and it may safely be conjectured that no writ for that purpose was ever issued to the burgesses, as the sheriffs exercised a discretionary power in such matters, and consequently only those boroughs, whose inhabitants seemed affluent enough to support the expenses of an election, were selected for the honour, amongst which it is scarcely likely Kirkham would be classed.

A market cross stood in the centre of the town, near to the ancient Moot Hall, about the beginning of this century, but has now, like the stocks, which originally had their place in the churchyard and afterwards were removed to a more public site, been long numbered amongst the memories of a past and less refined age. There is no allusion to a whipping post in any of the old documents, but we have the authority of a gentleman who witnessed the spectacle, that a man was publicly whipped in the Market-place fifty years ago.

The "Thirty Sworn men of Kirkham" was the name given to a council which took cognizance of parochial affairs, and of certain matters connected with the church, amongst other things appointing the churchwardens. This assembly was composed of representatives from the different sections of the parish, two

1. Paper in Bailiffs' Chest, dated 23rd October, 1676, and signed John Cestriens.

persons being elected from each of the fifteen townships as under :—

"Thirty Sworn Men in 1570.

"Kirkham :	Warton :
James Baine.	Wm. Platon.
James Clayton.	Robt. Fletcher.
"Clifton :	Bryning :
William Porter.	Robt. Croke.
Tho. Cardwell.	John Croke.
"Freckleton :	Ribby :
Hen^ry Colbron.	— Benson.
Rich. Browne.	Henry Shaw.
"Singletons :	Wesham :
James Davy.	Robt. Hornby.
Wm Smith	Henry Johnson.
"Larbrick :	Treales :
Robt. Johnson.	Wm Swarbrick.
Will. Fletcher.	Tho. Porter.
"Thistleton :	Hambleton :
Joh. Smith.	Robt. Bradshaw.
Robt. Cornay.	Wm Bamber."

The oath taken by the " Sworn men " was administered by the civil authorities, and their tenure of office was for life, or until they thought proper to resign. The origin of " Sworn men," or at least of the name, dates from the fourteenth century, and the institution itself seems to have been common in this part of Lancashire ; Preston, Lancaster, Garstang, and Goosnargh, having had assemblies bearing similar titles and performing similar duties, but consisting only of twenty-four men each.

In 1636 a serious dispute arose between the Thirty-men and the vicar, the Rev. Edward Fleetwood, owing to the latter requiring the council to subscribe to the following conditions :—

" 1st. They shall lay no gauld themselves without the consent of the vicar.

" 2nd. That the vicar shall have a negative voice in all their proceedings, and that they shall determine nothing without the consent of the said vicar.

" 3rd. They shall not put or elect any new 30-men without the vicar's consent.

" 4th. They shall not meet in the church upon any business whatever, unless they acquaint the vicar before.

" 5th. If there be any turbulent or factious person, that the rest of the company shall join with the vicar and turn him out." [1]

On the Thirty-men refusing to comply with his request, the vicar excluded them " by violence " from their usual meeting-

---

1. Records of the " Thirty-Men."

place in the church, and on the 5th of November, 1638, when they were called upon by the churchwardens to attend there in order to lay the necessary taxes for the repair of the sacred edifice, then much decayed, Mr. Fleetwood "locked himself in the church, as before he had many times done," and compelled them to conduct their business without the building.

Incensed at the persistent hostility of the vicar an appeal against his conduct was made by the "men" to the archbishop of York, and by him referred to the bishop of Chester, who replied :— "That the corporation or company of 30-men, not having any warranty from the king, was nothing in law ; but if the parish or township did delegate the power, to the 30-men as to church matters, then their acts relating thereunto were as effectual and binding as if they had the king's sanction ; and wishing to know the affection of the parishioners on this head, he issued an order on 22 Nov. 1638, that public notice sh^d be given in the church for all the parishioners to meet and give their voices whether they chose that the custom of the 30-men representing the whole parish two for every township, should continue, or they should be dissolved."[1]

Mr. Fleetwood having ignored this order, the churchwardens took upon themselves the duty of calling a general conference of the parishioners ; a great multitude assembled in the churchyard, where the meeting was held, the vicar having locked the church door, and declared in favour of their ancient custom being continued and preserved to their posterity as it had come down to them, freely giving "their power and strength to the said 30-men, to confer and determine all church matters."

To this resolution were appended the signatures of four hundred and ninety-four persons, amongst whom were Thomas Clifton of Westby and Clifton, John Westby of Mowbreck, Thomas Hesketh of Mains, Edward Veale of Whinney Heys, John Parker of Bradkirk, and Edward Bradley of Bryning.

The bishop of Chester, having received an official report of the result of the meeting, communicated with the archbishop of York, as below stated :—

"Chester palace, 14 Dec. 1638.

"Seeing the vicar (whom I have used with all gentleness and lenity), continues

1. Records of the "Thirty-Men."

still in his contempt, and addeth daily more forwardness thereunto, I must return the petitioners to my lord's grace of York, to be ordered by the high commissioner according to his grace's intimation signified in his * * * . I wish well to the sillie wilful man, but he makes himself incapable thereof.

"John Cestriensis."[1]

This effort to obtain redress for their grievances does not appear to have been attended with a success equal to the expectations of the "thirty," for a little later they instituted a suit in the consistory court at Chester against the vicar, " and, having proved their practice good, had sentence against him and £20 7s. 6d. allowed towards their expenses."[2] The "Thirty-men" were admitted into the church on Easter Tuesday, 1639.

During the period that Edward Fleetwood was vicar of Kirkham an event occurred in the parish which furnishes a forcible example of the superstitious feeling in religious matters existing amongst all ranks of the people at that time. The whole of the details of the circumstance are embodied in a pamphlet entitled " Strange Signs from Heaven," and by way of an introduction, the tract contains this certificate, " under the hand of Mr. Edward Fleetwood, minister of Kirkham parish in Lancashire, concerning the monster brought forth by Mrs. Haughton, a papist, living in that parish :—

"As we must tell no lie, so we should conceal no truth; especially when it tends to God's glory : There was a great papist, and of great parentage, within the parish of Kirkham, and his wife's mother, being of the same religion, did usually scoff and mock the Roundheads, and, in derision of Mr. Prinne and others, cut off the cat's ears, and called it by his name : But behold an example of the justice and equity of God in his judgements; as Adonibezec was repaid in his own kind; Haman hanged upon the same gallows that he had prepared for Mordecai ; and Pharoah and all his host drowned in the sea, into which he had thought to have driven the Israelites. And likewise one of the popish prelates, who said he would not dine till Ridley and Latimer were burnt, was burnt in his own entrails. So it fell out with this man's wife, a popish creature, who being great with child, when the time of her delivery came, she brought forth a monstrous child without a head, ugly and deformed, myself eyewitness thereof.

Edward Fleetwood, pastor.
W. Greenacres, midwife.

The tract itself informs us that in the course of a conversation with some gentlemen, Mrs. Haughton observed with great warmth that " the Puritans and Independents deserved all to be hanged," and concluded her uncharitable remarks by uttering a

1. Records of the Thirty-Men.   2. Ibid.

fervent wish that neither she nor any one belonging to her might ever become Roundheads; upon which "answer was made to her, that her children, if she had any, might (if God so pleased) have their eyes opened, and see that good which she was ignorant of. Mrs. Haughton retorted in these words: *I pray God that rather than I shall be a Roundhead, or bear a Roundhead, I may bring forth a child without a head.*" In course of time, as we learn from the pamphlet, she was delivered of a monster child, being attended in her confinement by "widow Greenacres, the midwife, formerly wife to Mr. Greenacres, some time vicar of this parish," who, "being a godly woman, could not be eased in her mind until she had discharged her conscience in making it known to Mr. Fleetwood." "For better satisfaction Mr. Fleetwood caused the grave to be opened, and the child to be taken out and laid to view, and found there a body without a head, as the midwife had said, only the child had a face on the breast of it, two eyes near unto the place where the paps usually are, and a nose upon the chest, and a mouth a little above the navel, and two ears, upon each shoulder one."

The certificate of the vicar relating to this discovery, together with a manuscript account of the circumstances connected with it, were "brought up to London by Colonel Moore (of Liverpool) a member of the House of Commons, and shewed to divers of the House; who commanded the tract to be printed so that all the kingdom might see the hand of God therein; to the comfort of his people, and the terror of the wicked that deride and scorn them."[1]

In the context are enumerated a few records of the "Thirty men," in order that the reader may have a clearer conception of their duties, and gain some information, not devoid of interest, respecting the more common-place matters associated with the history and regulation of parochial and church affairs in the town :—

"1571.

"Nov. 2. Rec^d for burial of a child of Mr. Veale (of Whinney Heys) in the church XIId.

---

1. According to the *Parliamentarie Chronicle*, "Mistress Haughton was the wife of Master William Haughton of Prickmarsh in Kirkham, the Fylde," and the child was born on the 20th of June, 1643.

" Paid for a scholar verifying the ch'wardens' acct.ᵃ

" The great bell taken down this year and a new one put up."

"1577.

" The churchwardens were ordered by the vicar and 30-men to continue in office another year, by way of punishment, because they had not repaired the bells or levied the gauld of xˢ per township."

"1586.

" Charge of the churchwardens for making the vicar a seat xiiᵈ.

"An order that each householder having a youth with a plough having 4 beasts shall pay ivᵈ

" Every one that married with another iiₐ, and every cottage iᵈ."

"1595.

" The churchwardens charged xiiᵈ for tarrying with Mr. vicar when he gave warning to all housekeepers not to sell ale during the time of service."

"1603.

" Rushes to strew the church cost ixˢ viᵈ. The churchwardens went through the parish to warn the people to come to church."

"1618.

" Pᵈ to Isabel Birley 3 weeks diet for 3 slaters at iiiˢ ivᵈ per week, xxxˢ."

"1634.

" The church was flagged this year."

"1643.

" Pᵈ for slating Mʳ Clifton's quire £1 5s. 3d., and for organ pipes which had been pulled assunder by the souldiers, 3s. 4d.¹ The churchwardens were demanded to attend the prime sessions at Weeton. 12 June they were ordered by the captains and other officers to make presentment of all recusants in the parish. In August they were employed several days at the parish cost about the covenant, and giving notice through the parish for them to take the covenant."

"1666.

" Spent on going perambulations on Ascension day, 1s. 6d."

"1679.

" The bishop ordered a bone-house to be built."

"1683.

" Spent upon the ringers upon the 9th of Sept., being thanksgiving day for his majesty's deliverance from the fanatick plot 2s. 6d.²

" Paid for whip to whip dogs out of church, 2s. 0½d.

" Paid for magpies and sparrow heads £10 12s. 4d."

"1746.

" 28 March. Paid for hiding registers, vestments, plates, etc., at the rebels coming 2s. 6d. ; same day paid for ringing when the Duke of Cumberland came to Preston, and when he retook Carlisle, 6s."

1. During the war between King and Parliament.   2. The Rye-house Plot.

" Apr. 18. Ordered that the curates of Lund, Warton, Ribby, and Singleton shall not exceed 2 qts. of wine each day they administer the sacrament until further orders."

The first church of Kirkham is commonly said to have been erected by the Saxons on Mill Hill, and subsequently rebuilt on its present site, but as this statement is unsupported by any more reliable evidence than tradition, we give it simply for what it is worth. The earliest authentic word of Kirkham church is in 1512, when the edifice was in part rebuilt ; and at that time, and doubtless for centuries before, it occupied the same situation as to-day. After the alterations and renewals had been completed, the building comprised a nave, chancel, and side aisles, separated by stone pillars, on which rested pointed arches. At the west end of the church, throughout its entire width, was erected a gallery, another of less extent being placed at the east end for the accommodation of the organ. The north aisle contained a small gallery belonging to the ffrance family, the private chapel of the Westbys of Mowbreck, and a spacious room or vestry, in which the "Thirty-men" held their meetings. In the south aisle was located the private oratory of the Cliftons, of Westby and Clifton. The chancel extended the width of the nave and south aisle, and in 1780 the Clifton chapel was, with the consent of its proprietor, enclosed within the communion rails. The reading desk stood against the central pillar of the north side of the nave, and immediately above it was placed the pulpit. The north wall was low, and contained several large windows. The whole of the building, with the exception of the chancel, which possessed a double-gabled roof, was covered in by a single roof, which slanted from the south to the north wall, and was pierced at each end with dormer windows. The main entrance was protected by a massive porch.

The tower was probably erected but little later, if not, indeed, at the time the church was rebuilding, as appears from the will here quoted, bearing the date 29th of July, 1512 :—" I, Cuthbert Clifton, Squyer, desire to be buryed at Kirkham in the tombe where Rychard Clifton, my great grandfather was buryed ; I bequeath £6 13s. 4d. towards buyldyng of the steple of the saide churche."

This tower was embattled with a short pinnacle at each corner, and stood about sixty feet high ; on a stone in one of the buttresses were carved the arms and name of Cuthbert Clifton. In the inside wall of the present tower there is fixed a stone bearing traces of an inscription, and it is probable, from the remnant of a name still discernible upon it, that this is the stone here referred to.

From the records of the "Thirty-men" are learnt several things of interest with regard to the church, and amongst them, that during the seventeenth century the edifice was used occasionally for scholastic purposes, thus :—

"1653-54.

"6 Jan. It was agreed (by the "Thirty-men") that no scriffener be suffered to teach in the church, unless he procure some honest townsmen of Kirkham to pass their word that whatsoever his scholars do, either in breaking glass or in abusing men's seats—and that they meddle not with the bells—he shall make good what they abuse."

In 1662 a font was erected at a cost of £2 5s. 4d., and most likely is the one now stationed in the tower entrance to the church. A bone house was built in 1679 in the recess or corner formed by the west wall of the north aisle and the north side of the tower, in obedience to the order of the bishop of the diocese. In 1724 gates were placed at the entrance to the churchyard, and in 1799 the old tithe barn which formed the westerly boundary of this plot of ground was blown down and destroyed ; the stone for the gate pillars was obtained from Ribchester. The following lists of persons buried in the Clifton and Westby chapels, or quyres, as they were called, were given in an old document which was copied in 1790 by Mr. W. Langton, who described it as "much defaced and torn :"—

"In the Clifton Quire

"1597, sir Geo Cowbrone and Mr. Cuthbert Clifton ; 1598, Henry Colbron of Frekleton ; 1601, Mr. Skillicorne ; 1604, ould Dorothie Skillicorne, Mr. Skillicorne's daughter ; 1602, Mr. Skillicorne, his wiff, Mr. Skillicorne, his son, and Henry Brown of Scales ; 1604, Lawrence Cowbrone, eldest son of above ; 1616, Henry Porter of Treales ; 1621, Mrs. Jane Anderton, died at Westby ; 1625, Mr. John Sharples, of Frekleton ; 1630, uxor Arthur Sharples, and Matthew Colbron of Frekleton."

"In the Westby Quyre.

"1605, Mr. Westby and Mr. John Westby (Mr. Thos. eldest brother) ; 1622, ould Mr. Hesketh ; 1623, Mr. Hesketh of Maines."

In a note we are told that when Mr. Skillicorne died in 1601, "and was to be buried, Seth Woods of Kirkham and another with him stood at Mr. Clifton's quyre dore to keep them from making a grave, and William Hull of Singleton did run at the door with wood and break it open—how it ended is forgotten, but he was buried there."

In 1822 the nave of the church was pulled down and rebuilt by aid of a rate imposed on all the townships; an inscription commemorating this event was placed over the arch of the old chancel. The tower and spire as they now exist were erected in 1844, whilst the present chancel was built in 1853. The spire and tower together have an altitude of one hundred and fifty feet, and the foundation stone of the latter was laid by Thomas Clifton, esq., of Lytham, on the 21st of November, 1843. The tower contains a peal of eight bells, but none of them are of ancient date, those alluded to in the records of the "Thirty-men" having been sold and replaced by fresh ones. The modern church of Kirkham, which, like its predecessor, is dedicated to St. Michael, is a large and handsome structure, built of Longridge stone, and capable of holding about eighteen hundred persons; the chancel is ornamented with a castellated parapet and fluted cornice. A stone coffin, which may be seen outside the church at the east, was taken out of the ground when the chancel was rebuilt. In 1725 the sum of £500 was left in trust by William Grimbaldson, M.D., to be expended in the purchase of land and other property, the income from which had to be devoted to providing a suitable person or persons to read prayers twice every day of the week except Sunday, in the parish church of Kirkham; in the event of this condition of the bequest not being fulfilled, it was decreed by the will that the annual interest of the money should be distributed amongst the poor housekeepers of Treales; so far, however, the requirement of the trust has been conformed to, and prayers are still read twice daily in the church.

Within the ancient church of Kirkham, doubtless in the Clifton chapel, was a chantry founded during the fifteenth century by Richard Clifton, of Clifton, who married Alice, the daughter of John Butler, of Rawcliffe Hall; and called the chantry of the "Holy Crucifix," as well as that of "Our Blessed Laydy." The commissioners of Henry VIII. issued the following report concerning it :—

"The Chauntrie in the paroche Church of Kirkeham.

"Thomas Prymbet preyst Incumbent there of the foundation of the antecessors of Sr Thomas Clifton, knight, to celebrate there for their sowles and all crysten sowles.

"The same is at the altar of our lady wt hin the paroche church of Kirkham, and the said Incumbent doth celebrate there accordinglie."

Sum totall of the rentall...... ....£6 os. 11d.,

"Whereof—

"Payde to Sir Henry ffarington, knight, as farmour to the kynge, our Sovereigne lord, of Penwarden-fee, for chief rente goynge forthe of the lands in ffryklyngton, by yere . . . . . 4d.

"Payde to the Kinges Majestie, to the handes of the receyvour of his late Monasteyre of Vale Royall, goynge forthe of the burgages in Kirkeham, by yere, in Christenmes and Mydsomur, ... 7s. 6d.

"Sum of the reprises ....7s 10d.

"And so remayneth......................................£5 13s. 1d.

This chantry was in existence in 1452, for in that year, when the abbot and convent of Vale Royal presented Dom. Edmund Layche to the vicarage, the archdeacon instructed John Clarke, the chaplain of the chantry, to induct him.[1] Thomas Prymbett, the officiating priest, was sixty years of age in 1548, and at that date the town and parish of Kirkham contained 1700 "houselinge people." Five years later Thomas Prymbett received a pension of £5.[2] His death occurred in 1564.

At the dissolution of monasteries, the chantry of Kirkham church was mulcted in an annual rent of 6s. 2d., which was ordered to be paid to the receiver of the Duchy. A lease of the lands appertaining to the chantry was granted to Lawrence Pembroke for a term of sixteen years.

In 1291 the living of Kirkham church was estimated in the *Valor* of Pope Nicholas at £160 per annum, but at the dissolution aforesaid it was valued at no more than £21 1s. 0½d. per annum.

In 1586 the advowson of the church was leased to James Smith, yeoman, of Kirkham ; and in 1591 it was granted for a period of twenty-one years by the authorities of Christ Church, Oxford, to John Sharples, of Freckleton.[3]

Within the church are several inscriptions, the oldest and most curious of which is to be seen on a stone forming part of the

1. Canon Raine's Hist. of Lanc. Chantries.
2. Willis's Hist. Mitr. Abb. vol. ii., p. 108.
1. Records of the Dean and Chapter, Christ Church, Oxford.

floor of the vestry, and covering the grave of vicar Clegg :—

> " R^d. Clegg came : V : M. : J666.
> Began poo^r loaves : E : J670.
> Ux^r Jennet nup^t E : j672.
> Mary n^t 9^r: j673 : nup^t, FEB : 96.
> Doro n^t. M. j675 : ob. j677.
> Abraham. n^t J : j677 : ob. j677.
> Doro : n^t : S : j678.
> Henerey n^t : J : j680. ob. j683.
> Eliz : n^t : M : j685. nup^t Feb. 1713.
> R^d Clegg V^r. ob j720. Æt. 85.
> W : Jennet ob : j7 . . . Æt . .

Others are in memoriam of Thomas, the son of Sir Thomas Clifton, of Lytham, died 1688, aged 20 years ; the Rev. John Threlfall, B.A., for " 56 years head-master of Kirkham School," died 1801, aged 84 years ; the Rev. Phipps Gerard Slatter, M.A., " head-master of the Free School," died 1815, aged 25 years ; the Rev. Charles Buck, M.A., for 27 years vicar of the parish, died 1717 ; the Rev. Humphrey Shuttleworth, vicar of Kirkham, died 1812, aged 76 years ; Richard Bradkirk, esq., of Bryning Hall, died 1813, aged 60 years ; Henry Rishton Buck, B.A., " lieutenant 33rd Regiment, who fell in battle at Waterloo, June 18, 1815," aged 27 years ; and James Buck, lieutenant 21st Light Dragoons, died January 7, 1815, aged 19 years.

In the church yard there are sundry inscribed stones, which, although little interesting on the score of antiquity, are worthy of mention as marking the burial places of persons of note in the parish at one time ; as—James Thistleton of Wrea, the founder of Wrea school, who was interred on the 27th of February, 1693 ; William Harrison of Kirkham, gent., interred January 12th, 1767, aged 60, who " left an ample fortune to poor relations, and £140 to be vested in land, the yearly income to be distributed in pious. books to the poor of Kirkham, Little Eccleston, and Larbrick : may the trustees dispense with integrity and effect the sacred dole " ; Edward King, esq., fourth son of the Very Rev. James King, D.D., dean of Raphoe, " formerly bencher of the honourable society of Gray's inn, and for above twenty years vice-chancellor of the Duchy of Lancaster " ; the " Rev. Charles Buck of Kirkham, A.M., died 4 Jan. 1808. Aged 54," also his two sons ; the Rev. Robert Loxham, vicar of Poulton, died in 1770, aged 80 years ; and John Langton of Kirkham, died in 1762, aged 71 years ; also many other members of the same family.

VICARS OF KIRKHAM.

IN THE DEANERY OF AMOUNDERNESS AND ARCHDEACONRY OF RICHMOND.

Date of Institution.	NAME.	On whose Presentation.	Cause of Vacancy.
1239	Dn's Will de Ebor	Duke of Cornwall	
Between 1272 and 1307	Simon Alley	Convent of Vale Royal	
1354	William de Slayteburn		
1361	William Boulton		
1362	Phil de Grenhal		
	Dn's Roger Dyryng		
About 1377	Robert de Horneby		
1418	Dn's Will Torfet		
1420	Dn's John Cotun		
1450	John Hardie		
1452	Edmund Layche	Convent of Vale Royal	
1512	Thomas Smith		
1558	James Smith		
1586	James Smith	James Smith	
1591	James Sharples, B.A.	Christ Church, Oxford	
1594	Nicholas Helme, M.A.	John Sharples	Death of J. Sharples.
1598	Arthur Greenacres, M.A.	Cuthbert Sharples	
1627	John Gerrard, M.A.	Christ Church, Oxford	
1629	Edward Fleetwood, M.A.	Exchange with	John Gerrard
1650	John Fisher		
1660	Richard Clegg, M.A.	Christ Church, Oxford	Death of J. Fisher
1720	William Dickson, B.A.	Ditto	Death of R. Clegg
1744	Charles Buck, M.A.	Ditto	Death of W. Dickson
1771	Humphrey Shuttle-worth, M.A.	Ditto	Death of C. Buck
1813	James Webber, D.D.	Ditto	Death of H. Shuttle-worth
1847	George Lodowick Parsons, M.A.	Ditto	Death of J. Webber
1852	Will. Law Hussey, M.A.	Ditto	Death of G. L. Parsons
1862	George Rich. Brown, M.A.	Ditto	Death of W. L. Hussey
1875	Hen. William Mason, M.A.	Ditto	Death of G. R. Brown

The parish registers furnish us with the subjoined information, which has been arranged in a tabular form :—

	1600—1601		1700—1701		1800—1801	
Baptisms	91	103	106	100	149	139
Marriages	20	19	15	25	40	45
Burials	69	44	103	86	157	112

Respecting Kirkham's less antiquated days it may be stated that Messrs. Thomas Shepherd, John Birley, and John Langton were the earliest to commence manufacturing on any large scale there, which they accomplished during the first half of the eighteenth century by establishing conjointly the flax spinning mill still existing, but with many additions, as the firm of John Birley and Sons.   John Langton was descended from John Langton, of Broughton Tower, through his fourth son, John, who resided at Preston, and of whom Cornelius Langton, of Kirkham, was the third son.   On the 31st of March, 1696, Cornelius Langton paid 30s. for his trade freedom in Kirkham, where he married Elizabeth, daughter of Zachary Taylor, M.A, head-master of the Grammar School, by whom he had issue John, Abigail, Zachary, and Roger.   Abigail died in 1776 ; Zachary entered the church, and espoused the daughter of Alexander Butler, of Kirkland ; Roger died in 1727 ; and John, the eldest, opened, in conjunction with the two gentlemen just named, a mercantile house in Kirkham, and left issue by his wife Elizabeth, daughter of Thomas Brown, of Ashtree Hall, Kirkham, —Anne, Sarah, Cornelius, Thomas, of Kirkham, and five other children.   The children of Thomas Langton, by his wife Jane, the eldest daughter of William Leyland, of Blackburn, were Elizabeth, Leyland, Cornelius, Zachary, Cicely, and William, of Kirkham, born 1758, died 1814.   John Birley was the son of John Birley of Skippool, and the ancestor of the large families of Birley, at Kirkham, Manchester, etc.   The mills at present standing in the neighbourhood of Kirkham are the flax mill of Messrs. John Birley and Sons, employing about 1,600 hands ; the weaving shed of Messrs. Walker and Barrett, 400 hands ; the cotton mill of Messrs. Harrison and Company, 150 hands ; the cotton mill of Messrs. Richards and Parker, 180 hands ; the weaving shed of Messrs. Richards Brothers, 84 hands ; and the Fylde Manufacturing Company in Orders Lane, a newly-established concern.   John Langton, who started in business at Kirkham as a flax spinner, purchased, in company with Ann

Hankinson, in 1760, two years before his death, two closes of land, with their appurtenances, in Freckleton, called Bannister Flatt and Freckleton Croft, containing by estimate 1½ acres, and 12 beast-gates upon Freckleton Marsh, all of which they conveyed by indenture in four months to John Dannet, Thomas Langton, and William Shepherd, in trust for the educating, teaching, and instructing, free from all charge, of such young girls within the township of Kirkham, as they in their discretion should make choice of, to read, knit, and sew ; and that they should for that purpose meet twice a year, on the 25th of December and the 24th of June, at Kirkham, to make choice of proper subjects, and keep a book, wherein should be entered the accounts of the receipts and disbursements. During the ten years which elapsed after 1760 additional benefactions were received amounting to £440. By indenture, dated 2nd of March, 1772, Joseph Brockholes and Constantia, his wife, conveyed to William Shepherd and Thomas Langton, trustees of the school, their heirs and assigns, for the sum of £425, two cottages, with appurtenances, in Freckleton, with a garden containing 36 perches ; a parcel of ground in a meadow in Freckleton, called Birl Brick Meadow, embracing 30 perches ; one cowgate in Freckleton Marsh ; five closes in Freckleton, named the Two Baker Meadows, the Two Lamma Leaches, and the Bank, holding six acres of customary measurement. From 1772 to 1813 further donations (£130) were received. The trusteeship of the school appears to have descended in the Langton family, and was held by the late Thomas Langton Birley, esq., whose father, Thomas Birley, had married Anne, the daughter and co-heiress of John Langton, of Kirkham. Clothing, as well as education, is supplied gratuitously to the scholars, who usually amount to 40, or thereabouts. A new building for the purposes of the school was erected on a fresh site a few years ago, in place of the former one, which had stood since 1761.

The Roman Catholics, through the munificence of the Rev. Thomas Sherburne, built a magnificent church at the Willows in 1844-5. The edifice comprises a nave, side aisles, chancel, south porch, and an elegant spire, having an altitude of 110 feet. On the south side of the chancel is the lady chapel, and opposite to it that of the holy cross The high altar is beautifully sculptured in Caen stone, and the reredos and tabernacle are covered with rich guilding. The walls contain several noble windows of stained glass. This church superseded one which had been erected in the same locality in 1809, anterior to which the chapel attached to Mowbreck Hall had been used by the Romanists of the neighbourhood for their celebrations and services. The Independents and Wesleyans also have places of worship in the town, situated respectively in Marsden and Freckleton Streets. The chapel of the Independents was constructed about 1793, and rebuilt in 1818, but that of the Wesleyans is of more recent origin. At the Willows, it should be mentioned, there is a school, open to all denominations, but under Roman Catholic supervision, which was established about 1828. Kirkham was first illuminated with gas in 1839. It contains a County Court House[1] and the Workhouse of the Fylde Union,[2] in addition to several other public buildings, as a Police Station, Waterworks' Office, National and Infant Schools, etc. The town is governed by a Local Board of Health.

No papers have so far been discovered throwing any light upon the origin of the Free Grammar School, and the earliest intimation of its existence is in 1551, when Thomas Clifton, of Westby, bequeathed "towards the grammar scole xxˢ." Thirty-four years later it was arranged amongst the "Thirty-men" that " 40s. taken out of the clerk's wages should be paid to the schoolmaster, and that 4 of the 30-men in the name of the rest should take possession of the school-house in right of the whole parish, to be kept in repair by it and used as a school-house;" also that "Richard Wilkins, now schoolmaster," should be retained in his office for a year or longer. In 1589 the above assembly "agreed that the 10s. a year pᵈ by Goosnargh to the church shᵈ in future be paid to the schoolmaster, and for every burial (except one dying in childbed) he shᵈ have such sum as was agreed by the 30-men, and also such sum as hath heretofore been paid for the holy loaf, which is of every house 3d., every Sunday successively towards repairs of the schoolhouse and help of his wages." In 1592 this order, as far as regards the holy-loaf contributions, was rescinded, the money as in former times going to the vicar.

The following is from the copy of an ancient manuscript

1. See Court of Requests page 209.　　　2. See Chapter XVI.

account of the school, from 1621 to 1663, formerly in the possession of Thomas Martin, esq., of Lincoln's Inn :—

"Isabell Birly, wife of Thomas Birly, born in Kirkham, daughter of John
Coulbron, an alehouse keeper all her life, and through that employment attayned
to a good personall estait above most in that towne of that calling, being moved
with a naturall compassion to pore children shee saw often in that towne, was
heard to say dyvers tymes she would doe something for their good, and in the
yeare 1621, having gotten a good stock of money in her hands, was moved to put
her sayings into action. The 30-men of the parish being assembled at the church,
she, with £30 in her apron, came to them, telling them she had brought that
money to give it towards the erecting of a free schole for pore children to be
taught gratis, whose parents were not able to lay out money for their teaching,
wishing them to take it and consider of it. They were the men especially trusted
by the parish for the common benefits of the church, and therefore were the most
like persons to move their severall townships to contribute every one something
towards the accomplishment of so charitable a work, and not doubting that their
good examples in their contributions would be a strong motive to excite others.
This gift was thankfully accepted, and wrought so with them that every one was
forward to promote it, especially Mr. Jno. Parker of Bredkirk, an eminent man in
the parish and one of that companie, being at that tyme one of the earl of Derbie's
gentlemen and somewhat allied to the said Isabell ; he forwarded it very much,
sparing neither his paynes of his bodie nor his purse ; for that end he travelled all
the parish over to every particular towne and house earnestly persuading them to
contribute to so good an use. Sir Cuthbert Clifton gave £20, Maister Westby of
Moulbreck £10, Mr. Parker £5, Mr. Langtree of Swarbreck £5, Mr. Hesketh of
Maines 40s., Mr. Greenacres, vicar of Kirkham, £4, and the several townships in
the parish gave as followeth :—Kirkham near £30, but not out; Ribby and Wray
£3 8s. 6d. ; Westby and Plumpton 16s. 4d. ; Weeton £7 2s. ; Singleton £1 13s. 6d.;
Little Eccleston and Larbrick 4s. 4d. ; Greenall and Thistleton £4 16s. ; Roseacre
£7 2s.; Wharles £1 13s.; Treales £8 4s.; Medlar and Wesham £1 5s.; Hambleton 4s. 6d. ; Salwick £3 5s. ; Clifton £3 7s. ; Newton and Scales £3 5s.; Freckleton £8 ; Warton £1 8s.; Bryning and Kellamer £4 13s.—in the whole £170 14s.'

When the time came for the selection of a suitable person to
undertake the charge and education of the pupils, it so happened
"that at that instant a young man, an honest, able scholar of good
gifts and parts, having a lingering sickness upon him, was come
over to Kirkham to Mr. William Armesteed (the curate of Kirkham), his cozen, for change of air, his name being Thomas Armesteed, and he was moved by some of the towne whether he would
accept to be schole master if suit were made to the 30-men to
elect him ; he, in regard to the weakness of his bodie then yielded
to the motion, otherwise he was a man well qualified for the
ministery and a moving preacher."[1]

1. Ancient Manuscript.

At the meeting of the "Thirty-men" to fill up the appointment there were two candidates, Mr. Armesteed and Mr. Sokell, but the former was elected. About the year 1628, when this gentleman resigned, Mr. Sokell was elected to the vacancy after a contest. Until 1628 the management of all matters connected with the school had rested with the "Thirty-men," but at that date the Roman Catholic gentlemen, who had been most liberal in their contributions, came to the conclusion that "it was not for their reputation altogether to leave the care of it to others and they to have no hand in it, therefore they took upon them to have a hand about it, and upon their doing so the 30 men, being tenants most of them to some of them, or dependant someway upon them, left it to them ; only Mr. Parker was not bound to the *gentlemen*, and he joined in with them."[1]

Isabell Birley and others had brought out a candidate, named Dugdall, at the recent election of schoolmaster, and were so incensed at his defeat by Mr. Sokell, a Romanist, that they drew up a petition to the bishop of Chester, complaining that "the gentlemen of the parish, being recusants all saving Mr. Parker, had intruded themselves to order all things" about the free school, and begging his lordship to issue an order how the future election of feofees for the school should be made, which he accordingly did, as follows :—

"Apud, Wigan, 31 July, 1628.

"At which day and place diverse of the Town and Parish of Kirkham appeared about the ordering of a schole master thereof for the time to come. At their request it is therefore ordered that the whole parish, or as many as shall appear at some day prefixed, after public notice given the Sunday before, shall elect six or nine lawful and honest men feofees for that purpose, whereof a third part to be chosen by the towne of Kirkham, and the two other parts by the parishioners generally, of which feofees Isabell Wilding's (late Birley) husband and her heirs, because she gave £30 to the schole maister, shall be one.

"Johannes Cestrensis. Edw[d] Russell."

The command of the bishop to call a public meeting was carried out, and in answer to the summons, read in church as directed, only seven persons presented themselves in "the parlour of Mr. Brown the curate," viz., Sir Cuthbert Clifton, knt., Mr. Thomas Westby, Mr. Thomas Hesketh, Mr. Langtree, Mr. John Parker, gentleman, and of the parishioners, "not one man saving Richard

1. Ancient Manuscript.

Harrison of Freckleton, and John Wilding of Kirkham ; and then and there the gentlemen elected themselves feofees, as also they elected Mr. Edward Fleetwood, the vicar."[1]

After the death of John Wilding in 1634, as his widow, Isabell, found herself growing more infirm, she waited on the feofees with the intention of supplementing her original donation of £30 with an additional one of equal value, if she found them "favourable to her in something she willed of them, whereas Mr. Clifton gave her harsh words and such as sent her home with much discontent and passion." When she died in 1637, it was discovered, as the manuscript from which we have been quoting informs us, that she had "left the £30 by will to buy land with, and the yearly rent to be divided to the poor of the town and parish of Kirkham."

During the struggles between king and parliament, the school was closed for several years, and re-opened with fresh governors or feofees. At that epoch the inhabitants were kept in a state of constant excitement and alarm by visits from either the royal or parliamentary forces, but fortunately no collision ever took place in the neighbourhood.[2]

By the will, dated 1655, of Henry Colborne, of London, a native of Kirkham, his trustees were requested to purchase the lease of the rectory of this town, and invest the profits, with the exception of £100 per annum, for sixteen years, in lands for the benefit of schools ; the purchases were to be settled on the Drapers' Company of London. In 1673, £69 10s. was obtained for the school, being the rent of lands bought in the metropolis by the Colborne trustees, £45 of which sum had to be paid to the head master, who was required to be "a university man, and obliged to preach once a month at least in the parish church or in some of the chapels ;" £16 16s. of the remainder was apportioned to the second master ; and £8 to provide an usher.[3]

In 1673 it was decreed by the Court of Chancery that the expense and duty of preserving the school-house in proper repair should devolve upon the township of Kirkham, whilst the election of masters should rest exclusively with the Drapers' Company.[4]

1. Ancient Manuscript.   2. See pages 61, 63, and 66.
        3. Charity Commissioners' Report.   4. Ibid.

In that year also lands, etc., at Nether Methop in Westmoreland to the value of £530 were purchased, according to the directions of the will of the Rev. James Barker, rector of Thrandeston, Suffolk, which required his executors to buy lands sufficient to yield an annual rent of £30, and to settle such property on ten trustees, elected by the bailiffs and principal burgesses of Kirkham; the trustees were ordered to apply the rental to the following uses :—£10 yearly to the schoolmaster ; £12 yearly in half-yearly instalments, as an "exhibition or allowance to such poor scholer of the towne as shall then be admitted to the university," such exhibition to be open to any pupil born in Kirkham and educated at the school, and in case no scholar was ready and fitted to take advantage of it the sum was to be used in binding out poor apprentices ; £5 for the purpose of binding apprentices ; and the remainder to be expended in defraying the cost of an annual dinner for the trustees when they met to "enquire concerning the demeanure of the scholler at the univerty," in whose case it was appointed that if they should find him "to be riotously given, or disordered and debauched, they should withdraw the exhibition."

In 1701, the Drapers' Company issued the following order touching the admission of girls to the benefits of the charity :—
"From henceforth no female sex shall have any conversation, or be taught, or partake of any manner of learning whatsoever in the free school at Kirkham, any former custom to the contrary notwithstanding."

In 1725 £400 was bequeathed to the trustees of the school by William Grimbaldson, M.D., to be invested in lands, and the rental to be added to the stipend of the head-master, if "he should be a scholar bred at Westminster, Winchester, or Eton, and a master of arts," but if not the rental to be devoted to binding apprentices, for which purpose it is used at present. In addition this physician left £50 to be similarly invested, and the income to be spent in buying classical books for the school. The management of the school has been in the hands of trustees from the time of Barker's bequest.

Since the establishment of the exhibition under Barker's trust twenty-eight youths have been assisted in their university careers by its means.

HEAD MASTERS OF GRAMMAR SCHOOL SINCE 1800.

Date of Appointment.		Name.		By whom appointed.	
1801 to 1806.		Rev. Thos. Stevenson.	*pro. temp.*	Company of Drapers.	
In	1806.	Jas. Thos. Halloway, D.D.		"	"
"	1808.	Rev. Henry Dannett, B.A.		"	"
"	1814.	Rev. Phipps Gerard Slatter, M.A.		"	"
"	1815.	Rev. Jas. Ratcliffe, M.A.		"	"
Before 1837.		Rev. Rich.d Martindell Lamb, M.A.	*pro. temp.*	"	"
In	1837.	Rev. Geo. Thistlethwaite, M.A.		"	"
"	1845.	Rev. S. E. Wentworth, M.A.		"	"
"	1866.	Rev. Jno. Burrough, M.A.		"	"
"	1874.	Rev. J. Young, M.A.		"	"

From the vestry book of Kirkham, we learn that the charity known as "Bread Money" originated from the vicar and "Thirtymen," who, on the 5th of April, 1670, "with the consent and countenance of some of the gentlemen and of the present churchwardens, with some neighbours of repute in the respective townships," held a meeting, at which it was unanimously decided to raise £80, such sum to be laid out on good security, and the interest to be expended in providing "a dozen penny loaves for every Sunday in the year, Christmas and the king's birthday, and for every other holiday, to be given to so many of such poor as shall use to frequent the church and to those of distant townships." The resolution continued :—" These loaves shall not be given to strangers or vagabonds, nor to children that shall but play about the church till sermon be passed, and then come in for a loaf, nor to any of the town of Kirkham in summer, but only in winter." In order to raise the fund agreed upon, it was resolved that "what could be got by contribution of the communicants at Easter should be thus employed;" vicar Richard Clegg promised £5, and stated that if he remained at Kirkham during the rest of his life, and had the means, he would at some future time give £15 more for the same object, an intention which appears subsequently to have been carried out by his daughter, Mrs. Mary Nightingale, who some years after his decease, contributed £20 towards the fund. £5 given for the use of the poor by Jane, wife of John Clifton ; arrears of rent due from Goosnargh ; and funeral doles were all devoted to this purpose. In 1867 the fund amounted to £102 2s., yielding an annual income of £5 13s. 3d.

A sum of £12 was given by vicar Clegg, the interest to be paid to the clergyman preaching a sermon in Kirkham church on Easter Tuesday.

Richard Brown, by indenture dated 1639, conveyed for a term of 999 years a close called New Moor Hey with appurtenances, in Kirkham, to James Smith, upon condition that he, his heirs and executors, should pay the yearly rent of 20s. at Martinmas. " It is witnessed, that the said Richard Brown, in consideration of the good will he bore to the town of Kirkham, and the inhabitants thereof, and out of his zeal to God, and the charitable relief of the poor, needful and impotent people within the said town, granted to William Robinson and three others, their heirs and assigns, the said yearly rent of 20s., to hold the same upon trust, and to dispose of it amongst so many of the people of the said town, as the bailiffs thereof for the time being should, in their discretion, think most needful, on St. Thomas's day."[1]

By indenture, dated 1734, Joseph Hankinson, of Kirkham, in consideration of £45 released and conveyed to Robert Hankinson, and four others a close in Kirkham, called Swarbreck's Old Earth, containing, by estimate, 1½ acres, to hold the same to themselves and their heirs for ever ; and in the deed it was declared that the consideration money belonged to the poor of the township, and that the grantees were only trustees of the same, and had laid it out by direction of the inhabitants for the benefit of the poor according to the wish of the benefactors. The indenture is endorsed :—" Conveyance of Swarbreck's Old Earth, for the use of the poor of Kirkham, purchased by monies given by Mrs. Clegg, widow of the Rev. Richard Clegg, vicar, and Mrs. Phœbe Sayle, wife of Mr. Charles Sayle, to wit £20 by the former, and £20 by the latter."

Thomas Brockholes, by an indenture of 1755, conveyed for £50 to John Langton and William Shepherd, their heirs and assigns, a close called Moor Hey, with appurtenances ; and subsequently

---

1. Indenture in Bailiffs' Chest.

in 1768 William Shepherd conveyed the close then denominated the Bailiffs' Moor Hey to Henry Lawson, yeoman, of Kirkham, who in the following year being moved by " divers good causes and considerations " sold to the Rev. Charles Buck, vicar of Kirkham, and twelve others, all of Kirkham, gentlemen, for the sum of five shillings, two plots of land in Kirkham township, one of which, called Moorcroft, contained a rood and four perches, and the other, Swarbreck's Old Earth, comprised an acre and an half. The conditions were that all profits or income accruing from the lands · should be used for the relief of the poor of the aforesaid township.[1]

On the 1st of December, 1739, a legacy of £40 was bequeathed to trustees by Elizabeth Brown, to be invested, and the interest applied to the relief of the poor and necessitous widows of Kirkham, or the neighbouring townships, at Michaelmas.

The sum of £140 was received under the will, dated 1767, of William Harrison of Kirkham, to be invested, and the interest to be expended in Common Prayer books, Bibles, etc., two-thirds of which were to be given to the poor of this town, and the remainder to the poor of Little Eccleston and Larbrick.[2]

In 1816 Mrs. Mary Bradkirk placed £320 in the navy, five per cents. in her own name and that of Zachary Langton, esq., of Bedford Row, London; and subsequently trustees of this fund were appointed, whose duty it was to distribute the interest as follows :—

That of £100 amongst five necessitous persons in the township of Kirkham for life, and each vacancy to be filled up immediately after the death of the former recipient.

That of £20 to Joseph Brewer, then parish clerk of Kirkham, for life, and after his demise to the person filling the office of sexton at the same place.

That of £100 to five poor persons of Ribby-with-Wrea, and that of the last £100 to five poor persons of Bryning-with-Kellamergh, the vacancies to be treated as in those of Kirkham.

The only requirement on the part of the pensioners being that they should be members of the Church of England. The income of this charity, which amounts to more than £10 a year, like those of the five preceding it, forms part of the bailiffs' fund.

---

1. Deed in Bailiff's Chest.   2. Report of Charity Commissioners, 1824.

CHAPTER XIII.

PARISH OF KIRKHAM.

FRECKLETON.

IN the Domesday Book Freckeltun is stated to contain four carucates of arable soil. During the reign of Henry III. Richard de Freckleton, Allan de Singleton, and Iwan de Freckleton, with three others, held land in Freckleton from the earl of Lincoln. In 1311 the heirs of Adam de Freckleton held Freckleton from Alice, the daughter and heiress of the earl of Lincoln, shortly after which Ralph de Freckleton was lord of the manor. Gilbert de Singleton had a house with 12 acres of land and a mill there in 1325. In 1349 the manor was held under the earl of Lancaster as follows :— Robert de Freckleton, 1 messuage and 3 bovates ; Nicholas le Botiler, 1 messuage and 11 bovates ; the heirs of Robert Sherburne, 2 bovates ; the heirs of Sir Adam de Banastre, 2 bovates ; and Thomas de Singleton, 1 bovate. During the first half of the 16th century the Botilers or Butlers retained property in Freckleton, whilst the Sherburnes held estates there until the early part of the 17th century. Hugh Hilton Hornby, esq., of Ribby Hall, is the largest territorial proprietor at present, but there are several resident yeomen.

In 1834 a temporary episcopal chapel was erected, and 5 years later the existing church was built, being a neat brick edifice, with a spire at the west end, and containing an ancient pulpit from Kirkham church. The Rev. G. H. Waterfall, M.A., was the earliest incumbent, and the Rev. Walter Scott, appointed in

1861, is now in charge. In 1718 a Quakers' burial ground was opened, but was closed in 1811. A meeting house was also established by the same sect in 1720, and pulled down after standing nearly a century. A Wesleyan chapel was erected in 1814 ; and in 1862 the Primitive Methodists opened another. A National school was built in 1839, and is supported mainly by subscriptions.

The village is long and irregular, but contains sundry better class houses, and a cotton manufactory, belonging to Mr. Sower-butts, holding 320 looms. The inhabitants are chiefly employed ployed in making sacking, sailcloth, ropes, etc. There is also a shipbuilding yard, of which Mr. Rawstorne is the proprietor, where vessels, mostly for the coasting trade, are constructed.

POPULATION OF FRECKLETON.

1801.	1811.	1821.	1831.	1841.	1851.	1861.	1871.
561	701	875	909	995	968	879	930

The township comprises 2,659 statute acres.

Andrew Freckleton and two more gave, about 1734, certain sums of money for the poor of Freckleton, the interest from which, together with 10s. per annum left by Lawrence Webster for the same object, amounts to £2 5s. a year. The township shares in a bequest of £5, with Clifton and Newton-with-Scales, from Elizabeth Clitherall, of Clifton, for the use of the poor.

WARTON. Wartun is entered in the survey of William the Conqueror as comprising four carucates, and later, when in the fee of the earl of Lincoln, the township was held by the manorial lord of Wood Plumpton. During the reign of King John, Thomas de Betham had the third of a knight's fee in Warton. Sir Ralph de Betham held Warton in the time of Edward III., and in 1296 Edmund Crouchback, earl of Lancaster, had a rent charge of 3s. 4d. there. Gilbert de Singleton was possessed of a messuage with six bovates of land in the township about 1325. The manor was held by Johanna Standish and Richard Singleton in 1515. John Talbot Clifton, esq., of Lytham Hall, is now the most extensive owner of the soil.

The church of Warton, dedicated to St. Paul, was completed in 1722, but not consecrated until 1725. Within recent years it has been apportioned a distinct parochial district under Lord Blandford's act.

CURATES AND VICARS OF WARTON.

Date of Institution.	NAME.	Cause of Vacancy.
Before 1773.	Wilfred Burton.	
In 1789.	Charles Buck, M.A.	
,, 1790.	James Fox.	Resignation of C. Buck.
,, 1823.	James Fox, B.A.	,, J. Fox.
,, 1840.	George Wylie, M.A.	,, J. Fox.
,, 1844.	Thos. Henry Dundas, B.A.	,, G. Wylie.

Warton school was built many years ago at the cost of the township, and in 1810 the sum of £277 was raised by subscription as an endowment. In 1809, William Dobson, of Liverpool, bequeathed £500 to the trustees, and another sum of £500 was also bequeathed by Mrs. Francis Hickson. In 1821 a new schoolhouse was built.

POPULATION OF WARTON.

1801.	1811.	1821.	1831.	1841.	1851.	1861.	1871.
376	445	468	531	522	473	446	444

The area of the township contains 3,939 statute acres.

BRYNING-WITH-KELLAMERGH. The earliest allusion to this township occurs in 1200-1, when Matilda Stockhord and others held two carucates in Briscath Brunn and one carucate in Kelgmersberg. A few years later Robert de Stockhord had the fourth of a knight's fee there. In 1253 Ralph Betham held Brininge, Kelgermsarche, etc.; and during the reign of Edward III. Sir Ralph de Betham possessed the fourth of a knight's fee in the same places, at which time John de Damport also held an eighth of a carucate. In 1311 John Baskerville had 3½ bovates, and Thurstan de Norley 4 bovates, in the hamlet of Kilgremargh.

In 1479 Sir Edward and William Betham had land in Bryning and Kellamergh; and two years afterwards half of the manor was granted by Edward IV. to Thomas Molyneux and his heirs. Thomas Middleton held both Bryning and Kellamergh in 1641. The Birley, Langton, Cross, and Smith families are now the chief landowners in the township.

Bryning Hall and Leyland House are the only places of interest amongst the scattered habitations. The Hall, now a farm-house, was formerly the seat of the Bradkirks, whilst Leyland House, also converted to farm uses, was the residence of the Leylands, of Kellamergh, during the 17th and part of the 18th centuries.[1]

POPULATION OF BRYNING-WITH-KELLAMERGH.

1801.	1811.	1821.	1831.	1841.	1851.	1861.	1871.
105	131	145	164	152	126	116	115

The area of the township in statute acres is 1,043.

RIBBY-WITH-WREA. In Domesday Book *Rigbi*, for Ribby, is entered as comprising six carucates. Roger de Poictou gave the tithes of "colts, calves, lambs, kids, pigs, wheat, cheese, and butter of Ribbi and Singletone" to the priory of Lancaster to serve as food to the monks who celebrated mass in that monastery. This grant was afterwards confirmed by John, earl of Moreton.[2] In 1201 Adam and Gerard de Wra paid two marks to King John in order to gain protection from the sheriff, who, it seems, was in the habit of unjustly molesting them in their tenements.[3] The manors of Preston, Riggeby, and Singleton were presented by Henry III. to Edmund, earl of Lancaster, who in 1286 became engaged in a dispute with the abbot of Vale Royal, which ultimately led to a mandate being issued by Edward I., at Westminster, to the sheriff of Lancaster, commanding him to draw a proper and just boundary line between the lands of the disputants, because the abbot complained that the earl had taken more territory than he was legally entitled to by his fee, thereby encroaching on the conventual possessions in Kirkham parish.[4] In 1297 earl Edmund's rents from Ribby-with-Wrea amounted in all to £19 19s.[5] per annum.

During the life of the first duke of Lancaster, Ribby contained twenty houses, and twenty-one and three-fourths bovates of land held by bondsmen at a rental of £19 16s. 4d. ; and at that time there were the following tenants in Ribby and Wrea :—Adam, the son of Richard the clerk, who held five acres, and paid 4d. per annum ; Adam, the son of Jordani, one acre for 12d. ; Roger Culbray, three acres for 9d. ; Richard de Wra, half a bovate for 5d. ; Adam de Kelyrumshagh, half a bovate for 4d. ; William de Wogher, six acres for 2d. ; John de Bredkyrke, half a bovate for

1. For "Leyland of Leyland House" see Chapter VI.
2. Regist. S. Mariæ Lanc. MS. fol. 1 and 4.   3. Rot. Cancell. 3 John. m. 5.
4. Harl. MSS. No. 2064.   5. Escaet. 25 Edw. I. n, 51.

9d. ; William le Harpour, one bovate for 15d.; Giles, two acres for 10d.; John de Bonk, one bovate and one acre for 10d.; John le Wise, eleven acres for 7d.; and Adam de Parys, two bovates, which were those of John le Harpour, for 3s., of free farm and two marks. After the demise of a tenant it was the recognised custom for his successor to pay double rent.[1] The rent days were the feasts of the Annunciation of the Blessed Mary and of St. Michael. H. H. Hornby, esq., of Ribby Hall, is the present lord of the manor.

The remains of the ancient manor house on Wrea Green are now used as a cottage ; Ribby Hall, the seat of the Hornbys, is a modern mansion, and was erected rather more than half a century ago. The church of Ribby-with-Wrea owes its origin to the trustees of Nicholas Sharples's charity, who purchased a piece of ground on Wrea Green in 1721, and, having subscribed sufficient funds amongst themselves, erected a small chapel upon it. The following year they obtained a license to hold divine service in the building, and on the 20th of June, 1755, it was consecrated by the bishop of Chester. At that date the church was endowed with £400, half of which came from Queen Anne's bounty, and the other in equal portions from the charities of Thistleton and Sharples. In 1762 the whole of this fund was invested in land in Warton, and other sums amounting to £600, including a legacy of £100 under the will of Thomas Benson in 1761, and further donations from the Royal bounty before mentioned, were expended in the purchase of land at Thistleton.[2]

In 1846 the township of Westby, with the exception of Great and Little Plumptons, was joined, by order of Council, to that of Ribby-with-Wrea, and the whole converted into an ecclesiastical district. In 1869 the title of the incumbent was changed from that of perpetual curate to vicar.

The old church was pulled down and the foundation stone of the existing structure laid in 1848, by the Rev. G. L. Parsons, vicar of Kirkham. On the 23rd of September in the ensuing year, it was opened for worship, but remained unconsecrated until the 4th of May, 1855. The church is dedicated to St. Nicholas.

1. Lansd. MSS. No. 539. f. 15.   2. MS. Church Records.

CURATES AND VICARS OF RIBBY-WITH-WREA.

Date of Institution.	Name.	Cause of Vacancy.
Before 1733.	Robert Willacy.	
„ 1756.	Samuel Smith.	
„ 1762.	James Anyon.	
In 1770.	— Watts.	
„ 1791.	John Thompson.	
About 1823.	James Fox.	
In 1845.	George Thistlethwaite, M.A.	Resignation of J. Fox.
„ 1846.	Stephⁿ Exuperius Wentworth, M.A.	Death of G. Thistlethwaite.
„ 1866.	Ralph Sadleir Stoney, M.A.	„ S. E. Wentworth.

The Rev. George Thistlethwaite was the son of the Rev. T. Thistlethwaite, incumbent of St. George's, Bolton-le-Moors, and in 1837 officiated *pro. temp.* as head master of Kirkham Grammar School. The Rev. S. E. Wentworth held the headmastership of the same school from 1845 to 1860, as well as his curacy.

The free school of Ribby-with-Wrea owes its existence to the frugality and benevolence of a tailor, named James Thistleton, of Wrea, who, although his daily wages averaged no more than 4d. and his food, managed, by great care and self-denial, to accumulate a sufficient fund to establish a school at his native place, an object to which he had in a great measure devoted his life. At his death in 1693, it was found that, after a few small legacies, one being "10s. to Mr. Clegg, vicar, to preach at my funeral," and another 6s. 8d. to each of the townships of Kirkham, Bryning, and Westby, for the use of the poor, he had bequeathed the remainder of his property "towards the making and maintaining of a free school in the township of Ribby-cum-Wrea for ever," stipulating only that his surviving sister should receive annually from the profits of his estate a sum of money sufficient for her support during the rest of her life. The executors appointed were Thomas Benson, Richard Shepherd, and Cuthbert Bradkirk, whilst the money designed for the foundation of the school amounted to £180.

The work thus commenced by Thistleton received, a few years later, substantial assistance under the will, dated 10th September, 1716, of Nicholas Sharples, who is described as a "citizen and innholder of London." The bequest in this instance amounted to £850, and the two executors, Richard Wilson and Robert Pigot, were directed, "with all convenient speed to apply such sum of money towards the building or finishing of a school-house for educating of boys and girls in Ribby-cum-Wrea," and in the purchase of land for the benefit of such establishment, and the remuneration of the master, "for educating such a number of boys and girls as nine of the most substantial men, chosen and elected out of Ribby-cum-Wrea for governors or elders, or the major part of them, shall think fit ;" also that his name should be inscribed in some prominent place on one of the school walls.[1]

In 1780 a girls' school was established in a building separate from that of the boys, but in 1847 the trustees of the foundation gave the "materials of the boys' school" and the plot of land as a site for the new church, and in return the ecclesiastical party erected, according to agreement, another school-house on a piece of ground adjoining the girls' school.[2]

POPULATION OF RIBBY-WITH-WREA.

1801.	1811.	1821.	1831.	1841.	1851.	1861.	1871.
307	398	500	482	442	406	444	446

The area of the township amounts to 1,366 statute acres.

WESTBY, WITH GREAT AND LITTLE PLUMPTONS. Gilbert de Clifton held the manor about 1280, and subsequently his son William de Clifton was in possession about 1292. During the reign of Edward III. John Fleetwood was lord of Little Plumpton, and in 1394 his descendant, John Fleetwood, resided there. John Talbot Clifton, esq., of Lytham Hall, whose ancestor was the Gilbert de Clifton just mentioned, holds the manor of Westby with Plumpton, by right of inheritance.

Bowen, the geographer, who wrote in 1717, alludes to a spa in Plumpton, and states that it was impregnated with sulphur, vitriol, ochre, iron, and a marine salt, united with a bitter purging salt. The site of the spa has been lost in the lapse of time.

Westby Hall, the seat of the Cliftons, has been supplanted by a farm-house. The old chapel connected with it was opened in 1742 to the Romanists of the district, but closed about a century later. The present Catholic chapel was built in 1861. In 1849

1. Vestry Book.   2. Ibid.

a school, free to all denominations, was established by Thomas Clifton, esq., of Lytham, but there seems to have been such an institution existing before, as Ann Moor, of Westby, bequeathed, in 1805, £40 to Plumpton school, and the interest of £20 to the poor of Great Plumpton.

POPULATION OF WESTBY-WITH-PLUMPTONS.

1801.	1811.	1821.	1831.	1841.	1851.	1861.	1871.
623	692	771	686	643	707	601	535

The area of the township is 3,426 statute acres.

WEETON-WITH-PREESE. On the arrival of the Normans Weeton contained 300 acres of arable land. In the 9th year of King John, Matilda, wife of Theobald Walter, obtained certain inheritances in Weeton, Treales, and Rawcliffe. Theobald le Botiler, or Butler, held Weeton in 1249; and in 1339, James, son of Edmund le Botiler, earl of Ormond, had possession of it, together with Treales, Little Marton, and Out Rawcliffe. The manor descended in the same family until 1673, when it passed to the 9th earl of Derby on his marriage with Elizabeth, daughter of Thomas Butler, the Lord Ossory. The present earl of Derby is now the lord of the soil, and holds a court baron by deputy. There is a fair for cattle and small wares on the first Tuesday after Trinity Sunday.

Preese is the Pres of Domesday Book, and comprised at that time two carucates. Henry, duke of Lancaster, held Preese at his death in 1361. In the reign of Henry VIII. the manor was in the hands of the Skilicornes, who for many generations were the coroners of Amounderness. Preese Hall, the ancient seat of this family, was much damaged by a fire in 1732, which destroyed the private chapel. In 1864 that portion of the mansion, which had survived the conflagration and been repaired, was pulled down. The site is now occupied by a farm-house, belonging to T. H. Miller, esq., of Singleton, who owns a large amount of the land.

The church of Weeton is dedicated to St. Michael, and was built in 1843 by subscription, to which the late earl of Derby contributed generously. In 1852 the edifice was enlarged, and in 1861 the township of Weeton-with-Preese was united with the Plumptons and Greenhalgh, to form an ecclesiastical parish. The Rev. William Sutcliffe, when curate at Kirkham, performed the duties at Weeton church, and was appointed incumbent there in

1861. In 1862 he was succeeded by the present vicar, the Rev.
William Thorold. A National school was erected by subscription
and a grant from the National Society of £30, in 1845. A
Wesleyan chapel was built about 1827.

POPULATION OF WEETON-WITH-PREESE.

1801.	1811.	1821.	1831.	1841.	1851.	1861.	1871.
384	508	473	477	545	465	465	433

The area of the township is 2,876 statute acres.

MEDLAR-WITH-WESHAM. The abbot and brethren of Cockersand
Abbey became possessed of this township at an early date, and
retained it until the dissolution of monasteries, when the manor
of Medlar passed, by gift or purchase, to the Westbys, of
Mowbreck Hall. The estates of the Westbys were confiscated
by the Commonwealth, and only redeemed on the payment of
£1,000. The estate and Hall of Mowbreck are still held by
the same family.[1] The mansion preserves many evidences of its
great antiquity, including the old chapel and priests' room.

Bradkirk, in Medlar, belonged to Theobald Walter in 1249, but
in the reign of Edward III. it was held by a family bearing the
name of Bradkirk, a title acquired from the estate. The Bradkirks
resided there as proprietors until somewhere about the opening of
the 17th century, when the earl of Derby had obtained the soil.
In 1723 Bradkirk was bought by John Richardson, of Preston,
from Thomas Stanley, of Cross Hall, in Ormskirk parish, who
held the manor by right of his wife Catherine, sister and heiress
of Christopher Parker, of Bradkirk, deceased, unmarried, a few
years before.[2] From John Richardson the manor passed successively by will to William Richardson, Edward Hurst, of Preston,
and James Kearsley, of Over Hulton, by the last of whom it was
sold in 1797 to Joseph Hornby, esq., of Ribby, and his descendant,
H. H. Hornby, esq., of Ribby Hall, is the present holder. The
original Bradkirk Hall, the seat of the Bradkirks and Parkers, has
long since disappeared, and the edifice now bearing the name was
erected or rebuilt by Edward Hurst in 1764.

In 1864 an Independent Day and Sunday school was built by
Benjamin Whitworth, esq., M.P., of London, on land given by
R. C. Richards, esq., J.P., of Kirkham, and presented to the

1. For "Westby of Mowbreck" see Chapter VI.
2. For "Parker of Bradkirk" see Chapter VI.

trustees of the chapel belonging to that sect at Kirkham. The railway station and several weaving sheds and cotton mills are situated in this township.

POPULATION OF MEDLAR-WITH-WESHAM.

1801.	1811.	1821.	1831.	1841.	1851.	1861.	1871.
216	230	215	242	209	170	563	860

GREENHALGH-WITH-THISTLETON. Greenhalgh is stated in the Domesday Book to contain three carucates of soil. The township was held by the Butlers of the Fylde at an early epoch, and retained until 1626 at least, when Henry Butler, of Rawcliffe, was lord of Greenhalgh and Thistleton. During the sovereignty of Edward I. the abbot of Cockersand had certain rights there, including assize of bread and beer.

Henry Colbourne, of London, bequeathed, in 1655, £5 10s. to establish a school at Esprick in this township, but his wishes were not properly carried out before 1679, at which date his legacy was supplemented by gifts from 41 yeomen in the neighbourhood, and a school erected to provide free education to the children of Greenhalgh and Thistleton. Further endowments of £60 in 1766 from John Cooper, and £80 a little later by subscription, were given to the institution ; and in 1805 Mary Hankinson left £200, and Richard Burch, of Greenhalgh, £200, to the same object. The original school-house, formed of clay and thatched with straw, has been pulled down, and a fresh one built. Subsequent donations have been received under the wills of the Misses Ellen and Hannah Dewhirst, the former of whom left £200, in addition to a gift of £100 during her lifetime, and the latter the residue of her estate.

The interest of £20, bequeathed for that purpose by a person named Lawrenson, is distributed annually to the poor of Greenhalgh.

POPULATION OF GREENHALGH-WITH-THISTLETON.

1801.	1811.	1821.	1831.	1841.	1851.	1861.	1871.
378	403	409	408	371	362	383	365

The township embraces 1,821 statute acres.

GREAT AND LITTLE SINGLETONS. At the Domesday Survey, Singletun contained six carucates of arable land, the lord of the manor being Roger de Poictou, who gave the tithes at the close of the eleventh century to the priory of St. Mary's, Lancaster ;

this grant was subsequently confirmed by John, earl of Moreton.[1] During the reigns of kings John and Henry III., Alan de Single-ton held a carucate of land in the township by serjeanty of the wapentake of Amounderness.[2] In 20 Edward I. (1292) Thomas de Singleton, a descendant of Alan, proved to the satisfaction of a jury, when his right to certain offices was called in question, that the manor of Little Singleton had belonged to his family from time immemorial, and that the serjeanty of Amounderness with its privileges and duties, was annexed and appurtenant to that manor. Thomas de Singleton admitted, however, when called upon by the king's attorney to show by what title he held the manors of Singleton, Thornton, and Brughton, the same having been amongst the possessions of Richard I. at his death, that he did not hold the whole of Singleton, as Thomas de Clifton and Caterina his wife had one third of two bovates there ; and urged this fact as a plea why he could not be summoned to answer the demand as made on behalf of Edward I. His objection was allowed.[3] In 1297 Edmund, earl of Lancaster received annually £21 from Singleton and 20s. from Singleton Grange. At the opening of the fourteenth century Little Singleton had passed into the hands of the Banastres, for the " hamlet of Singleton Parva " was one of the estates of William Banastre at his death in 17 Edward II. (1323-24).[4] Towards the end of the reign of Edward II. Thomas, the son of the notorious Sir Adam Banastre, held little Singleton and the serjeanty of Amounderness, and by the latter of these had a right to the services of two bailiffs and a boy to levy executions within the wapentake.[5]

The following notice of Singleton in the time of Henry, duke of Lancaster, who died in 1361, occurs amongst the Lansdowne manuscripts :—

"In Syngleton there are 21 messuages and 26 bovates of land held by bondsmen, who pay annually at the feasts of Easter and St. Michael £21 9s. 3d. And there are 11 cottages with so many inclosures, and one croft, and one piece of land in the hands of tenants-at-will, paying annually 21s. 6d. All the aforesaid bonds-men owe talliage, and give marchet and heriot,[6] and on the death of her husband a widow gives one third part of his property to the lord of the manor, but more is claimed in cases where the deceased happen to be widowers. And if any one

---

1. Regist. S. Mariæ, Lanc. MS. fol. 1-4.   2. Testa de Nevill. fol. 372.
3. Placita de Quo Warr. 20 Edw. I. Lanc. Rot., 13a.
4. Escaet. 17 Edw. II. n. 45.   5. The Birch Feodary.   6. Ancient feudal taxes.

possesses a male fowl it is forbidden to him to sell it without a license. The duke of Lancaster owns the aforesaid tenements with right to hold a court. It is to be noted that each of the above mentioned bovates of land is to pay at first 2s. 7d. per annum, with work at the plough and harrow, mowing meadows in Ryggeby, and carrying elsewhere the lord's provisions at Richmond, York, Doncaster, Pontefract, and Newcastle, with 12 horses in Summer and Winter. But afterwards the land was freed from this bondage, and paid per bovate 14s. 3d. ob."

The lands of Thomas Banastre, before named, in "Syngleton Parva, Ethelswyk, Frekulton, Hamylton, Stalmyn," etc., were escheated to John of Gaunt, duke of Lancaster, in 1385, after the death of Banastre.[1]

Edmund Dudley, who was attainted in 1509 and afterwards executed, held Little Singleton, as well as lands in Elswick, Thornton, Wood Plumpton, Freckleton, etc.;[2] and in 1521 Thomas, earl of Derby, held the manor of Syngleton of Henry VIII.[3]

In the reign of James I. Great Singleton appears to have belonged to the crown, for amongst a number of estates purchased from the crown by Edward Badbie and William Weldon, of London, for the sum of £2,000, is the "manor or lordship of Singleton, alias Singleton Magna," the annual rent of which is stated to have been £16 17s. od. Subsequently the manor passed to the Fanshaws, and from them to the Shaws; William Cunliffe Shaw, of Preston, esq., sold it to Joseph Hornby, of Ribby Hall, esq., and afterwards it was purchased by Thomas Miller, esq., of Preston, who greatly improved the property by draining the low lying lands known as Singleton Carrs, which in former days were frequently in a state of partial or complete inundation. Thomas H. Miller, esq., the present owner and eldest son of the late Thos. Miller, esq., has recently erected a noble mansion on the estate, where he resides during most of the year.

The earliest notice to be discovered of Singleton Grange is in an old schedule of deeds, in which the land is mentioned as having been granted by King John in 1215. In 1297, during the reign of Edward I., Edmund Crouchback, earl of Lancaster, received yearly the sum of 20s. from the estate. Subsequently the Grange passed into the possession of the abbot and convent of

1. Duchy Rolls.   2. Duc. Lanc. vol. iv. Inq. n. 13.   3. Ibid, vol. v. n. 68.

Cockersand ;[1] and at the dissolution of monasteries it became the property of Henry VIII., who in 1543 granted it to William Eccleston, of Eccleston, gentleman.[2] The Grange descended to Thomas, the son, and afterwards to Adam, the grandson, of William Eccleston. Adam Eccleston died sometime a little later than 1597. The estate after his decease passed through several hands in rapid succession, and in 1614 was sold by William Ireland, gent., to William Leigh, B.D., clerk in holy orders and rector of Standish. Theophilus Leigh, the eldest son of that gentleman, resided at Singleton Grange, and married Clare, daughter of Thomas Brooke, of Norton, Cheshire, by whom he had one son, named William. William Leigh succeeded to the Grange on the death of his father in 1658, and espoused Margaret, daughter of Edward Chisenhall, of Chisenhall, Lancashire, and had issue, Charles and Edward.

✛ Charles Leigh, the elder of the two sons, became celebrated as a physician and student of natural history and antiquities. He was born at the Grange in 1662, and at the age of 21 graduated as B.A. at the University of Oxford ; afterwards he removed to Cambridge to study medicine, and in 1690 obtained the degree of M.D. In 1685 he was elected a Fellow of the Royal Society. He married Dorothy, daughter of Edward Shuttleworth, of Larbrick, and practised as a physician both in London and in the neighbourhood of his birthplace, on one occasion, according to his own version, performing a wonderful cure on Alexander Rigby, of Layton Hall. His published works were—*Physiologia Lancastriensis*, in 1691, and the *Natural History of Lancashire, Cheshire, and the Peak of Derbyshire, with an account of the British, Phœnician, Armenian, Greek, and Roman Antiquities in those parts*, in 1700, of which latter Dr. Whittaker remarks :— " Had this doctor filled his whole book, as he has done nearly one-half of it, with medical cases, it might have been of some use ; but how, with all possible allowances for the blindness and self-partiality of human nature, a man should have thought himself qualified to write and to publish critical remarks on a subject of which he understood not the elementary principles, it is really difficult to conceive."[3]

1. Baines's Hist. of Lancashire.   2. Duchy Records.   3. History of Whalley.

Somewhere before the commencement of the eighteenth century, the estate of Bankfield was separated from the Grange, which, during the latter portion, at least, of the lifetime of Dr. Leigh, who died shortly after the publication of his "Natural History," was held by a person named Joseph Green. In 1701 the executors of Joseph Green sold a portion of Singleton Grange to Richard Harrison, of Bankfield, yeoman. The remainder of the Grange land was held by widow Green until her death, when it passed by her will, dated 1716, to her two sons, Richard and Paul Green.[1]

Richard Harrison, of Bankfield, obtained the whole of Singleton Grange in 1738, and left it on his decease to his son Richard, from whom it descended about 1836 to his only surviving child, Agnes Elizabeth, the wife of Edwards Atkinson, of Fleetwood, justice of the peace for the county of Lancaster. Mrs. Atkinson died childless in 1850, and bequeathed Singleton Grange to her husband, who in his turn entailed the estate upon his eldest son, Charles Edward Dyson Atkinson, still a minor, the offspring of a second marriage, with Anne, daughter of Christopher Thornton Clark, of Cross Hall, Lancashire, by whom he had issue two sons and a daughter,—Ann Elizabeth Ynocensia, John Henry Gladstone, and the present heir. The old Hall of Singleton Grange has been modernised and converted into a farm-house.

It is very probable that there was a chapel in Singleton during the earlier years of the fourteenth century, for in 1358-59, Henry, duke of Lancaster, granted to John de Estwitton, hermit, the custody of the chapel of St. Mary, in Singleton; and in 1440 a license was granted to celebrate mass to the inhabitants of Singleton in the chapel at the same place for one year. Twelve years afterwards another license was granted by the archdeacon of Richmond for an oratory to be established in the chapel for the use of the people of the township; and in 1456 the license was renewed by archdeacon Laurence Bothe to John Skilicorne, of Kirkham. The chapel, with all its appurtenances, passed to the Crown at the Reformation; and in the report of the Commissioners of Edward VI., it is stated that "A Stipendarye is founded in the Chapelle of

1. Title Deeds.

Syngleton, in Kirkeham, by vertue of a lease made out of the Duchie to Sr Richarde Houghton, knight, the 26th day of Februarie, in the ffirst yere of the raigne of our soveraign lorde the kinge, that nowe is (1547), unto the ende of 21 yeres the next following; wherein the said Sr Richarde covenanteth to pay yerely duringe the said time to a Pryest celebrating in the said Chapelle the sum of 49s. The said Chapelle is distant from the parishe Church of Kirkeham 4 myles; Richarde Godson, the Incumbent, of the age of 38 yeres, hath the said yerely salarie of 49s." Thomas Houghton, of Lea, the son of the knight, appears to have had some difficulty in inducing sundry of the Singleton tenants to recognise his right of proprietorship after the death of his father, for we find him pleading in the duchy court in 1560-61 that he held the "lands of the late kynge in Singleton, also a house called the chapell house, with three acres of land in the tenure of Wm Yede, a chapell called Singleton chapell, in Singleton aforesaid, with the chapell yarde thereunto belonging, one house or cottage called Corner-rawe, and a windmill; and that the tenants thereof, Robert Carter and James Hall, had never paid any rent, and refused to do so."[1]

In 1562 the Charity Commissioners of Edward VI. founded a "stipendarye in the Chapelle of Syngleton in Kyrkeham."

At the archiepiscopal visitation of the diocese of Chester in 1578, the following list of charges was brought against the curate of Singleton :—"There is not servyse done in due tyme—He kepeth no hous nor releveth the poore—He is not dyligent in visitinge the sycke—He doth not teach the catechisme—There is no sermons—He churcheth fornycatours without doinge any penaunce—He maketh a donge hill of the chapel yeard, and he hath lately kepte a typlinge hous and a nowty woman in it."[2]

From that time we hear no more of the old chapel of Singleton, but the chapel-house, alluded to above, was at a later period flourishing as an inn, and bearing the same name; at the Oliverian survey, in 1650, it was stated that there was a newly erected chapel at Singleton, but that it had no endowment or maintenance belonging to it, and that the inhabitants prayed that it might be constituted a parish church with a "minister and

1. Record Office. Pleadings, 3 Eliz.   2. Church Presentments at York.

competent mayntenance allowed."[1] It is probable that after
the decline of the Commonwealth this chapel fell into the
hands of the Catholics, for Thomas Tyldesley, of Fox Hall,
a Romanist, in his diary of 1712, 13 and 14, speaks several times
of going "to Great Singleton to prayers"; and doubtless it is
the one alluded to in the following indenture, bearing the date
29th August, 1749 :—"William Shaw, esq., lord of the manor of
Shingleton in y⁰ parish of Kirkham, gave a chapel belonging
to him at Shingleton aforesaid, then used as a popish chapel, to
be used for y⁰ future as a chapel of ease to y⁰ mother church of
Kirkham, for y⁰ benefit of y⁰ inhabitants of Shingleton and of the
adjacent townships ; and that the said Wᵐ· Shaw proposed to give
£200, to be added to a similar sum from Queen Anne's bounty,
for y⁰ endowment of y⁰ said chapel, in consideration whereof
Samuel, lord bishop of Chester as ordinary, the dean and chapter
of Christ Church, Oxford, as patrons, and Chas. Buck as incumbent,
by virtue of an act of George I., grant and decree that y⁰ said
William Shaw and his heirs and assigns for ever shall have y⁰
nomination to and patronage of y⁰ said chapel, as often as it is
vacant."

This chapel was dedicated to St. Anne, and in 1756 it was
agreed " by all parties that the chapel of Singleton should be
always considered a place of public worship according to the
liturgy of the Church of England, and the chapel yard always
appropriated to the burying of the dead and the support of the
minister "; further, the chapel living was declared a perpetual
curacy, separate and independent of the mother church of
Kirkham, " save and except" that the curate must assist the vicar
of the latter place on Christmas day, Easter day, Whitsunday,
Good Friday, and each sabbath when it is customary to administer
the sacrament ; also the tythes, Easter dues, funeral sermons, and
all other parochial rights and duties belonged to the vicarage of
Kirkham."[2]

The above is an authentic record of the way in which the
chapel of Singleton passed out of the hands of the Romanists into
those of the Protestants, but the Rev. W. Thornber, to whom
this document was evidently unknown, has given in his *History*

1. MSS. Lamb library.
2. Records of the dean and chapter of Christ Church, Oxford.

of Blackpool and its neighbourhood, a different version of the matter. He states, with apparently no greater authority than tradition, that after the suppression of the rebellion of 1745, the protestants of the village celebrated the 5th of November more zealously than usual, raising contributions of peat at every house, and amongst the rest had even the presumption to call at that of the priest. The refusal of the ecclesiastic to provide his share of fuel so incensed the villagers that they ejected him both from his house and the church ; and the lord of the manor seized this opportunity to convert the chapel into a protestant place of worship.

Singleton chapel was a low building with a thatched roof, the eaves of which came within a short distance of the ground ; the priest's house was attached to the chapel and communicated with it by a door into the sacristy. In 1806 this ancient building, having become much dilapidated, was pulled down and replaced, through the liberality of Joseph Hornby, of Ribby, esq., by a neat gothic structure, having a square tower at one end, in which was placed a peal of six bells ; in 1859 the latter edifice was levelled to the ground, and the present handsome and commodious church erected on the site, chiefly through the munificence of the late Thomas Miller, esq. The few mural monuments within the church are not of any great antiquity, and are *in memoriam* of the Harrisons and Atkinsons, of Bankfield. There are no inscriptions of interest in the churchyard, beyond those on the stones surmounting the vault belonging to the Bankfield families just named. In 1869 a separate district or parish was assigned to this cure, and the present incumbent of the church acquired the title of vicar.

THE CURATES AND VICARS OF SINGLETON.

Date of Institution.	NAME.	Cause of Vacancy.
About 1545.	Richard Godson.	
,, 1562.	Thomas Fieldhouse.	
In 1651.	Cuthbert Harrison, B.A.	
,, 1749.	John Threlfall, B.A.	
About 1809.	Thomas Banks.	
Before 1843.	William Birley, M.A.	
In 1843.	Leonard C. Wood, B.A.	Resignation of W. Birley.

The Rev. Cuthbert Harrison was the son of Richard Harrison, of Newton, in Kirkham parish, and appears to have been the progenitor of the Harrisons, of Bankfield, being the first of the name on record as holder of that property. It is doubtful whether this minister was ejected from Singleton, as generally believed, or not, for in 1662, the date of the Act of Uniformity which drove so many of the clergy from their cures, he was in Ireland, holding the office of minister at Shankel, near Lurgan; so that if his ejection ever did take place from Singleton it must have been anterior to, and consequently unconnected with, the obnoxious Act. According to a letter from his son, however, he was ejected from Shankel, and it is probably that circumstance which has given rise to the supposition and assertion that he was one of those who suffered in the Fylde for conscience's sake in 1662. After leaving Ireland he opened a meeting-house at Elswick in 1672 by royal license, for the use "of such as do not conform to the Church of England and are of the persuasion commonly called Congregational." This place of worship was closed shortly afterwards by a decree of parliament, and Cuthbert Harrison, to escape persecution, was compelled to hold his services "very privately in the night" in his own house, or in one belonging to some member of his congregation. "He practysed physic," says his son, "with good success, and by it supported his family and gained the favour of the neighbouring gentry. He baptized his own children, with many others."

Vicar Clegg, of Kirkham, seems to have grown very wrathful at what he doubtless regarded as the presumption of Cuthbert Harrison, in taking upon himself the right to baptize children and solemnize matrimony, and presented him before the ecclesiastical court on a charge of "marrying one James Benson, of Warles, and baptizing a child of his." The inquiry resulted in both Harrison and Benson being excommunicated; but the former was not deterred by this ban from repairing to the church of Kirkham, much to the indignation of Mr. Clegg, who on one occasion was so much disturbed on seeing the irrepressible excommunicant in the chancel, whilst he engaged with the sermon, that he lost the thread of his discourse, and being unable to find the place amongst his notes, "was silent for some time." Smarting under the additional annoyance the vicar ordered the churchwardens to eject Mr. Harrison from the building at once, but that gentleman refused to leave unless Mr. Clegg in person performed the duty of turning him out ; incensed at his show of obstinacy, the vicar appealed to Christopher Parker, esq., of Bradkirk Hall, a justice of the peace, who was seated within six feet of Mr. Harrison, to remove him, but the magistrate refused to act in the matter, and Mr. Clegg was obliged to descend from the pulpit and undertake the unpleasant task himself. He walked up to the offender, and, taking him by the sleeve, desired him to go out from the church ; Mr. Harrison went peaceably with the vicar, but had no sooner passed out through the chancel door than he exclaimed in a loud voice " It is time to go when the devil drives."

Shortly after this episode Mr. Clegg sued Cuthbert Harrison for the sum of 120s., being a fine of 20s. per month extending over six months, for non-attendance at the parish church. The defendant pleaded that when he had attempted to attend the service at Kirkham he had been ejected from the church by the plaintiff himself, and the judge who summed up the evidence in favour of the defendant, remarked—" There is fiddle to be hanged and fiddle not to be hanged." The verdict went against Mr. Clegg, who reaped only the payment of his own and defendant's costs from this piece of persecution.

Cuthbert Harrison died in 1681, and "a great entreaty," writes his son, "was made to Mr. Clegg to suffer his body to be buried in the church ; he was prevailed with, and Mr. Harrison was interred a little within the great door, which has since been the burial place of the family." The first epitaph below is said, by his son, to have been fixed upon " Cuth. Harrison's grave by Mr. Clegg"; the second one is a retaliation, reported to have been substituted by some local rhymester, after effacing the original one :—

1	2
" Here lies Cud,	" Here lies Cud,
Who never did good,	Who still did good,
But always was in strife ;	And never was in strife,
Oh ! let the Knave	But with Dick Clegg,
Lie in his grave,	Who furiously opposed
And ne'er return to life."	His holy life."

In 1768 another chapel was erected by the Romanists at Singleton by subscription, and almost immediately the officiating priest, the Rev. Father Watts, renounced his creed, publicly recanting at Kirkham; he died in 1773, when minister at the episcopal chapel of Wrea-green. According to Mr. Thornber, the priests of Singleton could seldom assign a better reason for desiring a removal to another sphere of labour, than that they were surfeited with wild ducks from the "carrs." The chapel was rebuilt subsequently, but closed when the present one at Poulton had been completed and opened a few years.

Mains or Maynes Hall is situated in the manor of Little Singleton, and appears on ancient maps as Monk's Hall. The original Hall was built in the form of a quadrangle, the chapel being on the right and the kitchen on the left; the latter, taken down rather more than half a century ago, was roofed with tiles, about six inches square, piled thickly upon one another, and contained several secret recesses or hiding places, one of which was situated near the mantel-piece, and another, entered from the floor above by means of a ladder, showed manifest evidences of having been occupied. The present Hall is less antique in its construction and arrangements than its predecessor. In 1745 a party of Scotch rebels feasted there; and George IV., when Prince of Wales, is said to have been an occasional visitor at the mansion. The mantel-piece of the drawing-room was formerly adorned with a family painting of the Howards, dukes of Norfolk; and adjoining that spacious apartment is a small room, which appears to have been an oratory, containing relics of distinguished saints. The outside wall of the old chapel bears the date 1686, and within are a gilded altar in a state of dilapidation, a large picture of the 'Virgin and Infant,' a coat of arms, and various scraps of scriptural texts and ordinances of the church of Rome.[1]

Cardinal Allen, of Rossall Hall, the brother-in-law of William Hesketh, who was living at Mains Hall at the opening of the seventeenth century, is said to have frequently secreted himself in the hiding places there, during the time he was engaged in endeavouring to alienate the loyalty of the catholics of this district, and induce them to assist the invasion of Philip of Spain, whose forces were expected to land at Peel in Morecambe Bay.

The Heskeths were the first tenants of Mains Hall of whom we have any notice, and the above William was the first of the family

1. This description is of Mains Hall forty years ago, as seen by Mr. Thornber.

to reside there ; a full account of the descent and intermarriages of the Heskeths of Mains will be found in the chapter on ancient families of the Fylde.

The Hall and estate are now the property of Thomas Fitzherbert Brockholes, of Claughton, esq.

POPULATION OF GREAT AND LITTLE SINGLETON.

1801.	1811.	1821.	1831.	1841.	1851.	1861.	1871.
325	396	501	499	391	293	338	317

The area of the township comprises 2,860 statute acres.

LITTLE ECCLESTON-WITH-LARBRICK. The *Testa de Nevill* records that Adam de Eccleston and William de Molines, with three others, had part of a knight's fee in Eccleston and Larbrick, about 1300. In 1500 Richard Kerston had 60 acres in Little Eccleston, a portion of which passed on his death in 1546 to John ffrance, who had married one of his daughters. The ffrances retained their possessions until 1817, when they were bequeathed by the last of the line to Thomas Wilson, of Preston, who adopted their surname.[1] Larbrick was held in 1336 by William de Coucy, of Gynes, but in 1358 it belonged to Sir William Molyneux, of Sefton, in whose family it remained until about 1601, at which date William Burgh, of Burgh, near Chorley, died, holding it. Subsequently the manor passed, through the daughter of William Burgh, to Edward Shuttleworth, of Thornton Hall, who had espoused her grand-daughter. The last proprietor here named died in 1673, and the estate was divided, a moiety going to Dr. Charles Leigh, who had married one of his two daughters and co-heiresses, and the second mediety to Richard Longworth, who was the husband of the other. Dr. Leigh mortgaged his share, which eventually was obtained by Richard Harrison, of Bankfield ; whilst that of Richard Longworth, passed, about 1700, to the Hornbys, of Poulton, and afterwards to the Pedders, of Preston, who held it for more than a century. Mr. Whiteside, who purchased it from the Rev. Jno. Pedder, is now owner. Larbrick Hall, for long a seat of the noble house of Molyneux, is at presented represented by a farmhouse. Dr. Leigh mentions an extremely cold well in Larbrick, in which fish were unable to survive beyond a few seconds.

1. For "ffrance of Little Eccleston" see Chapter VI.

In 1697, William Gillow left 10s. a year, the rental of some land, to be given to two or more poor persons of the township at Christmas, and in 1720, a further annual sum of 20s. was left for the same object by George Gillow.

POPULATION OF LITTLE ECCLESTON-WITH-LARBRICK.

1801.	1811.	1821.	1831.	1841.	1851.	1861.	1871.
178	192	224	230	199	215	209	192

The area of the township is 1,198 statute acres.

CLIFTON-WITH-SALWICK. As early as 1100 William de Clifton had lands in Clifton and Salwick, and from that date to the present time, with one short interval, the manors have descended in the same family, of which Jno. Talbot Clifton, esq., of Lytham, is the head.[1] Clifton and Salwick Halls, the ancient residences of the Cliftons, are now comparatively modern buildings. The church of Lund is situated in Salwick, and possessed a chantry so far back as 1516. The first notice of any connection between Kirkham church and Lund chapel occurs amongst the records of the "Thirty-men" in 1701, thus:—"Matt. Hall, ch warden, of Kirkham, in 1688, set up a scandalous trough for a font in Lund chapel; and 4 sackfuls of moss he then carried from the church to repair the said chapel, and so it first began to be repaired at the parish charge." The old chapel was pulled down in 1824, and a stone church erected. In 1852 a chancel was added, and more recently a tower. Lund and Newton-with-Scales were constituted an ecclesiastical parish in 1840. The church is dedicated to St. John, and the dean and chapter of Christ Church, Oxford, are the patrons.

CURATES AND VICARS OF LUND.

Date of Institution.	NAME.	Cause of Vacancy.
Before 1648.	Joseph Harrison.	
,, 1732.	Thomas Cockin.	
,, 1769.	Benj. Wright.	
In 1790.	Charles Buck, B.A.	
Before 1818.	Thos. Stephenson.	
In 1820.	Richard Moore, M.A.	Death of T. Stephenson.

The Rev. Jos. Harrison, brother to Cutbert Harrison, was

1. For "Clifton of Lytham" see Chapter VI.

ejected in the year 1662, for refusing to comply with the Act of Uniformity.

Alice Hankinson, left in 1680, £5 for the use of the minister, and Alice Clitherall a like sum for the same purpose. Thomas Smith bequeathed, in 1685, the annual interest of £20 to Lund chapel. The sum of £10 is received yearly under a trust of 1668, 50s. being for the vicar, and the surplus for the poor. The school was established about 1682, by a legacy of £60 left by John Dickson, half the interest to go to the minister of Lund chapel, providing he belonged to the Church of England, and the other moiety to the master of the school. The interest of £10, origin unknown, is paid each year to the trustees of the school.

POPULATION OF CLIFTON-WITH-SALWICK.

1801.	1811.	1821.	1831.	1841.	1851.	1861.	1871.
552	575	608	508	538	471	447	447

The township contains 3,776 statute acres.

TREALES, ROSEACRE, AND WHARLES. The ancient manor of Treales embraced the three estates of Treales, Roseacre, and Wharles, being computed in the Domesday Book to contain two carucates of arable soil. In 1207 Treales was granted to Robert de Vavassour, the father-in-law of Theobald Walter, and subsequently it descended in the Butler family until 1673, when the 9th earl of Derby acquired it with his wife, the daughter of Thomas Butler, the lord Ossory. The present earl of Derby is lord of the manor, and holds a court annually.

The church, a plain stone building with nave and chancel only, was erected in 1853, and endowed five years later by the dean and chapter of Christ Church, Oxford. The Rev. J. Hodgkin is the incumbent.

William Grimbaldson, M.D., left £300 in 1725, the interest to be used for binding out poor apprentices in Treales, whose parents received no parish relief. Boulton's and Porter's charities are rentals amounting to about £12 a-year, to be given to poor persons of the township. Bridgett's charity is the interest of £15 for the poor of Wharles.

POPULATION OF TREALES, ROSEACRE, AND WHARLES.

1801.	1811.	1821.	1831.	1841.	1851.	1861.	1871.
675	671	760	756	709	696	632	625

The township has an area of 4,015 statute acres.

NEWTON-WITH-SCALES. Newton appears in the Domesday Book as containing two carucates. In 1324 William de Clifton had 60 acres in Scales; and in 1354 Adam de Bradkirk held land in Newton. John Hornby, of Newton-with-Scales, left in 1707, the residue of his estate, after certain bequests, to six trustees to found and endow the present Blue Coat School; and in 1809 the funds of the institution were increased by a legacy of £800, under the will of James Boys, of London, an old pupil. The principal soil owners are the Rev. R. Moore, and the Westby, Swainson, Bryning, Hornby, and Loxham families.

POPULATION OF NEWTON-WITH-SCALES.

1801.	1811.	1821.	1831.	1841.	1851.	1861.	1871.
269	336	380	381	324	299	286	292

The area of the township is 1,525 statute acres.

HAMBLETON. Hambleton was held during the reign of King John by Geoffrey, the Crossbowman, or de Hackensall, from whom it descended to his son-in-law Richard de Sherburne, and afterwards to Robert de Sherburne, the son of the latter. The manor was held successively by different members of the Sherburne family until 1363, when it passed to Richard de Bailey, who had married the daughter and heiress of the last male Sherburne, and adopted the maiden surname of his wife. Hence the title of the manorial lords remained unchanged up to 1717, when the property became the possession of the Duchess of Ormond, the sole child of Sir Nicholas Sherburne, who died at that date. After the decease of the Duchess of Ormond, without issue, Hambleton passed to Edward, the son of William Weld, of Lulworth Castle, by his marriage with the sister of Sir Nicholas Sherburne. The descendants of Edward Weld still retain some portion of the soil, but a considerable proportion has been sold in recent years.

Bishop Gastrell affirms that the episcopal chapel of Hambleton was consecrated in 1567. In 1650 the Parliamentary Commissioners reported :—"There is no allowance to the minister, but only £5 per an. payd by Richard Sherburne, esq., lord of the manor, and £40 per an. by order from the committee for plundered ministers. The inhabitants desire it may be made a parish, and the township of Rawcliffe, lying within a myle of it and four miles from their parish church, may be annexed to it."

The present church was erected in 1749, and is a plain white washed building, without a tower or any attempt at architectural display. Attached to the south wall within are three tablets inscribed thus :—

" Beneath this marble are deposited the remains of Mary Ramsden, daughter and heiress of the rev. Christr. Westby Alderston, late vicar of St. Michael's in this county, and wife of Rowland Ramsden of Halifax. She was born Aug. 17th, 1768 and died Nov. 6th, 1764."

" Sacred to the memory of George Bickerstaffe of Hambleton, gent., died May 3rd, 1766 ; Jenny Alderston, his granddaughter, died May 16th, 1770 ; and Agnes, wife of the rev. Christr. Westby Alderston, widow of Richd. Harrison of Bankfield, and daughter of George Bickerstaffe, died March 14th, 1820."

" Sacred to the memory of the rev. Thomas Butcher, B.A., for 39 years the respected incumbent of this chapel. Erected by the voluntary contributions of his parishioners."

On the aisles of the church are three gravestones, bearing the following incriptions :—

" In this aisle lie the remains of the rev. John Field, B.A. and minister of this place, who died 21st April, 1765 ; also his wife and children."

" Here lies the body of Dorothy, wife of Richard Carter of Hambleton, who died 14th May, 1807."

" William, son of James Norris of Liverpool, buried the 29th of June 1692— Though Boreas' Blast and Neptune's Waves have tost me to and fro, yet a spite on both by God's decree I harbour here below : Here at anchor I doe ride with many of our fleet, yet once again I must set sail my Generall Christ to meet."[1]

1. This stone was in the yard until the rebuilding of the church, when it was enclosed within the new and more extensive edifice ; it is supposed to mark the grave of a sailor washed up on the banks of the river Wyre.

In earlier days, when the church was held by the Roman Catholics, the burial ground was evidently of much greater extent than at present, and surrounded by an immense moat, between six and seven yards wide, and of a considerable depth. In a field lying to the east of the church can now be seen the ancient limits of the ground in that direction, bounded by a long stretch of the old moat in a very fair state of preservation, but of course somewhat contracted by accumulations of vegetation ; and in another plot of ground to the west, may be traced by a slight depression the course of the same trench, marking the westerly extent of the yard. The northerly length of the moat passed behind the present churchyard, and a portion of it, about two yards wide, is still to be seen there, the remainder of its breadth being filled in and included in the cemetery. The southerly stretch of this ancient ditch or fosse ran just within the railings, protecting the burial ground in front. When the existing walls were built round the yard great difficulty was met with in forming a good foundation over the site of the moat at different points, as it was found to be filled in with fragments of bricks, mortar, and general rubbish, which seems to indicate that it was abolished when the church itself was in course of reconstruction, and that the old building materials and *debris* were used for the purpose of raising it to the common level, indicating that the work must have been accomplished either at the rebuilding of 1749, or at some previous and unrecorded one. The moat would be crossed by a bridge of fair dimensions, which was probably situated on the west side, as the sexton lately discovered the well-preserved remains of a straight footpath, paved with long tiles, and running from the church for some distance towards the site of the moat in that direction ; the path was between two and three feet below the surface of the ground.

The church was separated from the mother edifice of Kirkham, and had an independent district assigned to it in 1846. The incumbent has the title of vicar.

CURATES AND VICARS OF HAMBLETON.

Date of Institution.	Name.	Cause of Vacancy.
About 1648.	Robert Cunningham.	
Before 1662.	William Bullock.	
About 1725.	William Whitehead, B.A.	
In 1735.	John Field, B.A.	Resignation of W. White-head.
,, 1765-86	Mr. Parkinson.	
,, 1796.	Thomas Butcher, B.A.	
,, 1835.	Mr. Howard.	Death of T. Butcher.
,, 1836.	William Hough.	Resignation of — Howard.

An Independent chapel was erected by subscription a few years since, and schools subsequently added.

From the report of the Charity Commissioners, we learn that long before the commencement of the nineteenth century there was a school at Hambleton, but no attempt to elucidate more particularly its origin or date of erection can be hazarded. In 1797 the only endowment it can boast of was left by Matthew Lewtas, a native of Hambleton, and consisted of £200, the interest of which had to be given to John, the son of George Hall, of Hambleton, until he reached the age of twenty-one; and if before or at that time he was appointed master of the school he had to continue to receive the whole of the income whilst he held such mastership, but if, although he was willing to accept the post, some other person should be selected for it, then when he came of age, half of the income passed from him to the school, and he retained the other moiety until his death, when it also went to increase the stipend of the master. The other condition of the will applied to the master, and obliged him in return for the interest or income of the £200, to teach as many poor children of Hambleton as the money would pay for. John Hall never obtained the appointment, so that the present master receives the full interest of the bequest, which is invested on mortgage.

The poor of Hambleton have £2 annually distributed amongst them through the generosity of Sir Nicholas Sherburne, of Stonyhurst, who in 1706, when lord of the manor of Hambleton, charged his estate of Lentworth Hall with this charity.

The yearly interest of £10 was given for the benefit of poor housekeepers in Hambleton by Mary, the daughter of vicar Clegg, of Kirkham, and the wife of Emanuel Nightingale, of York, gent., who was born in 1673.

POPULATION OF HAMBLETON.

1801.	1811.	1821.	1831.	1841.	1851.	1861.	1871.
252	273	338	334	349	346	366	351

The statute acres of the township amount to 1,603.

CHAPTER XIV.

PARISH OF LYTHAM.

LYTHAM.

T the commencement of the Norman dynasty, when William I. instituted a survey of his newly-conquered territory, the name of the town and parish which will occupy our attention throughout the present chapter was written *Lidun*, and was estimated to contain two carucates of arable land. How long this orthography continued in use is difficult to say, but it could not have been for much more than a century, as amongst certain legal documents in the reign of King John, the locality is referred to under the style of *Lethum*, an appellation which seems to have adhered to it until comparatively recent years. The derivation of the latter title is apparently from the Anglo-Saxon word *lethe*, signifying a barn, and points obviously to an agricultural origin, whilst the more antique name of *Lidun* is possibly a corruption of the Anglo-Saxon *lade*, implying a river discharging itself into the sea, that is, its mouth or estuary, and *tun*, a town.

Shortly before the termination of the reign of Richard I. in 1199, Richard Fitz Roger, who is supposed to have belonged to the Banastre family, gave all his lands in Lethum, with the church of the same vill, and all things belonging to the church, to God, and the monks of Durham, that they might establish a Benedictine cell there to the honour of St. Mary and St. Cuthbert.[1] The following is a copy of the document by which the

1. Richmondshire, vol. ii. p. 440.

transfer was effected :—"Richard Fitz Roger, to all men, both French and English, who may see this letter, greeting : Let all and each of you know, that I, with the consent and wish of my wife, Margaret, and my heirs, for the Salvation of my lord, Earl John, and for the souls of my Father and Mother, and mine and my heirs, have given and granted, and with these presents confirm as a pure and perpetual offering to God and the Blessed Mary and St. Cuthbert, and the monks of Durham, all my estate of Lethum, with the church at the same vill, with all things appertaining to it, in order to build a house of their own order ; namely, within these divisions—From the ditch on the western side of the cemetry of Kilgrimol (Lytham Common) over which I have erected a Cross, and from the same ditch and Cross eastward, going along the Curridmere (Wild Moss or Tarns) beyond the Great Moss, and the brook, as far as Balholme (Ballam), which brook runs towards Snincbrigg (Sluice Bridge). Likewise from Balholme directly across the moss, which my lord John, earl of of Moreton, divided between himself and me, as far as the northern part of Estholmker (Estham), going eastward as far as the division of the water which comes from Birckholme (Birks), and divides Etholmker and Brimaker (Bryning), following this division of water southward as far as the middle point between Etholme and Coulurugh (Kellamergh), and thus returning towards the west and going southward across the Moss as far as la Pull from the other side of Snartsalte (Saltcoats), as it falls upon the sand of the sea, and thus going southward across to Ribril to the waterside, and thus following the line of the water to the sea on the west, and so to the ditch and across aforementioned," etc., etc. In a charter dated 1200-1, it is specified that the whole of the lands of Lytham, amounting to two carucates, had been presented by King John when earl of Moreton, to Richard Fitz Roger, by whom, as just shown, they were immediately conveyed to the monks of Durham.

There are unfortunately no means of ascertaining the extent or appearance of the Benedictine cell established at Lytham, but its site would seem to have been that now occupied by Lytham Hall, in the walls of some of the offices attached to which remains of the ancient monastic edifice have been incorporated. Dr. Kuerden alludes, in a manuscript preserved in the Chetham library, to an undated claim of feudal privileges in Lytham, by which the prior of Durham asserted his right to have view of frankpledge in his manor of Lytham, with waif, stray, and infangthefe[1]; emendations of the assize of bread and beer ; wrecks of the sea ; exemption for himself and tenants in Lytham from suit to the county and wapentake, and from fines and penalties; to have soc, sac, and theam ;[2] and finally, to have free warren over all his lands in Lytham, and all royal fish taken there. During the reign of Edward I. the legality of the ecclesiastic's assumption of the sole right to wreckage was called in question, ultimately ending in litigation, and at Trinity Term, York, the verdict of the jury was given against him. In the twenty-third year of his sovereignty, Edward I. granted the wreck, waif, and stray of Lytham to his brother Edmund, the earl of Lancaster. Amongst the Rolls of the Duchy is the record of an agreement, entered into in 1271, between Ranulphus de Daker, sheriff of Lancaster, Richard le Botiler, and others, for arranging and fixing, with the consent and approval of Stephen, the prior of Lytham, the boundaries between the land of Lytham and Kilgrimol, and that of Layton. The priors of Lytham were entirely dependent on the parent house until 1443, when they solicited and induced Pope Eugenius to issue an edict declaring the prior of that date and his successors perpetual in their office and no longer removable at the will and dictation of the monks of Durham. Afterwards, in the same year, letters patent were received at the Lytham cell, pardoning the application to the papal See and granting the request ;[3] but the union between the two houses was not absolutely dissolved, for we find that, in addition to the various properties at Lytham and Durham continuing to be valued together, the cell and domain of the former place were granted in 2 Mary, 1554, to Sir Thomas Holcroft as part of the possessions of the Durham convent. In

1. Infangthefe.—The power of judging of theft committed within the manor of Lytham.

2. {
   Soccum.—The power and authority of administering justice.
   Saccum.—The power of imposing fines upon tenants and vassals within the lordship.
   Theam.—A royalty granted for trying bondmen and villeins, with a sovereign power over their villein tenants, their wives, children and goods, to dispose of them at pleasure. This badge of feudal slavery was abolished in England during the reign of Charles II.
   }

3. Rot. Lit. Pat. 22 Hen. vi. p 1, m. 6.

1606 the knight transferred his rights and lands in Lytham to Sir Cuthbert Clifton, in exchange for certain estates on the opposite side of the river Ribble. John Talbot Clifton, esq., of Lytham Hall, a descendant of the latter gentleman, is the present lord of the manor. Reverting to the Benedictine cell it is seen from an ecclesiastical valuation, taken in the reign of Henry VIII., probably about the time of the Reformation, that the annual income of the institution was derived from the following sources:—

"Cella de Lethum in com' Lancastr'
Rad'us Blaxton prior Ibd'm

	£	s.	d.
Situ celle pdce cum pt' pastur' & terr' arabilib 3 p annu	8	8	0
Redd' & firmis in divs' villis viz—villa de Lethum, £21 11s. od.; Esthowme, £3 7s. od. ; Medholm, £7 2s. 8d. ; Pilhowes cum Bankehousse, 12s. 11d. ; Frekkylton cum Ranklysse, 7s. 3d. ; Bylsborrow cum Carleton, 13s. od.; Warton, Goosenargh & Kyllermargh, £1 1s. 8d.	34	15	6

Total ....£43   3   6"

It is evident from the wording of the foundation-charter of the cell of Lytham that a church existed there at that date, and Reginald of Durham affirms that the grand-father of Richard Fitz Roger pulled down the original church of Lytham, which had been built of shingle, and erected another of stone, dedicating it to St. Cuthbert.[1] This event must have taken place anterior to the establisment of the Benedictines in the locality, and is possibly related by the Durham ecclesiastic as a brief account of the stone church standing there when the grant of lands, etc., was made to his monastery by Fitz Roger. Amongst the number of historical fragments collected by Gregson is a notice to the effect that Thomas de Thweng was rector of the church of Lytham in 22 Edward III. (1349), and founded a chantry of twelve in the parish church "to pray for the good estate of himself and Henry, Lord Perci, and for the souls of their ancestors." Thomas de Thweng was descended from Lucy, granddaughter of Helewise, the eldest sister of William de Lancaster, and in 1374, very likely the year of his death, held the manor of Garstang.[2] The edifice existing until 1770, when another church, also dedicated to St. Cuthbert, was erected on its site, was a low building, constructed of cobble stones, the walls being more than a yard in thickness and penetrated by five windows, one of which was

1. Chet. Soc. Series, No. xxx. Penwortham.   2. Escaet. 49 Edw. III. n. 28.

situated at the east end, and the others at the sides. The main entrance was protected by a porch. From the scanty description preserved of the general features of this antique specimen of ecclesiastical architecture, it has been conjectured that its origin might be traced back to the time of Henry VIII. Within the erection the seats, which were of black oak, ornamented with scrolls, were arranged in four rows, two running down the centre and one down each side, whilst the north side of a small chancel was set apart for the choristers. The pulpit was fixed against the south wall ; and the Cliftons possessed an old canopied seat, the precise station of which cannot be ascertained.

On the demolition of this church in 1770, its successor arose with a somewhat more pretentious exterior, having a low tower abutting the west extremity. The interior of the latter structure contained several objects of interest, amongst which may be noticed two tables fastened to the wall and inscribed as under :—

FIRST TABLE.

" Charities to Lytham church.
" 1765.
" The honourable Countess Dowager Gower, one hundred and fifty pounds. Governors of Queen Anne's Bounty, two hundred pounds.
" 1768.
" Ryheads in Goosnargh, purchased with the above four hundred pounds. Thomas Clifton, Esq., added seven pounds per annum, to be paid of Bamber's estate in Layton, to the old stipend of twenty pounds per annum. Governors of Queen Anne's Bounty purchased six acres and three perches of land with the above two hundred pounds, from Barker's estate ; it adjoins Ryheads.
" 1770.
" This church was rebuilded. John Gibson, minister. William Silcock and William Gaulter, churchwardens."

SECOND TABLE.

" 1801.
" Subscriptions in the parish, two hundred pounds. Governors of Queen Anne's Bounty laid out the above two hundred pounds in the purchase of a rent charge of five per cent. per annum, payable off Bamber's estate in Layton.
" 1814.
" John Clifton, Esq., one hundred and thirty-one pounds. William Hornby, Esq., sixty-five pounds eight shillings. Joseph, Thomas, and John Hornby, Esqs., ten pounds each, making thirty pounds. Rev. Robert Lister, fifty pounds. L. Webbe, Esq., ten pounds. Joseph Benbow, five pounds. Captain Thomas Cookson, ten pounds. Richard Cookson, ten pounds. Cornelius Crookall, ten pounds. John Cardwell, ten pounds.

"Smaller subscriptions in the parish, sixty-eight pounds twelve shillings. Governors of Queen Anne's Bounty, six hundred pounds.

Total amount, one thousand pounds.

" Purchased five acres, one rood, and two perches of land, of eight yards to the perch, in Layton-cum-Warbreck, with the above one thousand pounds.

" Rev. Robert Lister, B.A., minister.   Thomas Cookson and John Cookson, churchwardens."

On each side of the altar, at the east end of the church, were several mural marble monuments erected in memory of certain members of the Clifton family, whose remains had been interred within the walls of the sacred edifice. Thomas Clifton was the first of this family buried at Lytham, and on his tomb was inscribed: —" Here lie interred the mortal remains of Thomas Clifton, of Lytham, esquire; who died on the 16th of Dec., 1784, in the 38th year of his age. Requiescat in pace."

Another monument, near to the former one, bore the following inscription :—" D.O.M.   Here lies dead the body of Ann Clifton, wife of Thomas Clifton, of Lytham, esq. ; daughter of Sir Carnaby Haggerstone, Baronet : but her name will live to future ages. Wonder not, reader ; in her was seen whatever is amiable in a daughter, wife, mother, friend, and Christian. Admire her, man; a pattern to her sex. O ! woman, imitate. She died in the 37th year of her age, on the 22nd day of February, 1760. Requiescat in pace."

The memorial writing over a third tomb ran thus :—" Here lies the body of Thomas Clifton, of Lytham, esq.; who departed this life in the 56th year of his age, on the 11th day of May, 1783. R.I.P.;" whilst a fourth monument had these lines upon it :— " Here lies the body of Jane Clifton, wife of Thomas Clifton, of Lytham, Esq.; daughter of the Right Hon. the Earl of Abingdon, who departed this life in the 61st year of her age, on the 14th day of Feb., 1791. R.I.P."

A white marble tablet fixed against the south wall, contained the annexed notice :—" In memory of Elizabeth Clifton, wife of John Clifton, of Lytham, Esq.; and daughter of Thomas Horsley Widdrington Riddell, of Swinburne Castle, in the county of Northumberland, esq.; who departed this life in the 63rd year of her age, on the 19th day of November, 1825. Requiescat in pace."

Sixty-four years from the date of its erection this church was also pulled down, having become unable to accommodate the increasing influxes of visitors during the summer ; and on the 20th of March, '1834, the foundation stone of the existing pile was laid by the late Thomas Clifton, esq., of Lytham Hall, who contributed £500 towards the cost of the building. Mrs. Fisher, the widow of a local physician, contributed £300, and the subscriptions for the necessary work were further augmented by a grant from the Church Building and Extension Society. The church, which comprises nave, side aisles, chancel, and embattled tower, contains the monuments of the Cliftons already enumerated, and three additional marbles, one of which, at the entrance to the chancel, records that " in the family vault near this place lies the body of Hetty, daughter of Pelegrine Treves, esq., and widow of the late Thomas Clifton, esq., of Clifton and Lytham ; she died on the 4th of June, 1864, aged 68 years. The other attached to the opposite side of the entrance is *in memoriam* of " Thomas Clifton (eldest son of John Clifton, esq., by Elizabeth, his wife) of Clifton and Lytham, who died 17th February, 1851, aged 63 years " ; whilst the third, in the chancel itself, is to the memory of " John Clifton, of Lytham, esq., who departed this life on the 25th of March, 1832, aged 68 years. Requiescat in Pace." Against the wall of the south side aisle is a tablet surmounted by a cross and inscribed thus :—" In memory of Richard Barton Robinson, born July 28 : A : D : 1804, died August 9 : A : D : 1872, vicar of Lytham for 36 years. This cross is gratefully erected by his parishioners, A.D. 1875." A similar tablet in the north aisle is erected to the " memory of Edward and Sarah Jane Houghton, by their only surviving son. E. H. born April 23 : 1807 : died December 15 : 1869. S. J. H. born September 26 : 1803 : died April 21 : 1872." The east window, beautifully emblazoned, "is dedicated by her friends and neighbours, to the memory of Ellen Fisher," born 1759, died 1837. Similar windows, north and south, in the chancel, were given by Thomas Clifton, esq., in 1845, also a second, on the south side, by Lady Eleanor Cecily Clifton, in 1871. The north side aisle contains six handsome windows inserted respectively to the memories of Anne Shepherd Birley, died 1872 ; James Fair, died 1871, by J. T. Clifton, esq. ; Sarah Agnes, wife of W. C. Dowding, clerk, M.A., died 1869, by her maternal aunt, Agnes Newsham ; her mother and sisters, by Anne Wilson, 1871; Margaret Hornby, died 1866 ; William and Agnes Birdsworth and of their father and mother, by their surviving relatives.　In the south side aisle are two memorial windows, one being to Henry Miller, died 1859, aged 46 years, and his infant son, died 1852, by his wife Caroline A. Miller ; and the other to John Stevenson, died 1872, aged 78 years ; Jane Stevenson, died 1872, aged 64 years ; William Elsworth Stevenson, died 1869, aged 31 years ; and Jane Stevenson, died 1872, aged 25 years.　The clerestory of the church is lighted by twelve single windows, each bearing the representation of a saint, all of which were presented by private individuals.

PERPETUAL CURATES AND VICARS OF ST. CUTHBERT'S.

Date of Institution.	NAME.	On whose Presentation.	Cause of Vacancy.
1379	William de Aslaby, monk.	Prior and Chapter of Durham	
1413	William Patrick, monk	Ditto	
1678	James Threlfall		
1701	Josiah Birchall		
1717	Timothy Pollard	Chancellors, Masters, and Scholars of Cambridge	Death of Josiah Birchall
1741	Ashton Werden	Alexander Osbaldeston, of Preston, esq.	
1743	Robert Willasey Thomas Place	Ditto	
1760	John Gibson	Abigail Clayton, of Larkhill, Blackburn, relict and executor of Thomas Clayton, who was surviving executor of Alexander Osbaldeston, of Preston, esq.	
1800	Robert Lister, B.A.	John Clayton, of Little Harwood, esq.	Resignation of John Gibson
1834	Richard Barton Robinson, M.A.	Thomas Clifton, esq.	Resignation of Robt. Lister
1870	Henry Beauchamp Hawkins, M.A.	John T. Clifton, esq.	Resignation of R. B. Robinson.

In 1872 the chancel was enlarged and a new vestry erected, whilst the solitary gallery at the west end, formerly used for the choir, was converted into commodious sitting accommodation for the congregation. During the same year half an acre was added to the north of the burial ground, and a fresh boundary wall, facing Church Road completed, the iron work being given by the late John Stevenson, J.P., of West Beach, and the stone work by the late John Knowles, proprietor of the Clifton Arms Hotel. The tower contains a peal of eight bells. John Talbot Clifton, esq., of Lytham Hall, is the patron of the living. The parish register begins in 1679.

The churchyard, which is encircled by a thick plantation of trees, possesses many very handsome monuments, but none of historical importance. The oldest gravestone still legible lies in close proximity to the ancient sun-dial, and bears the date 1672. The parish schools, erected in 1853, stand in Church Road.

Dodsworth informs us that in the neighbourhood of Lytham there existed, in 1601, a village called Waddum Thorp, and that eleven years previously the Horsebank was a green pasture for cattle. Dr. Leigh affirms that the hamlet in question was peopled by some Saxon fishermen. The locality alluded to in the foundation document as Snartsalte is now denominated Saltcoats, and was, like several neighbouring places, the site of a salt manufactory in remote days. Geoffrey Gillet worked the Saltcoats manufactory. Cambden in describing the extractive process says :—"They pour water from time to time upon heaps of sand till it grows brackish, and then with a turf fire they boil it into a white salt." Bowden wrote, in 1722, concerning the same subject :—On many places on the coast the inhabitants gather heaps of sand together which, having lain some time, they put into troughs full of holes at the bottom, pour water upor them, and boil the lees into white salt."

About 1800 the hamlet comprised several mud and thatch cottages, interspersed here and there with a fair number of habitations of recent origin, built with bricks and slated. There were also two inns in existence, the Wheat Sheaf and the Clifton Arms, besides two small licensed houses. The Wheat Sheaf was erected in Clifton Street during the year 1794, and almost simultaneously, but a little later, the Clifton Arms arose on the opposite side of the thoroughfare, facing the sea. There were several shops in the village, and in Douglas Street a house of confinement, containing separate cells, for the detention and punishment of any offenders against the law. The most pretentious dwellings stood upon the northern portion of the tract known as the Marsh, and all of them were newly constructed. One near the western extremity was a substantial house with gardens and plantation, inhabited by the clergyman of the parish, the Rev. Robt. Lister. In close proximity was a marine villa with a Chinese porch, belonging to William Hornby, esq., of Kirkham ; and a row of white cottages, called Lizmahago, after a race horse of John Clifton, esq., who had erected them for the accommodation of visitors. A pretty white villa was placed more to the rear, and several well-constructed lodging-houses studded the ground between those just mentioned and the old village, where clay and straw had been the time-honoured building materials. The beach afforded no more than three bathing machines, but sundry improvements, both in multiplying the vans and in the establishment of a warm sea-water bath, were in contemplation. No elegant promenade with its expansive sward, as at present, defined the landward margin of the beach, but the whole space, at one end of which Mr. Cookson had erected a windmill, was covered with miniature sand-hills and star-grass, unfolding a most uninviting and deterring aspect to the pedestrian. The church of St. Cuthbert's was built of rubble, rough cast and whitened, and certainly possessed, both externally and internally, no very extensive claims to architectural beauty. The instrumental part of the service was accomplished by means of a clarionet and a bass fiddle. The religious edifice stood in the midst of fields, and was approached by a footpath, sufficiently wide to admit the passage of bathing vans, which were occasionally had recourse to by visitors on wet Sundays, in order to attend the service with dry garments, being then, and for some time afterwards, the only covered vehicles in the place. Lytham Hall, embosomed in lofty trees and plantations, formed an imposing object, being situated half a mile inland, between the village and the church. This noble mansion, comprising three fronts, of which the east is the principal, was commenced in 1757 and completed in 1764, by Thomas Clifton, esq., and superseded the original Hall, erected about 1606, by Sir Cuthbert Clifton. At the date now under examination, its possessor, John Clifton, esq., had laid out a race-course for training purposes, of three miles and a quarter in circumference, in the fields to the north-west of the church; and close at hand were excellent paddocks and stables, filled with a considerable stud of fine blood horses. The residence of the trainer was an elegant villa near the stables, surrounded with a shrubery. Two steamers plied daily in the season between Preston and Lytham, but the larger share of the company arrived by the road, the journey having a few years previously been rendered more direct by the opening of a route across the marshes, past Freckleton, instead of the former circuitous one through Kirkham. In 1801 the population amounted to 920 persons.

During the ensuing twenty years Lytham made steady, if not rapid, progress. Buildings of modern and pretty designs sprang up along the beach, whilst others of substantial workmanship were visible in the lines of various thoroughfares, especially in Clifton Street. The two hotels already specified, underwent enlargements, owing to the growing pressure on their accommodation, and a fresh inn, the Commercial, was erected on the land behind the present Market Hotel, the front and main entrance of the house having an easterly aspect, overshadowed by several lofty trees. A little beyond the north gable end of the inn, in an westerly direction, were the old gates of the park attached to Lytham Hall, near to which, on the road side, was stationed the pinfold, constructed of cobble stones, in a quadrangular form, with an embattled tower rising about eight feet above the height of the walls. A small Baptist chapel, having a school-room connected with it, also existed, standing on part of the ground now occupied by the premises of Mr. Edmondson, draper, the remaining portion being covered by the residence and shop of that gentleman's father, who owned the chapel, and acted as its minister. The chapel would hold about thirty worshippers, and contained three or four rows of forms and a pulpit; whilst the school-room, of equal dimensions, was let to a person for a private day seminary.

During the summer months, hundreds of day visitors, in addition to the more permanent ones who constituted the company, found their way in carts, waggons, or lighter vehicles, to the coast at Lytham, from Preston, Blackburn, Burnley, and other inland towns, for the pleasure of enjoying once, at least, a year, an invigorating bath in the sea. The fortnightly spring tides were the signals which foretold the advent of these huge pic-nic parties, for such it seems appropriate to style them, who flocked down to the shore, generally bringing their own provisions with them, and after disporting themselves amidst the waves, and procuring amusement in various ways during the day, returned quietly or hilariously home to their several destinations, in the evening or following morning, in the manner they had arrived. Some from the more remote places prolonged their sojourn for three days. Races for the better class of farmers' horses were held annually on Wit-Monday, over the sward which runs from the windmill to the site of an old lime kiln about one mile distant, in the direction of Saltcoats, the course being round that spot to the starting point. These races, which are described as having been very fair contests, were kept up for many years. The prizes competed for were saddles, bridles, whips, etc. The bowling greens of Lytham amounted to two, which were attached to the Clifton Arms and Commercial Hotels, and were well patronised.

The following description of the attractions of Lytham, published in 1821, furnishes a pretty correct idea of the recreations afforded by the watering-place about that date :—" Lytham is a very salubrious place ; its walks are pleasant and diversified. You may walk for miles on the sand westward. You may trip to the Hey-houses and get bad ale. Common-side offers a journey, which, if you please, ends at Blackpool. The walks are many and various for those who love exercise ; the lazy will soon tire here, but the active will never be at a loss. The sands are fine—the sea breeze pleasant—the air is impregnated with health. Sailing may be had at tide time ; boats are occasionally going to Preston and over the water to Southport. There are baths, shower, cold, and warm for invalides. Old Hugh Holmes, the shaver, doctor, and shopkeeper, is an old man, thin and meagre, conceited to a tittle, and remarkably fond of chit-chat. The people here bathe not at all, whilst those from a distance think it a blessing. Holmes, the barber, said he had never bathed in his life, nor could I persuade him to do so. He said that he was sound in body, and if so, why dip in the briny sea at all."

In 1821 the population of Lytham amounted to 1,292 persons, consisting of 258 families ; and in 1825 the parish contained 258 houses, the occupants of 75 of which were employed chiefly in agriculture, and of 55 in trade, fishing, or handicraft, those of the remaining 128 being unclassified. Three years later the Wheat Sheaf Inn and a wide range of thatched buildings adjoining were demolished, and after leaving the spacious opening, called Dicconson Terrace, leading down to the beach, several improved dwellings and a billiard-room were placed on the remainder of the ground. The greater part of the marine frontage had been levelled, and efforts commenced to lay out a species of walk or promenade. The houses standing along the shore line were usually hired furnished by families for varying periods, at prices from one and a half to three guineas per week, their value being estimated by the number of bed-rooms, each of which represented ten shillings and sixpence a week. Other villas in the watering-place were similarly let, but lodgings could be procured amongst the humble cottages on a weekly payment of four shillings and sixpence by each individual. The prices at the hotels for board and lodging, exclusive of wine and liquors, were—at the Clifton Arms, seven shillings a day in private, and six shillings in public; the Commercial, five shillings and sixpence; and the Ship, a new inn erected since 1820, three shillings and sixpence. Of trades and professions in the village there were three milliners, six drapers, three boot and shoe makers, five joiners and cabinet makers, one druggist, two blacksmiths, one ship carpenter, one custom-house officer, one tide-waiter, one corn miller, three butchers, five grocers, two coal dealers, one confectioner, one surgeon, one attorney, and one clergyman. In addition it should be mentioned that a solitary ladies' seminary had been established within the previous twelve months. "I recollect," says Mr. Whittle, in his *Marina*, "visiting Lytham during July, 1824, when Mr. Lardner's troop of comedians were performing in what was termed the 'New Theatre, Lytham,' Cibber's admired comedy of a 'Journey to London, or a Bold Push for a Fortune,' and the laughable farce of the 'Irish Tutor, or New Lights.' The chief of the stage business was done by the Lardners, consisting of father, mother, son, and daughter. Likenesses were also taken in miniature by Mr. Lardner, senior, at from two to five guineas each! and the polite art of dancing taught by Lardner, junior. We saw in succession performed Morton's comedy of 'Speed the Plough, or the Farmer's Glory;' 'Lovers' Vows, or the Child of Love'; and Coleman's admired and excellent comedy of the 'Poor Gentleman'; all of which were tolerably got up, but the scenery was not of that kind which befitted a place of dramatic exhibition." During the season three coaches ran regularly from Preston to Lytham and returned, their times of departure being—from Preston, at 12 noon, 5 in the evening, and 7 in the evening; and from Lytham, at 6 in the morning, 9 in the morning, and half-past 4 in the afternoon. In addition to these coaches, occasional public conveyances and many private vehicles brought their loads of pleasure-seekers to the village, especially during Easter and Whit-tides. Letters arrived at half-past 9 in the morning and were despatched at 4 in the afternoon. In 1828 the buildings situated in the vicinity of the beach were, commencing at the eastern extremity of the line and travelling westward, a house, occupied by Miss Dennett, Rimmer's and Butcher's cottages, the Baths with a house adjoining, two newly erected dwellings, Cookson's cottages, Rawstorne's Marine Cottage, Craven's and Hampson's cottages, Clifton Place, Buck's cottages, Silcock's and Miller's cottages, Townend's and Captain Cookson's residences, Mr. Barton's house, Captain Fell's and Mrs. Birdworth's residences, Mr. Fisher's house, Lizmahago houses, Hornby's Chinese villa, the Parsonage, in the occupation of the Rev. Robert Lister; the Parish Church, situated more inland, and Church-house, a rural place. Mr. Corry, in his History of Lancashire, published about that time, states :—" That the increase of Lytham has not been so rapid as in many villages, where the people are engaged in manufacture; but a considerable part of the visitors and settlers within the last twenty years have been opulent individuals, who were induced by the beauty of the spot and the benefit derived from bathing in the sea water, to resort to this pleasing village." The houses were unnumbered and recognised by the titles bestowed upon them, or the names of their owners. Lamps for the autumn and winter evenings were unknown in the streets, whilst libraries, news-rooms, and livery stables were things of the future. The Clifton Arns Hotel had recently been overlaid with a thick coating of cement resembling stone, and the Commercial Inn had undergone sundry enlargements. An ornamental enclosure or garden had been formed on the land of the present Market-house, surrounded by a palisading and planted with flowers and shrubs. A carriage road also had been lately made from the village to the church of St. Cuthbert.

In 1831 the census of Lytham showed a total of 1,523 residents, being an increase of 231 over the population ten years before; and three years subsequently the ancient church of the parish was levelled to the ground and the erection of the present edifice commenced. The early growth of the summer resort was much retarded by the exceedingly short terms upon which building leases were granted. Previous to 1820 all land reverted to the lord of the manor forty years after its provisional purchase had been effected, so that there was little inducement for either the speculative or private individual to upraise habitations where the tenure was so unsatisfactory. About that date the duration of leases was extended to sixty years, and even this slight advance in a more liberal direction was not without influence in promoting the development of the place, but no great rapidity characterised the multiplication of houses until a later epoch, when periods of 99 and 999 years were offered to purchasers. In 1839 the Roman Catholics erected a chapel, dedicated to St. Peter, at the east corner of Clifton Street. Previously the members of this sect had worshipped in a small chapel belonging to Lytham Hall, which had superseded the domestic oratory of the Cliftons, in the days when they professed the Romish creed. The edifice in Clifton Street is of brick and has a priests' residence and schools attached, the whole being prettily encircled by willow trees and a low wall.

The returning seasons brought increasing streams of visitors to the shores of Lytham, and practically proved that the delightful and invigorating influences of the climate and sea were well and widely appreciated by the populace of the large inland towns. The marine esplanade and the firm sands left by the receding tide were ever alive with crowds of people, who either for health or pleasure, or a combination of the two, had arrived in the watering-place. The bathing vans were still unequal to the demands on their accommodation, and many were compelled to dispense with their decorous shelter, and unrobe themselves on the more secluded parts of the beach. To have returned home again without immersing their body in the buoyant sea would to most of them have been to omit the chief object of their journey, many, indeed, having such an exalted idea of the remedial and hygienic properties of the water that they imbibed huge draughts, and even filled bottles with it, for future use, or for friends who had been unable to come themselves. There were few amusements for the visitors beyond those enumerated earlier, but had there been none other, the exhilatering breeze and bath, coupled with the novel surroundings, would have possessed sufficient charm to insure a thronged season year after year.

In 1841 the population numbered 2,047 persons, being a rise of no less than 524 in the inhabitants during the preceding ten years, more than double the excess observed in the census of 1831 over its antecessor. During the previous twelve months the Clifton Arms Hotel, in Clifton Street, had been abolished and a stately building, bearing the same name, erected on the front, where it now stands, very considerable enlarged and beautified under the proprietorship of the late Mr. John Knowles, who purchased it on lease from the lord of the manor, and by whose representatives the Hotel and appurtenances were sold to a company of gentlemen in 1875.

The 16th of February, 1846, initiated a new era in the history and progress of Lytham, for on that day the branch line connecting this popular resort with the Preston and Wyre Railway was formally opened. At an early hour the town evinced manifest signs that the inhabitants were bent on doing full honour to the introduction of their invaluable ally ; flags and banners floated from the church and the residences of many of the inhabitants, and later in the day the streets were thronged with processions and spectators of all grades. The directors and a large party of the neighbouring gentry assembled by invitation at Lytham Hall, and after partaking of luncheon proceeded to the newly erected station, where the "opening train," consisting of an engine, gaily decorated, and fourteen carriages, awaited their arrival. Amongst the gentlemen who accompanied Thomas Clifton, esq., and Mrs. Clifton, on the formal trip to Kirkham and back, were John Laidlay, W. Taylor, J. Dewhurst, T. W. Nelson, Frederick Kemp, C. Swainson, James Fair, E. Houghton, W. H. Hornby, T. R. W. ffrance, P. Rycroft, W. Royds, and William Birley, esquires, the Revs. R. Moore and W. Birley, and Colonel

Rawstorne. The train departed amid a volley of cheers and discharge of cannon, and proceeded to Kirkham; the return journey was performed in fifteen minutes. The carriage station was 140 feet long by 53 feet wide, and covered by a somewhat unique roof of twelve wooden arches, put together in segments and secured by nuts and screws, all the timber ends butting upon each other like the stones of an arch, but as solid, from their peculiar construction, as if the whole had been cut out of a single block of timber. The Lytham line diverged from the main railway at a point about a mile to the north-west of Kirkham, and was nearly five miles in length. It passed within a short distance of the village of Wrea, where a station was built, and terminated in the immediate vicinity of the Roman Catholic chapel in this town.

The impetus given to the building trade of Lytham by the opening of the railway and the almost simultaneous extension of ground leases was soon visible in the erection of numerous houses. A Wesleyan chapel, capable of holding 200 hearers, was built, before the close of the year, in Bath Street; but this structure having, as time progressed, become inadequate to the wants of the congregation, the foundation stone of a new one was laid on the 12th of September, 1867, by T. C. Hincksman, esq., of Lytham, at the corner of Park and Westby Streets, service being first conducted there on the 23rd of September in the ensuing year, by the Rev. John Bedford, of Manchester. The chapel is faced with Longridge stone and white brick. In front are stone columns and pilasters nearly thirty feet high, surmounted by Corinthian caps, massive cornice, parapet, pediment, etc. It contains seats for about 500 persons. The old Wesleyan chapel is now used as a literary and social Institute, established in 1872. In 1847 the growth and prosperity of Lytham rendered it necessary that some form of local government should be adopted, and the inhabitants applied for and obtained an Improvement Act, by which the regulation of all public matters was placed in the hands of a board of commissioners elected from amongst the ratepayers. On the 13th of May in that year, the corner stone of a substantial lighthouse was laid on the "Double Stanner" bank, by Peter Haydock, esq., chairman of the Ribble Navigation Company, at whose expense the work was accomplished; but on the 20th of January, 1863, a heavy storm swept over the coast, and amongst other damages effected by its fury was the overthrow of this pile, which was subsequently re-erected on the Star Hills, far removed from the destructive influence of the waves, and perhaps more efficacious, from its greater elevation, as a beacon.   During the year 1848 a Market Hall was built on an open space, formerly the ornamental garden referred to in a late page.   In the month of June the edifice was completed and ready for use, being constructed of brick and supplied with stalls for various articles, such as fish, vegetables, toys, etc.   The tower was elevated in 1872 to receive a large clock, the gift of Lady Eleanor Cecily Clifton, and during the following twelve months additional dials and illuminative power were added.   The Hall is prettily situated in an enclosure of elm trees.

Another church, dedicated to St. John, was erected on the east beach in 1848-9, and consecrated on the 11th September, 1850. The site was granted by John Talbot Clifton, esq., who retains the patronage of the living, and the expense of construction defrayed by subscription.   The edifice is of stone, and includes a nave, side aisles, transepts, chancel, porch, and tower, surmounted by a lofty spire.   The side aisles are separated from the nave by pointed arches on circular columns.   The chancel has since been enlarged.   Within the church are several memorial windows, one of which, in the west end, is in memory of "James and Elizabeth Fair, who died August 16, 1871, and July 27, 1867," inserted by their children.   By the side of this is a smaller stained window to Mr. Bannerman by his widow.   The east window of the chancel is magnificently illuminated, and another, lighting the scholars' chapel on the south of that part, was placed by the Rev. W. H. Self "to his wife, Mary, ob. 1859."   The windows in the north and south transepts are, respectively, to "Thomas Miller, ob. 1865," and "Thomas Clifton, ob. 1851."   There are no mural tablets.   The organ was presented by William Bradshaw Swainson, esq., of Cooper Hill, near Preston, "as a tribute of affection, in memory of his mother, Catherine Swainson, who died at Lytham on the 1st of February, 1848."   The instrument was enlarged by the aid of public contributions in 1874.   The lectern was presented by Margaret Ellen Clifford, the second wife of the Rev. W. H. Self, *in memoriam* of her mother, Mrs. Hannah Biddell, in 1867.   The tower contains a peal of six bells.   An ecclesiastical parish was apportioned to the church of St. John in 1870. The Rev. William Henry Self, M.A., was the earliest incumbent and subsequently became the first vicar. The Rev. Gregory Smart, M.A., is the present vicar. The graveyard is a spacious area defined by a neat stone wall, and contains numerous elegant monuments. The vicarage house stands a very little distance to the east side of the church, and is a handsome villa residence. To the rear of the burial ground, and separated therefrom by a narrow street, are the parish schools erected in 1851 by subscription, and grants from the Council of Education and the National Society.

The want of proper illumination along the thoroughfares of Lytham during the long evenings of the autumn months, was a source of considerable inconvenience to the visitors, and induced many to vacate the place earlier than otherwise they would have done, so that the commissioners determined to erect gas works by loans on the security of the rates, and remedy the evil as soon as possible. On the 28th of October, 1850, the streets were lighted for the first time with gas. In 1851 the residents of Lytham amounted to 2,695, showing an increase of 648 persons since 1841. It was about this time that a lifeboat was stationed at Lytham, purchased by subscription, and named the "Eleanor Cecily," out of compliment to the lady of the manor. The boat-house stands on the promenade to the east, in close proximity to the old windmill, and is now occupied by a new and larger craft, presented by Thomas Clayton, esq., of Wakefield, in 1863.

Throughout the succeeding ten years the area of the town continued to expand with fair rapidity. Many graceful villas were added to those already existing on the front, whilst fresh shops and lodging houses arose along the different thoroughfares, plainly evincing a determination on the part of the inhabitants to keep pace with the spreading popularity of the place by creating ample accommodation for the crowds of visitors. A corps of Volunteer Riflemen was enrolled under Captain Lennox in 1860, during the month of January. The census of 1861 furnished a total of 3,189 residents.

The advisability of connecting the two watering-places of Blackpool and Lytham by a coast railway was now freely

discussed, and the scheme having been favourably entertained by
a number of affluent gentlemen, the requisite powers were sought
from Parliament for its formation. In May, 1861, the desired act
received the royal assent, and on the ensuing 4th of September
the first sod of the new line was cut by T. H. Clifton, esq., M.P.,
the son and heir of the lord of the manor, in Lytham Park. The
directors of the company were E. C. Milne, esq., (chairman), of
Warton Lodge ; John Talbot Clifton, T. Langton Birley, Charles
Birley, James Fair, Robert Rawcliffe, and Thomas Fair, esqrs.
The distance, about 7½ miles, was spanned by a single line,
stations being placed at the two termini and at South Shore, in
addition to which there was a gate-house at Andsell's road, near
the town, where it was proposed to have a booking office. The
railway was virtually finished in the autumn of 1862, but the
formal opening was postponed until the 4th of April, 1863. At
that date, which occurred on Saturday, flags and banners floated
from many of the windows, whilst the bells of St. Cuthbert's
church rang out merry peals at intervals throughout the day.
No further ceremony, however, was observed on the occasion,
than the running of a train to Blackpool and back with a select
party of invited guests. Regular public traffic commenced on
Monday. During 1871 this line was amalgamated with the
Preston and Wyre, of which the Lancashire and Yorkshire, and
the London and North Western Railway Companies are the
lessees. The track was doubled in 1874, by laying down another
length of metals, and connected with the Kirkham and Lytham
branch. In the same year on the 1st of July, a spacious and
handsome station which had been erected according to the design
of C. Axon, esq., of Poulton, was brought into service, and the use
of the original one belonging to the branch just specified discontinued for passenger traffic, the whole of which, both from Kirkham
and Blackpool, is now directed to the recently built central edifice.
It is expected that in course of time the coast line thus established
from Preston through Kirkham, Lytham, St. Anne's, South Shore,
to Blackpool will supersede the old route through Poulton to the
last named resort for the conveyance of passengers. Important
alterations, it should be noted, were effected in the course of the
branch from Kirkham to Lytham immediately preceding its
junction with the Blackpool and Lytham line, by which the

corner lying north of and between Kirkham and Wrea was cut off. The rails were also doubled.

Reverting to the town itself, we find that the day which gave the small coast communication between Blackpool and Lytham to the public use, also witnessed another event—the opening of the Baths and Assembly Rooms, situated on the beach, about midway between the Clifton Arms and the Neptune Hotels. The building is of brick, with stone dressings, and presents an elegant and rather imposing appearance. It comprises private and swimming baths for both sexes ; dressing-rooms, retiring-rooms, news and general reading-room, and a capacious saloon, able to contain 350 persons, used for concerts, balls, and other entertainments. Early in the same year a Congregational Church was completed in Bannister Street, the corner stone of which had been laid on the 17th of October, 1861, by Sir James Watts, of Manchester. The edifice is formed of Longridge stone, in the ornamental Gothic style of architecture, with a spire, and will hold about 500 worshippers. Within the enclosure wall surrounding the church are the Sunday schools connected with it. The first pile of the marine pier, extending into the estuary of the Ribble from the promenade, was screwed into the ground on the 8th of June, 1864. The structure was designed by E. Birch, esq., C.E., and is supported on hollow cylindrical columns, arranged in clusters. The length of the deck is 914 feet, the whole of which is encircled by a continuous line of side seats, whilst a lounging or waiting-room is stationed on the head. The entrance is protected by gates and toll-houses. Easter Monday, the 17th of April, 1865, was the day set apart for the ceremonious opening of the new erection. The town was gaily decorated with the bunting, and no efforts were spared to do full justice to the importance of so auspicious an event. Immense confluences of people arrived in excursion trains, running at greatly reduced fares, from the business centres of Lancashire and Yorkshire, and the streets and esplanade were literally inundated with spectators from all grades of society. To Lady Eleanor Cecily Clifton was delegated the honourable duty of declaring the pier accessible to promenaders, and at the selected time, that lady, accompanied by her son, T. H. Clifton, esq., proceeded to the spot, where the necessary form was gone through ; a large procession, headed by a marshall, and consisting of the mayor and corporation of Preston, the directors of the Ribble Navigation Company, naval and military officers, clergy, the several directors of the Lancashire and Yorkshire Railway, the Lytham and Blackpool Railway, the Blackpool and the Southport Pier Companies, and numerous gentry. Unabated prosperity continued to shine on the watering-place, whose limits were annually extended by additional buildings, and in all parts there was to be observed that aspect of recent improvements and embellishments which is ever indicative of a propitious fortune.

The population in 1871 had reached the high figure of 7,902, having more than doubled during the previous ten years, and if further evidence were required of the development of Lytham, none more irrefutable and convincing could be given than this wonderful multiplication of the inhabitants. On the 3rd of August, 1871, a neat Gothic cottage hospital, erected at the east end of the resort, in Preston Road, at the sole expense of the lord of the manor, was pronounced open for the reception of patients, and transferred to a committee of management. The building stands in three acres of land tastefully laid out, and comprises a central portion of two stories, with a wing on either side, containing two large wards (each with four beds), two sitting-rooms, surgery, bath-rooms, and laundry, on the ground floor; upstairs are four beds for invalids and a sleeping apartment for the matron. The hospital is intended for the poor labouring under disease or accidents. Luke Fisher, esq., M.D., is the physician in charge. From 1871 up to the present date (1876), there is nothing calling for separate comment beyond those matters in connection with the railway and station already noticed, with the exception of the beautiful park-garden, occupying the land formerly kown as Hungry Moor, and instituted through the liberality of J. T. Clifton, esq., who bestowed the name of the Lowther Gardens on the enclosure so gracefully designed and planted, and gave free access to the public on its completion, about three years ago. The progress of the town within the short interval at present under consideration, has been marked by even greater rapidity than that which shed such a halo of prosperity around the period more immediately preceding; and there is no apparent prospect that the powerful impetus which has thus far exerted its beneficial influence on the place is likely to experience any diminution. Indeed it may with reason be anticipated that when passenger traffic is more thoroughly established along the coast line from Preston to Blackpool, the demand for residential accommodation will be still greater than that which supplies abundant occupation to the builders to-day.

The original endowment of Lytham Free School was derived from the following sources :—In 1702, the Rev. James Threlfall, of St. Cuthbert's church, gave £5 ; and somewhere about the same time, William Elston, who died in 1704, presented £3 3s. 0d., for the use of the parish. Subsequently these sums of money were supplemented by a grant of £10 from John Shepherd, of Mythorp, and the whole invested, the interest being applied to local charitable purposes. The benefaction of John Shepherd was bestowed in trust upon Thomas Shepherd and his heirs, to the intent that the interest should be applied to the "use of such poor children's schooling, as they, with two or three of the most substantial men of the parish, whom they chose to consult, should think fit ;"[1] but it is doubtful how it was deposed of until 1720, when the three separate sums mentioned were incorporated, for a motive stated directly, with a collection made in aid of those who had suffered damage from a serious inundation in that year. The inhabitants were unable to agree upon an equable distribution of the collection specified, and decided, by way of settling the affair, to "make a free school,"[2] with it and the other sums. The total capital thus acquired amounted to more than £100. In 1728 £60 was derived from the residue of John Harrison's estate, by the direction of his will. William Gaulter gave to Lytham school in 1745 several securities for money, amounting in all to £99, and three years later bequeathed the residue of his personal estate, except 20s., to the same object, making a total benefaction of £335. The whole of the endowment fund has been invested in land, and the school has always been in the hands of trustees, who have control over the teachers and all matters affecting its interest and government.

Cookson's Charity is the interest of £10 bequeathed by Thomas Cookson at an unknown date before 1776, to purchase books for the poor children of the parish.

1. Charity Commissioners Report.   2. Ibid.

Leyland's Charity represents the sum of £60 left by Elizabeth Leyland to trustees, in 1734, in order that it might be laid out, and the annual revenue therefrom devoted to the assistance of the poor, either in relieving the elderly, or providing instruction for the young.

ST. ANNES-ON-THE-SEA. The locality in which the new watering-place is rapidly developing was indicated in the foundation charter of the Lytham Benedictine Cell as Kilgrimol. It has been suggested that the peculiar orthography of the word Kilgrimol points to there having been at some era a religious settlement, presided over by Culdees, the priests of Columba,[1] but it is more probable that the name is derived from the two British words *kilgury*, a corner, and *mul* or *meol*, a sand-hill. At a later epoch the district was known as Cross or Churchyard Slack, and tradition records that an oratory existed there until such time as it was swallowed up by an earthquake, long years ago. Mr. Thornber, in discussing the statement, advances the following fact as some evidence in favour of its veracity :—" Churchyard Slack is situated in a hollow, having on the north side a rising ground called Stony-hill, and at the distance of three-quarters of a mile a similar elevation, though not so marked. On these ridges are found innumerable small boulders of grey granite, having apparently been acted upon by fire ; but it is particularly remarkable that not one can be found amongst them entirely whole. Similar stones in less quantities are discovered in the intervening space, all more or less broken."

On the immediate outskirts of the embryo town is the small hamlet of Heyhouses, at which a school was established in 1821, and enlarged in 1853 ; and it was there that Lady Eleanor Cecily Clifton erected a church, in memory of the late James Fair, esq., of Lytham, on a site presented by her husband, the lord of the manor. The foundation stone of the edifice was laid in June, 1872, and on Wednesday, the 6th of August, in the ensuing year, the church and burial ground, occupying jointly 2½ acres, were consecrated by the Lord Bishop of Manchester. The interior contains accommodation for 300 persons, 145 seats being appropriated, and 155 free. The roof is of red tiles instead of slates.

---

1. See pages 15 and 16.

The building is at present a chapel of ease to St. Cuthbert's, Lytham, but will, when occasion requires, have a separate ecclesiastical parish of its own.

The whole of the land of St. Annes-on-the-Sea was leased to a company of gentlemen for a term of 1,100 years by John Talbot Clifton, esq., and on the 31st of March, 1875, the formality of laying the first stone of the future watering-place was gone through by Master John T. Clifton, the eldest son of T. H. Clifton, esq., M.P. The ceremony was accomplished amidst a large concourse of people, and was in fact the commencement of the handsome and commodious hotel near to the railway station, which has since been completed. The estate has been judiciously and tastefully arranged by Messrs. Maxwell and Tuke, architects, of Bury, and is intersected by broad streets with gentle curves. The houses are intended to be built either singly or in pairs with few exceptions, but in no case will any group comprise more than six ; gardens in each instance are to front the dwellings. A promenade, 3,000 feet in length and 180 feet in width, has been formed with asphalt along the marine aspect, and already between twenty and thirty villas have been raised on the sides of the recently made thoroughfares. A public garden with conservatories is also in course of formation, as well as efficient gas-works and other requisites.

CHAPTER XV.

PARISH OF ST. MICHAEL'S-ON-WYRE.

UPPER RAWCLIFFE-WITH-TARNACRE.

N the Domesday Book no less than three Rawcliffes are mentioned, and have been identified, respectively, with Upper, Middle, and Out Rawcliffes, the last being stated to contain three carucates, and the others two carucates each. In the *Testa de Nevill* it is entered that the grandfather of Theobald Walter gave four carucates of land in (Upper) Rawcliffe, Thistleton, and Greenhalgh, to his daughter Alice, on her marriage with Orm Magnus. William de Lancaster held Upper Rawcliffe at the time of his death in 1240; and in 1248 Theobald Walter, or le Botiler, had lands in Upper Rawcliffe and Mid Rawcliffe, as well as the manor of Out Rawcliffe, the principal portion of which had doubtless descended to him from his ancestor alluded to above.[1] An inquiry was instituted in 1322, during the reign of Edward II., concerning the possessions in land and mills of John de Rigmayden in Upper Rawcliffe, Wyresdale, and Garstang; and a similar inquisition, with the exception of Garstang, was made, three years later, in the case of widow Christiana de Coucy de Guynes.[2] In the succeeding few years Joan, the daughter and heiress of John de Rigmayden, and John de Coupland held Upper Rawcliffe between them. John de Coupland had married the widow of Sir William de Goucy, and was the gallant soldier who captured David II., king of Scotland,

1. Escaet. 33 Hen. III. n. 49.   2. Inq. ad Quod. Damnum, 16 & 19 Edward II.

on the battle field at Durham, and was rewarded for his bravery by Edward III., with the rank of knight-banneret and a grant of land. Joan de Rigmayden, the heiress, probably married William Southworth, as he is described as lord of Upper Rawcliffe a little later; Ellen, the sole child and heiress of William Southworth, became the wife of Robert Urswick, of Urswick, and their second son, Thomas, who succeeded to the estates of Rawcliffe, etc., and was knighted, left at his decease a daughter, who espoused, about 1430, John, the third son of Sir Richard Kirkby, of Kirkby. John Kirkby resided at Upper Rawcliffe Hall,[1] or White Hall, as it was subsequently designated, and was succeeded by his eldest son, William, who in his turn left the lands and mansion to his heir and offspring John Kirkby. The eldest son of the last gentleman, by his wife, the daughter of — Broughton, was William Kirkby; and he, in course of time, inherited the property, and married, in 1507, Elizabeth, the daughter of William Thornborough, of Hampsfield, by whom he had issue John, George, William, Richard, Henry, Anne, Elizabeth, and Jane. John Kirkby, the heir, was living in 1567, but died without offspring, as also did his brother George, so that Upper Rawcliffe Hall and estate passed to the third son, William Kirkby, who married Isabell, the daughter of John Butler, of Kirkland.[2] The Kirkbys continued in sole possession of the township until 1631, when Thomas Westby, of Mowbreck, purchased from them Upper Rawcliffe Hall and the estate attached, both of which he settled upon Major George Westby, the eldest son of his second marriage with Elizabeth, the daughter of Thomas Preston, of Holkar, and widow of Thomas Lathom, of Parbold. George Westby resided at White Hall, as the manor house was now called, and was twice married, being succeeded by John, the only child by his first wife, Margaret, the daughter of Thomas Hesketh, of Mains. Both George Westby and his third brother, Bernard, were royalist officers. John Westby, of Upper Rawcliffe, espoused, in 1684, Jane, the daughter of Thomas Bleasdale, of Alston, and had issue John, Joseph, James, and Alice, who became the wife of Thomas Gilibrand, of Dunken Hall, near Chorley. John Westby

---

1. St. Michael's Hall also belonged to the Kirkbys, and it is probable that one of the junior branches resided there before the Longworths of St. Michael's.
2. Flower's Visitation.

the eldest son, inherited the mansion and land on the death of his
father in 1708, and married, in the following year, Mary, the
daughter of Thomas Hawett, of Ormskirk, by whom he had Thomas;
George, who died in 1776, leaving several children by his wife
Mary, the daughter of — Field; John, died unmarried; Cuthbert,
died childless; and Jane. Thomas Westby came into the estate
in 1745, when his father was accidentally killed, and espoused
Margaret, the daughter and heiress of William Shuttleworth, of
Turnover Hall, and Bridget, his wife, who was one of four
daughters, the sole offspring of John Westby, of Mowbreck. The
children of Thomas Westby, of White Hall, and, ultimately, of
one fourth of Mowbreck, were John, who died unmarried in 1811;
William, died unmarried in 1811, just before his brother; Joseph,
died young; Robert, died childless in 1800; Thomas; Bridget,
an abbess at Liege; and two Marys, one of whom died in infancy.
Thomas, the fifth son, held Mowbreck, White, and Turnover Halls
and estates, on the decease of his eldest brother, and at his own
death in 1829, without issue, was succeeded, in Turnover, by Thomas
the only surviving son of his uncle, George Westby, whose death
occurred in 1776; whilst he bequeathed Mowbreck and White Hall
to George, the eldest son of this Thomas Westby, by his wife
Anne, the daughter of John Ashley, of London. The Westbys,
of White Hall and Mowbreck, sold their property at the former
place in recent years to the late John Stevenson, esq., of Preston
and Lytham. Reverting to the earlier Westbys, we find that the
active parts played by George and Bernard Westby in the Civil
Wars resulted in the confiscation of the White Hall estate by
Parliament; and in 1653 it was sold by the Commissioners of
State, being purchased for the Westbys again by, and in the
names of, some of their Protestant friends.

Upper Rawcliffe Hall was rebuilt about the time of its purchase
by the Westbys, who conferred upon it the new title of White
Hall. This mansion stood by the side of the river Wyre, and was
approached through a noble gateway. The windows were mul-
lioned, and two bays projected from the north-west front; within
were secret chambers and a private chapel. The Hall is now a
farm house. Turnover Hall, the ancient seat of the Shuttle-
worths, and afterwards one of the mansions of the Westbys, as
already shown, presents nothing of special interest to our notice.

St. Michael's Hall, the residence of the Longworths[1] during the seventeenth century, and probably of the Kirkbys before them, has since been rebuilt in an antique style, and converted into a farm house.

Tarnacre was claimed, amongst other places, by the abbot of Cockersand in 1292, during the reign of Edward I., and was, with Upper Rawcliffe, in early days, a feudal appendage of Garstang.

The township of Upper Rawcliffe-with-Tarnacre contains the ancient parish church of St. Michael's-on-Wyre, which occupies a prominent and picturesque station on the banks of the narrowed Bleasdale stream, in the midst of the rural village, to which its title has been extended. St. Michael's church, or *Michelescherche*, as it appears in the Survey of William the Conqueror, was obviously standing on the arrival of that warrior in 1066, being, with the exception of a similar structure at Kirkham, the only edifice of its kind existing in the Fylde at that time. There are no records amongst the meagre annals of Amounderness during the Saxon era, to assist us in establishing beyond question the antiquity of this church, but it may reasonably be supposed that its erection took place at no long interval after the year 627, when Paulinus was appointed bishop of the province of Northumbria, in which St. Michael's was situated. The zeal and piety displayed by Paulinus are said to have exercised an important influence in overcoming the pagan tendencies of the inhabitants of Lancashire, and although it is far from probable that the whole of the people of the Fylde at once became converts to Christianity, and renounced their heathenish and superstitious ritual, still it would be idle to deny that the ministrations of so earnest a prelate as Paulinus were fruitful to a considerable degree in our district, more especially when history proclaims the success of his efforts in other portions of his diocese. The small band of professed Christians would gradually extend their circle, and at no remote date a building would become necessary where divine worship could be conducted in a decent and orderly manner, according to the direction of the newly-adopted creed ; and it was, we opine, at such an epoch that the church of St. Michael's-on-Wyre was

1. See "Longworth of St. Michael's Hall" in Chapter VI.

first called into being. After the Norman Conquest the church formed an item of the princely estate of Roger de Poictou, acquired through the partial munificence of William I.; and possibly in 1094, or thereabouts, was conferred by him upon the priory of St. Mary's, at Lancaster, in like manner to similar ecclesiastical possessions which he held in Kirkham and Poulton. However that may be, it is learnt from the *Testa de Nevill* that rather more than a century after the foundation of the monastic house in the year just named, the advowson of St. Michael's was vested in King John, who presented Master Macy to the living,[1] then valued at £66 13s. 4d. per annum. In 1326, William de Walderston, rector of the church of St. Michael's, and the prior of Lancaster, were engaged in a controversy before the authorities of Richmond, respecting the forest and other tithes of Myerscough, and those of a place called Migchalgh, the suit being decided at Lancaster on the 13th of October against the rector.[2] Nineteen years later, Henry, earl of Lancaster, was patron of the living, and in 1411 Henry IV., duke of Lancaster, who had claimed and obtained the crown resigned by Richard II., conveyed St. Michael's church to the Master and Brethren of the College or Chantry of the Blessed Mary Magdalen, at Battlefield, near Shrewsbury, nominally established by himself.[3] The letters-patent by which the transfer was effected, bore the Duchy seal, and stipulated that Roger Yve, of Leeton, Keeper and Master of the College concerned (really its founder), and his successors, should, in return for the grant, make the following provision for the maintenance of a vicar at the church of St. Michael's :—

"The Vicar and his Successors to receive, have, and possess, the offerings and revenues which are and belong to the church of Michaelskirk, together with the fruits and offerings arising from Hay and Revenues ; the Tenth of Gardens dug with the foot, of Lambs, Calves, Young Foals, Poultry, Young Pigs, Geese, Eggs, Milk, Wool, Flax, Hemp, Mills, Apples, Garlick, Onions, Fishes, and Pigeons ; the first fruits of the Dead, otherwise called Mortuaries, whether they consist of Animals, Clothes, or any other thing whatsoever, together with our Pool and Mill, and also the Pool upon Wyre near the Rectory of Michaelskirk ; and further, the same Vicar and his Successors to have for their Dwelling the straw-thatched Porch below the Rectory, and the Door and House adjoining, with the Dovecote and Orchard near the Porch, and the Fishponds and Moats."

1. Fol. 401.   2. Regist. S. Mariæ de Lanc. M.S. fol. 68.
3. Rot. Pat. 4 Hen. VI. m. 10 per Inspec. Linc. Hen. IV.

The vicar on his part was required to pledge himself to pay all ordinary taxes and expenses incumbent upon the church, excepting "the covering of the chancel of the church, the payment of 40s. to the Archdeacon of Richmond, and the Tenths payable to the King for ever," for which the Master of the College agreed on behalf of himself and his successors to be answerable.[1] The foregoing grant and regulations were confirmed in 1425 and 1485 by Henry VI. and Henry VII. respectively. After the Dissolution the right of presentation was exercised by King Charles in 1629, who appointed Nicholas Bray to the vicarage. Subsequently the patronage of the living has descended through several private individuals, and is now centred in the present vicar, the Venerable Archdeacon Hornby.

The parish church of St. Michael's contained two chantries, one of which, dedicated to St. Katherine, occupied the chapel still existing in the north aisle. This chantry was founded some time about the middle of the fifteenth century by John Botiler, or Butler, lord of the manor of Out Rawcliffe. Canon Raines says that a portion of the body armour either of him or one of his immediate descendants remained suspended in the chapel until long after 1700.

Alice Butler, the daughter of Sir Thomas Radcliffe, and widow of Nicholas Butler, the eldest son of the founder, bequeathed by will, dated the 20th of November, 1504, "her sowll to God and hys Blessyd Mother and all the holye Cumpanie of heven, and her bodye to be beryd in Christian wyse in Saynt Katrine's chapel, where her husband laye;" also "to the lyght brenning there 20d; to Thomas Walton, or some wel dysposed priest to synge for my sowll for one yeare £1 13s. 4d., solemn mass of requiem, and other obsequies to be done as becometh one of my degree, but not too moche expendsive so that my executors let not (hinder not) my dowters advancement in marryage; and to Sr John Butler, Clerk, 40s. a yeare togider with meate and drynke whiles he is on lyfe."[2] In the reign of Henry VIII., William Harrison was the officiating priest of this chantry, and at that time its tenants, possessions, and annual rentals were, one

---

1. A copy of "The appropriation of the Vicarage of Michaelskirk," dated 1411, and now in the possession of the Ven. Archdeacon Hornby.
   2. E. Reg. Richmond.

tenement lying in Esprick, held by Thomas Dawson at 20s. per
annum; another tenement in the same place held by William
Hall at 19s.; a windmill in Stainall at 26s. 8d., and several parcels
of ground amounting to about an acre at 2s., held by Ralph Hull;
one tenement in Stainall with appurtenances held by Ralph
Hodgeson at 12s.; an acre of ground lying in a field at Stainall
held by William Hull at 2s. 8d.; two roods of land in Stainall
held by the wife of Christopher Hull at 12d.; divers plots of
ground estimated to comprise four acres in the same township
held by William Hull, the elder, at 19s.; one tenement with
appurtenances in Great Eccleston held by the wife of William
Stiholme at 13s. 4d.; and one tenement in Little Eccleston held
by Henry Wilkinson, at 20s.   Hence it seems that the gross
rentals amounted to £5 15s. 8d., out of which 5s. per annum was
paid to the wife of Robert Stannall for her jointure, leaving £5
10s. 8d. the actual yearly revenue of the chantry from its endowment.[1] At the accession of Edward VI., Henry Harrison was
the "Priest Incumbent at St. Katherine's Altar, being 54 years
old, and he taught a Grammar School according to his foundation."   When chantries were suppressed the educational
institution here alluded to was probably abandoned for want of
funds and a master; in any case it ceased to exist about that
time.   On the 29th of November, 1606, James I. granted to
Henry Butler, of Rawcliffe Hall, "all that Late Chantrie of the
ffoundation of John Butler, at the Aulter of the Blessed
Katherine within the Parishe Churche of St. Michaell-upon-
Wyre, in the Countye of Lancaster, lately dissolved, and all the
lands appertaining thereto."

The second chantry in St. Michael's church was founded
sometime during the fifteenth century by one of the earlier
Kirkbys, of Upper Rawcliffe, and in the reign of Edward VI. its
annual income from endowment property was £4 13s. 10d.,
Thomas Crosse, of the age of 40 years, being the priest who
celebrated there and "assisted the Curate."   Nothing more
precise concerning the origin of this chantry can be ascertained,
and even the situation it occupied in the church is unknown.   In
1553 Thomas Crosse received a pension of £4 13s. 10d. a year.[2]

1. Commissioners' Report before the Dissolution of Monastries.
2. Willis's Hist. Mitr. Abb. vol. ii p. 108.

VICARS OF ST. MICHAEL'S-ON-WYRE,

IN THE DEANERY OF AMOUNDERNESS AND ARCHDEACONRY OF LANCASTER.

Date of Institution.	NAME.	By whom Presented.	Cause of Vacancy.
About 1200	·Master Macy	King John	
,, 1377	William de Horneby	Duke of Lancaster (?)	
In 1411	Johannes de Daleby	College of Battlefield	
Before 1549	Michael Thorneborrow		
In 1549	Thomas Crosse.	G. Kirkby and Nich. Lawrenson, gents., patrons on this occasion only, by consent of John Hussey, master, and the Fellows of Battlefield College	Death of M. Thorneborrow
In 1628	Robert Carr		
,, 1629	Nicholas Bray	King Charles I.	Resignation of R. Carr
Before 1650	William Bray	King Charles I.	
About 1653	Nathaniel Baxter		
Before 1715	Thomas Robinson		
In 1715	Richard Crombleholme	Thomas Clitherall	Death of T. Robinson
, 1729	William Crombleholme	Edward Crombleholme	Death of R. Crombleholme
,, 1765	Robert Oliver	Richard Whitehead	Death of W. Crombleholme
,, 1768	Anthony Swainson, M.A.	Richard Whitehead	Cession of R. Oliver
,, 1784	Charles Buck, M.A.	John Swainson	Death of A. Swainson
1789	Hugh Hornby, M.A.	Joseph Hornby	Resignation of C. Buck
1847	William Hornby, M.A.	Himself	Death of H. Hornby

The Rev. Hugh de Horneby was the brother of Robert de Horneby, vicar of Kirkham, and it may fairly be inferred that they belonged to the family of Hornbys, whose descendants are now settled at St. Michael's, Ribby, and Winwick, but lapse of time has obliterated the connecting links. The Rev. Nathaniel Baxter was ejected in 1662, for refusing to take the oath required by the Act of Uniformity. Little only can be ascertained concerning the Crombleholmes, but it is conjectured that they were associated with the branch of that name seated at Goosnargh. The Rev. Richard Crombleholme had two sons— Edward and William, by the latter of whom he was succeeded in the vicarage, whilst to the former seems to have descended the patronage, acquired by purchase. The Rev. William Cromble- holme married the daughter of Alexander Butler, of Kirkland, and possibly had no offspring beyond the Elizabeth Cromble- holme, to whose memory the mural monument shortly to be noticed, was erected. The Rev. Anthony Swainson was the son of the Rev. Christopher Swainson, B.A., incumbent of Copp, and Elizabeth, his wife ; he was a Fellow of Worcester College, Oxford. The Rev. Charles Buck was the son of the Rev. Charles Buck, M.A., vicar of Kirkham ; he was afterwards curate of Warton and Lund. The Rev. Hugh Hornby was the sixth son of Hugh Hornby, esq., of Kirkham, whose eldest son was Joseph Hornby, esq., D.L., of Ribby Hall. He married Ann, daughter and co-heiress of Joseph Starky, M.D., of Redvales, and had issue, one son, William, now the Venerable Archdeacon Hornby, who succeeded him in the living, and is the present vicar and patron. The Ven. Archdeacon Hornby is an honorary canon of Manchester, and has been twice married, but further information respecting the family will be found in the pedigree of " Hornby of Ribby Hall."

The present church is a broad low building of rough stone, with a tower of similar character at the west end. Both the tower and church are surmounted and surrounded by a castellated stone parapet and ornamental pinnacles of the same material. The porch and the tower bear the date 1611 and initial letters H : B. upon their exteriors, but it is evident that much of the edifice can boast a considerably greater antiquity than that indicated by the corres- ponding inscriptions. It is also obvious from the varieties displayed in the architecture of different portions, more especially the windows, that the rebuilding of the church has not been accomplished all at once, but carried on at pretty long intervals, extending back certainly to the time of Henry VIII., and perhaps further. Within, the south side aisle is separated from the nave by a succession of stone arches running from east to west, whilst the north side aisle contains the chapel in which was placed the altar of St. Katherine, and where now is the following inscription :—" This Oratory, known before the Dissolution to have been a Chantry dedicated to Saint Katherine, and competently endowed with lands in the neighbouring townships, was repaired by John ffrance, esq., of Rawcliffe Hall, A.D. 1797, being an appendage to that ancient manor house." The tower opens directly into the nave without even the semblance of a partition, and on one wall is fixed a brass plate intimating that the large clock, whose huge pendulum vibrates opposite, and whose dials are visible without, was presented, in 1850, to the Ven. Archdeacon Hornby by his parishioners, as a mark of esteem. The mural tables occupying stations within the aisles and nave are erected to the memories of Edward Greenhalgh, of Myerscough Hall, died in 1823, aged 53, and Margaret, his widow, died in 1853, aged 92, also Mary, died in infancy, and Charlotte, died in 1823, aged 29, their daughters ; Thomas Westby, of White Hall, died in 1762, aged 47, and Margaret, his widow, died in 1802, aged 82, also their children—Mary, died in infancy, Joseph, in 1769, aged 16, Bridget, in 1786, aged 37, Robert, in 1800, aged 45, Mary, in 1805, aged 45, William, in 1811, aged 60, and John, in 1811, aged 65—Thomas, the only surviving child being the erector of the monument in 1812 ; Hugh Hornby, M.A., 56 years vicar of the parish, died in 1847, aged 81, and Anne, his widow, died in 1850, aged 81 years, also Joseph Starkey Hornby, born in 1839, died in 1858, and William Hornby, born in 1845, died in 1858—" They were lovely and pleasant in their lives, and in their death they were not divided"; Henry Hornby, late Captain in the East India Service, died in 1794, aged 54, "also near this place were interred the remains of his late father, Thomas Hornby, of St. Michael's, who died Mar. 8, 1785, aged 76, likewise Elizabeth, wife and mother to the above, who died May 14th, 1798, aged 84"; Elizabeth Crombleholme, daughter of the Rev. William Crombleholme, formerly vicar of the parish, " whose mortal remains were deposited in the graveyard of this church near those of her beloved parents on the 21st of May, 1817—Erected as a tribute of esteem by her affectionate relative Thomas Butler Cole, of Kirkland Hall." The Baptistry was restored in 1852 by the surviving children of John and Susannah Swainson, of Preston, and contains several tablets affixed to the north wall in memory of numerous members of that family, amongst whom may be mentioned the Revs.

Christopher Swainson, B.A., incumbent of Copp, died in 1775; Anthony Swainson, M.A., vicar of St. Michael's-on-Wyre, died 1784, aged 42 ; and Christopher Swainson, M.A., prebendary of Hereford, and vicar of Clun, Salop, died in 1854. The burial ground surrounding the church presents nothing of much interest to the antiquarian beyond an old sun-dial, and the Crombleholme grave lying under the shadow of the east wall. The living is a discharged vicarage.

The following extracts from the ancient vestry books will doubtless be interesting to our readers, although not of much importance as parish records :—

" April, 1683 : To Ann Raby for washing surplice, 4s.; to John Fisher for work for clock and bells, 8s. 6d.

" Ordered this 21st of June, 1683, that no person or persons for the future be admitted to bury any dead corpse in the church unless he or they, at whose instance such corpse shall be buried, do in hand pay to the sexton of the parish for the same, being 12 pence for the use of the parish, or sufficiently secure the same to him, the corpses of women dying in childbed only excepted, which are hereby intended to be free, as is usual in other parishes.—Thos. Robinson, vicar ; Rich. Longworth, Thos. White, gents. ; Jas, Raby, Rich. B. Hornby, Rich. Wilding, George Bennet, churchwardens."

" May 18, 1688 : It is ordered that the two former orders made, the one ffor destroying Magpie and Sparrow heads, and the other for allowing the churchwardens to pay * * * * * out of the parish money, be for the future suspended."

" July 4, 1729 : To ring one Bell at 7.0 ; to ring 2 Bells at 8.0 ; to ring and chime for Service in summer from half an hour past 10 o'clock, and in winter from Ten till half an hour after."

" Aug. 25, 1736 : It was ordered by ye Vicar and gentlemen of ye parish that another church lay after ye rate of 12d. in £1, besides ye 3 church lays before mentioned, be forthwith collected and gathered for repairing ye church. N.B : This church lay is collected for laying a new beam and erecting a new pair of principals between ye church and ye chancel at the joint charges of ye parish and Allen Johnson, esq., owner of ye chancel."

May 5, 1745 : Be it known that John Lewtas has cleared up ye difficulties about ye quakers' taxes for Rawcliffe.

" 1746 : Ringers' salary, 15s.; for 5th of November, 6s.; for sanding churchyard, 1s.

" November 6, 1780 : Agreed by the Vicar and gentlemen of the Vestry of St. Michael's, that each Ringer attending the church shall be allowed two tankards of ale, and each singer one tankard, together with each one their dinner."

" November 6, 1792 : It was determined by a majority of the gentlemen of the Vestry to raise the dues for opening a grave in the inside of the church to 6s. 8d.

" 1796 : At a meeting of the Vestry of this church it was unanimously resolved that the remainder of the profits arising from the estate called Terleways and the garden in Upper Rawcliffe, after defraying the expenses of a dinner and a quart of ale to each vestryman, churchwarden, the curate of Copp, and clerk of St. Michael's, at the respective days of Easter Tuesday and the 5th of November for 7 years ensuing, commencing with the present day (March 29, 1796), shall be suffered to accumulate during the above period towards purchasing an Organ for the Church of St. Michael's ; and that every Stranger introduced on the forementioned days at dinner, except it be on business of the parish, shall be paid for by the person introducing him."

"July 15, 1799 : To a Finger and Barrel Organ with the following stops— Open, Diapason, Stop do., Principal, Twelfth, Fifteenth, Sesqualtra, and Mixture,—£183 15s. od.

In 1708 Richard Cornall gave £40 to be invested, and the interest applied towards the maintenance of a schoolmaster for Upper Rawcliffe-with-Tarnacre, and in 1808 Joseph Fielding, of Catterall, was the sole remaining trustee of a sum of money, amounting to £60, of which the £40 doubtless formed part, for educational purposes. At that date Joseph Fielding induced the Rev. Hugh Hornby, vicar of St. Michael's-on-Wyre, and William Harrison, of Upper Rawcliffe, to undertake the trust with him on a fresh deed, the old one having been lost. A new schoolhouse was shortly erected on the site of the former building, and is now governed by the representatives of the trustees named. In 1813 Mrs. Elizabeth Crombleholme left £200 in trust to be invested, and the annual income therefrom paid to the master of St. Michael's-on-Wyre school for teaching three poor children of the parish to read, write, and cast accounts.

Bread-money was probably established during the lifetime of John ffrance, of Rawcliffe Hall, and arises from " two-sevenths of the clear rent of a close of ground lying in Kirkham, purchased with £20, to be distributed to the poor attending divine service in the parish church of St. Michael's, at the direction of John ffrance, esq., and his heirs ; Thomas Langton, gent., and his heirs; and the vicar of St. Michael's for the time being." [1]

Ralph Longworth, esq., of St. Michael's Hall, left £5 per annum to the vicar, and £2 10s. to the poor of Upper Rawcliffe.

Thomas Knowles, gent., left £2 10s., and John Hudson, gent., £2 a-year to the poor of the same township.

1. List of Benefactions within the Church of St. Michael's.

The Terleway's Lands were given by some one unknown at a
very early date " for the use of the parish, as the vicar and vestry
shall direct," and consist of lands in Claughton and a garden in
Upper Rawcliffe-with-Tarnacre.[1]

POPULATION OF UPPER RAWCLIFFE-WITH-TARNACRE.

1801.	1811.	1821.	1831.	1841.	1851.	1861.	1871.
494	617	643	665	671	697	682	700

The area of the township embraces 3,743 statute acres.

GREAT ECCLESTON. Great Eccleston was anciently held by
William de Lancaster as an appendage of the fee of Wyresdale.
William de Lancaster died without issue, and Wyresdale, with
its dependency Great Eccleston, passed to Walter de Lindsay, the
eldest son of his second sister, Alice. The Lindsay line terminated
in the heiress Christiana de Lindsay, living in 1300, who married
Ingelram de Guynes, Lord of Coucy, in France, whose eldest son
was created earl of Bedford in 1336, and whose second and third
sons, Sir William de Coucy and Robert de Coucy, held Great
Eccleston as part of Wyresdale, their inheritance, in 1346.
The widow of Sir William de Coucy conveyed her portion
of Great Eccleston in marriage to Sir John de Coupland, and the
remainder was then held by Baldwin de Guynes and Joan, the
heiress of John de Rigmayden. The whole of the township, with
the exception of certain lands rented by the convent of Deulacres,[2]
descended in the manner above described from William de
Lancaster, through the Lindsays and Guynes or Coucys, to
Coupland, Baldwin de Guynes, and Joan Rigmayden, and subsequently to their heirs. Amongst the *Familiæ Lancastrienses*
there are two families of Ecclestons, one of which is described as
of Eccleston, near Preston, and the other of Eccleston simply, the
latter doubtless being the Ecclestons who were seated at Great
Eccleston Hall anterior to the Stanleys, the occupants in the
seventeenth century, whose pedigree will be found, with others, in
a former chapter of this volume. The Ecclestons, of Eccleston,
near Preston, would belong to the place of that name in the
Hundred of Leyland. Thomas Stanley, an illegitimate son of
the fourth earl of Derby, settled, about 1600, at Great Eccleston
Hall, which, together with the estate, was probably purchased ;

---

1. List of Benefactions within the Church of St. Michael's.
2. Dugdale's Monasticon, vol. v., p. 630.

his descendants remained there until the death of Richard Stanley, in 1714, when Thomas Westby, of Upper Rawcliffe, obtained possession of the land and mansion, both of which have since descended in his line.

An Episcopal chapel was erected, in 1723, on the summit of a hill at Copp, almost a mile from the village of Great Eccleston, and near to Elswick chapel, "which," says Bishop Gastrell," being never consecrated and in the possession of the Dissenters, it was thought more proper to build a new one there than to seize upon that." Subjoined is a letter from John ffrance, of Little Eccleston Hall, to William Stafford, Commissary of Richmond, and Secretary to Bishop Gastrell, called forth by sundry matters in connection with the newly completed place of worship :—

"Eccleston parva, Aug. 3, 1724.

"Upon some discourse with Mr. Dixon (vicar of Kirkham) about Cop Chapell I will give you the trouble of this. When Subscriptions were desired towards building the said Chapell it was proposed and intended to be not only for the use of the Inhabitants of St. Michael's, but likewise for the use of several townships, which lye in the Parish of Kirkham, remote from their Parish Church ; and the Inhabitants of this township (Little Eccleston-with-Larbrick) have contributed more towards the Building than those of St. Michael's, and would have erected it within Kirkham Parish, if the situation had been thought equally convenient. And likewise the person, who promised to pay the hundred pounds towards the Queen's Bounty, gave a note touching the same, with conditions in favour of Kirkham Parish.

"Before the Chapell was erected the two Vicars of the Parishes aforesaid were together, seemed to encourage our proceedings, and talked amicably and agreeably about Nomination, etc. ; but since the Chapell was built several proposals have been made to which the Vicar of Kirkham has consented, but the Vicar of St. Michael's seems to dislike them. One of the proposals was that the determination of the affair might be referred to the Bishop of Chester, whose generous offer to procure £100 towards the Endowment of this Chapell gave great encouragement to our undertaking the building thereof. Some people have refused to pay their Subscriptions on pretence that the Vicar of St. Michael's has departed from former proposals ; but we hope (if these differences could be amicably settled to the satisfaction of the neighbourhood) that not only the old, but likewise several new Subscriptions might be procured, especially if our grateful behaviour for by-past favours may continue his Lordship's Countenance and Encouragement ; and we desire you to represent the matter to him as favourably as you think it will bear."

(Signed) John ffrance.

The chapel was a small plain brick building, dedicated to St. Anne, but in 1841 a tower was added, and at the same time a burial ground was enclosed and licensed in connection with it.

Great Eccleston, Elswick, and Little Eccleston-with-Larbrick townships were, in 1849, constituted a separate ecclesiastical district, known as the parish of Copp, of which this chapel is the parochial church. There is a vicarage house.

CURATES AND VICARS OF COPP.

Date of Institution.	Name.	Cause of Vacancy.
Before 1775.	Christopher Swainson, B.A.	
„ 1841.	Reginald Sharpe.	
In 1841.	Thomas Hathornthwaite, L.L.D.	Resignation of R. Sharpe.
„ 1864.	William C. Dowding, M.A.	Resignation of T. Hathornthwaite.
„ 1870.	William Bateson, M.A.	Resignation of William C. Dowding.

A new Catholic chapel was completed in 1835, and superseded one of considerable age. Three fairs are held each year on March 14th, April 14th, and November 4th, for cattle.

The origin of the free school at Copp has not been discovered, but the earliest endowment to be found dates from 1719, when William Fyld, yeoman, of Great Eccleston, left the remainder of his personal estate, amounting to about £250, to be invested in trustees, and the interest to be paid yearly "for a Master to teach Poor Children here, or in some other part of the township." By his will, dated 1st of April, 1748, William Gaulter bequeathed £242 14s. to certain trustees to augment the stipend of the master of this school, and directed that in case the educational establishment should ever be abandoned, or the terms of the will not be observed, the annual income derived from his bequest should be distributed amongst the poor inhabitants of the neighbourhood. In 1866 the school was temporarily closed, whilst the charity was under the revision of the Charity Commissioners; and in 1871 a new and more commodious building was erected. There is also another school in this township, called Lane Head school, held in a building erected by subscription on the site of the original one, which had collapsed through age. The only endowment is a rent charge of £5 supposed to have been left by Thomas Clitherall.

William Fyld, of Great Eccleston, bequeathed £2 annually to the poor of that township.

Ellen Longworth left the interest of £20 to be distributed in bread to the poor people attending divine service at Copp church.

POPULATION OF GREAT ECCLESTON.

1801.	1811.	1821.	1831.	1841.	1851.	1861.	1871.
455	540	648	624	661	631	641	565

The area of the township in statute acres is 1,412

OUT RAWCLIFFE. The manor of Out Rawcliffe was presented to Theobald Walter by Richard I., and from that time to 1715 remained in the hands of the same family. Theobald Walter, the son of the above-named gentleman, and *Butler* of Ireland, a title which, as elsewhere stated, he adopted as a surname, gave the whole of Out Rawcliffe, and one carucate of land in Stainall, to his relative, perhaps son, Sir Richard Butler, and from him sprang the long line of Butlers of Rawcliffe.[1] In 1627 the inquisition *post mortem* of Henry Butler, of Rawcliffe Hall, revealed that his possessions consisted of the two manors of Out and Middle Rawcliffes, and of lands in Upper Rawcliffe.[2] Henry and Richard Butler of Rawcliffe, father and eldest son, joined the ranks of the insurgents in 1715, and after the suppression of the rebellion, their estates were confiscated; Henry escaped, but Richard was seized, and died in prison at London in 1716, before the day appointed for his execution. The sale of Out Rawcliffe by Government was enrolled on the 19th of September, 1723, the purchasers being the Rev. Richard Crombleholme, (vicar of St. Michael's), John Leyland, Cornelius Fox, and James Poole ; and in the diary of the Rev. Thos. Parkinson, curate of Garstang, reference is made to the completion and terms of the transfer as follows :—

"April 1723.—* * * * At night I preached for T. Raby, of Tarnacre, at St. Michael's. His son paid me 10s. Mr. Crombleholm, the vicar there, came from London, whilst I was there, who, in conjunction with three more, had bought Rawcliffe demain and tenants, paying to the board £11,260. It cost them near £1,000 more in hush money, as they call it."

In 1729 the Rev. Richard Crombleholme, who seems to have bought up the shares of his co-investors, died, and five years later his heir, Edward Crombleholme, disposed of the lordship of Out

---

1. For "Butlers of Rawcliffe" see Chapter VI.   2. Duc. Lanc. vol. xxvi. n. 36.

Rawcliffe, with its courts, fishing in the Wyre, rents, etc., to Thomas Roe, whose only child and heiress married John ffrance, of Little Eccleston Hall. The only son and heir of John ffrance, of Rawcliffe and Little Eccleston, also called John, became lord of the manor on the decease of his father in 1774. He espoused Margaret, the daughter and heiress of — Rigg, of Lancaster, and, dying without issue, devised his property, after the death of his widow, to Thomas Wilson, of Preston, whose wife, the daughter of — Cross, of Shaw Hall, Chorley, was his nearest relative. Thomas Wilson assumed the surname of ffrance in addition to his own, and was succeeded, under the will of John ffrance, by his son, Thomas Robert Wilson-ffrance, who effected great improvements on the land by draining and re-covering the mosses, thereby increasing the value of the estate considerably. T. R. Wilson-ffrance died in 1853, and Rawcliffe descended to his only son, Robert Wilson-ffrance, who lived but six years afterwards, and bequeathed his estates to his sole offspring, Robert John Barton Wilson-ffrance, esq., at that time an infant, and now in possession. Rawcliffe Hall lies on the south of the township, in a park-like enclosure, leading to the banks of the river Wyre. The present mansion was built in the 17th century, but during more recent years has undergone material alterations. The remains of the Catholic chapel attached to it are situated at the rear.

The church of Out Rawcliffe was consecrated in 1837, and was erected by subscription and a donation from the late T. R. Wilson-ffrance, esq., who also gave the site, and retained the patronage. The style of architecture is said to resemble some portions of the ruins of Glastonbury Abbey, with a fine Norman arch over the west end. There are 250 sittings, of which 150 are free. The first incumbent was the Rev. W. Chadwick, who was succeeded by the Rev. Joshua Waltham. The Rev. James C. Home, M.A., is the third and present holder of the living.

There is a good day-school supported out of the Rawcliffe estate.

POPULATION OF OUT RAWCLIFFE.

1801.	1811.	1821.	1831.	1841.	1851.	1861.	1871.
413	484.	598	575	728	791	771	832

The area in statute acres of Out Rawcliffe is 4,340.

ELSWICK. From the *Testa de Nevill* it appears that about 1400 Warin de Wytingham and Alin de Singilton held respectively the eighth and sixteenth parts of a knight's fee in Elswick from the Earl of Lincoln. Edmund Dudley had the manor until his attainder at the beginning of the reign of Henry VIII.; and in 1521, Thomas, earl of Derby, held it of that monarch. The soil is now in the possession of several landowners.

In 1650 the Parliamentary Commissioners of the Commonwealth reported that the inhabitants, " being fifty families, and five miles from their parish church, had lately, with the voluntary and free assistance of some neighbouring towns, erected a chapel." The Rev. Cuthbert Harrison, who had been ejected from his benefice in Ireland for refusing the oath of Uniformity, procured a license from Charles II. in 1672 for the same chapel, " for the use of such as did not conform to the Church of England, commonly called Congregational." Parliament, however, decreed that the King's authority was insufficient, and forbade divine service to be held there a short time later. In 1702 the chapel seems to have been again opened, and continued in use amongst the Independents until 1753, when it was superseded by a new one, enlarged in 1838. The memorial stone of the present chapel, erected to commemorate the persecutions under the Five Mile Act of two centuries ago, was laid by Sir James Watts, of Manchester, on the 30th of July, 1873, and the building completed with all expedition. The chapel stands on a plot of ground presented by Mrs. Harrison, of Bankfield, adjoining the site of the former edifice, and is a handsome stone Gothic structure. The mortuary, with tower and spire, was given by R. C. Richards, esq., J.P., of Clifton Lodge, in memory of certain members of his family.

Elizabeth Hoole, by will dated 26th of April, 1727, charged a meadow in Elswick, which she gave to the Roman Catholic chapel of Great Eccleston, with the annual payment of £3 to the poor of Elswick.

POPULATION OF ELSWICK.

1801.	1811.	1821.	1831.	1841.	1851.	1861.	1871.
232	256	290	327	303	307	290	254.

The area of the township includes 1,009 statute acres.

WOOD PLUMPTON. In the Domesday Book Pluntun is entered as comprising two carucates of arable land. Robert de Stokeport died possessed of the manor in 1248, and his daughter and heiress married Nicholas de Eton as her first husband, and John de Arderne as her second. Robert de Eton, a descendant of her first marriage, obtained Wood Plumpton in 1340. Cecily de Stokeport, heiress of the Etons, conveyed the manor to Sir Edward Warren, of Poynton, in which family it remained until transferred, in 1777, to Viscount Thomas James Bulkeley on his marriage with Elizabeth Harriet, only child of Sir George Warren. The Bulkeley property ultimately passed to the Fleming-Leycesters, whence Lord de Tabley obtained the lordship. Charles Birley, esq., of Bartle Hall, is the present possessor of the manor. Wood Plumpton Hall was anciently the seat of the Warrens, whilst Ambrose Hall was occupied by a family of the same name, from which descended the Rev. Isaac Ambrose, who was ejected from Garstang by the Act of Uniformity. Richard Ambrose, of Ambrose Hall, left a son and heir, William, who married the daughter of — Curwen of Lancaster, and had issue a son, Nicholas. Nicholas Ambrose espoused Jane, daughter of John Singleton, of Gingle Hall, Lancashire, and left six sons and a daughter, the eldest of whom, William, resided at Ambrose Hall in 1567, and was twice married, first to Anne, widow of Lawrence Cotham, of St. Michael's-on-Wyre, and after her decease to Margaret, widow of Sir Richard Houghton. Flower's heraldic visitation, from which the foregoing is extracted, was made in in 1567, and consequently the pedigree cannot be traced further.

The church of Wood Plumpton is very ancient, being probably in existence during the earlier years of the 14th century. It was rebuilt in 1630, and has subsequently undergone numerous alterations, consisting now of nave, chancel, and two aisles. The communion table has the date and initials " W. A. 1635 " upon it, and a beam in the roof is carved with the year " 1639." An organ was obtained in 1849. The principal window, the gift of R. Waterworth, esq., of Preston, is beautifully emblazoned, in addition to which there are several other richly stained windows. A handsome monument of marble, representing a sailor mourning, is situated in the north aisle, and was erected in memory of Henry Foster, R.N., F.R.S., son of a former incumbent who was drowned in 1831, in the river Chagres, Gulf of Mexico. The church is dedicated to St. Anne, and the Rev. Isaac Mossop is the present vicar.

There is a Roman Catholic chapel at Cottam, erected in 1793, The date of the original one is unknown, but in 1768 it was almost completely destroyed by an election mob. A Wesleyan chapel was built in 1815, and another for the Primitive Methodists about 1819.

The township contains an auxiliary workhouse, connected with the Preston Union, which was erected in 1823. Annual courts are held for the manor of Wood Plumpton, which includes the hamlets of Catforth, Eaves, Bartle, and Wood Plumpton.

The school at Catforth was established by Alice Nicholson, of Bartle, who gave in 1661 the sum of £100 in trust for the maintenance of a free school within the manor of Wood Plumpton. Subsequent benefactions have been received as follows :—The same Alice Nicholson £10 by will, in 1664 ; John Hudson, of Lea, £20 by will, in 1676 ; John Hall, of Catforth, £20 by deed, in 1732; James Hall, of Catforth, £10 by will, in 1741 ; Richard Eccles, £100 by will, in 1762 ; Elizabeth Bell, £100 by deed, in 1813 ; Richard Threlfall, £20 by deed in 1813 ; and Ann Robinson, £90 by will in 1817. The total endowment up to 1813, amounting to £380, was invested on the 21st of April in that year, in the navy five per cents., in the name of the trustees. The further bequest of £90 was placed out at interest.

In 1817, Ann Robinson, the benefactress just mentioned, also left £90 in trust, the interest to be given to the master teaching the Sunday school at Wood Plumpton church.

Thomas Houghton gave, in 1649, the fourth part of the rental of an estate in Wood Plumpton to the poor of that township.

It is recited in an indenture, dated 9th January, 1709, that George Nicholson bequeathed the rents of several closes of land, which he stood possessed of for a certain term of years, in trust, for the poor of Wood Plumpton, and also left for the same charitable object, the sum of £200, to be retained by his executors, and the interest only distributed, until the expiration of the above term, when the sum should be paid to the churchwardens and overseers, and used as heretofore. The indenture further recites that on the death of George Nicholson in 1672, a Chancery suit arose out of the will, the result being that the poor were awarded £210 as a settlement of their legal claims upon the property of the deceased. The money was ordered to be invested, and the annual income bestowed as directed by the testator.

POPULATION OF WOOD PLUMPTON.

1801.	1811.	1821.	1831.	1841.	1851.	1861.	1871.
1,197	1,397	1,635	1,719	1,688	1,574	1,462	1,290

The township comprises 4,722 statute acres.

INSKIP-WITH-SOWERBY. In the Domesday volume this township appears as containing three carucates of arable soil. Richard Butler, of Rawcliffe Hall, obtained the manor of Inskip in 1281 as the dowry of his bride Alicia, daughter of William de Carleton. Inskip was held by Cuthbert Clifton, of Clifton, in 1512, from whom it descended to Sir W. Molyneux, of Larbrick and Sefton, who had espoused his sole child and heiress. In 1554-68 it was in the possession of Henry Kighley, and afterwards passed to William Cavendish, earl of Devonshire, on his marriage with the daughter and co-heiress of that gentleman.

The fishery of "Saureby Mere" belonged to William Hoghton in 1519, at which epoch Thomas Rigmayden and the earl of Derby had lands in Sowerby. The Stanleys have for long been lords of Sowerby and continue to hold a court-baron there. In Inskip also a court-baron takes place each year in June.

A church, dedicated to St. Peter, was erected in 1848 at the joint expense of the earl of Derby and the Ven. Archdeacon Hornby, vicar of St. Michael's-on-Wyre. The living, now a vicarage, is endowed with £100 per annum out of the corn rents. The Rev. A. Sharples, B.A., appointed shortly after the church was built, is the present vicar.

One-fourth of the rentals from certain lands in Goosnargh and Chipping was given by Thomas Knowles in 1686 to the poor of Inskip.

In 1750 John Jolly bequeathed the residue of his estate in trust, for the use of such poor housekeepers of Inskip-with-Sowerby as received no parochial relief.

POPULATION OF INSKIP-WITH-SOWERBY.

1801.	1811.	1821.	1831.	1841.	1851.	1861.	1871.
635	647	739	798	735	680	663	593

The area of the township in statute acres amounts to 2,888.

CHAPTER XVI.

PAUPERISM AND THE FYLDE UNION.

IN the fourteenth and fifteenth centuries it was not customary to recognise the pauper as a person whose misfortunes, however brought about, called for charitable aid, but all legislature was directed against his class under the common title of vagabonds. A statute of 1384 decreed that all vagrants should be arrested and either placed in the stocks, or imprisoned until the visit of the justices, who would do with them whatever seemed best by law; and in 1496 the punishment of incarceration was abolished, but the stocks were retained. The sixteenth century initiated a little more considerate state of things, and justices of the peace were authorised in 1531 to grant begging licenses to any necessitous persons in their districts unable to work for a livelihood. An act of 1547 ordained that any vagabond, not incapacitated by old age or illness, loitering and not seeking work for three days should be brought before a magistrate, who was directed to adjudge such vagrant to be, for two years, the slave of the person by whom he had been apprehended, in addition to which he had to be branded with the letter V on the breast. In case he ran away the law ordered that a further branding of the sign S should be inflicted, this time on his forehead or the ball of his cheek, and that slavery should be his perpetual portion. A third escape entailed death when re-captured. This enactment was never really enforced as popular indignation at its extreme severity was aroused at once, and after lingering two years it was repealed in favour of the stocks-legislature. In 1551 it was decreed that a register of destitute persons should be kept in each parish, and that alms should be collected in Whit-week, whilst on the Sunday following, during divine service at church, " the collectors should gently ask and demand of every man and woman what they of their charity would give weekly towards the relief of the poor." The funds so obtained were to be distributed amongst the poor " after such sort that the more impotent might have the more help, and such as could get part of their living the less." Eleven years later a statute ordained that if any person refused to contribute alms when called upon he should be summoned before a justice, who would determine the amount he had to pay, and commit him to gaol in case of further refusal. The legislative body of Queen Elizabeth passed " An Act for the punishment of vagabonds and the relief of the poor and impotent," by which justices of the peace were instructed to register the names of all the impotent poor who had been born within their several districts, or been existing there on alms within the three preceding years; to assign to them convenient places for dwellings or lodgings, in case the parish had not already undertaken that duty of its own free will; to assess the inhabitants to a weekly charge ; and to appoint overseers of the poor, having authority to exact a certain amount of work from those candidates for relief who were not entirely disabled from labour by age, sickness, or deformity. In 1575-6 it was ordered that a stock of wool or hemp should be provided in the different parishes for the purpose of " setting the poor at work," and that " Houses of Correction " should be established, in which vagrants or tramps were to be detained, the able-bodied being furnished with employment until a service was found for them, and the infirm transferred to an alms-house as soon as practicable. The " Houses of Correction," the origin of our workhouses, were directed to be built in large cities, or in the central towns of wide districts, thus the one for the Fylde was situated at Preston, an old college of Grey Friars lying to the south of Marsh Lane being converted to that use. Dr. Kuerden described this building more than two centuries ago as the " old Friary, now only reserved for the reforming of vagabonds, sturdy beggars, and petty larcenary thieves, and other people wanting good behaviour; it is the country prison to entertain such persons with hard work, spare diet, and whipping, and it is called the House of Correction." The present gaol of Preston was not completed until 1789, and by force of habit the expressive title of its predecessor has clung to it.

In 39 Elizabeth, 1597, an act came into force by which all previous legislation on the subject under consideration was repealed, and which decreed that overseers of the poor should be appointed in every parish, whose duty it should be to levy a rate upon the inhabitants for the support of the indigent, under the direction and with the approval of the local magistrates; in addition there were special regulations for the treatment of rogues, vagrants, and able beggars, for whom whipping and the stocks were ordered, after undergoing which punishments these idlers were to be returned at once to their native parishes and placed under the guardianship of the local authorities there.

Four years later certain modifications were made in the early part of the last statute, but the main principle of individual taxation by overseers, under the superintendence of justices of the peace, was retained unaltered. The chief objects of the law as it stood at the end of 1601 were—to relieve the lame, sick, aged, impotent, and blind ; to compel others of the poor to work, and to put out their children as apprentices.

At that time any one leaving his employment and wandering beyond the boundaries of his parish without any ostensible means of gaining a livelihood was liable to be arrested and punished as a vagabond, in addition he was compelled to return to his own district in disgrace ; so that whether a law confining labourers to their own neighbourhoods existed then or not, it is certain that they had little inducement to venture forth amongst strangers.

In 1662, during the reign of Charles II., the Law of Settlement was passed, by which all members of such classes as were likely to become at some period or other chargeable to the parish rates, were compelled to settle themselves on the parochial district to which they were connected by birth, marriage, apprenticeship, or similar ties; and upon which parish alone they would subsequently have any claim. In this way the unfortunate peasantry and labouring population were more securely than ever imprisoned within their parishes, for if they escaped the fate of the rogue and vagabond, and obtained work in another part of the

country, they were generally hunted out and driven home for
fear they should become burdens on rates to which they had no
title.   Such a condition of things went on with little change
for nearly two centuries, but the causes which finally brought
about a material alteration in the arrangement of pauper relief
will be noticed in the context.   The erection of workhouses for
the different parishes of the kingdom was sanctioned in 1723 by
the legislature, and three years later, as learnt from the following
extract out of the minute book of the bailiffs of Kirkham, the
inhabitants of that town determined to establish one :—

"22 May, 1726 :—Mem.   That the town of Kirkham was summonsed from
house to house, and the inhabitants unanimously agreed to the setting up of a
workhouse."

The act which decreed the building of workhouses for the
employment of the poor, stated that if any one refused to enter
those houses, or objected to perform his share of labour, no relief
should be apportioned to him.   There can be little doubt that
workhouses sprang up at Poulton and in the other parishes of the
Fylde about that date, as well as at Kirkham, but in their cases
there are no bailiffs' registers, or similar records, to fall back upon
for proof as to the accuracy of the surmise, and consequently we
are unable to speak with absolute certainty.   In the twenty-
second year of the reign of George III. (1782), it was enacted that
the guardians of the poor should employ the paupers of their
separate parishes in labour on the land at small remuneration,
and that the poor rate should be used only to increase the payment to a sum large enough for the subsistence of each pauper
thus employed.   Country justices, desirous of standing well in
the opinion of the peasantry, were not over scrupulous in the
discharge of their supervisionary functions, and granted or
sanctioned the granting of relief orders without any minute
inquiry into the merits of the cases.   Immorality was encouraged
by an allowance from the poor-rate to the mother for each
illegitimate child.   Practical responsibility for the proper
administration of the fund rested on no one, and about 1830
"the poor-rate had become public spoil, the ignorant believed it
an inexhaustible source of wealth, which belonged to them ; the
brutal bullied the administrators to obtain their share ; the
profligate exhibited their bastards, which must be fed ; the idle

folded their arms and waited till they got it ; ignorant boys and
girls married upon it ; country justices lavished it for popularity,
and guardians for convenience."[1]

In 1832 a Royal Commission was appointed to visit the different
parishes, and investigate the abuses which were being universally
carried on ; and in 1834 a bill was brought in to amend the laws
relative to the Relief of the Poor in England and Wales, and
passed that year, some of the main clauses being—an acknowledgment of the claims to the relief of the really necessitous, the
abolition of settlement by hiring and service, and of all out-door
relief to the able-bodied. The enactment provided for the union
of small and neighbouring parishes, the rating and expenditure of
the rates remaining a distinct and separate matter ; each union
was to have a common workhouse for all its parishes, in which
the men, women, children, able-bodied, and infirm must be
separated, and where the able-bodied inmates should do a certain
amount of work for each meal. The distribution of relief was
left to the guardians and select vestries, and to the overseers in
their absence. The whole system of unions and parish relief was
placed under the control of a Central Board, by whom everything
was arranged and settled, and to whom any appeals were to be
directed.

Shortly after the passing of this act, the following twenty-three
townships of the Fylde were banded together for parochial purposes, and denominated the Fylde Union :—Bispham-with-Norbreck, Bryning-with-Kellamergh, Carleton, Clifton-with-Salwick,
Little Eccleston-with-Larbrick, Elswick, Freckleton, Greenhalgh-
with-Thistleton, Hardhorn-with-Newton, Kirkham, Layton-with-
Warbreck, Lytham, Marton, Medlam-with-Wesham, Newton-
with-Scales, Poulton, Ribby-with-Wrea, Singleton, Thornton,
Treales, Roseacre, Wharles, Warton, Weeton-with-Preese, and
Westby-with-Plumptons. In 1844 the guardians erected the
Union Workhouse at Kirkham, at a cost of about £5,400, and in
1864 the building was enlarged so as to be able to accommodate
250 paupers. All small, local workhouses in the districts comprised in the union were of course closed on the opening of the
central one. The guardians of the different townships constitute

1. History of England, by H. Martineau.

a board, in whose hands rests the regulation of all matters concerning the union.

By a subsequent act, the original Central Board of Poor Law Commissioners was superseded by a controlling board composed of four members of the government, *ex officio*, and certain other commissioners appointed by Her Majesty in council, the inspectors, whom, it should have been mentioned, were provided under the previous act, were now invested with more extended powers ; workhouse visitors were appointed ; annual reports were ordered to be issued ; and a clause forbidding the cohabitation of man and wife in the workhouses was dispensed with after the parties had arrived at sixty years of age.

INDEX.

—:o:—

FLEETWOOD AND BLACKPOOL: PRINTED BY W. PORTER AND SONS.

LIST OF SUBSCRIBERS.

LIST OF SUBSCRIBERS.

—:o:——

Abbott, Christopher	Blackpool	Bamber, Joseph	Thistleton
Abbott, John	,,	Bamber, Nicholas	Greenhalgh
Abbott, Chris., jun.	South Shore	Bamber, Lawrence	Lytham
Ackroyd, Miss Annie	Blackpool	Bamber, W. F.	Stoke-u-Trent
Adams, John		Bainbridge, John	Preesall
Adamson, William	Liverpool	Banks, Henry	Little Carleton
Adcock, John	Blackpool	Banks, John	Blackpool
Addey, Jacob	Chorlton - cum -	Banks, W. B.	Thornton
	Hardy	Bannerman, Charles A.	Lytham
Akroyd, James	Preston	Barber, Thomas	Blackpool
Allmark,	Blackpool	Baron, Henry	South Shore
Anderson, Councillor	South Shore	Baron, J.	Lytham
Anderton, Robert	Kirkham	Baron, Robert	Blackpool
Anderton William	South Shore	Baron, Mrs. E.	,,
Andrews, John	Blackpool	Barrow, William	,,
Archer, Henry		Barrett, G. C.	,,
Archer, William	Bispham	Barton, Grimshaw	,,
Armstrong, John	Claughton	Barton, Henry	,,
Armytage, Rev. J.	Elswick	Barton, Thomas	,,
Arthur, Christopher	Kirkham	Barton, Henry T.	Stalmine
Ascroft, Alfred	Preston	Barton, Benjamin G.	Skippool
Ashforth, George	South Shore	Bates, William	Lytham
Ashworth, John J.	Pendleton	Bates, William	Blackpool
Ashworth, J. W.	,,	Bees, Enock	,,
Ashworth, William	Blackpool	Bell, John	,,
Ashton, J. F.	,,	Bell, Matthew	,,
Ashurst, William	,,	Bennett, James	Fleetwood
Aspden, Henry	,,	Bennett, Miss B.	Rock Ferry
Aspden, Thomas	,,	Bennett, Miss E.	,,
Atherton, Charles	,,	Bennett, William	Treales
Atherton, Daniel	,,	Bennett, James	Kirkham
Atkinson, James	Preesall	Benson, William	Catterall
Atkinson, John	,,	Berry, Charles J.	Blackpool
Atkinson, Thomas	Blackpool	Best, Thomas	,,
Atkinson, William	Lytham	Bickerstaffe, Thomas	,,
Axon, Charles H.	Blackburn	Bickerstaffe, John	,,
		Bickerstaffe, Robert	,,
Bailey, Councillor	Blackpool	Bickerstaffe, Councillor	,,
Balderson, J.	Poulton	Billington, William	Lytham
Ball, James	Blackpool	Billington, Thomas	Wrea Green
Ball, John	Fleetwood	Bilsbury, Miss	Poulton
Ball, William	Westby	Birch, Miss	Blackpool
Bamber, William	Blackpool	Birch, Henry	,,
Bamber, William	,,	Bird, Henry	Fleetwood
Bamber, George	Kirkham	Bird, P. H.,	
Bamber, James A.	Layton	F.R.C.S.,F.L.S.	Lytham

Birley, A. Leyland   Kirkham
Blackurst, William   ,,
Blackburn, Agnes   Blackpool
Blackburn, Edward   Out Rawcliffe
Blackburn, Mrs.   ,,
Bleasdell, Rev. Canon W.
            M.A., Kingston, Ontario
Blundell, W. B.   Out Rawcliffe
Boardman, George   Blackpool
Beardman, James   ,,
Boardman, William   Great Marton
Bolton, George   Blackpool
Bond Miss A.   Fleetwood
Bond, John   ,,
Bond, Charles   Preston
Bond, Whittaker   Blackpool
Bone, John W. Cromble-
    holme, B.A., F.S.A. London
Bonny, James   Fleetwood
Bonny, Councillor   Blackpool
Bonny, John   ,,
Bonny, Thomas   ,,
Bottomley, Wm. H.   ,,
Bourne, Col. James
    M.P., J.P., D.L.   Heathfield (3)
Bourne, Capt. J. Dyson
    5th Dragoon Guards   London
Bourne, Lady Marion   ,,
Bourne, Thomas R.   Bristol
Butler-Bowden, Lieut.-Col.
                         Pleasington Hall
Bowers, Thomas   Blackpool
Bowdler, Wm. H.   Kirkham
Bowker, George   Blackpool
Bowman, James   ,,
Bowman, Richard   Hambleton
Bowness, R. H., M.D.   Poulton
Boys, William   Catterall
Brade, John   Thornton
Bradley, Robert   Pilling
Bradley, James   Weeton
Bradley, John   Kirkham
Bradley, Miss   Out Rawcliffe
Bradshaw, William   Blackpool
Bradshaw, Alice
Bradshaw, Matthew   Elswick
Braithwaite, Councillor Blackpool
Braithwaite, Ralph W.
Brandon, Edward J.   Fleetwood
Brearley, Martha Ann   Blackpool
Breckell, Edmund   ,,
Brenerd, James   Fleetwood
Brewer, Miss   Lytham
Brewster, Charles   ,,
Bridge, James   Cheetham Hill
Brooks, A. Mrs.   Bournemouth
Brooks, John   Blackpool
Brook, John   ,,
Brown, William J.   ,,
Brown, Jonathan   ,,
Bryne, John   ,,

Bryning, John   Wesham
Bryning, Edward   Bispham
Bryning, John, J.P.   Newton
Burdekin, Elizabeth   Lytham
Burns, Rev. William   South Shore
Burridge, Stephen   Ardwick
Burton, Edward   Norbreck
Butcher, Paul   Blackpool
Butcher, R.   ,,
Butcher, James   ,,
Butcher, Thomas   ,,
Butcher, Robert   ,,
Butcher, William   South Shore
Butcher, Thomas   Great Marton
Butler, William   Fleetwood
Butler, James   Thistleton
Butler, James S.   Poulton (2)
Butler, Richard   St. Michael's

Callund, Alfred, J.   Fleetwood
Camotta, Josephine   Blackpool
Cannon, Joseph Lee   Lytham
Cardwell, Edward   Singleton
Cardwell, Gilbert,   Blackpool
Cardwell, Thomas   ,,
Cardwell, W. and Bros.,   ,,
Cardwell, E.   Lytham
Cardwell, William   Revoe
Cardwell, Robert   Little Marton
Carr, Thomas H.   Fleetwood
Carson, Alexander   ,,
Carson, Samuel   ,,
Carter, John   ,,
Carter, John   Wesham
Carter, T.   South Shore
Carter, Thomas   Larbrick
Carter, Miss A.   Blackpool
Carter, Mrs. E.   Lytham
Carter, Miss   ,,
Cartmell, N.   Westby
Cartmell, Richard   Little Carleton
Cartmell, George   Fleetwood
Cartmell, James   Freckleton
Cardwell, Elizabeth   Blackpool
Catlow, Mrs. Sarah A.   Lytham
Caton, Richard   Blackpool
Catterall, James   Larbrick
Catterall, Sarah A.   Kirkham
Catterall, Robert   ,,
Catterall, James   ,,
Catterall, William   Poulton
Causton, H. K.   Brigton
Charlton, Robert   Kirkham
Charnley, William M.   Blackpool
Chew, John   ,,
Clarke, John   Little Eccleston
Clarke, D.   Singleton
Clarke, Robert   Lytham
Clarke, Thomas R.   Blackpool
Clarkson, John   Kirkham
Clarkson, Thomas   Blackpool

Clarkson, James — Carleton
Clarkson, Mrs. Mary — ,,
Clarkson, Robert — Out Rawcliffe
Clarkson, Henry — Wesham
Clegg, Matthew — Kirkham
Clegg, Miss — Blackpool
Clifton, John Talbot — Lytham Hall (3)
Cook, George — Blackpool
Cookson, Richard — Wrea Green
Cookson, Mrs. R. — Lytham
Cookson, Thomas — South Shore
Cookson, Helen — Blackpool
Cookson, Miss — ,,
Cookson, William — Freckleton
Cooksley, Mrs. — South Shore
Crabtree. John — Blackpool
Cragg, William — ,,
Crestadoro, A., P.H.D. — Manchester
Crippin, William — Old Trafford
Critchley, P. — Singleton
Crombleholme, R. A. — Halifax
Cross, James — Fleetwood
Crossley, Thomas — Blackpool
Crossfield, W. P. — Freckleton
Croxall, Joseph — Blackpool
Crozier, Robert — Lytham
Crookall, Elizabeth — Fleetwood
Crookall, John — Springfield
Coop, William — Blackpool
Coop, John — ,,
Cooper, Henry — ,,
Cooper, Jane Miss — Kirkham
Cocker, Ald. Wm. H.,
  J.P., Mayor of Blackpool
Cockhill, Tom — ,,
Collins, George — Fleetwood
Collinson, Joseph — Lytham
Collinson, Elizabeth — Barrow
Cornall, Cuthbert — Blackpool
Cornall, Richard — ,,
Cornall, Robert — South Shore
Corless, Thomas — Pilling
Coulston, William — Blackpool
Coulston, Councillor — ,,
Cowl, George — ,,
Cowell, Joshua — Thornton
Cowell, David — Fleetwood
Crompton, Robert — Blackpool
Croft, John — Fleetwood
Croft, Thomas — Blackpool
Croft, Mary Ann — ,,
Crook, George — ,,
Crook, Robert A. — ,,
Crook, H. M. — ,,
Crook, H. — Newton
Crook, Thomas — Out Rawcliffe
Crook, Thomas — Inskip
Crookshank, Joseph — Blackpool
Cumming, W. C. — South Shore
Cunningham, J., J.P., — Lytham
Cunliffe, Ellis, J.P. — ,,

Cunliffe, Mary — Blackpool
Curtiss, Lawrence — ,,
Currie, Thomas — ,,
Curwen, John — ,,
Curwen, John — ,,
Curwen, Ann Miss — Lytham
Curwen, Robert — Birkenhead
Curwen, Henry — Liverpool

Dagger, William — Lytham
Dagger, William — Blackpool
Dagger, Richard — ,,
Dakin, John — ,,
Dalby, George B. — Preston
Daniels, John — Blackpool
Darlow, Henry — ,,
Davenport, Mrs. — ,,
Davies, T. R. — Kirkham
Davies, Alexander — Fleetwood
Davies, James N. — Poulton
Davies, William — Out Rawcliffe
Danson, William — ,,
Deakin, William — Blackpool
Dean, C. A. — Glasgow
Derby, the Right Hon.
  Earl of — Knowsley Hall
Desquesnes B. — Blackpool
Devonshire, His Grace
  the Duke of — London
Dewhurst, Edward — Blackpool
Dewhurst, William — ,,
Dewhurst, William — ,,
Dewhurst, John — ,,
Dewhurst, William — Great Marton
Dickinson, Mrs. — Rock Ferry
Dickinson, Robert — Blackpool
Dickson, W. J. — Kirkham
Dickson, William — Preston
Dickson, J. B. — ,,
Dickson, William — Bryning
Dixon, Mrs. — Wesham
Dixon, Thomas — Blackpool
Dixon, William — ,,
Dobson, John — Preesall
Dobson, Miss — Poulton
Dodgson, William — Westby
Dodgson, Brian — Catterall
Donnelly, John — Blackpool
Douglas, Robert — Fleetwood
Drewry, William — ,,
Drewry, Thomas — ,,
Drummond, Thomas A. — ,,
Dudley, Mrs. E. — Kingswinford
Dugdale, Richard — Blackpool
Dunderdale, Richard — ,,
Dunderdale, R., J.P. — Poulton
Dunkerley, John W. — South Shore

Eastham, Henry — Blackpool
Eaton, Ellen — ,,
Eaves, Robert — ,,

Hardman, Ald., J.P.,	South Shore (2)	Hosker, William	Lytham
Hardman, William	Blackpool	Horsfall, John	Lytham
Hardman, John	Little Marton	Holt, Richard	Roa Island
Harrison, J.	St. Michaels	Holt, James	Fleetwood
Harrison, Thomas	Blackpool	Holt, John W.	Blackpool
Harrison, Robert	,,	Howson, William	Blackpool
Harrison, John	,,	Howson, Thomas	,,
Harrison, Ainsworth	Fleetwood	Howson, Thomas	
Harrison, Edward	Norbreck	Hornby, Archdeacon	St. Michael's
Harrison, William		Hornby Mr.	Kirkham
F.S.A.,D.L., J.P.	Preston	Hornby, William	St. Michael's
Harrison, R. B.	South Shore	Hornby, John	Thornton
Harrison, Matthew	Catterall	Hope, Rev. S.	Southport
Harrison, William	Freckleton	Hope, Miss	Blackpool
Harrop, Miss A.	Manchester	Houghton, William	Kirkham
Halstead, Robert	Lytham	Houghton, Thomas	Stalmine
Hanby, Richard	Manchester	Houghton, Adam	Pilling
Hawkins, Rev. H. B.	Lytham	Hoyles, Thomas	Blackpool
Harris, Henry	Blackpool	Howard, Thomas	Fleetwood
Handley, Joseph	Bury	Hutchinson, William	Great Eccleston
Handley, Richard	Blackpool	Hull, William	Blackpool
Hayhurst, John	Preston	Hull, Richard	Thornton
Hayhurst, Thomas	Pilling	Hull, Thomas	Poulton
Haslem, D.	Singleton	Hull, Mrs.	Higher Lickow
Hatton, G. jun.	Blackpool	Hull, John	Blackpool
Hankinson, John	Lytham	Hull, Rev. John, hon. canon	
Hayworth, L.	Blackpool	of Manchester	Yarm
Hayes, Mr.	,,	Hull, Henry	Blackpool
Heap, Thomas H.		Humphrys, G. M.	Fleetwood
Heath, Edward	South Shore	Hunt, John	Cleveleys
Hemmingway, Edward	,,	Hughes, Rev. R. J.	Rossall
Hesketh, William	Fleetwood	Hughes, W. H.	Blackpool
Hesketh, R.	Treales		
Hesketh, James	Lytham	Ibbison, Edward	Blackpool
Hedges, David	Lytham	Ingham, Robert	
Heaton, T. W.	Blackpool	Ireland, Thomas	Westby
Hermon, Edward, M.P.	Preston		
Higginson, John	Out Rawcliffe	Jackson, John	Preston
Higginson, Thomas	,,	Jackson, William	Singleton
Hill, Henry	Blackpool	Jackson, Joseph	Garstang
Hill, Samuel	,,	Jackson, Thomas	Kirkham
Hines, William		Jackson, Mrs.	Blackpool
Hines, Rev. Frederick	Kirkham	Jackson, Robert	Hambleton
Hopwood, W. B.	Blackpool	Jackson, James	Stalmine
Holt, Alfred	,,	Jackson, Joseph	Blackpool
Hooton, William A.	,,	Jackson, Richard	Newton
Holmes, George	,,	Jackson, James	Out Rawcliffe
Hogarth, Thomas	Revoe	Jackson, Richard	,,
Hogarth, James	South Shore	Jackson, Jonathan	,,
Holgate, William	Blackpool	Jackson, James	Garstang
Holmes, John	,,	Jacson, C. R., J.P.	Barton Hall
Home, Rev. J. C.	Out Rawcliffe	Jameson, J. M.	Fleetwood
Hodgson, James	South Shore	Jenkinson, William	Pilling
Hodgson, W. S.	Freckleton	Jenkinson, Miss	Blackpool
Hodgkinson, T.	Great Eccleston	Jenson, Evan	Pilling
Hodgkinson Thomas	Out Rawcliffe	Jeffrey, Rev. N. S.	Blackpool
Hough, Rev. William	Hambleton	Jeffery, Ann	,,
Holden, James	Manchester	Johnson, Richard	Fleetwood
Holden, George	,,	Johnson, John	Out Rawcliffe
Holden, John	,,	Johnstone, Margaret	Fleetwood
Holden, Thomas	Pilling	Johns, Henry	Blackpool

Myres, J. J. junr.	Preston	Pickup, John	Blackpool
Myres, J. J.	Freckleton	Pickup, Henry	,,
		Pickop, John	,,
Newsham, Joseph F.	Great Eccleston	Pilling, Rev. W.	Lytham
Newby, James	Blackpool	Pilling, Thomas	Blackpool (2)
Newall, J. H.	,,	Poole, W. H.	Fleetwood
Nickson, Mary	Salwick	Poole, John	Bispham
Nickson, Joseph	Ballam	Poole A. M.	Out Rawcliffe
Nickson, Squires	Blackpool	Porter, Robert	Blackpool
Nickson, William	,,	Porter, J. E.	,,
Nickson, James	,,	Porter, John	,,
Nickson, John	,,	Porter, William	St. Michael's
Nickson, Richard	,,	Porter, Edward	Kirkham
Nicholson, Thomas	Pilling	Porter, Ralph	Dowbridge
Nicholl, William	Blackpool	Porter, James	Wigton
Noblett, Miss Dorothy	,,	Porter, Edmund	Fleetwood
Noblett, John	Thornton	Porter, Robert	,,
Nutter, Mrs. Elizabeth	Accrington	Porter, Miss	,,
Nutter, Wm. H.	St. Annes-on-the-Sea	Porter, William	Rossall
Nuttall, Ann	Blackpool	Pollitt, J. B.	Blackpool
Nuttall, John	Lees	Pountney, W. E., M.B. M.C.	
Nuttall, Richard	Warton		Lytham
		Pollard, Miss	Poulton
O'Donnell, Michael	Blackpool	Pratt, James	Fleetwood
Ormerod, Councillor	Newton Hall	Preston, Emma	Blackpool
Orr, J. A., M.D.	Fleetwood	Preston, Richard	,,
Oswin, Miss	Blackpool	Preston, George	,,
		Preston, Daniel	,,
Pakes, Rev. C.	Blackpool	Preston, Mrs	,,
Parsons, Mrs.	Nantwich	Prince, Daniel	,,
Parnell, Alderman	South Shore	Price, John	,,
Parker, William	Lytham	Preston, George	Out Rawcliffe
Parker, William	Blackpool	Preston, Joseph	Fleetwood
Parker, Peter	,,	Preston, Henry	Thornton
Parker, John	,,	Preston, James	Elswick
Parker, Thomas	,,	Proctor, Miss	Blackpool
Parker, Adam	,,	Pye, Edward	Out Rawcliffe
Parker, Michael	,,		
Parkinson, John	,,	Rawcliffe, Alexander	Fleetwood
Parkinson, Thomas	,,	Ray, John	Bispham
Parkinson, James	,,	Ramsbottom, James	Castle Hill
Parkinson, Nicholas	Fleetwood	Raby, Benjamin	Freckleton
Parkinson, Robert	Poulton	Radford, William	Blackpool
Parkinson, Robert	,,	Redman, John	Fleetwood
Parkinson, Robert	,,	Reynolds, Thomas	,,
Parkinson, Richard	,,	Reynolds, W. H.	Grappenhall
Parkinson, William	,,	Read, William	Blackpool
Parkinson, Richard	Wesham	Read, John	,,
Parkinson, James	Marton	Read, William	,,
Parkinson, James	Lytham	Rennison, Sarah	,,
Parkinson, James	Layton	Reason, William	,,
Parkinson, Robert	Hambleton	Ripus, D.	,,
Parkinson, Miss	Preesall	Rigby, James	,,
Parr, Thomas E.	Thornton	Rigby, John	Freckleton
Pearson, Rev. James	Fleetwood	Ridgway, Squire	Blackpool
Pearson, J. E. H.	Blackpool	Riley, Thomas	Singleton
Pearson, John	St. Michael's	Riley, P. D.	Blackpool
Phipps, Emma M.	Great Eccleston (2)	Riley, Mr.	,,
Phillips, Charles	Blackpool	Riley, John, J.P.	Oldham
Phillips, Rev. S. J.	Rossall	Rimmer, John, jun.	Blackpool
Pickup, Miss E.	Fleetwood	Rimmer, William	,,

Rimmer, Samuel	Blackpool	Singleton, George	St. Michaels
Richards, R. C., J.P.	Clifton Lodge	Singleton, Joseph	Layton
Richardson. Rev. W.	Poulton	Singleton, James	Poulton
Richardson, John	Warton	Singleton, Richard	Wardleys
Richardson, Edward	,,	Singleton, John	Lytham
Richardson, Robert	Freckleton	Singleton, John	Lytham
Richmond, Edward	Blackpool	Singleton, John	Heyhouses
Roskell, Robert	Hambleton	Singleton, John	Stalmine
Roskell, Robert	Out Rawcliffe	Singleton, Richard	L. Poulton Hall
Roskell, John	,,	Simpson, John	Blackpool
Rossall, Richard	Fleetwood	Simpson, W. E.	,,
Rossall, Robert	St. Michael's	Simpson, John	Fleetwood
Rossall, William	Little Bispham	Silcock, Richard	Thornton Hall
Rossall, Thomas	Blackpool	Simmons, Rev. J. F.	South Shore
Robinson, Roger	,,	Silverwood, Thomas	Blackpool
Robinson, J. H.	,,	Skelton, James	,,
Robinson, T. G.	South Shore	Slater, John	,,
Rowley, William	Blackpool	Slater, James	Kirkham
Rowcroft, William	Kirkham	Smith, Mrs.	Lytham
Royles. Thomas	,,	Smith, Robert	Blackpool
Roe, Miss	Hambleton	Smith, T. H.	,,
Ross, Thomas	Out Rawcliffe	Smith, Christopher	Bispham
Rossall, Richard	Little Marton	Smith, Robert	,,
Rushton, Theodica	Blackpool	Smith, John L	,,
Rushton, R.	,,	Smelt, Thomas	Old Trafford
Rymer, Thomas	,,	Snalam, George	Thistleton
Rymer, Thomas	Lytham	Sowerbutts, H. E.	Preston
		Southward, Ambrose	Rawcliffe
Sanderson, William	Carleton	Southward, John	Preesall
Sanderson, William	Bispham	Speakman, Thomas	Hghr Broughton
Sanderson, Peter	Carleton	Speak, W.	Blackpool
Sanderson, Robert	,,	Speak, William	Lytham
Salthouse, Thomas	Lytham	Spencer, James	Freckleton
Salthouse, Ezekiel	Blackpool	Stanton, Thomas	Blackpool
Sandham, William	Fleetwood	Stanley, Isaac	Fleetwood
Scott, Thomas	Lytham	Stephenson, Mrs	Lytham
Scott, John	Clifton	Stead, Edward George	Blackpool
Scott, Rev. Walter	Freckleton	Stirzaker, Matthew	Little Eccleston
Seed, Mrs. James	Lytham	Strickland, Thomas	,,
Seed, James	Freckleton	Strickland, Henry	Blackpool
Seed, G. L.	Poulton	Strickland, John	Marton
Seed, William	Fleetwood	St. Clair, J., M.B.,C.M.	Blackpool
Seed, Thomas	Liverpool	Stott, Samuel	Lytham
Seddon, Mrs	Lytham	Standish, Mrs	Kirkham
Sedgwick, Elizabeth	Blackpool	Standish, John	Lytham
Shepherd, William	Singleton	Stoba, William	Fleetwood
Shepherd, James	Blackpool	Stafford, Thomas	Out Rawcliffe
Sharples. George	,,	Stewart, Thomas	St. Michael's
Sharples, John	Lytham	Sumner, John	Poulton
Sharples, Councillor	South Shore	Sumner, Joseph	Preston
Shaw, William	Blackpool	Sunderland. T.	Blackpool
Sharp, Henry	,,	Sutcliffe, Gill	,,
Shee, Michael	,,	Swarbrick, George	South Shore
Shaw, Robert, J.P.	Colne Hall	Swarbrick, James	Blackpool
Sharp, John	Lancaster	Swarbrick, Edward	Great Eccleston
Shorrocks, James	Out Rawcliffe	Swarbrick, John	Poulton
Shawcross, James	,,	Swarbrick, James G.	Out Rawcliffe
Shorrocks, Miss E. S.	St. Michael's	Swallow, George	Cheetham
Sheffington, Edward	,,	Swann, Robert	Wesham
Singleton, William	Kirkham	Swan, John	Kirkham
Singleton, Richard	Out Rawcliffe	Swain, James	Fleetwood

Swift, James	Warbreck
Sykes, James, jun.	Liverpool
Sykes, Isaac	Blackpool
Sykes, Robert	South Shore
Sykes, B. Corless	Seaforth
Sykes, James Albert	Liverpool
Sykes, Thomas B.	,,
Sykes, James	Breck House
Sykes, Benjamin	Preston
Taylor, Miss N.	Out Rawcliffe
Taylor, Mr	Southport (2)
Taylor, William	Poulton
Taylor, Rev. Roger	Lytham
Taylor, Miss E.	Fleetwood
Taylor, Robert	,,
Taylor, A.	Blackpool
Taylor, Richard	,,
Taylor, James	,,
Talbot, William	,,
Terry, W. H.	,,
Thompson, William	Kirkham
Thompson, Joseph	Elswick
Thompson, Christopher	Blackpool
Thompson, Wm. C.	Fleetwood
Thompson, James	Kirkham
Thompson, James	Hambleton
Thompson, Stephen	Out Rawcliffe
Thornton, Mrs	Preesall
Thornber, P. Harrison	Poulton
Threlfall, Thomas	Blackpool
Threlfall, Richard	South Shore
Threlfall, George	,,
Threlfall, Richard	Rossall
Topping, Edward	Blackpool
Townson, Richard	,,
Todd, Eave	,,
Towers, John	Fleetwood
Topham, John	Kirkham
Tomlinson, Richard	Warton
Turner, Philip	Fleetwood
Turner, James	,,
Turner, Mrs.	Poulton
Turner, Capt. Henry	Stockport
Turnbull, Joseph	Blackpool
Tunstall, James	St. Michael's
Twigg, J. B.	Blackpool
Tyler, Robert	Thornton
Ulyeat, William	Blackpool
Underwood, Thomas H.	,,
Upton, Joseph	Blackpool
Valiant, Robert	Fleetwood
Valiant, James	Skippool
Ward, Robert	Blackpool
Ward, John	Kirkham
Ward, William	Fleetwood
Ward, John	Fleetwood
Walsh, Richard	Wardleys
Walsh, John	Upper Rawcliffe
Wade, Mrs. I.	Hambleton
Wade, Elizabeth M.	Blackpool
Wade, Thomas	,,
Wade, Thomas	,,
Waring, Thomas	,,
Waring, Robert	Lytham
Ware, Titus Nibbert	Bowden
Watts, Edward	Longsight
Warbrick, Richard	Fleetwood
Warbrick, John	Lytham
Warbrick, Richard	,,
Walmsley, Fred	,,
Walmsley, Thomas	,,
Walmsley, Joseph	Carleton
Walmsley, Joeeph	Fleetwood
Waddington, Miss M.	Kirkham
Walker, Dr. J. D.	,,
Walker, Thomas	Blackpool
Walker, William	Arbroath
Walker, Joseph	Eccles
Walker, Miss Alice	,,
Wainwright, Rev. C. H.	Blackpool
Waite, John	,,
Wayman, Rev. James	,,
Whatmough and Wilkinson	,,
Weston, D.	,,
Wartenberg, Siegfried	Lytham
Westhead, Mrs.	Lytham
Whiteside, John	Bispham
Whiteside, John, jun.	,,
Whiteside, John	Larbreck
Whiteside, John	Freckleton
Whiteside, Robert	Kirkham
Whiteside, George	Lytham
Whiteside, Jane	Blackpool
Whiteside, Ann	,,
Whiteside, Charlotte	,,
Whiteside, Robert	,,
Whiteside, Robert	,,
Whiteside, Robert	Ballam
Whiteside, Robert	Marton
Whiteside, Thomas	South Shore
Whiteside, William	Westby
Whiteside, Thomas	Ballam
Whiteside, George	Larbrick
Whiteside, Thomas	Little Eccleston
Whiteside, John	Fleetwood
Whiteside, John J.	,,
White, Ann	Blackpool
White, Evan	,,
Whittington, Mr.	,,
Whittaker, James	,,
Whittaker, John	,,
Whittaker, John	,,
Whittaker, Henry	Lytham
Whitworth, John	Alderley Edge
Whitworth, Robert	Manchester
Whitworth, Alfred	Rusholme
Whitworth, B., M.P.	London, (3)

Whitworth, Thomas	Withington (3)	Worthington, W. H.	South Shore
Whalley, John	Blackpool	Worthington, Thomas	Poulton
Whalley, Henry	South Shore	Worthington, John	Warton
Whalley, Charles	Kirkham	Worthington, Thomas	Trenton, Ontario
Whitehead, Edward	Bolton	Worthington, James	Stockport
Wild, James	Blackpool	Worthington, Henry	South Shore
Wilson, Henry T.	Blackpool	Wood, Rev. L. C.	Singleton
Wilson, William R.	Lytham	Woods, Richard	Kirkham
Wilson, George	Blackpool	Woods, George Butler	Fleetwood
Wilson, Thomas	,,	Wood, Robert	,,
Wilson, Thomas	Fleetwood	Woodcock, Miss	Blackpool
Wilson, Edward	Norbreck	Woodcock, Elizabeth	,,
Wilton, John	Freckleton	Woodcock, J. & M.	,,
Wiggins, W.	Blackpool	Wolstenholme Bros.	,,
Williamson, Robert	Out Rawcliffe	Woodley, Mrs. Jane	,,
Williamson, Thomas	,,	Woodhead, Miss M. A.	,,
Williamson, Thomas	,,	Woodhall, John	,,
Wilkinson, Miss Ellen	,,	Woodhouse, John	Stalmine
Wilkinson, Thomas	,,	Woodhouse, Charles	,,
Wilkinson, Joseph	Blackpool	Wright, John	Thornton
Wilkinson, Robert	,,	Wright, Joseph	Blackpool
Wildman, William	,,	Wright, William	Fleetwood
Wilde, Isaac	,,	Wright, Sarah	,,
Wilding, Richard	,,	Wright, G.	,,
Wilkinson, George	Bispham	Wright, Rev. Adam	Gilsland
Wilkinson, John	Blackpool	Wright, Miss Jane	Kirkham
Wilks, Christopher	Lytham	Wray, John	Blackpool
Winterbottom, Dr.	Manchester	Wray, John	,,
Wignall, John, J.P.	Fleetwood	Wylie, Robert	,,
Worthington, George	Lytham	Wylie, Jonathan	,,
Worthington, John	Blackpool		
Worthington, William	,,	Young, John	Kirkham

Printed in January 2025
by Rotomail Italia S.p.A., Vignate (MI) - Italy